MW00807655

Europe before history

The societies of the European Bronze Age produced elaborate artifacts and were drawn into a wide trade network extending over the whole of Europe, even though they were economically and politically undiversified. Kristian Kristiansen attempts to explain this paradox using a world-systems analysis, and in particular he tries to account for the absence of state formation. He presents his case with a powerful marshalling of the evidence across the whole of Europe over two millennia. The result is the most coherent overview of this period of European prehistory since the writings of Gordon Childe and Christopher Hawkes. One of the great strengths of his book is the broad European perspective, which allows him to address some of the larger questions that have been raised in the study of the Bronze Age. *Europe before history* captures the complexity of a prehistorical world at different levels of integration and interaction from local to global.

NEW STUDIES IN ARCHAEOLOGY

Editors
Colin Renfrew, *University of Cambridge*
Clive Gamble, *University of Southampton*

Archaeology has made enormous advances recently, both in the volume of discoveries and in its character as an intellectual discipline. New techniques have helped to further the range and rigour of inquiry, and encouraged interdisciplinary communication.

The aim of this series is to make available to a wider audience the results of these developments. The coverage is worldwide, extending from the earliest hunting and gathering societies to the colonial period.

KRISTIAN KRISTIANSEN

University of Gothenburg

Europe before history

PUBLISHED BY THE PRESS SYNDICATE OF THE UNIVERSITY OF CAMBRIDGE
The Pitt Building, Trumpington Street, Cambridge, United Kingdom

CAMBRIDGE UNIVERSITY PRESS
The Edinburgh Building, Cambridge CB2 2RU, UK   http://www.cup.cam.ac.uk
40 West 20th Street, New York, NY 10011–4211, USA   http://www.cup.org
10 Stamford Road, Oakleigh, Melbourne 3166, Australia
Ruiz de Alarcón 13, 28014 Madrid, Spain

First published 1998
First paperback edition 2000

Printed in the United Kingdom at the University Press, Cambridge

Typeset in Plantin 10/13 [VN]

A catalogue record for this book is available from the British Library

Library of Congress Cataloguing in Publication data
Kristiansen, Kristian, 1948–
Europe before history / Kristian Kristiansen.
    p.   cm. – (New studies in archaeology)
ISBN 0 521 55227 3
1. Bronze age–Europe. 2. Iron age–Europe. 3. Europe–Antiquities. I. Title. II. Series.
GN778.2.A1K75 1998
936–dc21   97–14350 CIP

ISBN 0 521 55227 3 hardback

CONTENTS

FIGURES

This book could not have been written without the support of my European colleagues working with the Bronze Age and the Early Iron Age. Without their willing
participation in an exchange network of manuscripts, off-prints and books I could
not have kept up with recent research during the past fifteen years, a time in which
my professional work has been a full time post in archaeological monument administration (since October 1994 replaced by the professor chair of archaeology at the
University of Gothenburg, Sweden). For that I owe a personal debt to most of the
names in the bibliography. I hope they will continue to send me their works even now
that they have seen how I made use of them, or rather a selection of them. During the
process of reading and writing several colleagues helped by providing me with up to
date bibliographies and manuscripts covering areas and periods with which I was less
familiar. I especially wish to thank Renate Peroni, Anna Maria Bietti Sestieri, M.
Almagro-Gorbea, M. I. Martinez Navarette, David Coombs, Alexander Palavestra,
Olivier Büchsenschütz and Georg Kossack. No less important was Eva Örsness of
the Royal Danish Library, who never spared any effort to provide the books I asked
for. I also received inspiration from a seminar about Europe in the 1st millennium BC
held in January 1989 in Copenhagen arranged by Jørgen Jensen and myself.

Special thanks go to those of my colleagues who took me out into the landscape
and taught me about site locations in areas with which I was less familiar: Antonio
Gilman in Spain, John Barrett in Scotland, Richard Bradley in southern England, J.
Briard in Brittany and John Collis in Czechoslovakia. Although this work is based on
published evidence, I am also grateful to the many colleagues who over the years have
helped me with my study and recording of Bronze Age material in the museums of
northern Europe. This has provided another necessary background; hopefully there
will come a time and an opportunity to analyse this material.

For archaeological inspiration, during my student years, to perceive the Bronze
Age from a larger European perspective I must mention the works of Henrik Thrane
and Jørgen Jensen. A special thank-you goes to the Centre for Research in the
Humanities, its leader Mogens Trolle Larsen and my colleagues there, for inspiration
during my two-year stay from 1987 to 1989. The centre was set up as a five-year
project between 1986 and 1991 by the Danish Research Council for the Humanities,
and my participation in working out a programme for the centre in early 1985 was the
direct occasion for formulating the project for this book. It followed on a nearly
ten-year period of stimulating interdisciplinary meetings and discussions with anthropologists, historians and archaeologists in Copenhagen and London, including

Jonathan Friedman, Mike Rowlands, Kajsa Ekholm, Lotte Hedeager and Mogens Trolle Larsen.

To write a book is an individual process, and a very joyful one, in which you build up a universe of the past in a silent dialogue between yourself and your colleagues through their works. To retreat from it in order to create a critical distance is difficult, but necessary. I have been fortunate to receive constructive criticism on select chapters from Antonio Gilman, Tim Earle, Heinrich Härke, Olivier Büchsenschütz, Ludwig Pauli and David Coombs. I also want to thank Nick Thorpe for improving the English, and for making useful comments on the text. Tove Woller and Alice Lundgren made all the drawings and prepared the illustrations. Eva Englund took care of all permissions to reprint illustrations, a most time consuming work. Ian Hodder inspired the title of the book in a late-night discussion about 'the best title'. Finally I owe my deepest gratitude to those funds that allowed me to take leave and complete the book. I received economic support for writing, drawings, language correction and travelling from E. C. Gads foundation, Professor Wimmers foundation and the Research Council for the Humanities.

The manuscript was written during 1988–9 at the Centre for Research in the Humanities in Copenhagen, and during a brief period of leave in the early summer of 1991, for which I wish to thank the National Forest and Nature Agency, Ministry of the Environment. Final revisions were made during a two-month stay as visiting professor at the Sorbonne in Paris during the spring of 1992, which also gave me an opportunity to present the book in lectures and to discuss it with students and colleagues there. Illustrations and bibliographical details were completed during 1992–3, and finalised in July 1993. I have attempted to add new literature in the text where possible, or have discussed it in the notes.

Every book has its biases and I shall not regret or excuse any except those due to language barriers, creating an information barrier. It will be apparent from the bibliography that my main readings are in German, English and French, while I can with some effort make myself familiar with texts in Dutch, Italian and Spanish. Regrettably I am dependent on translated summaries for works in the Slavonic and Balkan languages, except for the most common Bronze Age terminology. This regret should not only be on my side – I cannot help raising a slight critique against the lack of translated works from Eastern Europe and the Mediterranean, for these would place their archaeology more firmly in a Central and West European research environment.

The dedication is to my beloved wife and colleague Lotte Hedeager, and our now ten-year-old son Niels, for creating the social and intellectual environment in which I thrive and survive. I, or rather we, now understand the realities behind the apparent clichés of such dedications.

Copenhagen, July 1994

Due to various reasons, among them a complicated process of getting permissions to publish the many illustrations, and my own change of work to become professor at the University of Gothenburg in Sweden in the fall of 1994, the production process of this book became rather prolonged. I am grateful to Eva Englund for her invaluable assistance in administrating the 'permission process'. Between 1993–4, when the manuscript was finalised, and early 1997, we have witnessed a 'European Bronze Age Campaign', initiated by the Council of Europe, including a whole series of conferences, exhibitions etc., just as many new books and articles have appeared. They do not change my basic interpretations.

Gothenburg, May 1997

ACKNOWLEDGEMENTS

This book is published with the assistance of a grant from the Danish Research Council.

The following institutions and individuals have kindly granted permission to repro
duce illustrations for the book:

University of Chicago Press: 1; National Museum of Denmark: 36, 38, 39, 47;
University Library Uppsala: 6 (here based on Gräslund 1987); The Royal Library
Copenhagen: 2, 8; Institut für Ur- und Frühgeschichte der Christian-Albrechts-
Universität Kiel: 7 (here based on Jensen 1988, earlier in Hildegard Gräfin Schwerin
von Krosigk; *Gustav Kossina. Der Nachlass – Versuch einer Analyse*. Offa Ergänzungs-
reihe Band 6, Neumünster); University of Pennsylvania: 112a–B, 113; Römisch-
Germanisches-Zentralmuseum Mainz: 27a, 182, 183, 185; Peabody Museum of
Archaeology and Ethnology, Harvard University: 121A–B (based on O.-H.Frey and
S. Gabrovec; *Zur Chronologie der Hallstattzeit im Ost-Alpenraum*. Actes du VIIIe
Congrès International des Sciences Préhistoriques et Protohistorique vol. I, Bel-
grade); Hachette Publishers Paris: 52, 79, 134, 216; Akademie der Wissenschafte
Berlin, Zentralinst. für alte Geschichte und Archäologie: 106; Karl Wachholtz Verlag
Neumünster: 53; Villa Giulias Rome: 87A–B

F. Audouze and O. Büchsenschütz/Hachette Publishers France: 52 (from W.
Kimmig; *Buchau, Reallexikon der germanischen Altertumskunde* 4) 79, (originally in
T.C.M. Brewster, 1963, *The Excavation of Stable Howe*), 134 (originally in O.
Braassch and R. Christlein, 1982, *Das Unterirdische Bayern*, Stuttgart), 216 (orig-
inally in J. Rageth, 1986, *Wichtigsten Resultate der Ausgrabungen in der bronzezeitlichen
Siedlung auf dem Padnal*, Jahrbuch der Schweizerischen Gesellschaft für Ur- und
Frühgeschichte, Basel); J. Biel: 130 and 132; J. Bintliff: 194; I. Bodilsen: 29; I.
Bouzek: 49, 99, 103A, 223, 309; P. Brun: 3, 72, 157; Bruneaux/Editions Errance
Paris: 187; D.-W. Buch: 57, 60b, 109, 123, 159; S. Champion: 173; A. Coffyn: 64, 74,
75, 77; J. Coles: 35; J. Collis: 184, 189; J.H. Crouwel and J. Morel: 204; B. Cunliffe:
68, 156, 161, 162, 163, 165; S. Frankenstein and M. Rowlands: 137 and 138; H. Frey:
145; J. Friedman: 15; S. Gabrovec: 116; T.J. Gamito: 81; B. Gräslund/Royal Library
Uppsala: 6; B. Gibson: 98; A. Guidi: 70; A. Haffner: 177A; L. Hedeager: 167, 168;
University of Pennsylvania/H. Hencken: 86A–B, 112a; K. Horedt/Inst. of Arch.
Budapest: 200; Horst/Dept of Arch. Berlin: 106; L. Husty/A. Haffner: 177B; B.
Hänsel: 202, 212, H. Härke: 139; J. Jensen: 122, 167; A. Jockenhövel: 88, 89, 207; K.
Kaus: 114; I. Kilian-Dirlmeyer: 69; W. Kimmig: 133, 135, 136, 219; G. Kossack: 100,
101, 110, 126, 127A–B; K. Kristiansen: 30, 32A, 205A–B; K. Kromer: 104A–B, 115,
117, 118, 119, 140, 150; W. Lampe: 96; M.-T.Larsen/Royal Library Copenhagen: 2;
H. Lorenz/Römisch-Germanische-Kommission Mainz: 182, 183, 185; H. Müller-

Karpe: 31; A. Müller-Karpe: 171; D. Nash: 155, 176; J.W. Neugebauer: 198A, 199; J. Ostorja-Zagorski: 58D, 160; A. Palavestra: 144; C. Pare: 175; L. Pauli: 120, 141, 143, 186A; J. Paulik: 210; S. Pearce; 78; V. Pingel: 33B; R. Pleiner: 105, 108; V. Podborsky: 27B, 37; M. Primas: 197A, 215; F. Rötlichsberger: 12; A. Rapin: 188; C. Renfrew: 5; R. Rolle: 147, 148, 149; M. Ruiz-Galvez: 80; P. Schauer: 59A–D, 191, 195; J. Schibler: 197B; M. Shanks and C. Tilley: 16; A. Simons: 180; A. Snodgrass: 65; P. F. Stary: 71; T.P. Stepniak. 32B, 48; K.Struwe/Karl Wachholz Verlag Neumünster: 53; I. Strøm/Villa Giulias: 87A–B; R. Taylor: 76; H. Thrane: 42, 43, 76, 92, 93; N. Venclova: 186A–B; J. Vladar: 201; F.-W.von Hase: 193; J. Waldhauser: 178, 179A; P. Wells/Peabody Museum Harvard: 121A–B; U. Wels-Weyrauch: 206; H. Wüstemann: 91; R. Young/University of Pennsylvania: 112A–B, 113.

Drawings were done by Tove Woller of the following figures: 9, 13, 14, 17, 19, 20, 21, 22, 23, 24, 25, 26, 35, 41, 44, 54, 56, 58A–D, 61, 66, 67, 95, 98, 107, 110, 128, 154, 169, 179B, 198B, 213, 214, 217, 218, 220, 221, 222, 226. Drawings and supplementary artwork are by Alice Lundgren on the following figures: 10, 11 28, 34, 40, 45, 50, 51, 62, 63, 68, 73, 80A, 82, 83, 84, 87, 90, 97, 102, 111, 112, 115, 125, 129, 137, 142, 146, 151, 152, 170, 172, 174A–B, 181, 190, 192, 196, 206, 207, 208, 211, 219. Drawings were done by Catherina Oksen of the following figures: 18, 30, 32A, 224, 225.

Background to the inquiry

1.1 Introduction

Aims and objectives (the inquiry)

This book is about the prehistoric foundations of the historic Europe that emerged with the Roman Empire. In archaeological terms it encompasses the Bronze Age and the Early Iron Age – the 1st and 2nd millennia BC – two millennia that are still badly understood, although they are central to our understanding of what brought Europe into the mainstream of world history. The Bronze Age especially exerts a strange fascination on both the archaeologist and the layman. It represents the first industrialisation in the history of Europe – it produced some of the most stunning works of artistic and technical mastery in bronze and gold ever seen, and yet all this creativity was not employed to any significant degree in economic development, remaining within the sphere of social and ritual activities. From 2000 BC to the close of the 1st millennium social and economic institutions in Europe stayed at the level of developed prestate social organisation, on the very border of state organisation, despite the fact that these societies were engaged in a highly sophisticated and competitive long distance exchange of goods and ideas, covering most of Europe; and despite the fact that the apparent stability concealed multiple sequences of local and regional expansions and recessions. Yet the overall evolutionary balance did not tip into state organisation until the middle to late 1st millennium, although several of the necessary social and economic building blocks were already in place. What factors made it happen at exactly this moment, and not a thousand years earlier?

The idea of writing this book originated out of these and other unresolved questions that kept coming back to me during the last few years in which I have worked with the prehistory of northern Europe. It became increasingly clear that historical changes operated at a much larger scale than that covered by regional research traditions and by prehistoric cultures themselves. During the Bronze Age there emerged a truly international network of metal trade and exchange, making all regions dependent on each other, despite their different cultural traditions. The question of external versus internal factors in promoting change therefore became crucial. It demanded the development of interpretative theoretical frameworks that were able to account for this complexity – such as centre/periphery and world systems approaches. Second, the beginning of the Iron Age brought about a revolution that had significant long term implications and changed the nature of and potential for political and economic control, just as it favoured the development of new regional traditions. Northern and Central Europe from now on followed different evolutionary pathways. The explanation of these diverging developments is not to be sought solely within a North or Central European framework – they demand a much larger historical and geographical scale. My encounter therefore started with the following general questions and hypotheses:

(1) What is specific about the Bronze Age compared to earlier and later periods, and how are we to understand and explain this period in European prehistory? The question was already formulated by Gordon Childe (1930), who saw the Bronze Age as crucial for developing an entrepreneurial and competitive European tradition. To answer it, however, we have to re-evaluate the nature of social organisation, of constraints and possibilities, going beyond the traditional notions of tribes, chiefdoms and states (Chapter 3.2), and also going beyond the traditional barriers of chronological and cultural classifications (Chapter 2.1). Instead I shall begin with the social and economic building blocks of society (Chapter 2.3) to see what organisational patterns will emerge. It is my hypothesis that the Bronze and Early Iron Age displayed an organisational complexity spanning categories from developed tribal societies to archaic states, and that the regional and temporal balance between these variations was dependent on a complex interplay of centre–periphery relations and regional traditions (see Points 3–5 below).

(2) In Bronze Age Europe the organisational framework of society operated within a well-defined cultural framework at local and regional levels. It raises the question of the meaning and maintenance of cultural traditions, of ethnicity and of cultural change – taking place through alliances/trade or through the movement of people (various types of migrations). These are old questions in archaeology, which, however, have fallen into some disrepute. During the 1st millennium BC we are for the first time confronted with literary evidence about prehistoric people, so we cannot and should not escape such questions. On the contrary, we should take the opportunity it offers to test hypotheses about the meaning and identification of ethnicity and of migrations. To what extent do the historical sources merely reflect conditions in the literate societies describing 'the barbarians', and to what extent are these brief descriptions meaningful for understanding Celtic or Germanic people?

Based on this I shall make an attempt to project back in time some of the results concerning the meaning of cultural traditions and the identification of migrations. It is my hypothesis that migrations in certain periods played a much larger role than has normally been accepted in recent years (Kristiansen 1989). To test this it is necessary to define the conditions leading to migrations and the conditions to be met when identifying them (Chapter 7.1).

(3) To what extent can we speak of centre–periphery relations on a local and regional scale during the 1st and 2nd millennia BC? The Bronze Age introduced a new form of interaction and interdependence, which can only be fully grasped by considering the whole range of connections. Therefore an attempt is made in this book to explore the significance of applying a world system concept to the Bronze Age (the

theoretical background is described in Chapter 3.2). It will be argued that as a heuristic device it may help us to rethink the nature of international connections that characterised Bronze Age Europe and beyond. From approximately 2000 BC onwards the expansion of international exchange accelerated the pace of change in regional cultural traditions, and – by the very nature of bronze technology – created a dependency in terms of supplies of metal and know-how between different regions that added a new dimension to change and tradition. A changed balance of international exchange relations might now affect local and regional polities hundreds or even thousands of kilometres away. Although regional traditions were maintained by recontextualising new information into their cultural idioms (e.g. Nordic, Atlantic or Lausitz traditions), they rested on a common stock of metallurgical know-how and common traditions of social and religious value systems that accompanied the flow of bronze.

Thus the nature of regional and interregional dependency is a central theme for understanding and explaining change and continuity during the 1st millennium BC. (4) But, then, why was prehistoric Europe so resistant to state formation after having been incorporated into an international network of trade and alliances that had linked Central Europe to the states of the Eastern Mediterranean and the Near East from the beginning of the 2nd millennium BC? Was this rooted in the nature of the emerging world system, keeping the Bronze Age societies in the role of regional peripheries, suppliers of raw materials? Or was the resistance inherent in the social and economic conditions of European Bronze Age societies? This question, and the possible answers to it, are closely linked to another question: why was the resistance finally broken at the beginning of the Iron Age? Was it due to internal developments or to external forces? The answers to these increasingly complex questions of course depend on the outcome of the first two questions.

(5) What consequences did the regional traditions and structures that had emerged during the 1st and 2nd millennia BC have for the subsequent development of early states in Central Europe and the expansion of the Roman Empire?

This question cannot be answered fully, but it is my hypothesis that during the 1st and 2nd millennia there emerged in Europe a structural hierarchy involving northern, Central and southern Europe (the Mediterranean), characterised by different regional traditions, e.g. Celts and Germans. These historically embedded differences to a large degree determined the later expansion of the Roman Empire in the West. According to this theory the genesis of the Roman Empire, and consequently of much of later European history, is to be sought in the two millennia preceding it. I therefore conclude the book with a comparative chapter describing the historical and structural regularities that characterised the integration of Europe into a Bronze Age world system, which gradually transformed Europe north of the Mediterranean and created a structural hierarchy of regional traditions (Chapter 8.4; Kristiansen 1994).

These key questions cannot be answered in any simple or straightforward way; they turned out to demand a whole book, on the way leading to yet a new series of questions. Only in the final conclusion and epilogue shall I return to them. But it is the story of Europe before History, during the two millennia before Christ, that is the real source of fascination. And there is certainly more than one conclusion to be drawn – I am proposing two sets of conclusions, based on a cultural historical and an evolutionary perspective respectively, reflecting the structure of the book, which I shall briefly comment on.

To balance generalisation against contextualised interpretation I have organised the book into three parts: in the first part the theoretical and methodological framework is delineated (Chapters 1–3). The second part is the historical narrative and interpretations (Chapters 4–8.1). Each chapter presents a specific historical problem in its context. They can in principle be read on their own, and only some of the information they hold will be carried over to the final conclusions (Chapters 8, sections 2 and 3). This should allow the reader to follow my arguments from their point of departure in particular cases to the final construction of a model of a Bronze Age world system, and to come up with alternative models or refutations.

So it is on the one hand a book about understanding and explaining regional variation and interdependence in a long term perspective. But it is also a book about historical regularities (and variability) during the 1st and 2nd millennia BC, and about the historical forces governing them.

There are some obvious constraints on a book of this nature. It is written by an archaeologist with some anthropological training and a genuine interest in history, but it is written from the perspective of archaeology, trying to give social and historical meaning to material evidence. It follows from the scope of my venture that there will be numerous possible points of criticism, where I have not been able to penetrate all the relevant literature. However, I hope that my interpretations will command enough interest to make any factual omissions of less importance. The focus of debate will hopefully be at the level of interpretation and explanation. Such concepts, however, are also embedded in a tradition of learning. I shall therefore give a brief account of the intellectual framework that has shaped my thinking during the past ten to fifteen years, and thereby also the structure and scope of this book.

Archaeology, history and society

'Die Grenzen meiner Sprache bedeuten die Grenzen meiner Welt' wrote the philosopher Ludwig Wittgenstein. This is true not only in a conceptual sense, but also in a wider social and historical sense. The conditions of our existence determine to a large degree our ability to understand and interpret the conditions of others, whether in the past or in the present. Although scientific research traditions have developed to overcome such constraints, Europe's own intellectual and political history of the past 200 years has with increasing clarity taught us that humanistic, historical and social disciplines are undoubtedly determined by the history of the present (Chapter 2.1). This is not to deny that one can achieve knowledge about the past in ways that involve objective elements of historical truth, but the way we structure and use this knowledge is largely shaped by present concerns.

The interaction between past and present, between knowledge and interests, has become more widely recognised within the past twenty-five years (Habermas 1968).

It has happened during a period in which the global order of economic dominance changed, and thereby also challenged the role of anthropology and archaeology, due to internal social and economic restructuring in the centres of domination. This has also been reflected in the crisis of universities whose departmental structure was shaped during the consolidation period of capitalism in the late 19th century. It defined disciplines that had acquired specialised functions in maintaining the structure and hierarchy of the present – anthropology to understand underdeveloped and colonised people, archaeology and history to sustain the myths of civilisation and national identity, economy to underpin the capitalist world system, etc. The gradual formation of new interdisciplinary traditions of learning after World War II reflects changing conceptions, and the need to understand the complexities of both the past and the present in a period of major transformations, sometimes called the postmodern period. It is a symptom of these experiments, which have become more widespread during the 1980s, that this book was conceived and written during a two-year stay at a newly founded 'Center for Research in the Humanities' at the University of Copenhagen. And even more so it reflects the present condition of uncertainty and the resistance of old traditions and structures of learning that this institution was designed as an experiment, allowed to live for five years.

Archaeology, the past interpreted through its material remains, has more than most other disciplines, perhaps with the exception of anthropology, been subject to ideological reinterpretations in recent years. This is due to the role archaeology holds in most countries around the world, as national guardian of the cultural heritage. This gives archaeology a special profile and position tending to constrain its applicability as a social and historical discipline of a more general nature. Historically it can be explained by the role played by archaeology in the formation of European nation states and national identities during the 19th and early 20th centuries (Chapter 2.1). With few but notable exceptions, such as Gordon Childe, it is only during the past twenty-five years that archaeology has come to take a critical approach to this role and has developed a more general framework of social anthropological and historical theory. It is thereby entering the scene of world history rather than of national history.

Europe before History is a product of these developments and an attempt to demonstrate the significance of prehistory for understanding important aspects of world history. As such it is also situated within a tradition of learning and adopts a specific conceptual framework that has emerged during the past twenty years, partly as a response to the changes described above, but also as a reaction against dominant traditions within European archaeology (Chapter 2.1). It proposes that European prehistory has to be understood in terms of Europe's position for several thousand years as a region marginal to the centres of civilisation, both interacting with them and resisting their influence in a selective way. It further proposes that prehistoric societies were able to create the conditions for their own transformation, thereby allowing internal dynamics an essential place in understanding change. This, however, also resulted in expansions and regressions, in the formation and collapse of large-scale networks of exchange and trade, and in migrations. In this way prehistoric transformations created new conditions for interaction with other societies and regions, from the pastoral nomads of the steppes to the civilisations of the Near East and the Mediterranean. Therefore internal dynamics both affect and are affected by external factors, dissolving the dichotomy between internal and external.

In order to come to terms with European prehistory, we have to abandon the arbitrary and ideological basis of traditional research, considering Europe and its various regions as natural, self-sustaining units of research and instead setting them in a wider framework of interacting regional systems, in some periods forming 'world systems'. This obviously puts certain demands on the quality and representativity of the archaeological record. With a nearly 200–year-old archaeological tradition Europe is probably one of the most well-suited regions in the world for this type of research.

What meaning, then, can be given to the concept of world systems and centre–periphery relations in the past? Was the creation of ancient world systems already a special feature of Europe and the Near East from later prehistory (Rowlands, Larsen and Kristiansen 1987)? These questions have been made topical by the recent works of historical sociologists, such as Michael Mann (1986), John A. Hall (1986) and Gunder Frank (1991) in their attempts to rewrite and give new theoretical meaning to world history (and to sociology), attempts that follow in the wake of similar concerns within historical anthropology, exemplified by the writings of Fernand Braudel (1972), Eric Wolf (1982), Immanuel Wallerstein (1974), and Kajsa Ekholm and Jonathan Friedman (1979 and 1980). Hall has suggested that the basic feature of capitalism and industrialism, which distinguishes it from other social formations in world history, was the fragmentation into nation states and the competitive social interaction evolving from this, both horizontally and vertically (Hall 1989, 96).

In this book I explore the origins of competitive interacting regional networks, or world systems, in a European context, and the kind of basic social structures and dynamics underlying such systems. My objective is to restore faith in archaeology as a historical discipline that can contribute meaningfully to world history by unfolding and explaining the forces of history in a long-term perspective and at a geographical scale that allows the reconstruction of ancient world systems and their interaction. This is where archaeology can make a unique historical contribution to understanding processes of historical change beyond national and regional boundaries.

However, since archaeology is closely interwoven with European history of the past two hundred years, and since the question of European origins and traditions has played a significant role during this period, including the formation of national states and identities, it is not unproblematic to present an interpretation of the later prehistory of Europe that leads up to the formation of historic peoples and states, such as Celts, Germans, Illyrians, Etruscans, Romans, etc. They still play a role in the social and political transformations taking place in the present. And since archaeology has been undergoing a major theoretical change since World War II, in part due to these political issues, we cannot separate social theory, ideology and archaeological interpretations. I have therefore devoted the next two sections to delineating and critically discussing the ideological context of 'European origins'.

1.2 European origins

Civilisation and barbarism

It may be taken as a sign of increasing theoretical maturity within the discipline of archaeology that it is beginning to see itself as a product of the forces of history. Over the past ten to fifteen years there has been a change from an internal understanding of archaeology as the result of the work of archaeologists (Daniel 1975) towards a broader understanding that situates archaeology in its social and political context (Gathercole and Lowenthal 1989; Layton 1988). By the 1980s archaeology had lost not only its theoretical, but also its political innocence. This critical re-evaluation of traditional practices has assessed several areas, from the ideology of museums and conservation (Horne 1984; Cleere 1989; Shanks and Tilley 1987a, part I), to the social history of the discipline as a whole. It is often national in scope, due to the present organisation of archaeology, which was itself the outcome of the formation of national states and the development of a national past (Kristiansen 1981; Fowler 1987). In the following a very preliminary attempt will be made to go beyond such an internal framework by trying to relate it to changes in the conception of European origins and their relationship to economic and political strategies on a more global scale.

The development and international expansion of archaeology was intrinsically linked to the formation of modern national states and the modern world system during the 19th and 20th centuries, but with its roots in the 16th century (Wallerstein 1974; Wolf 1982). In accordance with this, a number of different archaeological traditions emerged that can be broken down into three major types: national, colonial and imperialistic (Trigger 1984). They ultimately sprang from the same source, the expanding nation states of Europe, defining the rest of the world according to their status in terms of Europe's colonial or imperialistic strategies during the previous two hundred years. How does the idea of European origins relate to the development of recent European history, including the role played by archaeology?

Myths of origin have played a large part in shaping our conceptions of the past, thereby giving order and meaning to the present. In Europe two myths have been dominant. They were both shaped by the classic dichotomy between Civilisation and Barbarism, reflecting the nearly universal ethnocentric categorisations of the dominated by the dominant, of the bad guys by the good guys (Harbsmeier 1986) (Figure 1). Recent research on this neglected subject suggests that the contradictions between Barbarism and Civilisation, and between indigenous European origins and cultural transmission from the centres of civilisation, have played a major role in shaping the political ideology of European nation states, thereby also implicitly influencing research objectives and interpretations (Larsen 1989; Rowlands 1989). It produced two dominant myths of origin – one that saw Europe as the barbarian destroyer of classical Rome, and one that saw European barbarism as a necessary revitalisation of a decadent civilisation.

According to the myth of barbarian destruction, the flame of civilisation was carried from the Near East, via Greece, to Rome, where it was destroyed by

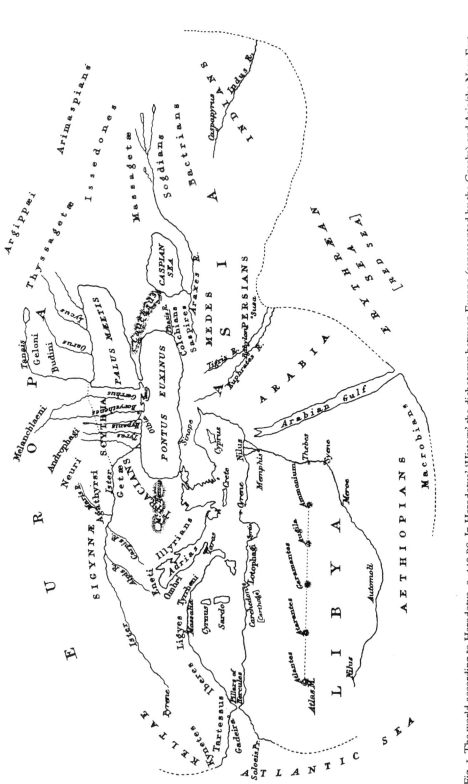

Fig. 1 The world according to Herodotus, c. 440 BC. In Herodotus' 'History' the dichotomy between Europe (represented by the Greeks) and Asia/the Near East (represented by the Persians) is played out in full, forming a dramatic world historical opposition between freedom and despotism, good and bad.

Fig. 2 An Assyrian bull statue from Nineveh on its way through the Dorian colonnade at the British Museum in 1850. From the *Illustrated London News*, reproduced after Larsen (1988,19), it shows the great public interest that Layard's findings aroused in Europe.

barbarians, only to be revived after the Renaissance. The new industrial empires of England and France saw themselves as the successors to classical civilisation, and their campaigns of archaeological excavation on classic sites in the Near East during the 19th and early 20th centuries were explorations of the roots of classical and biblical civilisations, and the exhibition of the evidence in new large museums in London and Paris is to be seen as part of this historical mission (Larsen 1988). During the 1840s the excavations had the character of a race between France and England in locating and bringing home treasures from what they both believed was ancient Nineveh (Figure 2). In the wake of this archaeological imperialism the leading European nations established archaeological institutes in the Mediterranean and the Near East, most of which still exist.

The historical and anthropological disciplines were also shaped during the late 19th century, at least in part by this civilising venture of expanding European imperialism. Social anthropology responded to a need to understand the 'primitives' according to their supposed place as historically and economically peripheral, while archaeology and ancient history were soon able to demonstrate the successful evolution of civilisation from Stone Age to Iron Age and Industrial Age with its climax in 19th-century Europe. In this way the discoveries in the 1850s and 1860s of the Old Stone Age, the Palaeolithic, in Europe showed, when contrasted to existing stone age people, that evolution had been successful and had led to civilisation only in certain regions of the world. Darwinian principles of selection could be applied to account for and to legitimise the superiority of Europe and its domination of the rest of the world.

At the same time, or slightly later, another tradition regarding barbarian Europe as the original source of uncorrupted freedom, maintaining communal life and free-dom, as opposed to the despotism of classical empires, developed in Middle Europe, especially in Germany. With the aid of historical linguistics, 'Volkskunde' (the study of traditional culture), and archaeology which had by this time laid down the fundamental chronological and cultural framework of the prehistoric roots of Euro-pean history, a national-historical framework was constructed to support the revived and expanding German nation. Through the ethnic interpretations of archaeological cultures by Gustav Kossinna direct ethnic links were postulated between the prehis-toric past and the present. This framework proved so successful that it was adopted in most European countries. It later served as a platform for racist constructions of a Germanic 'Urvolk' rooted in Indo-European tradition, which was adopted and transformed to serve the Nazi regime. It has to be stated, however, that its source was a common European tradition that rose to dominance around the turn of the century (Jensen 1988; Chapter 1.2 below).

As a consequence of this recognition of barbarian roots as a vitalising element in the formation of European dynamics (Figure 3), oriental origins were toned down. The notion of static oriental despotism was in part responsible for its falling into disrepute at a time when industrialism hailed innovations, free markets and individ-ualism. Greece, however, was 'saved' by the discovery of its Indo-European, that is European, origins, although this change was also clearly ideologically based (Bernal 1988). By the end of the 19th century barbarism had been recontextualised and rehabilitated through the combined efforts of linguistics, history, and not least archaeology (Rowlands 1989).

Thus the late 19th and early 20th century was the great period of the invention of tradition, with history and archaeology quite openly serving ideological functions that were transformed into national and international myths of origins and civilisa-tional superiority (Hobsbawm and Ranger 1983; Kristiansen 1993). One need not go through many books, newspapers or other popular literature of the time to realise the fundamentally racist outlook of these historical constructions. On the other hand, the past was also used to support the historical roots of basic free rights, as well as making aggression, expansion and warfare legitimate features of the European tradition. In a paradoxical way the violence and potential revolutionary outcome of class conflicts were also seen as barbarian traditions, so the concept was highly contradictory, as is the history of Europe itself. Nationalism served to channel such internal class contradictions into external aggression and expansion, e.g. colonialism and mass migrations.

The ideology of national independence, underlying the rise of the nation state, had, however, created another dilemma, since all peoples could reasonably make claims to such rights. In this situation history, archaeology and anthropology helped to prove that such virtues had been achieved through a long-term civilisational

Fig. 3 Early Iron Age warrior representing the early 20th-century myth of heroic European barbarism.

process culminating in European capitalism, now expanding to the rest of the world, which had to learn and earn the virtues of civilisation through imperialistic and colonial salvation. It was only after the collapse and transformation of traditional colonialism after World War II that academic interests turned to understanding and explaining the historical forces underlying this global transformation and the roles played by archaeology, anthropology and history (Ekholm and Friedman 1980; Trigger 1984).

'Civilisation' is thus an ideological concept, rooted in the cosmology of economic dominance and exploitation masked as a cultural virtue. It is therefore linked to state formation and the development of centre–periphery relations with dependent or just as often semi-independent and threatening 'barbarian' peripheries. Consequently the term can be more objectively described as a level of social and economic organisation, allowing a certain degree of cultural sophistication, as well as a certain degree of social oppression and economic exploitation. We should therefore abandon the traditional conceptual framework of 'civilisation' and 'barbarism' as it has been employed until today in both marxist and liberal writings and take a more unbiased view of European prehistory from the perspective of social and economic organisation. It was Engels, inspired by Morgan, who applied the unfortunate evolutionary framework of 'Savagery', 'Barbarism' and 'Civilisation' in his classic work *The Family, Private Property and the State*, later to be adopted by Childe in his highly influential and popular books, such as *What Happened in History* (Childe 1942/85). Whereas Childe explained the progress of civilisation in social and economic terms as an evolutionary process, thereby escaping the most obvious ideological biases of the terminology, none the less it implies that civilisation is the ultimate goal, reducing prehistory to the processes leading up to it.

Consequently, concepts such as civilisation and barbarism reflect culturally determined preferences and value judgements that may deprive us of the ability as historians to understand and to recognise significant features of both civilised and barbarian societies. This already happens insofar as the concept of civilisation defines the relationship between prehistory and history through the occurrence of scripts and the survival of written evidence. In this way prehistory is pushed ahead of the expanding frontier of civilisation, defining arbitrary borderlines of historical research and explanation. Although archaeology, history, anthropology and classical philology are increasingly employed in a synthetic study of history, both ancient and more recent, the institutional consequences of this theoretical integration of the disciplines have been taken at only few universities. As long as institutional categorisations, which are themselves the outcome of the ideological structure of civilisation, still dominate research, our ability to transcend these ideological barriers to reach new levels of historical understanding will be severely hampered. It can be argued that the concept of civilisation, when stripped of its ideological clothing, can be used merely as a convention, just like evolution, which has been subject to exactly the same kind of critique for being teleological and ideological. There is, however, a crucial difference: civilisation has a active form – to become civilised, or simply to civilise, implying a much more penetrating and widespread ideological function in daily language. Evolution has no such function – one cannot become evolutionised, it remains within academic vocabulary, and can therefore more easily be used as a convention.

The uniqueness of Europe

Since so-called barbarian societies persisted for millennia in contact with more stratified societies or states, this raises a number of questions as to the causes of such an apparent stability. Was it imposed by the dominance of centres as a form of underdevelopment, or is it the opposite situation – that barbarian or tribal societies display an inherent resistance to hierarchy, state formation being an abnormal development? This view has been forwarded both by anthropologists (Clastres 1977) and by archaeologists and historians, most recently by Mann (1986, chapter 2). Stuart Piggott has put it this way (1965, 23):

> All my study of the past persuades me that the emergence of what we call civilisation is a most abnormal and unpredictable event, perhaps in its Old World manifestations ultimately due to a single set of unique circumstances in a restricted area of western Asia some 5000 years ago.

Mann has reached a similar conclusion (1986, 105ff.).

Counterbalancing the view of tribal societies as inherently egalitarian and un-dynamic Jonathan Friedman has in several works argued that an egalitarian tribal social organisation is more often than not the result of cyclical devolutions, whereby ranked tribal societies have been cut off from larger social and economic networks. Exchange, expansion and ranking are thus to be regarded by him as the normal situation (1985, 64), implying that:

> the truly cold societies [referring to the Lévi-Straussian notion of 'hot' and 'cold' societies] of the world have been largely frozen by the expansion of our own civilisation. These primitive contemporaries who also serve as the bottom rung on the neo-evolutionist ladder have not refused history, but are some of its principal victims. They cannot be conflated with the real archaeological past.

The apparent resistance of European societies throughout prehistory to state forma-tion and 'civilisation' is therefore an interesting phenomenon that raises a number of questions, whose answers may also give important clues for understanding aspects of Europe's later history. Since capitalism, and more specifically industrialism, devel-oped in western Europe, it has posed the natural question: why Europe? What historical factors accounted for such a unique development? Did there exist historical conditions unique to Europe, or was it rather their specific combination at a given moment that created a situation which under the same circumstances could have happened elsewhere where the same conditions prevailed? And how far back in time can they be traced? I don't pretend to be able to answer such major world historical questions. What I propose to do, however, is to elucidate some of the ways in which European prehistoric societies both resisted and interacted with a larger world system during the 1st to 2nd millennia BC. I believe it is possible to point to certain organisational and structural features emerging during this historical sequence that exerted a lasting impact on later historical developments in Europe. This is not to say that capitalism can be explained by this, only that some of the framework within which it developed is rooted in later prehistory.

The genesis of capitalism has normally been the subject of historians looking at its immediate preconditions in the transformation of feudalism to mercantilism and ultimately capitalism and industrialism. While Marx delineated the theoretical framework for explaining the internal processes in *The Capital*, later work also tried to trace its historical roots in Antiquity (Anderson 1974) and to put it into a larger global framework (Wallerstein 1974), leading to important theoretical developments, e.g. centre–periphery and world system theories, exerting influences also on archaeology and anthropology (Rowlands 1987a; Champion 1989b; Ekholm and Friedman 1980, 1985). However, most works on the economic history of Europe and the Mediterranean do not extend back much beyond the Roman Empire and have only rarely taken into account archaeological evidence, even in the early medieval or feudal period where the archaeological evidence is very rich. While earlier European archaeology relegated itself somewhat from the mainstream of historical-sociological research in the late 19th and early 20th centuries, by serving ideological and nationalistic purposes, the later development of European archaeology has done little to transform the material evidence into historical accounts transcending national boundaries, as will be demonstrated below. It was the writings of Gordon Childe, Grahame Clark and their successors that helped to free archaeology from its nationalist, ethnic ideology, placing it in a larger social and economic setting of historical and evolutionary narrative and explanation, although obviously also constrained by the traditional archaeological framework.

Gordon Childe (Figure 4) was the first to trace the entrepreneurial European spirit back to the Bronze Age (Childe 1930). He saw Europe as receiving basic technological innovations from the civilisations of the Near East in a process of diffusion, at the same time opposing state formations and despotism. This resulted in the development of a new social dynamic in Europe:

> Among the Early Bronze Age peoples of the Aegean, the Danube Valley, Scandinavia and Britain, we can already recognise these very qualities of energy, independence and inventiveness which distinguish the western world from Egypt, India and China. (cited after Rowlands 1984a, 149)

Childe rejected ethnic and national interpretations, but rooted basic social and economic components of later European history in prehistory. Since the 1960s this tradition of an autonomous and unique European development has been modernised and raised to dominance under the leadership of Colin Renfrew (1973) (Figure 5), who even sees this tradition as extending further back into the Neolithic: 'The basic links of the traditional chronology are snapped and Europe is no longer directly linked, either chronologically or culturally, with the early civilisations of the Near

Fig. 4 Gordon Childe (1892–1957) was the first European archaeologist to present the prehistory of Europe and the Near East as a coherent, historical narrative for a wider readership.

Fig. 5 Colin Renfrew (1937–) re-established a new autonomous framework for a social and historical understanding of the prehistory of Europe after the partial collapse of the traditional cultural and chronological framework of European origins.

East' (Renfrew 1973, 116). In a recent article Larsen has focussed attention on the ideological basis of this view (1989), which is extended even to include the origins of civilisation on Crete and on the Greek mainland: 'I believe, indeed, that the first European civilisation was very much a European development, and that most of its features can be traced back, not to the admittedly earlier civilisations of the Near East, but to antecedents on home ground, and to processes at work in the Aegean over the preceding thousand years' (Renfrew 1973, 211–12).

The Indo-Europeans have been replaced by autonomous social and economic development, but this still fits well into the ideological tradition of creating a special European identity (see also Bernal 1988). Larsen added in his work the following comment (1989, 235): 'It is difficult to avoid linking this interpretation of the early 1970s with the political realities of the time, and especially with the strong desire felt in Europe to understand the subcontinent as an entirely autonomous entity.' In his most recent book Colin Renfrew has even leaned towards a more national historical approach as rooted in prehistoric traditions (1987, 6):

> These lands have been our lands, and those of our forefathers, for thousands of years longer than is widely thought. Many of the features, then, which define the Irish, or the Spanishness of the Spanish, or the Britishness of the British, go back very much deeper . . . This, I think, is a fundamental change in perspective, and one which carries many interesting implications with it.

I would replace 'interesting' with 'dangerous'. Here Renfrew is not far from Gustav Kossinna, although this, in all fairness, is not the tone of the book. But it does reveal and confirm the underlying ideology of a European perception of history.

Against this, claims are still made by scholars of ancient history for the dominance of classical civilisations in shaping and consistently influencing European developments. In a recent discussion in the journal *Symbol* the Near East has been recontextualised as the origin of European dynamics, in opposition to the traditional perception of static Asiatic regimes. Other ancient civilisations, such as China or Mesoamerica, however, are still denied such dynamics (Larsen 1989, 236). Larsen has taken a middle position in this debate about innovating 'hot' societies versus static 'cold' societies by referring to Mesopotamia as 'lukewarm' (1987). Most researchers, however, have focussed attention on the decline of the Roman Empire and the emergence of feudalism in order to explain the nature of capitalism. This is a classic area of debate among historians, recently reformulated by several researchers, among them Perry Anderson (1974). He traces the roots of feudalism and later capitalism to the unique mixing between Roman civilisation and Germanic tribalism after the fall of the Western Empire. This, of course, then raises the question, once again, about the nature and origin of Germanic traditions.

The old questions and dichotomies are thus very much still with us, as well as their underlying ideologies. Archaeological and historical research is ideologically biased from top to bottom, from its disciplinary divisions (infrastructure) to its basic interpretative terminology (superstructure). If we are to unwrap this constraining ideological clothing, it is necessary to engage actively in a critical historical analysis of its origin and use, as well as attempting to develop new theoretical and academic frameworks for research. Such analysis should also include basic archaeological frameworks and methods, as principles of chronological and cultural ordering likewise shape interpretations.

Background to the archaeology

2.1 Archaeological context

The heritage of Montelius and Kossinna
While the Swedish archaeologist Oscar Montelius (1843–1921) provided the cultural and chronological framework for much of the European Bronze Age (Gräslund 1987) it was the German philologist and archaeologist Gustav Kossinna (1858–1931) who added to it historical flesh and blood (Eggers 1959: chapter 4). As their contributions created a school of archaeological research that is still with us, although modernised (Klejn 1982 for overview) and, in the case of Kossinna, partly denied, we shall deal with the theoretical and methodological implications of their work for the history of Bronze Age research.

In 1885 Oscar Montelius (Figure 6) published the results of fifteen years of museum registrations and research on the Bronze Age chronology of northern Europe, thereby setting the standard for typological-chronological works in European archaeology. Matured through a debate with the Danish archaeologist Sophus Müller, who had challenged Montelius' previous findings, it stood up as a definitive work, in terms of both results and methods, and is still valid. It established for the first time a clear and well-defined culture in its geographical and temporal development, including absolute datings by cross-references to the classical world, where the major cultural impulses were located. In this way it also created the cultural-historical (diffusionist) framework for the interpretation of later European prehistory that has dominated the field up to the present day. Montelius continued his studies throughout Europe and the classical world, classifying metalwork and pottery in typological series and cultural groupings. All this was summarised with great clarity in his classic work from 1903, *Die älteren Kulturperioden im Orient und Europa*, whose first part, 'Die typologische Methode', remains one of the best written pieces of methodology in the history of archaeology. In Central Europe the German scholar Paul Reinecke summarised in a similar way his findings for Bronze Age cultures in a number of short articles without much documentation, but with a lasting impact on European Bronze Age chronology (Reinecke 1906–9, reprinted 1965). The terminology Bronze A to D and Hallstatt Culture A to D was introduced here. By 1910 the basic layout of Bronze and Early Iron Age cultures had thus been completed.

Around the turn of the century Gustav Kossinna (1858–1931) (Figure 7) formulated a set of theoretical propositions that was to influence European archaeology for many decades. Trained as a philologist he was, like many of his contemporaries, concerned with tracing the tribal names of ancient European peoples known from

Fig. 6 The Swedish archaeologist Oscar Montelius (1843–1921) established the first reliable chronological system for the Bronze and Iron Ages and developed the method of typology.

Fig. 7 The German philologist and historian Gustav Kossinna (1858–1931) was the first archaeologist to exploit the cultural and chronological systems of archaeology by formulating theories about their historical meaning.

classical texts, such as Celts, Germans, Illyrians, and particularly with the identification of the Indo-Europeans as they had been defined by linguistics. With archaeological cultural groups now emerging in the form of consistent distributional
patterns of material culture, and given the historical and linguistic data, there was
only a narrow gap between the two. They were combined most effectively by
Kossinna in published lectures from 1885 onwards, titled *The Prehistoric Distribution
of the Germans*, and *The Indo-European Question Archaeologically Answered*. They
rested on the following proposition: 'Scharf umgrenzte archäologische Kulturprovinzen decken sich zu allen Zeiten mit ganz bestimmte Völkern oder Völkerstam-
men' (cited after Eggers 1959, 211). This was followed by another proposition: that
continuity in archaeological cultures over time also implied ethnic continuity.

These highly provocative and stimulating propositions were soon applied to trace
the history of historically known peoples back into prehistory, or rather, to chart their
distributions from prehistory into historical times became a major research goal.
Diffusion and migrations were added to the theoretical repertoire in order to explain
the expansion of cultural traits or whole cultures. From 1900 up to the end of World
War II, this was the dominant archaeological framework, with archaeological cultures
as the basic foundation, and ethnic groups and their diffusion or migrations as the
historical superstructure. Social and economic changes were more or less relegated
from these explanatory concepts, since stable ethnic and racial characteristics (the
'folk spirit') were thought to be the driving forces of history. Much effort was expended
in defining regional and local cultural groups, and since metal objects were the starting
point, only later to be followed by pottery, burial rites etc., the simplistic one-
dimensional homogeneity of archaeological cultures was not really challenged, nor
was their historical interpretation. Although Scandinavian and English archaeologists
remained critical of the most obviously chauvinistic and nationalistic interpretations,
and pointed to political misuses, they were basically employing the same framework.
Gordon Childe's book *The Dawn of European Civilisation* made this patchwork of
cultures accessible in a simplified way between 1926 and 1958, when the last edition
appeared. In his own words, it 'aimed at distilling from archaeological remains a
preliterate substitute for the conventional politico-military history with cultures,
instead of statesmen, as actors, and migrations in place of battles' (Childe 1958, 70).

After World War II theoretical and interpretative scepticism became dominant. It
was realised that ethnic interpretations had been too simplistic and were open to
political and racist misuses. What was needed, therefore, was a re-evaluation of their
applicability and a development of basic archaeological methods. Critical 'tests' of
ethnic interpretations were carried out in a number of studies, where linguistic,
historical and archaeological data could be compared (Hachmann, Kossack and
Kühn 1962; Werner 1956, 1962; Eggers 1959, chapters IV, V). The results, however,
were never used to develop a more systematic framework of possible correlations
between material culture, language and ethnicity in areas and periods without
written sources. Nor have concepts such as migration, trade or exchange (diffusion)
been dealt with in a systematic way, not to speak of questions concerning social and
economic organisation (summary in Veit 1989).

During the 1950s there appeared, however, a methodological reorientation – a kind of new archaeology – that focussed on settlement studies, distribution maps and their potential, initiated by a group of German archaeologists, with Herbert Jahnkuhn and Rolf Hachmann being among the most influential. The new tradition was centred around the journal *Archaeologica Geographica* and had some influence on the development of settlement archaeology, e.g. Northwest European coastal archaeology (Kossack, Behre and Schmid 1984). This research tradition unfortunately never rose to dominance, although the approach was further developed by individuals in several areas, e.g. by Ostorja-Zagorski in Poland and Evzen Neustupny in Czechoslovakia to mention just two. Most Bronze Age research, however, has either avoided dealing with social and cultural history, instead concentrating on classification, or has uncritically continued the rather simplistic pre-World War II approach identifying ethnic groups and migrations in terms of culture groups and their diffusion or expansion, especially in East Central Europe and the Balkans (e.g. Hammond 1976; Kemenczei 1984). Only in recent years have we witnessed a more critical discussion of such problems (Crossland and Birchall 1974), including the possible integration of culture, ethnicity and social organisation and their 'ethnogenesis' (Herrmann 1988; Horst and Schlette 1988; Benac *et al.* 1991). The latter represents an interesting attempt to modernise the pre-war Kossinna proposition that ethnicity can be traced historically through the archaeological record. Personally, I am sceptical about the value of such endeavours, as ethnicity is a complex phenomenon which cannot be reduced to a homogeneous cultural concept, but should be linked to a treatment of social and economic strategies, a discussion to which I shall return later in the chapter about the Celtic migrations.

Another major goal following World War II was to make the empirical foundations of archaeology more scientific in terms of documentation and systematic classifications. Major works of chronology and classification were published, especially from the 1950s. European Bronze Age chronology had never been systematically worked out, and this was achieved in the works of Müller-Karpe (1959) and von Brunn (1968), which set the methodological standards for a whole generation of Central European scholars in the working out of local and regional chronologies. Since the 1960s this has been followed by major publication programmes of Bronze Age metalwork. The series *Prähistorische Bronzefunde* continues the typological tradition of classification and documentaton of single groups of objects: razors, axes, swords, etc. now occupying more than a hundred volumes, while series like that of Aner and Kersten for the Nordic area document the full context of all burials, hoards and single finds. To this we may add an increasing number of solid regional studies since the 1960s, such as Herrman (1966) or Gediga (1967). So the dominant research programmes have thus been either the full documentation of an archaeological culture in a smaller region or the documentation of a single type in larger regions. Only in recent years have settlement programmes come to play a more important role, to which we shall return below.

These research trends have only to a limited degree taken into consideration theoretical developments since the 1960s in North America, England and Scandinavia. Two research cultures have emerged, a Central European (the German- and French-speaking research culture) continuing earlier European traditions, and an Anglo-American (the English-speaking research culture). Communication between them has until recently been sporadic. There are, however, clear signs of a breaking down of barriers that will be discussed in subsequent chapters where they belong.

One effect of the numerous typological studies has been a multiplication of the number of local culture groups or variants. It has, however, become increasingly clear that the traditional concept of culture as a recurrent pattern of overlapping distributions cannot be maintained. Different aspects of material culture may produce varying distributional patterns according to their function and place in society, as proposed more than twenty years ago by David Clarke (1968, fig. 58) and demonstrated by Mats Malmer (1962) and Steve Shennan (1978). The full theoretical and interpretative implications of this still remain to be recognised in European Bronze Age research, although the problem is encountered and attacked in much recent research (e.g. Brun 1984; Lorenz 1985). Only in the few regions that are defined by natural topographical borders, such as the Nordic, may the classic, homogeneous, definition of culture as recurrent, overlapping patterns of material traits be applied. As the Nordic culture was the first to become well defined, this approach has been applied widely, without taking into consideration that the underlying topographical, social and historical conditions are very different in most of Europe.

If we accept the realities of the increasingly complex patchwork of cultures that has emerged in the European Bronze Age, especially in Central and Eastern Europe, then this reflects less homogenous, more disruptive and changing social and historical conditions. If we do not accept these patterns it raises the question of the theoretical status and methodological definitions of culture in European Bronze Age research. I suggest that we should critically re-evaluate the many cultural groups that have emerged, and discuss how they relate to the larger regional cultural groupings (Brun 1988a; 1991). In this way we may be able to reduce the number of cultures in Bronze Age Europe considerably. The larger cultural groupings, such as the Atlantic, the Nordic, the Lausitz Culture, etc., normally share some general characteristics in metalwork and rituals, whereas local groups are often defined in terms of pottery and local metal types. Such local groupings do not deserve the name of a culture, but should rather be considered in terms of patterns of social interaction and exchange at more local levels within the framework of the larger regional cultures. Plesl has put his finger on the problem in a recent critique of the many Urnfield cultural classifications, asking the question:

> Ob z. B. in der jungbronzezeitlichen Periode in Böhmen nebeneinander so viele nach ihrer Kultur unterschiedliche Menschengruppen gelebt haben konnten – d. h. die Kultur der Lausitzer Urnenfelder, Knoviz und Milavce-Kulturen, die Egergruppe, nach unsere zeitgenössischen Klassifizierung.

After pointing out the tendency to overlook shared cultural traits he concludes that instead of looking for differences:

> Gerade jene Merkmale und Züge hervorgehoben werden sollten, die sie in
> grössere Komplexe verbinden, so dass sie der angenommenen historischen
> Realität besser entsprechen wurden. (Plesl 1987, 11)

These questions will be treated more fully in later chapters when discussing the
nature of regional and local networks of social interaction. But let me finally add one
small observation: the employment of the culture concept to characterise local and
regional groups declines from East Central Europe to Scandinavia, where local and
regional groups are never named, except in northern Germany (the Sprockhoff
tradition), but here 'groups' replace 'cultures'.

In conclusion one may say that the Montelius tradition has won and has come into
full play. But by losing its theoretical framework, as represented by Kossinna, it also
became sterile, a continuing exercise in typological and documentary perfection,
since there were no clearly formulated theoretical and historical problems to define
relevance and orientation. Although the Kossinna approach has been rightly
criticised, it represented an attempt to give historical meaning to the archaeological
data. In a humorous essay by Michael Gebühr, describing an imagined meeting
between Montelius and Kossinna on a cloud north of the Alps in the 1980s to take
stock of the situation seventy-five years after their time, the frustration of Kossinna is
played out:

> 'Spezialisierung! Das ist es eben.' Kossinna platzt der Kragen. Er macht eine
> grosse Geste. 'Wohin wir blicken, der gleiche kalte Kaffee. Die Nadeln der
> frühen Lapatutti-Kultur! Die Riemenzungen im Blabla Gebiet, – man kommt
> sich vor wie in einem Kurzwarengeschäft. Fehlt nur doch: Die Drahtreste der
> augehenden Urnenfelderzeit . . .'
>
> '. . . im Neuwiederbecken. Habe ich gerade gelesen. Nicht uninteressant.'
> Ein nicht näher genannt sein wollender unlängst verstorbener Typologe
> flattert vorüber.
>
> '. . . dann wären wir komplett.' Kossinna starrt ihm verzweifelt nach.
>
> 'Was wollen Sie?' Montelius wird ernst. 'Typologie und Chronologie sind
> nun mal die Voraussetzungen für alle weiteren historischen Untersuchungen.'
>
> 'Aber nach Jahrzehnten wird es doch wohl . . . verdammt noch mal' –
> leichtes Donnern aus dem Alpenvorland – 'bei allen guten Geistern',
> korrigiert Kossinna, 'wird es wohl endlich möglich sein, mal über die
> Voraussetzungen hinauszukommen.'

After some more conversation Kossinna's frustration reaches a peak:

> 'Die Leute ersaufen im Material. Wer grosse historische überblicke und
> problemorientierte Zusammenfassungen gibt, schreibt doch meist die alten
> Schinken ab. Und wer arbeitet denn noch problemorientiert? . . . Immer das
> gleiche Schema: Was für Typen habe ich gefunden? Wie alt? Wie Verbreitet?
> . . . Jede Grabungstechniker kann das leisten. Jeder Mittelschüler, wenn er
> mal das armselige bischen Prinzip kapiert hat.'
>
> 'Aber Herr Kollege', erzürnt sich nun Montelius, 'ich muss doch bitten . . .

Mein Werk, die Methode betreffend . . .'

'Von wegen Methode', diesmal unterbricht Kossinna erregt den schwedischen Altmeister. 'Ja, Methoden haben die Herrschaften da unten noch. Das haben ich mir genau angesehen. Aber was für methoden.' . . . 'Nicht einen Schritt ist man über Ihren geschlossenen Fund hinausgekommen.' . . .

'Das muss ich Ihnen leider recht geben, Herr Kollege', seufzt Montelius zwar ein wenig geschmeichelt, aber im übrigen Traurig. 'Nenneswert weiter gekommen sind die nicht.' (after Gebühr 1987, with some abbreviations)

The constraints of the Three Age System

The Three Age System is a metaphor for any arbitrary cultural and chronological divisions, beginning when C. J. Thomsen (Figure 8) introduced the technological division of Stone, Bronze and Iron Ages in 1837. This is not to deny the necessity of chronological and geographical groupings. My aim here is to focus attention on the way in which such categories have implicitly formed, and to some extent distorted, historical conceptions of the past. This subject has been given a fuller treatment recently by Michael Rowlands (1984a, 1989), where it is pointed out that the major social and economic changes do not occur at the transitions between technological stages, as has often been implicitly assumed. Instead they occur some time after. In a summary of recent research he proposes that the Late Neolithic/Early Bronze Age form a continuum and the same is true of the Late Bronze Age/Early Iron Age. This points to some basic problems inherent in all periodisations.

Archaeologists, like historians, are trapped by a paradox: on the one hand the evidence is rich and suited for social reconstructions and historical explanations, on the other hand to do this properly makes it necessary to concentrate on rather short periods of time or to limit oneself to small regions. The sheer quantity of material that nowadays has to be ordered and analysed makes scholarly specialisation unavoidable. In this way most social reconstructions tend to become static, neglecting explanations of social and historical change on a larger temporal and spatial scale. The broader view is thus limited to a few common sense reflections at the end of a thesis, or is presented in popular books.

Another unintended consequence of chronological and geographical divisions is the inherent tendency to confine and define academic specialisation within such boxes. Over the past hundred years such specialisations have become increasingly narrow. The obvious problem is that the forces of history are not constrained by academic boundaries. To be understood they demand to be traced, both in time and in space, beyond cultural and chronological borders. It is exactly what happens between archaeological periods that has to be explained. The Urnfield period did not come out of the Urnfield period, it is not self-explanatory. Its genesis is to be located in changes preceding it, e.g. during the late Tumulus Culture. The problem is, however, that we can only perceive changes when they have taken place. This raises both methodological and theoretical problems.

In methodological terms major changes or transformations are often accompanied

Fig. 8 C. J. Thomsen (1788–1865) founded the first archaeological museum in the world in Copenhagen. By introducing systematic principles of find recording and recovery he laid the groundwork for archaeology, exemplified in his documentation of the technological and chronological evolution of Stone, Bronze and Iron Ages.

by similar changes in the archaeological record, e.g. from barrow burials to flat grave cemeteries, from hilltop settlements to lowland occupation, etc. It means that no unified methodological framework can be applied. In terms of settlement sites, catchment analysis can of course be employed irrespective of the nature of the settlement, whether it is upland or lowland. But we still have to adjust the parameters and change the underlying interpretative framework.

Most archaeological methods can only be applied within a specific social and cultural context that defines the significance of the observed variation. An analysis of burial wealth has to take into consideration that a change in burial ritual, e.g. from inhumation to cremation, may also entail a change in the conception of the significance of burial and of burial wealth. Therefore one cannot automatically compare a quantitative analysis of burial wealth if it encompasses a change from inhumation to cremation. Wealth often disappears from burials in periods of cremation, but does it mean that these people were poorer or rather that they did not want to deposit their wealth in this way any more? It could also be that instead it was deposited or consumed in other ways, e.g. through ritual hoarding or potlatches, as has been proposed for the Bronze Age (Hundt 1955; Kristiansen 1991, fig. 2.3).

This implies that one cannot fully understand and explain variations in burial rituals without considering their relationship to other types of ritual. Burials represent an archaeological and cultural context, but this is only part of a larger context of ritual and religion that may manifest itself materially in a number of other ways. A holistic approach is therefore necessary if we want to be able to translate archaeological evidence into social and historical categories, and if we want to explain variation in terms of changes in social organisation. In this respect theory is the only unifying framework that allows us to transcend and give social and historical meaning to major changes in the archaeological record (Chapter 2.3). The tendency in European archaeology for practitioners to specialise not only in certain periods and regions, but also in certain archaeological categories, such as burials or hoards, or even in single types of objects, is therefore disruptive for a social and historical interpretation of the results obtained by such work, if it is not counterbalanced by theoretical and historical anthropological insights into the nature of social organisation and change in pre-state societies (Chapter 3).

The explanation of change, as defined by archaeological periods and cultures, is also confronted by a theoretical and interpretative problem of a different nature. Social and cultural changes cannot be fully observed until they have actually taken place and have materialised. Their genesis in a preceding period is, however, difficult to observe. There is often little in the earlier period to suggest that a major change was under way. This is probably due to our definitions of archaeological periods and cultures in terms of ideological and ritual evidence. Most cultures and periods in the Bronze Age are defined by stylistic patterns on metal objects (prestige goods) and on fine pottery, plus recurrent combinations of such objects in burials. Changes in ritual are often used as supplementary diagnostic features. The difficulty of observing changes before they have materialised therefore suggests that ritual and ideological manifestations in the material record tend to conceal changes that are under way. As long as possible they try to convey the impression that everything is as it used to be. Indeed, the basic Marxist idea of contradiction implies that material culture should be able to reflect different and even opposing trends, e.g. between ideology and economy. The often contrastive changes in the archaeological record between periods and cultures are a reflection of these ideological functions, which may even continue some time after the social changes have taken place. Walter Torbrügge pointed to the problem in a discussion of the transition between the Early and Middle Bronze Age (Br. A2 to Br. B) (1976b9, 3):

> Unbestritten bleibt das späte A-Funde nicht mit dem sogenannten
> Hügelgräbermilieu der Stufe Bz B zu verbinden sind. Ebenso unbestritten ist
> die feste Verknüpfung aller B-Funde untereinander. Zwischen beiden Stufen
> bestehen als Folge eines komplizierten Wandlungsprozesses . . .
> unverkennbare Gegensätze. Diese Kulturhistorische Wechselerscheinungen
> lassen sich durch das antiquarische Ordnungssystem allein nicht aufklären.

It is therefore necessary to focus on settlement and economic evidence if one wishes to trace the genesis of change in the preceding period, as they will often show that things are not as they used to be, and that changes are already under way. Once again it points to the need to employ a holistic approach and to consider all the available evidence (Figure 9).

We may conclude that periodisations and specialisation are inevitable, a necessary

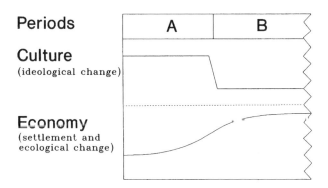

Fig. 9 Different modes of change in economy (economic practice) and material culture (symbolic and ideological order). While the economy gradually changes, ideological order is maintained through material culture.

outcome of the amount of data and the need to bring order to it. But this should not proceed blindly, as the tendency has often been, and the definition of cultures should be critically re-evaluated. After all, it is the answers to historical questions that ought to determine the relevance and nature of more fine-grained classifications of the evidence, rather than the reverse situation, where definitions of cultures and chronological periods are considered an independent exercise upon which interpretations can be built. It has to be realised by archaeology that culture-historical and social interpretations cannot be completely separated from the definition of cultures and chronologies (Navarette and Garcia 1983), just as it has to be admitted that in contrast to periodisations based on absolute datings, now becoming more frequent, those founded on typology cannot define periods shorter than some sixty years (Kristiansen 1985a; Eggert, Kurz and Wotza 1980). These problems are highlighted by the fine-grained Late Hallstatt and La Tène chronology, to which we shall return later.[1]

2.2 Geographical and chronological framework

Geography and climate
Geography defines the physical boundaries to history. Although erosion and historical changes of vegetation add important constraints that determine local economic conditions, the basic topographic framework has remained unchanged. At the macro-level we may profitably even consider some present vegetational variations as being relevant to our understanding of both the potential of, and the limitations to, prehistoric subsistance. In Figure 10 these basic parameters are presented. To begin with geography, the major river systems always served as routes of communication and transport. In northern and central Europe they define four recurring interaction zones:

(1) The western route connects southwest Europe north of the Alps with north-western Europe by way of the Weser and the Rhine. From here connections either lead on towards southeast Britain and the Thames or follow the North Sea coast up to Jutland and western Norway. To the south the Rhone leads on to the Mediterranean.

(2) The Elbe/Oder line connects Denmark and the western Baltic with Bohemia, the Carpathians and beyond. The lower Elbe, however, also played a part in the western interaction zone, giving the area around the Elbe 'knee' a central position throughout most of prehistory.

(3) Finally, southern Scandinavia and the central Baltic formed a lowland interaction zone with eastern Europe, stretching to the Black Sea and the area north of the Carpathians, with the Vistula, Dnieper and Dniester river systems as connecting lines.

Taken together, these three interaction zones linked northern Europe with both central and eastern Europe, the connections being reflected in recurring distribution patterns of both metalwork and settlement. In some periods one zone dominated, at other times another, but each was always active, since they were connected by such major, and usually stable, settlement concentrations.

(4) The main east–west communication vein in Europe is, of course, the Danube, connecting eastern and western Europe from the Black Sea to southwestern Europe north of the Alps. On its way the Danube links with both the Elbe and the Rhine, as well as sending important tributaries into the Balkans and the Carpathians. Again, this is reflected in recurring distribution patterns of metalwork and settlements. Other European river systems mainly served regional needs connecting coastal and inland areas.

Sea communications also played a major role in shaping cultural connections during the Bronze Age. The waters of southern Scandinavia and the Baltic undoubtedly helped to maintain the strong Nordic cultural traditions present throughout most of its history, just as the Atlantic seaboard was in certain periods unified by common cultural traditions based on maritime communication from Ireland to Iberia. The Mediterranean, on the contrary, was too vast and discontinuous to serve the same functions, and only the maritime skills of the Bronze Age civilisations of the Eastern Mediterranean allowed them to operate throughout the whole Mediterranean, and this systematically only from the 1st millennium BC onwards.

The major vegetational zones had an important influence on Bronze Age society (Figure 10). Of general economic significance are the geographical limits of certain trees and crops. One of the most important is the Mediterranean olive/vine complex, whose westward expansion and economic significance is linked to the Bronze Age (Renfrew 1972), but is only certainly present in the western Mediterranean from the 1st millennium BC. In temperate Europe the dry steppe environment in the Pontic area north of the Black Sea, and on the Hungarian plain, had important social and historical consequences in terms of pastoral expansion, as we shall see. The River Tisza represents the western limit to pastoral settlement, although temporary raids frequently reached further west. The light soils of the north European lowlands and of the upland British Isles also favoured the development of dry grasslands and heath vegetation, and thus animal husbandry, during the Bronze Age. To this we must add the location of the major copper and tin deposits in Europe (Figure 11).

Climate is another unstable constant (Figure 12). It remained largely stable within

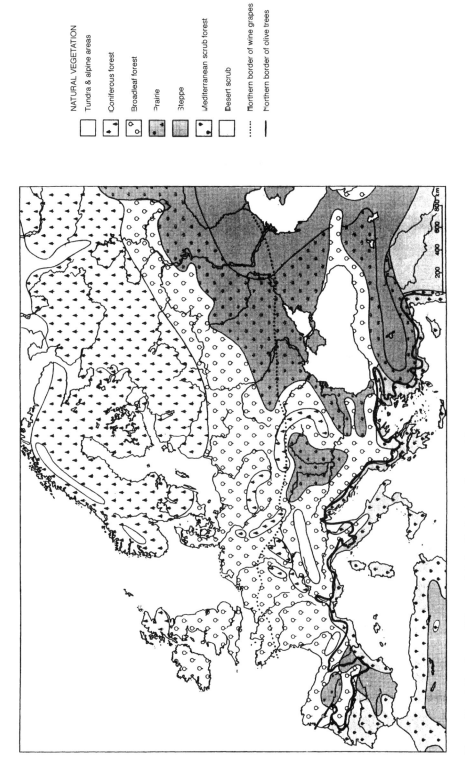

NATURAL VEGETATION

Tundra & alpine areas

Coniferous forest

Broadleaf forest

Prairie

Steppe

Mediterranean scrub forest

Desert scrub

Northern border of wine grapes

Northern border of olive trees

0   200   400   600   800 km

Fig. 10 Vegetational map of Europe, defining the basic environmental zones

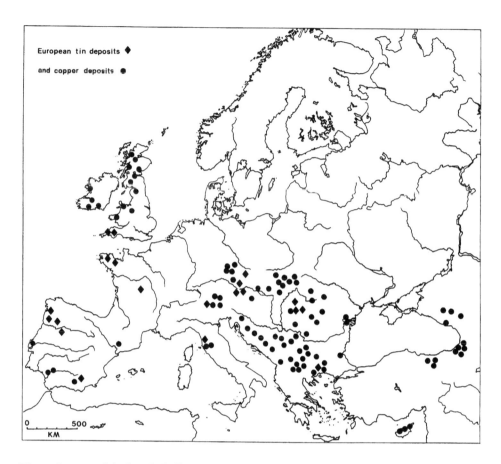

European tin deposits ◆

and copper deposits ●

0   500
KM

Fig. 11 Copper and tin deposits in Europe.

the period under study, but it has been subject to cyclical fluctuations, some of them with significant economic and historical consequences (Aabye 1976; Harding 1982; Wigley, Ingram and Farmer 1981). These have been discussed in several studies, especially those of Jan Bouzek (1982), who has linked dry/wet and warm/cool periods to expansions and regressions during the Bronze Age. The two most important dry periods were during the Earlier Bronze Age (Late A1–A2/B1) and in the Urnfield period. The general tendency in a primitive farming economy is for dry and warm periods to favour more intensive agriculture in lowland areas (reflected in riverine and lake shore settlement), while cooler and more humid conditions promoted upland grazing and flooded lake shore and riverine settlements, thereby preserving them. Recent research has filled out the picture of past climate, showing that there were also fluctuations during the dry and wet periods (Aabye 1976; Bouzek 1993). In general precipitation is high along the Atlantic seaboard and in the Alps, and lower to the east, with central and eastern Iberia and the steppe regions north of the Black and Caspian Seas being especially dry.

These general geographical observations may seem obvious, yet experience has

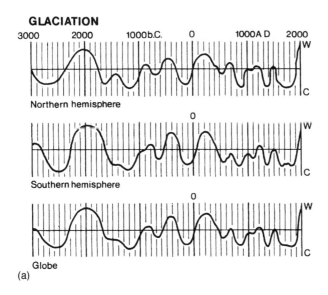

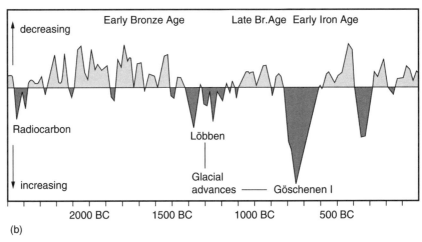

Fig. 12 (a)Climatic fluctuations based upon glacial advances and retreats, reflecting respectively cold (C) and warm (W) periods. (b) More detailed climatic fluctuations for the period 2500 BC–0, based on variations in C14, reflecting cooler and warmer periods.

taught us that they are too often forgotten. For example, the study of distribution maps may cross several geographical and climatic boundaries without any notice being taken of such variations in subsequent interpretations.

Chronology and dating

For the sake of convenience I shall summarise the cultural and chronological framework employed throughout the book in a separate section. Since there exist a number of regional chronological frameworks, it is necessary to compare them, which I have done in Figure 13A–C. I have restricted myself to the major regional systems – for the Nordic area that of Montelius, for central Europe the Reinecke framework in its

A

Absolute dates BC	Central Europe	Northern Europe	Western Europe	Northern Italy	Greece	
— 2300						
	Br.A1a EBA I	Late Neol. I	Middle Beaker Phase		Early Helladic III	
1950						
	Br.A1b EBA II	Late Neol. II	Late Beaker Wessex I	Early Bronze Age (antica)	Middle Helladic I/II	
	Classical Unetice		(Bush Barrow)		Middle Helladic IIIAB	(1775)
1700	Br. A2 EBA III	Period IA (Fårdrup)	Wessex II (Arreton)		Late Helladic IAB	(1700)
1600				Middle Bronze Age (media)	Late Helladic IAB	(1625)
	Br. B1 Tumulus	Period IB (Sögel–Wohlde)	(Acton Park 1)		Late Helladic IIA	(1550)
1500	Br. B2	IIa	Middle Bronze Age (Acton Park 2)		Late Helladic IIB	(1450)
1400		Period IIbc		"Terramare"	Late Helladic IIIA	
	Br. C		(Taunton)			
1300					LH IIIB	(1330)

B

Absolute dates BC	Central Europe	Northern Europe	Western Europe	Northern Italy	Greece
— 1300					
	Br. D	II Period III	Bronze Final I (Rosnoen/ Penard)	"Terramare"	Late Helladic IIIB
1200					
	Ha A1		Bronze Final IIa (Penard)	Late Bronze Age (recente)	Late Helladic IIIC
1100					
	Ha A2	Period IV	BF IIb (Wilburton)	Final Bronze Age/ (final)	Sub Mycenean
1000					
	Ha B1		BF IIIa (Broadward)	Proto– Villanova	Proto Geometric
950/900					
	Ha B2	Period V	BF IIIb	Este I Villanova I	Early Geometric
800					
	Ha B3		(Ewart Park/ Carps–Tongue)	Este II Villanova II	Late Geometric
750/700					
	Ha C	Period VI	Early Hallstatt (Llynfawr/ Armorican axes)	Este III AB Villanova III	Orientalizing
600					

Fig. 13 The major chronological systems for the Bronze and Early Iron Ages in Europe: (A) Early and Middle Bronze Age; (B) Late Bronze Age and Early Iron Age; (C) Early Iron Age.

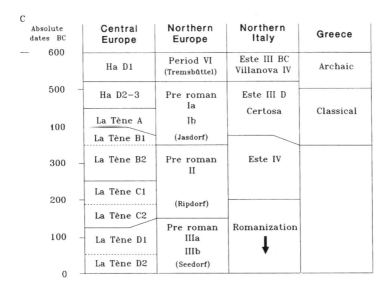

Fig. 13 (*continued*)

present form, for the Atlantic the combined French–British system, and for the Mediterranean the Greek and Villanovan chronologies. In eastern Europe there are several overlapping regional dating systems, but I have chosen to apply the Reinecke framework here as well. For the Iron Age I have further simplified matters by employing the La Tène scheme generally.

I shall not enter into a discussion of the details of each system, but rather point out some of the major areas of debate where adjustments have taken place, or where there are still unresolved problems. Generally the Bronze Age chronology is so well grounded that no major changes can be expected. The chronological system, and the absolute datings given to it, rest on three cornerstones: the typological method of relative chronology to establish regional chronological sequences; the historical-comparative method of cross-dating to establish chronological fixed points; and C14 and dendrochronological datings of samples of organic material to establish an absolute internal chronology. Each of these methods presents specific types of methodological problem, as does their combination. In general terms, the absolute datings provided by dendrochronology and C14 are used as chronological markers to which the regional cultural sequences can be linked by way of typology and cross-dating.

(1) The typological method is well established, and reliable when applied correctly. This is the case in most of Bronze Age Europe, due to the quantity of material and the consequent high statistical probability of eliminating random variation. Its weak points are at periods between transitions, when burial and rituals of deposition can change so drastically that it becomes difficult to define continuity. A cultural/ritual change may then sometimes be mistaken for a chronological change. For example, Early Bronze Age chronology, from being based on hoards and a few burial finds,

shifts its emphasis to burials with the advent of the Tumulus Culture. This makes it difficult to cross-date certain types of object. The transition from Ha B3 to Ha C represents another such change in burial ritual and material culture. Finally, there exist conserving and innovating areas, which means that overlaps between periods should be expected, e.g. Montelius II continuing on the Danish Islands after the beginning of Montelius III in Jutland (Randsborg 1968; Kristiansen 1985a).

The relationship between settlement chronologies and hoard/burial chronologies may also be problematic. Settlements depend on pottery dating, therefore periods with little pottery in burials represent a problem, making it hard to combine the two. We may add to this the problem that the duration of occupation phases at settlements is not always easy to determine.

(2) Historical cross-datings represent an absolute chronological anchor, although not as precise as once believed. The sample of datings is usually small and uneven, raising the degree of statistical insecurity concerning the representativity of the results obtained. Müller-Karpe's work is still the foundation for the Central European Bronze Age in relation to Greek and east Mediterranean chronology (1959, Abb. 64). There are fixed points connecting the two areas in the Early/Middle Bronze Age and from the Late Bronze Age/Early Iron Age onwards. The method raises a further methodological problem: the circulation time of imports before they are deposited fluctuates. Periods of economic expansion will see rapid deposition and short circulation time, while in recessions prestige goods are kept above ground for longer periods (Kristiansen 1985a). In most circumstances short circulation time ensures reliable cross-datings, and especially so because the speed of trade and information exchange in Bronze Age Europe was high, there are virtually no delays in the spread of trends across Europe. In a Dark Age, however, the prolonged circulation time of prestige goods may create dates that are too old.

Adjustments to the Greek chronology have taken place at the transition between Middle and Late Helladic, that is the beginning of the Shaft Grave period. New C14 dates suggest a higher chronology, setting the transition at 1700 BC, while the traditional dating favours 1600 BC (e.g. Warren and Hankey 1989, table 3.1). I have chosen the higher dating (Manning 1988; Dietz 1992, fig. 93), which corresponds well to the central and west European chronologies (Becker, Krause and Kromer 1989; Sperber 1987, except that I do not follow Sperber's redefinitions). Recently the chronology of the 'centuries of darkness' after 1200 BC has come under some attack (James *et al.* 1991). The suggestion is made by James *et al.* to extend the pre-Dark Age periods down into the Dark Age. This solution has been widely criticised, although the problem of the lack of material from the Dark Age in the Near East and the eastern Mediterranean has been generally acknowledged. In relation to Central Europe, one would instead expect the later Dark Age periods to become older, closing the gap from 'below' rather than 'above' the fault line. For now I have maintained the traditional datings, supported by C14 (Manning and Weninger 1992).

For the Hallstatt period the works of Zürn (1974), Parzinger (1988) and Pare (1989a) have created a fairly firm chronology, although there are still discussions about the overlap between sub-periods, which will be dealt with later in relation to the culture-history of the particular period. The La Tène chronology is widely accepted, due to the many fixed points.

(3) The debate over the calibration of C14 dates has now finally been resolved by the extension of dendrochronological dates back into the Bronze Age and the Neolithic, in combination with a more fine-grained calibration curve (Pearson 1987). Problems of individual C14 dates are still mostly linked to the lack of precise context and/or the own age of samples. However, we are now obtaining sequences of dates from both settlements and cemeteries, which have solved most of the earlier discrepancies (recently published extensively in Gonzalez, Lull and Risch 1992, tables A–E and chapter 3.2). Unfortunately, between 800 and 400 BC the calibration curve is flat, making calibration more or less impossible.

The Alpine lake dwelling dates represent the cornerstone of Bronze Age dendro-chronology (Becker *et al.* 1985; the main results are given in *Antiqua* 15, 1986 by Ryoff and Rychner, and by Gallay and Rageth; Bocquet, Marguet and Orcel 1987). I follow these dendrochronological dates, where possible, supplemented for the north by dendro-dates for the oak coffin burials of Montelius II, and recent archaeological adjustments of Early Bronze Age chronology (Vandkilde 1988, 1990, fig. 1; Randsborg 1991).

On the whole there is now a correspondence between traditional datings, well-defined C14 dates and dendrochronology. Today the Central and North European chronology is the most reliable, compared both to the Mediterranean and to western Europe. The most radical change to the traditional chronology is the extension of the prelude to the Bronze Age (Early Reinecke A1) back to 2300 BC, while the classic Unetice Culture (Late Reinecke A1), as represented by the princely burials of Leubingen and Helmsdorf, has been dendrochronologically dated to around 1900 BC (Becker *et al.* 1989). This marks the beginning of the Bronze Age proper. From here there is a good match between the three dating methods until the Late Bronze Age, where the later Urnfield sequence has been set between fifty and a hundred years older than generally suggested. In Scandinavia C14 dates are following a similar pattern, e.g. the princely burial from Håga in Central Sweden, of developed Period IV, is now dated to c. 1000 BC (Lamm 1989, fig. 3). In general the good old typologists Müller-Karpe and Montelius have been proven right in their once rather controversial absolute datings.

3

Theoretical context

3.1 Contextualising archaeological theory

As long as archaeology remained a small discipline operating within a rather well-defined and homogeneous framework of museums and a few university departments theoretical and methodological consensus could be maintained. With the expansion of university departments, the increase in the number of students and not least the popularity of conservation archaeology, placing archaeology firmly within a political context of legislation and administration, the conditions of archaeological work changed, and with that also the possibility of maintaining a unified framework. The theoretical and philosophical debates of other humanistic disciplines, such as history, sociology, anthropology etc., began to make their impact, just as the uses of the past in the present became a major concern. As archaeology developed into a rapidly growing academic industry market forces also came into play, both in terms of popularisation and in terms of promoting new and more interesting approaches, new journals, etc. – all healthy signs of an expanding discipline. In this sense archaeological theory can be seen as a marketplace offering a variety of approaches to the past. However, such approaches are not free-floating commodities to be chosen at random, they bring with them a number of social and historical implications, since they are rooted in different perceptions of the world and in different historical traditions. It is this relationship between practice and perception that determines the relevance and usefulness of the various approaches. Instead of starting a theoretical battle of incompatible arguments for one approach against another, they should be contextualised historically and philosophically, as this determines the relevance and meaning of arguments.

The theoretical cycle
Within the past ten years archaeology, along with other anthropological and humanistic disciplines, has witnessed attempts at deconstructing basic theoretical categories and their underlying premises, especially evolutionary and functionalist/ecological paradigms. They are replaced by contingency and historical particularism, by individualism and culturalism. It has to be realised, however, that this is neither unique nor to be understood within a purely academic rationality.

During the past 150 years we can observe a cyclical shift between generalising, teleological frameworks and particularising, non-deterministic frameworks, with middle positions in the form of functionalism and structuralism (Figure 14). Thus the second half of the 19th century was dominated by evolutionary frameworks,

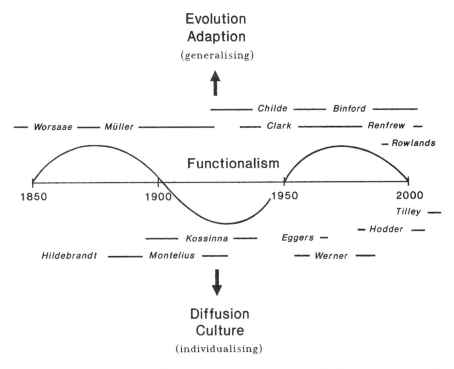

Fig. 14 The theoretical cycle oscillating between evolutionary and diffusionist, generalising and particularising interpretations of the past and the present.

based on the new insights of natural science (Darwinian selection and evolution, geological principles), and the social and archaeological disciplines (progressive evolution from Stone Age to Civilisation). In the context of the imperialistic expansion of western capitalism, it was applied to support an ideology of the superiority of the west. With the consolidation of the global world order new forms of colonialism and nationalism came to dominate. Academically it led to a new focus on the particular, identity, variation and diffusion. In anthropology it was originally presented as a reaction against the exclusion of historical and cultural variation from the evolutionary framework, an attempt to give voice to the cultural context and its underlying ideas and beliefs (e.g. the Boas school). Very soon, however, it was applied in a national-historical context to support claims for continuities between past and present, and in support of diffusionist claims about the spread of civilisation. As demonstrated in Chapter 2, this framework was dominant until recently in Europe, though stripped of its theoretical superstructure. The new optimism after World War II, however, set the climate for a reintroduction of evolutionary and ecological frameworks, which in archaeology became linked to positivism in order to create a scientific basis for social and ecological regularities. It is this framework which is now under attack in a climate of lack of faith in the future, economic fragmentation and ethnic revivals.

With this short summary I have intended to set the scene for a discussion of the underlying academic rationality of these opposing trends and the way they may be seen to be linked to global changes in ideological climate and economic conditions. In recent works Friedman has proposed that the dominance of one or the other is determined by civilisational cycles of hegemony and cultural identity (1989). At a macrohistorical level he sees a cyclical regularity between historical conditions in the present and our perception of culture and history. Modernism and homogeneous perceptions (evolutionism, universalistic categories) come with periods of centralisation and political hegemony, whereas pluralism, and stresses on cultural identity occur in periods of decentralisation, fragmentation and lack of confidence in overriding or universalistic perceptions (Figure 15).

Obviously this is a gross generalisation, the aim of which is to situate academic traditions in their historical context, implying that academic developments and internal rationalities are related, at a deeper (or higher) level, quite naturally, to conditions in the present. There are deviations, of course, as in some disciplines or regions old traditions may continue due to specific historical conditions, e.g. marginalisation and exclusion from the general trends of academic change, as in the case of archaeology in Central Europe. We have to forge an interaction between two perceptions of history, culture and society that are complementary, but have been separated by different research traditions. It follows from this that we should pay some attention to the potential social and ideological implications of different academic research traditions. Having made this point, we can continue to explore their underlying rationalities and social implications. By doing so we soon learn that both traditions have been criticised for being reactionary and manipulative in their world views. Particularists criticise generalists for trying to impose a western world hegemony on the rest of the globe by insisting on understanding all cultural and historical variation within a western, universalistic framework of evolution, positivism or whatever. This deprives other cultures of their identity and deprives us of the possibility of understanding new aspects of 'the other' whether they are long dead or still alive. Attempts to make the world accessible in more systematic and objective ways (positivism) are branded as denying the object of study its historical and cultural particularity. In similar ways the particularists and culturalists are criticised for deconstructing the wholeness into so many different parts that it ultimately deprives us of the ability to understand the conditions of social and historical change. The creation of particularised, local or national identities further serves reactionary forces, preventing people from understanding the real conditions of their own lives and the forces governing them. So in a paradoxical way the attempts to restore local cultural identities that had been lost during the process of colonisation run the risk of leading on to a romantic or even a constructed historical understanding, mystifying historical conditions.

Thus the intellectual history of the past few hundred years has taught us that history is shaped by the conditions and interests of our own time. This has in recent years led to a dangerous relativism and pessimism in learning. But we have to accept the subjective foundations of knowledge without losing faith in the possibility of creating knowledge that is real and not subject to any kind of manipulation. I do not propose to return to a kind of rather naive or innocent optimism of the

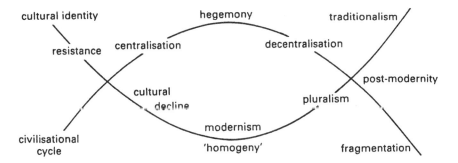

Fig. 15 Civilisational cycles of hegemony and cultural identity.

positive role of the humanities in supporting the present; the social and humanistic disciplines have quite clearly come to play the role of the critical voice in the present. With this comes a self-reflective awareness of the intellectual history and ideological frameworks that have shaped our traditions of learning and knowledge (Chapter 2). But it does not deny the possibility of contributing to our understanding of the past in more objective ways. This implies the employment of general theoretical categories, a search for historical regularities in all their variation and an attempt to explain them within a general framework of social theory, without falling into the deterministic trap of reducing all variation to a universal set of causes. At a certain level of analysis social and economic regularities are undeniable realities, but this does not reduce their explanation to a single or recurrent set of causes. Consequently I consider the critique against general theory as giving the answers beforehand to be both misleading and mistaken. It may be true in some cases, either because of bad research or because the evidence is not good enough to resist theory and therefore cannot enter into a dialogue with it. But neither bad research nor bad evidence should be the standard by which we judge the validity of our scientific approaches and procedures, nor should we abandon them uncritically; on the contrary, it should lead us to improve them. By this I do not want to deny some of the problems created by employing general theoretical categories (Kristiansen in press). But I refuse to naively abandon theoretical and historical insights achieved over the past hundred years, since all theories and explanations are to some extent dogmatic, deterministic and ideological. If they were not they could be neither historic nor scientific.

The current trend towards deconstruction, particularism and culturalism entails some important insights when coupled with and balanced against its apparent opposition – general theory and materialist perspectives. But taken at face value, as a one-sided oppositional strategy, it has to be rejected, both for theoretical and for ideological reasons, since it represents a revival of approaches which historically have proved to be only too well suited for reactionary, nationalist and chauvinistic purposes, due to the fact that the significance of historical transformations of social and economic structures is relegated to a secondary position at the expense of cultural continuities and traditions.

The position offered here implies that explanation and interpretation proceed in a dialectical interaction between data and theoretical concepts enabling us to frame the evidence and link it to the underlying principles and historical dynamics producing it. It rejects relativism and subjectivism, as well as scientific absolutism and objectivism. It takes a 'realistic' middle position, where knowledge is constituted in a systematic and dialectical process, a series of successive approximations that are subject to some degree of verification, falsification and interpretative rigour that transcends subjectivity and objectivity (Rowlands 1984b; Wylie 1989). Although it may be claimed with some justification that historical knowledge is an accumulating process, or at least has been so during the past hundred years, its nature and direction form part of competing historical cycles of ideological and political interests, embedded in different research traditions characterised by different approaches to basic epistemological problems of relevance and historical priorities. In that sense the choice of theoretical framework is not neutral. It stresses the importance of understanding the historical context of theory, but it also recognises the need to transcend such constraints in an attempt to establish a meaningful dialogue of theoretical principles that is not governed by strategic and competitive opposition.

To overcome some of these constraints I propose to consider research traditions not only within their social and historical setting, but also in terms of their academic context, as defined by their efforts to come to terms with and solve certain kinds of problem. In the next section I therefore provide a short theoretical background to the context underlying this work.

The theoretical context
Theoretically this book situates itself within the general reorientation of archaeology often called 'processual' or 'New Archaeology'. It deviates from it in its rejection of the more extreme positivist claims to developing and testing ahistorical so-called general laws and of its mechanistic perception of the world. In similar ways it deviates from the contextual claims to historical particularism and from its cultural reductionism.[1] There is no easy way to reduce the complexity of interpretation, and certainly not on the geographical and temporal scale of this book. The theoretical framework serves as a background, as a conceptual set of tools to think with. They are not to be used as boxes into which to fit data according to a test procedure, but as tools with which to understand data. For the same reason there will be no formulation of deductive hypotheses followed by test criteria, although this may be useful in other circumstances. Generalisations are useful shorthand for much more complex historical processes, whose interpretation is an intellectual process that cannot be reduced to a simple one-dimensional test procedure, or to the identification of a predefined social typology. My aim is to identify regularities in the archaeological record that correspond to a number of basic social and economic strategies, vertically in terms of the internal structure of the evidence, horizontally in terms of cultural distributions. This includes the identification of migrations versus exchange mechanisms as agents of expansion, acculturation and change. The approach is holistic, trying to employ all

categories of evidence. There will thus be little methodological rigour in the articulation of data and interpretation, except in a few case studies; the book is basically an
interpretative and explanatory sketch, a kind of first approximation to a historical
understanding of the Bronze Age and Early Iron Age. Although I have attempted to
let the particular properties of the various regional and temporal sequences come into
play, reduction is inevitable, as in any historical interpretation. I present here the
theoretical background, which gives the general guidelines to interpretation, enabling the reader to confront the two and make up his or her own mind.

The theoretical approach is rooted within the tradition of structural marxism[2],
supplemented by later developments. I shall briefly discuss some basic concepts
before proceeding to a presentation of social theory.

Social reproduction   Social reproduction is considered the object of analysis.
It is derived from the discussion of production and reproduction in the later works of
Marx (*Grundrisse*, *Critique of Political Economy*, *The Capital*), where production/
appropriation, exchange/distribution and consumption were seen as interlocked
processes that allowed of no priority of one over the other, as discussed by Friedman
(1976b). The object of analysis then becomes systems of social reproduction, which
are not defined a priori, neither theoretically as social formations containing various
modes of production nor in terms of boundaries. However, they have to be constituted in concrete analyses which specify those relations 'that dominate the processes of production and circulation and which therefore constitute the socially
determined form by which populations reproduce themselves as economic entities'
(Friedman and Rowlands 1977, 203).

Determination   The concept of determination is introduced to account for
constraints that do not allow the system to reproduce itself within its given social and
ecological environment: these may result in the emergence of contradictions between
different social groups (intra-systemic contradictions) and between different functions, e.g. a given social strategy and the economy necessary to support it (inter-
systemic contradictions). Such constraints, however, are often the result of social
strategies whose unintended consequences in the long term create new conditions of
production (e.g. a changed ecology) that are incompatible with the dominant social
organisation. In this way a society may create the conditions for its own transformation. Thus it is the social relations of production that dominate and hence determine the formation of such constraints and their impact on social developments. It
follows from this that the location and definition of contradictions between the
various 'levels' is crucial in order to define those historical moments where incom-
patibilities, e.g. those between a certain social strategy and its economic basis, can be
observed or implied. Likewise the consequences of such 'systemic' contradictions for
social organisation, e.g. in terms of increasing economic exploitation, warfare etc.,
represent an important focus of research. This is not to say that all change is to be
explained by contradictions, although social life is never as smooth as we are taught

to believe. Also, external factors may impose new conditions, which however, only shifts the problem of locating its causes and underlying contradictions to another area, once again stressing the need to consider change in terms of larger interacting structures.

Transformation   In a historical and evolutionary sense determination can be seen as resulting from the interaction between local, regional and global processes of reproduction defining a set of determining historical conditions with a range of evolutionary options, suggesting that prediction (or postdiction) in a non-rigorous statistical sense is possible. There are choices and options, but in principle their range of variation should be definable, at least at the level of macrohistory. There is no determination in that certain stages must be passed through, only the starting point remains universal. Evolution is multi-linear and multi-directional, constituted by cyclical processes of evolution and devolution. The historical and geopolitical balance between processes of evolution and devolution determines when transformations take place. It represents a cluster of qualitative changes that are able to dominate and reorganise the structure of ancient world systems. Such a definition implies that transformation is a result of multiple changes on a large geographical scale, which cannot be reduced to a predefined set of levels of organisation. Change is a historical process that can only be understood in a long-term perspective, as it results from the accumulation of multiple small-scale changes over time in a large geographical area. When it takes place, however, the effects are far reaching and may occur very quickly. Thus most of the building blocks of a new level of social organisation already exist, though without the possibility of realising their potential. We shall return to a critical discussion of these questions in the concluding chapter of the book hopefully with new insights gained along the way.

Culture and identity   To this theoretical framework of the operating and transformation of social structures in time and space we must add a *theory of culture* that allows us to understand the way in which symbolic meaning is constituted and employed in social strategies, including the formation of social identities in terms of material culture. We need to come to terms with the meaning and function of symbolically coded networks and the ways they are related to changes in social and economic conditions. Historically they may be used in both innovating and conserving: innovating by new elites to define themselves as opposed to others, by groups resisting such claims, by larger tribal entities in an expansive strategy of migration and/or ethnic inclusion; conserving by elites or larger tribal or regional entities to consolidate themselves or even to resist pressure from outside (Hodder 1978b; 1982a; 1986; Shennan 1989). In some regions during the Bronze Age regional identities may persist for millennia, raising questions of ethnicity and language, since social norms and rules certainly did change throughout these time spans.

Symbolic meaning is thus defined by boundaries of exclusion and inclusion, vertically and horizontally. It is always relational and structural; it can never be

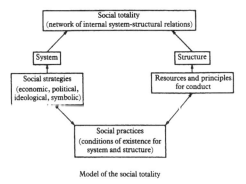

Model of the social totality

Fig. 16 Relationship between meaning and function in the archaeological record.

determined in isolation, only within a given context. But it is also determined by its role or function, and once it has been instituted it takes on a life of its own that tends to constrain change. The instituting of tradition is what allows the archaeologist to acknowledge pattern and regularity in the material record, which further suggests a rather close relationship between material form and meaning. The difficulty is to explain the emergence and transformation of structures of symbolic meaning, and their relationship to social and economic changes. Whose identities are reflected in the evidence, are there contradictory social strategies and identities displayed, how do local and regional identities relate to larger organisational structures, is there local resistance to change, etc.? Such questions can only be answered by employing a holistic framework of both meaning and function, linked to structured principles of conduct and functional systems of maintenance that interact with each other. It corresponds to what I have earlier called cultural representation and material function (Kristiansen 1984a), but I have not used these concepts here since they do not adequately express the active function that material culture possesses as a symbolic practice of its own, which was probably much stronger in pre-industrialised societies than we can imagine.

In conclusion: we have to deal with two interdependent dimensions of historical interpretation and practice – a structural/symbolic one defining meaning and principles of conduct, and a functional/systemic one defining social strategies. The relationship is demonstrated in Figure 16. To me it indicates that we are entering a more productive, pluralistic phase of theoretical and interdisciplinary dialogue. The recent attempt within history, anthropology and sociology to create a more historical understanding of social and economic history, as represented in the work of Mann (1986) and Wolf (1982), works that in less dogmatic and more pragmatic ways combine elements from various research traditions, would seem to support such a view. I am not advocating concealing all differences by a pragmatic attitude, as there are obvious contradictions, both intellectually and ideologically, between some of these approaches. But there remains more room for integration and dialogue than the current debates suggest.

3.2 Systems of social evolution

In this section I shall unfold the general theoretical position defined above in its application to an evolutionary framework relevant to this study. It defines two areas that need further theoretical specification: the possible variation in social hierarchy (level of social organisation) and the spatial interaction between such structures.

The range of variation in social complexity relevant to Bronze Age Europe is broadly speaking covered by the tribal/chiefdom and early state categories. Although attention will be focussed on the processes of change in subsequent chapters, we need some arbitrary theoretical fixed points between which such processes can be seen to operate. The categories of chiefdoms and states represent such ideal types. They are, however, neither neutral nor well defined. I shall therefore begin with a discussion of their definition and meaning.

Chiefdoms and states – a critical assessment

In recent years several works have stressed the inadequacy of our present evolutionary typology, emphasising that individual types, such as chiefdoms, span too broad a range of variation (e.g. Feinman and Neitzal 1984; Upham 1987; Spencer 1987). Although some propose wholly abandoning evolutionary theory (Hodder 1986; Shanks and Tilley 1987b, ch. 6) it remains a highly useful theoretical framework at a general level of explanation. We need instead to revise and redefine it in accordance with the emergence of new historical and theoretical insights.

Attempts to redefine evolutionary typologies have specifed variants in terms of complexity and scale, e.g. simple and complex chiefdoms (Earle 1978; Steponaitis 1978), in terms of organising principles of the political economy, e.g. staple and wealth finance (D'Altroy and Earle 1985; Earle 1987b), in terms of ecological conditions (Sanders and Webster 1978) and in terms of underlying structural dynamics (Friedman and Rowlands 1977).

Although each redefinition has introduced important new concerns, we are quickly becoming mired in a proliferation of terms without much attempt to relate these terms to each other systematically. For example, how do prestige goods systems, as defined by Friedman and Rowlands, relate to wealth finance in chiefdoms, as defined by Earle? How should we compare apparently alternative types such as the stratified society, defined by Fried (1960; 1967) or 'Militärische Demokratie', originating in the work of Engels (1977, originally 1891). In addition the chiefdom concept has been applied to a range that many would see running the gamut from tribal to state societies. Complex chiefdoms, as defined by Earle and Steponaitis, comprise elements of what Fried and others would term archaic states or stratified society. Has the chiefdom concept lost its heuristic value?

In my opinion the reason for this state of affairs is that a few organising principles have been studied without due consideration of their implications for the social organisation of production. Thus, cross-cultural studies of diagnostic traits, such as those by Peebles and Kus (1977), Claessen (1978), or Feinman and Neitzal (1984), employ correlations between variables such as population size, levels of decision-making, settlement hierarchy, status distinctions etc. to define levels of social complexity. In this way apparently similar traits can be lumped together without due consideration of their cultural and material functions in organising production and distribution. One may thereby overlook significant differences in structure, such as the nature of tribute/taxation, ownership, labour mobilisation, social classes etc. Such phenomena are often not visible or subject to direct observation, but can only be inferred through interpretation of the cultural and structural whole that makes up society. What on a comparative scale of traits may look like a continuum without clear dividing lines can, when considered as an organisational whole, turn out to reveal significant differences e.g. in terms of economic and social control. Thus organisational properties cannot be treated in comparative isolation, except in an exploratory phase of research, since their cultural meaning and material functions depend on their place and function in society (the definition of which we shall return to later).

The above critique calls for a critical reassessment of organisational properties and their articulation in intermediate societies between tribes and state. Since states are in a number of ways distinctively different from other forms of social organisation their definition determines the definition of chiefdoms in a negative sense, by defining what they cannot be. I shall therefore proceed with a discussion of the basic features of state organisation.

To Fried the transition to a state form of organisation was a fundamental one . He termed a first phase of that process a *stratified society*, in which 'Man enters a completely new arena of social life.' (Fried 1960, 721). Most authors have overlooked the fundamental character of this change by focussing on the general description stating that 'stratified society is distinguished by differential relationships between the members of society and its subsistence means' (Fried 1960, 721), while de-emphasising the social and political changes in organisation and exploitation that accompanied this differentiation (Fried 1978). The transformation to a stratified society must be recognised as the structural change that underlies the evolution of states (e.g. Sanders and Webster 1978; Hass 1982).

I believe that stratified societies represented an archaic form of state organisation, between chiefdoms and fully developed states, a genuine phase on the road to fully fledged states (Claessen and Skalnik 1978). In order to highlight the qualitative differentiation taking place during this phase it is necessary to discuss in more detail some of the characteristics and some of the variability of such incipient states in prehistory.

Stratified societies possess the basic features of state organisation, such as strong social and economic divisions and an emphasis on territory (rather than kinship), but they lack developed bureaucratic institutions. As stated by Fried (1960, 722):

> The decisive significance of stratification is not that it sees differential amounts of wealth in different hands, but that it sees two kinds of access to strategic resources. One of these is privileged and unimpeded; the other is impaired, depending on complexes of permission which frequently require the payment of dues, rents, or taxes in labour or in kind. The existence of

such distinctions enables the growth of exploitation, whether of a relatively simple kind based upon drudge slavery or of a more complex type associated with involved divisions of labour and intricate class systems.

The emergence of new power relations cross-cutting traditional, communal, networks is redefined in terms of economic obligations, with the requirement to pay tribute or tax, replacing traditional social rights and obligations. Economic exploitation is formalised, enforced by military power and sanctioned legally as well as ritually. Complexity, scale and other institutional and political traits are thus secondary and variable traits to these structural transformations (see the discussions in Claessen 1978; and in Johnson and Earle 1987).

Variants of stratification have been recognised by Fried (1960) and others (e.g. Claessen and Skalnik 1978; Haas 1982). I have chosen two variants of archaic state organisation that seem to cover a majority of cases, which for convenience I will call the centralised and decentralised archaic state. These general terms replace older eurocentric or more historically specific terms such as the 'Asiatic State', 'Militärische Demokratie', or the 'Germanic Mode of Production'. This stresses the world historical significance of archaic state or stratified society formation.

The decentralised archaic state   In his classic work *The Origins of the Family, Private Property and the State* of 1884 (revised version 1891), Engels developed a historical case of the transition from decentralised stratified society to archaic state under the name of 'Militärische Demokratie' or the 'Germanic Mode of Production'. He saw 'Militärische Demokratie' as a transitional stage towards civilisation, the highest level of barbarism, in which contradictions between the traditional community-based society and a new social and economic order separated from this were played out. In 'Militärische Demokratie' war leaders sustained themselves through plunder and territorial conquest. Hermann (1982) has elaborated on this concept in the light of modern research.

The decentralised archaic state can be described in the following terms. Subsistence production is decentralised with village communities or individual hamlets scattered over the landscape. Chiefs and kings set themselves apart from the agrarian substratum through a retinue of warriors. Freed from kinship obligations, the warrior chiefs and king control, undermine and exploit the farming community through tribute and taxation. Ownership of land is formalised, and a landless peasant class develops in that process. Government is carried out through regional and local vassal chiefs who also provide warriors and ships in periods of warfare. Similar structures may develop in pastoral societies in their interaction with state societies or under internal contradictions of blocked expansion (Bonte 1977; 1979; Irons 1979; Krader 1979; Sáenz 1991).

Towns are absent. Instead we may find trading communities or ports of trade, controlled by the central government (Hodges 1982). Specialised craft production is performed by both slaves and free specialists. Centres for craft production may co-exist with local settlements, but the craftsmen are attached to elite patrons. Such trading and production centres may develop into small towns, and the control and/or taxation of long-distance trade may indeed play a significant role in the development of decentralised archaic states.

In Europe, but also in cases in Africa and Asia, the ritual role of kingship as an economically legitimating factor seems to be replaced by secular and ideological functions, corresponding to the new forms of social and economic control (Mair 1977; Wallace-Hadrill 1971).

Central to this new social form of stratification must be formalised ways to extract tribute, tax and labour. This income can then be supported by territorial conquest to create larger polities or kingdoms. Although bureaucracies are not institutionalised, written script may be employed by specialists to record transactions. Thus it is the interaction between warfare (plunder and territorial conquest), control of trade and the formalising of landholding and taxation that leads to decentralised state formation.

I see particularly in Europe a development from more generalised to more specific ways of surplus extraction linked to emerging markets and private landholding, allowing increasingly formalised forms of tribute, tax and rent to develop. Without private landholding and taxation linked to it, the state cannot be permanently sustained in a decentralised economic setting. The latter, however, also constrains and 'checks' kingship and the formation of centralised political institutions. In the decentralised archaic state, the basic features of the feudalised state are gradually formalised. I suggest that it is mainly linked to secondary state formation in Europe, Africa and Asia (see the case studies and discussion in Claessen & Skalnik 1978; Service 1975, II, also Earle 1991b; Tsude 1988).

The centralised archaic state   The second variant is the centralised archaic state, or the 'Asiatic State'. It was identified by Marx, although it never occupied an important position in his works. Basically he took over the notion of a centralised ritually sanctioned government based on state 'ownership' of land administered through various kinds of tribute ('temple economies' – for a full discussion see Sofri 1969/75). The historical implications of the Asiatic State have been widely discussed and criticised (Bailey and Llobera 1981; Wickham 1985), and it is now clear that there is always an interaction between a private and a public sector in these societies, 'feudalisation' processes being linked to the collapse of centralised polities (Bintliff 1982). On the other hand, general features of this kind recur in initial state formation, as the principles of the theocratic chiefdom are formalised (Webb 1975; 1987). The formulations by Friedman and Rowlands (1977) may be used as a second, alternative, path to state society, in contrast to the decentralised archaic state.

The centralised archaic state formalises the tribal structure of the conical clan into a ruling elite, legitimised by controlled ritual access to the supernatural. The centralised archaic state develops in regions of high productivity where surplus can be generated and controlled. Through a formalised system of tribute, surplus production is converted into large-scale ritual activities, building ceremonial centres, organisation of craft production and centralised trade. Slave labour, obtained by capture in warfare or through debt, and the division of labour e.g. along lines of kinship, evolve into new classes/ethnic groups in communities performing special activities. A primitive bureaucracy emerges to administer production, trade and religious activities.

The internal economic structure consists of a tribute/corvee relation between local lines and local chiefs and between the chiefs and the paramount, and chiefly estates and royal estates are maintained by debt slaves and captives.

The centralised archaic state formalises the basic components of a developed bureaucracy to administer production, trade and religious activities. In its further development both warfare for control of essential resources and commercialisation of production for trade play an important role (Gilman 1991; Ferguson 1991). In comparison with the decentralised archaic state the major difference lies in the centralised economy with its potential for sustaining a state apparatus and the ritualised genealogical structure of the ruling class.

Evolutionary antecedents to the archaic state and stratified societies
Contrasting with my characterisation of stratified societies, here termed archaic state organisation, chiefdoms should be considered a tribal form of social organisation.[3] Economic and political processes are organised along lines of kinship (or kinship relations are defined along lines of production and exchange). Control, embedded in kinship, has not yet transformed social groups into classes. Nevertheless, even within tribal structures hierarchy and exploitation may still be a major factor. By gradually eroding traditional rights and increasing exploitation the road may be paved for a reorganisation into the more permanent order of the state (Gledhill 1988, 11ff; Spriggs 1988). We are dealing with a progression in which the state represents a formalising of hierarchy and exploitation that makes the process, if not irreversible, then hardly reversible to a tribal level. Thus a state–class structure rarely disappears entirely in periods of political fragmentation. We should rather speak of state systems that may alternate between a number of organisational forms, such as centralisation versus decentralisation, feudalism versus commercialism, empires versus city states, etc.

In Figure 17, I indicate two evolutionary trajectories which evolve from the tribal structure. The centralised archaic state represents a continuous development of the tribal structure (evolution), whereas the decentralised archaic state is rather the outcome of devolutionary processes (Friedman 1975, 186 ff.; 1979, chapter VII). Following Earle I have defined two types of chiefdom organisation based respectively on staple finance/control over subsistence production and on prestige goods/control over valuables. Wealth finance as defined by Earle has much in common with prestige goods economies as defined by Friedman and Rowlands, just as staple finance and tributary systems represent another, if not opposing, strategy of economic control. In both cases wealth, movable or staple, is considered to be the basic economic factor. Staple finance, however, is dominated by vertical relations of production and exchange, prestige goods being a dependent variable, whereas in prestige goods systems horizontal relations dominate and are sufficient to establish

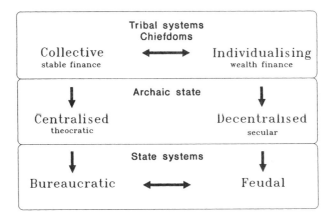

Fig. 17 A temporal model of evolutionary trajectories.

control of labour and production. These two principles are not mutually exclusive and may be combined in various forms of social organisation, although in pre-state societies prestige goods economies are mostly linked to individualising, segmentary, 'pastoral' societies, while staple finance is generally associated with collective, territorial and 'agricultural' societies (Figure 17). In essence it seems reasonable that different sources of income will result in different internal developmental characteristics in stratified societies. Thus chiefdoms based on staple finance may develop into centralised archaic states, and those based on wealth finance, into decentralised archaic states (Friedman 1979; Friedman and Rowlands 1977).

It should be stressed that the stratified society or archaic state is not to be considered a static, well-defined, level in social evolution. Its definition embodies change; it represents the historical processes that transform a tribal structure into an early state. Although described as an ideal type it is better characterised as a transformational process that may last several hundred years. It might also be expected that its various characteristics will not develop at once, but rather in several stages of change and transformation. The concept of archaic states and stratified societies thus blurs the great divide between pre-state (tribal forms) and state societies, and it offers a chance for archaeologists and historians to trace some of the most decisive transformational processes in world history in some detail.

Conclusion The theoretical implications of the above discussion can be summarised as follows:
(1) A basic distinction can be made between a tribal and a state form of social organisation.
(2) The formation of early states is a historical process that gradually undermines and changes the conditions of tribal organisation and develops new institutions to control and exploit production. The concept of archaic states or stratified societies is applied to represent this transformational process, whose organisational variability is summarised in Figure 17 in two ideal types.

(3) Tribal social organisation is a general form of social reproduction spanning a wide range of social forms (segmentary, territorial, etc.) and with a range of developmental trajectories. Chiefdoms are considered to fall within the range of tribal social organisation. Two dominant variants and their trajectories have been summarised in Figure 17.

(4) Such variation is a result of long-term changes in social and ecological conditions of production and the geographical variation in basic resources. This creates different conditions for development and interaction at different points in time and space.

(5) We should consequently avoid too rigid institutional categories and rather try to consider and interpret the observable evidence as a continuum of organisational variability in time and space. The comparative study of institutional characteristics (e.g. of tribes or chiefdoms around the world), can only serve as a starting point, never as a definition nor as an interpretation of the actual properties of the social system and their internal articulation.

Evolutionary trajectories and systems of social evolution

In the preceding section I have considered the internal structure and articulation of two ideal types of social organisation without implying anything about the conditions of their transformation. To do so we have to give up the traditional notion of evolution as a unidirectional sequence of transformations taking place within bounded social units (Ekholm 1980 & 1981; Friedman 1976a; Friedman and Rowlands 1977). Evolution is both a spatial and a temporal process. We therefore need to consider the temporal and spatial framework within which evolutionary processes operate. This demands, according to Friedman (1976a, 54):

> that we consider the total space within which reproduction occurs as a process. Within that space we must consider the social structured properties that determine the nature and intensity of flows and thus the rate of reproduction in the larger system. Finally we must deal with society not as consisting of actual societies, but of structures of temporal processes.

If we are to consider chiefdoms within such a larger framework we need to understand the principles that lead to and distinguish various social formations. We need to look behind the prevailing evolutionary typology of tribes and chiefdoms to define the structuring principles which create spatially dependent social formations. The theoretical premises of my understanding of processes of evolution and devolution are as follows:

1 Tribal social organisation may generate several evolutionary trajectories, including variants of chiefdom organisation.

2 Their direction and potential depends on their place within a world system.

3 Such a world system can be very large and structurally diverse, including centre–periphery relations from states to tribes.

4 Consequently, tribes, chiefdoms and states may be understood as parts of a contiguous structure defined in space.

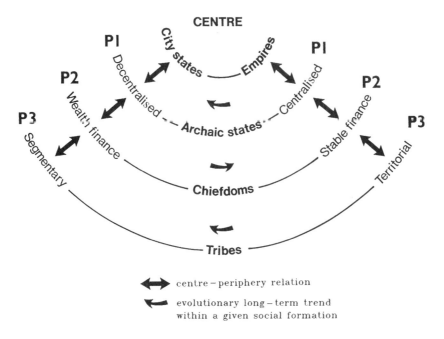

Fig. 18 A spatial model of centre–periphery relationships among evolutionary types. The arrows mark long-term evolutionary trends within a given social formation.

5 From this it follows that chiefdoms are, more often than not, dependent in some way on their place in larger historical cycles of evolution and devolution.

Such an approach has a number of theoretical implications (Rowlands 1987a). One of them is that the dichotomy between internal and external is dissolved, or becomes relative. The traditional polarisation of production and exchange, production being primary and internal, can no longer be maintained. Instead we have to put them on equal terms and consider them within a framework of systems of social reproduction where production, circulation and accumulation of wealth are considered as inter-locked processes in time and space. The complexity of such world systems – whether based on core–periphery relations (Friedman and Rowlands 1977; Wallerstein 1974; Rowlands, Larsen and Kristiansen 1987; Champion 1989a), or on interacting re-gional systems (Renfrew and Cherry 1987; Schortman and Urban 1992) has yet to be explained.

Within such systems there are no unidirectional evolutionary processes, only multiple interacting processes of evolution and devolution whose local, regional and global developmental trends determine the reproduction and transformation of the larger system. Figure 18 gives a schematic outline of such a world system, forming a structural hierarchy. In the centre city states and empires have evolved. They are then linked economically and politically to peripheries at increasing distances. This may give rise to a variety of direct and indirect forms of dependency and interaction that have to be worked out in their historical setting. Perhaps more significantly, it proposes that after the emergence of state systems it is no longer possible to talk about independent developments. This does not deny autonomous developments, but since interlocked regional exchange systems have been in existence since the Neolithic, we have to consider the implications of this for processes of change on a larger scale than the local and regional system. According to this, tribes and chiefdoms are often dependent for their reproduction on larger systems that they do not control. Consequently, chiefdoms are in many cases, perhaps in most, a secondary development. Such an approach naturally also has consequences for the conception of the ethnographic present. Many autonomous tribes and chiefdoms may simply be devolved societies, the result of core–periphery collapse, the outer periphery being temporarily cut off from the larger system and reverting back to a tribal organisation (Cohen 1978, 54 f.; Ekholm and Friedman 1980/1985).

Within such a world system, the regional systems maintain a degree of relative autonomy (Renfrew and Shennan 1982). Despite their dependency on remote regions for supplies of metal, prestige goods and ritual information, regional long-term trends may determine the interaction and eventually the course of development within the larger system. If we can identify such long-term regularities on a regional scale we are in a better position to understand and to explain major changes and transformations of interacting regional systems, such as the Lapita complex in Oceania (Kirch 1987), the Midwestern Hopewellian in North America (Braun 1986), or the Corded Ware/Bell Beaker complex in Europe (Shennan 1986b). The crucial question is when and under what conditions does regional interaction become a driving force? We should also be prepared to face the possibility that less complex, peripheral, regions may be decisive for developments in more complex core regions, dependent on the spatial and structural location of threshold levels.

As a heuristic device I define some possible relationships between centres and peripheries, based mainly on Friedman (1979, 12f.):

(1) Centre–periphery structures are based on an exploitative relationship between centres of accumulation and supply-zone peripheries. Such structures may take on various forms, where one can distinguish between dependent and independent structures.

(2) Dependent structures rely for their reproduction on their relationship to centres. There may be specialist producers supplying agricultural products, raw materials or specialist products to various centres. They may be trade states, pastoral states/ chiefdoms. They are often dependent on the import of subsistence requirements from either centres or their peripheries of 'independent' tribal or chiefdom structures (e.g. the need of pastoralists and city states for agricultural produce), placing them in a vulnerable middle position between two social systems. The import of prestige goods from the centre to maintain their exploitative position is another characteristic feature (e.g. the Hallstatt chiefs in relation to Greek and later Etruscan city states, or the Germanic societies in relation to the Roman Empire). Such dependent structures may act as centres or catalysts to further peripheries, which will, however, often be beyond their immediate control.

(3) Independent structures are not directly dependent for their reproduction on centres (which to them may be the above dependent structures), although they may be heavily influenced by them, ideologically or in terms of their social and political strategies. They may supply slaves and mercenaries to centres and develop warlike elites. Often they are expansionist, characterised by internal regional cycles of accumulation, expansion and regression. In the Bronze Age their relative autonomy is defined culturally in terms of symbolic and ritual norms and practices defining regional traditions differing from those of the centres, although influenced by them. They may also supply basic forms of wealth, such as metal. In that case their independence is relative. Sometimes they expand temporarily into archaic states or 'barbarian empires' (nomadic empires or larger tribal confederations such as the Germanic), especially in periods of decline of the centres, which they may overrun, leading to 'Dark Ages', as happened several times during the Bronze Age.

(4) A variant of independent structures are so-called 'primitive' structures, disintegrated tribal groups that have been cut off from their networks by dominant centre–periphery structures (e.g. Nugent 1982), which may still exploit them. They may also be social groups that have avoided dominance, for a variety of reasons, and maintained an egalitarian, autonomous social organisation. They are often described as family groups, 'Big Man' societies, with a village organisation, characterised by the lack of larger polities (Johnson and Earle 1987, chs. 3–8). Such societies are of course dependent in the sense that their history and social organisation are linked to the dominance of other societies, and they may define themselves in opposition to them, just as they may interact with them, e.g. hunter-gatherers selling special products to trading farming societies, as in Northern Scandinavia during the Bronze Age (Olsen 1985; Kristiansen 1987a).

When applying this global approach to concrete studies one should avoid institutional concepts that are too rigid and instead try to identify and explain the underlying organisational properties spatially and temporally. Institutions, like social types, always represent a cross-section of complex processes creating variation in time and space. Whether such processes are to be considered a continuum or whether abrupt, even catastrophic, changes and transformations may occur, will be discussed in the last section.

One can ask if it is possible to identify and come to terms with such large-scale processes in archaeological terms. Since archaeologists are used to dealing with changing distributions of material culture, we are in a better position than either historians or social anthropologists to understand processes of large-scale change (see Chapter 2.3). A major task is to study the way material culture is employed in social strategies to define processes of expansion/resistence and to form local, regional and international identities (Gailey and Patterson 1987). The consumption of wealth in time and space may also give important clues to identifying processes of centralisation/ranking when compared with the organisation of production. This should be linked to studies of the way values are established and employed in such processes as a means of creating power and dependency (Earle 1982). This way of establishing value is often linked to cosmologies where power resides in the ability to travel and create alliances and links with distant chiefdoms/centres of ritual superiority (Helms 1986; 1988a; 1988b). Exchange and political power are linked to one another in creating and reproducing local and regional power structures.

3.3 Societies as organised networks

By now it should be clear that there is no such thing as a society. There are multiple overlapping networks of interaction that define various local and regional identities or cultures within which people and goods move in networks of social obligations, dependencies and economic transactions. There are individual hamlets, settlement compounds and larger fortified central places, whose structure helps us to define basic elements of social and economic organisation. Ritual, warfare and exchange are the mechanisms by which these social and economic components or strategies are operated and set in motion. The way they articulate locally and regionally defines various organisational profiles, some of them overlapping, some not.

Such organisational complexity cannot be perceived in advance by a social typology. A theoretically informed inductive strategy is necessary in order to link the properties of the archaeological record to the basic properties of social and economic organisation. One may call it a kind of 'middle range' strategy. We must therefore begin our analyses of the Bronze and Early Iron Ages by defining the basic components – or building blocks – of society and their relationships to each other. They include both the social and economic properties of society. Social properties include vertical and horizontal relations of organisation.

Social properties

Vertical relations of organisation   The fact that the destruction and deposition of wealth is a major characteristic of the Bronze Age and Early Iron Age should focus our attention on the role of ritual consumption in social strategies. This has been the aim of some recent studies (Bradley 1990; Levy 1980; Kristiansen 1978; 1991). We can observe that:

1 Rank was mostly ritualised.
2 Prestige goods of bronze and gold were used in social strategies, including their destruction and deposition.
3 Such depositions were subject to cyclical fluctuations and contextual changes in time and space.

Ritual is a powerful way of legitimating and institutionalising new positions of rank, but having done so ritual also constrains further developments towards power and hierarchy (Bloch 1977). This dialectic is probably decisive for understanding the permanence of European Bronze Age societies and it should also lead us to focus attention on those periods and regions where attempts were made to disconnect rank and ritual, by separating claims to social and economic power from direct ritual sanction, which may pave the road to state formation. It can be suggested that during

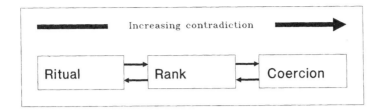

Fig. 19 Strategies for establishing and maintaining order and control vertically.

the Bronze Age we see repeated moves back and forth between the formation of ritually sanctioned rank and attempts to separate rank and ritual.

Ritual sacredness may also be employed in creating centre–periphery relations, by linking ritual and social superiority together. When access to outside exchange networks and to mythical power is unified, a powerful combination of ritual, social and economic dominance is established (Helms 1979; 1986; 1988).

The ritualised formation of rank, however, cannot be separated from the potential and factual use of force (coercion), as reflected in the dominance of weapons in certain regions and periods in burials and hoards. As has been demonstrated, they were also used (Kristiansen 1984b).

Ritual, rank and coercion are thus intrinsically interlinked in pre-state societies (Figure 19) and should never be studied in isolation. The balance between them defines different phases in the formation of power and in the playing out of social conflicts, indicated by the arrow defining a continuum from more peaceful to more contradictory strategies. It may thus define organisational structures ranging from ritualised to institutionalised political/military power (Figure 21).

Horizontal relations of organisation   Metalwork defines overlapping networks of social interaction at various levels. Some of these distributions form recurrent patterns that define regional cultural identities, while others point to interregional exchange. Typological studies have provided an empirical framework for understanding and explaining such social and economic processes when combined with relevant theoretical insights. However, we have yet to learn how to understand the ritual and social values of different objects and their place in a hierarchy of exchanges. As a starting point we can make the following observations:

1 Weapons, tools and ornaments of bronze and gold were employed not only functionally or as local status symbols, but also as prestige giving goods that were exchanged as gifts in alliance formations, thereby creating obligations and dependency.

2 Such exchanges, which included the movement not only of goods but also of people, overlapped with or were embedded in more commercial transactions and considerations.

3 This may lead to the expansion of political or commercial spheres of influence, sometimes followed by migrations.

4 Despite this, the emerging exchange networks or cultures are always larger than the political units which make them up.

Thus there exists a continuum from the exchange of goods through political expansion to migrations (Figure 20). The exchange of gifts represents a universal element in social reproduction, which may, however, take on expansionist forms, leading to more competitive strategies, which may finally be concluded in migrations or social movements of people, whether traders or larger groups. I propose that these strategies are intrinsically interlinked in pre-state societies, defining a continuum from peaceful interaction to more competitive and contradictory strategies, where one strategy cannot be defined nor understood without the other (Figure 21).

The last observation, that political entities were always smaller than the cultures they defined, deserves some reflection. It implies that political entities were dependent on maintaining open, competitive systems; there could be no closure if bronze was to be distributed. It defines an interesting difference to the subsequent Iron Age, as iron is more widely available locally, at least in small quantities. Only later industrial production created a new situation. It also defines a similar kind of difference to the Neolithic, where most raw materials were available locally. Bronze Age societies in comparison had to break through local and regional barriers of social interaction, which defined a whole new framework for the international spread of social and ideological value systems, technological advances, new techniques in warfare, etc., although these changes were normally recontextualised locally and regionally. In this respect the Bronze Age may be seen to represent an intermediate stage between a traditional tribal social organisation and a state form of organisation, whose characteristics beyond those of evolutionary stage theory are still to be explored. The Bronze Age is in certain aspects historically unique. For nearly two millennia it unified Europe within a common framework of interacting exchange networks, a repetitive dialectic between maintaining regional traditions and interacting across their boundaries, between sharing international value systems and recontextualising them locally and regionally, between openness and closure. In some ways this is a dynamic it shares with Europe today (the EC), though under completely different social and economic conditions.

Economic properties

Subsistence strategies and settlement components   During the past two decades settlement excavations all over Europe have changed our perception of the social and economic organisation of the Bronze and Early Iron Ages (Audouze and Büchsenschütz 1992): from the hillforts of the Atlantic Bronze Age and Early Iron Age (Cunliffe 1982b) through the newly discovered citadels of the El Argar Culture (Gilman 1991) to La Tène oppida (Collis 1984b). It has led to a new and better understanding of settlement hierarchies both in Central Europe and the Mediterranean (Figure 22). In accordance with this, palaeobotanical evidence and landscape surveys have shown that Bronze Age societies were able to organise the landscape on a grand scale as early as the 2nd millennium BC (Fleming 1988). Some marked

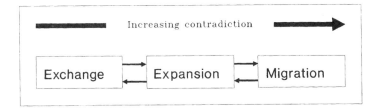

Fig. 20 Strategies for extending social relations and control horizontally.

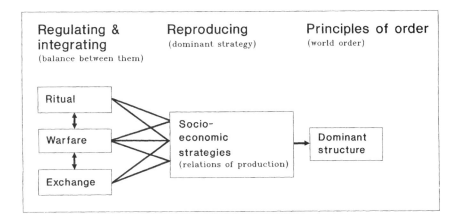

Fig. 21 Types of relationships between strategies of vertical and horizontal control defining dominant strategies and structures.

Fig. 22 Basic settlement components, which in various combinations define different types of hierarchy and contradiction.

temporal and regional cycles in subsistence and settlement can be observed through the two millennia – e.g. from extensive to intensive farming, from upland to downland. Most farming practice, however, combines different strategies, defining a dominant type. As a starting point we can make the following simplified observations:

1 Fortified settlements and settlement hierarchies are characteristic throughout the Bronze Age and Early Iron Age only in some periods and regions.

2 They alternate with regions and periods with no or few fortified settlements.

3 The economy fluctuates between agrarian (intensive) and pastoral (extensive) strategies, linked to a predominance of lowland or upland settlements.

Figure 23 gives the relation between dominant subsistence strategies and the subsequent organisation and ritualisation of the landscape. It hypothesises that predominantly pastoral and agrarian strategies result in different settlement structures and in different ideological manifestations of control over the landscape (Fleming 1972). They should therefore be studied in relation to each other. In the subsequent analyses such variations will be traced. For the settlement evidence Collis has formulated a typology of different types of settlement developments which I shall employ (Collis 1982: 9.2, 9.3). According to this the development of fortified settlements may reflect either a situation of expanding hierarchies or the reverse – fragmentation and collapse, when all settlement is concentrated within fortified villages, as in the Late Lausitz Culture (Ostorja-Zagorski 1982). Consequently it can be suggested that the lack of fortified settlements in some situations may testify to political control, securing peace and preventing destructive warfare, at least at the local level.

In Figure 24 I have summarised what I consider to be the dominant strategies for explaining social organisation and change during the 1st and 2nd millennia BC. This suggests both the actual range of each strategy (e.g. from ritual control to coercion/warfare), and their interaction, which may define a number of different organisational profiles and developmental trajectories. Production–distribution–consumption defines the flow of goods, services and people within such structures, e.g. tribute, rent, etc., from hamlets to chiefly centres, to be employed in ritual consumption, warfare or in producing prestige goods for exchange. Such flows and their 'channels' define a dominant set of social relations of production (a dominant structure). These are the components to be applied in the concluding chapters.

'Societies' are thus defined in two ways: in terms of regional cultural codes or identities within which certain norms and practices dominated, and in terms of the principles that structured and organised the strategies and institutions described above. The first definition is basically descriptive – it can only be given meaning in terms of structuring principles, and in terms of the functions they performed. As archaeologists are primarily dealing with the interpretation of spatial distributions of material culture, from settlements to burials and hoards, in scale from local to regional or even 'global' distributions, we must consider the above strategies in their relationship to *power as a spatial phenomenon*. In Figure 25 I have defined what I consider to be the two extremes relevant to Bronze Age social organisation: a tribal and an early state form.

Power as spatial networks

Tribal systems (Figure 25A) are characterised by extensive exchange networks, that may develop into regional cultural traditions. Confederations and tribal groupings of various kinds are surely hidden behind these networks. But their wider significance in terms of ethnicity and language is still a matter of dispute, to which we shall return. Political power, however, is diffused and can only be practised with economic efficiency, as control of land and labour, at the local level of chiefly followers. Military power may be extended beyond that, but mostly as raiding for slaves, cattle, etc., or

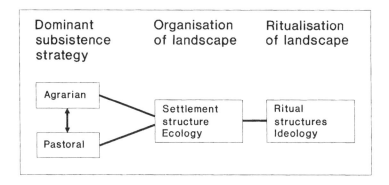

Fig. 23 Types of relationships between dominant subsistence strategies and the subsequent organisation and ritualisation of the landscape.

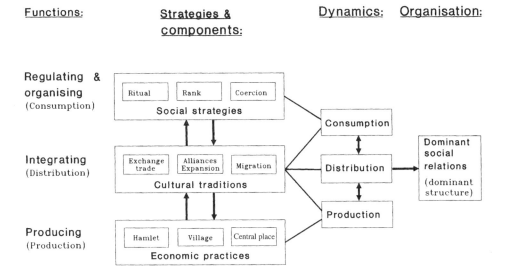

Fig. 24 Summary diagram of strategies and dynamics constituting Bronze and Iron Age social organisation.

in warfare over the control of important alliance and trade networks. Territorial control is not the objective, warfare is rather heroic and ritually instituted. Ritual remains the dominating integrating mechanism through which all transactions have to pass, whether social, economic or even military. Therefore ritual or sacred power can play an important role in mobilising larger followings and in creating alliances that extend far beyond the local setting. This may define local and regional relations of centre–periphery where goods and people are moving towards the centre in exchange for ritual services in a system of unequal exchange, a kind of ritualised tribute.

The different strategies thus have different spatial distributions, reflecting different levels of influence. No political control of larger areas from a single centre is

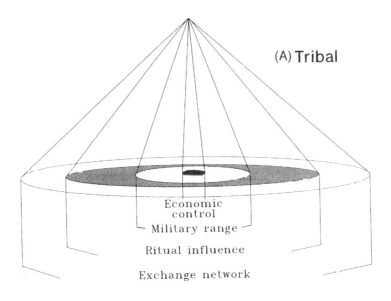

(A) Tribal

Economic
control
Military range
Ritual influence
Exchange network

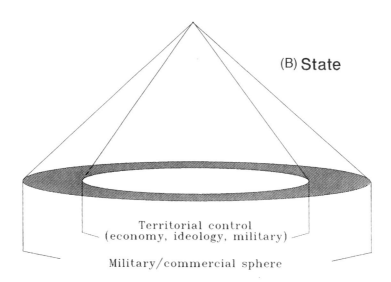

(B) State

Territorial control
(economy, ideology, military)
Military/commercial sphere

Fig. 25 Two ideal types – tribal and state forms – of overlapping power networks.

possible, whereas networks may be extensive. In an intermediate position to early state systems one may find confederations between chiefly centres that control trade routes, but not the territories beyond. These are peer polities between nodal points in a decentralised political setting (Renfrew and Shennan 1982).

Early state systems (Figure 25B) are characterised by a much closer connection between ritual, exchange and economic and military/political control. However, two types of control are at work, that over a territory and that over a larger commercial network. Territorial control unifies political, military and economic control. Ritual is often relegated to an ideological institution with little impact on the execution of power that is channelled through landholding and tribute/tax. Military force is used against attempts to escape obligations. Beyond the region under territorial control there extends a wider area where nodal points of trade may be controlled and protected by military force if necessary. Such commercial/military power networks are important characteristics and they may sometimes be swallowed up in empire formation, or unified in confederations. Under normal conditions, however, military striking power and commercial networks tend to be larger than territorial control, defining various types of centre–periphery relations.

Most of the variation to be seen in the Bronze Age to Early Iron Age falls within these extremes, probably defining a number of variations related to early state formation and the development of complex centre–periphery relations. These relationships and their range of variation will be traced in the subsequent analysis of Bronze Age society.

Discussion and conclusion

Although the model presented here owes much to Mann's theoretical programme, as reflected in the borrowing of the chapter heading, there are also divergences that need to be spelled out. Some are due to the nature of Bronze Age society by comparison to state societies, which are Mann's major object of analysis, others concern principles of theory.

Mann dismantles a number of traditional concepts: society as a unified concept, on which we agree, and also levels, dimensions, etc. He then introduces a group of categories, freed from their former constraining relationship to 'society', which he conceives of as basic power organising factors. They are: ideological, economic, military and political (the IEMP model). Mann's reason for doing so is the observation that the spatial range of these factors rarely coincides; they define power networks of different geographical scale. The real dynamics of history are therefore rooted in understanding their distribution and their interaction, which is always bigger than society. The same observations could be made for the Bronze Age, leading to the defining of similar organisational categories. Although this may then seem warranted for historical and heuristic reasons, it raises some problems as to the theoretical and explanatory status of the organising factors. Here Mann has not yet presented a theoretical framework for the articulation of his IEMP model in different types of social and historical settings, as it awaits the conclusion of his historical analysis. Are there recurring structural and spatial relationships between these components that allow us to define more general organisational types and regularities in the way they interact? In the concluding chapter I shall demonstrate that this indeed is the case.

I thus consider my models of organising factors relevant to Bronze Age society, like that of Mann's IEMP model, to represent a heuristic application relevant to the societies under study. These building blocks enable us to characterise the organisational complexity, and to discover regularities, without being constrained by preconceived social types or other theoretical models. It represents a first level of analysis of societies in their concrete historical settings.

At the next level of analysis an attempt must be made to define the socially organising principles according to which the societies under study operated. Are there recurrent features that allow us to define dominant structures, and are there recurrent spatial relationships between them that enable us to define structural hierarchies, centre–periphery relations or other types of macro-structural interaction and dependency? Finally, are there historical developments in the relationship between these structures that permit us to define, or at least to characterise, developmental regularities, whether cyclical, devolutionary or evolutionary? To do so we need to confront results achieved at the first level of analysis with theoretical models, as presented in the previous sections, in order to characterise and define observed regularities. This may also lead to modifications of the general models.

At the final level of analysis an attempt must be made to locate forces of change within the historical structures and transformations. Is it possible to locate one or several sets of determining factors operating at certain levels of organisation and under certain historical conditions? This leads us back to discussing universal constituents of social change, constraints and determination.

This stepwise exposition of increasingly generalised historical processes and structures implies a similar exposition of abstract categories to handle these problematics. No honest researcher can of course ignore the problem of being 'blinded' by preconceived concepts, but this remains a basic existential problem that is not solved by choosing a secure position of either letting general categories organise the evidence no matter its variation or burying oneself in a hermeneutic illusion of becoming one with the object of study. I have tried to overcome these problems, first by describing and discussing the historical and ideological context of theory and interpretation, and second by exposing the theoretical structure of the project, from general principles to applied models, and their place in the subsequent analyses. Theories are tools to think with, not boxes to fit evidence into. Concrete analyses and interpretations will therefore be carried out inductively, each chapter being defined by a specific historical context. In this way I hope to allow all relevant variation to come into play. Only in the last chapter will I try to identify the larger macrohistorical regularities. This structure allows the reader to follow my arguments from their point of departure in particular cases to the final construction of a Bronze Age world system, and to balance and to evaluate critically my proceedings against the theoretical prescriptions presented above. By thus exposing the full theoretical and interpretative strategy I invite active participation and dialogue with the reader.

4

Regional systems: the social and cultural landscape in Europe in the Late Bronze Age, 1100–750 BC

4.1 The social and cultural landscape

Regional traditions

Around 1100 BC Europe was characterised by a number of quite distinct regional traditions or cultures, rooted in or influenced by the Urnfield tradition of shared burial rituals and religion. It was strongest in Central Europe, as at the ritual peripheries the Urnfield phenomenon was more integrated into older traditions (Figure 26). To begin with the latter area: along the Atlantic façade, from England to Iberia, there emerged a rather unified tradition in metalwork and ritual depositions, which reached a climax towards the end of our period, to be discussed in the next chapter. The various chronological and regional phases have been characterised in terms of industrial traditions, but I prefer the neutral categories of the French, Bronze Final I–III. Our period is covered by BF IIa–IIIb. In the north the Nordic culture adopted elements of Urnfield ritual without giving up basic Nordic traditions in both metalwork and ritual, reflected in the continuous use of earlier Bronze Age barrows for secondary urn burials. No urnfields appeared until the beginning of La Tène. In Central Europe the Urnfield culture, despite remarkable similarities from east to west, is also characterised by regional traditions: a west European, called the Rhine-Swiss-French group (RSF), extending its influence further southward into northeastern Iberia; a northeast European, termed the Lausitz Culture; an Alpine; and a Danubian/Carpathian. Within the Alpine tradition we should also include northern Italy, which during the Proto-Villanovan and Villanovan periods fell within the Urnfield orbit. We can, however, speak of a common Urnfield area that included the above regional traditions, leaving us with three major groups (for the time being excluding the Mediterranean and eastern Europe around the Black Sea): the Nordic, the Atlantic, and the Central European Urnfield proper.

At the interface between these large regional traditions transitional or mixed local traditions appeared – in northern Germany between the Nordic and the Lausitz regions and in the Alps between Italy and Central Europe. Some of these 'buffer' cultures will be discussed later.

These regional cultural traditions formed a system, in the sense that the frequency of interaction between them was high enough to maintain a common pace of change both in metal and ceramic production, and also in rituals, without one region dominating the other. This has been demonstrated in the development of fibulae and pins of different types and regions (von Brunn 1968, figs. 6 and 10), razors (Jocken-

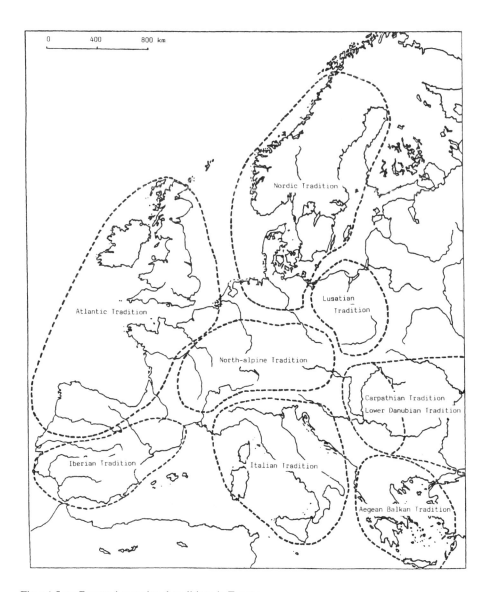

Fig. 26 Late Bronze Age regional traditions in Europe.

hövel 1972) and swords (Cowen 1955; Müller-Karpe 1961; Schauer 1971), to mention just a few types. There was a vivid and rapid exchange of ideas over large
distances, often switching from one medium to another, e.g. from ceramics to
metalwork and back again. For example, a common base motif on pots during HaB1,
over large tracts of Europe, was a star design formed by bands of parallel lines,
sometimes with protruding lines from the centre. Originating in Ha A2, it appears on
different vessel form shapes both in France and in Central Europe, whereas in
the Nordic region it was adopted for metal hanging vessels, but not on pottery
(Figure 27).

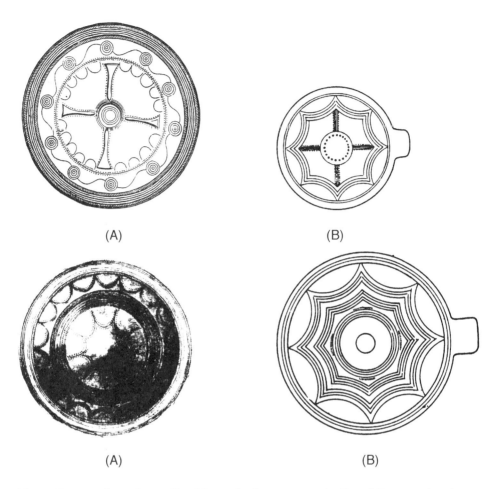

(A)   (B)

(A)   (B)

Fig. 27 Common decorative motif and its application on pottery in Central Europe and on bronze ornaments in the Nordic region during HaB1: (A) from Nordic hanging vessels; (B) from Moravia.

In order to understand such similarities it is necessary to consider the mechanisms that produced them and their manifestations in local, regional and interregional traditions. We can approach the problem in two ways: either we can examine what constitutes regional or even supra-regional traditions, sometimes called a 'koine', a 'complex', or even a 'techno-complex' after Clarke (1968, ch. 8) and then dissolve them into their components; or we can begin by examining what constitutes local groupings, and then proceed to see how they eventually make up larger regional traditions. The two strategies may produce rather different results, as we shall see. I shall employ both, but choose first to discuss regional traditions.

We have to distinguish between two types of regional traditions: one that is linked to a specific culture (e.g. the Nordic Bronze Age or Germanic Iron Age) displaying geographical and spatial continuity; and another that is linked to a recurring emergence of such cultural traditions within the same region in a long-term perspective.

To take the latter first, we can observe a general Nordic cultural tradition from the

Neolithic onwards that encompasses the region of present-day Denmark, northern Germany and southern Sweden. In some periods it extended further northwards, e.g. during the Late Neolithic (dagger period), to encompass most of Scandinavia. In other periods there are interruptions, as new cultural traits intrude into parts of the region. Then the Nordic tradition re-emerges, as is the case from the Early Bronze Age. During that period it expands to include most of Scandinavia, except the far north and the interior of Scandinavia, encompassing a region that stretches 2,000 km from north to south and 1,000 km from east to west (Kristiansen 1987a). Behind the major social and economic changes taking place from the Neolithic to the Iron Age, when we can identify a Germanic, Scandinavian, language within the Nordic region, there appears to exist a regularity in cultural distributions that withstands most social and cultural changes.[1]

In the following, however, I shall explore the first and most common variant – the regional traditions of the later Bronze Age (Figure 28).

A culturally specific regional tradition defines an area within which regular production and exchange of metalwork and pottery creates a stylistic regularity – general norms for how a sword or a neck ring should look and social and ritual norms for what they signalled and how they were used. Certain norms and ideas spread all over the European continent, but they were soon adapted into regional clothing styles, allowing archaeologists today, and prehistoric people in the past, to distinguish where they belonged, both vertically (farmers or chiefs) and horizontally (settlement groups and tribes). Thus the major stylistic zones defined by archaeologists are not arbitrary, but reflect real similarities and differences. What is arbitrary, of course, is our interpretation of them. To overcome that we should as the first thing avoid lumping together phenomena that had different social meanings in the past. Difference depends on context – who is signalling? Is it local farming communities or local or regional elites? They define different spheres of interaction. But it also depends on the archaeologists of today. The Nordic culture exemplifies the creation of a large-scale regional tradition by integrating different spheres of interaction, so creating local groupings as well (Baudou 1960; Larsson 1986; Sørensen 1987). It further exemplifies a research strategy which began by defining the overall criteria of a regional tradition before dissolving it into smaller components.

There are certain preconditions for the rise of a regional tradition in material culture, some of them general, some of them linked to Bronze Age technology. They are:

1 A technological ability to master metallurgy.
2 A social and economic ability to obtain supplies of bronze and to develop and maintain specialist skills.
3 An innovative ability that is linked to a need to signal one's own identity as opposed to the identity of others, and a priority of indigenous over foreign cultural traits.
4 A regular social interaction based on shared norms of conduct and communication (language).

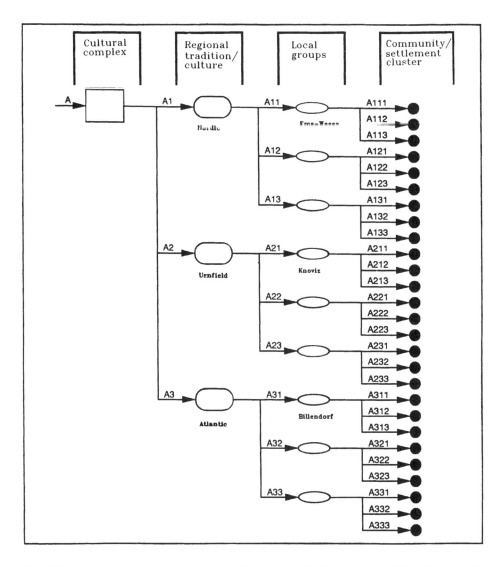

Fig. 28 Terminology employed to characterise different geographical levels of cultural identity in material culture in Bronze Age Europe.

These preconditions imply that the formation of cultural identities in the Bronze Age demanded a degree of economic and social compatibility or equality between the regions involved in the circulation of bronze. The process of developing a cultural identity that is not based on a migration thus entails two stages:

1 Acceptance of new materials and value systems linked to them. In this phase the consuming region is dominated by the producing region and local production of rather simple tools (mostly imitations) takes place. This may be replaced by the second phase.

2 Integration and transformation of new and traditional social and cultural components, including the development of local or regional specialist workshops, allowing the former consuming region to interact with the former dominating region on equal terms.

According to this, the rise of cultural identities in the Bronze Age was conditioned by a high degree of economic, social and ritual correspondence – a structural compatibility – between large regions in Europe (cultural complex). Among other things, the rise of cultural identities represented the regional formation of social self-consciousness, signalling this to former dominating groups. Internally it represented the formation and consolidation of a new dominant ideology, in the case of the Nordic Bronze Age an elite ideology. In regions and periods with strongly organised village and peasant communities pottery may take on the role of social and cultural identification for this group, replacing containers of wood and hide. There were, however, always certain elite products, such as beaten cups and amphorae, that were accepted widely across Europe as specific elite objects. Thus when defining regional cultural traditions it is necessary to consider what constitutes them: elite products versus everyday items, pottery versus metal, foreign versus local. What is the relationship between foreign prestige objects that are not imitated and locally produced elite products? Are there differences linked to male/female or other selective mechanisms that may give clues to the internal properties of social organisation and their internal and external legitimation (Sørensen 1987)? The balance between these factors defines the nature and the rate of change, but we may conclude that major breaks in cultural continuity are always related to social changes of one kind or another.

The Nordic region   The Nordic tradition emerged during the Bronze Age around 1500 BC and is recognisable until c. 500 BC. Nordic Bronze Age culture is constituted by elements of general European origin (tumulus barrows, and later on urn burials) and elements of genuine Nordic origin. Their synthesis defines a new social and cultural tradition, which can be traced for 1000 years, despite developments and changes in form and style (Figure 29). Basic ritual and social traditions, and their material correlates, however, display continuity throughout the period. To give a few examples:

1 The paired use of war axes and lurs in ceremonies, the lurs being a genuine Nordic product.
2 The employment of Nordic swords, razors and tweezers as male chiefly symbols, and belt ornaments as female symbols (Figure 29).
3 The continuous employment of the same chiefly barrows for burials.

These traditions are essentially Nordic, but certain foreign prestige goods are accepted, among them swords and hammered bronzes, as the Nordic metallurgical tradition was based on casting. Throughout the Bronze Age new Central European symbols and ritual practices are integrated into the Nordic tradition. When it was finally dissolved around 500 BC (but already beginning to break up from 700 BC with

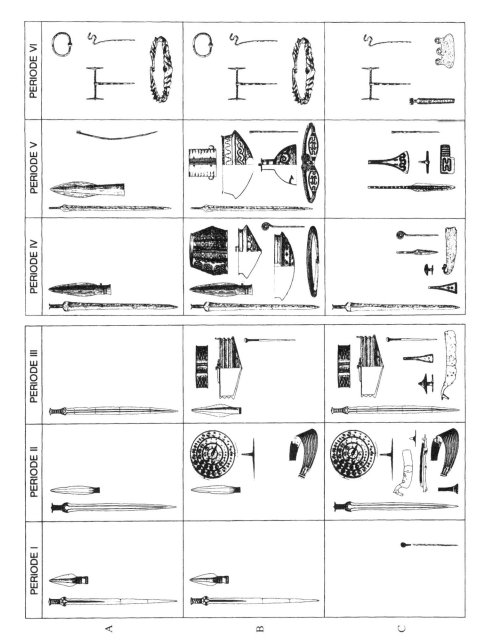

Fig. 29 The basic Nordic chiefly symbols during the Bronze Age, as represented in (A) prestige goods depositions of single pieces (one type hoards); (B) prestige goods depositions of several pieces/sets (multi-type hoards/personal sets); and (C) burial depositions. Axes, which are numerous in hoards, do not appear in burials (see also Figure 34).

the advent of HaC), it is accompanied by major social and economic transformations (Kristiansen 1980, 24ff.; Jensen 1994; Sørensen 1989). The first phase of that process is the taking over of new non-Nordic prestige goods of Hallstatt type, indicating a weakening of social and cultural traditions and identities.

The basic components of Nordic social and cultural tradition define the larger Nordic group. Within that, however, regional and local territories can be documented, linked to minor variations in style and ritual, but still within the basic Nordic idiom. They reflect interacting elite networks, behind which we may also see the contours of tribal divisions, as suggested by Baudou (1960), and Larsson (1986). The smallest local groupings are around 40 by 40 km in size (Rønne 1986), while larger ones, characterised by inter-chiefly alliances, encompass regions up to 100–200 km in diameter. Beyond that, alliances took place with distant regions for ritual and commercial reasons.

Within the northern Scandinavian region, however, there existed another social and cultural complex of hunters and fishers, belonging to an Arctic tradition, which maintained a distinct culture. They interacted with the coastal Bronze Age farmers throughout the period, and it has been suggested that this social/economic relationship represents the genesis of Lapp ethnicity (see Olsen 1985, in contrast to Odner 1985, who places it in the Iron Age). In Figure 30 I have outlined the basic distributions of these cultural traditions, which interacted in a chain of centre–periphery relationships. From the Arctic culture Bronze Age communities borrowed the tradition of rock carving, enabling us to define ritual centres of domination, towards which surplus production and metal were directed in a process of unequal exchange. They also served as central meeting places for alliances and trade (Kristiansen 1987a).

In conclusion the Nordic Bronze Age tradition was based on a continuity of basic social and ritual traditions, within a common language universe,[2] which was able to adopt and transform new impulses over a period of nearly 1,000 years. It was finally dissolved as the outcome of basic social and economic transformations of society that laid the groundwork for developments throughout the next millennium, to which we will return later.

Middle Europe   In Middle Europe it is more difficult to come to terms with what constituted regional traditions (Plesl 1987). If we maintain that it is the integration between social, ritual and symbolic practices, the whole Urnfield complex is one tradition, consisting of a number of local and regional variations in metalwork and in pottery. These should be considered as variations on a common theme, which is also exemplified by similar series of objects, such as pins, found over larger regions (Figure 31). The most basic distinction is probably that between an Alpine western tradition and a Danubian/Carpathian eastern tradition, influencing various local groups at their peripheries.

One reason for the difficulty of coming to terms with larger cultural traditions, and their relationship to regional and local variations, is a research tradition that either separates the cultural components (studies of single types) or, where that is not the

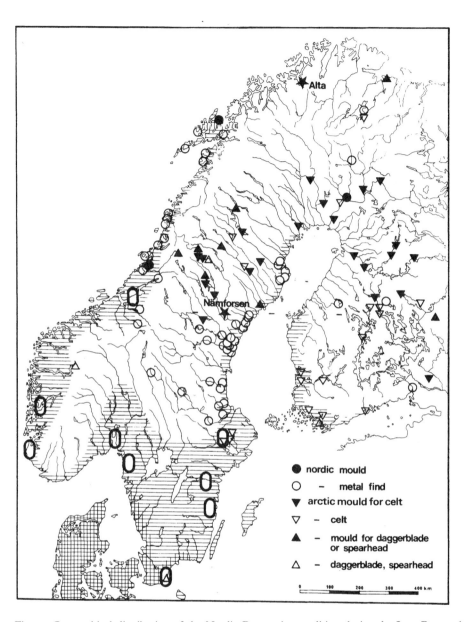

Fig. 30 Geographical distribution of the Nordic Bronze Age tradition during the Late Bronze Age, defined by the use of barrows (double hatched), cairns (horizontally hatched), ritual centres of rock carvings (ovals) and Nordic and Arctic bronzework.

case, bases itself upon highly local studies of all available material. This means that we possess a detailed knowledge of local traditions and subgroups, which we shall attempt to employ in following sections. With the exception of Müller-Karpe (1959) and von Brunn (1968), however, there have been very few studies of the relationship between local and regional traditions, although the problem is well understood and discussed, most recently for the Rhine-Swiss-French complex of the Urnfield

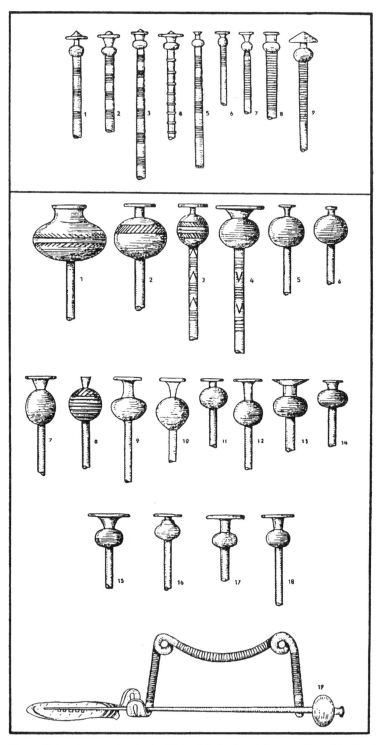

Fig. 31 Cultural interaction in the Alpine Urnfield tradition as reflected in the similarity of pins: 1–9, vase-head pins of the western Alps; 10–19, vase-head pins of the eastern Alps.

Culture (Brun and Mordant 1988). The unresolved discussions during the past forty years of what constitutes the Lausitz Culture exemplify the problem (see most recently Bukowski 1988). The reality may be that a regional tradition within the Urnfield culture, characterised by much local variation at its border with the Nordic culture tradition, was given the status of an independent culture at a time when the Urnfield culture was less well defined (Gediga 1988). In opposition to the Urnfield culture, the Atlantic tradition is today well defined in its regional and local contexts (Coffyn 1985; Brun 1991).

In conclusion A regional system is made up of a number of regional traditions that are culturally distinct, but follow the same developmental pulse in terms of metalwork, the spread of new ideas and institutions. According to this definition Europe formed a regional system during the Late Bronze Age, from the Atlantic to the Carpathians and from the Mediterranean to Scandinavia. The regional traditions shared certain prestige goods, and through elite exchange shifting patterns of inter-regional (international) exchange networks were formed, keeping the system together. Within each regional tradition local groups of more restricted circuits of exchange developed (typically 100–200 km in diameter), defined by specific local types or by variations in the execution of the common regional repertoire. Below that level small community networks of local political territories may sometimes even be defined (summarised in Figure 28). The balance between such local, regional and interregional networks determined the maintenance of the system, sometimes leading to the formation of new local groups, which might change and dominate the regional tradition. These dynamics have led to much terminological confusion in Bronze Age studies, as described in the previous chapter.

Since European Bronze Age specialists have not been able to reach a consensus on these matters I shall not make a new attempt, but shall instead consider the various social and economic strategies as they can be traced in the evidence. As a beginning I believe it is profitable to consider some cases of how boundaries were defined and how interaction and exchange took place across them. However, it is necessary first to discuss the nature of metal consumption or deposition, since it represents the evidence for reconstructing patterns of exchange and interaction.

The consumption of wealth

Metalwork was deposited in enormous quantities during the Bronze Age. There are, however, temporal and regional variations that are not random, but reflect historical changes in production, distribution and deposition, which we will trace in subsequent chapters.[3] In order to do this, we must understand the context of metal consumption and its spatial and temporal variations (for a general survey see Bradley 1990).

Cycles of hoarding and burial deposition In earlier works I have proposed certain regularities in the relationship between burial and hoard deposition, based on comparative historical sequences from Denmark (Kristiansen 1978; 1991). They can be summarised as follows (Figure 32A):

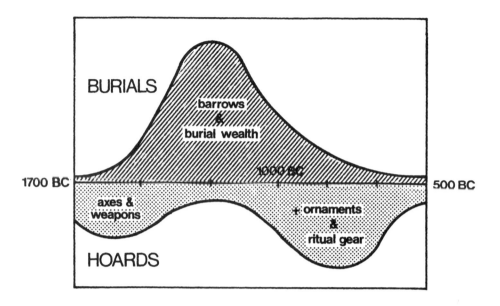

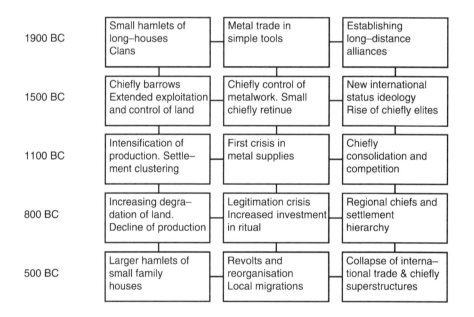

Fig. 32(A) Ritual variations through time: patterns of investment in wealth deposition and monument construction during the Nordic Bronze Age.

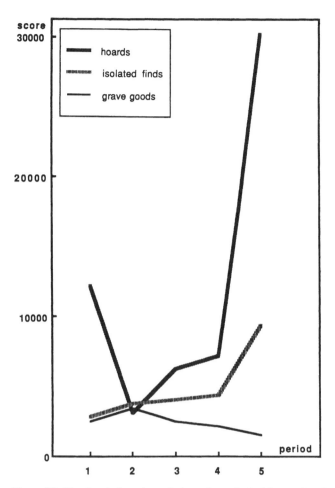

Fig. 32(B) Ritual variations through time: chronological fluctuations in the amount of metal deposition by weight scores in hoards, isolated finds and burial finds in the Lausitz Culture during Montelius I–V.

(1) The deposition of prestige goods in graves reflects the formation of new elites, often buried in large barrows. Burial ritual is used by the living to enforce the ritual and social significance of a chiefly lineage, by establishing a visible monument. The early phase is characterised by a dominance of weapons, while the increasing deposition of female ornaments represents the onset of consolidation.

(2) The deposition of prestige goods in hoards reflects the consolidation of elites, who are now offering gifts to the gods (often personal prestige goods such as swords or ornaments) in return for their support. The ceremonials may be communal, but the gifts are hidden and returns are paid by establishing the chief's sacred position as representing the gods. Burials are mostly sparsely equipped with metalwork. In this phase we may also find widespread hoarding of tools from the farming population.

(3) The intensity of deposition is governed by economic factors of production, supply and distribution, as well as by ritual considerations. Changes in quantities of deposition can be expected to reflect changes in political and economic conditions.

The above propositions suggest a complex interplay between social strategies, ritual practices and economic conditions. However, I do not claim that they cover all variation, only that they serve as an interpretative point of departure for examining temporal and spatial variations on a regional scale (e.g. Barrett and Needham 1988, table 12.1). But they do suggest that the consumption of metalwork, whether in hoards or burials, must be considered as variations on a common theme, the ritualised formation and reinforcement of power. We can therefore expect cyclical regularities in the relationship between different modes of deposition in time and space. This is indeed the case, as revealed by changes in hoarding frequencies in Middle Europe during the Late Bronze Age.

Two trends can be observed: first a shift in the deposition of bronze hoards from east Central Europe (Ha A2–B1) to western Europe (Ha B2–3) during the Late Bronze Age (Furmanek and Horst 1982b, Karte 5–6). Second, in both areas the hoarding of personal prestige goods, weapons and ornaments, was preceded by a period of chiefly warrior burials (Wegner 1976; Bradley 1990, fig. 22). What we see, then, is a change in the depositional context of prestige goods from burials to hoards, often in rivers, corresponding to the sequence outlined above for the Nordic and Lausitz regions. It suggests changes in the way metal was employed in social strategies. It may reflect either a period of consolidation, or a period of intensified social and economic competition. For reasons to which we shall return, I assume that the change of deposition reflected both a more hierarchical (consolidated) and open (competitive) society whose internal dynamics were played out through competitive exchange and the deposition of metalwork at all levels – from chiefs to farmers and smiths. It is indeed the rise to dominance of a social group of farmers that is responsible for the large-scale hoarding of tools – axes and sickles – during Late Bronze Age Europe. In northern Europe the change from chiefly to farming depositions can be represented graphically (Figure 34). By Ha C all hoarding had come to an end, and warrior elites were once again buried in barrows, a change that cannot solely be ascribed to the employment of iron. A new social order and a new elite had been established.

Within these general trends in the consumption of wealth we find local and regional cycles that correspond to changes in economic conditions and in long-distance exchange, which will be illuminated in subsequent chapters.

The representation of content and context Hoards cover a broad spectrum of types in terms of content and context, which may not necessarily correspond to a single model of the ritual deposition of prestige goods. I shall therefore make an attempt to delineate a systematic method for understanding the content and context of hoarding. It will make it easier to characterise and interpret hoarding in subsequent chapters without too much repetition.[4]

It may be that the question of the nature of deposition – ritual or secular – may in the end not be so decisive, if we can characterise and define hoards in terms of their content. After all, different causes of deposition may be closely related, although it may not look that way at first sight. If we take warfare, it represents the conclusion of

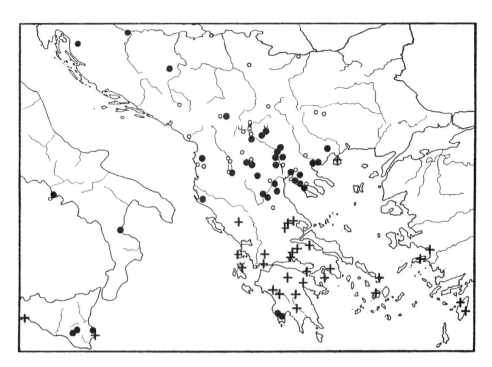

Fig. 33 Ritual variation in space: distribution of Balkan or Macedonian pendants in burials (circles) and sanctuaries (crosses).

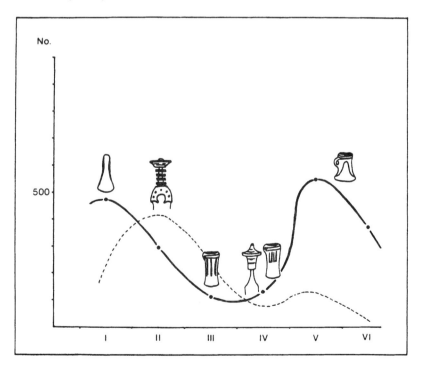

Fig. 34 Axe and sword frequency in Southern Sweden over the six Bronze Age periods.

social and economic conflict; both may lead to an increase in hoarding. Ritual depositions may increase in periods of social stress in order to legitimate the existing order, and warfare may lead to similar depositions, either to hide valuable items from raiders, or to hide the booty. Most important, therefore, is the characterisation of hoards, their composition, find contexts and distributions. I propose a four-step strategy of analysis (Kristiansen 1974b):

(1) Whom do the hoarded objects represent? For example, personal equipment (one or several sets of ornaments), a metalsmith/trader (many similar objects, scrap), farmers/peasants (single objects such as axes or sickles), or the collective gathering of the metal of a village or hamlet (all types mixed together).

(2) What do they represent? This question overlaps with the above, but represents a further analysis of regularities that can be linked to social groups and to the nature of hoards: were they prestige depositions, or did they rather represent capital intended for payment and distribution? The answer may depend on where in the process – from production to final destination – the hoarding took place (to be discussed below).

(3) Who deposited the objects and how? Those represented by objects in the hoard may not be those who deposited it. In the case of ritual hoards it could be a public act of the family on behalf of a dead chief. We only need to assume correspondence if the act of deposition was secret and hidden, meant to be recovered. Therefore contextual analysis of the find circumstances is important: are there traces of ritual to suggest public deposition, was it possible to recover the deposition, how were the objects ordered, etc.?

(4) Where and why? This overlaps with the above, but stresses the location of finds – in wet or dry conditions, in settlements or at their fringes in inaccessible places, etc. They may help in understanding the relationship between landscape, settlement and ritual places. Here we can finally approach the question of why, but it seems less important if we are able to determine points 1–3.

When these questions have been analysed we have a point of departure for understanding hoarding as relating to the use and function of bronze in society. From here regional analyses of social and economic dynamics of distribution and consumption of metal can start. Von Brunn has stressed the different roles metal played in the economy in Central and northern Europe, based primarily on an analysis of points 1 and 2. The dominance of tool hoards in east Central Europe stresses the importance of bronze in subsistence and the significance of metal production and distribution, while the dominance of ornaments and weapons in the north should point to their employment in prestige building. This may be partly true, but it should be pointed out that it does not rule out ritual motives for hoarding in Central Europe although their deposition close to or within settlements suggests that many hoards were originally stored only for a period of time, to be recovered when needed (e.g. von Brunn 1958; see, however, Jannsen 1985). Hungarian scholars, such as Kemenczei (1984) and Mozsolics, have in several publications stressed that hoarding occurred in waves that can be linked to major social and historical changes of population (Mozsolics 1957; 1967), although Mozsolics has retreated from a simplistic cause-and-effect interpretation (1985). Mandera (1985) has further suggested that most hoards represent secondary deposition in periods of unrest of the votive gifts from sanctuaries above ground, a hypothesis yet to be confirmed.

If, however, it was common to store metal seasonally until it was needed for distribution or use, for example as payment (Pauli 1985b), the lack of retrieval may indicate warfare and disruption. It could also be, however, that hoarding represented a ritualised way of getting rid of seasonal overproduction, to prevent inflation; and in terms of personal prestige goods it represented not only a way of limiting the amount of prestige goods (inflation), but also competition for prestige through destruction (potlatch). Since basic components of ritual and religion were more or less similar all over Europe, I assume a ritual motive underlies most hoarding episodes. It should be noted as well that the hoarding of prestige goods is quite common in Central Europe (Schumacher-Matthäus 1985), challenging the former interpretations of Mozsolics (see also Wanzek 1989).

The conclusion is that whether hoards were deposited for ritual or for secular reasons, their composition is the most important parameter for understanding their function, to which I shall now turn.

The representation of sequence: production, distribution and consumption When discussing the production and exchange of metal, hoards play an important role, because their deposition was not fixed – they could, in principle, be deposited at any time and at any point during the sequence from production to regional and local distribution and final consumption (whether for recycling or for ritual deposition). Their content may further represent persons or groups of people, functions and uses of metal, that are found neither on settlements nor in burials. Burials and settlements represent by comparison a fixed context in time and space. Hoards are dynamic and changeable – they represent, potentially at least, what happened from production to use in settlements and burials. In sum, they record some of the economic activities that linked settlements and communities together (Figure 35).

Some hoards represent the content of traded goods, corresponding to what a single person could carry. That is most clearly demonstrated by the north German hoard from Koppenow, which was found in the wooden box it had travelled in (Sprockhoff 1956, 39). Most hoards were deposited in an ordered way, in pots, stone cists, in wooden or other now vanished containers. Whereas burials indicate a more permanent presence of the individuals buried, and therefore can be used to delineate ethnic and settlement boundaries, hoards may tell us about trading visits to foreign territories, or they may testify to an exchange for the metalwork of another group. Only when depositions of hoards are dominated by indigenous metalwork of personal prestige sets can they be paralleled with burials in signalling ethnic and cultural traditions.

Let us, however, assume that hoards and their composition can be used to

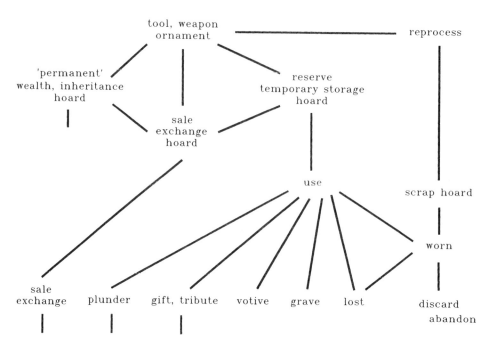

Fig. 35 The circulation of metal and some methods of deposition or discard of metal objects in the Bronze Age.

characterise the production and distribution of metalwork. We may therefore distinguish different types of hoards depending on the stage in the distribution process at which they were deposited, but independent of the causes of hoarding:

(*1*)   *Scrap hoards for recycling/melting down* (Figure 36)   These are less common than normally postulated, as many hoards containing broken pieces do not belong in this category, since the broken pieces are not dominant, are often rather large and can be fitted together to define original objects. They belong then to the categories defined below of distribution hoards or personal hoards. Scrap hoards occur in Central Europe during Ha A2 and B1, and in western Europe during HaB2–3, as well as during the early Urnfield period.

(*2*)   *Production hoards* for trade   These consist of one or several series of identical objects, most of them new (Figure 37). They may be on their way to local or distant groups, gradually becoming mixed with local types, defining the next variant.

(*3*)   *Distribution hoards*   These consist of smaller hoards for trade and further distribution, often mixed with new local types or a little scrap/raw material. This is a very common type, useful for identifying trade relations. We may distinguish between hoards for local distribution, mixed up with local types and often rather small, and hoards for long-distance trade, which often maintain their original composition over longer distances (Figure 38).

Fig. 36 Scrap hoard for recycling from Eiby, Zealand.

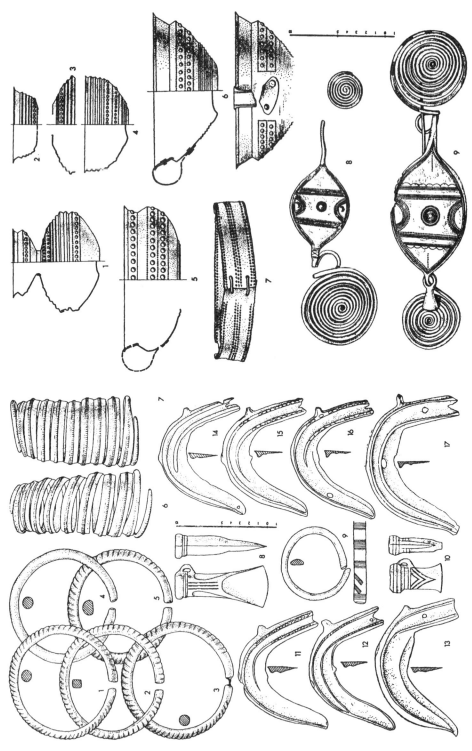

Fig. 37 Set of personal valuables, and trading goods, from the central site of Stramberk-Koptouc in Moravia.

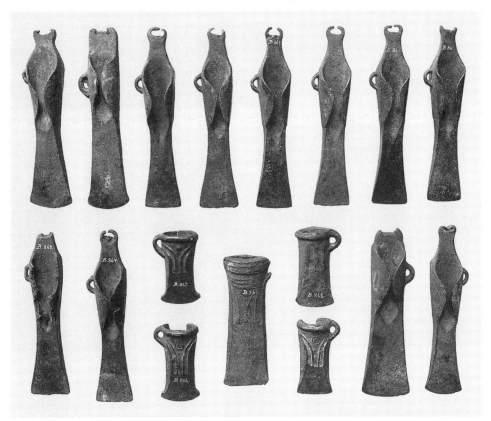

Fig. 38 Distribution hoard of identical Central European winged axes from Ørbæklunde, Fuen, Denmark.

(4) *Personal hoards* These consist of sets of personal ornaments, weapons or tools (Figure 39). This category is much larger than normally believed, as it often contains sets from several persons that have to be separated out by careful examination, e.g. employing wear analysis. They may contain supplementary symbolic objects of wagon/horse equipment, depending on regional traditions for the decision of which elements to deposit (horse harnesses/phalera in eastern and northern Europe, wagon and wheel fittings in western Europe). Series of single objects may also belong here, if they are worn, representing a group of people (e.g. sickles or neck rings), just as many single finds belong here. What social bonds or circumstances made several persons, or often two, deposit their personal ornaments together it is difficult to know. But it suggests that there existed specific ritual or social relations between groups of people, often two, during the Bronze Age.

(5) *Community hoards* are of two types: ritual hoarding of costly ritual gear, normally not linked to other forms of metal deposition (e.g. lurs and shields); and composite hoards of the hamlet or village, representing a mixture of the above types in various combinations, often containing many objects.

Fig. 39A Personal hoard consisting of two sets of female ornaments from Rannered, Northern Jutland.

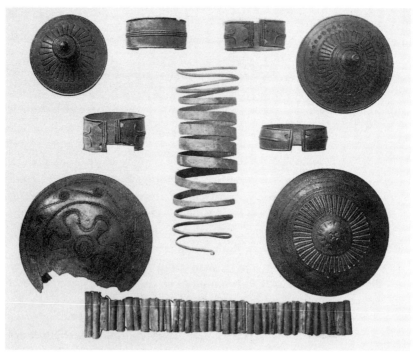

Fig. 39B Personal hoard consisting of two sets of personal female ornaments, from Kirkendrup, Fuen, Denmark. The hoard also contained imported metal vessels of the type found in Stramberk-Koptouc (Figure 37). The arm spiral is a Lausitz type, and reveals the exchange route (see also Figures 42–45).

As most hoards are to be considered as closed finds, except those where repeated deposition could take place (e.g. in rivers and caves), they are extremely valuable in both chronological and cultural-historical studies, because they often define the limits of trade (spatial interaction) and the time limits of what was in circulation at a given time (chronological interaction). This is normally restricted to a single period, generally its early and late parts, which can often be determined by an analysis of wear on the items. It is a myth that hoards normally contain objects from different periods – rather, that is the exception, reflecting periods of extreme scarcity of metal, or simply the random discovery of hoards during the Bronze Age itself.

It should be noted that none of these categories can be defined absolutely, only statistically by combination analysis. They represent ideal types varying around a norm. It should also be noted that elements from one type may be found in another type, e.g. some scrap metal in distribution hoards. Ritual destruction is a common phenomenon not to be mistaken for scrap hoards, just as selective hoarding of neck rings, for example, should not be confused with distribution hoards if there are worn pieces among them.[5]

We have today a series of regional Late Bronze Age hoard analyses allowing us to employ some of the above categories and considerations in subsequent chapters. I shall therefore not go into a discussion of the literature at this point.

After these reflections we can now turn to an analysis of boundaries and interaction, employing hoards, burials and type distributions.

Boundaries and interaction
The maintenance of boundaries and interaction across them are characteristic of Bronze and Early Iron Age Europe. One of the classic examples of boundary formation and maintenance in the Bronze Age was given by Eggers in his textbook (1959, Abb. 30), exemplifying the proper use and interpretation of distribution maps to define different cultural identities (Figure 40). The figure shows several characteristic features:

1 A buffer zone that separated the two cultural traditions – they are defined by different burial traditions.
2 An exchange network across the boundary defined by non-local types that also occur in the buffer zone between the two cultures.
3 The deposition of hoards and single finds in and around the buffer zone, where burials and settlements are rare.
4 To this we may add the recent evidence of a few fortified settlements in the buffer zone during the later Bronze Age (Horst 1982, Abb. 2), where trade could be carried out.

Such boundary formation is a recurrent feature of Bronze Age societies, but has been given little systematic attention. A recent study by Patrice Brun (1993) illuminates in more detail the specific features of boundary maintenance in Late Bronze Age societies, in this case between the Urnfield and Atlantic traditions (Figure 41). It shows striking similarities to the above pattern and establishes boundary studies as an

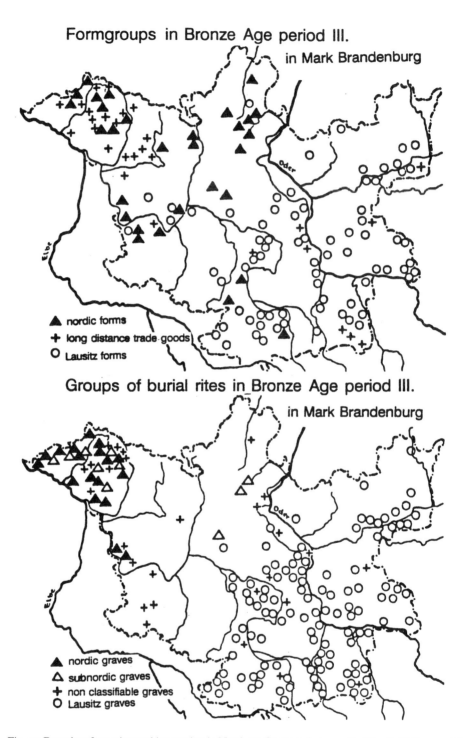

Fig. 40 Boundary formation and interaction in Northern Germany between the Nordic Culture and the Lausitz Culture.

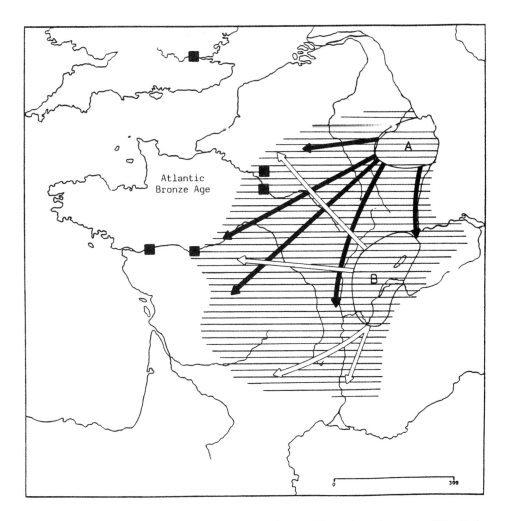

Fig. 41 Two phases (A and B) of later Urnfield expansion into France from the western Rhine-Swiss group, followed by boundary formation between the Urnfield tradition (hatched) and the Atlantic tradition (unhatched), characterised by concentrations of hoards (squares).

important new concern in Bronze Age archaeology. Also in this area the 'buffer zone' (some 60 km wide) was characterised by hillforts and an agglomeration of metal depositions (hoards and single finds) in rivers and along ancient roads. In some periods the buffer zone may develop its own cultural identity by taking over control of the trade between two regional traditions. This happened in northern Germany and in the Alps during Ha B3. Boundaries may thus be characterised as a neutral zone between two regional traditions where exchange took place at specialised settlements (e.g. hillforts). Local (mixed) boundary cultures may develop over time, just as the boundaries may shift in a process of political expansion. The latter phenomenon is well known from the Nordic tradition in northern Germany, the expansion of the Lausitz groups and the westward expansion of the Urnfield tradi- tion. On a time scale of 100 years it may be impossible to distinguish a gradual political expansion of settlements and social institutions from a more rapid migration.

But the question that remains unanswered is, how did exchange between different cultural groups take place? At what distances and at what level of organisation were those long-distance exchange networks operating that connected the regional traditions and their local groups? To answer that we must consider the nature of trade/ exchange as exemplified by the composition of hoards, the nature of border maintenance (cultural groups and traditions) as reflected above in Figure 40, and the distribution of international prestige goods across regional and local cultures.

Extensive research within the last generation into the distribution of international prestige goods has significantly widened our knowledge of the scale of long-distance exchange. Taken together with distributions of more localised types, it enables us to make some tentative suggestions as to the scale and organisation of long-distance exchange. Based on the classic investigations of von Mehrhardt, a later generation of scholars (Pal Patay, Olga Kytlicova, Henrik Thrane, Albrecht Jockenhövel, Peter Schauer) has been able to refine our knowledge of specialist workshops, especially those making hammered bronzes (drinking services and body armour), examining their manufacturing methods and the distribution of their products. The literature is extensive, so I shall confine myself to tracing the lines of long-distance exchange in Ha B1 between Hungary and southern Scandinavia via the territory of the Lausitz culture.

Let us begin by considering a map of Ha B1 bronze vessels, produced by Thrane, whose work on Nordic–Central European connections is the cornerstone of this chapter (1975; 1977). Figure 42 shows the distribution of large Ha B1 elite bronze vessels, with two marked concentrations, one in the area of production in Hungary and a more diffuse one in Denmark/northern Germany. The map suggests that the primary market of these costly buckets was the north, and that they were too valuable to be deposited on their way through the Lausitz culture for example. In fact they passed through several local cultural groups on their way north (Furmanek and Horst 1982b, Karte 3). How did this transmission take place – from village to village, or over larger distances in more directed ways? Looking at the map, one might be tempted to infer a rather organised exchange system. Different deposition habits in the intervening zone cannot explain the evidence, since other types of imported objects were deposited in the regions between Hungary and the north. Additional factors have to be looked for.

The hoarding evidence may give a clue, since we have quite a good knowledge of the composition of hoards containing products from the same workshops. Along with the large buckets belonged hammered drinking cups, whose distribution is more widespread (Figure 43), demonstrating a much larger market and more frequent deposition, this time also in intervening regions on their way north. The two distribution maps demonstrate that certain areas developed specific preferences, and that the workshops in Hungary/Czechoslovakia supplied both the western and eastern Alps and Italy, although a western, Swiss, workshop produced Jensovice drinking cups as well (Thrane 1975, 138 ff.). The latter region became increasingly

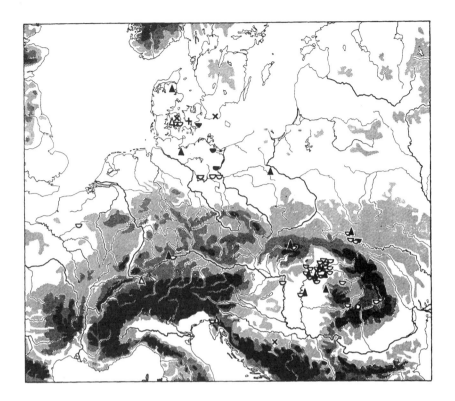

Fig. 42 Distribution of Ha B1 hammered bronze vessels, showing areas of production and consumption.

important, together with Italy, during the subsequent period. Several distribution hoards from Denmark and northern Germany containing Jensovice cups suggest that the trade was highly organised and could pass across the intervening Lausitz region without much change in composition (Thrane 1975, figs. 82, 83). That it did pass through the Lausitz region is testified by a Danish find of Jensovice cups together with a pair of Lausitz arm spirals at Kirkendrup (Figure 39). The work of Kytlicova (1967; 1985, Abb. 1) has clearly demonstrated the gradual change in composition of hoards from one region to another, but the pattern also includes many local distribution hoards.

We have to envisage a long-distance network of exchanges from one central fortification to the next, as shown by the production/distribution hoard with Jensovice cups from the large fortification of Stramberk-Koptouc in Mähren controlling trading further north (Podborsky 1970) (Figure 37). It implies the organisation of trading expeditions, protected by retinues of warriors, travelling sometimes 100–150 km from one political territory to the next. From the central fortifications, some of the material, which may also include other objects – tools, sickles, etc. – was distributed locally, accounting for smaller mixed hoards of the type carried by single individuals or a small group (summarised in Figure 44).

We can thus distinguish between long-distance distribution hoards moving from centre to centre, and local distribution hoards passing to their territories, the latter

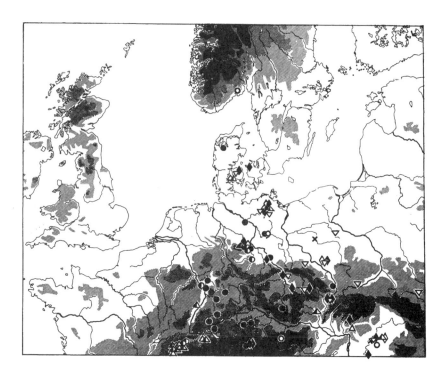

Fig. 43 Distribution of hammered bronze vessels: Fuchstadt type variants 1 (solid circle), 2 (open circle), and 3 (half-filled circle); Jensovice type variants 1 (open triangle), 2 (half-filled triangle), 3 (rhombus), 4 (open inverted triangle), 5 undecorated (open rhombus), uncertain type (cross).

dominated by local types, or sometimes by single series of foreign types, producing the kind of regional variations in hoard composition, with some overlap, demonstrated by von Brunn and Kytlicova. We can substantiate these propositions further by considering the distribution of a number of locally produced types found mostly in burials. It is objects such as fibulae and knives whose distribution reveals patterns of personal travel and contacts at the chiefly level. The route from Hungary to the north, or one of them, passed through Moravia, following the Oder river to the Baltic. Small clusters of similar fibula types in Moravia and the lower Oder demonstrate close personal interaction between these two regions (Betzler 1974). The gap between the two regions can be filled by other personal types, such as knives of Silesian type, forming one cluster on the upper Oder and another further north on the lower Oder. Here they overlap with another local distribution of Phatten knives, of a type that is also found in Denmark, on Zealand. These few examples of localised distributions, which can be supplemented by many others, form a chain of personal exchanges between local cultural groups or political territories, sometimes over rather long distances.

We can specify further the nature and impact of such elite exchange by considering relations between Denmark, especially the Danish Islands, and the mouth of the river Oder, where Nordic and Lausitz cultural traditions in settlement and metalwork

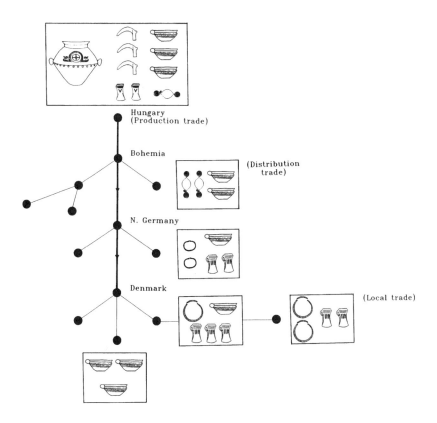

Fig. 44 Model of the regional and local distribution of metalwork from Central Europe (Hungary) to Denmark.

met. In this region the political alliances were formed which secured supplies of metal and elite goods (while another alliance system was linked with the northwest and the River Elbe). We shall therefore consider the social and cultural context of this exchange relationship. Alliances involved marriage exchange among the elite, establishing ritual friendships between chiefs (as in Dark Age Greece), and the transport of shiploads of metal products, together with some movement of metalsmiths. This is reflected in the occurrence of hoards and burials of Nordic character around the Oder, and a similar occurrence of objects produced around the Oder in hoards and graves in eastern Denmark, especially Zealand (e.g. armrings, as shown by von Brunn 1968, map 15). Miniature swords from Zealand also have a localised distribution around the mouth of the Oder (Sprockhoff 1937, map 7), and Phatten knives have a similar distribution in graves on Zealand, as shown in Figure 45.

There were regular ship connections across the Baltic between these regions. A hoard in a pot from Mandemark on the Danish island of Møn (Thrane 1958) contained a complete ornament set of Lausitz manufacture, of the personal type, which surely belonged to a woman married off to a Danish chief. We likewise find on the Oder a hoard from Nassenheide with a Danish set of ornaments from Zealand or

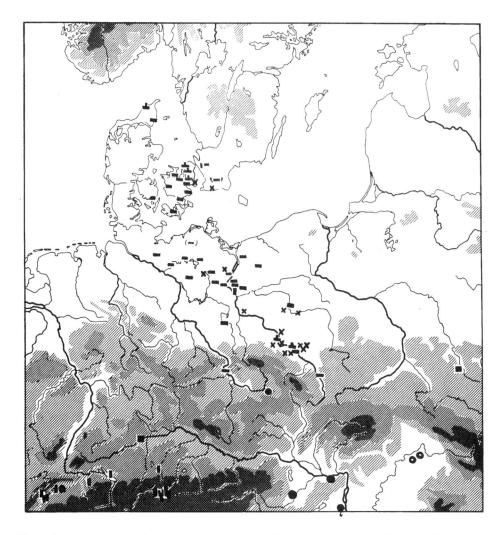

Fig. 45 Local chiefly networks of personally exchanged objects in burials between Lausitz and Zealand, represented by local variants of Phatten knives.

Fuen (Sprockhoff 1937, Tafel 16, 3–5). That the Lausitz impact during this period originated in intermarriage is perhaps best documented in pottery. As demonstrated by Jørgen Jensen, when analysing a find from Gevning on Zealand, the Lausitz influence on Danish and Nordic pottery during this period is very significant (Jensen 1967a; for Sweden see Jaanusson 1988; Mogielnicka-Urban 1989).

It seems, however, that intermarriage, with the exception perhaps of eastern Denmark, is on the whole more frequently testified from the Nordic region to southern neighbours than the reverse, at least in metal types, reflecting the dominant ideological position and expansive strategy of Nordic chiefdoms. Along the Elbe we find settlement clusters of local cultural groups, with an influx of Nordic types (Struwe 1979, Taf. 62). In several personal hoards one can follow the process from the arrival of a full Jutish ornament set, freshly deposited, towards gradual intermixing through time with new local forms, while the remaining Nordic items become worn. The last Nordic objects to be replaced were the fibulae, as they had a special significance. Another hoard on Bornholm, Grisby, is interesting in testifying to a rather direct connection between northern Germany/Lausitz and Bornholm, within an otherwise Nordic context (Broholm 1946, 182–3). The hoard consisted of two groups of objects that were separated: a collection of scrap bronze; and a group of finished products, mainly ornaments, of Nordic type, representing three personal sets. One ornament, however, is especially interesting. It combines the plate of a Lausitz Spindlersfeldt fibula with round Nordic end plates cast on to it. This is a unique hybrid form that also has chronological implications for Early Montelius IV/Ha A2. In the hoard there were several north German sickles and the personal objects of a man, a razor and an arrow head of Lausitz type. The finds suggest either that a Lausitz smith was at work for a Nordic settlement, or that a Nordic smith had returned from northern Germany with some of their products. But as the razor is a distinctively personal status object I prefer the first interpretation.

Thus a frequent interchange of people, both male and female, took place during Ha B1 between eastern Denmark and the mouth of the Oder and from there on to the Lausitz Culture. Lausitz influence was mainly felt in pottery, and in some metal forms, but these only rarely occurred in the Nordic context as imports. Instead we find high-quality prestige goods from the Hungarian plain and workshops of the Knoviz culture in Moravia, as outlined above. Social and ritual value apparently increased with distance from the source, a general phenomenon also observed in later periods (Hedeager 1978b). Elite drinking sets were a common European phenomenon. Their social and ritual importance in the north is demonstrated by the production of a specific Nordic type of golden drinking cup with horse heads attached to them. They occur either alone in ritual depositions or together with high-status male, or more often female, ornaments, such as belt buckles. Feasting, drinking and ritual seem to have been closely interwoven. In the south buckets for sieving the wine were used. In the north this was either not needed or not understood and a sieving bucket (from Kostraede) was simply lined with resin, to be employed as a normal amphora. Thus very explicit rules of foreign versus indigenous values were at work. Women particularly signalled Nordic tradition, but the basic male status symbols also remained Nordic, except for a few foreign swords testifying ritual friendship and alliances (these are more common, however, in subsequent periods, as we shall see). Nordic prestige goods were apparently valued more highly by neighbouring local groups south of the Baltic than vice versa, suggesting political and perhaps ritual superiority. It was at the level of ritualised elite feasting that high-value foreign objects had a specific pan-European significance.

These elite drinking sets indicate a chain of exchanges over rather long distances, from the large production/distribution hoards in Hungary, such as Hajdu Bözmer, to various types of distribution hoards in the northern region. Body armour belonged together with the group of elite prestige goods, originating in the same workshops in Hungary, but with a wider westward distribution and production (Goetze 1984). Chains of personal exchange relations also stretched out from the Hungarian plains towards northern Yugoslavia/Italy and the Alpine/west European region (Thevenot 1991). They were part of a major regional distribution system of metal originating in Transylvania, where we find very large hoards, especially during the preceding period (Rusu 1982; Petrescu-Dimbrovita 1977). Centres of high-quality production, however, were concentrated in Hungary, mostly, on the upper Theiss river and west of the Danube (Mozsolics 1985). The distribution of Transylvanian/Hungarian products to the north is demonstrated by the westwards and northwards spread of bronze sickles and celts/axes in hoards, some of them reaching the Nordic region and inspiring local forms (Thrane 1975, 111ff.). Tools were the medium for trading larger quantities of bronze, rather than ingots, of which there are very few in hoards. The regional variations in hoard composition thus suggest the operation of a highly complex system of production/distribution originating in the Carpathians (Transylvania). From here large quantities were exported in the form of axes and sickles. In Hungary and Czechoslovakia specialist workshops created a series of high-value prestige objects for further export to northern and southwestern Europe, sometimes accompanied by local forms (Novotna 1987; Kytlicova 1967). These workshops probably represent political confederations that were able to exploit sources of metal in the eastern Carpathians during this period, controlling the production and further distribution of prestige products – a regional division of labour (Figure 46) . Lines of exchange demonstrated the principles of overlapping spheres of power networks (community territories, chiefly alliance networks and international elite styles), reflected in the changing composition of burials and hoards.

Conclusion 1

Regional traditions, wealth consumption and elite exchange characterised Late Bronze Age Europe. How did they relate to each other? We have been able to demonstrate that the formation and maintenance of regional identities in material culture were strong in terms of metalwork. Exchange and deposition of metalwork was most intense within regional boundaries. It suggests a tight correspondence between social and cultural norms of conduct, to such a degree that foreign imports were soon remelted or recontextualised. Exceptions were personal belongings (small gifts), and ritualised prestige goods of hammered drinking buckets and cups.

Imported goods were thus accepted:

1 when elite or prestige goods had a special ritual significance linked to their type and origin (and belonged to a tradition of hammering not mastered locally);
2 when they belonged to individuals who had acquired foreign objects on a personal basis, through gift exchange, as the result of trading expeditions (for males this would involve swords and small possessions, such as knives and pins), and through intermarriage to establish or maintain alliances. In the latter case they were gradually replaced by local types. Only in pottery do we see the real impact of such

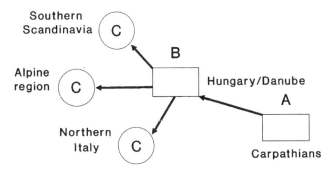

A: Large-scale metal production ⟶
   large production and distribution.
   Hoards.

B: Specialist workshops for elite
   products in Hungary/Danube
   ⟶ trade hoards (beaten cups/
   amphorae).

C: Markets/areas for elite consumption
   ⟶ mixed hoards.

Fig. 46 Model of the regional division of metal production and distribution in Europe during Ha B1.

cross-border movement (for comparative ethnographic evidence see Hodder 1982a).

This pattern suggests that exchange was couched in forms of alliance formation between elites with the aim of maintaining or increasing the supply of metal needed for producing local types of prestige goods. Rowlands has expressed this in a vivid and clear outline of the system (1980, 46f.):

> Relations of dominance and hierarchy depend directly on the manipulation of relations of circulation and exchange, and not control of production per se. But circulation and exchange cannot be separated from the production of surplus and hence the resources required to produce them . . . Since alliances are established through exchange, involving material goods, women and symbolic knowledge, success depends on maintaining flows of these resources. However, alliances in themselves do not bring prestige, but instead form the support base for local leaders to compete with each other in ceremonial displays of feasting and fighting, in the recitation of heroic deeds, and in claims to ritual and genealogical ties with ancestors and the supernatural world.

There is, then, both a ritual and an important economic side to exchange, with the bulk of material probably being tools for remelting, some of them turning up in hoards. Lines of long-distance trade were maintained with distant regions over several generations, suggesting, if not a directional trade, then something close to it, jumping over local settlement units by travelling distances sometimes of several hundred kilometres. Economic motives must have played a role, and a knowledge of regions and conditions far away must be assumed. The political and economic organisation of long-distance exchange should make us expect competition and shifts in trade routes according to changes in economic and political conditions along the routes, which we shall see demonstrated in Chapter 5. The patterns of exchange further testify to the existence of different spheres of influence – trading routes sometimes extending far beyond the actual political territories. Regional polities can be discerned in the ability of Hungarian elites (confederations or archaic states) to maintain a monopoly of specialist skills, exploiting the rich and cheap supplies of the Carpathians, and trading them further west and north as costly prestige goods. It suggests the operation of rather complex and well-organised polities.

There are, however, other important aspects of chiefly expeditions and travels to more distant regions. What was acquired was not only metal and prestige, but perhaps even more important, sacred ritual knowledge of distant regions and religions, myths linked to the performance of chiefly or community rituals. The beaten buckets and cups were nothing without information on their ritual use and social importance. Mary Helms has in several articles, recently summarised in a book (1988b), demonstrated the importance of distance in granting specific ritual status to sumptuary goods. Chiefs who travel to faraway mythical places and return not only carry with them prestige goods, but themselves becoming sacred and heroic. The travels of Odysseus are indeed a classical myth of this type. Bronze Age ideology was preoccupied with the ritual importance of heroic travels and the transmission of myths and ritual of distant origin.

We are lucky to have preserved, in the Nordic region, rock carvings of ritual scenes (ritual cartoons) and sets of bronze figurines, illuminating the use of ritual gear in large-scale communal ceremonies performed by the chiefly elites, both male and female (Figure 47). Large fleets of ships are a recurring theme testifying to the importance of trading expeditions, and in the Baltic islands groups of chiefly burials are in ship-shaped stone settings. Although there is continuity in Nordic symbolism throughout the Bronze Age, we can observe the cumulative addition of new symbols and rituals, linked to the formation of new long-distance exchange networks. During this period the bird sun-ship (*Vogelsonnenbarken*) was introduced in a standardised form along with the new hammered buckets and drinking sets, and the duck motif soon found its way onto Nordic razors.

The specific religious meaning of the symbolism need not detain us here, our concern is with the ritual context of elite exchange and consumption. Status information was ritualised and linked to elite exchange. We must therefore assume that chiefly centres had key ritual functions linked to them, and that some of the major centres were drawing people to them from far away to sacrifice (hoarding) and to receive sacred information, along with other more secular matters of metal trade and exchange. Such a pattern can be demonstrated for the Nordic region (Kristiansen 1987a). In Central Europe we must assume similar functions for some of the large

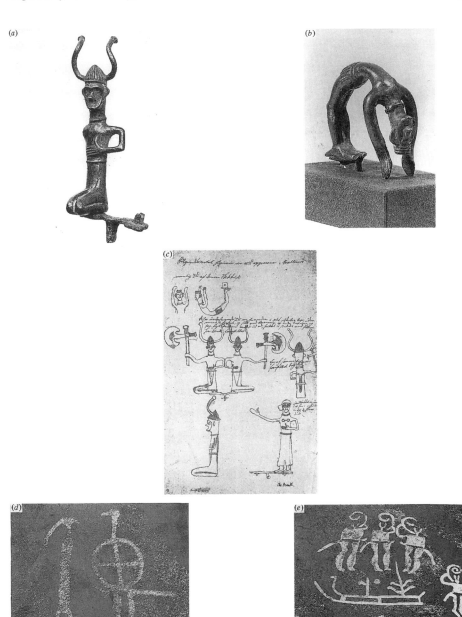

Fig. 47 Rock-carvings and statuettes showing ritual performances by the chiefly elite of common Bronze Age myths: (a) male warrior chief with horned helmet and ritual axe (originally a pair); (b) female priest in a short corded skirt doing ritual acrobatics; (c) drawing from 1779 of the complete set of bronze figures of which (a) and (b) are the only surviving pieces; (d) rock carvings from Buhuslän, Sweden, of a ritual wedding; and (e) lur-blowing men with horned helmets and a ship with a life tree. These ritual cartoons hold a potential for reconstructing ritual scenes which can be compared with written and archaeological evidence from Central Europe and the East Mediterranean.

fortified settlements and for ritual central places at rivers and lakes, or in caves, characterised by clusters of hoarded bronzework. At the local level ritual holy places, such as bogs and other inaccessible areas, with taboos linked to them, were employed for ritual depositions. This leads on to the role of consumption – the regular deposition of metalwork in hoards and graves.

As we have maintained a double ritual and economic function for elite exchange we shall do the same for wealth consumption. Economically it was a way to control the circulation and value of prestige goods; socially it was a method of enforcing dominance by ritual means, whether at a personal level in burials or as gifts to the gods in hoards. We can observe a macro-historical geographical shift in the employment of hoard deposition from eastern to western Europe. It represented increased competition, inflation of value and attempts at consolidating the existing social order by ritual depositions. Thus hoarding was linked to competition and conflict under conditions of growing pressure on established hierarchies, eventually leading to their collapse or transformation, while burial consumption was instead linked to the emergence and consolidation of new elites. The balance between the different hoarding categories may also give a clue to these historical changes. A dominance of ritual hoarding of personal prestige goods is suggested as representing the consolidation of elites (gifts to the gods), whereas increasing frequency of production and distribution hoards rather points to increasing competition, inflation and perhaps warfare. Thus I see no opposition between the various interpretations of wealth depositions, they need not assume different types of society, as recently suggested by Bradley in an interesting outline of the problem (1984, 101 ff.). Rather they emphasise different phases within historical sequences of change. In order to throw more light on the basis of change, we shall consider demographic and economic trends in the Late Bronze Age.

4.2 Demographic and economic trends
After the expansion and acculturation of the Urnfield culture over most of Central Europe the subsequent consolidation from c. 1100/1000 BC is characterised by population increase, reflected both in settlements and in the number of cemeteries.

Cemeteries and settlements
Urnfields and village organisation belong together. The urnfield is the cemetery of a larger community. When talking about demographic trends we can therefore employ the number of urnfields and their size in parallel with actual settlements as indicators of settlement size and density. This is necessary, since in many regions urnfields are better known and excavated than settlements, which are not a homogeneous category. We can distinguish between regular farming communities in villages, small groups of farms or hamlets, larger defended sites with specialist functions of various kinds and seasonal or specialist settlements, e.g. in caves or mining communities.[6]

Before discussing the internal organisation of settlement and individual cemeteries let us consider some general demographic trends as reflected in regional surveys. In a recent quantitative summary of the Polish evidence the increase in the number of

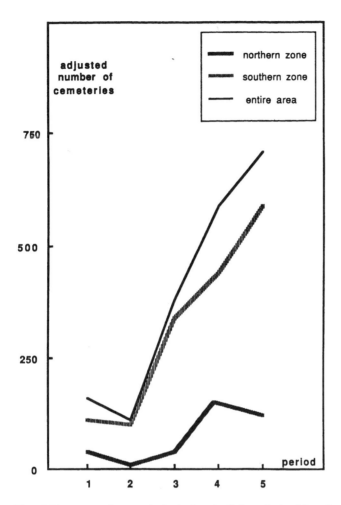

Fig. 48 Frequency of cemeteries in the Lausitz Culture during Montelius I–V.

cemeteries is very significant (Figure 48), occurring earlier in the south than in the north (Stepniak 1986). If we compare this with a diagram of settlement numbers in the Knoviz group, that displays a similar picture (Figure 49). An analysis of settlement, burials, hoards etc. in a smaller region of Poland demonstrates in a more detailed way the build-up of settlement in relation to topography and soil types (Figures 50, 51). Settlements of the early Urnfield period were scattered, but concentrated at the best soils (period III, Ha A1–2). Later settlement expansion was located mainly on second- and third-category soils along river valleys in periods IV and V (Ha B1 and Ha B2–3), and in the central area clustering is evident. Gediga's maps demonstrate the build-up of settlement during the later Urnfield period, and the inclusion of increasingly poor soils. Other regions display basically similar trends (e.g. Gedl 1992; Mordant and Gouge 1992). In the Nordic area there is both increasing clustering and also settlement expansion onto more marginal soils in eastern Scandinavia (Welinder 1976; Kristiansen 1978). In the Swiss region lake

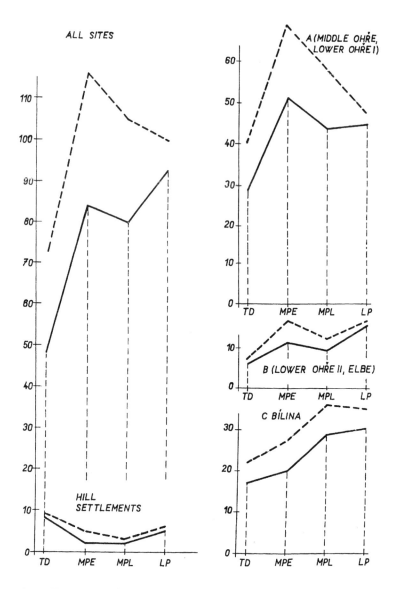

Fig. 49 Frequencies of settlements from the Knoviz group during Br. D (TD), Ha A1–2 (MPE), Ha B1 (MPL) and Ha B2–3 (LP) for the whole settlement area, and for three local areas.

shore settlements witness dense populations towards the end of our period, and the employment of both lowland riverine/lake-shore locations as well as mountain settlements testifies to a dry climate and intensive exploitation of all available resources due to population clustering (Primas 1990). The occupation of caves and rock shelters in mountainous regions is widespread (Bouzek 1982; Petrequin 1988).

In conclusion, there can hardly be any doubt about the build-up of population and settlement density as a general trend during the 300 years in question, although one has to consider the internal structure and size of both settlements and cemeteries.

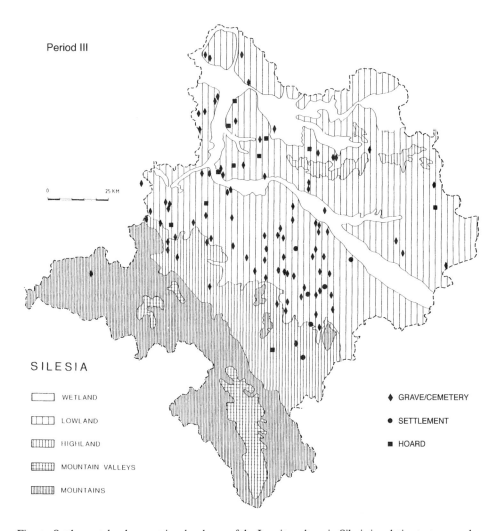

Fig. 50 Settlement development in a local area of the Lausitz culture in Silesia in relation to topography during the Late Bronze Age, Montelius III–V, showing expansion and increasing settlement density. Symbols: rhombus = grave/cemetery; circle = settlement; square = hoard.

One should also be aware of the inter-regional dynamic of settlement: an increase in one region can often be linked to a decline in a neighbouring area. Such dynamics can of course reflect economic change, as seen in less bronze being deposited in hoards and burials, but they can also result from an actual decline in population and eventual expansion or slow migration into other regions. Therefore one needs to take into consideration cemeteries, metal depositions and settlements to evaluate the nature of change. This has been done by Furmanek for Slovakia, demonstrating that a build up of both population (number of cemeteries and settlements) and economy (metal depositions) in the Lausitz group corresponds to a similar decline in more southerly neighbouring regions, especially those earlier inhabited by Tumulus culture groups (Furmanek 1985, Abb. 12–14). It suggests that the Lausitz region

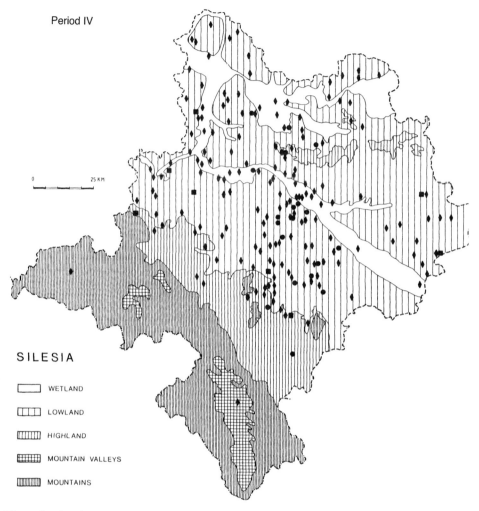

Period IV

0   25 KM

SILESIA

☐ WETLAND

▥ LOWLAND

▥ HIGHLAND

▦ MOUNTAIN VALLEYS

▨ MOUNTAINS

Fig. 50 (*continued*)

received populations from the Central European Danubian region, rather than the reverse, as was believed earlier. Similar regional dynamics have been demonstrated for the Nordic regions, where a decline in western Scandinavia is counterbalanced by expansion in the East (Kristiansen 1978), and we must recognise that such cyclical processes of expansion and decline were an inherent feature of Bronze Age societies at both local and larger regional levels, as we shall see later. On a larger regional scale the Western Urnfield tradition (RSF) experienced consolidation and boom in terms of both settlement and metalwork during its final period Ha B2–3, leading to increasing social differentiation, e.g. in terms of fortified settlements and elite burials (Brun 1988a, figs. 7, 18).

The three centuries from 1100 to 750 BC (the Middle and Final phases of the Urnfield culture) therefore witnessed an overall trend towards settlement concentration, population increase and social and political hierarchisation. These processes,

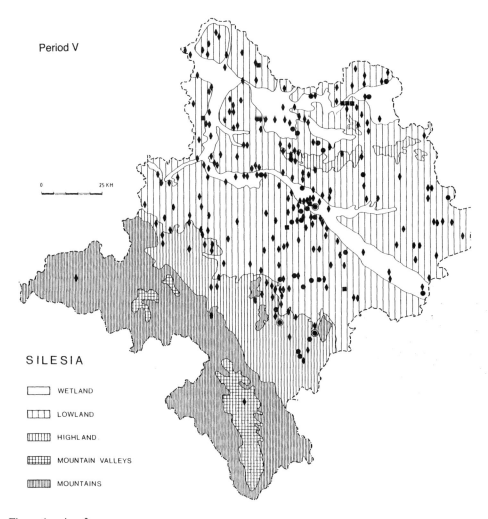

Period V

0   25 KM

SILESIA

☐   WETLAND

▥   LOWLAND

▦   HIGHLAND

▦   MOUNTAIN VALLEYS

▥   MOUNTAINS

Fig. 50 *(continued)*

however, were seen to operate in an east–west direction. In Ha A2–B1 expansion took place towards the northeast and southeast, stimulating developments in the Lausitz culture and in the Villanovan of northern Italy, as we shall see later. During Ha B2–3 similar processes took place in the Western RSF groups (Figure 41), while the Danubian/Carpathian region was in a period of transition, to be discussed in the next chapter. On the whole the period must be characterised as stable, despite local ups and downs, witnessed in the many continuously occupied settlements and urnfields. The build up of population in large organised communities (Figure 52), however, demanded an intensive exploitation of the landscape, which in the long run could lead to degradation of the soil and economic collapse. In such a situation small changes in climate, rainfall or other factors could prove disastrous. We shall therefore turn our attention towards production and the economy.

Classification of Agricultural soils	Cemeteries 20 40 60%	No.	Cemeteries 20 40 60%	No.	Cemeteries 20 40 60%	No.
Class II		29		29		31
Class III		33		47		71
Class IV		14		32		29
Class V		19		22		45
Marshes		1		9		4
Forest		5		8		13
Bronze Age	Period III	101	Period IV	147	Period V	193

Fig. 51 The development of settlement location, as represented by cemeteries, in relation to soil quality, in Silesia from Montelius III to V, demonstrating the increased use of poorer soils.

Subsistence and economy

In many regions the Urnfield period represented one of the most densely populated eras of later prehistory, only paralleled by medieval and historical settlement. One therefore has to ask, with Harding (1987, 37): 'What new production methods were adopted and what new resources tapped to feed the extra mouths which the field evidence seems to attest?' First of all, the expansion of settlement into less densely settled areas, the inclusion of new ecological niches, in itself created economic potentials. But most settlement areas already had a long history of activity, and they now became more heavily settled. Landscape and land use were well organised, as reflected in land divisions, and the systematic layout of settlement, still best documented in England; the landscape inhabited by the people of the later Urnfield period was therefore an open one in most regions. Forests had virtually disappeared in all settled areas, and what was left was exploited in a controlled way for grazing, fencing, leaf foddering, etc. There were still large tracts of more marginal land that were covered by forests or had been abandoned due to over-exploitation and degradation, but the settled areas were open and intensively exploited, and settlement now occupied most land suitable for farming/fishing, both upland and downland. The dry climate allowed the settling of low-lying, fertile soils along rivers and lakes, e.g. the River Thames, the northwest European lowlands and the Swiss lake dwellings.

This is the parallel evidence provided by pollen diagrams, settlement surveys and palaeobotanical research. Although most pollen diagrams are still from northern Europe and Switzerland (summarised for Denmark in Hedeager and Kristiansen 1988; for Sweden in Berglund 1991, 405ff.; for England in Bradley 1978 and 1984; for Middle and northern Europe in Audouze and Büchsenschütz 1989, ch. 9, plus case studies: Kloss 1986; Lise-Kleber 1990; Girard 1988), diagrams are also now appearing from Spain and Portugal and the Mediterranean. They all point to an open landscape of pastures and agriculture. In many regions husbandry based on large

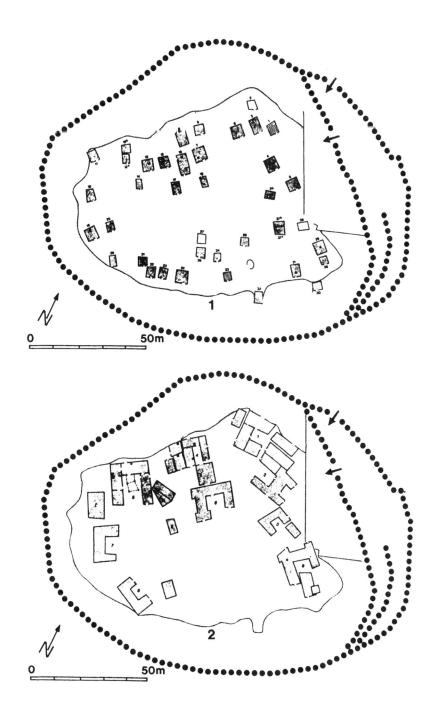

Fig. 52 Plans of the Urnfield settlements Wasserburg, Buchau in Baden-Württemberg. The early phase at Wasserburg from 1100 BC comprised thirty-nine blockbau houses, while the later phase comprised nine large two-winged houses and several ancillary structures.

free-grazing herds remained the dominant subsistence strategy. But in comparison to earlier periods intensive agriculture played an increasingly important role, especially in Central Europe, but also influencing the Nordic and Atlantic regions, e.g. through new crops and farming practices, including more efficient ploughing methods (the composite ard).

The stable agrarian communities had adopted a range of new cultigens to add to barley and wheat that were to continue into the Iron Age (summarised in Jocken-hövel and Ostorja-Zagorski 1987; Körber-Grohne 1987; Willerding 1970). Millet, oats and horsebean became important (Küster 1988b; Jäger 1987), as well as legumes, while rye began to appear. The naked variant of barley became common, as well as bread wheat. Barley was on the whole dominant in northwest and northern Europe (England and Scandinavia) while wheat was more frequent on the intensively tilled valley and flood plains of Central Europe. However, there was much local variation. Barley was employed due to its suitability on most soils, including more sandy ones, and its use in beer production. The use of oats reflected the importance of the horse, which also appears in the bone material in larger numbers than before, perhaps with the exception of eastern Europe, where it became common earlier (Bökönyi 1986). The new crops, millet and rye, were well suited for more sandy soils, which to a large degree had now been settled in northern Europe, especially in the region of the Lausitz Culture, but also in western Europe. Horsebean, the expansion of which is primarily linked to the Urnfield period (Jäger 1987), was valuable in crop rotation as it re-established nutrients, and several oil-bearing plants such as flax and the poppy were also exploited systematically for the first time. All over Europe, weeds, such as goosefoot or gold of pleasure, were systematically collected on fallow fields, to be included in the diet (Willerding 1988). A division of crop husbandry strategies between intensive arable farming and extensive farming appeared (Veen 1992).

When we consider the production of metal tools we find a good correlation with the above evidence. During the Urnfield period agricultural tools of bronze were for the first time mass produced, increasingly replacing stone, bone and antler, which were, however, still widely used for many purposes. Sickles and axes now appear in great quantities, especially in the Carpathians, but soon in most regions, leading to regional types (Lausitz, Middle German, Nordic, etc.) (Figure 53). The numerous sickle hoards testify to their massive trade and circulation, and the importance of grain production. It may even be that some groups of sickle hoards, containing used pieces, should be seen as belonging to central settlements, hoarded by the community or its leader, either for ritual purposes, or simply as a mean of storing the sickles over the winter (Brunn 1958). The occurrence of sickles mainly in female burials (e.g. Furmanek and Stloukal 1986, Tabelle 7) suggests that harvesting was carried out by women, as in historic times. The many axes demonstrate the importance of wood working and carpentry (house and boat building), whereas most axes would seem to be too small for felling primary forest. Cutting of secondary forest and leaves for cattle fodder was probably the most common practice in this period of prehistory. Another indication of the importance of grain production is the widespread occur-

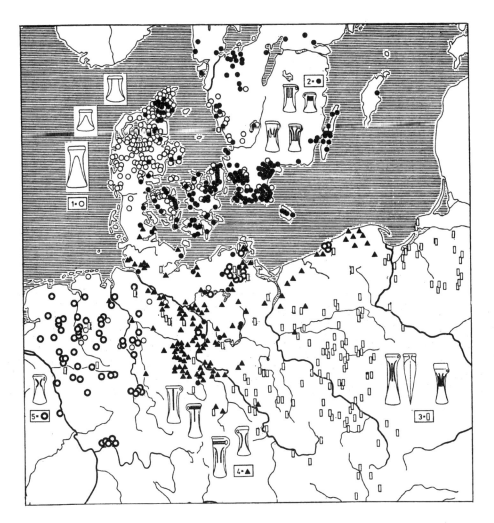

Fig. 53 Local cultural groups in lowland Northern Europe during Montelius V, as represented by axes.

rence of deep storage pits, as in the Knoviz culture; they are later also well documented in England (Audouze and Büchsenschütz 1989, 129), just as raised storage huts on four solid posts are common in most settlements. In a simulation study of a Lausitz economy, plant production is thought to account for 66 per cent of daily calorific intake, and husbandry only 20 per cent (Rydzewski 1980).

If we consider husbandry, cattle was in most regions still the major meat supplier, but significant changes had taken place in the relative balance of animals in several regions. Compared with earlier times sheep/goat and pig are more common, a trend which continues during the La Tène period. But regional variations are considerable. In the northwest, in the marshlands, cattle were still dominant although on the retreat compared to sheep (Ijzereef 1981, 194), whereas in southern Scandinavia, where large treeless commons had emerged, sheep/goat and pig became increasingly important during the Final Bronze Age (Figure 54). This trend seems to apply to a

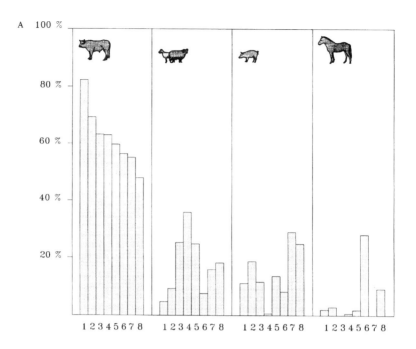

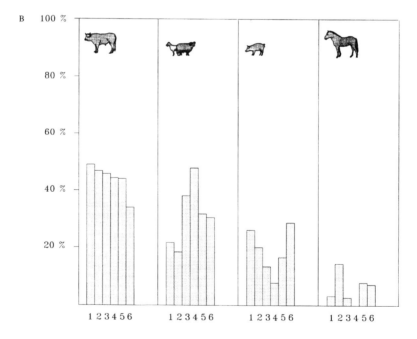

Fig. 54 Animal bone frequencies at South Scandinavian settlements from (A) Late Bronze Age IV/V to (B) Late Bronze Age V/VI, showing the increase of pig and sheep over time. (A) (1) Kirkebjerget, (2) Voldtofte, (3) Fosie IV, (4) Bulbjerg, (5) Hötofta, (6) Kvarnby, (7) Haag, (8) Veddelevvej. (B) (1) Kolby, (2) Andala, (3) Veddelevvej, (4) Fosie IV, (5) Hasmark, (6) Abbetved.

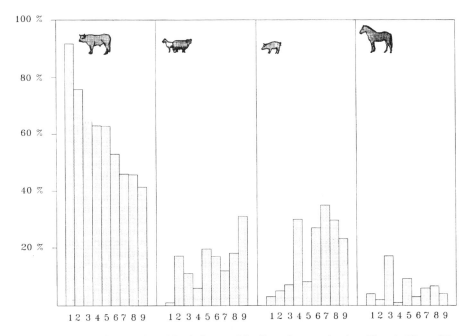

Fig. 55 Animal bone frequencies at North German/Nordic settlements (1, 2) and Lausitz/Central European Late Bronze Age/Early Iron Age settlements (3–9). 1 Kratzeburg, 2 Gühlen-Glinenick; 3 Smolenice-Molpir, Slovakia (HaCD), 4 The Heuneburg (HaD), 5 Lübbenau (Lausitz), 6 Wüste-Kunersdorf (Göritzer Group HaC), 7 Dresden-Coschütz (fortified Lausitz settlement), 8 Tesetice, Moravia (HaCD). According to Figure 54, 1 and 2 should represent chiefly settlements.

larger region in Central Europe (Figure 55) (Jockenhövel and Ostorja-Zagorski 1987, 46; Teichert 1986; Ambros 1986; Kokabi 1990), as well as in the Alpine area (Figure 56) (Chaix 1986; Ostorja-Zagorski 1974, fig. 6),[7] Iberia, Italy (see Chapter 8.2) and the Balkans (Greenfield 1988). It reflected both ecological changes, dry open land becoming more common, and shifts in exploitative strategies, sheep now being producers of wool rather than meat and milk (Ryder 1988).

There are, however, also internal variations to be observed. In one of the large chiefly settlements in Denmark, Lusehøj/Voldtofte on Fuen, to which we return in the next chapter, 80 per cent of all animal bones were cattle (Figure 54, A1). This represents a new economic division between chiefly settlements dominated by cattle (cattle were also the prestige animal in social and economic transactions, as later recorded by Tacitus), and normal settlements dominated by sheep/goat and pig. The latter must have supplied wool for the chiefly settlement, along with other products. Similar variations can perhaps be detected in some of the Lausitz fortifications, dominated by cattle, as opposed to settlements with mostly pig (Figure 55) (Ostorja-Zagorski 1974, Table 2), although ecological conditions, nearby forests for pigs to roam in, are decisive as well. Another type of economic diversification occurs with seasonal transhumance between upland and downland grazing, e.g. in Switzerland (note 7), as also proposed for eastern Europe, especially Rumania (Comsa 1988).

On the whole there is a general European tendency towards more sheep and fewer

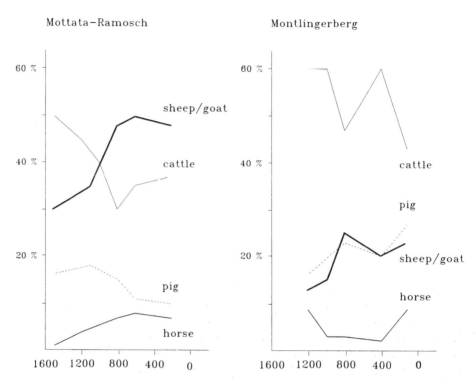

Fig. 56 Changes in the relationship between cattle, sheep/goat and pig from Middle to Late Bronze Age and Early Iron Age at two Alpine settlements – Mottata-Ramosch and Montlingerberg.

cattle during the Bronze Age, although the evidence is still scanty and uneven. As the Voldtofte case demonstrates, in this period we can expect local variation due to social and economic diversification. More generally cattle dominated in the west of Europe in the marshes and on the large pastures of northwest Europe. Moving towards Central and eastern Europe the ratio of pig to cattle increases. A temporal trend is the decline of cattle at the expense of sheep/goat and pig, continuing during the La Tène period, as an adaption to new ecological and economic conditions, e.g. the stalling of cattle (Figures 56).

Recent studies have demonstrated the impact of Urnfield settlement on soil formation and erosion in Central Europe (Jäger and Lozek 1982) as being so massive that it can be compared with the early medieval expansion of Slavs and later Germans (Jäger and Lozek 1987). The studies of Jäger and Lozek have further demonstrated that the Urnfield period was rather dry, following a more humid phase during the Tumulus culture (Bouzek 1982).

The Urnfield economy was thus favoured by a rather dry continental climate that allowed the exploitation for agriculture of fertile low-lying river and valley land that under more humid or colder conditions was less attractive. This meant on the other hand that regions with low annual rainfall became less attractive for agriculture. Urnfield settlements had even expanded into regions of less favourable soils and built up large populations there, as in the Lausitz culture. All in all the Urnfield economy was vulnerable to soil degradation and climatic change, especially to a more humid or colder climate which began at the transition to Ha C or even earlier, to which we return in Chapter 6.

Settlement and political systems

If we next consider the internal structure of settlements and cemeteries, they correspond to each other in displaying a hierarchical structure, at least in a number of central regions. At the top we find fortified central settlements for a larger region (in general Chropovsky and Herrmann 1982). Below that were villages or hamlets of farmsteads, sometimes also chiefly compounds, replacing the fortified settlements (Torbrügge 1988, 284). The full structure has been best documented in the west Lausitz region (Bukowski 1991), but is also emerging in south Germany (Jockenhövel 1974; 1982; 1991, Abb. 8–9), England, to which we return in the next chapter, and Central eastern Europe (Saldova 1981; Bandi 1982; Soroceanu 1982). Normally their size does not exceed 10 ha, on average they are rather smaller, in contrast to the much larger Hallstatt central places, both in eastern (Horedt 1974, Abb. 2) and western Europe (Cunliffe 1982b). There are, however, some larger examples, like Hradiste, which also distinguish themselves by a more marginal position and long distances to the nearest large central place, which may suggest different functions or hierarchies among fortified settlements.

The nature of fortified settlements as central places with specialist functions (bronze casting and trade, e.g. hoards) and central economic functions for a larger region (storage huts) has been documented in numerous excavations, although these are always partial (e.g. Coblenz 1967; 1978). In the Billendorf group in eastern Germany Buch has demonstrated a settlement system in which a fortified settlement served a settlement zone of 100–200 km^2 (Buch 1979; 1985b), which, however, mainly belonged to Hallstatt C. Open settlements sites (hamlets and villages) normally held 60–180 people, fortified settlements 600–1,000 (Bukowski 1991, 101). Similar results were obtained in Bohemia for Ha B (Saldova 1981). That fortification was a serious matter is shown by the heavily fortified wall constructions and entrances, of which there was normally only one (Figure 57). At some locations there even seems to be a special residence or acropolis for an elite (Buch 1986b, 104ff.; Bandi 1982). While most fortified settlements seem to have had central economic and political functions in a local settlement system, some, such as the Wittnauer Horn in Switzerland, are also linked to the control of trade routes along important mountain passes or rivers. A temporal development is observable, as the number of fortified settlements seems to increase towards the end of our period, at least in western Central Europe (Jockenhövel 1982, Tabelle 2; Bradley 1984, fig. 6.2; Brun 1987, 56). During the same periods open settlements seem to become larger, taking the form of villages rather than hamlets[8] (Figure 52). In a study of Polish fortified settlements a trend could be demonstrated from larger multi-functional central places with an open space in the middle for cattle etc., surrounded by numerous open settlements, towards increasingly smaller and more densely occupied fortified settlements with less related open settlement, suggesting increasing conflicts that forced more people

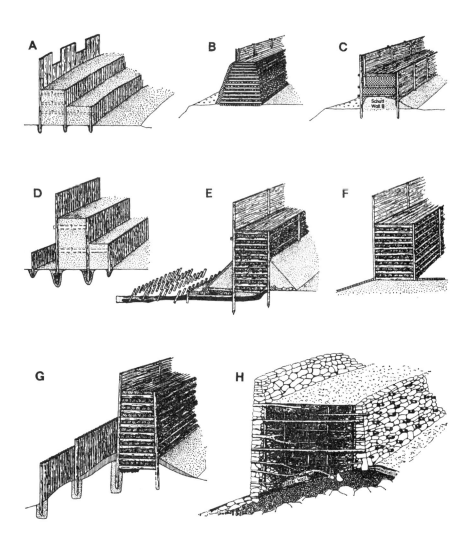

Fig. 57 Reconstruction of defence works from the Lausitz Culture, illustrating their variety and complexity.

into fortified villages, culminating in Biskupin-type sites (Niesiolowska-Wedzka 1974).

The internal structure of burials corresponds in general to the hierarchy suggested by settlements, but with much local variation. In regions with large settlements and fortified settlements we also find the largest cemeteries with 1,000 graves or more and the richest burials. Hoards also seem to cluster in such regions, as seen in Transylvania, in Rumania (Soroceanu 1982), and in the Lausitz culture (Brunn 1968). In regions with less dense and hierarchical settlement systems urnfields, and probably also settlements, are smaller, as observed by Torbrügge for Bavaria (1988) and

Mordant for France (Mordant and Gouge 1992), but small cemeteries belonging to single farmsteads or hamlets are well documented in the Lausitz culture as well (Buch 1986b, note 27). Whether this reflects a political structure of central settlement areas controlling more peripheral sites, or whether it instead denotes regional differences in social and economic complexity, remains to be analysed. There are virtually no in-depth studies of the internal political structure that try to answer questions about scale of political control and complexity.

The ritual of urnfields signals egalitarian village societies, and differentiation in grave goods is normally minimal. Some well-analysed urnfields, such as Oblekovice (Rihovsky 1968) and Klentice (Rihovsky 1965), suggest that the number of pots and their decoration were used to signal minor differences in status, although small groups of richer burials with swords or razors occur, reflecting village chiefs or local chiefs of some kind. They are paralleled at traditional settlements by a frequent occurrence of a single large farm (Audouze and Büchsenschütz 1989, figs. 110, 111). Demographic studies are still very rare, but can hopefully be expected to increase in number, as many large urnfields have been excavated in recent decades (Figure 58). In northern Germany and the Lausitz culture anthropological determinations from large urnfields of age and sex suggest a demographic structure much like that of the Iron Age, with high child mortality and rather few old people, although around 20 per cent died after the age of forty (between forty and sixty) (Bukowski 1991, Tabellen I–IV). Average life expectancy was for men thirty-four and for women thirty. (Figure 58B). Similar figures are found at Svarte in Southern Sweden (Figure 58C). At the Radzovce site (Figure 59A) belonging to the Eastern/Carpathian Urnfield culture an analysis has been carried out of 1,000 burials, representing approximately 70 per cent of the cemetery (Furmanek and Stloukal 1986). The average life expectancy was 22.4 years; of the dead population, non-mature individuals, i.e. children and young people, made up more than 44 per cent. These figures are comparable to the Iron Age, and to peasant populations in pre-industrial times (Figure 58D). The size of the living population has been calculated for the various phases at Radzovce, providing figures of 60 to 100, depending on which method of calculation is preferred, and they apply well to the Lausitz cemeteries (Bukowski 1991). This may correspond to a typical Urnfield village, which the lack of prestigious grave goods perhaps supports. The few interments with razors or weapons match quite well with a figure of one burial in each generation. It should be noted that although children were on the whole buried in rather low-quality pots with few grave goods, a small number of male children were equipped according to the rules of male chiefly graves, suggesting permanent and inheritable social differentiation.

Elaborate elite burials, however, are more often separated from the urnfields and characterised by sets of drinking services, weapons and armour. Kytlicova has divided elite burials into two groups: a higher-ranking group with complete sets of beaten metal drinking services, and a lower-ranking group with only one or two cups (Kytlicova 1987; 1988 with catalogue). To the higher elite should also be assigned burials with wagons and body armour. The elite burials are characterised by their

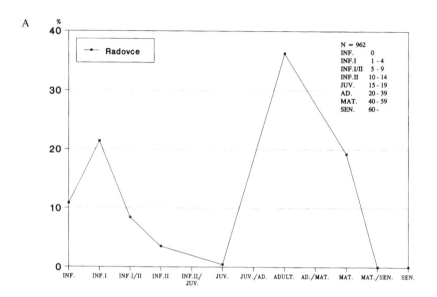

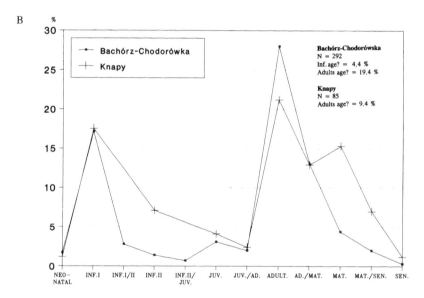

Fig. 58 Comparative diagrams of age structure at Late Bronze Age cemeteries: (A) Radovce, Slovakia, (B) two Lausitz cemeteries, and (C): Svarte in Scania, Sweden.

great similarity over the whole Urnfield region, despite local variations in culture and burial ritual. This group quite clearly signalled distance from their own people and equality to their peers (Schauer 1984b). Body armour, however, is only rarely found in complete outfits – these were apparently too costly. If we look at distribution maps of armour it clusters in the central regions of the Urnfield culture, where the production of high-status metalwork also took place (Schauer 1975; 1978; 1979/80; 1980; 1982a). An exception to this pattern is the Nordic area, where shields are more common. There is little doubt, however, that the ideology of a warrior elite

C

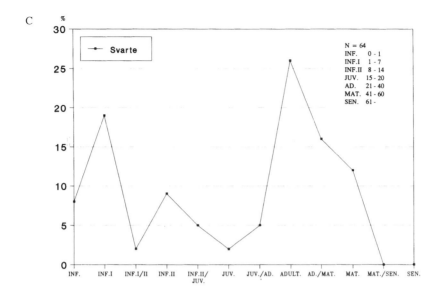

D

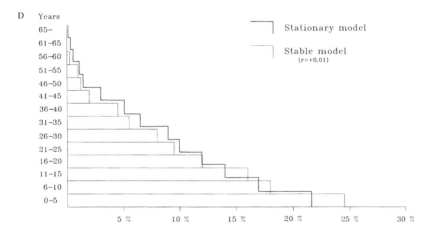

Fig. 58(D) The age structure of a living Hallstatt population based on evidence from Polish cemeteries.

dominated throughout Europe, as reflected in the distribution of swords and lances in combination with occasional finds of body armour.[9]

A warrior elite, as first defined by Müller-Karpe (1958) and refined by Schauer (1975), thus represented the political leaders of metal production and trade based at the largest central places (Figure 59A–D). They controlled a region whose size we still can only guess at, although we shall make an attempt in the next section. Below them in rank we can envisage groups of local chiefs as reflected by the richer graves in urnfields with weapons or a single beaten cup, or in ritually deposited hoards, perhaps also residing in smaller fortified settlements. Below them again were farming communities and hamlets of four or five houses with storage pits and a small urnfield. Between twenty and sixty hamlets were controlled by each fortified settlement. But

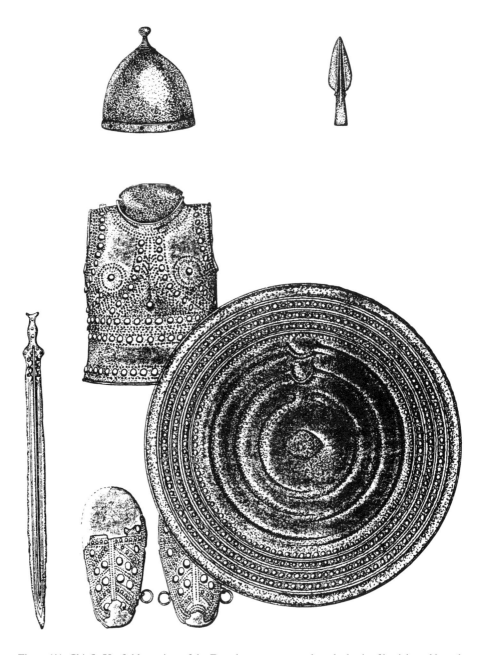

Fig. 59(A) Chiefly Urnfield warriors of the Danube, reconstructed on the basis of burials and hoards.

this was apparently not the bottom social level. In the settlements of the Knoviz culture human bones from casual burials in settlement pits (as opposed to structured burials at cemeteries) are quite numerous (Bouzek *et al.* 1966, 83ff. and 111f.), suggesting that people of low social status, landless serfs or slaves, were also part of Urnfield society.[10] In a recently published Knoviz settlement at Brezno (Pleinerova and Hrala 1988) it could be demonstrated that the skulls had been subjected to a

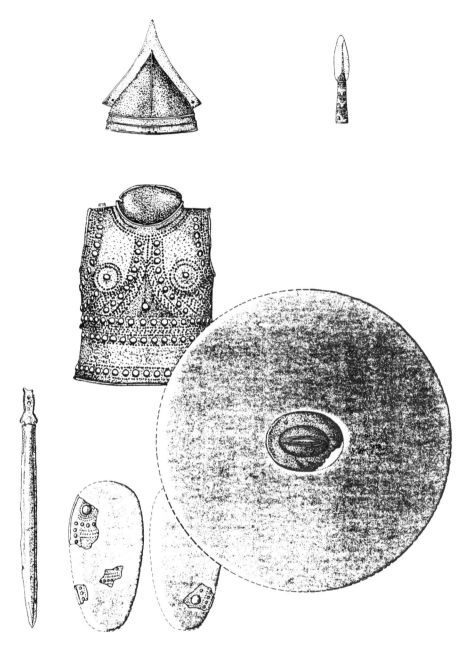

Fig. 59(B) Chiefly Urnfield warriors of the Northwestern Alps, reconstructed on the basis of burials and hoards.

series of blows, probably from stoning. It suggests that slaves supplied the labour force in mines, and that some of the upland hillforts marginal to farming could have housed such populations. As we know from the classic work of Pittioni (1951), large work groups of up to 200 people were needed in some mines, while in other regions mining was on a smaller scale, with open cast quarrying predominating. To this we

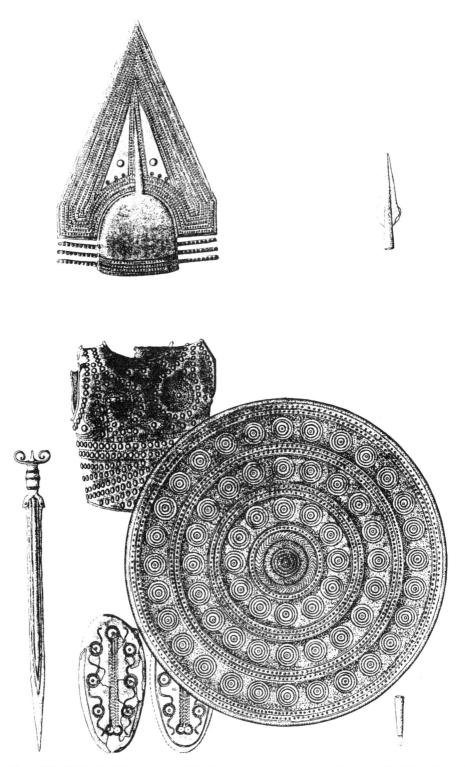

Fig. 59(C) Chiefly Urnfield warriors of Northern Italy, reconstructed on the basis of burials and hoards.

Fig. 59(D) Chiefly Urnfield warriors of Western Europe, reconstructed on the basis of burials and hoards.

should add further processing of the raw material, smelting, and the production of tools and weapons which then had to be traded and distributed.

It thus seems that the division of labour in some regions was rather highly developed, while in others villages and cemeteries were small and with little indication of hierarchy. We therefore have to discuss how social organisation and the politics of power operated. Let us first consider territories.

Today we have quite a good knowledge of the local components of Urnfield society, due to a large number of relevant studies. They all suggest the existence of well-defined settlement territories made up of clusters of settlements ('community groups', Figure 28), separated by 'buffer zones' formed by natural divisions (mountains, wetlands, etc.) Larger settlement concentrations in open land are normally 20–25 km in diameter, sometimes surrounded by smaller clusters, and in river valleys settlements are grouped in long lines, often forming a nearly continuous band. Local characteristics in pottery styles developed within these settlement clusters, suggesting that they formed a local tribal group (Figure 60). Such tribal territories, made up of a group of local tribal groups or community clusters, are typically 150–200 km in diameter, suggested by the distribution of local types of bronzework (Figure 53).

Regular inter-tribal communication was maintained at local levels, as seen in the dispersion of pottery motifs over wide regions, studied in some detail by Herrmann for the Hessen group (1966, Abb. 8), and at elite levels over longer distances, as demonstrated above. Burials and hoards with elite goods suggest that settlement clusters could have been under the political control of a single fortified settlement, with vassal chiefs distributed among smaller fortified settlements. But no systematic analysis of the interrelation between all these components has yet been carried out. We have to infer the structure of political organisation and control from the parallel indications given by settlement and burial hierarchies. In Figure 61 I have summarised the political structure of Urnfield society. It raises the question of internal relations between the components, economically (tribute/trade), militarily (the size and range of warrior groups) and ritually/socially.

Conclusion 2

The outline presented above is incomplete, as it deals with a partial historical sequence that began two centuries earlier. Our conclusions will therefore have to be incomplete and partial. A fuller understanding of the later part of the Urnfield culture also requires a discussion of its origin and spread. Only then will it become clear that what look like evolutionary changes are actually part of recurrent processes of expansion and change beginning several centuries earlier, which we shall discuss in Chapter 8. For the time being we shall confine ourselves to sketching the nature of social organisation and processes of social change. To understand change we must situate the basic components of Urnfield society in terms of our previous theoretical models (Figure 25). Let us begin with the smallest element – the village.

Villages are peasant communities, divided into family units, not farms, although smaller individual farmsteads also occur. Animals were generally kept and reared outside the actual settlement, although at some they could be fenced in behind the palisades, or were kept in enclosures, as in England. Land was divided into blocks of fields, now known from Central Europe (Brun 1987, 45), and we must think of use rights as being granted to individual families in the villages, although the overall planning of production was in the hands of the community. Hamlets and villages were dependent for their reproduction on supplies of metal, and perhaps on military

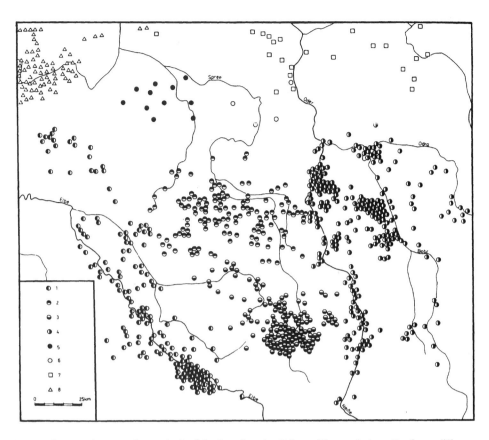

Fig. 60 Community areas (25–40 km) of the Late Lausitz Culture. The symbols 1z–8 refer to different community areas or regional subdivisions, based on local variations in material culture.

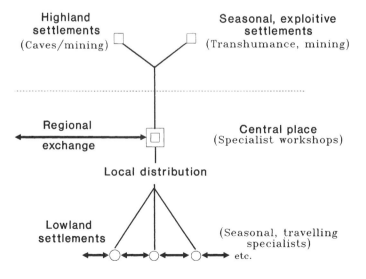

Fig. 61 Model of the Late Urnfield settlement system.

protection offered by fortified sites or larger chiefly settlements. In return they provided tribute and services to the centres.

Thus Urnfield farming communities can be suggested to represent, if not yet a class, then socially distinct peasant groups, in the process of being separated from the elite as a social class, yet strong enough to organise themselves as a group with a social and ritual identity (urnfields). Urnfield society was thus highly stratified, to be characterised as complex chiefdoms or archaic states (Engel's 'Militärische Demokratie'). In opposition to this view, Wells, in his recent study (1989), has characterised the Urnfield period as socially rather unstratified, dominated by small hamlets and villages, only to develop a hierarchy in the Early Iron Age, due to individual entrepreneurs who were offered new possibilities with the rise of city states and trade centres in the Mediterranean. The perspective is evolutionary: Iron Age chiefly centres must arise from something less stratified. In this way the evidence for hierarchy during the Urnfield period is distorted. Brun (1987), although theoretically more sophisticated, also suggests a model of evolutionary development which may be applicable when only considering the west, as he does. However, if one includes eastern Central Europe, and the 2nd millennium BC, as we shall do later, it becomes clear that simple straightforward evolutionary models do not work when dealing with Bronze Age Europe.

The nature of military organisation is crucial for understanding Urnfield society. The development of military retinues marks a significant evolutionary change in all tribal societies. When chiefs are able to mobilise young warriors in a retinue, fighting for their chief rather than their kin group, the road is paved for a breaking up of the solidarity of kinship society. How far had Urnfield society proceeded along that road? First, it has to be realised that military retinues span a wide range of types, from rather simple tribal warrior retinues that temporarily serve their chief in periods of warfare to the Viking and medieval type of permanent retinues maintained by the king, later to develop into armies (Steuer 1982). Second, we should expect regional variations.

We can approach the organisation of warfare from two angles: by considering the kind of military organisation needed to attack and defend the large fortified settlements, and from the evidence of weapons in graves and hoards, discussed above. From the structure of settlements and burial equipment it seems fairly safe to conclude that warfare had reached the level of fighting for territories with the possibility of gaining access to tribute from farming populations and from trade. Command hierarchy and specialised functions were in force, at least at the level of chiefly officers, the leaders employing costly body armour (Figure 59). The archaeological evidence suggests they had a following of young chiefly warriors, armed with lances and spears (Figure 62). Below them we must envisage a larger group of peasant warriors equipped with slings, bow and arrows, needed for the defence of, as well as attacks on, fortifications.

Urnfield social organisation and hierarchy demonstrate the interlocked processes of agricultural intensification, organised settlement expansion and massive demographic growth allowing the rise of political and military hierarchy on a territorial

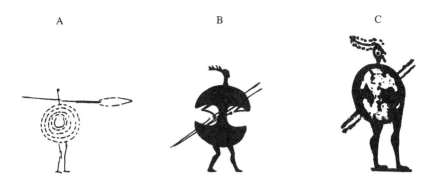

Fig. 62 Depictions of Bronze Age warriors with shield and spears, the military backbone of chiefly retinues throughout the 1st and 2nd millennia BC. (A) Nordic warrior from the Wismar bronze horn (period III); (B) Mycenaean warrior from an amphora; (C) Greek warrior from Geometric krater.

scale. Industrial production and trade in metal, however, necessitated the maintenance of open elite networks and alliances, preventing territorial closure, fostering the formation of political centres and confederations of strong chiefdoms. When expansion came to a halt, we may predict that continuous demographic growth would increase the scale of political and territorial conflict, ultimately leading to ecological and economic collapse and social transformations.

Hierarchy and fortification culminates in the west during Ha B2–3, as recently summarised by Brun (1987). It is reflected in the increasing production, distribution and deposition of metal in graves and hoards, in further fortification and the rise of new elites over larger regions. In the east there is a concomitant decline in the use and deposition of bronze (Furmanek 1973). Three interpretations are possible, any one not necessarily excluding the others: economic decline, increasing use of iron, or the expansion of conflict and of nomadic peoples, which also followed in the west during Ha C. This raises questions of increasing regional divergence and the formation of new centres of production in the south, leading to the reorganisation of trade and political centres. In the next section we shall examine some of these regional processes in greater detail.

5

Regional divergence: the Mediterranean and Europe in the 9th–8th centuries BC

During the later 9th and early 8th centuries BC the regional traditions of the Late Bronze Age began to show signs of increasing divergence – some areas suddenly witness an accelerating pace of social and economic change, while others continue older traditions. This drastic development was due to a number of new factors altering the old patterns of interaction, severing them or intensifying them. The old systems were for some time resistant to change and the consequences were therefore not seen in full until subsequent centuries. But it is in the Final Bronze Age, at the advent of the Iron Age, that the foundations were laid which determine and explain later events. The changes can be attributed to at least three factors, whose impact we shall trace in subsequent chapters: the spread of iron; the foundation of Phoenician and Greek colonies in the western Mediterranean – Italy, Iberia and North Africa; and the expansion of nomadic influences, perhaps also nomadic groups, into parts of Central Europe. The way in which these factors interacted with local and regional trajectories of change was decisive for later history.

5.1 Economic take-off in the Mediterranean: the Phoenician and Greek expansion

The Phoenicians
After the collapse of the Mediterranean commercial system around 1200 BC (Liverani 1987) and the subsequent Dark Age in Greece, commercial activities in the western Mediterranean were for some centuries of little significance. In Iberia as well it led to a kind of Dark Age, a complete change of settlement and social organisation in most regions that was followed by resettling in open villages for farming, where plough agriculture was added to irrigation. There were few bronzes, and tin bronze only appears with the emergence of the Atlantic Bronze Age and the reappearance of the Mediterranean trade network.

The Phoenicians were the first to take up economic exploration in the western Mediterranean, sometime after 1100 BC (Schauer 1983; Niemeyer 1984). However, it was not until the beginning of the Greek expansion after 800 BC that major social and economic changes made themselves felt over larger territories and led to the forma-tion of new orientalising cultures in Iberia and Italy during the 7th and 6th centuries, when the Greek city states and colonies rose to dominance. This reflects an import-ant difference between Phoenician and Greek engagement: while the Phoenicians established trading colonies in the classic sense, factories with family trading houses that left the local elites to govern their own affairs, the Greek expansion was basically a migration, setting up new Greek settlements/city states that in the long run had a much more profound effect upon local social and economic developments. The results of these divergent approaches on later historical trajectories in Iberia and Italy (Iberian and Etruscan cultures) have been pointed out recently by Frankenstein (1979; 1994), and we shall return to some of them in the next chapter. They also reflect different geopolitical strategies, the Phoenicians exploiting the far west, Iberia and North Africa, while Greek expansion was instead directed towards Italy and Central Europe, closer to their home base and traditional exchange partners. The changeover from Phoenician to Greek domination after 600 BC in the western Mediterranean therefore led to major changes in exchange networks and in wealth accumulation in the European hinterland, as we shall see. Since both Phoenician and Greek expansion in the western Mediterranean has been summarised in several recent publications (Niemeyer 1984; Harrison 1988; Kimmig 1983; Rouillard 1991; Aubet 1993), I shall only give an outline of its implications for European Late Bronze and Early Iron Age societies.

The Phoenicians had been active in the western Mediterranean, both east and west of Gibraltar, since the later 2nd millennium (Schauer 1983, 2), but from the 9th century onwards their presence began to make a more profound impact in the west, which can now be documented in some detail thanks to major excavations carried out in the past fifteen to twenty years (Schubart 1982; Niemeyer 1982; 1984, 29 ff.). We can distinguish two phases. In the early period Phoenician traders simply acted as middlemen manipulating existing exchange networks, drawing the Atlantic exchange system into the Mediterranean (Frankenstein 1979, 278 ff.; Almagro-Gorbea 1989). This 'parasitic involvement', to use a phrase of Frankenstein's, is reflected in the use of Oriental goldwork and metalwork, as well as Atlantic metal, as gifts for gaining access not only to the metallurgical riches of the Atlantic region, but also to the gold mines of western and silver mines of southern Iberia (Ruiz-Galvez 1989). Other examples of the involvement of local elites in prestige goods exchange are the introduction of east Mediterranean weapons and shields, as depicted on grave stelae, which then spread further along the Atlantic coast (to be treated in a later chapter).

The second phase, which marks a heavier involvment, begins in the 8th century. Based on their previous experiences and explorations the Phoenicians set up trading colonies and factories, exploiting the silver mines of south Iberia, especially in the Huelva area. Beginning with a few stations in the 8th century, a whole series was established and from the 7th century flourished on the southern coast (Harrison 1988, fig.; Schubart 1982). Through their factory sites, where specialised craftsmen also worked, they established trade relations with the local elites who probably took care of the mining, which triggered a rapid social and economic development, characterised by the orientalising influences coming from the Phoenicians, and innovative responses from the indigenous population. In only a few generations a radical transformation of local societies took place (Aubet Semmler 1982; Arteaga 1987; Gamito 1988; Almagro-Gorbea 1988b), leading to the formation of a proto-urban culture (traditionally named Tartessian), characterised by rich tumulus chamber burials and large structured villages up to 40 ha in area. From the 6th century, now under strong Greek influence in southeast Spain, the Iberian culture and city states developed further, including the creation of a script, in many ways a similar process to that bringing about Etruscan culture (Almagro-Gorbea 1986; Arribas 1964; Harrison 1988, 95 ff.).

The Phoenician presence in the western Mediterranean was governed by political conditions in the eastern Mediterranean. It has been suggested that their expansion of commercial activities beyond the eastern Mediterranean was linked to the need for tribute to pay the Assyrians, who left them free to trade, but imposed their demands upon them (Frankenstein 1979; for a general summary see Schauer 1983; Aubet 1993). After 900 BC the Phoenicians had specialised in luxury production – metal vessels, glassware, inlaid furniture, alabaster and ivory carvings. Due to their maritime skills (Almagro-Gorbea 1988a) and trading colonies and partners all over the Mediterranean, they could make a profit by moving commodities to places where they were rare and in great demand (Figure 63). Essentially they were able to manipulate value differences within this larger trading system. Silver was one of their major tradegoods obtained in exchange for luxury articles, since the Assyrians had a high demand for silver to be used in economic transactions, which expanded with the growth of their empire. Therefore, silver mining came to be the major economic activity in Iberia after 700 BC, probably because the Phoenicians could not obtain enough silver from other sources in the Mediterranean. When the Phoenician city states were finally incorporated into the Babylonian Empire, their trading activities waned and came to a halt after 573 BC. These were taken over by Carthage and its colonies, but these events opened up the possibility of a more massive Greek expansion, to which we shall return later.

The historical and archaeological implications of the two phases of Phoenician involvement on local and regional cultures are rather different. During the early phase Atlantic metalwork was distributed, probably by the Phoenicians, or by their trade partners, to Sardinia and as far afield as Etruria and Sicily (Ruiz-Galvez 1986). The famous Huelva hoard, interpreted as a sunken cargo of Atlantic metalwork containing more than 400 objects, is taken to represent the Atlantic trade, whereas Phoenician goldwork, armour and bronze buckets were entering the Atlantic circuit through exchange by the 9th century BC (Coles 1962; Gräslund 1967a; Hawkes and Smith 1957), probably already during the 10th century, according to recent C14 dates (Ruiz-Galvez 1995, ch. VI) placing it between 850 and 950 BC for the Huelva hoard (remains of the wooden haft of a spear) which seems to correspond with other C14 dates of the Atlantic Bronze Age (Coffyn 1985, ch. III). In accordance with this, recent adjustments of the Atlantic chronology to the Central European (Burgess 1979; Coffyn 1985, ch. III; Ruiz-Galvez 1986; Gomez 1991), place the emergence of the Mediterranean/Atlantic trade in Bronze Final III safely within Ha B2–3 (950–750 BC), perhaps with some late depositions in Ha C.

The further spread of Atlantic bronzes to the western Mediterranean – especially to Sardinia and Italy – and the appearance of some Italian objects in Iberia, can be seen either as resulting from the traditional Phoenician trading system of exchanging

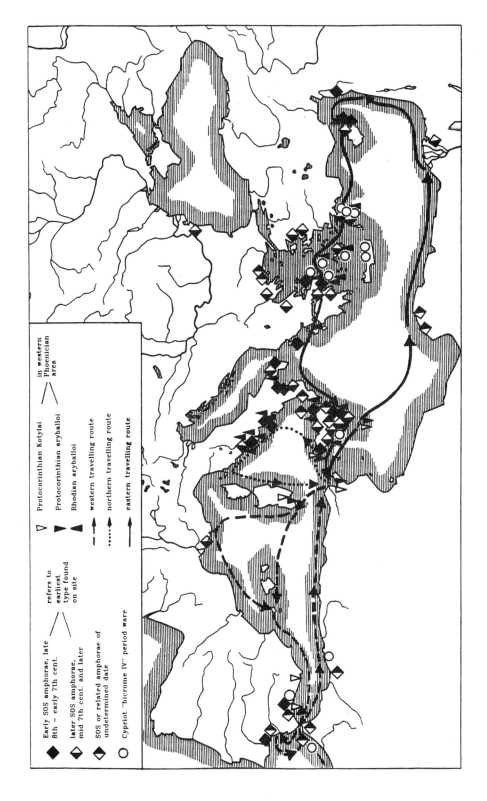

Fig. 63 Phoenician trade routes in the Mediterranean (arrows) and map of 'Phoenician' objects/trade monopoly in the late 8th and early 7th centuries BC.

the products of one region for those from another area, or as a result of Iberian/ Atlantic trade now expanding into the Mediterranean (a few Atlantic bronzes were entering the area across land from western France, e.g. the group named after the Venat hoard (Coffyn 1985, carte 11)). As the Phoenicians were also trading with Sardinia (as testified in written records back even to the 11th century BC) and Italy they were probably responsible for these distributions, although it remains a matter of discussion (Ruiz-Galvez 1986, 21 ff.). If we may take fibulae to represent personal belongings, exchanged on a reciprocal basis rather than as a trading commodity, the presence of Cypriot fibulae in the western Mediterranean – on Sicily, in Italy, on Sardinia and a little group in Iberia (Coffyn 1985, carte 24) – would seem to support such an argument (Figure 64). In general the Atlantic exchange networks did not extend beyond the southwestern tip of Portugal, except for specially traded goods. This may give us a clue to how and where the Atlantic and the Mediterranean exchange systems came into contact, to which we shall return later.

The Greeks
The Greek expansion is closely linked to internal processes at home during the 8th century: population growth, improved methods of agriculture, developments in specialist production and iron technology all taking place within the emerging framework of the first centralised settlements and cities (Snodgrass 1971; 1980; Morris 1987). But first we must say a few words about the preceding period.

As is well known, the Dark Age was only dark by comparison to the palace society of the Mycenaean period. Looking at it in its own terms it can be seen as a peaceful and flourishing period, at least according to recent excavations at Lefkandi in Euboea (Calligas 1988). From the 11th to the 9th century a pastoral economy prevailed; habitation was rather dispersed, mainly on hilltops (discussed in Snodgrass 1987, 187 ff. ; Cherry 1988, 26ff. ; Skydsgaard 1988). The social structure has been interpreted as patriarchal, with local leaders living each as the head of his family, and chiefs of their kinsmen, in sometimes rather large megaron houses (up to 48 m long). Trade with the east, especially with the Phoenicians, gave increasing access to foreign luxuries and skills (Coldstream 1982). Overlooked by the hill settlement was the burial place, where the chiefly warriors were buried with their swords and spears under a tumulus, along with their families, in the late Urnfield tradition.

Some time in the late 9th century this structure was transformed. The traditional economy and social organisation were abandoned and the population moved into new fortified sites. A complex interplay of factors lay behind this change, as outlined by Snodgrass (1980): the intensification of agriculture, leading to higher productivity and population with an increasing need to reallocate land. This is when iron comes to dominate both tools and weapons, and the need for iron must have risen drastically to meet agricultural and other basic demands (Snodgrass 1989). Snodgrass has traced the change from a dominantly pastoral to an agricultural economy by the falling frequency of ox and sheep figurine dedications at Olympia over the 10th to the 8th century (Figure 65).

From that time the pace of change accelerated. Population grew rapidly, although

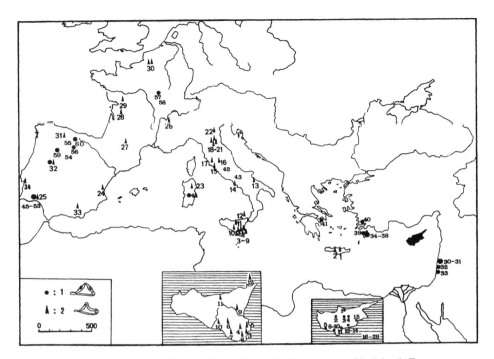

Fig. 64 Distribution of Cypriot and related fibulae in the Mediterranean and in Atlantic Europe.

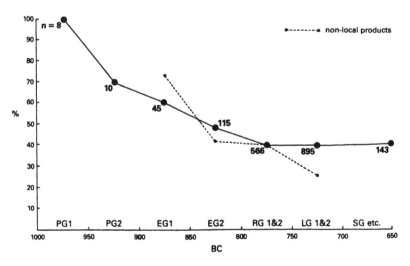

Fig. 65 Ox and sheep figurines as a percentage of all animal figurine dedications at Olympia, showing a gradual decline from the 10th to the 8th century.

we must wonder if what can be observed in the cemeteries was instead the visible effect of a major rise in population preceding the reorganisation of society around 800 BC. New communal cemeteries replaced the old family ones, reflecting the rise to dominance of new social groups, as argued recently by Morris (1987). The change in burial rite, allowing the identification of new population groups, should probably be seen as the major factor behind the steeply rising numbers of burials, rather than a sudden increase in population. This certainly took place, but was a more gradual process, as shown by settlement studies (Morris 1987, fig. 54) (Figure 66). New places of worship, later to develop into temples, were brought into use, especially after 750 BC; by the end of the century most settlements had one, providing an important ritual and communal identification of the new polis organisation (Mazarakis 1988). It meant a separation of the ritual and political power combined by the former chiefly leaders, who had taken care of ritual in their houses. Central to that had been the sacred dinner with privileged members of society, with sacrifices taking place outside in the open. It was basically similar to practices in Late Bronze Age Central and northern Europe.

The decline of the old order and the formation of new ritual centres connected to major settlements marked the beginning of a new era – that of the polis with its communal government. It brought about the overthrow of the old aristocratic leaders, and the formation of a new and much larger ruling class of landowning free citizens, introducing a new element of competition for government, and competition between city states, whether in terms of trade, temples or dedications (votive offerings). Later on this was recognised by many for what it was, a rapid and drastic change of a centuries-old social order, which led to nostalgic feelings, exemplified by Hesiod in the early 7th century (Works and Days II, 174–8):

> Would that I did not live in this fifth generation, but had either died before it or been born afterwards! This is now truly a generation of iron; for men never stop toiling and wailing by day, and perishing by night. The gods will give them sore troubles.

This apparent nostalgia found an expression in hero-worship at old Mycenaean tombs. Hero-cults began in the Dark Age, but spread rapidly during the 8th century, at the same time as the many new cemeteries and burials appeared. This supports Morris' argument (1989a; 1989b) that these changes reflected the formation of new social groups, employing old ideology as well as new burial rituals in the process, (Figure 67). In such a kaleidoscopic turmoil of change one needs something to provide assurance that some part of the old order is still intact – an anchor to the past – and the hero-cult fulfilled that desire. Old tombs fired the imagination, as well as chance finds, and even excavations, as the written sources tell us. Old finds or imitations of them turn up in offerings or in burials, most notably the golden death masks in the princely tombs of Trebeniste in Macedonia (Palavestra 1994). But they also influenced the style of certain ornaments and weapons, e.g. the reappearance of flange-hilted swords with a T-hilt, as well as appearing on vase paintings (e.g. shields), which also depicted scenes from heroic myths, as proposed by Snodgrass (1981, 70 ff.). The hero-cult originated in the new land divisions and the subsequent disputes arising from them, where references to ancestors were used to legitimate claims to land. Thus, historical continuity with the past was constructed to legitimate a new social and economic order. Soon the hero-cult led to the formation of regional

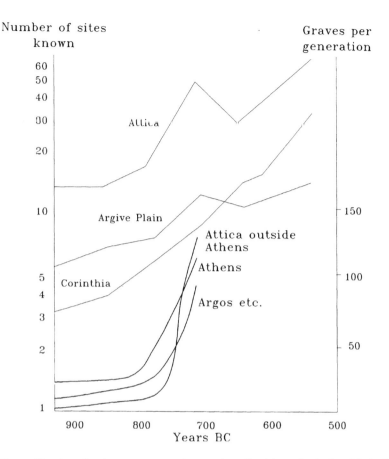

Fig. 66 Number of settlements compared to number of burials on the Argive plain in Greece.

heroes – Odysseus of Ithaca, Menelaus of Sparta, etc. – and took on a wider significance.

It is in this context that the classic epics of Homer should be seen, as they were written down some time during this period. While it can be disputed as to what extent the epics represent Dark Age society or retain elements of Mycenaean society (but see E.S. Sherratt 1990), their active function of mobilising and recontextualising the past for purposes in the Archaic present cannot be disputed (Morris 1989a). The epics were, along with the hero-cult, used to maintain common values, highly needed and relevant in a period of dramatic social change, adventurous migrations and expanding trade and warfare.

During the 8th century we can thus observe a number of diagnostic traits of early state formation in the Aegean:

1 The separation of ritual and political power, and the emergence of temples and state religion.
2 Literacy, at first employed in heroic contexts, increasingly in administrative, commercial and legal matters.

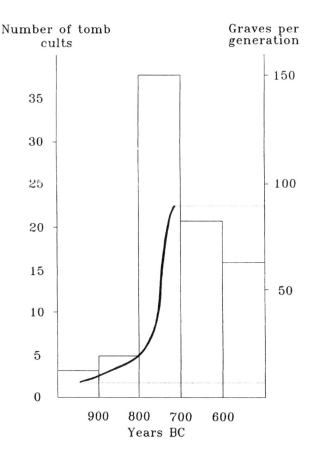

Fig. 67 Number of strong archaeologically known tomb cults compared to number of burials.

3 Ritual and heroic myths are transformed into written texts, replacing oral traditions.
4 The development of the chiefly retinue into an organised army of the city or the
state.
5 Institutionalised government, the polis and class formation.

When we link all these elements together they would seem to support the rather
far-reaching interpretation by Morris of the period as one of social revolutions,
triggering both a new social order and migrations of those who could not have their
expectations fulfilled at home. But it is also true that layers of former social and ritual
practices were carried along in new functions or as mere relics, softening the
transformation, and illustrating its complexity (Ferguson 1991). From the mid-8th
century this early state structure was in operation, and began to expand. The rapid
population increase, in combination with the large numbers of people who had
gained new social status without corresponding economic possibilities, was soon
channelled into colonial migrations, with the formation of new settlements from
mother cities. After the first foundations in southern Italy, e.g. on the island of Ischia

at the northern end of the Bay of Naples, in the early 8th century, new colonies were rapidly established in the Aegean and southern Italy (Graham 1982). From 600 BC the western Mediterranean was also included, after the decline of the Phoenicians, as well as the Black Sea coast, to which we shall return later (Figure 68).

After 700 BC southern Italy had been transformed into an extension of the Greek world, having a profound effect upon developments in central Italy and the Villanovan/Etruscan region. Until the Persian Wars of the early 5th century when Greece rose to empire and as rapidly declined, the colonies had a dominant role in influencing developments in the Mediterranean. It is remarkable that their impact was greatest during the period of city states, and declined as they reached what is traditionally considered the zenith of Greek society. But as we shall see demonstrated again and again, the observable climax of a development is not when it really happened, instead it means that it is all over.

'The trade explosion' was Collis' (1984a) way of summarising developments in the Near East and the Mediterranean from 700 BC. The magnitude and extension of commercial and political interaction is demonstrated by votive offerings in the major Greek sanctuaries. It is an interesting way of describing what came to Greece (not necessarily 'who') rather than the usual concern with how far Greek products can be traced. A recent quantitative analysis of the origin of depositions by Kilian-Dirlmeir (1985) showed that at Perachora 74 per cent of the offerings were of Phoenician origin, apparently testifiying to a trading colony, while Olympus was dominated by material from the Greek provinces, and Samos was characterised by depositions from all over the known world, including Macedonia, the Balkans, Italy, Egypt, Assyria, and even regions further afield in the Near East (Figure 69). Greek products and their associated pottery were also now widely distributed. Large quantities of pottery occur from Spain to the Near East, traded by the Phoenicians as well as by the Greeks themselves, but only as a secondary effect of more basic economic interests in minerals, especially silver, gold and iron. As stated recently by Gill in a critique of the importance attached to Greek pottery, which was a low-value commodity:

> A picture of ancient Greek artefacts is emerging which is less idealized than the 19th century view. It was a society which cared much more for gold, silver and obviously precious things than for painted pots, for ivory or metal sculpture rather than for stone – a society, in short, which is very much more like the texts rather than the imagined world of timeless philosophers and aesthetes. (Gill 1988, 741)

In material culture this international interaction is reflected in the spread of the orientalising style, originating in Asia Minor (Curtis 1988; Piotrovsky 1969).[1] The large cauldrons with animal heads, and shields or lids with friezes of lions and other animals, became especially popular items, copied widely. One may compare shields in 7th-century Etruria directly with those from Urartu (e.g. Collis 1984a, 11a with Stary 1981, Beilage 2). As has been demonstrated in several recent studies by Schauer (1978; 1980; 1982a), changes in body armour and probably also military organisation

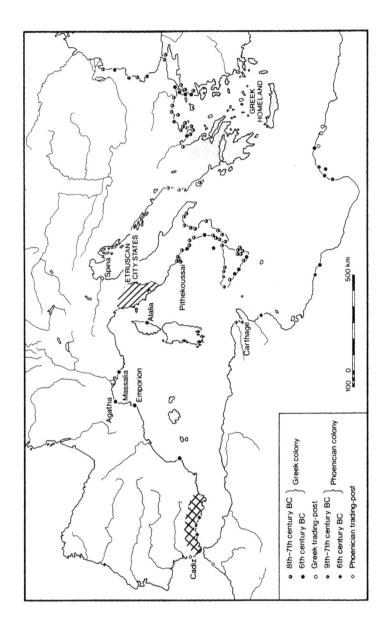

Fig. 68 The foundation of Greek colonies in the Mediterranean. Double hatched: Phoenician/Iberian interaction; hatched: Etruscan Culture.

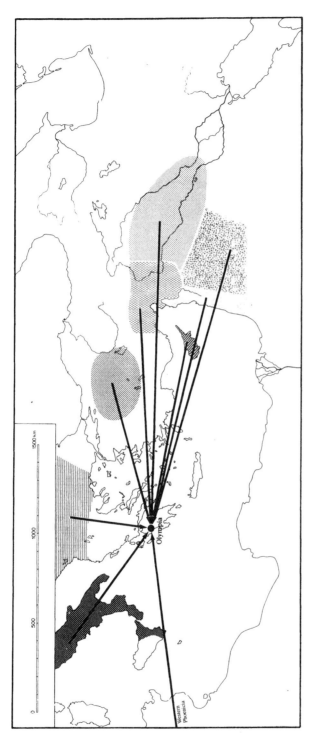

Fig. 69 Foreign dedications at Olympia during the 8th–7th centuries BC.

originated in the Near East as well, at an early date. What is important to note, however, is the organisation of warfare after 700 BC, when the Near Eastern phalanx was introduced, making possible military action on a very different and larger scale. It rested on the duties of the landowning citizens of the city state, wealthy and numerous enough to provide military service, and from that time armour began to appear in larger quantities at sanctuaries as votive dedications/offerings, while burial wealth was reduced (Morris 1987, 183 ff.). This is a pattern of social consolidation which we shall see repeated throughout Europe during the Bronze and Iron Ages. The phalanx and hoplite are yet further signs of a developed state society. With the advances in shipbuilding, enabling ships to carry larger loads of goods and men, the foundations were laid for the commercial empire of the Greeks.

Italy

In central and northern Italy we can observe a development towards early state formation during the 9th-8th centuries with many parallels to Greece (Bietti Sestieri 1981; Peroni 1979; 1989, 426ff.; Dietz 1982; Barker 1988; Bartoloni 1989; Stoddart 1989). During the final phase of the Mediterranean commercial system during the 13th century BC northern and central Italy had developed close connections with the Urnfield culture, as demonstrated by the spread of Peschiera daggers (Peroni 1956) and other objects (Müller-Karpe 1959). It is important to note that these exchange relations north of the Alps were maintained throughout the following period, after the collapse of the Mediterranean economy, as we shall see later.

During the Proto-Villanovan period settlement and economy conformed to the traditional Bronze Age pattern: settlements consisted of clusters of small houses on natural high-points which were easy to defend, surrounded by fields where the traditional grains were grown along with legumes. Defensive consideration became increasingly important from Middle to the Late Bronze Age (De Grossi Mazzorin and Di Gennaro 1992, fig. 1), leading on to an organized territorial settlement pattern in the late Bronze Age (Agostini *et al.* 1992; Ceci and Cifarelli 1992). As in Iberia, sheep were the dominant animal, whereas pigs were important as meat suppliers, normally butchered at an early age (between one and three years). Cattle were raised for milk and traction, and their numbers declined from the Middle to Late Bronze Age, though with local diversification, suggesting a specialized economy (De Grossi-Mazzorin and Di Gennaro 1992, figs. 3, 4). As in Spain and Greece, pollen analyses have demonstrated that the landscape was still covered with productive mixed oak forests, with pastures at higher elevations. The evidence suggests a mixed agriculture with a strong pastoral component, much in the same way as in Iberia and Greece. Local transhumance, where sheep were taken to the uplands for grazing during the summer, is already probable from the Middle Bronze Age. This farming practice was favoured by the rather dry and warm climate that prevailed during the Urnfield period. The change towards a more humid climate from the 8th century BC provides an interesting correlation with the major social and economic changes taking place throughout the Mediterranean. Recent research in Etruria suggests that the rise of the early Etruscan state was linked to a reorganisation of rural settlements into larger 'villa-like' farm units and to a major intensification of farming practices, especially during the 8th century, although the agriculture of this transition period is still not well known (Barker 1988). Tree crops became particularly import-ant. Chestnut was exploited systematically at least from 1000 BC, while the tradi-tional Mediterranean polyculture of the vine–olive complex was present from the 8th century, probably introduced by Greek colonists, and in full swing by 700 BC. The documentation of these changes in farming practices is crucial, as they allowed the feeding of substantially larger populations, as well as the development of an indus-trialised processing of agricultural produce into luxury products (textiles, oil, wine, etc.) for the growing elites.

In accordance with this we can observe a marked population increase during the 9th and 8th centuries, greater clustering of settlements, and the formation of central-ised sites with special economic and political functions (Bietti-Sestieri 1985; 1993, 239ff.; Guidi 1985). Systematic surveys in southern Etruria have demonstrated this very clearly: before 1000 BC 28 settlements are known, from 1000 to 700 there are 79, increasing to 314 between 700 and 500 BC. The central settlements emerging after 900 BC are very large compared to earlier ones, and can reasonably be termed proto-urban (Peroni 1979, 24 ff. and 1989, 462ff.) (Figure 70). They imply a reorganisation of settlement structure and a nucleation of population comparable to Greece, and were accompanied by technological improvements in pottery manufac-ture, metalworking and farming. Regional cultural groups evolved, identical to later political and language territories (Bietti Sestieri 1993, 244ff.). In Etruria the five largest Villanovan settlement centres later became the five major Etruscan cities in the region (Ceci and Cifarelli 1992). The site hierarchy of the early state thus emerged during the 10th–9th centuries, a development illuminated by rank-size graphs (Guidi 1985).

Thus, from the 9th century there developed in Italy new centres of metal produc-tion for the growing local elites and for international exchange and trade north of the Alps, in return for amber and other products. At first, the workshops produced in the Urnfield tradition, as it had developed in Hungary, and we can see in the distribution of certain types of metal how the frequency of exchange with the Danube intensified during this period, presumably involving an actual movement of Danubian metal-smiths to Italy. At one of the Hungarian Late Bronze Age/Early Iron Age hillforts, Sopron, domesticated grapes were found in refuse pits, indicating the intensive and wide range of exchange between the Mediterranean and Central European chiefly elites (Facsar and Jerem 1985; Jerem *et al.* 1985).

With the advent of trade with the Phoenicians (Rathje 1979), and later, in the 8th century, with the Greek colonies (Ridgway 1992), especially Pithecusa (Ischia), Greek and orientalising influences became dominant in Italy, as reflected in armour and the appearance of Greek pottery in burials (Buchner 1979). The settlement of Vejo, to which we return later, may have been particularly instrumental in developing these new relations. Changes were now accelerating at such a pace that we may assume the presence of Greece traders and craftsmen in Etruria (Fredriksen 1979) at the same time as the Etruscan city states emerged, adopting the new orientalising

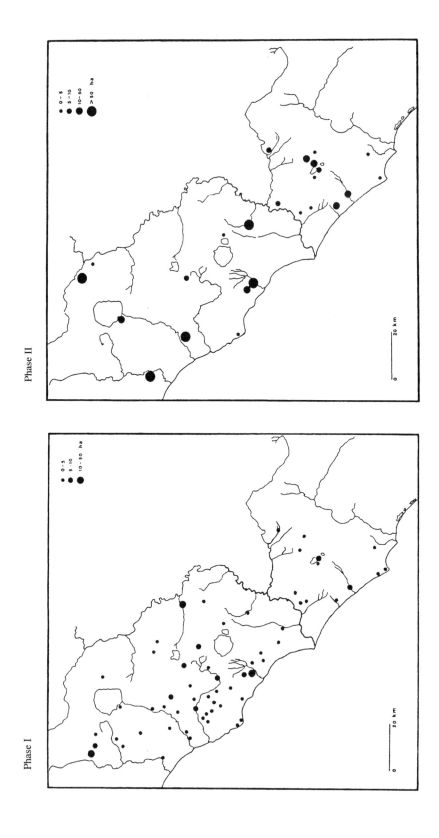

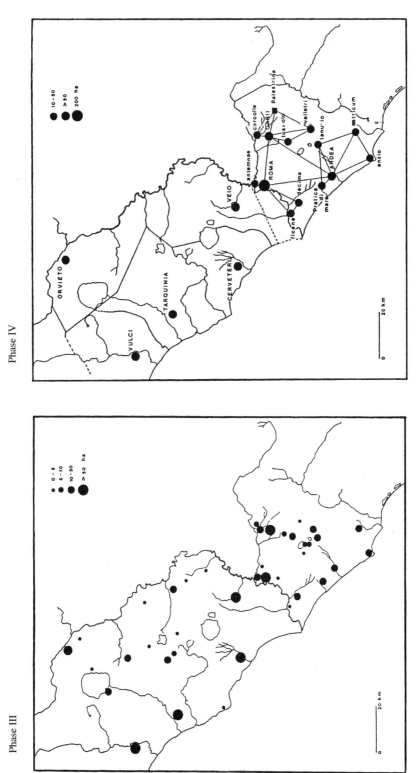

Fig. 70 The evolution of settlement in Etruria and Latium, showing an increasing trend towards centrality, followed by urbanisation. Phase I = 10th century BC, Phase II = 9th century BC, Phase III = 8th century BC, Phase IV = 7th century BC.

style, as well as other characteristics of state formation as observed in Greece. The economic basis was the greatly increased production due to the introduction of olive–vine cultivation, as well as the exploitation of the rich iron ores in Tuscany from 800 BC, the only major iron ore source in Italy south of the Alps. From the 6th century the well-established Etruscan city states already had a wealthy middle class of landowning merchants, as testified by burial monuments and texts. Wine and olive, textiles, iron and luxury goods in bronze were widely exported, as we shall see in the next chapter.

What we witness, then, is a process towards state formation leading to cultural and social identification with a political territory. It is accompanied by similar diversification in burials, where warrior elites are characteristic. Stary (1981) has demonstrated how the warrior aristocracy of the 9th and 8th centuries is replaced after 700 BC by collective warrior burials with few effective iron weapons (Figure 71). It must represent a change in the organisation of warfare, from chiefly retinues and the use of war chariots to an army of more professional warriors of free citizens as in Greece. The political leaders therefore did not need to boast of their position as warriors any longer. The few rich warrior burials of the 7th century are now extraordinarily rich (the so-called princely graves), reflecting a new and higher level of political organisation. Recent mortuary studies have further detailed the picture of social change. Bietti Sestieri (1985; 1993) has demonstrated a change from individual identities expressed in burial ritual to groups of burials corresponding to new descent groups – the *gens* – from which the new aristocracy originated. This development would seem to correspond to changes in Greece, where they signalled the rise of the *polis* (Morris 1987).

From the 7th century we can thus chart the emergence of political territories formed by confederations of city states in several regions of the Mediterranean. The Etruscans, Iberians and other groups can be identified by distributions of material culture and language, as reflected in inscriptions, although the Etruscan and Iberian languages still defy decipherment. This gives a strong clue to the parallel formation of political, cultural/ethnic and language identities, as discussed earlier for the European Late Bronze Age. It is remarkable, however, that despite regional differences in material culture, army equipment and military organisation follow a parallel trend all over Italy, presumably due to frequent interaction, alternating with warfare, especially in the late 8th century, during the period of social and political reorganisation. It is also at this time that we find both the highest frequency of warrior graves and the greatest diversity in weapon equipment. After 700 BC, with the development of infantry units of archers and fighters using sword/spear, chariots are replaced by cavalry. From the 6th century Etruscan armies were able to confront the Greeks in battle and defeat them. By then a new political balance had been achieved in the Mediterranean, and the building blocks for empire formation were in place, although this was not yet the case in Central Europe, as we shall see.

Conclusion 3

Collis (1984a, 39ff.) has characterised the beginning of Mediterranean expansion, initiated by the Phoenicians, as a 'reawakening in the west'. On the other hand, I would stress, along with Snodgrass (1980), Barker (1988), Peroni (1979) and others, that the process of change in the Mediterranean, especially from the 8th century, is a general phenomenon. It took the form of a kind of cluster interaction between demographic and economic growth, stimulating social and technological changes, and ultimately also leading to increasing demand for goods and trade. So we cannot really separate internal and external processes. Morris (1987, 196ff.) has most recently stressed that internal class conflict was at the root of change in Greece: the peasant population rebelled against their aristocratic lords (chiefs), taking over new land. To establish the new social order they founded villages/small towns and the democratic ideology of the polis was shaped during the process. Later in the Archaic period new kings or 'tyrants' took over control, finally leading to rebellion and democracy of the free citizens at the expense of the slave and serf groups that had emerged. We see at work here the recurrent opposition between aristocratic absolutism and republican rule, favouring farming/peasant populations, as is later manifest in the history of Rome. What makes it interesting from an archaeological point of view is that here written sources allow us to compare the historical sequence of changing power relations with changes in the archaeological record, which may allow us to extrapolate from the known to the unknown in Central and northern Europe.

How significant was trade during these processes of change – was it a secondary phenomenon or did it play an active economic role? The Phoenicians were obviously trading for gain in the modern sense of the word, while the profitability of Greek trade is more debatable during the early phase. The debate over the nature of the ancient economy is an old one (Finley 1973; Garnsey, Hopkins and Whittaker 1983). Traditionally, trade was considered in modern economic terms as having played a major role, but during the past twenty years a new orthodoxy has risen to dominance under the influence of Moses Finley, pointing out trade's social embeddedness. We shall approach the problem again when discussing the rise of the Hallstatt kingdoms and the Greek/Etruscan trade with Central Europe in the 6th and 5th centuries. I suggest, however, that this old dichotomy is now obsolete. The social and ritual embeddedness of trade during the 2nd millennium BC has been illuminated by Zaccagnini (1987) and Larsen (1976), but, like the ritual of diplomacy today, it was an ideological curtain behind which profit calculations were operating. To unveil it we have to document the quantity of traded commodities and how far they were moved.[2] We know for instance that early in the 2nd millennium BC Assur maintained a well-organised bulk trade with Kanesh based upon strict profit calculations and in quantities comparable to the later Venetian and English trade in textiles (Larsen 1987a). The figures given in the late Mycenaean palace records for quantities of bronze leave no doubt as to the economic significance of trade in metals at the time, which is confirmed by sunken cargoes such as that at Cape Gelidonya. We have no reason to believe that the trade of the earlier 1st millennium BC in the Mediterranean was any less organised, as has now been proved by the documentation of Phoenician factories in Iberia. But this also confirms the embeddedness of trade and prestige goods in manipulating local elites by introducing not only new status symbols, but

CENT.

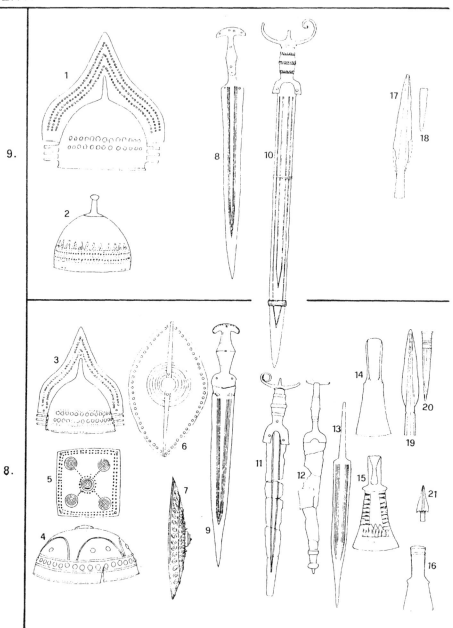

CENT.

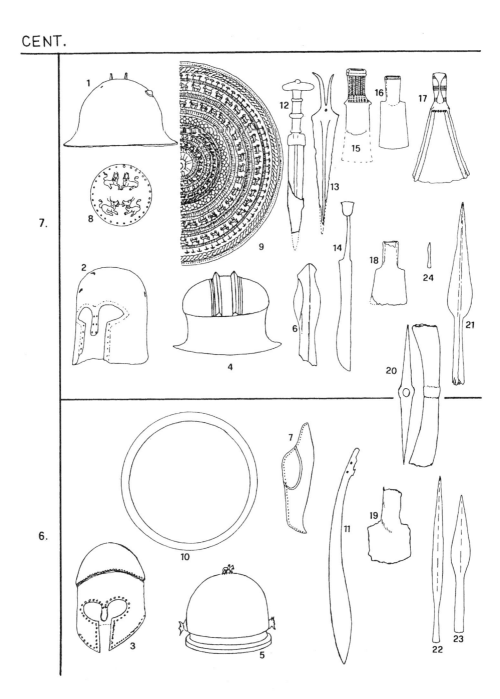

Fig. 71 The development of armour from the 9th to the 6th century BC in Italy.

also new value systems (needs) and corresponding new technologies with which to implement them (Almagro-Gorbea 1992).

The Phoenicians may have been the first to re-establish the old commercial contacts in the Mediterranean, but what happened afterwards was due to a tremendous interaction between local processes of change, spurred by a receptiveness to technological innovations and social change, leading to the explosion of trade from the 7th century onwards. It was further stimulated by the rapidly expanding demands from the larger and wealthier populations. I therefore suggest that we should consider the spread of Greek and Phoenician prestige goods in Italy and Iberia, including pottery, as the tip of a trade iceberg. So let us now consider how this initial take off in the Mediterranean influenced, or was influenced by, developments in Central and northern Europe.

5.2 Interaction along the Atlantic façade

Social and economic interaction along the Atlantic façade has been a recurring phenomenon since the Early Bronze Age for a number of obvious reasons. Tin is a scarce resource only available in a few places, among them Cornwall in southern England, northern Portugal and Brittany, and perhaps also Ireland. In fact tin can only be extracted here or in Central Europe. Gold and silver are also scarce metals, gold being available in Ireland, gold and silver in Portugal. Add to this the more frequent occurrence of copper ores, rather easily accessible, and it seems obvious that connections should develop between these regions. But that need not imply a large-scale interaction zone along the whole of the Atlantic façade, indeed in several periods there was contraction and regional closure.

The emergence of the Atlantic network

The societies along the Atlantic façade, from England to Iberia, underwent major changes after 1200 BC (Burgess 1988; Harrison 1988). Old settlement traditions and hierarchies collapsed or were given up, in many regions metal production and trade declined, and settlements were reorganised into open villages with a strong emphasis on agriculture, much in the Urnfield tradition. The collapse, however, also corresponds to the decline of the Mediterranean commercial system. When we consider what its reappearance after 1000 BC meant for developments in Iberia and along the Atlantic façade, it is clear that these two systems were to some extent dependent upon each other. To *what* extent, we shall attempt to evaluate later.

Due to remarkable progress in Bronze Age research during the past twenty years in England, France, Portugal and Spain it is possible to reconstruct in some detail the Atlantic Bronze Age as a cultural tradition in itself, its relation to Urnfield inland traditions in France on the one hand and to Phoenician and Greek trade on the other. Although the Atlantic Late Bronze Age culture, especially its late phase, the Ewart Parks and Carps-Tongue Complex, had been defined by earlier archaeologists, such as Savory (1949), it was the classic work of Briard (1965), followed by Burgess (1968) that started a new and successful phase of research, with the systematic classification, combination analysis and mapping of finds, supplemented by metallurgical analyses. With the latest major works by Coffyn (1985) and Ruiz-Galvez (1987) on Iberia and Coffyn, Gomez and Mohen (1981) on the Venat hoard, we have today a quite complete overview of metal production and distribution. We can add to this the many large settlement excavations, which have drastically altered our conception of the social and economic background (Cunliffe 1982b; Almagro-Gorbea 1986; Martins 1988a; 1988b). There are, however, still only a few attempts at integrating this evidence into a reconstruction of social organisation (Rowlands 1980; Pearce 1983).

The Atlantic Bronze Age was made up of a number of distinct regional centres of metal production, unified by the regular maritime exchange of some of their products. The major centres were southern England/Ireland, northwestern France and northwestern Iberia (Portugal). These regions were also linked to Central European exchange networks, which explains why the Atlantic bronzes, especially swords and spears, follow general European trends, although with a distinct character of their own – a conservative, archaic, approach, and simplicity. One cannot escape noticing the lack of sophistication in the metalwork, it is plain and straightforward – there is none of the stylistic artistry of the Nordic tradition or the technical mastery of the Urnfield specialist workshops. Quantity rather than quality, with some exceptions, seems to be the rule. We can only guess at the other, perishable, materials that were the objects of artistic creativity, perhaps textile production and wood working.

We can trace the beginnings of the Atlantic networks in Bronze Final II from the 11th century down to 900 BC, first emerging in southern England and northwestern France, to their forming a regional system of exchange. It is from this centre that the network is extended to include the whole Atlantic front in BF III, as a result of new techniques and greatly increased production, circulation and consumption of metal. Not until this period are stable tin bronze alloys characteristic over the whole region (Harrison and Craddock 1983). It is further characterised by an influx of metalwork from Late Urnfield Europe, especially hammered bronze buckets (Hawkes and Smith 1957), from the Nordic Bronze Age mostly ornaments (O'Connor 1980; Herity and Eogan 1976, 212 ff.), and from the Oriental/Mediterranean culture mostly weapons/cauldrons (Hawkes and Smith 1957; Coles 1962; Eogan 1990; Burgess 1991, 32ff.). The diversity is most clearly demonstrated in Ireland, testifying to its central position in the Atlantic network (Eogan 1969; 1981). It should be noted, however, that the exchange network consisted of a number of discrete regional and local circuits (Figure 72) – the West Iberian groups (Coffyn 1985, 189ff.), the French Venat groups and English local variants of the Ewart Park complex (Burgess 1968). Above these local groups, mainly defined by tools, there was a unified diffusion of elite goods, especially swords, cauldrons and spits, with, however, some marked concentrations (Figures 73–75). These suggest that southeast England, western France, Ireland and Northwest Portugal were centres of elite display and consumption. Outside these centres we find generalised distributions of tools, swords and spears, circulating more widely. The distribution pattern can be explained as the result of two different methods of operation:

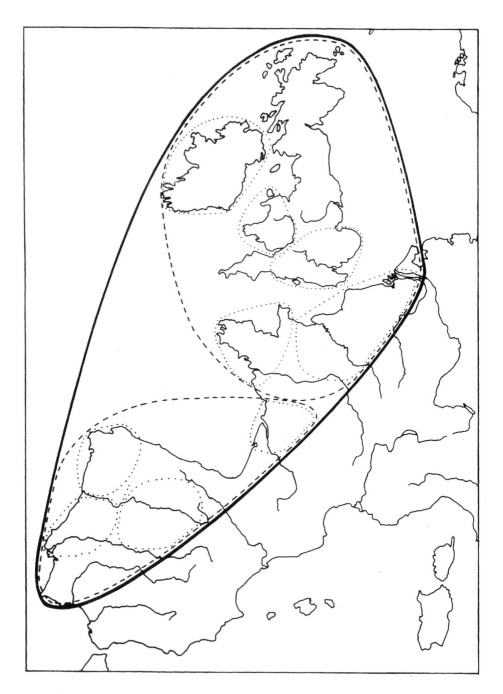

Fig. 72 Schematic outline of the Atlantic tradition and its regional/local groups.

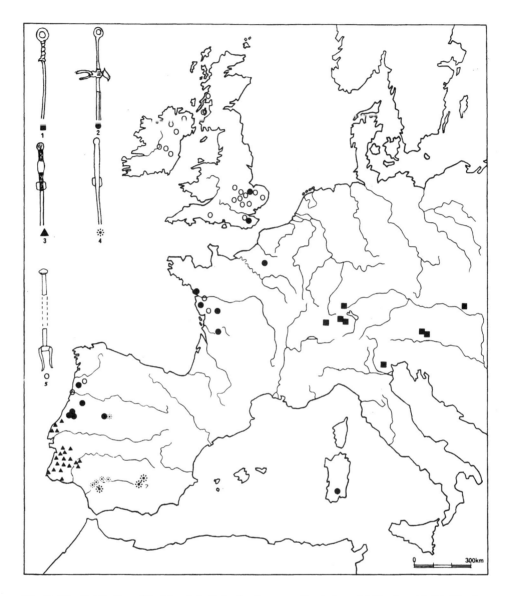

Fig. 73 The distribution of flesh hooks/spits for feasting according to type: (1) Continental, (2) Atlantic, (3) Southwest Iberian, (4) Southeast Iberian, (5) Irish-English.

(1) By long-distance trade in elite goods between regional clusters of chiefdoms, cross-cutting local settlements. This should be seen as linked to the trade in metals, as both Ireland/Wales and northwest Portugal are rich in minerals, while southeast England and western France may have been favoured by access to the Central European network.

(2) By chains of short-distance exchange circulating all types of metalwork; some regions richer in metal and therefore characterised by more competition hoarded prestige objects, while in other regions they were considered too valuable for that.

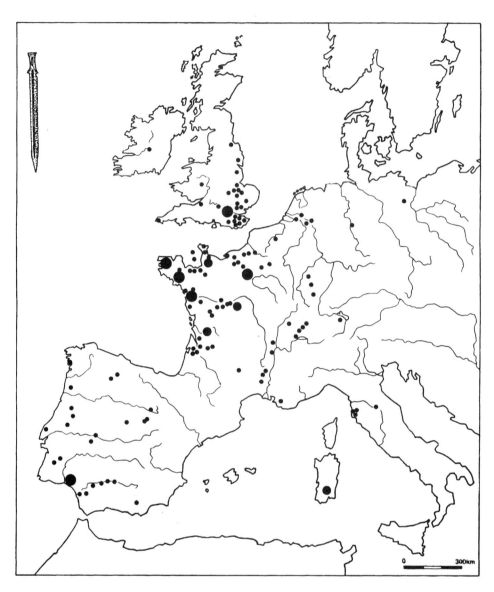

Fig. 74 The distribution of carps-tongue swords. The larger symbols indicate hoards with several swords.

According to the distribution of specific high-status items, such as Irish cauldrons (Figure 75), long-distance maritime journeys must have been undertaken from Ireland to Portugal, 1,500 km apart, although exchange also took place via Wales to the Thames valley and the Continent. And from Portugal to Sardinia is another 2000 km. Given the maritime skills of the period I propose that the first distribution method was practised. But below that level there were still multiple chains of short-distance regional exchange at work, both up and down the Atlantic and with Central Europe, as we shall see. Rowlands (1980, 44), based on the work of Franken-

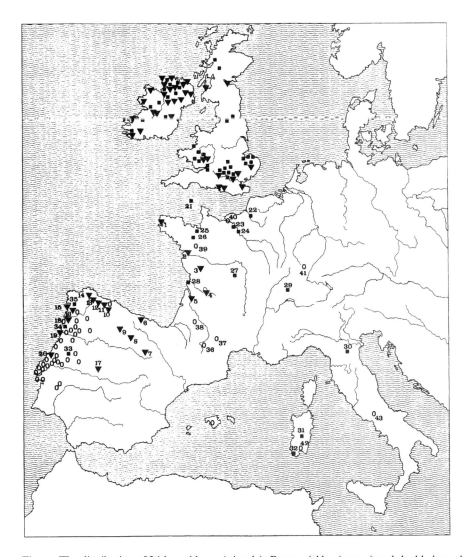

Fig. 75 The distribution of Irish cauldrons (triangle), Breton sickles (square) and double looped axes (circle).

stein, has suggested a temporal development from short-haul maritime exchange (BF II) to long-distance trade that bypassed previous links (BF III). The latter development is seen as the result of Phoenician intervention, their maritime skills being employed in the initial phase and later taken over by the new regional centres. It presupposes a substantial (and early) Phoenician involvement in the Atlantic, trading fine textiles, pottery and wine, which may perhaps be inferred from some Atlantic settlements in Portugal (Martins 1989; in press). Analyses of alloying and trace elements may be of help in solving the question of the nature of metal exchange. Briard (1965; 1988) and Northover (1982) have demonstrated a close connection between typological/chronological sequences and metal composition, suggesting that exchange circuits were regional, and that our typologies are in accordance with the realities of the past.

Two observations deserve further discussion: while centres in Ireland and Portugal were located according to mineral resources, the groups in southeast England and western France were located at the periphery of mineral resources, but with easy access to Central European networks. In southeast England, with centres of consumption along the Thames (Needham and Burgess 1980; Needham 1990), local Bronze Age societies were also in contact with northwestern and Central Europe along the Rhine. An analysis of wear and damage on Late Bronze Age metalwork in southern England has demonstrated that they increase with distance from the Thames (Taylor 1982 and 1993) (Figure 76), underpinning the suggestion of its centrality. In western France the Venat hoard exemplifies this region's central position, giving access to most of the European exchange networks at the time, although clearly dominated by the Atlantic. Figure 77, showing the extension of the Venat network, should be compared with the distribution of sanctuaries in Greece in Figure 69, suggesting that Europe north of the Mediterranean was truly international at this time.

Given this evidence I venture to propose that there existed in southeast England and in western France groups of chiefdoms strong enough to exploit their neighbouring mineral-rich regions, or, alternatively, that they could do without them. This proposition gains further momentum when we consider Brittany. It is a peculiar fact that most distributions avoid Brittany, despite its being so rich in minerals. Only Carps-Tongue swords and a few other types enter this region. Against this there are nearly 300 hoards of Armorican axes with more than 32,000 axes known from them. This destruction of wealth is so remarkable that we must assume overproduction and inflation, leading to a spiral of desperate internal competition and ritual destruction. This crisis has traditionally been linked to the collapse of the Atlantic network following in the wake of the introduction of iron and the founding of Phoenician factories in Iberia, which from then on could satisfy their commercial demands locally. But could it be that Brittany had been deliberately excluded from the major trade routes, as part of the regional politics of competition? It depends on the dating of Armorican axes, which is still problematic, and often assumed to go down into Ha C (Ruiz-Galvez 1991; Rivellain n.d., chap. 5). This would explain overproduction and support the traditional hypothesis. However, I propose as an alternative that regional rivalry led to the exclusion of Brittany from international exchange during the last phase of the Atlantic Bronze Age (Carps-Tongue swords are probably earlier). It would also explain why Armorican axes are rarely distributed south of Brittany. In the next chapter we will review similar patterns of regional rivalry and avoidance, suggesting that regional politics were a reality in Late Bronze Age Europe. This, of course, is also suggested by the consistent maintenance of certain cultural borders, as previously discussed, as also seen between the Atlantic and the Urnfield culture, taking us back to the question of what kind of identity was being signalled. Obviously it was one different from modern ethnicity, but important enough to be consciously and continuously marked, and strong enough to demand that most imports were melted down and recontextualised.

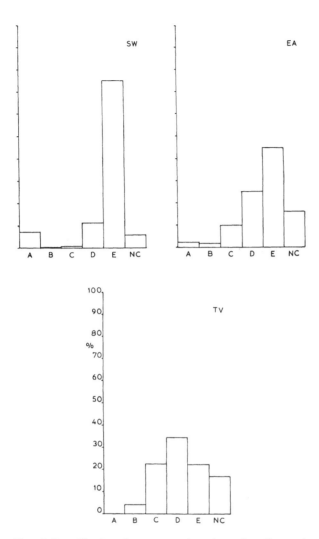

Fig. 76 Quantification of use wear and repairs on Late Bronze Age metalwork from Southwest Britain (SW), East Anglia (EA) and the Thames Valley (TV). A = no wear, B = slightly worn, C = worn, D = well worn, E = heavily worn, and NC = not classifiable.

As for the Nordic/Lausitz region there appear to have been some ports of entry and exchange/trade, defined by clusters of hoards at central points of communication on the borders (Figure 41). As in the case of the Nordic region, we can assume that communication within the Atlantic tradition was facilitated by a language unity, probably already divided into regional groups.

We should, however, also consider settlement evidence and social structure, as they may give important clues to the functioning of the system.

Social organisation of the Atlantic tradition
Let us begin by discussing the major categories of metalwork and their potential social significance:

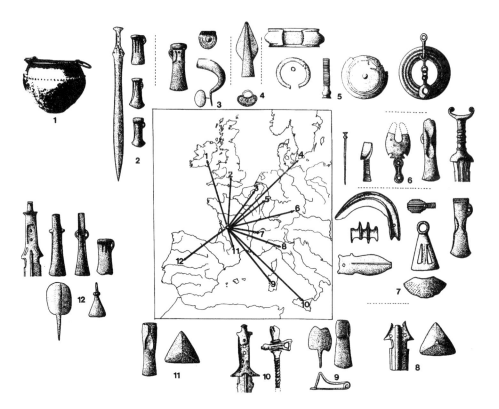

Fig. 77 The European relations of the Venat hoard.

(1) Tools, among them axes, are the most common. Does this imply forest clearings and settlement expansion, or more specialised woodworking? Although it is evident that clearings took place, I propose the latter, since most axes are suited for wood-working, ship- and house-building, rather than heavier uses. Leather knives (Roth 1974) may also point to the importance of husbandry, whereas sickles are rather few in number compared to Central Europe.

(2) Weapons testify to the importance of warfare. The employment of shields and helmets, although only rarely deposited, places at least some of these warriors in the group of warrior elites. Coombs' analyses have demonstrated recurrent combinations of weapons from BF II onwards (1975). To this elite level also belong the many different fragments and elements of wagons and horse harness.

(3) Feasting and ritual at the elite level are demonstrated by the massive Irish cauldrons and the Atlantic roasting spits or flesh hooks, whose wide distribution from Ireland to Portugal indicates their generalised elite functions. They were inspired by Near Eastern/Mediterranean types which had ritual functions as well, symbolising high rank, and form part of the Phoenician/Atlantic exchange sphere (Figure 73).

The relative weighting between these categories in hoards, at regional and local levels, may indicate their social and economic significance, as an echo of the messages people in the past wanted to transmit. It is clear, then, that objects relating to feasting and ritual are the most exclusive, and tools the most common, with weapons in a middle position. When we consider the group of large composite hoards an analysis has been carried out suggesting that there were two groups, those with and those without ornaments (Coffyn, Gomez and Mohen 1981, tables 5–7). If we consider the smaller, more common hoards, they are mostly dominated by tools or weapons, tools being the most common.

If we put these observations together, and add the expanding production, distribution and hoarding of metal over time, we may conclude that we are dealing with well-organised warrior elites, whose major occupation as an elite activity was the production and distribution of metalwork, some of it for their own internal prestige-building, some for their farming communities and some for trade. The hoards and their composition testify to most of the hoarding types suggested earlier, with a rather small group of large hoards, either mixed communal/central place (trading?) hoards of Venat type, or a series of single types, as at Huelva (production/distribution hoards). They are surrounded by a larger group of local production and distribution hoards, often difficult to distinguish from personal hoards. It seems that most were tool or weapon hoards, as in the Middle Bronze Age, in contrast to the Nordic region where the picture is just the opposite, with Central Europe in a middle position (in the north, however, axes were mostly deposited as single pieces (Jensen 1973), while some axe distribution hoards are also found).

According to hoard composition Atlantic Bronze Age societies were patriarchal, with little room for demonstrating female status positions. In Central Europe and the north, with a heavier emphasis on agriculture and old traditions of displaying female status positions, much greater investment was made in female ornaments. Women apparently played important roles in alliance formations, and could bring wealth and status with them. The Atlantic Bronze Age gives the impression of a society where women did not have the same key position in alliance formations and ability to accumulate wealth. Wealth was gained and displayed by men. If this was so, we might expect that the economy was dominated by husbandry – or that husbandry was a central means of accumulating wealth, besides contributing to subsistence and production. Much in the evidence would seem to support such a proposition: a marked shift occurred in the relative balance between cattle, pigs and sheep/goat from the Late Neolithic/Copper Age to the Bronze Age. Pig, dominant in the Neolithic, was replaced by cattle as the major animal, supplemented by sheep and goat, whose importance increased further with the Early Iron Age (Tinsley and Grigson 1981; Turner 1981; Bradley 1978, 3:1). It suggests a shift in subsistence strategy towards pastoral farming. The increase of sheep can be linked to the appearance and development of wool production, which cannot be demonstrated earlier (Ryder 1988). During the Middle Bronze Age the large upland pastures and field systems accord with this scenario, but with their partial collapse and the subsequent reorganisation of settlement in the Late Bronze Age towards more heavy soils in many regions, we may assume a more integrated pattern of transhumance between upland and lowland – that is, a change from a dominance by upland economies towards a dominance by lowland economies, at least in southern England.

Looking at settlement evidence, the 8th century BC is characterised by numerous foundations of fortified settlements (hillforts in English terminology) (Bradley 1984, fig. 6.2), and this also goes for Iberia, where several recent excavations have uncovered large stone-built fortifications (Martins 1988a; 1988b). Field surveys suggest that in northern Portugal fortified settlements were regularly spaced with only a few kilometres between each – although most of them still await closer dating (Martins 1989). The English evidence suggests that hillforts became more numerous and complex during the Early Iron Age, but again many of these late sites may well have had an earlier foundation, as at Danebury (Cunliffe 1983). The problem as far as England is concerned is that hillforts are more numerous in regions with less metalwork, perhaps arising out of competition and warfare under increasing stress. So what we may be seeing is a division between hillfort-dominated pastoral farming and areas of agrarian farming with the stress on metal consumption, a split originating in the late second millennium, where the system has been illuminated in great detail by Ellison (1981). In the uplands it has been possible to demonstrate separate settlement compounds for male and female activities, with the males linked to leather working and husbandry, similar male/female divisions being visible in cemeteries. Stock raising and its products formed the dominant economic activity. Enclosures can be seen, together with settlement compounds, to form modular patterns of hierarchical social organisation, with large enclosures as centres for production and distribution (Bradley 1978, fig. 4.2 ; case studies in Brown 1988; Barrett, Bradley and Green 1991, ch. 6). Rowlands (1980, 34) used the dichotomy between upland and lowland to construct a model of the social dynamic of these economic variations:

> In fact it seems more fruitful to view these upland settlements as forming one sector within a large regional division of labour. Perhaps their location would best be understood as the result of demand for upland products by communities situated in lowland river valleys or on the coast?

This view is supported by the arguments that lowland communities were in charge of cross-Channel trade. What circulated between these regions were not only metal for inter- and intra-chiefly exchange and rivalry, but also women, slaves and cattle.

The evidence of settlements and economy thus does not support a simple, homogeneous model of a hierarchical, patriarchal society with a heavy emphasis on pastoralism. It rather suggests more complex relationships between different local and regional economies, forming local and regional centre–periphery relations linked to divisions of labour and control over the flow of metal, dominated by the coastal lowland communities. The argonauts of the Atlantic Late Bronze Age demanded an economic base at home, but to maintain that they also had to engage in trade and exchanges that were from time to time concluded by ritual depositions, the destruction of wealth, a ritualised demonstration and regulation of their prestige as chiefs. In other cases hoards were the result of attempts to extend their power base through warfare, but whether depositions were due to warfare or ritual, they testify not only to the importance of production and distribution of metal, but more so to competition and fighting for prestige and power. This obviously also had to be demonstrated in hundreds of other ways that we can only try to infer – with more or less certainty: large feasts and redistributions to mobilise warriors and followers both to maintain local power and to organise and carry out prestigious trading expeditions. There emerges a clear division between the lifestyle of an elite, living inside fortified central settlements, using flesh hooks for their meat consumption, large cauldrons for feasts or simply feeding a large household, and that of peasants, whose diet was based on corn products and some meat, prepared in earthen ovens and using heated stones for cooking, reflected in heaps of fire-cracked stones from Ireland to Sweden (Buckley 1990), as well as cooking pits over most of Europe.

If we are to become more concrete about the components of the social system and their interrelations, we can turn to Susan Pearce, who, in an illuminating study, has made a well-argued attempt at social reconstruction (1983). She traces a development from rather small-scale territorial groups, characterised by land divisions and integration between upland grazing and lowland agriculture, in the late second millennium, towards the emergence (or re-emergence) of warrior elites, central settlements and client relationships after 1000 BC. The embryonic appearance of social divisions defined by divisions of labour and economic obligations later leads on into the archaic states and elite peasant relationships of the Iron Age and later historical time, although Pearce stresses the lack of really effective central authority in the Late Bronze Age (Figure 78). Smiths worked under the patronage of chiefs or lords, while farmers were entering into a redistributive relationship with chiefs, the reality of which was one of tribute and clientship (also Jorge 1992; Ruiz-Galvez 1994). These new exploitative relations were probably furthered by conditions of worsening climate and the need to intensify agricultural production and protection of produce, as well as by chiefly competition for maintaining control of alliances and the flow of prestige goods and metal. In much the same way Coombs (1975, 77) has concluded in an analysis of weapon hoards that they reflected:

> A period of unrest caused by an increased pressure on the available land due to population growth and climatic decline. Within the hoards an aristocracy is embraced, with the right to possess horse and wagon equipment, a cauldron and possibly a sword, also having a retinue of spearmen using the short javelin and long thrusting spear and a smith at their command. Other hoards suggest the artisan class of this society, especially metalworkers, woodworkers and leatherworkers.

Thus the emergence of lance and spear dominated hoards during the Ewart Park phase and later suggests the growing importance of spear-fighting warrior retinues, being part of a concomitant development in large parts of Europe.

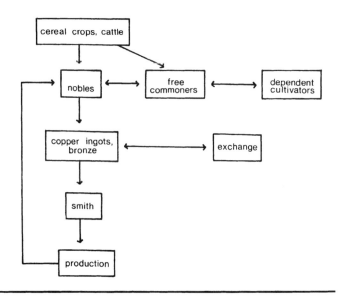

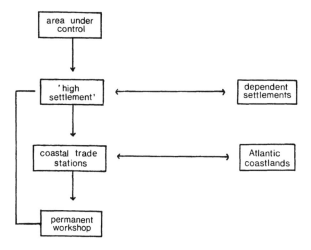

Fig. 78 Model of the social organisation and the corresponding settlement structure of the Late Bronze Age of Southwest England.

It is remarkable that the Atlantic Bronze Age, although maintaining contact with Urnfield society and southwestern groups of the Nordic culture, demonstrated a distinct identity, most clearly seen, perhaps, in the maintenance of the round house/ settlement compound tradition, peculiar as it must have looked, at least from the Continent (Figure 79). Very few exchanges were accepted, most foreign metal being melted down and recontextualised. In this respect the Atlantic groups maintained a strategy of cultural resistance and boundary maintenance of the same nature as the Nordic and the Urnfield traditions. One may even characterise the Atlantic Bronze Age as being deliberately archaic and conservative, producing old types in slightly altered new versions, in much the same way as later Celtic archaism. This character-

Fig. 79 Reconstruction drawing of palisaded farmstead from Staple Howe, Yorkshire. Although from the Early Iron Age, it represents the tradition of the Late Bronze Age farmsteads.

istic perhaps gains in significance when we consider that the Atlantic network continued classic Bronze Age traditions under increasing pressure from changes occurring elsewhere, resulting from the beginning of iron use – a development that the Atlantic tradition had to refuse to accept, because its very existence was based on the trade in tin, copper and bronze.

Tartessos and Atlantic–Mediterranean interaction

Southern Iberia is a key area in Atlantic–Phoenician interaction. Where did this interaction take place? If we consider the distribution of grave stelae they form a pattern, which I suggest is the representation of an evolving centre–periphery structure (Figure 80). Its centre is at the southwest corner of Portugal, the Alentejo/ Algarve region, a perfect point of entry for a trading chiefdom, exploiting the rich mineral resources in its hinterland. Here we find a group of Late Bronze Age cist gravefields, which mark the early distribution of chiefly polities. At its periphery is a concentric distribution of stelae some 100–200 km from the centre. They cover a rather long period from the 9th to the 7th centuries (Gamito 1988; Almagro-Gorbea in press; Domingo 1993) reflecting a stable structure. It is important to note, however, that the stelae near the centre in Alentejo are the oldest, going back to the 10th century or earlier, just as we find the latest, with writing, here, which point to its continuous and long-lasting role as a centre. We also find here a special type of the ritual roasting spits or flesh hooks, elsewhere linked to elite food consumption (Figure 73). The political/economic nature of the centre–periphery structure is further demonstrated

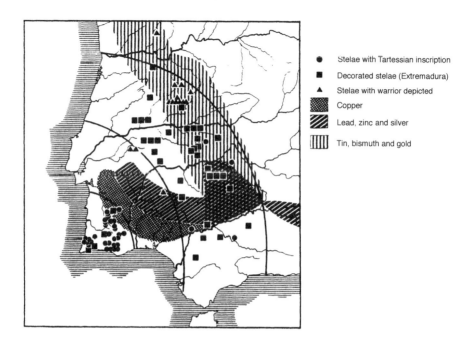

Fig. 80(A) Distribution of grave stelae and mineral resources, forming a centre–periphery relation between coast and inland areas.

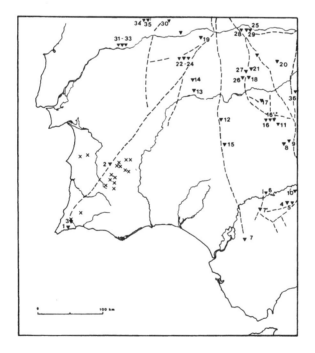

Fig. 80(B) Stelae and old road systems, suggesting an ancient communication system between coast and inland areas, and between inland settlements.

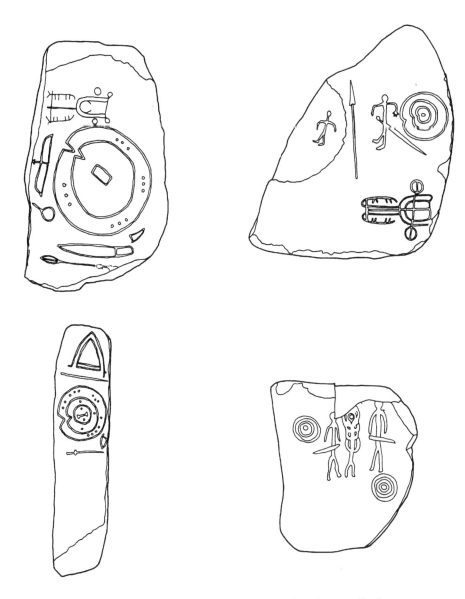

Fig. 81 Examples of grave stelae from the Late Bronze Age of southwestern Iberia.

by the distribution of goldwork (Coffyn 1985, Carte 46), the earliest probably going back into the period of early stelae. It occurs in the same area and exemplifies the richness of this culture and its peripheries.

I thus propose that a centre, or rather a group of chiefdoms forming a polity, arose in the Algarve area in the early part of the Atlantic culture, due to its gold and mineral riches (Figure 80). It acted as a trading partner for the early Phoenician expeditions, as reflected in some of the goldwork, but especially in the armour brought from the east Mediterranean, along with helmets and the V-notched shields on the stelae (Figure 81). They combine elements from the Atlantic and the east Mediterranean world.[3] From here selected Mediterranean skills and products were transmitted to the Atlantic network, along with the ideology of warrior elites as depicted on the slabs and stelae and reflected in the finds, e.g. shields from Portugal to Ireland (Coles 1962; Gräslund 1967a; Almagro-Gorbea 1992). Other elements were derived from Urnfield cultures through France and Germany, spreading as far west as the Thames in southern England. The pictures on stelae and gold finds suggest elite exchange from kings or high chiefs to vassal chiefs in exchange for services, slaves and minerals, as also suggested by Almagro-Gorbea (1986, 421–38). I do not propose that there was a unified political structure of centre–periphery relations, rather an expanding alliance network joining the coastal centres to the hinterlands, where local elites adopted the new warrior elite ideology. The process may exemplify the formation of warrior elites at the peripheries of centres, as known in other cases, supplying goods and services to the centre in return for prestige goods (Frankenstein and Rowlands 1978; Nash 1985). It coincides with a remarkable intensification of land use (Stevenson and Harrison 1992, fig. 9). Due to a different ritual tradition, and perhaps also due to their extreme prestige value, shields and weapons were depicted on stelae rather than buried with the dead.

The above must be considered a working hypothesis, but it has the virtue of making sense of a pattern of evidence, both in terms of its internal organisation and in terms of its interacting role between two regional networks, the Atlantic and the Mediterranean. The interpretation of a strong centre or archaic kingdom, located in the southwest corner of Iberia, would explain why Phoenician colonies do not appear further west than Cadiz near Huelva. If there was a Phoenician Tartessos, it should be here, to the southwest (note 3); later it could perhaps have moved towards the Huelva region (Aubet Semmler 1982, Abb. 2–3). The legend of Tartessos, as known from the Old Testament, is linked to early Phoenician trading expeditions in the late 2nd millennium beyond Gibraltar. It also figures in later Greek texts where it was renowned as a rich metal-producing region. There is an account of a Greek fifty-oared ship from Ionia that reached Tartessos, where the mariners were received in a friendly manner by the king, whose name was Arganthonios. This visit should date to between 640 and 550 BC. Another Greek visit is recorded in which the ship returned home with a huge profit, and had a bronze cauldron made in honour of the goddess Hera. Normally, however, Tartessos is located in the Huelva area, where a rich orientalising culture developed under the influence of the Phoenician colonies, and this may well be the later Greek Tartessos (Niemeyer 1984).

The precise location of Tartessos is not important. What is significant, however, is that as a myth it testifies to the early Phoenician engagement west of Gibraltar due to its mineral resources, and it records an apparently stable and rather organised society, which was able to attract the commercial attention of the Phoenicians and Greeks for several hundred years, beginning in the 10th century BC. On archaeological grounds I suggest that this 'kingdom' was located in the southwest corner of Iberia, rather than around the Guadalquivir River and Huelva.

5.3 From Villanova to Fuen: the Phahlbau connection

The emergence of the Phahlbau connection

Looking at distribution maps of selected types of metalwork enables the archaeologist to discover both regional traditions and international connections and regularities that were unknown to prehistoric people, although they might have been aware of considerable parts of such networks from combined personal experience and myth (Helms 1986; 1988b). Their knowledge would thus be contextualised and localised within a social and ritual framework at a specific point in space within the network. Although the abstraction of the distribution map summarises large-scale geographical interrelations, it may also make us forget to ask the most relevant questions such as: how far did people travel when they married, when they traded, etc., and how far did their knowledge about the world around them reach? What context do the finds come from – burials, hoards, etc. – and what social groups did they belong to? In a world of rapid and widespread international communication of ideas and objects everybody may eventually in principle meet everybody else, in a chain of exchanges. To enable such rapid exchanges as the archaeological record suggests, they cannot have passed through all settlements, although obviously some objects did. In the Bronze Age there was already a well-organised hierarchy allowing exchange to be carried out over longer intervals, thereby speeding up the pace of change and the spread of news (Jockenhövel 1991; Larsson 1985). To explore the nature of such long-distance exchange, the length of travels, and the nature of local distribution and exchange, let us first examine some distribution maps and their testimony to a regular long-distance network from Italy to Denmark during the 8th century BC. This will be followed by an analysis of the internal context and structure of some selected chiefly centres along the route.

By the 8th century Central and Northern Italy had taken over the production of elite metalwork from Hungary. Items from Italian workshops were distributed northwards and eastwards to establish long-distance trade relations, among others with the Nordic region. Here amber was one of the commodities that was in demand, as Italy was also beginning to manufacture and distribute amber, e.g. to Yugoslavia where we find amber used in increasing quantities on fibulae, e.g. at Glasinac and Vergina, as well as in Italy itself. The rise to dominance of the Phahlbau route to northern Germany and Fuen should be seen as resulting from these changed conditions. But they are to be understood within the framework of the general westward move and flourishing of metal production.[4]

An overall impression of the exchange networks of the period is given in Figure 82. It defines the major characteristics: clusters in the Phahlbau region in Switzerland, south of the Elbe bend, an old centre, and from there further on to the Oder, where there is one line of exchange towards Pomerania and the River Vistula and another to the Danish islands. A subsidiary line went up the Elbe to Jutland, at least for part of the period.

We note two characteristics of the distribution maps. First, prestige goods, such as swords and horse gear, are directional – they move along well-defined lines with marked depositional concentrations along the way. As other find types (e.g. pins) fill in the empty spaces between the clusters we can assume that the concentrations reflect political centres that were able to control both the exchange and the consumption of certain types of prestige goods. The clusters thus derive from the distribution of prestige goods to local chiefs or vassals. Müller-Karpe's regional sword types (1961, Tafel 98–101) give a good indication of the chiefly centres (Figure 83), supporting Figure 82.

According to this model, chiefly centres were able to organise trade expeditions over distances of sometimes several hundred kilometres. As we shall see later, the average distance was rather less than that. Blurrings of the pattern occur, and can be explained by alternating lines of exchange and/or the local redistribution of prestige goods. Figure 84, showing the distribution of Phahlbau and Nordic spears, is illuminating in demonstrating the directional nature of exchange and the rapid change of style on entering the Nordic zone at the Elbe. It further suggests that exchange took place over longer distances in the Urnfield culture than in the Nordic culture.

The second characteristic of the distribution maps is the avoidance of the Lausitz region with its strong fortified settlements (Figure 82). That it represented a well-considered strategy is apparent from the fact that it is quite a detour to reach Pommerania by way of the Elbe and Oder. Instead of continuing directly through Lausitz territory, the route continues northwards to the Oder, to turn towards the east. In this way the route remained within the territory of Nordic/North German Culture, which must have been the decisive factor. We may conclude from this that the amber trade had now started to exploit the rich Pommeranian resources, and that this trade was in the hands of Nordic merchants, competing with and avoiding the Lausitz region. The reasons for this could be many, but it suggests that polities above local levels were realities in Late Bronze Age Europe, supporting the picture we have drawn of the highly organised nature of trade and exchange, not to mention local populations.

Warriors and women: exchange and the transformation of meaning
What was being exchanged northwards? Basically bronze, in the form of winged axes (Thrane 1975, fig. 55) and prestige goods from Italy and the Alpine region, such as wagons/horse gear, buckets and weapons/armour (including hammered shields). Other types such as pins, relating rather to personal and reciprocal relationships, are more widely spaced, although generally conforming to the distributional pattern of prestige goods (Thrane 1975, fig. 103). They suggest that women moved in the formation of local marriage alliances, being responsible for distributing Phahlbau pins all the way to Denmark, while only occasional Nordic ornaments moved south from the Nordic cultural sphere (Thrane 1975, 223ff.) What we see at work here is apparently a recurrent Bronze Age pattern, which in earlier chapters has been interpreted as representing a two level exchange: long-distance, directional elite exchange between political centres versus short-distance, chiefly and common, reciprocal exchange from settlement to settlement.

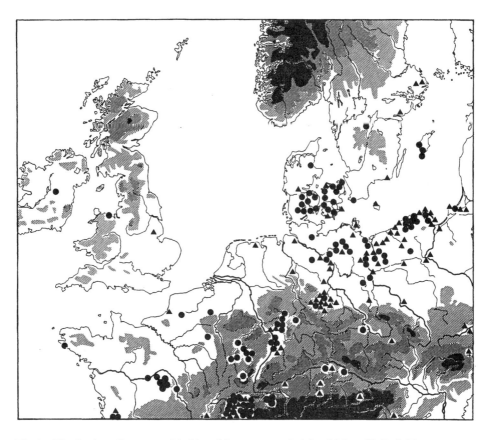

Fig. 82 Distribution of horse gear (circle) and Antenna swords (triangle) from Ha B3 in Europe.

That women were used in expansionist policies is demonstrated by the increase in Nordic ornaments between the Rivers Oder and Vistula, and south of the Elbe, not to mention northwestern Germany, with links extending as far as the Netherlands, where trading colonies seem to have been in existence throughout most of the Bronze Age (Butler 1986), or (to use a less modernistic terminology) sites in exchange relations with Nordic settlements on the Elbe (this may point to the existence of Nordic settlement along the now drowned coastal strips of the Bronze Age land-scape). On the Baltic coast we also find weapons, suggesting a real settlement expansion whereas female ornaments extended further to the south than did Nordic weapons, stressing the employment of women in the formation of alliances (Thrane 1975, fig. 128). The increasing Nordic engagement in long-distance trade is not only reflected in the expansion of Nordic metalwork, but also in the development of local and regional metalwork styles under Nordic influence from the Vistula to the Ems and Weser, as demonstrated by Sprockhoff (1956) and specified in several studies by Tackenberg (1971) and Horst (1972). What we can see at work is Nordic expansion-ism at the expense of the former Lausitz/Hungarian connections. It was probably a process of elite expansion, as local metalwork forms and pottery seem to testify to

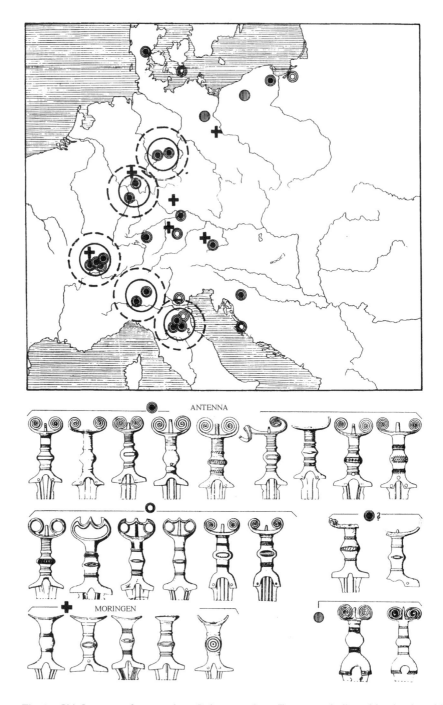

Fig. 83 Chiefly centres from northern Italy to northern Europe, as indicated by the deposition of the Antenna sword and the Moringen sword. Suggested political catchment areas are circled. The swords represent a select group of prestige objects which all cluster in the same areas, representing cultural and political centres.

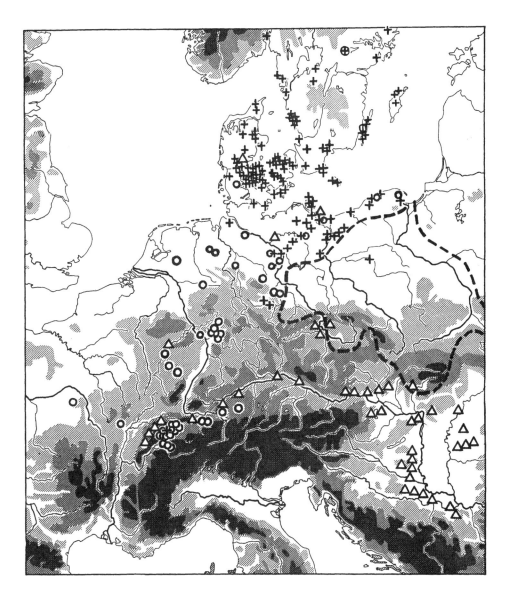

Fig. 84 Distribution of Phahlbau spearheads (open circle) and West Baltic spearheads (cross) in relation to Cimmerian bridles (triangle) and the full distribution of the late Lausitz Culture (dashed line).

local continuity and mixing (Kostrzewski 1958; Dabrowsky 1968; Fogel 1988, Karte 8). The Nordic area of influence between the Oder and the Vistula was a 100 km-wide coastal zone, whereas to the west of the Oder it extended further south. It is remarkable, however, that the Nordic finds form distinctive clusters at the major commercial entry points, e.g. at the mouths of the Oder and the Vistula, with distinct demarcation lines with local cultures, at the Oder the Middle German-Görtizer group (Griesa 1989, 341). The southern shores of the Baltic had become an area of filtering and experimentation with Nordic and foreign forms. After 700 BC the development of local cultural traditions accelerated, giving rise to the Pommeranian culture to the east (Luka 1966; Malinowski 1988a; 1988b). It reflected the increasing dominance of the north German/Polish area in trade and exchange with the Hallstatt culture to the south and southern Scandinavia, especially Sweden, to the north.

To the south, in Italy, we see a similar expansion of metalwork and trade at important transition zones, leading to the formation of new elites and regional cultural traditions in the southern Alps at nodal points of transfer between Italy and the Alpine region. These come to form the Este and Golasecca cultures (Pauli 1971; Ridgway 1979).

The intensity of north–south exchange is shown in many, often unexpected, ways. As noted earlier, at the boundary with the Nordic zone cultural selection was operating to recontextualise new forms and elements into Nordic design (Sørensen 1987). High-status prestige goods were accepted, especially within the male sphere, such as weapons, wagons and amphorae/drinking vessels, but the true impact of foreign influences can be detected hidden in Nordic metalwork forms or in pottery and bone-working. We have already noted this for dress pins. In Nordic bone-working geometric designs were adopted, whereas in metalwork they were transformed into softer curvilinear motifs (Figure 85). This forms part of a general European trend, in which elements of Greek Geometric style were adopted in metalwork and in pottery and wood/bone-working as seen not only in Italy, but also in the Phahlbau settlements. We can indeed speak of a common European 'geometric koine', integrated into local styles in various ways. A strange dichotomy developed between the soft rolling lines of the Phahlbau and Nordic styles on the one hand and geometric patterns, which apparently preceded the Phahlbau style, beginning in HaB1. The meander motif was especially popular all the way from the Mediterranean to Denmark. A rather more direct influence is manifested in burial ritual by the employment of house urns in the north, some of them being very close to their prototypes, along with the manufacture of miniatures (especially swords and spears). Only later, when new lines of long-distance trade were opened up between Pommerania and the Alpine/North Italian region, did house urns and face urns become standard burial containers in Pommerania. We can also detect regional variation in the mechanisms of selection or filtering: in northern Germany and northern Jutland there developed a tradition of plastic decoration in metalwork on hanging vessels, found also in goldwork, and linked to a similar Villanovan/Italian style (Sprockhoff 1961; Hencken 1968).

Sometimes peculiar changes of context occurred: in Villanovan burial tradition male warriors had their helmet employed as a lid on top of the urn. Often a replica in clay (a pottery helmet) was produced for the occasion, developing its own more solid style. This, it turns out, served as the prototype for the strange Nordic belt buckle, being part of that peculiar set of high-status female ornaments that included a hanging vessel (carried on the back) and belt buckle (to close the belt), making many kinds of practical work impossible, not to speak of direct body contact. Recurrent patterns of wear indicate their use as ornaments (Kristiansen 1974b). In Figure 86A and B I have selected some examples of this strange parallelism, spanning HaB1–B3, which must imply a direct knowledge of the pottery helmets, since they have a

Fig. 85 Geometric motif (meander) on a bone tool (belt?) from an urn grave in northern Jutland, Denmark, late period IV (Ha B1/ B2).

distinct style of their own, not quite identical to the metal prototypes. This transformation from a warrior helmet to a protective female belt buckle, was, however, not accidental. The belt box, attached to the belt at the back, originated from Italian bronze shields. A nearly identical pattern of ornamentation is seen on an Italian bronze shield and a belt box from late Montelius IV/late Ha B1 (Figure 87A). During Ha B2–3 this shield ornamentation was imitated on a series of belt boxes from northern Germany and north Jutland (Figure 87B). To complete the picture, the same transformation of male armour into female ornaments or motifs is seen in the decoration on the large breast fibula. Its oval fibula plates are covered with variations on the ornamentation of metal shields (Gräslund 1965–66).

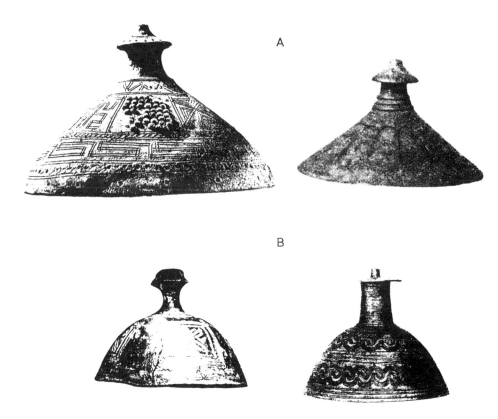

Fig. 86 Villanovan pottery helmets (replicas), used as urn lids and Nordic belt buckles of bronze. A = late period IV/Ha B1. B = late period V/Ha B2–3.

These symbolic transformations obviously merit further consideration. First, we can observe that only protective weapons were transformed, suggesting some kind of transfer of protection, not only to the woman, but perhaps mainly to her husband. It surely lends a new significance to the male/female relationship in the Nordic Bronze Age, and to our perception of female ornaments. As hanging vessel/belt buckle and fibula represented the highest female status kit, the fibula only occurring with hanging vessels (Kristiansen 1974b; Levy 1982, fig. 6.1), and since male weapon burials had virtually disappeared, sometimes to be replaced by miniatures, it may further be suggested that it was in this way that the wives of high-status warrior chiefs signalled their specific relationship and the position of their husband. It raises interesting questions concerning the status of women, both socially and perhaps also economically, including their ability to transfer goods and land through inheritance.

Along the routes of chiefly long-distance exchange there circulated not only goods but also specialists in hammered metalwork, as well as large quantities of prestige goods to be further distributed from the chiefly centres. Let us therefore in the following section consider the internal structure of such centres, as a precondition for understanding the operation of elite exchange and its cultural and social context.

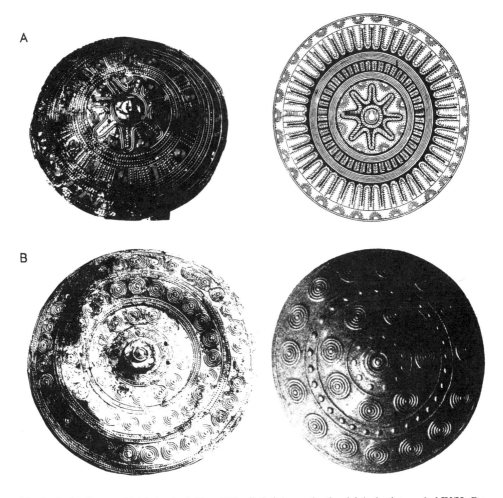

Fig. 87 Italian bronze shields (to the left) and Nordic belt boxes (to the right): A = late period IV/Ha B1 (B2), B = period V/Ha B2–3. The shields are reduced in size for ease of comparison.

Princely burials and the context of elite exchange

If one travelled from Villanova to Fuen, or in the opposite direction, during the 8th century BC, which some adventurous individuals of the day may even have done, they would have met familiar social and cultural practices, at least if they happened to belong to the elite which was able to travel. To illuminate this let us take as our point of departure an amphora from a rich warrior burial at Vejo in Central Italy (Figure 88, upper part) and expose the history of its production and distribution, along with the products of related workshops (Jockenhövel 1974). Originating from one of the specialist workshops that developed in Italy under Hungarian/Urnfield influence, it belonged to the aristocratic lifestyle of chiefly dining and drinking. The symbol of the 'Sonnenbarkenvogel' (sunship bird), which appears from Italy to Scandinavia, and from France to the Carpathians, signifies the ritual *koine* of the Urnfield culture (Figure 89), as well as stressing the ritualised nature of social conduct and legitimation.

Fig. 88 Amphorae from Vejo in Italy (above) and Gevlinghausen in northern Germany (below).

When we consider the distribution and social context of these amphorae, nearly all of them are found in aristocratic burials, as at Vejo. In an analysis of the whole group of amphorae and buckets Albrecht Jockenhövel has made a number of important observations (1974, 32 ff., Abb. 6) allowing us to distinguish between South and North Alpine traditions. One workshop was located in southern Etruria, while it is more difficult to locate the Central European workshops to a more precise area than Hungary. Among the amphorae there appears a parallel to the Vejo piece in an aristocratic burial from Gevlinghausen in Northwest Germany (Figure 88, lower part), demonstrating once again how close contacts were at the chiefly level. It is interesting, however, that on the basis of technical details Jockenhövel suggests that the amphora from Gevlinghausen was made north of the Alps, as an imitation of pieces like that from Italy, perhaps by an 'imported' fine metalworker, travelling between the chiefly courts. It has long been recognised that during the 8th century BC there emerged in northern Germany a group of hammered metal cups in 'Punkt-Buckel' (point-buckle) style that was locally made (Sprockhoff 1956). As the Nordic tradition only employed casting techniques it suggests that specialists were imported from Central Europe or Italy to the chiefly centres of northern Europe. Another plainer amphora was found in the 'royal' burial in Seddin on the Elbe, which has a parallel in a piece from Rørbæk, northern Jutland in Denmark, both probably made within a north European chiefly context (Jockenhövel 1974, Tafel 6). The recent find of fourteen hammered Herz-sprung shields in a bog at Lake Vänern in Sweden may support such a hypothesis (Hagberg 1988). It offers a rare glimpse of a highly developed system of production and distribution, beyond that of traditional gift exchange, but in accordance with an organised system of elite exchange and trade. So does the deposition of nine bronze corselets from Marmesse in France (Mohen 1987).

When these elite burials with amphorae and buckets are considered, they demon-strate an astonishing similarity in burial ritual, ranging from small details, such as wrapping the burnt bones up in linen, as described by Homer (*Iliad* XXIII: 252), to the Dionysian drinking rituals and the employment of standardised symbolic motifs and figures on the amphorae (Figure 88).

Fig. 89 The common Urnfield sunship bird motif from a selection of hammered works: (1) Unter-glauheim, Kr. Dillingen, (2) Gevlinghausen, Kr. Meschede, (3) Vejo, Quattro Fontanili.

Elite burials during the 8th century BC, from Italy to Denmark, and from France to the Balkans and Greece, thus share:

1 Drinking and dining habits linked to common social and ritual traditions.
2 The exchange of prestigious drinking services (amphorae, buckets and cups), and sometimes also of specialist metalworkers (Kytlicova 1988).
3 The employment of costly four-wheeled wagons for social and ritual purposes (Pare 1987b), sometimes seen in miniature metal wagons taking part in ritual processions, found in Italy, Iberia, and Central Europe (Figure 94).
4 The use of metal horse equipment – harnesses, bridles, phalerae (Thrane 1975, ch. 5).
5 The exchange of prestige weapons and metal body armour, sometimes in large quantities.
6 The construction of monumental barrows, a practice confined, however, to northern Europe, Italy and southeast Europe.

Let us now consider in more detail two examples of the internal context of such elite burials, in order to establish the level of social organisation of the group.

Seddin   In the Seddin region of the Elbe, several chiefly centres emerged during this period, regularly spaced some 80 to 100 km from each other (Figure 90). Above them all stands the Seddin area, possessing a remarkable concentration of rich graves, with the 'royal' burial at the apex of the whole group, situated in one of the largest barrows of northern Europe – 80 m wide and 11 m high, enclosing a stone-built chamber with a vaulted roof. An analysis of all the burials and hoards by Wüstemann (1974) has made it possible to give an outline of the structure of metal depositions, as well as burial ritual. The region is defined by clusters of barrows and urnfields within an area north of the Elbe, just above its southward bend, extending approximately 60 km both east–west and north–south (Figure 91).

Wüstemann's analysis of the top-level burials, mainly from barrows, has revealed significant differentiation within this stratum of burials. Some of it may be chronological, with one group of burial goods being later in date. Perhaps a more important ritual differentiation is seen in the use of either barrows or cemeteries. Urnfield burials are generally poor, as only 17 per cent contain burial goods. To this may be added a spatial separation between the two otherwise contemporary rites, suggesting that people buried in barrows wanted to distinguish themselves from the commoners by taking up the archaic tradition of barrow burial, as well as by furnishing their graves with sometimes extraordinary riches. In accordance with this interpretation of the ritual demonstration of social differentiation, in the Seddin area barrow burials total 320 in 240 barrows as against 1,000 burials in urnfields. The latter represent traditional village communities with village chiefs above which a ruling elite had established itself.

The barrow group, however, also signalled diversification and internal ranking: a larger group of cairns (made of stones) with rather sparse burial goods stands out against a smaller set of sometimes rather large barrows (made of turf and earth) with

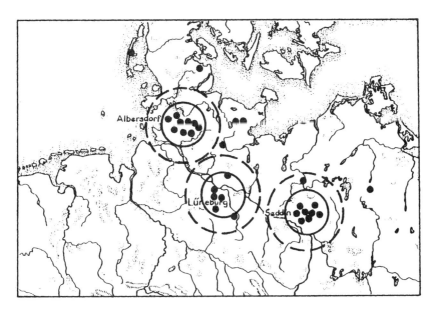

Fig. 90 Chiefly centres along the Elbe, defined by richly ornamented Nordic razors. Proposed political/commercial catchment areas are circled.

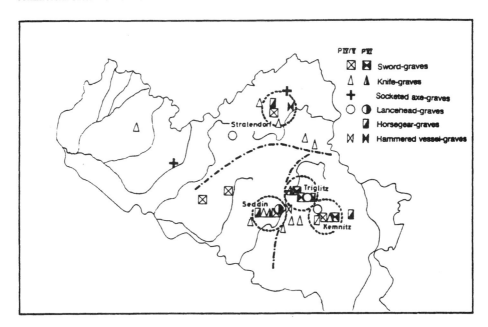

Fig. 91 Map of the Seddin area with centres of chiefly burials circled and local political boundaries marked.

stone packing surrounding a cist. Nearly half the cairns and barrows contained burials with metal grave goods, often of high quality. Among them a few burials stand out as extraordinary, in terms of both the grave goods and the size and construction of the barrow and burial chamber, especially a group of large and richly furnished 'royal' barrows in Seddin with unique features, such as the vaulted roof of the burial chamber in the largest. Parallels have been drawn with Bulgaria and the Balkans by Sprockhoff (1957). The stones for these mounds were specially selected or imported, while in some cases unusual treatments are seen – in the royal Seddin chamber the walls were covered with plaster on which beautiful red, white and black designs were painted. The Seddin paramount chief was buried along with two women, also accompanied by grave goods and thus most probably his wives. His bones were put in an amphora, accompanied by a sword, metal vessels and Nordic razors and tweezers, as well as a miniature spear and a decorated knife, both Nordic, and by several unique pottery types. In general these burials often contain unique items specially produced for the paramounts. Other chiefly burials display variations on the ritual of the royal burial, a few of them apparently belonging to the paramount group, and they all displayed Nordic paraphernalia of chieftainship – razors/tweezers, knives and pins.

The Seddin region thus provides evidence of the concomitant expansion of Nordic trade and the rise of new paramount elites in nodal points of exchange, employing barrows to impress and to demonstrate their new positions as regional chiefs above the level of traditional chieftains. The latter were reduced to vassal chiefs within the local network of political control and redistribution, and at the lowest level we find village headmen buried in the urnfields. This new three-level structure probably approached archaic state formation. However, despite differentiation and separation in burial goods and ritual, both village headmen and paramount chiefs employed metalwork in the same, mostly Nordic, tradition, but with qualitative differences. It appears as if there still existed a continuum of kinship relations between top and bottom, appearing in the burial evidence, but separation and potential class distinctions were probably not far away. This remains speculation, but the next case study will add more evidence to the picture of the internal structure of such chiefly centres.

The rise of the Seddin region during Period V can only be explained by its strategic position as the point of entry to the Nordic and north German region, controlling trade westwards along the Elbe and towards Jutland, further northwards to the Danish islands and eastwards towards the Oder and further on to Pommerania. This nodal position emerges from all distribution maps of prestige goods. We can thus link control of long-distance trade in prestige goods to the emergence of centres of wealth accumulation and the formation of social and political hierarchies that approached archaic state formation. The society was characterised by paramount chiefs controlling tributary vassal chiefs in smaller tribal centres by redistribution of prestige goods. I thus prefer to interpret the evidence presented by Wüstemann as representing a single hierarchical structure, perhaps with some spatial shifts of paramount centres, rather than autonomous tribal territories, each with their own paramount. Although this is possible, especially if they formed a confederation, it does not seem compatible with the kind of control of long-distance trade suggested by the archaeological evidence. For several generations the Seddin region was able to maintain a central

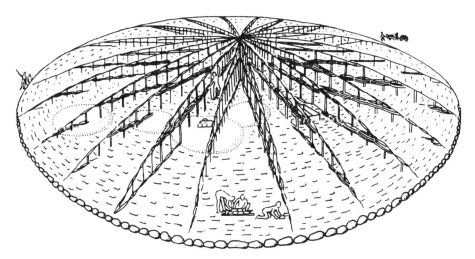

Fig. 92 Construction of the Lusehøj barrow in sections, using fences to stabilise the sod. The two rich graves are marked and the earlier, smaller, barrows picked out.

position in the north–south trade network, preventing competing centres arising in its vicinity, until the monopoly was finally broken in period VI by the takeover of long distance trade from Pommerania and eastern Scandinavia to northern Italy and the eastern Alps by the Billendorf culture and other Lausitz groups, experiencing a last flourish (see next chapter). It is signalled by a break in the use of cemeteries and barrows (Wüstemann 1974, Abb. 10). Whether or not Seddin declined peacefully has yet to be determined.

Voldtofte   The Seddin centre was a rare, but not unique, phenomenon in the north. A similar centre, Voldtofte, has been documented on southwest Fuen in eastern Denmark, exhibiting the same basic characteristics, but with the advantage of recent excavations and an excellent standard of publication (Thrane 1984), which enables us to illuminate in some detail the construction of a royal burial and the formation of a centre.

The Voldtofte region has for the past 100 years been known for outstanding burials and hoards, as well as rich settlements. The wealthiest burials came from a group of five large barrows or tumuli, which yielded rich finds some 100 years ago, but only the recent excavation by Henrik Thrane (1984) of one of them, Lusehøj, has made it possible to contextualise the earlier finds.

The barrow   Modern excavation techniques enabled the documentation of its construction principles. The barrow, originally 7 m high and nearly 40 m wide, had been erected in sections, divided by wattles stretching out from a central pole. The wattles served to keep in place the grass turves, which had been cut quite large – 20 × 40 cm, sometimes 40 × 40 cm, weighing about 30 kg each (Figure 92). An area of approximately 7.3 ha was stripped to provide the turf. The building of the barrow can be estimated to have taken 12.9 person-days of 10 hours' length each. If we add the area needed to provide the necessary turf for building the two neighbouring barrows it amounts to 33 ha of grassland – not an insubstantial area. From the barrow there is a wide view over the sea, on a clear day even across to southern Jutland.

The barrow area had formerly been cultivated, as field systems were documented (Thrane 1984, fig. 106), but the most significant feature is the fact that the barrow was erected over four small barrows from the previous period. These were of a common Late Bronze Age burial type that is common, especially in areas with no existing Early Bronze Age barrows (see also Stjernquist 1961; Menke 1972; Olausson 1987). These small mounds or cemeteries reflect influences from northern Germany and the Lausitz region. What we see then is the formation of a traditional settlement in Period IV with small family barrows/cemeteries. They contained nineteen identifiable burials, 42 per cent of them being infants, thus corresponding to the general picture of age composition and child mortality during later prehistory (Olausson 1987, fig. 19; Bukowski 1991, Abb. 41). Two interpretations of the subsequent sequence of events are possible: one of the families rose to dominance, and demonstrated its link to the ancestors by placing the princely barrow of its 'nouveau riche' chief on the family cemetery; alternatively, a new chiefly family wanted to destroy the memory of a former local competitor. As things stand I prefer the first interpretation. No matter which explanation one chooses, it is unquestionably clear that the giant barrow was a demonstration of newly achieved chiefly power, overruling the former families, and demonstrating the ability to mobilise sufficient manpower and grassland to build a large barrow that can only have amounted to a small corner of the chiefly land. This becomes even more clear when considering the burial evidence. In opposition to the small family mounds only a limited number of selected people were buried in the large barrows.

The Lusehøj burials   The primary burial consisted of a cremation pit with accompanying pyre. The grave goods had been placed on the fire, and only burnt fragments survived. Around the pit a wattle fence was erected (Figure 93). Like the sections in the barrow mound, it could be reconstructed completely by filling in the holes left by the decayed twigs with plaster – a remarkable technical achievement. After the pit and the fence were finished with, a straw mat was laid out to cover the ground and the pit (Thrane 1984, fig. 82).[5]

The fragmentary grave goods testify to the extraordinary character of the burial: they consisted of nails and fittings from a Central European Hallstatt wagon, sections of chain with rectangular rattle pieces, as known from lurs, fragments of a sword or dagger, and pieces of iron and gold. The cremation pit containing the pyre material is also unusual in a Nordic context, where the bones were normally sorted and cleaned before deposition in an urn. Grave goods were normally not burnt. The ritual is reminiscent of the Homeric tradition, and is known from some of the earlier Central European princely burials, such as Caka, with a strong Mycenaean influence in burial goods (Paulik 1962). Who was buried here? Thrane suggests a man, but in that case the traditional equipment is missing (razor/tweez-

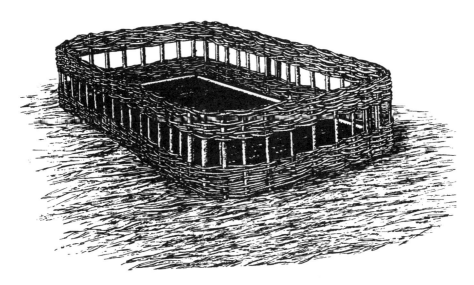

Fig. 93 The Lusehøj burial reconstructed. A straw mat covered the burial pit, surrounded by a fence.

ers). In hoards horse gear and harness are usually found along with high-status female ornaments, also missing from the burial. Arguments both for a male and for a female burial can be put forward, although the fragment of a sword points to a man, as well as the chain, normally associated with lurs, and found in another extraordinary burial in Schleswig-Holstein (Menke 1972, Taf. 59, Nos. 34–36 and 46–53), which also contained four buttons, like those found in the other Lusehøj burial described below. Due to the ritual relationship between women and wagons in Nordic hoards an interpretation of a buried woman can be supported. In Central Europe, however, wagons are normally associated with chiefly male burials. The latter piece of evidence may be decisive, considering the otherwise strong foreign impact, and the fragment of a sword.

The secondary, or parallel, burial was no less remarkable. Unfortunately it was excavated by King Frederik VII around 1860, and we therefore cannot safely determine its relationship to the primary burials. Thrane considers that it was placed on the old ground level, in a stone cist, before or at the same time as the central burial. A Central European hammered metal vessel served as the container for the burnt bones and the burial goods. A curved, hammered bronze lid, covered in resin with small pieces of shining amber, covered the urn, which again was wrapped in a large linen cloth and furthermore a hide. Outside the urn, inside the linen wrapping, there were two small hammered bronze drinking cups. The burial goods were no less remarkable: four buttons, two of them of gold, a golden 'Eidring' (oathring) (now lost), two razors (one richly decorated), and an ornamented socketed axe. There may have been two male burials here, a not uncommon event during the Nordic Bronze Age. The quality of the burial goods is superb – they belong to a local southwest Danish workshop (Baudou 1960, Karte 18 and 50; Thrane 1984, fig. 109) whereas the bronze vessels and the lid were probably imported or made by a foreign specialist. According to Thrane, the bronze lid has its only parallel in Italy, in Bologna, (Mehrart 1952, Pl. 4,3) where it covered a metal urn of the same type, just as the use of linen to wrap round the urn conforms with other princely burials.

Interpretation If we accept the above interpretations the barrow contained the exclusive members of a chiefly lineage: two male chiefs (twins?); and a female high priest – or, more likely, a male of extraordinary position, demonstrated by the imported wagon, the belt buckles and the bronze chains, very rare in Scandinavia (Thrane 1984, fig. 109). Both burials stand out against the traditional Nordic burial rites. They demonstrate a break with tradition, except for the Nordic bronzes, a deliberate attempt to introduce foreign high-status customs and prestige goods. This was of course accompanied by a whole new ideology and etiquette of ruling elites. It is in accordance with the interpretation of the deceased as belonging to a newly established elite, stronger and more wealthy than seen before in the region as a whole. They shared more similarities with other chiefly elites outside the area such as those of Seddin and Albersdorf (Figure 89), with whom close contacts and the exchange of prestige goods and specialists were maintained. This new ideology, however, was also shared with a group of followers, comprising vassal chiefs in the local area, who helped to support and provide the necessary political and economic back-up. If we examine the local context of the princely burials, we find, as at Seddin, a whole group of chiefly barrows, some of the excavated examples containing rich burials. Rich votive deposits are also found nearby. In the Egemose bog fittings and nails of a Central European Hallstatt wagon, like the one in Lusehøj, were found (Jacob-Friesen 1970), suggesting that this was no singular or unique phenomenon. The whole area around Voldtofte must have shared in the riches coming into the centre, conforming to the pattern from Seddin (Thrane 1984, figs. 112, 113). This wealth is demonstrated in an accumulation of foreign imports and gold (Thrane 1975, fig. 132; Jensen 1966, Karte 4).

If we consider burials and hoards as part of a single structure of ritual depositions that was consciously employed in the social strategies of the elite, it is remarkable that nearly all the rich burials are male, while almost all the hoards are dominated by high-status female ornaments. High-status women belonged to, and were identified in, a ritual sphere of deposition, while men would more often be manifest in burials. On the whole male status symbols had disappeared from burials and hoards, except for some sword and spear depositions (Kristiansen 1984a, fig. 12), whereas women continued to signal their importance in votive depositions of one or several sets or ornaments (Kristiansen 1974a, fig. 13), sometimes associated with horse gear and wagons. This can be linked to the ritual wagon processions shown in miniature from Italy and Iberia (Figure 94). I consider this change in depositional practices during the Late Bronze Age to reflect the consolidation and withdrawal of the chiefly elite from actual warfare (in contrast to western Europe and the Atlantic region, where weapon depositions still dominated). By contrast, women were an object of alliances and they remained an important medium of competitive deposition. In this way they were used to present

Fig. 94 Cult wagon from Strettweg, Austria, found in a princely Hallstatt burial in 1851. The wagon was probably produced in the 7th century BC, but has parallels throughout Late Urnfield and Early Iron Age Europe.

gifts to the gods on behalf of the chiefs. In the subsequent Period VI/Ha C the full consequences of this development are seen, as all votive depositions are linked to a standardised set of double neck-rings.

Economic background New ideas and valuables may come from the outside, adding international prestige to local chiefs, but wealth has to be financed from some source, and the first and most obvious place to look for it is locally. We may discuss which came first, local or foreign control, but once in operation a chiefly centre demanded the exploitation of a larger community or group of settlement units to maintain itself. Trading expeditions, ships and warriors, not to mention large feasts, were expensive. How was all that provided for? And what did the Voldtofte centre have to offer in return for all the foreign prestige goods?

We are lucky enough to know a little about the local background to the Lusehøj princes, as the chiefly settlement has been partly excavated, along with a number of traditional settlements. An excavation early this century revealed a settlement at Voldtofte, lying close to the Lusehøj barrows. The accumulated cultural layers were unusually thick and rich in finds. Several large pots containing stored grain were found, as well as an abundance of animal bones and high quality bronzes, the latter not usually found at settlements. All in all the settlement belonged to a special category. This has been confirmed by partial rescue excavations in recent years, supporting the picture of a complex chiefly settlement (Berglund 1982). It could be demonstrated that the wall plaster of the houses had been painted white and covered with red curvilinear decoration, apparently in the Nordic style (Berglund 1982, figs. 9, 10). It is reminiscent of the painted plaster inside the Seddin burial chamber.

Among the bronzes, most of them fragments, we find several of the types known from richer burials.

The most striking feature of the Voldtofte settlement was, however, the domestic animal bone assemblage. In an analysis of a larger group of Late Bronze Age settlements mostly from eastern Denmark/southern Sweden by Nyegård (1983) (Figure 54A) it could be demonstrated that sheep and pig were dominant compared with cattle – with one exception: Voldtofte. Here, nearly 80 per cent of all animal bones were from cattle. This points to at least two things: first, the importance of cattle as a prestige animal, to be used in exchange, as well as in subsistence; second, the ability of the chiefly centre to monopolise cattle, suggesting control of the local economy, which provided wool and pork meat to the centre, as well as other services. The settlement evidence thus conforms to the pattern demonstrated by the burials and hoards of a social and economic hierarchy dominated by the ritual and economic superiority of a centre. As long as gains were favourably balanced against risks for vassal chiefs and their followers when taking part in trade expeditions and raids to supply the necessary goods for the centre (Figure 95), the structure could be reproduced. It was supported by a massive ritual legitimation, as reflected in ritual hoarding and ceremonies. What was traded? Amber, textiles, women, mercenaries, well-bred cattle and horses (in several Late Bronze Age settlements they make up 15–20 per cent of the bone material) and perhaps slaves for the emerging Italian city states. A known high-status commodity was the disks of raw pitch/resin, processed by heating and subsequently formed (Hayek *et al.* 1989). In some cases also amber and incense were added, the last element identified in a recent analysis of the Seddin disk carried out by Rausing (1984). Most disks have been found on moors, often several together (Becker *et al.* 1989, fig. 9). This is the only Nordic commodity, except female hair, also found in bogs, that can be documented in the north, whereas amber is recorded in its final context in burials far to the south. Finally, hides and exclusive furs and skins from Central Scandinavia may have been a sought-after commodity, as well as sea salt (Jaanusson and Jaanusson 1988).

Conclusion 4

Within a brief period in the 8th century BC two princely burials took place in Lusehøj at the new royal court at Voldtofte on southwest Fuen. The rich grave goods reflect the operation of an international princely network linking Italy, via Switzerland and Seddin, to Voldtofte, mapped in Figure 82. We must assume that connections were rapid and well organised, otherwise wagons could not have been imported. Also details such as the hammered metal lid, with a parallel in Bologna, testify to close personal connections over long distances.

Within the local social and economic environment we observe the employment of similar objects linking Seddin with Voldtofte, made within the same 'workshop tradition' and during a short period of perhaps fifty years in late Period V/Hallstatt B3 (Höchmann 1987). This suggests the existence of close dynastic and commercial links between the princely families around the western Baltic, situated at distances of 75–100 km apart. Visits could be carried out in a one- or two-day trip, within

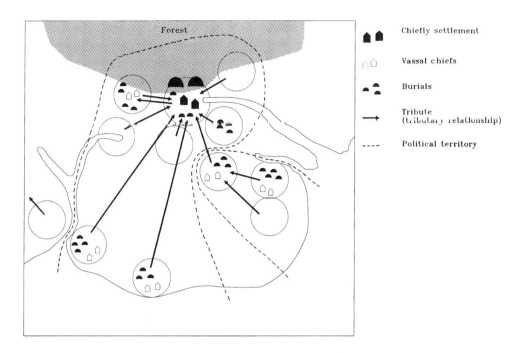

Fig. 95 Model of the local settlement hierarchy within the Lusehøj/Voldtofte chiefly territory on South-western Fuen.

boundaries protected by chiefly vassals. The group is further characterised by the employment of horse gear (Figure 82) for horse harness (Figure 96), in which a western and an eastern group can be distinguished (Larsson 1975, Abb. 27; Lampe 1982, Abb. 11), just as some of the phalerae are hammered and some are cast (local imitations). The latter phenomenon suggests that specialists mastering hammering were only available to the chiefly centres. Horse gear and wagons, the latter normally not deposited, were linked to the high-ranking chiefly women, whereas golden 'eidrings' were a symbols of male high chiefs. They cluster in the same area around the Baltic (Figure 97). Among the male chiefly regalia we also find razors and tweezers, as well as richly ornamented knives. In areas of traditional urn burials and the votive deposition of weapons and ornaments, they symbolised the chiefly stratum just below the high chiefs.

It is remarkable that the custom of building monumental barrows is only seen in a few places on the western fringes of the Baltic, at Seddin and Voldtofte, whereas traditional ritual hoarding was the rule elsewhere. It supports the interpretation of these barrows as an abnormal demonstration, representing the emergence of new ruling elites basing their power and wealth on the control of long-distance trade with Italy and Central Europe. It may also be, however, that the barrows reflect their closer contact with these regions, taking up new customs more rapidly.[6]

High-ranking women took up an important position in Late Bronze Age society in Central and northern Europe. Much of the metalwork in hoards was actually made

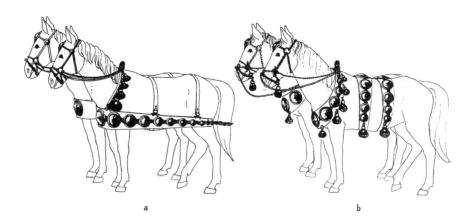

a   b

Fig. 96 Two reconstructions of the possible employment of phalerae in horse harness based on the hoard from Ückeritze, Northern Germany.

up of ornaments, and we can also distinguish here a number of social levels (Kristiansen 1974b; see Levy 1982 for the north) although few attempts have been made to reconstruct social differences and functions according to gender (Sørensen 1987). The combination of horse gear and high-ranking sets of female ornaments in several North European hoards recalls Tacitus' description of the goddess Nertheus, driven round on a ritual wagon with a female priest and her slave. If we consider the elaborate ornaments and what wearing them implied, it immediately becomes clear that many of these high-ranking woman could not have performed much work while adorned with them. And they did put them on, as shown by recurrent wear patterns, although some of them had to stay on permanently, like the huge ankle rings (Kristiansen 1974b). Others, like the large fibulae constructed as metal brassières, were perhaps reserved for ritual functions. We know from bronze figurines in the Nordic region that female priests took part in rituals wearing only a cord skirt and ornaments, while performing ritual dances and ceremonies (Figure 47). They also had elaborate hairstyles, in both the Early and Late Bronze Age (Wels-Weyrauch 1994), suggesting a life without much labour for the highest-ranking women. Lower down the ranks, however, women surely had specific tasks; not least, harvesting was female work, as shown by sickles in burials and hoards, although they may also in some cases have a ritual significance relating to fertility.

The evidence of ranking among woman thus corresponds to the analyses of male equipment, and further suggests that women gained importance in political alliances as marriage partners and in social and ritual life towards the end of the Bronze Age.

The picture sketched of Late Bronze Age society by the evidence of hoards and burials is illuminated by Scandinavian rock carvings and metalwork, including sets of figurines (Figure 47). This alternative evidence testifies to the role of complex rituals preceding and accompanying all major events in life. The geographical structure of metalwork and rock carvings indicates an accumulation of metalwork, ritual gear and high symbolic complexity in rock carvings at regional chiefly centres throughout Scandinavia (Figure 30). We can observe a local hierarchy of declining ritual com-

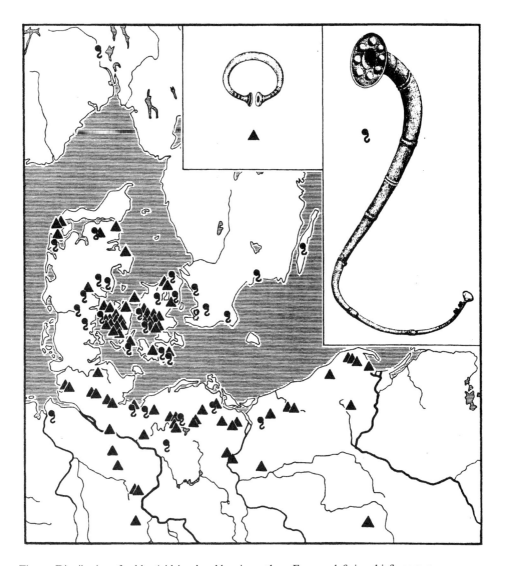

Fig. 97 Distribution of golden 'eidrings' and lurs in northern Europe, defining chiefly centres.

plexity with distance from the centres (Nordbladh 1980; Bertilsson 1987). Thus the ritual superiority of chiefly centres was employed to manipulate and direct wealth from local peripheries into the centre in a process of unequal exchange. The ritualised structure of Bronze Age society can be summarised as follows. At the top we find the ritual twin warrior chiefs performing large-scale public ceremonies, involving lur blowing, ritualised axe and spear combats, and various ritual games and dances. Rituals were linked to weddings, burials and the preparation of trading expeditions (ship motifs, sometimes with rituals being performed on the boats or in connection with them) and warfare (symbolic axe processions and war games). As in Greece, Italy and Central Europe wagons played an important role in ritual processions, probably including burials (Pare 1989b). We should envisage ritual plays in which the high chiefs and priests (always in pairs), together with the high-ranking priestly women, performed the myths of the life cycles of the gods. On some occasions ritual gear was deposited in hoards, confirming the scenes on rock carvings, while at other times it was not deposited but instead carved, (e.g. individual weapons). Also meals and feasts are testified to by the ritual hoarding of bronze cauldrons and golden cups. At the local level we find fertility rituals, from sun worshipping to simple symbols, such as cup marks, being employed widely. They correspond to the ritual hoarding of single objects, mostly tools from local farming communities (Jensen 1973). We can thus identify the whole sequence from chiefs to warriors, farmers and craftsmen, in the composition of hoards and burial. The development and maintenance of common religious and social value systems was due to the operation of long-distance exchange networks operating through chiefly centres, in a complicated process of acceptance, recontextualisation and the rejection of new influences.

The basic factor keeping the system together was the gift – between royal families maintaining dynastic links and alliances, from rulers to vassals, and as gifts to the gods presented by the chiefs or kings in votive offerings. In all cases social bonds of loyalty were established. The gift was the principal form of exchange in archaic society (Marazov 1989, 91):

> There was hardly any area in the life of archaic man that was not coded through an appropriate exchange of gifts: for making friends, for marriage, funerals, initiation etc. Since the king's behaviour was ritualised to the highest degree, it is precisely in the relations among the rulers that this feature of archaic customary law can be expected to be best reflected.

This is true of Thrace, described by Marazov, as well as in northern Europe, as we have seen. In Thrace one can flesh out the archaeological finds with the historical sources describing gift-giving among the Thracian kings and their neighbours, the Greeks. The archaeological reconstruction of the connections between Villanova and Fuen, however, entails all the basic elements of heroic or Archaic Greek society, as it was practised in Italy and the north. Shared norms of social and ritual conduct from Greece to Denmark were the basis for maintaining these royal and chiefly networks of elite exchange and trade. We may therefore assume that they operated according to the archaic traditions of gift-giving, as known from Homer, Hesiod, Thucydides, etc.

Seddin and Voldtofte reflected the opening and take-over of a western trade network along the Elbe, in opposition to the earlier network from Zealand across the Baltic to the Oder and further south, described in the previous chapter. New political and economic conditions in the Lausitz culture and beyond had closed this route, or reduced its importance, giving way to the Elbe–Phahlbau–Villanova network. Did the Lausitz culture block Nordic trade, or was the decline of the workshops in Hungary and their movement to Italy the decisive factor? And can we really suppose such controlled actions at a supra-local level of political interaction, demanding a knowledge of conditions hundreds of kilometres away? After having penetrated the

Italian–Nordic network and made interpretative visits to their archaeological remains at Seddin and Voldtofte the answer is in the affirmative.

5.4 The nomadic connection: the Thraco-Cimmerians

Background to the problem

The question of Thraco-Cimmerian influences in Late Bronze Age Europe (mainly
Ha B3/Late Period V/Late Atlantic III) is part of the long-standing debate in
European archaeology about the proper interpretation and explanations of external
factors in cultural change, especially those originating in the steppe region of Eurasia.
We shall take up the discussion of migrations in Chapter 7, but it is already
appropriate at this stage to present the problem, and plan for a solution. It has become
commonplace in Anglo-American archaeology to dismiss migrations in a rather
high-handed manner by stating that they belong to a primitive archaeological past
and so do not merit serious consideration – as if they had already been subject to such
serious and critical analyses (see Champion *et al.* 1984; Renfrew 1987). That is in fact
not the case. No systematic analysis and discussion of the criteria for identifying the
existence and causes of migrations versus internal change and information exchange
have been presented for the Bronze Age, nor for any earlier period, by either pros or
contras. A few careful analyses in restricted regions, such as that of Shennan (1978)
for Corded Ware in Central Europe, are more or less all we have. There have,
however, been many persuasive attempts to account for the evidence by reference to
other types of processes, most notably Colin Renfrew's territorial analyses (1973) and
Andrew Sherratt's Secondary Products Revolution (1981). These should not be
dismissed, as they represent vital insights – a necessary social background. But neither
should the possibility of various types of migration be ignored. A primary objective
must therefore be to establish some criteria for evaluating the impact of cultural
change, to allow us to assess where on the scale from information exchange to
migrations we should place the Thraco-Cimmerian phenomenon.

During the 9th and 8th centuries BC we can observe two major changes in the
eastern Urnfield region: the deposition of bronze comes to an end, while it reaches its
height in the west, and at the same time new technological and social elements are
introduced – iron and components of a nomadic life style (new types of horse gear
and wagons). The flourishing Hungarian production centres of elite bronzes declined during the same period, and moved to Italy and the Alpine region (Mozsolics
1972; Fekete 1983). Earlier research saw all these changes as forming a single chain of
historical events – warring nomads conquering the rich centres of Bronze production, bringing with them new weapons and iron technology and forcing skilled
metalsmiths into exile. However, the pattern has turned out to be more complex, and
it is clear that no single or uniform explanation accounts for the changes in the
evidence. We have to adopt a more holistic approach that takes into account all
factors, internal as well as external. Instead of considering primarily the evidence for
new styles of horse gear in Europe, we should make an attempt to understand
changes in the region whence the new so-called Thraco-Cimmerian influences

originated. Only then can we assess the validity of the earlier hypotheses – did a Thraco-Cimmerian cultural complex exist that can be characterised in archaeological terms, and were internal conditions in this region such as to support and eventually explain a westward expansion? Likewise, we must discuss whether there are internal changes in Central Europe that may account for an openness to new developments or eventually a need for change. In short: are the forces of change to be located in the pastoral region or in Central Europe? It should be remembered that a migration must begin somewhere – as a solution to a problem. What from the perspective of Central Europe may look like external intrusions or influences are, at the same time, part of internal processes of change in the nomadic region. Thus migrations are to be understood in terms of internal processes, but often we forget to consider the region of their origin, leading to a false definition of the problem as one of external causes of change.

Pastoralists and agriculturalists

We must first discuss in more general terms the relationships between pastoralists and agriculturalists, as a background for assessing the historical conditions prevailing from the 9th and 8th centuries BC. Pastoralists depend on agriculturalists for their reproduction, just as agriculturalists often obtain foreign goods from trade with nomads, who due to their mobility are able to link wide areas by trade and exchange. The symbiotic relationships between them may take several forms: from balanced coexistence, as described for the Pathans and the Baluchi by Barth (1956 and 1967c) to exploitative relationships with pastoralists forming a warring elite extracting tribute from peasant populations, as in the case of the Maasai in Africa (for a comparative typology see Goldschmidt 1979). The latter relationship may take the form either of spatial coexistence or of spatial separation, e.g. as defined by steppe environments bordering farming environments (valley/forest regions), as was the case north of the Black Sea in eastern Europe. Although pastoralism can adopt a wide range of forms from rather egalitarian to highly stratified societies, there are a number of common traits, recently summarised by Goldschmidt (1979) from a conference on pastoral production and society. Among them I list:

1 Task demands: control and movement of animals (to secure water and grass), danger and hardship. This demands military prowess and protection. Raiding is part of the game.
2 Social nexuses: stock linkages including inheritance, brideprice, wergild and clientship (contracts). Segmented patrilineages (*obok*) and age sets.
3 Career factors: herd building (high mobility), network formation, military skills (especially among young men), animals used to buy wives and therefore produce progeny. Here individual action leads directly to status.
4 Attitudes: self-determination and independence, explicit self-interestedness, concern with high status; the objectification of persons, and the acting out of hostile impulses.
5 Religious rituals: rites of passage such as initiation with body mutilation, physical endurance, spirit placation, and divination.

To this we may add the extremely conservative nature of pastoral ideology and behaviour, making generalisation possible in time and space, despite variations in both ecology and social complexity. Therefore pastoral states were never durable, otherwise they led to the dissolution of pastoral life.

There are, however, a number of factors making pastoral nomads subject to stratification, state formation and temporary territorial expansion into neighbouring regions, that would seem to be characteristic of the steppe nomads of Eastern Europe and Central Asia (Krader 1979; Burnham 1979; Sáenz 1991):

(1) Due to their symbiotic/exploitative relationship with farming communities on the one hand and their herds on the other, the factors determining pastoral social and economic life are more variable than in farming communities. Although pastoral life offers possibilities of economic manipulation, wealth accumulation and social mobility enforcing hierarchy, and implies a long-term political advance (dominance) for pastoralists over agriculturalists, it also entails a basic element of unstable, fluctuating social and economic conditions. Herds may both grow and decline more rapidly than agricultural production. The balance of the ecology and economy is thus delicate as it depends upon the proper adjustment of both a herding and a farming economy. In favourable periods it may lead to the build-up of herds and people, which in periods of changing climate or environments (e.g. overgrazing) then hit back with double force. These risk factors are compensated for in a number of ways, e.g. partnerships and wide distribution of the herd, ensuring the flow of animals and the formation of extensive social networks. It follows from this that pastoral economies with a balanced reliance on both farming and livestock are most likely to develop and maintain complex hierarchical political systems. Figure 98 proposes a regularity between the reliance on livestock/farming, ecological conditions and social hierarchy. Although mainly based upon African conditions, it shows that the Eurasian region falls within the range of developing social complexity.

(2) Pastoral nomads often employ long-distance exchange to maintain both internal polities and alliances and exchange with peripheral communities. Such exchange and trade relations typically originate in well-organised state societies, which the nomads supply with a number of exotic goods, ranging from metal to special breeds of horse and slaves from their peripheries or from tribute-paying societies. In periods of weakening state organisation the nomads are tempted to gain direct access to the sources of wealth, as shown by the recurrent nomadic attacks, sometimes successful, on both China and the Near East (Lattimore 1979). In periods of imperial expansion or changing trade routes, traditional nomadic trade monopolies may be cut short, or trade may even be directed away from their traditional lands, leading to migrations or attempts to take over trade by military means.

(3) Due to these highly complex social and economic relationships, which tend to form fluctuating structures of centre and periphery, ranking and political stratification evolve, forming a vital component in internal confederations and competitive feuding for economic and political control. In Central Asia the conical clan, or *obok*, which is linked to stratified social formations based on inherited ranking and order of

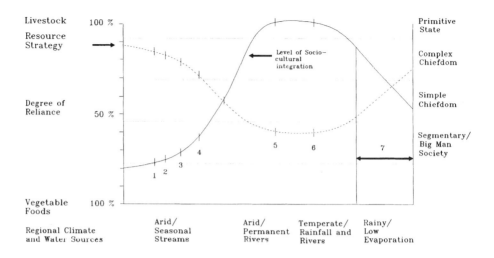

1   Southern Turkana
2   Maasai
3   Nuer
4   Mandari
5   Fulani States 18th &
      19th century
6   Ankole Kingdom
      19th century
7   Irish Chiefdoms 8th –
      9th century AD

Fig. 98 Relationship between rainfall/climate, resource strategy and social complexity in nomadic societies from later history.

birth, consequently came to characterise social organisation (Krader 1963, 323). It meant that stratification was the basis of social organisation.

(4) As a result of their military potential, pastoral chiefs and their retinues/armies were employed as allies or mercenaries in periods of unrest between the dominant state powers in southwest Asia from the 1st millennium BC onwards, as seen, for example, in the use of the Scythians and Cimmerians by both the Assyrians and the Greeks. This policy entailed a degree of risk, as warring tribes would sometimes continue raiding, as happened with the Cimmerians. Another common variant leading to hierarchical pastoral social formations emerged in situations where mobile warriors controlled and levied tribute on caravan routes or trading centres, or simply robbed merchants, while their serfs and client groups took care of animals and eventually of agricultural production. This was a common pattern in North Africa (Sáenz 1991), and similar conditions existed along the Black Sea and in the Caucasus.

When considering the interaction of these factors there are good reasons why pastoral social organisation, more than other social forms, tends to expand and dominate farming communities when possible. Their social organisation is generally open to incorporation, and clientship offers a potential for social advancement (Haaland 1967). This explains the evolutionary potential of pastoral social forms when confronted with stable farming communities, or even state societies in periods of fragmentation and decline. But just as characteristic is the lack of durability of such expansion if it extends beyond the ecological frontiers of nomadic life. Due to the delicate balance of factors within which pastoral nomads operate, they were doomed either to be incorporated, or to retreat to their core regions throughout Central Asia once these had been established and defined by states and empires to the south and forests to the north. It was perhaps the effect of successful incorporation, and its impact on social organisation through the acculturation of basic pastoral components, which in the long run had the most profound influence on social evolution, as well as the spread of Indo-European languages, in later European prehistory.

The formation of pastoral social organisation in Eurasia

After these rather heavy categorisations it should be stressed that although pastoralism forms one end of a subsistence range where the other is represented by sedentary agriculture, mixed forms were widespread throughout prehistory and history. During later prehistory the formation of large upland pastures in Central Europe/the Mediterranean and heathlands in northwest Europe created ecological conditions that made pastoral husbandry an integral part of the subsistence economy (Fleming 1972; Sherratt 1981) over large areas from the later 4th and the 3rd millennia BC. Shifts in dominance from pastoral towards agricultural strategies occurred, depending on long-term economic trends, but from the Late Bronze Age to the Early Iron Age both strategies seem to have coexisted, forming local patterns of seasonal migration between lowland and upland grazing (Comsa 1988; Greenfield 1988; Hammond 1982). This localised vertical transhumance, characteristic of mountainous regions, differs from the horizontal movement of herds and livestock in steppe environments, which in its classic form is mounted. In Central Europe upland pastures alternated with lowland pastures and mixed forests. An important consequence was that Central Europe formed no ecological barrier to the steppe region north of the Black Sea and further east during later prehistory. On the contrary, a familiar environment of pastures and open land in the Hungarian plains, extending into a steppe environment, made contacts with nomadic groups and their expansion westwards a natural extension of their original habitat, forming a circum-Pontic interaction zone, as suggested by Mallory (1989, 261).

Two natural routes were available: through the lowland zone north of the Carpathians, where the Dnieper, Bug and Dniester rivers flow into the northeast European plains, making contact with the River Vistula and its tributaries; and a southern route that could either bypass the Carpathians to the north down to the River Tisza or follow the Danube from the Black Sea, with offshoots into the Balkans. But how and when were the steppe cultures formed? After all, parts of the Asian steppe region, especially the Eurasian, included some of the most fertile soils in the world (black soils) that were allowed to be solely exploited by an extensive pastoral way of life for several millennia.

The formation of pastoralism and large-scale steppe environments in eastern

Europe seems to be a result of two interlocked processes: a long-term transformation in the forest zone leading to the creation of pastures, and an expansion of population groups from this zone into the natural arid steppe environments of eastern Europe north of the Black Sea and Caspian Sea, the so-called Pontic–Caspian region, and probably also into the Hungarian Plain at an early date. As summarised in recent works by Anthony (1986), Telegin (1986), Bökönyi (1986), Dergachev (1989) and Mallory (1989, chs. 7, 8), these processes were well under way during the 4th millennium BC, when horse domestication developed. This was a crucial innovation, as the horse could be employed for meat, traction and riding, the last demonstrated by cheek-pieces for fixing the bit from the 4th millennium and by indirect evidence from tooth-wear studies (Anthony and Brown 1991). By the 3rd millennium the steppe environment and the bordering forest zone in the Pontic–Caspian region were already inhabited by pastoralist groups, defined as the Yamna culture, characterised by the building of *kurgans* (barrows), and the use of horses and wagons (Dergachev 1989). These were the populations that under various names are thought to have formed the Indo-European core groups, spreading westwards and eastwards in a number of 'waves' from the 4th millennium, according to Gimbutas (Gimbutas 1979; for an opposing view see Renfrew 1987; while for a balanced middle-of-the-road assessment see Mallory 1989, 1991b). From the early 3rd millennium they contributed to the formation of the Corded Ware/Battle Axe cultures in Europe, with a major social and economic pastoral component (Kristiansen 1988; Mallory 1989) that provided the social and economic basis of Early Bronze Age societies (Shennan 1986a; 1986b).

It should be noted that as early as the 3rd millennium BC a number of recurrent features in the interaction between the steppe zone and Central and northern Europe had emerged:

(1) An interaction zone in eastern Europe, the circum-Pontic area, but also including the Balkans, where trade and prestige goods exchange alternated with migrations along the lines of entry mentioned earlier. Its existence meant that nomadic groups were familiar with at least some of the people and environments further west.
(2) From an early time migrations normally stopped at the River Theiss (1979), a pattern we shall see repeated, while in northern Europe the River Vistula seems to be the limit, although small groups may have found their way further north and west.
(3) Horse management and trade in horses seems to have formed an important element of trade and exchange from the Bronze Age onwards (Bökönyi 1986; Sherratt 1987). In much the same way regular contacts, trade alternating with migrations, towards the south through the Caucasus, transmitted influences and prestige goods from Anatolia in exchange for copper and perhaps tin, and later iron (Cernych 1976; Kohl 1987; 1988).

The appearance of horse riding in the 4th millennium BC brought about a revolution in communication and territoriality, as it expanded the size of potential exploitative territories by a factor of five, although seasonal movements of families and livestock employed much slower ox-drawn wagons. The horse could be used to explore new territories, in raiding and trading. This innovation is therefore crucial for understanding the exploitation of the steppe environment during the 4th and 3rd millennia and the subsequent formation of new types of political organisations, based on extensive alliance networks (Anthony 1986, fig. 3), that had the evolutionary potential to form confederations and later short-lived nomadic empires. The emergence of an extensive Pontic–Caspian cultural area from the later 4th millennium (the Yamna Culture) was due to these factors, which also tended to develop and maintain a common language, especially during the formation period. Riding meant that warring groups could strike militarily over vast distances with rapid movements that could be followed up by migrations, or by a speedy retreat if more convenient. Nomadic groups were further able to settle in resource-rich niches in otherwise indigenously populated habitats. At the local level raids and looting gained new importance as they could be carried out quickly and efficiently, initiating a new age of warring and shifting territoriality. The nature of military and settlement expansion of course depended on the level of social organisation and not least on military technology and organisation.

These new conditions changed significantly the nature of communication and warfare in large regions of prehistoric Europe (Sherratt 1981), although it was only in the steppe regions that full advantage could be taken of them. Here a mobile, warring, ideology prevailed, spurred by the need to move the herds between resource-rich valleys, often separated by large stretches of less fertile arid grassland, imposing a long-term trend towards mobility. In Europe the agricultural economic basis remained a stabilising component, imposing a long-term trend towards sedentism and more fixed territoriality. Farming and pastoral societies thus ultimately represent two different world views (Goody 1976), whose blending in later European prehistory added a special evolutionary component to it.

Archaeological orthodoxy has in recent decades tended to identify itself with the ideology of sedentary farming, paying less attention to the social and ideological potential of pastoral societies. Within a nomadic framework it would be quite natural to consider a large-scale military operation and subsequent migration to rather remote regions, if profits were likely and the environment favourable. The capacity for such movements and military operations of course depended on the level of social and military organisation. While territorial expansion during the 4th and 3rd millennia BC was still based on a tribal organisation of mixed farming dominated by stock breeding, economic specialisation towards true pastoralism and larger polities evolved no later than the Bronze Age, when the steppe was fully opened up from Altai to the Danube (Dergachev 1989). From 2000 BC or earlier, regional specialisation and division of labour emerged, with some regions focussing on horse breeding (the Don area), others on cattle husbandry and some on farming (the Caucasus), while still others were mainly herding sheep and goats, with some cattle and horses (the lower Volga), such variations relating to environmental conditions (Shilov 1989). During the 1st millennium BC archaic nomadic state formation was a reality, according to literary evidence concerning the Scythians and Cimmerians in their dealings with Urartu, Assyria and the Greeks (Khazanov 1978; Barnett 1982), but it may well have been under way much earlier. Thus the development of fully mounted nomadism was a long-term process, as was the diffusion of its various components. Although horse riding may already have begun in the 4th millennium in the Pontic region, it is not until the 2nd millennium that secure archaeological evidence testifies to it in the form of cheek-pieces from Central Europe (Hüttel 1982). This was followed by the employment of two-wheeled war chariots from about 1600 BC across a vast area from Europe to the Far East (Piggott 1983, 87ff. and figs. 52 and 55; Zaccagnini 1977). Only in the late 2nd millennium, from approximately 1200 BC, do we find metal bridles and thrusting swords, which may suggest the employment of mounted cavalry or perhaps more probably wheel-borne warriors.

In conclusion, there already existed from the 3rd millennium BC a circum-Pontic interaction zone in which pastoral farmers and pastoralists interacted with settled Bronze Age communities to the south in the Caucasus and the Balkans. From the 2nd millennium onwards we can identify a Carpathian–Danubian interaction zone (Cernych 1978; Gergova 1987) that pushed the frontier of stable, highly organised Bronze Age cultures eastwards. After the breakdown of Bronze Age civilisations, the beginning of the Iron Age and subsequent migrations from the 12th/11th century BC onwards, more archaic forms of social organisation emerged in the Balkan/Black Sea area based upon transhumance and true pastoralism, leading to the formation of a new Thraco-Pontic interaction zone or *koine*, forming close relations with the Caucasian area (it was from here that some of the early influences between the Pontic region and Central Europe originated in the 11th century (Ha A1–2)), which formed the background for the intensification of contacts around the Black Sea from the 9th century BC, to be considered in the following section.

With these introductory remarks making up a basic historical and theoretical baggage let us approach our period and people: the Thraco-Cimmerians. Who were they and what place do they occupy in the patchwork of changing nomadic alliances, wars and migrations?

Who were the Thraco-Cimmerians?

According to Greek tradition as recorded by Herodotus (The History 4.11ff.), the Cimmerians were known as the people who preceded the Scythians north of the Black Sea, the latter driving them out of this territory, whence they moved into Asia Minor in the late 8th to early 7th century BC. Archaeologically, this would account for some of the westward expansion of nomadic cultural influences recorded from the 9th and 8th centuries. The history of the Cimmerians and the later Scythians, however, is also closely linked to their relationship with the Assyrians and the state of Urartu, located to the south of the Caucasus and north of the Assyrians in the mountains around Lake Van. The importance of Urartu in Near Eastern history has been re-emphasised in recent decades due to many new archaeological discoveries (Akurgal 1968; Barnett 1982; Piotrovsky 1969), as well as magnificent royal nomadic burials in the Caucasus and Pontic region with costly oriental gifts or imports from 'Cimmerian', pre-Scythian and Scythian contexts (Kossack 1983; Galanina 1987; Rolle 1977). It should also be observed that the pastoral zone stretched far into Iran, thus creating a dynamic centre–periphery relationship with the civilisations of this region, influencing each other's material culture (Akurgal 1968, 112 ff.; Kossack 1983; 1987, Abb. 22). From 900 BC rich, well-organised, 'kingdoms' or 'chiefdoms' developed in the Caucasus, interacting with the civilisations to the south (Kossack 1983). Here we also find typical horse bits and cheek-pieces of early Thraco-Cimmerian type (Kossack 1983, Karte 1).

Urartu flourished from 900 to 600 BC in competition with the Assyrians, and the wars fought between them gradually led to the participation of the pastoral peripheries on both sides. Written records from the time document this, as well as archaeological sources, especially in the Caucasus and beyond (Rolle 1977; Barnett 1982; Kristensen 1988). For example, Cimmerians served as Assyrian troops in Sargon's campaigns against Urartu in 715/714 BC. Mostly, however, like the Scythians, they seem to have been allied with the Medes against Assyria (Piotrovsky 1969, 128 ff.). The references to Cimmerians further state that they swept into Asia Minor, where they sacked the citadel of the Phrygian King Midas, who was said to have taken his life in the ruins (Barnett 1982). These accounts show clearly that well-organised pastoral warriors were on the move during the 8th and 7th centuries, and, perhaps more important, were in close contact with the dominant states of the time, which we may expect to have had consequences for their material culture, to which we shall return.

Like the Scythians the Cimmerians seem to have been roaming around over great distances as warring groups/mercenaries. During the early 7th century they attacked Lydia and Greek coastal cities along the Aegean Sea, and according to Herodotus were later expelled from there. Place names in Scythia show that they must have been in this region as well at some time. During their turbulent migrations they were also at one point allied with the Thracian tribes of the Threres and the Edoni, according to Strabo, suggesting that some of their attacks on the Lydian towns originated from there. It further suggests a close social and cultural relationship between at least some Cimmerian and Thracian tribes, which is confirmed by archaeological discoveries. In Asia Minor the Cimmerians have apparently left no clear archaeological traces, except for 'Cimmerian' arrowheads, perhaps symptomatic of the brief warlike nature of their presence in this region.

Attempts to identify the Cimmerians on archaeological grounds have been, and should perhaps also be expected to be, fruitless. What we can observe is a grouping or complex of related cultural traits which during the 9th and 8th centuries were expanding into Central Europe. The distribution map (Figure 103) corresponds to the philological evidence, as this cultural complex originates in the Caucasian region, bordering on Urartu. Instead of looking for a concrete archaeological identification, I suggest we should accept a general definition by which we link pastoral nomadic cultures from the Caucasus and westwards to the Cimmerians, using the concept in the sense of an archaeological culture, rather than as a specific historical people, accidentally referred to at various times in history, and in several places, none of which was their original homeland.

We must also briefly discuss the Thracian component (Hoddinott 1981; Hellström

1980; Venedikov 1980; Nilsson 1980): who were the Thracians, and what do we know about them? Although in early history the Thracians inhabited a region in the northeast Balkans (in present-day Bulgaria), just south and north of the Bosphorus, we should also include the wider lowland region around the Danube, present-day Romania, on the Black Sea coast, in the Thracian cultural complex, as it was known to be under Thracian influence during this time (Gergova 1982; 1987). The Thracians emerge in history in Homer's accounts of the Trojan war, already renowned for their richly adorned armour and their bravery (Nilsson 1980). For the later Greeks Thrace was the home of the myth of Orpheus, an old Thracian king, and of Jason with the Golden Fleece. It was also the land of magnificent gold- and silverwork (amply testified archaeologically Nikolov 1989, 16; Gergova 1988) and of strange customs of polygamy and a religion very different from their own. Homer mentions Thracian kings as being allied with Troy, so at that time their social organisation must have been well developed, as well as their cultural identity (Hoddinott 1981). It was, however, the rich mineral resources, and especially the rich iron ores, which laid the foundations for developments during the 1st millennium BC. As in the Caucasus, the Balkans and Italy, there emerged during this period local kingdoms, whose territories were characterised by minor local variations in material culture and by a group of royal tumuli (in Greece the polis was likewise characterised by local variations in style, e.g. Coldstream 1983). Thracian kings and nobles were buried either in rock-cut tombs or under barrows. The Thracians were renowned for their horses and as mounted warriors, and they remained independent until the expansion of Philip II of Macedonia in the later 4th century BC, at which time some of the large treasures were buried.

The metallurgical riches of Thrace were the primary reason behind the Greek settlement, leading them to found some of their earliest colonies there from the late 8th century BC, a process accelerating in the 7th century when they settled round the shores of the Black Sea (Bouzek 1990, 19ff), whence Herodotus later made his observations and accounts of the Scythian tribes. The highly developed metallurgical skills of the Thracian kingdoms are seen in the famous silver treasure from Rogozen (Nikolov 1989; Marazov 1989; Fol 1988), as well as other rich hoards, such as Vulchitrun, (Venedikov 1987), which should be dated to this period.[7] From this time – the 6th and 5th centuries onwards – the Thracian kingdoms and their metallurgy are firmly placed in both the written and archaeological records, influenced by both Greek and Anatolian traditions in metalwork (Moscalu *et al.* 1989). Metal vessels were part of royal gift exchange (Marazov 1989), as was usual throughout the Near East. They belonged to the drinking and dining equipment of the royal elites, as demonstrated in the magnificent royal tumuli of the Phrygian kings at Gordion in Asia Minor from the late 8th century BC (Young 1981). Here the whole repertoire of forms, functions and styles is displayed, from the large cauldrons with bull attachments to metal vessels for drinking and dining. This complex spread throughout the Mediterranean, even to the Atlantic zone, although mostly in locally produced forms, a development we shall return to in the next chapter.

The raiding of Thraco-Cimmerian warbands in Lydia during the 7th century

(Herodotus 1.15–16) and the later expansion of the Persians (where Darius in 512 BC passed through the Thracian lands with his army to conquer the Scythians north of the Danube, a campaign which ultimately failed, as we know) exemplifies the central position of the Thracians at the crossing of the Hellespont, which both earlier and later resulted in cultural contacts with Asia Minor. Thus the development of the later Thracian culture took place in much the same way as the Iberian and Etruscan cultures – under strong influence from the Greeks, leading to the formation of archaic kingdoms. Classical sources mention between fifty and one hundred Thracian tribes, but they were united under royal rule. Before the colonisation of the Greeks, however, Thracian culture was heavily influenced by the Pontic cultural *koine* around the Black Sea, by Macedonia, and by the neighbouring states on the coast of Asia Minor. This takes us back to the 9th and 8th centuries.

Archaeological definition of the Thraco-Cimmerian horizon
In a survey of Macedonian and Thracian bronzes Jan Bouzek (1973; 1974) demonstrated the emergence of a circum-Pontic or Thraco-Cimmerian cultural koine from 800 BC (Figure 99A, 99B). Here old Urnfield traditions in metalwork mixed with new Cimmerian influences originating in the Caucasian region, and Macedonia represented a dynamic centre of production integrating the new influences, linked to horse equipment (for arrangements of straps for harnesses) and ritual purposes (various types of pendants). This cultural complex presupposes close contacts between the regions in question, the nature of which is still debated. It corresponds to the introduction of a new ceramic style, the Basarabi culture (Vulpe 1965), representing a complete break with former Urnfield traditions, with its geometric encrusted designs instead prefiguring later Hallstatt pottery. That Cimmerian mounted nomads were expanding their activities westward is undoubted; the question is the nature of that expansion: was it conquest, migration, or extensive trade, eventually combined with the control of important trade colonies on the Black Sea? Herodotus (1.15–16) mentions the Cimmerians' reign over the kingdom of Sardis in Asia Minor, which they held for some decades, with the exception of the citadel. We must therefore envisage well-organised societies, probably at the level of archaic state formation, at least in their home region of the Caucasus, where they were interacting with Urartu and various city states (Rolle 1977), and in Thrace. This interaction – trade alternating with raids and plunder – is manifested in the appearance of Anatolian/Urartian imports in burials in the Caucasus and the Pontic region (Galanina 1987; Kossack 1986, 128 ff.).

The westward expansion of the Cimmerians represents a recurrent feature of nomadic history on the western steppe – in periods of drought or due to internal warfare, large groups would move at the expense of other groups, who were then pushed further on. Successive westward tribal moves towards the Black Sea are known from late prehistory into historical times – the Cimmerians, followed by the Scythians, in turn followed by the Sarmatians (Sulimirski 1970), just to mention those known from the 1st millennium BC. Considering the nature of Cimmerian and Scythian military history, as recorded in ancient texts, and given the warring nature

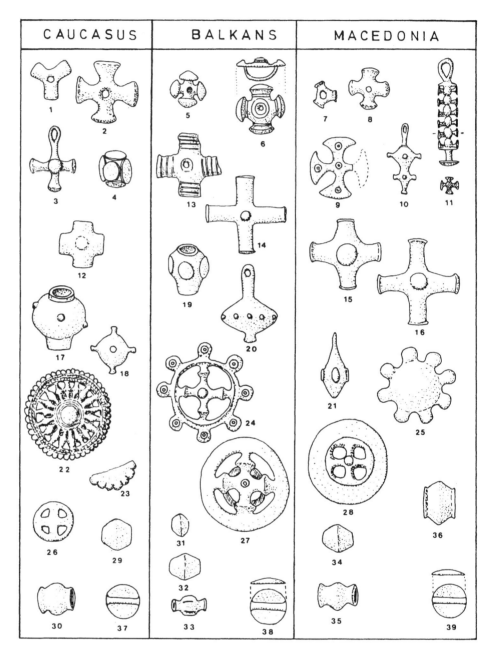

Fig. 99(A) Comparative chart of bronze types from the Northern Caucasus, the Balkans and Macedonia.

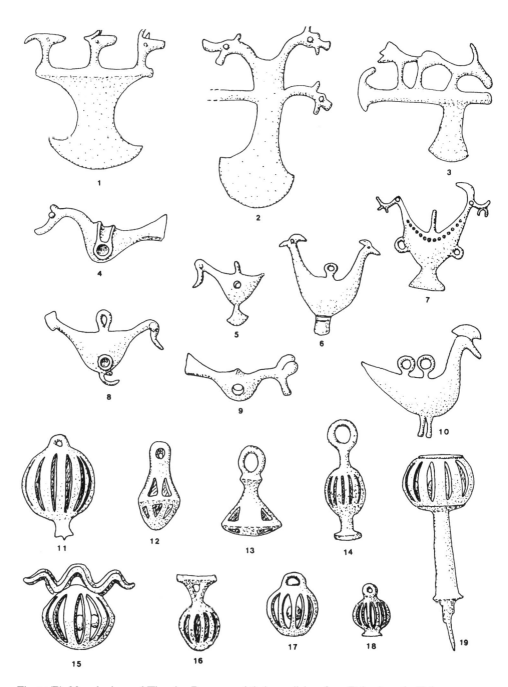

Fig. 99(B) Macedonian and Thracian Bronzes and their parallels: 1 from Bulgaria, 2 the Kuban area, 3 Stara Zagora, Bulgaria, 4 and 9 the Kuban area, 5 Stip, 6 near Rila, 7 Transylvania, 8 Radanja, 10 Prozor, 11 Luristan, 12 northern Armenia, 13 upper Kuban, 14 Glasinac, 15 Bohemia, 16 Glasinac, 17, 18 Switzerland, 19 Staraja Mogila near Kelermes.

of nomadic social organisation and its well-trained mounted archers, also armed with daggers or short swords, we should imagine a series of conquests into eastern Europe, to gain access to tribute in the form of agricultural produce and trade. Let us consider to what extent the archaeological evidence can illuminate the problem, first in the Pontic-Caucasian region, then in Central Europe.

In a number of works Kossack has delineated the Cimmerian horizon in Europe (1954a; 1980), and has in recent years traced its origin in Asia (1983; 1986; 1987; see also Bouzek 1983 for a useful overview). It seems possible to describe a cultural complex of well-defined burials spanning the 9th to late 7th centuries, when Scythian culture takes over. It ranged from Siberia to the Caucasus (Figure 100), and it has even been possible to suggest a three-stage chronological sequence (Kossack 1983; 1986; 1987). This cultural complex originated in Central Asia/Siberia, where its basic components occur – large well-bred horses, royal burials with large numbers of sacrificed horses and part of the royal retinue, stelae with animal and warring motifs, early animal or zoomorphic style, and daggers and swords with cross-shaped hilts, e.g. at Arzan. The same complex emerges later in the Pontic/Caucasian region, e.g. in Tli and Kelermes (Kossack 1986; Galanina 1987). In reality we may be seeing the gradual development and westward expansion of the Scythians and their culture, which then reached its final form with the use of animal style etc. through Iranian and Urartian influences received as a result of their participating in the Assyrian–Urartian wars of the late 7th century. According to this, the pre-Scythian style developed during the 7th century (Ha C; Kossack's Phase 2, with its beginnings in the late 8th century), while the Scytho-Iranian style flourished from 600 BC onwards (Kossack Phase 3) (Figure 101). It represents another aspect of the orientalising styles that spread throughout Europe and the Mediterranean with the intensification of trade and migrations, in part due to Assyrian expansionism (Kossack 1987). With these new, earlier, datings the Central European and Caucasian/Russian evidence has been brought into correspondence. It should be noted, however, that there already existed an old tradition of contacts with the Iranian region through the Caucasus, the central role of which was emphasised by its rich metal ores, supplying both the steppe and the Assyrians (and later the Urartian state).

Thus between the 9th and the 7th centuries BC there appeared on the Pontic-Central Asian steppes a new cultural complex of a more hierarchical, warring nature, employing iron for its weapons, as well as early animal motifs. The Cimmerians represented the first phase, with only a few animal heads, mainly on sceptres, dominated by geometric designs, and openwork metalwork (pendants, belt fittings) (Figure 99). We should imagine a rich tradition of wood carving, which has not been preserved, translated into metalwork from the 7th century onwards. The formation of the Scytho-Iranian animal style reflected the rise of new ethnic and religious identities among the pastoral chiefdoms of the Caucasus and beyond, resulting from intensified centre–periphery relations with Urartu and later with Assyria. Beginning with intensified trade and the establishment of political relations the pastoral chiefs were increasingly drawn into the politics of Urartu and Assyria as mercenaries and allies, leading to a rapid cultural exchange and change. A close parallel to this process

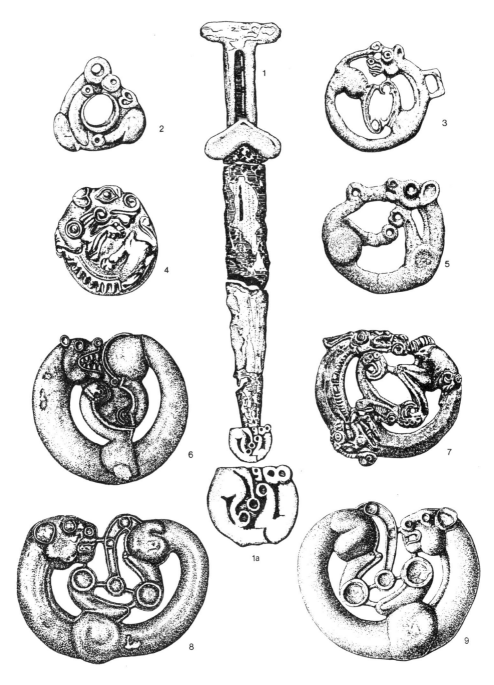

Fig. 100 Rolling animals from Siberia (6, 8, 9), northern Caucasus (1) and the Crimea (2, 7). (6) is from Arzan, Tuva. (1) is made of iron and bronze, (2) of bone, (3, 5, 8) of bronze, (4, 9) of gold.

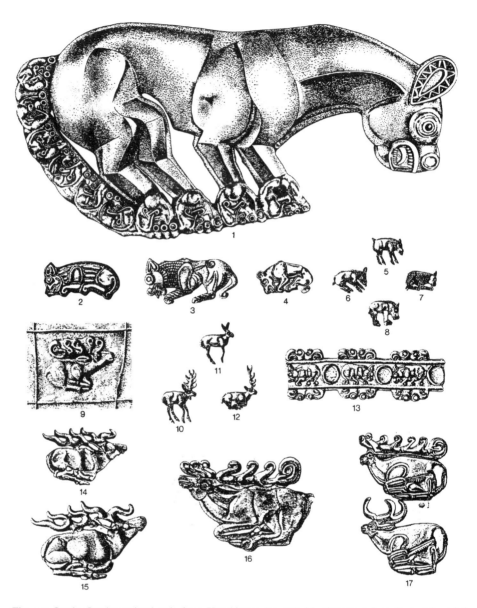

Fig. 101 Scytho-Iranian animal style from Kazakhstan (14, 15), Northwestern Iran (2, 3, 13) and the Kuban area (1, 4–12, 16 and 17).

is the development of Late Hallstatt and Early La Tène culture in relation to the Greeks and Etruscans. Also the Germanic zoomorphic styles emerged through their interaction with, and opposition to, the later Roman Empire, forming new and larger political entities and applying new technological skills in the process.

Likewise we find in the Pontic region new breeds of horse, new horse equipment, as well as Iranian/Urartian and later Greek imports, suggesting a higher level of specialisation in terms of military tactics and techniques, which was coupled with more developed horse breeding and management. This enabled military campaigns over greater distances as well as the control of long-distance trade. Its genesis was on the one hand the animal style/ideology of the Central Asian region, on the other interaction with the emerging Urartian state and control of the rich metal ores in the Caucasus (Kossack 1983). The changes leading to this new cultural complex then represent one aspect of its penetration into Central Europe during the same period. Another is the tradition of trade and exchange around the Black Sea region, which also included the Danubian/Carpathian area on its eastern fringe, as demonstrated above (Figure 99). How were these two strategies played out?

Horses, wagons and mounted warriors

I shall begin by presenting the interpretative framework of this chapter. It rests on two observations made earlier: new elites tend to signal their identity by depositing specially selected prestige goods in burials, often in barrows; consolidated elites do not deposit large amounts of prestige goods in burials, and eventually only deposit small symbolic pieces, but instead present gifts to the gods in hoards or at sanctuaries (the Greek parallel to this ritual). The picture is rarely as clear cut as this, and can be blurred by hoarding due to warfare, by a lack of prestige goods, etc. If, however, we apply this simple generalisation it becomes possible to explain the distribution of horse gear and wagon fittings during the 9th–8th (Ha B3) and 7th (Ha C) centuries BC, as well as the development of Ha C warrior burials.

Let us start by considering the distribution map Kossack produced nearly forty years ago in a classic study of the 'horse and wagon complex' (Figure 102). Although it can be supplemented, especially in the east, it still gives the basic picture for Central Europe. According to my hypothesis the zone with depositions of horse gear represents a 'frontier of change'. It was here that the new Thraco-Cimmerian social order of mounted warriors – the horse/wagon complex – was expanding westwards, leading to the formation of new ritual and social norms of conduct, reflected in the widespread appearance of new wagon types, metal adornments and fittings for horses and wagons, belt fittings, etc. To the east, in the Black Sea area and the Balkans, it had already been enforced and integrated, represented by the circum-Black Sea–Pontic cultural *koine* of Figure 99. If we add Bouzek's mapping of Caucasian/Thraco-Cimmerian finds around the Black Sea (Figure 103), it becomes apparent that in the Caucasus we have another area of new, more settled, pastoral elites interacting with Urartu. Then we have three more centres on the major rivers: the Don, Dnieper and Dniester. It is clear, however, when considering the characteristic Caucasian horse bits, daggers and sceptres (Podborsky 1970, Abb. 27) that the two major concentrations are in the Caucasus and in Central Europe between the Carpathians and the Denarian Alps. It was here that the new elites were formed and settled, while the steppe areas were not subject to similar transformations. One might of course suggest that these were areas of pastoral migration and movements, whereas in the Caucasus and the Danube area the Cimmerian chiefs settled as overlords by elite conquest and during the social transformation produced by settling down deposited their symbols, or local chiefs adopted part of the new complex. It is

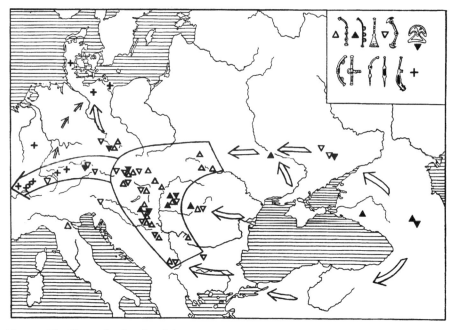

Fig. 102 The Cimmerian frontier of change.

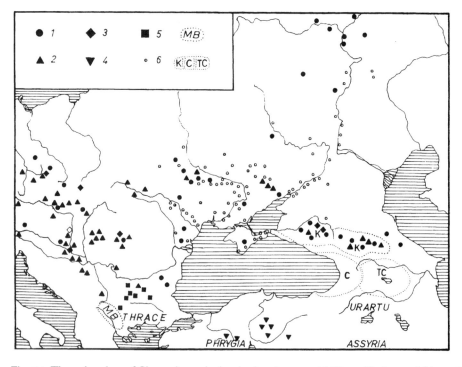

Fig. 103 The archaeology of Cimmerian and related cultural groups: (1) Bimetallic dagger, (2) horse bits of North Caucasian types, (3) sceptres, (4) Cimmerian arrowheads in Asia Minor, (5) Thracian bronzes, (6) other Cimmerian finds from the Pontic area. MB = area of earliest canonical Macedonian bronzes; K = Koban and Kuban culture; C = Colchis culture, TC = Central Transcaucasian group.

clear both from the context of finds and from the study of sceptres by Hancar (1966) that the sceptre was an item of royal regalia, just as the daggers and horse bits belonged to warrior chiefs. However, the significance of the parallels between the Caucasus and the Denarian Alps, (acting as barriers that were not crossed), may rather be that in these areas the new pastoral chiefs were able to exploit economically a position between the steppe and the more developed states, Urartu in the east and Greece/Italy in the west.

In Figure 102 I have suggested several lines of expansion. By this I stress with other researchers that the Thraco-Cimmerian expansion was not the unified movement of a single tribe. On the contrary, it has been shown that there existed significant local and regional differences in material culture within the Pontic/Balkan cultural *koine*, representing local political territories, these held together by a common social and ritual framework. The spread of this complex therefore took place in a mixture of trade and elite conquest, soon leading to the acculturation of the intruding groups as settled overlords. It was favoured by changing ecological conditions of cooler and wetter climate which produced a crisis in many Urnfield lowland settlements, just as it favoured upland grazing and transhumance. I propose three routes: a northern one from the rivers Dniester and Bug going through the Carpathians from the north (or proceeding northwards as later on the Scythians did), a Danubian route, and finally a Thracian-Balkan route. Only the two northern routes were truly pastoral, distinguished not only by horse gear, sceptres etc., but also by special types of iron spears and other weapons (Stegmann-Rajtar 1986, Taf. 5). The Thracian-Balkan route was probably later, as pastoral *kurgans* with typical horsegear are known there from the 7th century (Tonceva 1980; Tasic 1971), but Macedonian bronzes were on the other hand transmitted via this route northward to the Hungarian Plain (the Danube and the Tisza) during the 8th century (Kemenczei 1988b).

During the past generation Hungarian scholars have carried out an important task in defining chronologically and geographically the various phases of pastoral expansion in the Pannonian Plain from the 9th to the 6th centuries BC (summarised recently by Kromer (1986, 37 ff.). From the earliest phase we find the pattern repeated many times during the following centuries (and known even since the Later Neolithic): genuine pastoral traditions in burial ritual, material culture and economy stopped at the River Tisza. From here elements of the material culture spread westwards and southwards by way of exchange, especially the horse/wagon complex, although some burials with genuine 'Cimmerian' bronzes further northwest along the Danube into Moravia and Austria may be accepted as resulting from the continued expansion of warrior groups which were soon assimilated (Stegmann-Rajtar 1986, Taf. 5) (Figure 104B). East of the River Tisza, however, we observe a complete replacement of the traditional Late Urnfield culture (Patek 1974, Abb. 1; Kemenczei 1986, Abb. 1): a new burial ritual of slightly flexed or stretched out inhumations, often with animal sacrifices and new types of burial equipment. The horse gear is mainly found in hoards (e.g. Kemenczei 1983), probably belonging to burials, in the same way as the later Scythian burials often practised a vertical separation of burial goods from the buried person (Figure 104A). At the same time

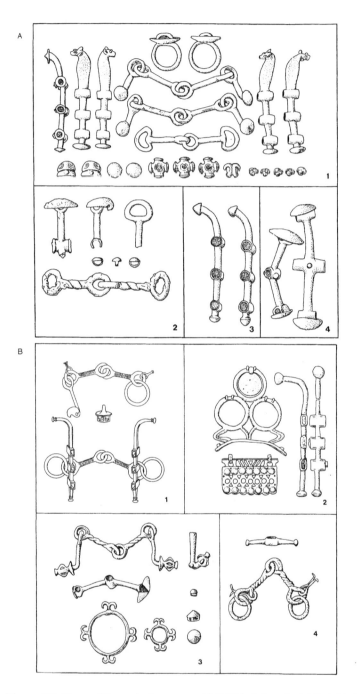

Fig. 104(A) Thraco-Cimmerian horse gear: (1) Stillfried, Austria, (2) Steinkirchen, southern Bavaria, (3) Szanda, Hungary, (4) Tolna, Hungary.

Fig. 104(B) Hallstatt horsegear in local imitation of 'Thraco-Cimmerian' types: (1) Hradenin, Bohemia, (2) Mindelheim, southern Germany, (3) Frög, Kärnten, (4) Statzendorf, Austria.

Urnfield settlements come to an end. All in all there are clear signs of a new ethnic group with a different lifestyle and material culture. Two further observations support the picture of a demarcation between different ethnic groups:

1 The area between the Tisza and the Danube is virtually without finds, representing an apparently empty buffer zone, west of the Danube.
2 The Late Urnfeld and Hallstatt cultures continued their social and economic traditions centred around large fortified settlements forming a solid group west of the Danube (Patek 1986).

It is clear, then, that the fortified elite residences of the Late Urnfield/Early Hallstatt period served not only internal but also external defensive purposes. As we can see from the distribution maps, and from finds in *kurgans* during the 7th century, a peaceful interaction and borrowing developed between the Thraco-Cimmerian complex and its neighbours, leading to the assimilation of its technological and social innovations throughout Europe.

Wagons and horses had long been known within the Urnfield culture. What distinguished this new complex from previous ones? As I have suggested, this was mainly its social and military dominance, which was integrated into ritual, adding new beliefs and myths to Urnfield religion. But there was a very real background to this dominance, which makes it easier to understand. In several studies Kossack has demonstrated the technological and economic implications of the new horse/wagon complex (1988). First, the new bits were of the two-joint type, meant for riding, as opposed to the rigid Urnfield bits, which were more suitable for traction, as they are hard on the mouth of the horse. Today they are used to keep down the head of the horse in dressage, in combination with the two-joint/part bit. The cheek-pieces ensured that the bit could not be drawn out of the horse's mouth. Second, compared to Urnfield bits with a diameter normally of 7 cm, the new types are 10–11 cm, implying larger breeds of horse. Third, the wagons and wheels demonstrate a newer and more complex technology (Piggot 1983, 168ff.). From this we may conclude that riding had now become fully developed in warfare, demanding the specialised breeding and training of horses. We may further conclude that this whole complex demanded the presence of new specialists for wagon construction and for horse breeding and training, which presupposes either highly organised elite exchange and trade, or the intrusion of a new overlord with his retinue and court. That trading in horses took place between the Scythians (Sigynnians) and the Venetians on the Danube is known from ancients texts e.g. Herodotus (Harmata 1968). (As we have seen above, these larger breeds originated on the Central Asian steppes at an earlier time.) All in all this major social change was not possible without an influx of specialists and horses. It had a strong secondary impact on Late Bronze Age societies all over Europe: wagons, horses and horse gear became objects of metal production and consumption, but with various emphases.

The transformation of warfare and of male prestige goods thus represented a new technological and social complex linked to new forms of riding/military tactics demanding better control of horses. It was accompanied by new types of weapon, together with new types of prestige wagons/war chariots. The horse bits clearly indicate the highly specialised nature of riding and dressage (in its original function as war training). All the main functional types known today are found fully developed in the Thraco-Cimmerian complex. In line with this, new light weapons such as daggers and axes were introduced, to become the prestigious weapons of the Hallstatt period, first in the eastern Hallstatt culture and in Italy (Stary 1981 and 1982). The old heavily armoured Urnfield warrior, eventually mounted or on a chariot, was not effective against mounted warriors with light efficient weapons. The Urnfield warrior could hardly fight effectively from horseback, in opposition to the Thraco-Cimmerians. The new military complex did not spread overnight, and it was resisted in both Italy and the west. But it led to a change in male prestige weapons and equipment, first in the eastern Alps and Balkans, later in the western Alps, from traditional heavy weapons and armour to light weapons, axes and daggers; just as dress fittings, especially the belt, became a new area of display. This change reflected a profound social transformation in the role of the warrior chief, who increasingly retreated from heavy fighting and rather displayed the symbols of warfare and strength – dagger and belt. Instead he employed warriors, that is effective armies, to do the fighting, employing the spear, bow and arrow. In the votive deposits at Fliegenhöhle of the 8th century BC the balance between chiefs and ordinary warriors may perhaps be seen in the deposition of more than 200 spears (rank and file) against 11 swords (officers/chiefs). The belt also reflected the introduction of trousers and new male dressing habits taken over from the steppes, where they were a functional outcome of horse riding.

The process was highly complex, trade alternating with elite conquest. Some burials clearly contain foreign Cimmerian chiefs, while others are those of local chiefs adopting some of the inventory through trade. In general it seems that in Hungary pastoral overlords brought with them both a new burial ritual and a completely new material culture (Kemenczei 1986), while in Slovenia and along the southern frontier in the Yugoslavian highlands there was more of a mixture of foreign and local traditions (Eibner 1986). At the 'frontier of change' a new princely social organisation emerged in the 8th century, characterised by large fortified settlements and tumulus burials, as at Stična, Ödenburg/Sopron (Patek 1981) and Novo Mesto (Knez 1981). This complex stretched from the Danube and the eastern Alps southwards along the Denarian Alps to the Balkans, where similar rich burials at Glasinac, and later on at Atenica, Novi Pazar and Trebeniste, testify to the presence of new elites. The many new, large, fortifications reflect the conflicts following in the wake of the social and political transformations. They may also be seen as strongholds against their warring pastoral neighbours.[8] Whether or not the new elites were Thraco-Cimmerian overlords or indigenous chiefs adopting the new ideology, a new hierarchical social organisation grounded in easy-to-defend elite fortifications in valleys, very different from the open steppe-like landscapes of Thrace and the Hungarian plains, rapidly developed. Large tumulus barrows, another aspect of the new eastern ideology, were raised outside the new royal courts at Stična and Novo Mesto (see next chapter) to signal the presence of new elites, as at

Seddin and Voldtofte in the north during the same period (see previous chapter). When considering the imports found in princely burials we must assume that trade both with the Greeks in the southern Adriatic and with Italy across the Adriatic soon developed, horses being one obvious article of trade, as well as slaves. Further to the south, contacts and influences from Greece and Italy were much stronger (to be discussed in the next chapter).

How do we explain the different ways this new complex was manifested in ritual depositions (burials or hoards) in other parts of Europe? From the 'frontier of change' the new complex spread by way of elite exchange and trade to western and northern Europe. Here it did not lead to major social changes, but was integrated into existing wagon and horse ritual (which, after all, had been known for a long time) that was reinforced. Deposition was likewise integrated into existing patterns. In the north phalerae were chosen for symbolic representation, although horse bits were sometimes deposited, but never the wagon, while in the west and south symbolic pieces of wagon fittings or fittings from horse harnesses are found mostly in hoards (Jockenhövel 1972; Pare 1987b). The production in bronze of ornamental pieces like the phalera in itself stresses the increased social and ritual importance of the horse and wagon, just as the first bronze handles for whips reflect the same tendency . Only in Italy did full wagon burials take place (Woytowitsch 1978).

Having considered the whole social and cultural landscape of the Thraco-Cimmerians[9] we should no longer be surprised by their expansion and ability to establish new chiefly or royal centres in east Central Europe. They were from the same mobile warring substratum that participated in the Assyrian–Urartian conflict; later they are recorded as roaming around Asia Minor for eighty years, leading to the downfall of the Phrygian Empire (Barnett 1967). Neither their northern routes into Central Europe in the late 9th and 8th centuries BC, nor their southern route into Asia Minor, were accidental. They followed old established routes of political alliances and trade – to the north between the Pontic steppe and the Balkans/east Central Europe and to the south between Urartu and Phrygia, which were old allies, as were Phrygians and Thracians/Macedonians (according to legend the Phrygian aristocracy originated in Macedonia). The Thraco-Cimmerian cultural *koine* represented a new dynamic phase of mounted pastoral warfare and social organisation, spurred by a closer interaction with developed states through the Caucasus, that spread rapidly around the Black Sea, extending their influence into both the civilised states of Asia Minor and the agrarian chiefdoms of the Balkans and east Central Europe.

Conclusion 5

During the 9th and 8th centuries BC developments in the Mediterranean, Central and eastern Europe display a number of similarities. This seems to have been a period of demographic growth and increasing social differentiation across large regions of Europe. Basic components in social organisation were much the same – chiefly organisation, combining political and ritual functions, the use of votive offerings, which developed rapidly in Greece as burial goods disappeared, was apparently governed by the same religious structure, and in many ways may help us to understand Late Bronze Age ritual hoarding in Central and northern Europe. Social and ritual norms of conduct were exchanged along with body armour, metal vessels, amber and other commodities during the 9th and 8th centuries BC. Thus Greece and Italy shared with the rest of Europe the basic social and religious building blocks of archaic society. More generally we can also observe the recurrent inverse relationship between votive offerings and burial wealth in Greece. Analysing international exchange connections reveals the same kind of internationalism in both Central Europe and Greece. We could even see how during the 8th century the elites of northern Europe were adopting specific Mediterranean styles. Why is it, then, that the Mediterranean was suddenly able to 'take off', while Central Europe maintained its basic structure?

First of all Europe north of the Alps had not yet transcended the barriers of traditional primitive farming systems, and although social differentiation developed rapidly in some regions, as we shall see in the following sections, there soon appeared the first signs of crisis, which from the 7th and especially in the 6th century BC led to large-scale regional collapse and reorganisation. Whereas the Greek population expansion could be mobilised in large-scale migrations and trading ventures, such possibilities were not open to continental Europe, except in the steppe region of eastern Europe. It may be, then, that more productive agriculture in the Mediterranean, coupled with technological advances within the economic sector that could not be taken advantage of in Central Europe, represented a crucial obstacle to state formation. That is one possibility, but there are obviously others to be discussed. One of them is the human factor, as suggested by Snodgrass (1980, ch. 1). The nature of social reorganisation in Greece led to the emergence of a large class of free citizens and craftsmen, who were open to experimentation, and this atmosphere spread to other aspects of social life, including commerce. So traditions of equality and communal government were combined with a new individualistic, enterprising spirit, that broke through the barriers of traditionalism so strong in European Bronze Age societies. Even if we find enterprising traders and argonauts of the Atlantic they did not challenge their traditions, on the contrary they recontextualised innovations into a traditional framework upon their return. This is even true of the later Hallstatt chiefs, who took the old system to its limits, and eventually paved the way for later transformations.

The social and economic constraints of European Bronze Age societies thus tended to undercut trends towards major social and economic diversification. When plugged into international commercial networks, social hierarchies were inflated, but returned to normal when commerce ceased. Only a true economic transformation that could improve the productive base would be able to secure a long-term maintenance of new social forms. Such a social and economic transformation took place in the Mediterranean, and paved the way for economic take-off and state formation. From now on the demands of the new wealthy middle classes in the Mediterranean exerted an increasingly strong force in their relationships with Bronze and Early Iron Age societies north of the Alps and the Balkans. This is not to deny that the major economic sector was agrarian and basically self-sufficient, but it served rather as an exploitative basis for building up these larger commercial activities feeding the needs of the expanding wealthy middle classes. Trade in the modern sense of the word was a reality from now on.

Obviously a major component in long-distance trade, especially in the European hinterland, was high-value, small bulk commodities, such as amber, gold, tin and silver. Later textiles, women and slaves followed. The strategy was basically the same as that used up to the present day: the extraction of scarce raw materials that were refined at home and sold back to the suppliers as 'prestige goods'/diplomatic gifts to secure access to the sources of silver, gold, amber, etc. Finley (1973, Chap. II) pointed out that status and consumption were two dominant operators in the ancient economy, something it shared with European Bronze Age societies. But status and consumption changed direction – in the city states they were relegated from the individual to sanctuaries, which marked a formalisation that freed the individual to dispose more freely of surplus according to political motives, subsumed under economic motives. This change did not take place north of the Mediterranean. Thus, the evolutionary trajectory of the Mediterranean was from now on separated from that of middle and northern Europe, leading to the formation of centre–periphery relationships between the two regions, the consequences of which we shall consider in the next chapter.

6

The new economic axis: Central Europe and the Mediterranean 750–450 BC

6.1 Interlude and change: the beginning of the Hallstatt Culture

I have now delimited the European world system of the Late Bronze and Early Iron Age, based on an interpretation of regional traditions and their interaction during the first three centuries of the 1st millennium BC. This has ranged from the Atlantic in the west to the Pontic steppes in the east, and from Scandinavia to Italy. Having thus set the scene, and to avoid repetition, I shall now proceed a little faster, concentrating on what I consider to be the major sequences of change in Central Europe during Ha C and Ha D, that is from 750/700 to 450 BC.

The interpretative model to be applied in this chapter consists of three components, requiring a brief description:

I propose that the spread of Ha C warriors in Central and western Europe reflects the formation of a pastoralised chiefly elite, creating a more decentralised social and economic environment, reflected in a heavier emphasis on animal husbandry and transhumance. It led to a concomitant decline in north–south trade in the west, whereas the eastern Hallstatt flourished during this period, maintaining exchange networks with the Lausitz, Pommeranian, culture on the Baltic (particularly through amber) as well as with Italy. The Hallstatt thrusting sword and wagon burials are diagnostic of western Hallstatt, the axe and dagger of eastern Hallstatt. Western Hallstatt is decentralised, eastern Hallstatt hierarchical and centralised.

These changes coincided with the formation of Etruscan culture and the consolidation of Greek settlement in southern Italy, leading to rapid economic development and more intense trade relations with Greek and Phoenician colonies and factories. In Iberia the Tartessian culture, the forerunner of Iberian culture, developed. This meant that the need for silver, gold, copper and iron could be satisfied largely by mining activities in Iberia and Italy at a time when copper was less in demand. Consequently there was no need for the Atlantic network, which collapsed (creating the Armorican hoards), just as it led to internal disruption and the building of many new hillforts. In the north, also, trade relations with the south declined although not as drastically, but the old Bronze Age social and ritual order was still transformed.

Thus there formed during the 7th century a centre–periphery relationship of both contact (to the east) and apparent opposition (to the north and west), between an emerging Adriatic cultural *koine* of expanding city states and a Central European warrior zone encircling it from the Denarian Alps round the northern Alps and down towards the Rhône, with lines of expansion westwards along the Seine and Rhine to southern England (Figure 111). The eastern Hallstatt maintained and developed trade relations with the Italian/Adriatic *koine*, while the northern and western warrior zone, representing a new frontier of change, was instead defined by its opposition to the new centres of civilisation, a situation that did not change until Ha D, when the Greeks and Phoenicians traded roles in the western Mediterranean, leading to a new expansion of Greek colonisation and trade in this region.

Many factors were responsible for these changes in the social landscape of late Bronze Age societies, which were now finally entering the Iron Age, having postponed it for several hundred years. In the following we shall trace some of them in more detail.

The spread of iron technology

It is one of the theses of this book that the significance of the Bronze and Iron Ages respectively are not determined primarily by the ability to produce bronze or iron objects, but rather by the impact of that production upon the economy and its social organisation. By that I not only mean as tools in production, for the impact of regional and local changes in metal production were just as important. The exploitation of new ores may lead to major shifts in the economic balance. For bronze-producing societies there was an additional factor: they needed tin as well as copper, and while the latter occurs rather widely, although it is geographically restricted, tin is only found in a few locations in Europe. Therefore international exchange was a prerequisite for maintaining a Bronze Age society. Iron is different, as it is locally available in many moorland regions, a difference which in the long term, with the spread of knowledge of iron processing, tended to undermine the social system of the Bronze Age. Thus the suggestion may be made, and can be supported by empirical evidence, that iron was produced in situations where bronze was lacking. This can be seen to be the case in several instances, from Greece to Scandinavia. After the collapse of the centralised palace economy, with its heavy demand for bronze (Snodgrass 1989 refers to a stock of 800 kg recorded on a palace tablet), long-distance exchange of bronze came to a partial halt, and iron technology developed to replace it. The same situation was repeated 600 years later in the Nordic region, where iron was known for at least 200 years before it was finally adopted at the time when supplies of bronze ceased. Let us, however, consider the spread and impact of iron in more detail, as the process of change from bronze to iron technology was complicated, and led to an entirely new system of metal production and distribution. It is therefore important to consider its implications as a background for the interpretation of the regional divergences that characterised the social landscape of Europe during the 8th century (as described in preceding sections).

When Reinecke originally set the beginning of the Hallstatt period in the 12th century BC this reflected the first appearance of iron and the changes in social organisation following from the Urnfield migrations. Today we know that it was only in Greece that an iron technology developed at that time (Snodgrass 1989), while in eastern and Central Europe the process was more drawn out (Figure 105). In the circum-Pontic zone of eastern Europe iron came into use during the 11th century when bronze depositions fell substantially (Chernykh 1978). A pattern of declining

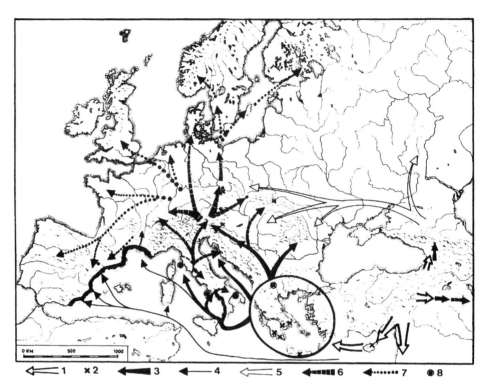

Fig. 105 The spread of iron in Europe: 1, second half of the 2nd millennium BC in Asia and Eastern Mediterranean; 2, sporadic occurrence of iron objects; 3, the area of Greece with earliest finds and the primary directions of the spread of iron; 4, Phoenician influence; 5, Cimmerian and Scythian influence; 6, iron in Central Europe and Italy in the Late Bronze Age and earliest Iron Age; 7, spread of iron in North and West Europe about 500 BC; 8, important early metallurgical activity.

depositions of bronze and the increased use of iron characterised eastern Central Europe after 1000 BC (Furmanek 1973; Furmanek and Horst 1982b, Karte 5–6), while bronze hoarding increased towards the west and north. When iron technology was introduced in west Central Europe after 750 BC imported iron objects accumulated in burials in the northern Hallstatt zone, without entering the Nordic region (Figure 106), where they appeared only after 500 BC (Bukowski 1986b).[1]

Two factors smoothed the transition from bronze to iron technology. In the Mediterranean the need for prestige goods, such as bronze vessels, cauldrons and complex ornaments, helped to maintain a specialised bronze industry, while this was not possible in most of Europe North of the Alps. Here, however, the introduction took place gradually, beginning with imported iron objects/ingots and rather simple locally produced types, only later to be followed by a more developed iron technology. This dualism persisted in most of Central Europe until the 7th century, with iron objects becoming increasingly common, but most still weapons and simple tools (Brun 1987, 54; Buch 1989, fig. 91). There was certainly no Iron Age revolution taking place. This has been demonstrated effectively by Laszlo (1977, Abb. 2), Pleiner (1980, fig. 11.3) and Levinsen (1989, 446 and fig. 104), who distinguish several phases, full-scale iron production on the whole occurring very late in Europe

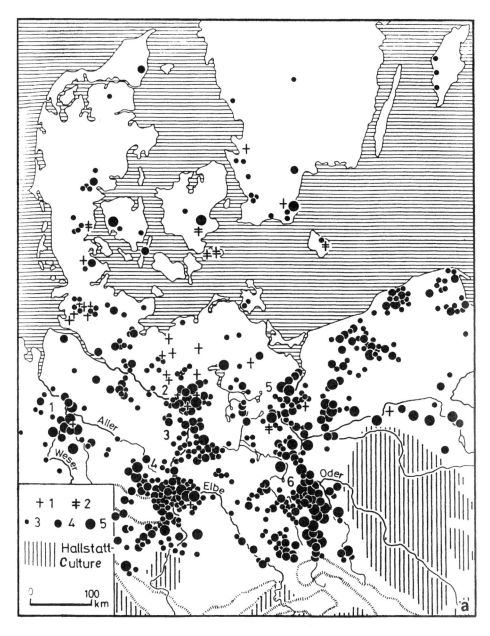

Fig. 106 Distribution of iron objects from the Late Bronze Age and the Early Iron Age in Northern Central Europe: 1 = Period III–IV (HaA); 2 = Period V (HaB); 3–5 = Period VI (3 = one object; 4 = two to four objects; 5 = five or more objects).

north of the Alps (Figure 107). Thus the introduction of iron was a complex and long-drawn-out process, whose social and economic consequences depended on existing regional trajectories (Geselowitz 1988). Taylor (1989) has recently presented an interesting additional argument, suggesting that full-scale iron production and the development of blacksmithing proper occurred in connection with the mining of salt

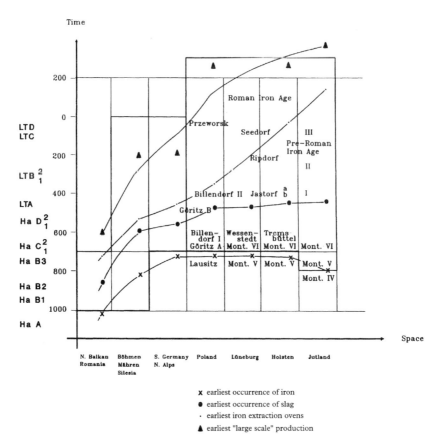

Fig. 107 The geographical and temporal spread of the components in iron use and production: cross = earliest occurrence of iron; large circle = earliest occurrence of slag; small circle = earliest iron extraction ovens; triangle = earliest 'large scale' production.

and the first industrial mining of iron ores, often located in the same regions (1989, fig. 10). He also argues for a late flourishing of full iron production. While iron then may be locally extracted in many areas, ores suitable for large-scale mining and salt mining are more restricted (Pleiner 1980, 11.7; Peschel 1985a: Abb. 3) (Figure 108). Also, the full development of iron technology is highly complex and labour intensive compared to bronze metallurgy (Geselowitz 1988).

From the 8th/7th centuries, salt and iron extraction through mining laid the foundations for a new economy in Central Europe. Before that time ironsmithing had largely been an activity supplementary to bronze metallurgy, the situation changing after 800/700 BC. It had several important consequences: it meant that copper and bronze production declined, making it difficult to maintain a class of specialised bronzeworkers north of the Alps, although local production of simpler tools and ornaments continued for some time yet (Figure 109). As central settlements were now primarily looking for iron ores and attempting to control their exploitation, large-scale copper and tin mining was gradually reduced in scope, or

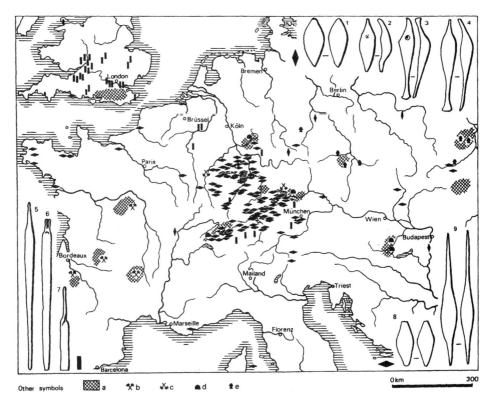

Fig. 108 Iron bars in Central Europe and main iron mining and smelting centres of the Early Iron Age. Iron bars dating from the Late Hallstatt period (1–4), Late Hallstatt/La Tène period (5–9) depicted as examples. Explanation of symbols: a = iron smelting centre; b = Celtic iron mining known from written sources; c = site with archaeological evidence; d = domed furnace; e = furnace with slag pit.

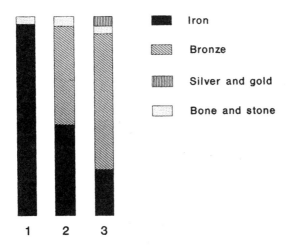

Iron

Bronze

Silver and gold

Bone and stone

Fig. 109 Relationship between the use of iron, bronze, silver/gold and bone/stone in the Billendorf Culture in the production of 1 = tools; 2 = weapons; and 3 = ornaments.

given up. This again produced a change in settlement structure and the collapse of traditional lines of exchange. Taylor (1989) has taken the argument further by suggesting that mining and iron production demanded large quantities of charcoal, so favouring new upland settlements, which were combined with sheepherding. Salt production leading to large-scale food conservation made such year-round upland settlements possible.

This scenario explains the (partial) displacement and decentralisation of settlement during Ha C in western Europe. While these were the immediate effects of the metallurgical transition around 700 BC in Central Europe, it is probable that in the long run central polities were able to control production at a distance, as also happened during the Bronze Age after an initial phase in which mining and chiefly settlements were located together. Second, and highly important for the development of new centre–periphery relations, the decline in specialist bronze craftmanship north of the Alps created a new market in this area for the metal vessels and other prestige goods still being produced in the Mediterranean, but no longer locally available further north after the 6th century. Traditional bronze metalworking continued, however, until the 5th century and of course as a small-scale activity during the subsequent centuries (Waldhauser 1986a).

We may immediately test the first of our propositions: if in the initial stage mining and production were increasingly monopolised and industrialised around a relatively few large ore sources, we should expect this to be reflected in the distribution of iron objects and ingots compared to bronze through time. Figure 111 shows the distribution of Ha C swords of bronze and iron respectively. It clearly demonstrates that iron swords were kept within the central area of Hallstatt settlement and were not distributed further afield. Only the bronze sword was exchanged into the secondary zone, where this highly effective new sword was also locally imitated, but only in bronze. Effective mining and iron production were still restricted to the Hallstatt zone proper. This development becomes even more clear when we consider Ha D (Figure 108). Here the distribution of iron bars coincides exactly with the royal Hallstatt centres, including the later centres in the Hunsrück Eifel. Iron production had now become truly industrialised and controlled, suggesting the importance of iron for the economy of the princely centres of Ha D. Another area of production was in southern England, where similar chiefly centres arose. By now chiefly polities had become strong enough to control production at a distance through a hierarchical system of control and redistribution, to which we shall return in the next chapter. Second, the loss of local specialist production of prestige goods of hammered bronze and more complicated castings had made this area a perfect market for such products from Greek colonies and the Etruscans. This process obviously also took on other important aspects, such as the introduction of a new elite ideology linked to foreign prestige goods, which we shall discuss below.

In the long run these monopolies could not be maintained, as more and more local areas began to master the whole technological process of mining and production. This technological decentralisation took place during La Tène times, from the 5th to the 4th century (Bukowski 1986a; Piaskowski 1986; Waldhauser 1985). Local copper

General process of centralised/decentralised metal production.

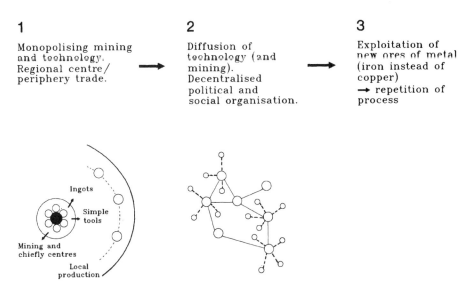

1

Monopolising mining and technology. Regional centre/ periphery trade.

➡

2

Diffusion of technology (and mining). Decentralised political and social organisation.

➡

3

Exploitation of new ores of metal (iron instead of copper)
→ repetition of process

Fig. 110 Model of the spatial and temporal development of metal production, suggesting a cycle of centralised/decentralised production.

production also continued (Waldhauser 1986a, Abb. 5). Thus, explanations of the collapse of the Hallstatt royal courts should also take this diffusion of technological skills into consideration, although, of course, it might also be a consequence of the collapse.

We may conclude then that:

(1) The spread of the use and processing of iron was a long drawn out process taking place at first within the framework of existing social formations. It was not a revolutionary process, nor did it create a new class of individual entrepreneurs (Wells 1989). They were already there.

(2) During the first phase of use iron supplemented bronze production, and was channelled through existing trade relations as a prestige commodity, often found in burials.

(3) Iron-producing regions tended to monopolise production and know-how during the early phase, leading to the formation of centres of wealth, and peripheries of supply. As bronze production gradually declined this tended to undercut the social system of Bronze Age societies, increasing their dependency on iron.

(4) With the spread of mining, processing and production techniques to wider regions, the original monopolies would tend to break down, as iron could be obtained locally in many areas. Local communities could satisfy their own needs, which further undermined the authority of traditional Bronze Age chiefs, who would see themselves cut off from both the top (the exchange of bronze) and the bottom

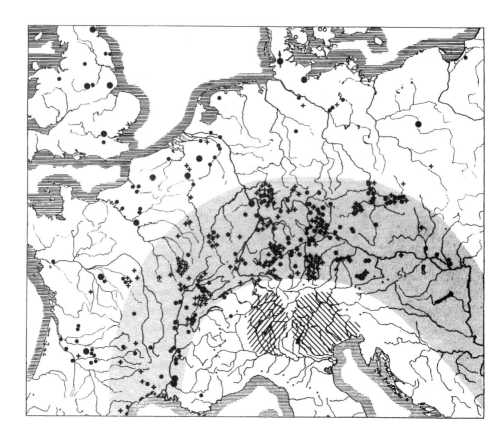

Fig. 111 The initial phase of centre–periphery formation during the early Hallstatt period, a warrior zone being formed around the Adriatic cultural *koine* of early city states, reflected by the distribution of the Hallstatt iron sword (the western Hallstatt) and fortified chiefly centres in the eastern Hallstatt (not mapped). Buffer cultures define the border zone between centre and periphery (Este and Golasecca). Beyond the periphery bronze weapons still dominate: solid circle = bronze sword; cross = iron sword; hatched = Este and Golasecca.

(new local iron production). This, however, was a gradual process, during which bronze metalwork declined, as supplies and specialist workshops could not be maintained in competition with ironsmiths.

(5) New, more rigid forms of social control gradually developed, based on land ownership and taxes, backed by military force rather than by ritual superiority and ideological force, as had been the rule during the Bronze Age.

These processes are not necessarily specific to the introduction of iron (Figure 110). I suggest that they may have worked in rather similar ways during the introduction of bronze, implying that archaic state and initial class formation was already taking place in several areas during the Bronze Age. Some of these processes were then repeated during the early phases of the Iron Age. The introduction of iron was therefore not revolutionary in the short term. In the long term it increased the economic range and capacity of society, as well as the potential for social control and hierarchy. In evolutionary terms this was a quantitative rather than a qualitative development. In subsequent chapters I shall attempt to trace and illuminate the processes of change suggested above.

The Hallstatt culture and the formation of centre–periphery relations

Like most researchers I employ the term Hallstatt culture to refer to Ha C–D, that is the period 750/700–500/450 BC, because it is in accordance with the material culture at the type site of Hallstatt. The previous period was likewise defined as that of the Urnfield culture, as urnfields remained the dominant cultural characteristic in Central Europe until Ha C.

The Hallstatt culture is not easy to characterise as a culture, even less so to explain. It could be defined by its burial rite as a tumulus culture, distinguishing its burial practices from the predominant urnfields of the previous period. In that sense it can be seen as an extension of a circum-Pontic chiefly burial tradition within an elite culture. It can also be characterised by its material culture in metalwork and pottery. It represents a break with former Urnfield traditions, from Scandinavia to the Alps, by introducing new types of openwork bronzes (fittings for wagons, belts etc.) and a new geometric/rhombic style differing slightly from the Greek/Urnfield geometric *koine* by being broken up into separate geometric designs, whereas the Urnfield and Geometric styles are more continuous. Technically, the pottery took up painting and inlaid patterns from Italy/Greece, and became highly refined in some areas. As with the former geometric *koine* it represented a barbarian adoption of certain design elements of the Near Eastern/Mediterranean orientalising *koine*, described in Chapter 5.1. In the western Hallstatt, however, it possessed a strong creative individuality, while in the eastern Hallstatt it kept closer to its prototypes (Frey 1969, Abb. 40–44). Finally, it can be characterised by its social and economic organisation, which differed from the Urnfield tradition by being primarily an elite culture, allowing only princes, chiefs and their followers visible burials, the last category being numerous at the large royal residences. In economic terms it relied more heavily on cattle husbandry, characterised by a displacement of settlement towards upland regions, at least in the west. In several of these respects parallels can be drawn with the Tumulus culture of the Middle Bronze Age, which also represented a period of more humid climate that favoured upland grazing, only at that time the movement went from west to east (see Chapter 8).

Depending on which criteria are chosen, the Hallstatt culture may be said to cover different areas. Its core, however, is a zone north of the Alps encircling the northern Italian/Adriatic region. Some of its cultural and social elements spread further north and west, creating a secondary Hallstatt zone. To the north its limit was the Nordic area, which still manifested itself in a special version of the new cultural trends, characterised by large hollow ankle rings and pairwise neck rings with elaborate twisting. Other aspects, however, were fully accepted. To the west, along the Atlantic façade, primary Hallstatt influences were accepted more willingly.

The eastern Hallstatt is rather difficult to characterise, as it originated in the previous period, and is less strongly based on a homogenous material culture except in its northeastern part, Slovenia and Carpathia (Frey 1969; Kromer 1986). Here the employment of the iron axe and dagger in burials, which extends the region further south to include Yugoslavia (Stary 1982, Abb. 1), may be decisive. It stresses the impact of Italian/Greek and Balkan influences, as the axe and dagger were the new international status symbols from the Near East to Italy and Iberia. If we choose tumulus burials and central fortified settlements as indicators there is geographical continuity right down to Macedonia and Thrace. According to Palavestra, however, in the Central Balkans 'different cultural influences merged here, creating a more or less uniform type of Hallstatt culture of Balkan provenance' (1984, 103).

The nature of the Hallstatt C Culture as a warrior zone peripheral to the emerging city states in Italy and the Adriatic is an important precondition for understanding its cultural make-up. Contacts northwards were filtered through the Este and Golasecca cultures (Pauli 1971; Ridgway 1979), northern provinces of Etruscan culture that developed a flourishing metal industry. Drawing these cultures together on one map (Figure 111), the structure of the centre–periphery relations becomes clear immediately, and may explain in part why so few genuine imports ended up in the ground in the primary Hallstatt zone. This shared with Italian/Greek culture the social and ritual norms linked to wagons, as well as the associated material culture, including belts (Pare 1987a). In this respect we may compare leather and openwork bronzes in the Hallstatt culture with similar products from an area spanning Gordion in Asia Minor to Italy (Figure 112B). This cultural matrix spread remarkably unchanged, most probably through Italy, although it could also have been derived from either the Thracian or the Pontic region, with their close contacts with Asia Minor. This route mostly brought horse gear and weapons, but we cannot exclude the possibility of more wide-ranging influences. Figure 112 presents some examples of parallels between Asia Minor, (represented by Gordion), the Mediterranean, and south Germany, which also included geometric designs and technical details in leatherwork. It was part of the gradual spread of the Orientalising style (including a new status kit) out of Asia Minor from the 8th century onwards, first by the Phoenicians, later by the Greeks and finally by the Etruscans. On the whole, the eastern Hallstatt area more willingly adopted Villanovan/early Etruscan designs and practices (coming through Este and by cross-Adriatic sea trade) in pottery, metalwork and ritual than did the western Hallstatt, which maintained a strongly autonomous tradition during its early phase (Ha C). Figure 112A illustrates characteristic design motifs from Asia Minor and Villanova, to demonstrate the common design *koine*.

Ha C and D culture thus only took up certain elements of the orientalising style, mainly those linked to the chiefly horse–wagon complex, including symbols of warfare (especially the dagger/axe to the east). Royal burials from Gordion in Phrygia to Salamis on Cyprus illustrate the royal context of large cauldrons with protruding heads, metal vessels and belts (in the *Iliad* the value of a cauldron is described as corresponding to twelve oxen), whereas the axe/dagger symbols were those of warrior chiefs. At Gordion, nine large belts had been hung on the wall of the burial chamber (Figure 113) testifying to the special significance attached to them as royal symbols of

Fig. 112(A) Identical design motifs (swastikas) on Villanovan pottery from Tarquinia (upper group), and belts from the royal tumuli at Gordion, Asia Minor (lower group).

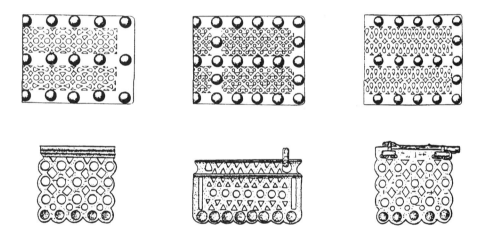

Fig. 112(B) Leather and open-work bronzes with identical design structures on belts from the royal tumuli at Gordion, Asia Minor (upper group), and from early Hallstatt C burials in Bavaria (lower group).

power. In Central Europe not only the symbols and their royal ideology were adopted, but during Ha C their style was copied and applied to other items, e.g. mountings for wagons (Figure 112B). The filtering and transformation from the east Mediterranean, Italy and Golasecca to Hallstatt is illustrated by the metal cup with a duck-headed handle – a local adaptation and development of the east Mediterranean/west Asian dipper.

The overland network from the eastern Hallstatt through Macedonia/Thrace to Asia Minor is demonstrated by the circum-Pontic/Balkan *koine* of metalwork from

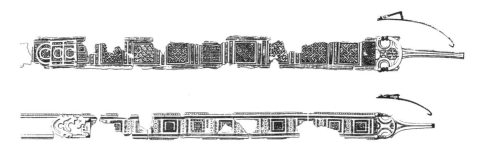

Fig. 113 Two belts from the royal tumuli at Gordion.

the 8th century (Kemenczei 1988b), relating to the expansion of openwork bronzes from belts and wagon fittings, to which we may also link Asia Minor and Gordion. Here the breast plates (Young 1981, fig. 28), provide a further connection to the Balkan/Adriatic tradition. During Ha D the interaction between the Mediterranean centres and the princely peripheries accelerated, bringing a large amount of southern imports to the Hallstatt princely residents, in both the western and eastern Hallstatt. Although this had some impact on the Hallstatt culture, e.g. in the development of goldwork, the basic cultural matrix in pottery and local metalwork remained loyal to tradition. The foreign imports served as prestige goods, whose value was linked to their exclusive character. Therefore they were not copied, except at the elite residences, thereby remaining under control. There is a clear parallel here to the Roman–Germanic interaction of the first two to three centuries AD. Only with La Tène did the development of a new style that integrated foreign and local traditions begin.

Industrial centres of the eastern Hallstatt[2]

Trade and hierarchy Consolidation and continued change characterised the eastern Hallstatt. It was still based on the combination of: (1) Italian/Greek prestige goods (metal vessels and armour); (2) Illyrian/Balkan traditions (e.g. clan burial mounds); and (3) Danubian/pastoral traditions in horse gear and weapons. These influences were a product of the trade between the steppes (horses), the Hallstatt zone (iron, salt, amber) and the Italian/Adriatic (prestige goods). It was controlled and organised by barbarian overlords in the intermediate zone, living at their royal courts and burying their clan members, clients and retinues in large tumulus grave-fields. Their wealth rested on the needs of the rapidly growing urban populations in Italy and the Adriatic for basic subsistence products, prestige goods and perhaps also slaves. Daily subsistence practices became increasingly dependent on salt for conserving food in the new urban centres and for the trading fleet, and on iron for tools and weapons. The Hallstatt region could supply both products, as well as some prestige goods, such as amber, traded down from the Baltic, to which we shall return later.

The hierarchical nature of society is clearly reflected in the cemeteries. At Klein-

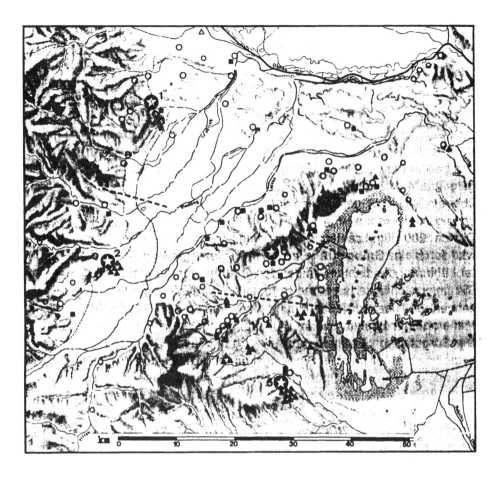

1 Mödling–Kalenderberg

2 Bad Fischau–Malleiten

3 Purbach–Burgstall

4 Eisenstadt–Burgstall

5 Ödenburg–Burgstall
   (Sopron–Várhely)

✪ Hilltop settlement (fortified)

○ Settlement

▲ Burial mounds

■ Flat graves

--- 'Border' between territories

Fig. 114 Territorial settlement structure in Eastern Hallstatt (Kalenderberg group) based on the regular spacing of fortified hilltop settlements, surrounded by ordinary settlements and flat graves.

klein 685 small mounds for 'commoners' should be compared with 15 large 'princely' barrows (Dobiat 1981). Even this buried population was privileged, representing commoners of social standing earning their living at the royal court, as opposed to those living on the many small open settlements. The settlement system was highly organised, even at the local level, with fortified sites at regular distances from each other, within visible signalling distance, i.e. 20–30 km apart (Figure 114) (Kaus 1981). Analyses of the grave goods from Slovenian/Pannonian chiefly gravefields

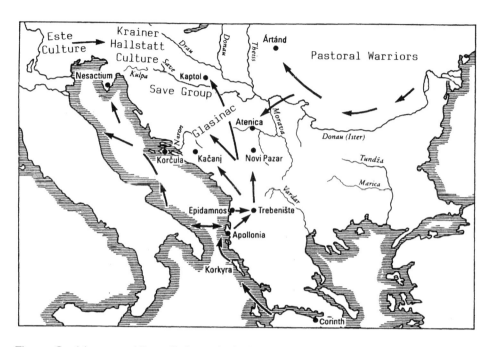

Fig. 115 Greek imports and lines of influence in the Balkans during the Early Iron Age.

have detailed the social structure of this period (Terzan 1986): three or four group-ings of grave goods can be recognised, with male warrior burials accompanied by imports forming the richest element. A social hierarchy running from 'kings' or 'paramount chiefs' to vassal chiefs, warriors (the king's retinue) and a larger group of commoners or clients was by now well established. The high-status males were matched, however, by an outstanding group of rich women, present in all cemeteries, corresponding well to the later pictorial evidence from the *situlae*, where high-status women play an important role (Eibner 1986).

How far did this zone of chiefly residences extend? The eastern Hallstatt is traditionally defined as the area from the eastern Alps to the Danube, including Slovenia to the south (Kromer 1986), which, however, only represents the northern part of the zone defined by the Hallstatt pottery tradition. The Hallstatt system of princely social organisation extended down through the Denarian Alps, including such important centres as Glasinac (Benac and Covic 1957), Novi Pazar and Trebeniste, to which we shall return (Figure 116). To the north, in Czechoslovakia, Bohemia instead belonged to the western Hallstatt (Dvorak 1938), although with some eastern connections (Saldova 1974), while Moravia fell within the eastern Hallstatt (Podborsky 1974). The eastern Hallstatt was fed commercially by the Greeks (Figure 115) through their colonies in southern Italy and by the Este culture (the Venetians), linking Etruria and Slovenia by trade, which was the basis of its wealth (Ridgway 1979; Egg 1980, Abb. 4 and 1985, Abb. 39–40). It is therefore an extension of Etruscan civilisation, rather than of Hallstatt culture, owing its riches to its central position, like the Golasecca culture to the west. There were also direct

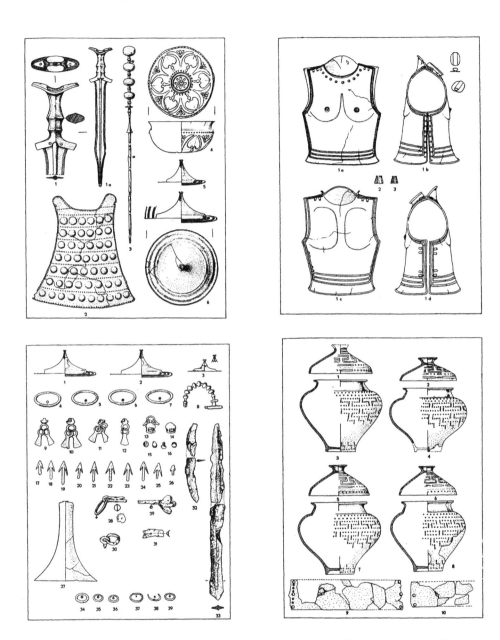

Fig. 116 'Princely' burial at Stična from Hallstatt C, showing a mixture of Late Bronze Age and Early Iron Age traditions, and Greek/East Mediterranean and Cimmerian influence.

connections across the Adriatic, where rich coastal settlements belonging to the Italian/Adriatic *koine* organised inland trade with the Hallstatt chiefs in the highlands (Alexander 1962, fig. 3; Kromer 1986, Abb. 7, 8), especially from 600 BC onwards.

It is characteristic, however, that during the 7th century (Ha C) only a small selection of high-value imports were deposited with chiefly burials, exemplified by the warrior chief from Stična in Slovenia with Greek armor (Figure 116) and similar

Greek and Italian imports to the south in Glasinac and Kaptol, acquired from the Greek colonies. Greek imports may then have been generally exclusive and scarce, whereas other foreign products such as amber were quite common, as were the metal vessels from Este. It is from the 6th century BC (Ha D) that trade and acculturation – the civilisation process – exploded, due to the intensification of Greek and Etruscan trade to feed the accelerating demands of the wealthy new urban populations. During the 7th century, however, the traditions of the previous century continued and developed, including iron and salt production, laying the groundwork for the intensification of trade from the 6th century. We can, however, indirectly attest that other Greek and Italian imports were circulating among the elite during the 7th century, such as the large cauldrons with protruding gryphon heads, as these were imitated in pottery (Figure 117) (Frey 1989).

We can thus observe that by the 7th century BC the chiefly residences of the eastern Hallstatt, from the eastern Alps to the Denarian Alps in the central Balkans, were consolidating their position between an acculturated pastoral eastern Europe and the evolving city states in the Adriatic. The economic basis of the chiefly residences of the eastern Hallstatt consisted of at least three major elements: industrialised production of iron and salt, trade in horses between the Pannonian 'Sigynnians' and the Venetians in Este, and trade in amber with the Baltic.

The horse trade hypothesis relies on a combination of archaeological and written evidence, and has been promoted mainly by Hungarian scholars (Harmatta 1968). In his history Herodotus (Book 5, 9) refers to a people named the Sigynnians, living beyond the Istos (the Danube), with a territory stretching towards the Venetians at the Adriatic (or, alternatively, the Drava). They drove in wagons, dressed according to Median style, and traded horses to the Venetians, who sold them on to Sparta (here they were entered in horse races among other uses). As has been demonstrated by Bökönyi (1983) the Hungarian horses of this period were of the larger steppe type, known from chieftain *kurgans* beyond the Black Sea in large numbers from the 9th century BC onwards (Kossack 1983). Since western and Mediterranean horses were small, steppe horses were much in demand from Urartu in Asia Minor to the Mediterranean, where their presence has been documented osteologically, both in Este (among the Venetians) and in Urartu, where both the small and large breeds were found. Archaeologically, this trading relationship is reflected in the appearance of Greek imports in Hungarian chiefly *kurgans* (Romsauer 1992), e.g. the helmet at Vaskeresztes (Fekete 1983, Abb. 8; 1985), and other close connections between Hungary and eastern Hallstatt/Este. The presence in the Adriatic of the Greeks and their influence on local societies can already be detected during the 7th century BC, as was documented by Herman Frey (1966 and 1969; Siegfried-Weiss 1979); many of the Slovenian bridles and cheek-pieces reflect Greek/Italian tradition (Dehn 1980). During the following century we even find a Spartan *hydria* in a Scythian burial (Parducz 1965).

There can be no doubt about the historical existence of a trade in horses between Pannonia and the Este, once again demonstrating the economic relations between centres and peripheries, pastoral nomads being part of this structure. The

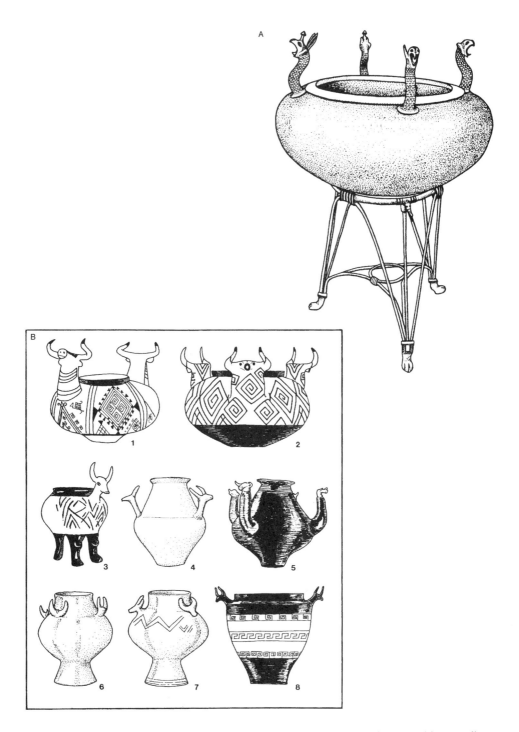

Fig. 117 Transformations of orientalising influences: (A) Tripod-cauldron of bronze with protruding heads; and (B) pottery imitations from the Eastern Hallstatt, Kalenderberg group.

acculturation resulting from this relationship is reflected in material culture by the taking over of Italian motifs, but with an increasing degree of 'barbarisation' with distance from the centres (Figure 118). That contacts were still maintained across the steppes to the Caucasus is reflected in the appearance of East Hallstatt pottery in one of the Kelermes burials (Kossack 1986, Taf. 2). At the same time, or perhaps a little later, pre-Scythian groups were moving westwards, appearing in the Carpathians.

Industrial production Industrial production is exemplified by the two well excavated industrial centres: that at Hallstatt itself (lying at the border between eastern and western Hallstatt) (Kromer 1959), and that at Stična in Slovenia (Gabrovec 1974). Both have been the subject of a recent analysis and interpretation by Peter Wells (1981; summarised 1984, ch. 3). Hallstatt was a mining community that flourished from approximately 750 to 450 BC. After a modest beginning around 1000 BC the mining activities, and with that the wealth of the community, took off after 750 BC. More than 4,000 m of galleries providing 2 million cubic metres of salt testify to the scale of the activities, and these figures only include what has already been detected. Both excavations of galleries, which were discovered during modern mining activities, and excavations of the large cemetery of 2,000 burials, of which some 1,100 are well recorded, make Hallstatt one of the most illuminating sites of the period (Kromer 1958). Mining techniques and the living conditions are well known due to the preserving ability of salt and the frequent accidents. The most famous is the body of a miner, fully clothed, that was found in 1737. Long pointed bronze picks were used in the galleries to break up the salt, and wooden mallets and shovels to collect the hammered-out chunks of salt. They were carried out on the back in skin knapsacks, each holding some 45 kg, supported by wooden frames which were easy to turn over when they were to be emptied (Figure 119). Everything testifies to considerable skill, experience and a division of labour, as one might expect from a society with previous experience of copper mining. The miners were well fed according to the food remains – beef, pork and bread – but remnants of fabric bore many signs of clothes-lice, just as the miners suffered severely from worms. It was hard, unhealthy work, the deepest galleries being 300 m below the ground surface, and life expectancy was shockingly low, as demonstrated at Dürrnberg, a neighbouring salt mining community (Figure 120).

Underpinning these mining activities, which involved hundreds of people, there must have been a strong central organisation supplying food and other necessities to this remote and narrow valley lacking suitable farmland. To set up the activities demanded several years of hard work until the salt ores had been reached and the galleries established. Not only actual mining but also transport had to be organised. That it was a large and rich community is shown by the cemetery, which rates among the richest during the Hallstatt period in terms of the average score of wealth, and in terms of the many different regions that provided the goods found in the graves, although most objects were locally produced. Several attempts have been made to analyse the grave-goods structure, from quantitative counts showing the unequal distribution of wealth to combination statistics and sociological analyses (Kromer

Fig. 118 The acculturation of Adriatic/Mediterranean motifs and their 'barbarisation' from Este to Sopron in Hungary. 1 = Ödenburg/Sopron; 2 = Kleinklein, Steiermark; 3 = Vace, Slovenia; 4 = Magdalenska gora, Slovenia.

Fig. 119 Reconstruction of a miner carrying chunks of salt at Hallstatt.

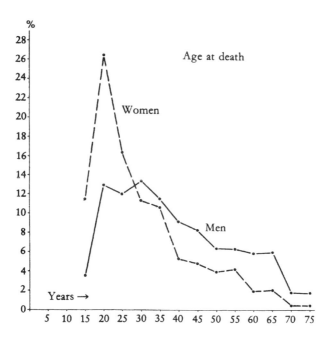

Fig. 120 Graph showing the age of death (and life expectancy) of adults in the Iron Age graves of the mining community at Dürrnberg, above Hallein. The difference between men and women is manifest.

1958; Wells 1984, fig. 20; Hodson 1986). Kromer suggested a social layout of the cemetery with warriors at the wings, surrounding the more ordinary graves of commoners, women and children, although many of them were rich. It would rather seem, however, that the cemetery is divided into a Hallstatt C and a Hallstatt D section, characterised by inhumation and cremation respectively. During Ha C 73 per cent of all bronze vessels were from sword graves, defining their outstanding position. During Ha D the group of wealthy burials increased, suggesting demographic growth of the leading families. The largest group of burials, apparently the miners and commoners, were poor. The presence of Hallstatt swords so far east is remarkable, and may suggest that Ha C warrior chiefs had been called in to protect and lead the community, as part of its wide-ranging contacts. It suggests that the real organising power lay outside the valley, at one of the chiefly residences. Also, the large number of commoners receiving a burial is highly unusual, pointing to a stronger social integration or solidarity within the community.

The increasing industrialisation of salt mining from Ha C onwards (other nearby salt-mining communities were Dürrnberg at Hallein, and further north on the Saale and the Halle) reflected the increased need to store food for the new urban populations, not only in Italy, but also at the central princely residences, some of which held rather large populations. The mining activities, their organisation and specialisation testify to a division of labour and social complexity of a kind which we would expect from emerging state societies. This new organisation is detectable in the princely or royal residences, such as Sopron and Stična. They were established in areas rich in iron ore (Wells 1984, fig. 21) and acted as commercial centres, the graves at Stična being rich in Baltic amber. The large cemetery at Stična suggests a population of 500 people or more, but if we consider the area enclosed by defence works, 800 by 400 m, the number of inhabitants could easily have been in the thousands (Figure 121). Wells carried out a comparative analysis of the tumulus cemeteries of the East Hallstatt residences, reaching rather low population estimates, leading him to construct a model of social organisation based on family groups allowing individual entrepreneurs to rise to dominance. However, due to the lack of wealth in burials Wells makes the false assumption that late Urnfield society was rather undifferentiated. Instead, wealth was deposited in hoards, burials not being the focus of social competition. His model rests on two important observations/interpretations: (1) barrows were used repeatedly, suggesting a social organisation based on family groups; (2) the burial wealth does not define a clear hierarchy, unlike in the west during Ha D, where paramount chiefs exhibit extraordinary wealth (see however Terzan 1986). In the eastern Hallstatt chiefly wealth appeared in several barrows at the same time, suggesting that leadership was not permanent, but shifted between families. This picture goes against most of the other evidence – the question therefore becomes whether the burial evidence is sufficiently representative to allow such far reaching conclusions.

If one considers the burial statistics presented by Wells (1981, table 11), they can hardly be representative of whole populations, but rather of wealthy groups/families/clients attached to the paramount chiefs, including craftsmen and traders. Wells' analysis does show differential access to wealth both internally and between the central settlements, Stična being among the richest (Wells 1981, tables 8–10). It could suggest either some sort of regional political hierarchy, or different attitudes towards wealth deposition. The fact that Hallstatt rates among the richest, and could hardly be socially autonomous, while some central residences are without rich sword burials, may indicate that burial wealth is not a representative parameter for social hierarchy and political organisation (or that the evidence is not representative). Wells' own demonstration of the importance of industrial production and of specialised long-distance trade points towards more complex societies with a developed division of labour and a consolidated elite with little opportunity for entrepreneurs to rise to the chiefly level. Also, imitations of Italian products, e.g. ceramic *oinochoes* (jugs) and kraters (for mixing wine), indirectly suggest a much larger influx of foreign products, especially prestige foods and wine, than is reflected in burials, as pointed out earlier. This assumption makes sense when considering the development of situla art from around 600 BC and its reflection of Italian elite life style and ritual.

I therefore conclude that the East Hallstatt centres controlled specialised production and long-distance trade, as well as the local hamlets and settlements, who paid tribute in the form of food to the centres. As Stična is the best-excavated chiefly residence, I suggest that Wells' hierarchical model for Stična (1981, fig. 29) should be generally applied. Only future excavations and better publication of the data will enable us to give more definitive answers to the questions discussed above, as Wells also noted; the source material currently available is simply on too unequal a footing to permit safer conclusions based on comparative analyses.

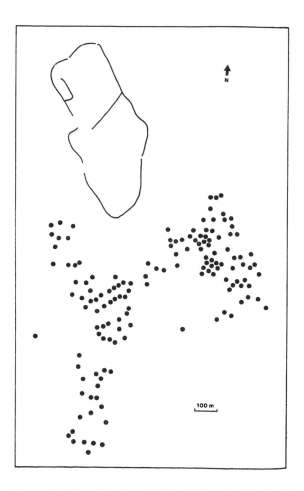

Fig. 121(A) Plan of the site of Stična in Slovenia, showing the course of the walls around the hilltop settlement (upper left) and the burial mounds (black circles) still visible.

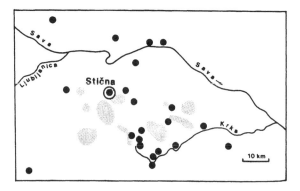

Fig. 121(B) Schematic map showing density of surface iron ore deposits and evidence for prehistoric iron production in Slovenia. Stippled areas are sedimentary deposits containing iron ores; black circles are prehistoric iron smelting sites; the site of Stična is marked.

From the Baltic to Este: the Pommeranian connection

Baltic amber has played a major role in discussions about the relations between the Nordic region and Central Europe/the Mediterranean from the early Bronze Age. However, in a critical study of the economic significance of the amber trade during the Late Bronze Age in Denmark, Jørgen Jensen(1965a) concluded that there were virtually no indications of amber being an important item of trade; quite to the contrary worked amber from southern Europe appeared in Period VI burials in Denmark, corresponding to Ha D (6th century BC). This was a period of cultural change across the whole of northern Europe, due to strong influences from the Hallstatt centres in Central Europe, leading to the final decline of the Nordic Bronze Age metalwork tradition, although the process had already begun in Ha C (7th century) (see also Jensen 1965b; 1967a). Jensen therefore reversed the traditional picture and proposed that the rich Italian, Balkan and Central European amber finds were local, or came from Sicily.[3]

Since Jensen's important work it has been established that the Hallstatt amber is of Baltic origin, both at Hallstatt (Beck 1982 and 1985) and in the Balkan groups (Palavestra 1987 with references), forcing us to reevaluate the question of north–south contacts during this period. As I have already suggested, Pommeranian amber was being exploited from Ha B2/3 (Chapter 5.4). With the collapse of the elite trade route from Villanova to Fuen in the late 8th century due to social change and disruption in western Europe, the west Danish/north German Bronze Age chiefs lost control of the Pommeranian trade. Instead a more direct route was established between Pommerania and the eastern Hallstatt/Balkan chiefly residences, which has been the subject of much Polish and Yugoslavian research. Two recent articles exemplify the different schools of thought: Malinowski (1983) has presented a rather straightforward case of trade relations, southern imports being exchanged for amber. This is reflected in the occurrence of large amounts of Baltic amber in the eastern Hallstatt area and in Italy, whereas Italian/East Hallstatt products are found on the route towards Pommerania, leading to a new flourishing of local cultures in the East Hallstatt tradition (Malinowski 1983, figs. 1–3). Kossack (1982) has raised some objections to this picture, pointing out that only a few products are genuine imports and that there existed a variety of contemporaneous, competing, exchange networks linked to several areas of the Alps. Thus there was not one trade route, but rather many chiefly networks. What is the solution?

It can be established that from the 8th century BC amber becomes more and more abundant in Italy, the eastern Hallstatt and the Balkans, employed on pins, *fibulae* and necklaces (Este II/Bologna II onwards: Müller-Karpe 1959; Ridgway 1979), first supplied through the 'Villanova–Seddin–Fuen' network (Chapter 5), later through the 'Pommeranian–Lausitz/Silesian–Slovenian' network, where the princely centres in Slovenia/western Balkans, such as Stična, played a central role for further distribution. However, it is particularly during the later phase, in the 6th century, that amber is employed in a lavish 'nouveau riche' manner never seen earlier or later. In Italy specialist workshops of amber carvers emerged, developing a unique figural art, supplying the peripheries with their products; once again demonstrating the old

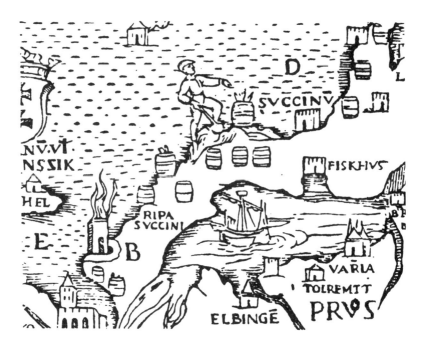

Fig. 122 Section of a map from 1539 showing the amber-rich coastal area of Samland in former Eastern Prussia. The amber is collected and stored in barrels for transport and sale.

imperialist strategy of importing raw materials cheaply, refining them into prestige products that are sold back at high values to the periphery (also to Denmark itself, as observed by Jensen 1965b). We must therefore assume that new rich deposits of amber had become available, considering the much larger quantities being circulated. As the Balkan/Italian amber from the Early Iron Age was Baltic, it would primarily have come from the bay of Gdansk (Danzig), which today produces 4,000 kg a year (compared to the Jutish west coast with an estimated yield of 1,000 kg a year, but this figure could have been higher in prehistory). In historic times the richest area was east of Gdansk, in Samland, Russian Kaliningrad, where industrial production took place from the 16th century (Figure 122) and in the 19th century the yearly production was 500–600 tons, used in lacquerwork and for cigarholders. The traditional method, still employed today, is to collect the amber in nets as it washes in after storms with other light material. Especially large amounts of amber appear on exposed coastlines with heavy erosion during storms, such as the west coast of Jutland and the Pommeranian coast, where the amber-rich layers are washed out. After a single storm in 1862, 2,000 kg of amber was collected from a 7-km stretch of coast at Palmnicken in the eastern Baltic (for a general discussion see Jensen 1982, 13ff.).

Thus, although we should not attribute too great an economic significance to amber, it is justifiable to relate the enormously increased consumption of Baltic amber in the Adriatic/Italian city states and the Hallstatt princely burials to developments on the east Baltic coast, when other archaeological indications point in the same direction, and when the Danish lines of exchange seem to have faded, as demonstrated by Jensen. Although Kossack may be correct to argue that a complex network of exchanges supplied a large geographical region from southern Germany to the eastern Hallstatt, certain shifts in the direction of the trade and the distribution of amber over time can be observed. Second, marked changes took place in the Lausitz groups involved in the trade, even affecting developments in eastern Scandinavia. Let us first consider the exchange network and its influence on local culture.

From Hallstatt C onwards several Lausitz regions were influenced by the eastern Hallstatt. This has been demonstrated in great detail in well-excavated and published cemeteries in Poland (Gedl 1973) and in the former East Germany e.g. the Billendorf Culture (Buch 1979 and 1982a). Elements of acculturation include a distinct chiefly elite buried in timber graves, although normally without metal vessels and horse gear (Bönisch 1988; Buch 1986a), stylistic elements on pottery, including painting, specific forms such as pottery boots, known from Urartu in Asia Minor to Italy and the eastern Hallstatt, as well as a series of imports or local imitations e.g. drinking vessels (Figure 123). Due to the traditional scarcity of metal in the Lausitz culture a practice had developed of imitating metal vessels in pottery, and during Ha C small cups with duck-headed handles were especially popular in pottery form, as well as bird *protomes*. Finally, we may note the presence in Pommerania, in the amber-producing area, of house urns (which were most probably introduced during Ha B2/3 via the Villanova/Seddin network, according to both their dating and their distribution in Villanova, the Elb, Pommerania and Denmark/Sweden (Kossack 1954b, Tafel 23A)), and from Ha D onwards cist burials with face urns (Figure 124). Both types were directly inspired from Italy, but the face urns soon developed their own style (Luka 1966; Malinowski 1988a). It seems, though, that while Ha C contacts were of the normal type of elite exchange/alliances, bringing some amber along with them, from Ha D onwards large amounts of amber were transported south and more specific Italian influences moved northwards to the Pommeranian culture, including Mediterranean cowry shells (Malinowski 1983, fig. 3), just as the lines of exchange become greatly narrowed. An echo of the new amber network can perhaps be detected in Herodotus (Chapter 3/115), referring to the sea to the north of Europe whence amber was obtained. It has further been proposed that the mentioning of the Venetians by Ptolemy (Ptol. III 5,7,8), and later Jordanes (Jord. Get. 34) as a people living on the Weichsel should indicate a relationship with the Italian Venetians of Este, rooted in the exchange network of the Early Iron Age, or even going back to the diffusion of the Hungarian Late Urnfield metal workshops to northern Italy, which is at least archaeologically well attested (Vekony 1982). All this remains obscure, and we are on safer ground when tracing the archaeological evidence for exchange.[4]

The lines of exchange during Ha C covered, as already mentioned, a range of Hallstatt groups from Bavaria to Slovenia and further south. They can, however, be divided into more distinct lines or networks of chiefly exchange, taking place between central or chiefly fortifications (Gediga 1979; Karte 1) Gediga's study illustrates the geographical connection between southern imports, Hallstatt-influenced pottery

Fig. 123 Drinking service and bird protomes from the late Lausitz Culture (a, b) and drinking scene (c) from a situla in Austria. The pottery boot, known from the Near East to Este, was also adopted in the late Lausitz Culture.

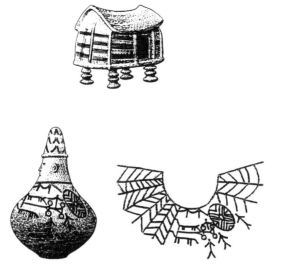

Fig. 124 House urn and face urn from Pommerania.

and fortified settlements in Silesia, leaving little doubt as to the rather well-organised nature of exchange between local political centres. We may select certain types of object with a more widespread distribution to illustrate the various exchange routes. The spectacle *fibulae* reflected an old line of exchange with the Central Balkans, now reaching Pommerania, where a local variant was produced (Betzler 1974, Taf. 82). Other local Pommeranian forms, such as the 'Schleifenringe' (Sprockhoff 1956, Karte 25) were also inspired by similar Balkan types. Kossack's old map of pottery with bronze nails and harp *fibulae* (1954a, Tafel 22) still gives a good illustration of the network from Italy/Slovenia via Pannonia and Silesia to Pommerania (Figure 125). These few types indicate an exchange network that supplied the eastern Hallstatt/Slovenia and the Central Balkans with raw amber, employed on *fibulae* and pins at the major cemeteries. At Stična 32 per cent of all graves contained amber (Wells 1981; 1989, 271).

We may perceive the west Balkan/Slovakian group of princely residences as central foci for the amber trade, both to the Este and Italy and further on to the Central Balkan group of princely burials, with Glasinac as an import centre on the way (Benac and Covic 1957). Certain changes seem to have taken place in Ha D; it looks as if more direct connections were established between Pommerania and Este/Italy, where the carving workshops now flourished. Perhaps the eastern line was cut for a brief period by the Scythian expansion. Thus, the lavishly furnished royal tombs in the Central Balkans from the 6th century BC contained imported amber figures from workshops in central Italy (Palavestra 1984; 1987; 1993). At the same time in Pommerania we find a group of Certosa *fibulae*, as well as Mediterranean cowrie shells (Malinowski 1983, fig. 3), as evidence of the intensification of Italian contacts (Jensen 1965a, fig. 2). The very clear Italian inspiration behind the Face Urn culture in Pommerania could suggest that a fairly direct trade organised from Italy (or Slovenia?) had replaced the traditional chiefly exchange of the Ha C/early D period, although this cannot be substantiated by an abundance of direct Italian evidence, but rather by indirect evidence. This may seem strange considering the enormous amounts of amber traded southwards. The explanation must be that the lack of centralised control of production in Pommerania, and the quantities available, inflated the exchange value of amber. With the La Tène period the Pommeranian amber trade seems to have come to a partial halt, not to be resumed until the Roman period.

The increased importance of Pommerania in north–south trade also affected and intensified relations across the Baltic to Sweden from Ha B3/Ha C, as Sprockhoff (1956) has demonstrated. Along the east Swedish coastline, up to Mälaren (the Stockholm region), a final flourishing and deposition of Nordic metalwork took place, and several (East) Ha C metal vessels were deposited during this period in Sweden (Stjernquist 1967). Most significant, however, is the evidence from settlement pottery of frequent and intensive contacts across the Baltic, which must have included regular marriage alliances reflected in the pottery (Jaanusson 1981; 1988, Abb. 2a).[5] One possible effect of these contacts was the early introduction of iron into eastern Sweden, which probably derived from Hallstatt influences on the Lausitz

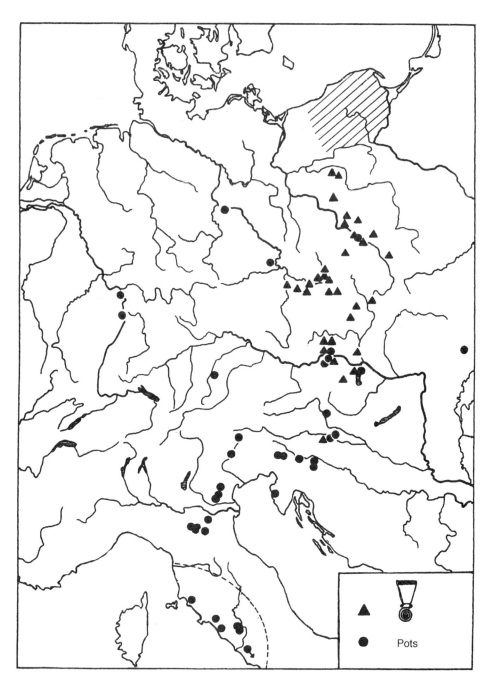

Fig. 125 The distribution of harp fibulae and pots with bronze nails, showing the exchange network connecting Italy, Eastern Hallstatt and Pommerania: hatched area = Pommeranian Culture; dashed line = Etruscan Culture.

Culture (Bukowski 1986b, Abb. 11; Hjärthner-Holdar 1986). Sea salt may also have been traded across the Baltic (Jaanusson and Jaanusson 1988). By the inclusion of the Baltic in exchange networks tied to eastern Hallstatt and Italy, taking over from the western network of Ha B2/3, described earlier, this area experienced a cultural flourishing of archaic Late Bronze Age cultures, in Pommerania mixing with Hallstatt and Late Villanovan/Etruscan influences. This explains the continued or delayed production of traditional Nordic bronze metalwork in eastern Sweden, the latter becoming a melting pot, maintaining far-flung exchange networks, not only with Pommerania, but also with Central Russian groups (Meinander 1985; Hjärthner-Holdar 1993, figs. 2, 3)

The development and expansion of the Pommeranian culture during Late Hallstatt C–D/Early La Tène (Malinowski 1988b, Abb. 1–2) reflected a new cultural and social identity in the wake of cultural influences brought by the amber trade network, and as a consequence of social and economic growth in settlements and improvements in farming techniques (Ostorja-Zagorski 1982; 1986). Similar conditions characterised central Sweden during the Late Bronze Age (Welinder 1976, fig. 3; Welinder 1974, 198; Wigren 1987; Jensen 1989). It seems to have been linked to an expansion of animal husbandry, taking in low-lying grazing areas of raised seabed and higher sandy soils (Bertilsson and Larsson 1985; Larsson 1989, fig. 9). We may thus link the expansion of metal trade and consumption in the eastern Baltic during Montelius V–VI (Ha B3/Ha C) to a demographic and economic expansion, leading to the inclusion of more marginal soils in southern and central Sweden (Welinder 1976) and from the Oder to the Vistula south of the Baltic. The development of local cultural traditions and identities (Sprockhoff 1957), including the Pommeranian culture, was part of this social and economic high point, signalling local identity and strength to their partners both to the north and to the south in the Lausitz culture (comparable to the development of the Este and Golasecca cultures in northern Italy). The social and cultural ethos was based on maintaining archaic Bronze Age traditions in metalwork and consumption. Although iron objects were taken up, and there was even some primitive iron working, iron was not used as a prestige object for deposition, and settlement evidence suggests that its general use was fairly restricted (Horst 1989). This resistance to iron in the Scandinavian/west Baltic region thus reflected the maintenance of Bronze Age traditions in the employment of prestige goods in exchange and ritual consumption (Figure 106). When these local cultures were later transformed during the social and economic changes taking place during Late Ha D and early La Tène, the Pommeranian culture strengthened its cultural image against both the Lausitz culture (which collapsed) and the expansion of the Early Iron Age Jasdorf cultures of northwestern Europe, but even then some archaic Bronze Age traditions in ritual deposition were maintained as an anchor of tradition in a period of rapid social transformation.

If we consider developments in the Baltic region during the Late Bronze Age from both an economic and political/commercial perspective a correlation appears between economic expansion and the intensification of foreign exchange relations/local metal consumption on the one hand and economic regression and the decline of

foreign exchange relations/metal consumption on the other. What is then the economic significance of the amber trade? It would seem that amber in itself was not
enough to develop or maintain a certain economic level. On the contrary, it was only
after the colonisation of the east Pommeranian coast, spurred by Nordic traders and
settlers (Sprockhoff 1957), in conjunction with local economic expansion and intensification, that an economic and social basis was established allowing exchange
networks to be created through which the amber could then be circulated. We are
dealing with a cluster of causes and effects, where the archaeological chronology is
not sufficiently fine-grained to give historical priority to one single factor, which may
indeed reflect the historical reality more accurately. Social and economic development was a necessary basis on which to build the political and commercial networks
that fed new social dynamics back into the system, leading to the formation of a new
social and cultural identity.

I have earlier linked the decline of foreign exchange and metal consumption in
western Scandinavia to an economic regression due to overexploitation and soil
exhaustion in western and northern Jutland during the Late Bronze Age, especially
Period V (Kristiansen 1978). It led to a prolonged circulation time for bronze, a
gradual decline in deposition and an increased use of bone and antler to replace
bronze. It explains why the Villanova–Seddin–Fuen network did not include western
Jutland, but instead was linked to the areas of more fertile soil in southern Jutland
and Fuen. Here, however, we cannot postulate an ecological crisis as a prime reason
for the loss of trade in the late 8th century BC. Changes occurring in west Central
Europe are a more likely cause, as I shall argue.

Chiefly warriors of the west
The western Hallstatt differs in nearly all respects from its eastern counterpart, except
in sharing the same burial tradition and some common elements in pottery. Since the
classic analysis by Georg Kossack (1959) of the south German Hallstatt period in
Bavaria, the main features of the western Hallstatt have remained clearly defined and
little changed (although his Ha C2 has been incorporated into Ha D1). Much new
evidence has been accumulated concerning regional groups, especially to the west in
Germany (Torbrügge 1979a), France (Lambert and Millotte 1989), Belgium (Marien
1989; Warmenbol 1989). Burial rituals and wagons have been described in great detail
(Kossack 1970; *Vierrädige Wagen* 1987), just as the Hallstatt sword has been given a full
treatment (Gerdsen 1986). Systematic regional settlement projects going beyond
central sites are unfortunately rare. My account relies mostly on Härke (1979)
supplemented by some more recent surveys (e.g. Simons 1989).

The sword has become the diagnostic type of Hallstatt C in western Europe
(Figure 126). It is employed across the whole of Central and western Europe in
burials, while depositions in rivers come to a complete end, except in the Atlantic and
Nordic traditions (Bradley 1990, fig. 35). This represents a significant change compared to the Late Urnfield period, when most swords and other prestige goods were
deposited in rivers or in hoards (Torbrügge 1970/71; Wegner 1976; Kubach 1978/
88). According to our hypothesis about the implications of the sudden appearance of

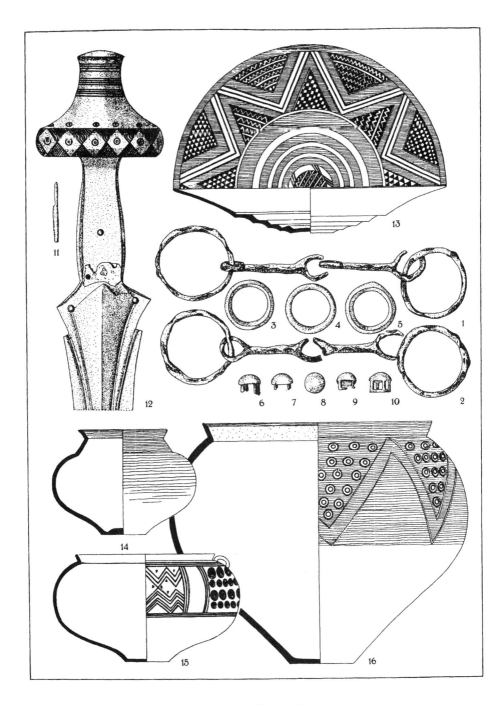

Fig. 126 Chiefly burial from Mindelheim, Bavaria, Hallstatt C.

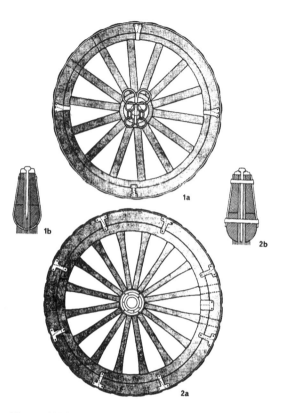

Fig. 127(A) Wheels with board felloes and iron attachments: 1. Hradenin, Bohemia; 2, Grosseibstadt, Lower Franconia.

rich male burials in barrows, this change in burial ritual signalled either the formation of new chiefly elites, or a new definition of their role. The employment of the sword, in opposition to the more exclusive dagger, suggests the development of a chiefly warring group, where actual participation in warfare was an important aspect of the chiefly role, as opposed to the princely burials with daggers in Ha D. The Hallstatt warrior chiefs were mounted, as reflected in the employment of one-edged swords, these being the fighting sword of a mounted warrior, known since the earlier 2nd millennium in Asia Minor, now for the first time making its appearance in Central Europe (Gräslund 1985).

More detailed local variations can be discerned from regional studies. In some areas small barrow groups appear, exclusively holding high status individuals, mostly warrior chiefs. The social identity and exclusiveness of the warrior chiefs is further seen in the appearance of purely male barrow groups, as at Underfranken (Kossack 1970), where a group of male warriors aged between twenty-five and forty-five were buried with wagons. Both the separation of the cemetery and the use of identical rituals suggest that the buried men were closely linked as a chiefly group, separating themselves from the rest of society. In other areas larger cemeteries appear, containing a small number of rich chiefly graves and a larger group of more ordinary graves, as at Oberfalz (Torbrügge 1979a), where, of 224 burials, only 5 were accompanied by

Fig. 127(B) Assyrian war-chariot, Til Barsib (Tell Asmar), second half of eighth century BC.

swords. This may suggest a higher degree of social integration. However, the cemeteries never approach the numbers buried in the larger urnfields; they seem to represent a select group of people, perhaps the followers of the chiefs. On a regional basis it appears that warrior graves on the whole make up some 10 per cent of all burials (Kossack 1959), which is the proper background for evaluating their significance and exclusive character within a region.

Another important feature of the chiefly group is the wagon burials. They normally featured larger chambers and richer burial goods (Kossack 1970, Tab. 4–6), and were accompanied by more complex rituals. The wagon was primarily for prestige and ritual (burial?) processions, as reflected in both the later Situla art of the eastern Hallstatt and the model wagons fashioned in both bronze and clay (Chevillot and Gomez 1979). It thus continued traditions introduced during the Late Urnfield period, whereas the technology, as mentioned earlier, was new. As Kossack (1970, 129 ff.) has pointed out the Ha C wagons were a result of new specialist skills introduced by the Thraco-Cimmerian complex, originating in Assyrian/Elamite workshop traditions (Sandars 1976; Piggot 1983, figs. 104, 105) (Figure 127). The same technology, however, is also found in Italian wagon burials during the 7th century BC (Pare 1987a), just as cheek-pieces with rectangular loops of western Hallstatt type are also found in the eastern Mediterranean (Canciani 1970, Taf. III). So the new technology could have come both through the Mediterranean area/Italy and overland through eastern Europe, as demonstrated by both art styles and weapons (e.g. Stegmann-Rajtar 1986). The major shift is the placing of the wagon in the burial, which perhaps suggests a new, more individual, role for the wagon in chiefly ritual (Kossack 1970, 155 ff.).

When summarising variations in gravefield structure and wealth two larger regional groups appear: a western one where wagons are rare, and an eastern or west Central European group with wagon burials and more prestige goods (especially toilet equipment). On the whole, the burial ritual is standardised, and the accompanying grave goods are few in number, except for pottery. Among 567 sword burials recorded by Gerdsen (1986), only 62 contained horse gear, and figures for other grave goods were of the same order – metal vessels, knives and toilet equipment only occur in 10 per cent of the graves. With the exception of metal vessels, most of the richer graves are in the eastern group, that is the region north of the Alps around the Danube/Rhine.

A further clue to understanding the nature of the western Hallstatt chiefs is the location of burials. Although both low-lying and upland locations occur, there is a tendency towards upland settings or locations that favoured the control of upland resources (Kossack 1970, fig. 3), suggesting a heavier dependency on animal husbandry and perhaps also in some regions the control of iron production. It corresponds to an interpretation of the Ha C phase as representing the expansion of a new social and economic order, in which mounted semi-pastoralised warrior chiefs achieved local authority, eventually forming chiefly groups or small-scale confederations, but apparently not larger political hierarchies. Such a picture conforms well with a 'pastoral warrior ideology' of autonomous, competing groups, and is in accordance with the structure of barrow groups, where Ha C warrior chiefs had the highest status in local cemeteries. They distinguished themselves by larger mounds, but rarely by special prestige goods. The sword and the barrow were the essential symbols. The social setting appears decentralised: no hierarchy beyond the local level can be established, although a more developed social hierarchy has been suggested for Bohemia (Koutecky 1968). It raises the question of how we might explain the employment of wagons and horse gear in the eastern group, forming a series of clusters from Bohemia towards the Danube and westwards towards the Rhine (Pare 1987b, Abb. 1). The wagon burials occur in areas with the highest density of warrior graves. We may therefore assume that they reflected a higher degree of competition and chiefly rivalry, as wagons were also known outside the area where they were employed in burial ritual. This competitive situation could be linked to the control of iron production, but the areas also lay on important communication routes towards the Elbe (Bohemia), the Rhine and the upper Danube. It is therefore remarkable that the later princely Hallstatt residences moved further to the southwest, leaving behind the former Ha C centres as satellites around its northern and eastern periphery, later to rise again during Early La Tène (Figure 129).

The formation and spread of the western Hallstatt C warrior complex still remains a puzzle, presenting archaeologists with a theoretical as well as a methodological challenge. Considering the social organisation of the eastern Hallstatt and Italy, as well as that of Ha B3 in Central and western Europe, we should have expected the development of more hierarchical forms, as well as more 'modern' weapons (axes and daggers). Instead we observe the rapid expansion throughout western Europe of an archaic warrior elite without princely chiefs and without central fortified sites, at least not in the main areas, leading to a cultural cut-off from the Italian/East Hallstatt tradition of weapon forms (the Antenna sword). Virtually no southern imports came from Italy to the western Hallstatt, where they cluster along the Rhine (Roymans 1991, fig. 16), and they are also rare in the Golasecca culture (Marinis 1988, Carte 2). It is not known if the reasons for this should be sought north or south of the Alps, but by Hallstatt D Italian traditions are once again taken up, reintroducing the Antenna dagger. In fact if we put Ha C and D together the picture would look as expected: high chiefs retreated from warfare into their residences, employing daggers and prestige goods in burials (metal vessels in Ha D, etc.), supported by vassal warrior chiefs employing simpler and more effective weapons (long swords and the one-edged sword for mounted warfare in Ha C). The changes in the settlement pattern are just as abrupt from both Ha B to C as from Ha C to D. Härke (1982; 1989) pointed out recently that there is continuity in general settlement location (although not for individual settlements) in many areas between Ha B3 and Ha D. Again the picture would fit if we joined at least part of Ha C and D together. This was actually proposed by Torbrügge (1979a, 207 f.; 1988, Tab. 1), who raised the methodological issue: Ha C is defined exclusively as a burial group with few stratigraphical observations and few overlappings with Ha D (and Ha B3). Therefore Ha C settlements might well be of Ha D character. It seems, however, that both C14 and some settlement evidence confirm Ha C as an independent chronological phase of at least 100 years.[6]

It is not possible to define the precise origin of the western warriors/wagon elites geographically, probably because there is no precise origin, or because it happened too rapidly to be traced archaeologically. It represents an extension of trends already under way during the Late Urnfield period, leading to both continuities and discontinuities. In the following pages I shall examine more closely these changes and their social and economic significance. In material culture the long sword and pottery represent continuity, although new orientalising geometric motifs took over both on pottery and in some of the metalwork. In horse gear the east European cheek-pieces with three loops remained in use down to 750/700 BC, e.g. in the Hungarian hoard of Fügöd with HaB and Ha C types occurring together (Kemenczei 1988a), which explains the development of the Hallstatt version (with square loops instead of round) from that time (Figure 104). Since part of the Thraco-Cimmerian complex had already spread westwards during the 9th and 8th centuries, we should rather see the development of Ha C as a local transformation of this substratum (Pautreau 1989) – a conscious creation of a new cultural code, perhaps inspired by the eastern Hallstatt, but with a western identity. It signalled the takeover of a new ideology of mounted warrior elites breaking with former agrarian traditions of social equality. Although an elite had resided above in the fortified chiefly settlements, the village as a social and economic unit represented the basic building block in the farming economy during Urnfield times and was represented ritually in the urnfield cemeteries. During Hallstatt C the warrior chiefs and their followers became the primary focus in burial ritual, and it seems that village communities were on the whole made ritually invisible, except those serving the chief (larger cemeteries with small mounds may of course have been subject to destruction, but this was equally true of the urnfields).

The rapid, almost drastic, changes in ideology and material culture suggest profound social and economic changes over large areas, although with many local variations, especially in the peripheries, as we shall see in later pages. Continuity apparently increased with distance from the central Ha C region (Roymans 1991, note 6). The western Ha C was therefore most probably triggered by an economic crisis due to population pressure and a climatic change that lowered the carrying capacity of the traditional economic strategies within the western Urnfield region, whereas the Atlantic economy, with its stress on animal husbandry, might profit from it. It should also be borne in mind (see Chapter 2.2) that the climatic change towards higher precipitation began during Ha B3. At that time west Central Europe was more densely settled than ever before and therefore highly vulnerable to changes in both climate and ecology, which might lead to a decline in lowland productivity. The areas in question were those where higher ground water or sea levels could make settlement and traditional farming impossible, that is in lake and river valleys. This would especially affect the old Urnfield core areas centred around the large river valleys and lakes, such as the Thames, the Rhône, the Danube and the Alpine lakes (e.g. Arnold 1992, figs. 1 and 7). According to dendrochronology the Swiss lake dwellings were already abandoned during the 9th century BC (Becker *et al.* 1985; *Antiqua* 15), while there are widespread foundations of upland settlements throughout Europe, implying that the exploitation of the landscape was approaching a critical level at the transition to Ha C (Dunning 1992).

A general transformation in ideology and lifestyle towards a more warring and pastoral society would be well suited to supporting a shift in the balance between lowland and upland settlement economies, with the upland settlements rising to dominance. Such a change in the economy opened up new opportunities for changing the social and ideological balance as well. We need not assume widespread migrations according to this hypothesis. We must assume, however, that the rapid spread took place through the existing Late Urnfield network, triggering local changes in a kind of chain reaction. We should consequently expect most of the settlement pattern to remain intact during the early phase, supplemented by new upland settlements, while in areas with abrupt changes in settlement pattern, we may perhaps expect this to be due to disruption and migrations. To test these propositions we have to consider the settlement evidence, which has been excellently analysed by Heinrich Härke (1979; summaries 1982; 1989).

Härke has made two significant observations: (1) a nearly universal break in settlement continuity occurs between Late Urnfield and Early Hallstatt settlements, interpreted as a collapse of settlement structure and social organisation (1979, fig. 47); (2) very few settlements are datable to Ha C, none of them fortified. In Late Ha C the reappearance of several medium to large enclosures or hillforts takes place, as well as the first chiefly settlements (1979, fig. 50).

Härke argues for a shift in local dominance in Ha C, away from the main settlement areas and communication lines, which supports the impression of disruption and local warfare (Härke 1979, diagram 5):

> The substratum of open settlement consisted in Ha C of single huts, farmsteads and small hamlets . . . They were supplemented by enclosed settlements of hamlet and village character on slopes and forested mountains . . . a very thin scatter of medium sized to large refuge forts of up to 30 hectares and more were located on hilltops and high plateaux at the fringes of some population clusters. (Härke 1979, 237)

On the basis of this late Ha C evidence he proposes a dominance of upland livestock economies, and it is noteworthy that, according to his map, the two areas with structured hillforts correspond to areas of wagon burials and numerous warrior graves (compare Härke 1989, fig. 57 with Gerdsen 1986, Karte 16).

Let us supplement this picture by settlement evidence from a few other areas. In England, on the Thames, there is a break in continuity and a reorganisation of settlement towards a livestock economy (David Miles, personal communication; Barrett, Bradley and Green 1991, 239 for southern England), and the same is true of several areas in the western Hallstatt region. In the Rhine area two micro-regions have been intensively surveyed due to brown coal open mining (Simons 1989). Here an interesting difference can be observed between a valley area with some settlement displacement and a well-drained lowland area with continuity in settlement location. A general continuity in settlement location is also observed at the lower Rhine, the Ha C rather representing the appearance of a new elite ideology as reflected in warrior burials (Roymans 1991). Thus, there appears to be a complex pattern of local and regional changes. To account for the drastic displacements and changes from Ha B3 to Ha C in the West Hallstatt area Härke (1989) has recently applied a 'Dark Age' model (following Renfrew) to explain the evidence. It includes: the disappearance of settlement hierarchy, a dispersed settlement pattern, changes in burial rite, discontinuity of specialist craft production, unrest and population movements, and the reappearance of hillforts after a gap of 100 years. He finds that the Ha C evidence corresponds in nearly all respects to the proposed model.

Summarising the settlement and burial evidence it appears that Ha C was a period of large-scale disruption and local warfare in many areas of western Europe, breaking off the trade routes between Italy and northern Europe/Denmark, and leading to a prolonged period of cultural isolation. A new elite ideology of warrior burials was introduced. We cannot exclude on these grounds the existence of some migrations, or a sequence of small-scale migrations, in the western Hallstatt, in combination with a relocation of settlement. Other factors could also be responsible for this decline of long-distance exchange, as the introduction of iron weapons and tools reduced the scale and intensity of exchange. Already during Ha C we can observe the formation of a centre and a periphery in terms of the employment of iron and bronze. The Ha C iron sword was not produced and distributed outside the central Hallstatt area, in contrast to the bronze sword (Figure 111). This may imply a certain degree of monopolisation of ironworking, but it also reflects the way that bronze production was now primarily maintained on the 'peripheries'.

Conclusion 6

The different developments that characterised East and West Hallstatt were due to a combination of internal and external factors. Late Ha B society embodied two contrasting economic and ideological trends. One was centred around stable farming communities with an egalitarian ideology and ritual traditions of fertility, expressed in thousands of votive depositions by single households of their work axes/small ornaments (pins). Another manifested itself in the chiefly elites laying down their arms for the gods. Both landscape and settlement were highly organised and heavily exploited. Chiefly centres of craft production, ritual and redistribution held together the territorial organisation, supported by a group of spear-bearing warriors, with the sword-bearing and armoured paramount chief at the top. During the late 9th and early 8th centuries BC this economic and ideological balance was gradually eroded and disturbed: demographic pressure and climatic deterioration forced more settlements into upland regions, gradually changing the focus towards animal husbandry and perhaps a more mobile economic strategy. This in turn demanded larger areas for pasture, leading to tensions and competition for land. Second, pastoral nomads expanded westwards in a series of conquest migrations that reinforced the ideology of mounted warriors over most of Europe. In the east it led to a transformation and strengthening of political hierarchy along the frontier, manifested in princely residences, while large areas of east Central Europe were taken over by pastoral nomads. In the west the new warrior ideology at first sustained the elite, but gradually undermined existing social and ritual traditions. It is interesting that the areas of the wagon/horse ideology of Ha B3 were those later dominated by Ha C swords. Finally, the introduction of ironworking changed the balance of settlement and trade networks. In the west the old social and economic order could no longer sustain a sedentary elite, and a new warrior ideology of raiding took over, disrupting the old pattern, based on the pastoral element in the economy, which in itself led to competition for land, containing an inherent tendency towards expansion. No communal ritual consumption or hoarding played a part in this ideology, instead sanctuaries were above ground (Lambot 1989). The social and ritual spheres were integrated, accumulation of wealth was personal, and so was its consumption. Therefore burial depositions of weapons replaced ritual depositions to the gods. There was no concept of solidarity with the peasants, who were an exploited class. Social bonds became individualised, in the form of clients and a personal retinue of the chief, owing their loyalty to him personally.

Ha C was therefore a period of social mobility in the west, as well-organised long-distance trade was replaced by long-distance raiding and the establishment of alliances and trade relations on a more direct personal basis, well suited to satisfy short-term personal needs, but not long-term investments from Mediterranean traders. It explains in part the decline of trade with Italy and the Mediterranean. A second characteristic of warrior societies, according to Daphne Nash, whose description of the Celts (1985) I rely on, is their territoriality and cultural exclusion from others, distinguishing themselves from farming communities, which they exploited if possible. This makes their culture highly recognisable, perhaps at the expense of that of farming communities. Third, as exchange was personal and linked to inter-chiefly contacts and to establishing a following of clients, especially young warriors, no market exchange or urban settlements for production and trade appeared. Finally, territorial expansion could be rapid and far reaching if it was fuelled by access to plunder and the extraction of tribute from weaker farming communities. Due to their competitive nature, warrior societies tended to keep political centralisation to a minimum.

These characteristics, which we encounter in the relationships between warring pastoral nomads and sedentary farmers ranging from Africa (the Maasai) to the Iron Age warrior societies of the Migration period, as known through literary evidence, represent a universal ideological and social strategy, which appeared and disappeared at regular intervals throughout history. It was in constant competition with the more hierarchical organisation of sedentary farming communities, with their potential for producing enough surplus to allow more complex social and political organisations to emerge. In some periods the hierarchical sedentary organisation dominated, enrolling the warrior organisation into its framework; in other periods, as we have seen, warrior societies took over. Later we shall probe more deeply into the relationship between the two, and the conditions for the dominance of either strategy. For the time being it suffices to note their differences, in terms of social organisation, ideology and geographical distribution. This distinction can explain much of the social and geographical transformation of the following centuries, as well as during the 2nd millennium BC.

6.2   The royal dynasties

Prestige goods and the intensification of centre–periphery relations
During the 6th and early 5th centuries BC (Ha D) three groups of princely or royal residences appeared around the Italian/Adriatic *koine*: northwest of the Alps, northeast of the Alps (mainly in Slovenia), and in the central Balkans (in the southern Denarian Alps). They all resulted from Greek and Etruscan commercial expansion establishing centre–periphery relations with mineral rich areas. The northwest group was served by Marseille and the Golasecca area, the northeast group via Este and the northern Adriatic by new Greek colonies, and the central Balkan group from Greek colonies and cross-Adriatic trade. Due to the different levels of archaeological documentation, only the northwest group has been fully described and acknowledged. Here we have both settlement evidence and burials, while in the Balkans the evidence is on the whole less well documented and there are as yet no settlements. As I shall try to demonstrate, there can, however, be no doubt about the similarities between the East Hallstatt (especially the Balkans) and the West Hallstatt groups. Before attempting that it is necessary to introduce the concept of prestige goods and their role in social change (see also Kossack 1974; Fischer 1973).

Prestige-goods societies, as a special type of archaic state formation dependent on the employment of foreign prestige-giving valuables to develop and maintain internal hierarchies, were first described by Friedman and Rowlands (1977), relying on case studies from Africa by Ekholm (1977). The model assumed a centre–periphery relationship, the centre supplying prestige goods to the periphery in order to establish its dependency. It was soon applied in case studies of the internal structure of Late Hallstatt culture by Frankenstein and Rowlands (1978) and of the Roman Iron Age by Hedeager (1978b; 1987), followed by other studies (Brun 1987), but it was also applied more generally to describe the social dynamics of Bronze Age societies based on the control of the circulation of wealth (Kristiansen 1978; 1987a; 1987b).

We should distinguish between the employment of prestige goods in tribal chiefdoms (traditional Bronze Age societies) and in archaic states or complex chiefdoms (developed Bronze and Early Iron Age societies). In the former, prestige goods were used horizontally between peers, although some forms of dominance might be established locally. They circulated through traditional kinship relations, and although these could be manipulated they did not break down. Relations of centre–periphery were often indirect (see generally Chapter 4). In the second case prestige goods were primarily used to establish a direct relationship of dependency from the centre to the periphery, and internally from chiefs to their subordinates, cross-cutting traditional social and ritual lines of kinship. Prestige goods relations of the second type are therefore thought to represent a new type of dependency and control that characterised the transformation from a tribal to a state form of society. These are of course ideal types between which variations fluctuate (Figure 128). In the following I describe the classic situation in which a more developed centre uses prestige goods to introduce new value systems and to establish political relations with a less developed periphery.

Foreign prestige goods are part of a process of change, giving them a limited duration. They represent an external value system used by an elite to create a new platform for power. If successful this has to be followed by a consolidation phase in which the new norms of social and ritual conduct are transformed into a local idiom, establishing an indigenous tradition. In this process old myths are rewritten, and new royal genealogies established. It explains why old royal myths and narratives are often preserved on the peripheries (e.g. *Beowulf* in England, although it is about early Danish and Swedish kings) and not in the centre, because here they were replaced and thus forgotten when new dynasties took over. An alternative development is of course to adopt the foreign elite culture, thereby transforming the local culture into a copy of the centre. However, as we shall see, if the elites did not in due course establish a locally founded legitimacy they were normally unable to survive by themselves, if no longer backed by the centre. Thus prestige goods systems were often expansive and short lived.

A second characteristic of prestige goods is that they have to be used and consumed to be effective. They are given to vassals, to the gods, securing their support, and to the dead, to demonstrate newly acquired positions to the living (as well as to the dead ancestors and the gods). Conspicuous consumption is therefore part of the

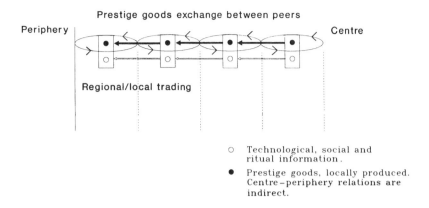

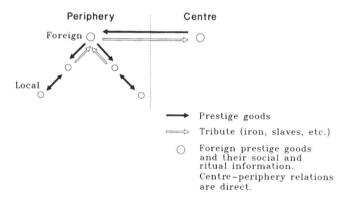

Fig. 128 Two models of prestige goods exchange, one based on exchange between peers (peer-policy interaction, with indirect centre–periphery relations) and one based on direct exchange between centre and periphery.

process of change. It also represents a way to regulate the exclusiveness of valuables. In the initial phase foreign prestige goods are mostly employed in burials as individual status symbols, in the subsequent consolidation phase consumption changes direction towards the gods, symbolising a relationship between the elite and the supernatural. From this it follows that periods of change where prestige goods were employed are much more visible archaeologically than periods of consolidation, a warning against too simplistic an interpretation of grave goods and social organisation. They should always be balanced by other types of depositions (in hoards or sanctuaries), because they are part of the same religious structure (as in Pingel 1980, Abb. 2).

Finally, prestige goods and the rules of gift-giving cannot be separated. The gift is in all pre-state societies the basic way of establishing a social relationship, whether one of dependency, equality or dominance – vertically between different social levels within a group, or horizontally between different groups, which may also develop into an asymmetrical relationship of dependency and dominance. The potential for establishing asymmetrical relationships is encoded in the universal rules of gift giving: the giver is always in a dominant position, as any gift has to be repaid in equal measure or with more. The gift is a social contract – e.g. through marriage and bridewealth – but at the same time a potential creator of dependency if you cannot return it, or if the value of what you receive is worth more than you can give back. In this way a chief may establish dependent vassals and clients – paying him back by political or military services instead. Ultimately, if unable to meet the demands, the client may be enslaved. Thus behind the rules of gift giving the realities of political strategy and of economy are operating, but which comes first is often difficult to establish.

A much debated point about prestige goods is their ability to establish new status positions and relations of dependency without prior economic dominance. We should probably acknowledge that prestige goods are the visible symbols of a complex process of change, some of it archaeologically invisible. They were primarily used to introduce new social and religious value systems. As described in Chapter 3.2 ritual is a powerful way of establishing new claims to power. Since rank in Bronze Age society was ritually sanctioned, new and stronger rituals, eventually coupled with force, were necessary to break down old norms and introduce new ones. Therefore the rise of new social groups to power, or allocating more power to existing chiefs, demanded heavy and visible investments in ritual, often in the form of monumental barrows and the deposition of wealth in burials. Although the economy cannot be separated from the social and ritual forces of change – there had to be something to exchange and invest both locally and externally – I maintain that the manipulation of prestige goods was in itself often sufficient to change the economy to serve new needs. The West Hallstatt royal residences were established on the basis of a warrior aristocracy with a chiefly ideology, but whose social complexity was lower in fact than in neighbouring areas. I shall therefore in the following make an attempt to trace in more detail the rise of royal centres of political and economic dominance.

We can begin by making three observations with implications for our understanding of the nature of prestige goods during Ha D. First: they were not imitated locally or lower down the social scale, only the real thing counted. It meant that value was attached to the exclusiveness and 'foreignness' of the goods. It further implies that the elite was able to control local production. Second: no accumulation of capital, e.g. in hoards or royal treasure chambers, took place. It demonstrates that foreign prestige goods had no purchasing power, their value was tied to a specific and well-defined social and ritual context, where they could be used as gifts in the formation of alliances between chiefs and vassals. They symbolised the chief's familiarity with the Greek and Etruscan lifestyle. Finally, foreign prestige goods did not form sets (except functionally), defining a specific social status or position: they were rather symbols of wealth and lifestyle, where the number and size of goods was an important measure of successful economic relations with the Greeks and Etruscans, and internally with the royal family (the typical 'nouveau riche' syndrome).

Commercial competition in the western Mediterranean

The western Mediterranean was dominated by three political and commercial powers during the 6th and early 5th centuries – the Greeks, the Etruscans and the Carthaginians/Phoenicians – while the Iberian culture was not fully formed until the 5th century (Ridgway 1980; Boardman 1984b; Harrison 1988, ch. 7; Almagro-Gorbea 1989). Their internal competition, alliances alternating with warfare, led to some regional shifts which had an impact on Europe north of the Alps. The Greeks gradually came to dominate the sea trade and the western shores of southern France and Iberia, while the Etruscans controlled land trade northwards to the Alps as well as towards the Balkans. It should further be noted that we are dealing with city states capable of carrying out both colonisation and planned commercial politics, including their dealings with the Hallstatt region.

During the 7th century BC the Etruscans had become a political and economic power (Ridgway 1980; Bonfante 1986), being in command of both a war fleet and a commercial fleet of trading ships. Greek, Euboean and Phoenician craft specialists and traders resided for periods in their cities, giving rise to the orientalising style (Strøm 1971) derived from Asia Minor and the Near East; crafts, towns and burial wealth flourished. The richly furnished tombs reflected the Greek ideology of the 'Hero', just as Greek or Greek-inspired armour was in use. After 600 BC a wealthy middle class of merchants and landowners was consolidated, reflected in a more modest display of burial wealth, with family tombs replacing monumental barrows. Once again we see demonstrated the relationship between ritual display and the rise and consolidation of a new elite class. The very same processes, but with no consolidation, and therefore no happy ending, from now on unfolded on the periphery of the Hallstatt culture, incorporating the western Hallstatt into the social and cultural realm of the Mediterranean city states. That it had not happened before was due to the takeover by warrior societies of the West Hallstatt, but how then could it happen now?

By 600 BC the Greeks had established themselves as a dominant commercial and acculturating force in the western Mediterranean, in competition with the Etruscans and the Carthaginians. The activities of their by now well-consolidated colonies in southern Italy were supplemented by new colonising groups from the Ionian coast of Asia Minor, fleeing Persian domination. Phocaean traders and settlers were especially active. They founded Marseille (Massalia) around 600 BC with the aim of exploiting the Rhône and its hinterland, as well as the southern shores of France. This was well chosen from a strategic point of view, as it also gave access to the Atlantic, and served as a central focus for coastal trade down to eastern Iberia and with the Etruscan cities. The coastland around Massalia was already a magnet for trade and colonisation during the late 7th century BC according to the distribution of Etruscan Bucchero vessels (Kimmig 1982, Abb. 6), but activity now accelerated, with several Greek trading stations being founded along the coast, as seen from the distribution of Greek pottery (Kimmig 1982, Abb. 25–29). Attic Black-figure and Red-figure vases appeared all over the western Mediterranean, carried by both Phoenicians and Etruscans, testifying not only to the acculturating force of the Greeks, but also to the economic impact of their trade, most of which is not traceable, except for oil and wine. What made this expansion possible in the face of the now firmly established Etruscan city states?

Apparently neither the Etruscans nor the Iberians were aiming at distant colonisation – they both stayed within their confined political territories and, in the case of the Etruscans, extended their economic power commercially, supported by a strong fleet. Competition at sea was inevitable, and two sea battles, in 537 and 474 BC, are seen as crucial for changing the balance of sea power and trade in favour of the Greeks and the Carthaginians. Politically the Etruscans expanded by taking over or colonising neighbouring 'city states', leaving long-distance colonisation to the Greeks. They expanded inland southwards, to Rome (in 616 BC) and northwards, through the Apennines to the Po Valley, during the second half of the 6th century, perhaps already beginning around 575, when the founding of twelve cities is attributed to this. Archaeologically it is reflected in finds of Attic pottery and bronze vessels (Marinis 1988). This gave the Etruscans direct access both to Este and the eastern Hallstatt in Slovenia and to 'Celts' north of the Alps, through Golasecca, as testified by written sources. On the Adriatic coast Adria and Spina were the key ports. Etruscan metalwork flourished under Ionian craftsmen between 550 and 475 BC, producing *Schnabelkannen* and other products for trading widely north of the Alps. It may have compensated for their declining sea power in the west Mediterranean. But this is taking us too far. During the 6th century the Rhône valley was therefore an important part of Greek trade activities, and so slightly later were the Alps for Etruscan northward trade, the bulk of it moving through the Este and Golasecca cultures.

The internal structure of Hallstatt residences

The western Alps   We can now return to the western Hallstatt. At the same time as Massalia was founded by the Greek Phocaeans, a chiefly defended residence, The Heuneburg, was founded on the Danube, located where the east–west communication routes met with the north–south routes from the Rhône Valley and the Alps. Thus the founding of Marseille and The Heuneburg, archaeologically and historically well attested, may be said to symbolise the beginning of a new era of interaction between the Mediterranean and west Central Europe. Within a few decades there emerged a group of princely or royal residences stretching from The Heuneburg in the east to Vix and Mont Lassois in the southwest (Figure 129). They are characterised by the presence of Greek/Italian imports at the central residences, these being surrounded by a group of large 'royal' tumuli with burials in chambers accompanied by wagons, foreign prestige goods and often gold, when not plundered in antiquity (following the definition in Brun 1988b) (Figure 130). The rapidity of this development calls for an explanation: was the Hallstatt periphery colonised, and by whom?

Given the nature of Ha C warrior society, which did not invite foreign traders, it is likely that there was an active trading policy directed from north Italy and Massalia

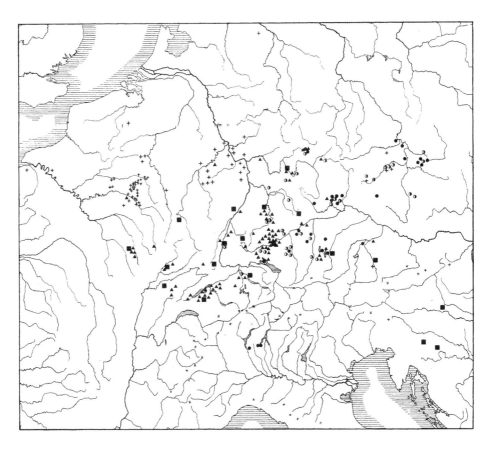

Fig. 129 Wagon graves of the Hallstatt and Early La Tène period, and central settlements ('Royal residences' or *Herrensitze*) of the Late Hallstatt period: filled circle = Early Hallstatt (HaC); triangle = Late Hallstatt (HaD); half-filled circle = uncertain dating; cross = Early La Tène, square = royal residences of the Late Hallstatt (HaD).

towards the Hallstatt hinterland. But contacts with the East Hallstatt region are also probable – the structure of western Ha D residences is very much like those of the eastern Hallstatt, as well as some of the burial traditions in the early phase (e.g. Magdalenenberg). This does not contradict the continuity in pottery production, representing the lower level of the population (Zürn 1970). Finally, indigenous developments must have played a role, but what? It is remarkable that the area covered by the Ha D residences avoids the areas of rich Ha C wagon burials (Figure 129). The pendulum had swung back from warrior societies towards agrarian, hierarchical societies, in the Ha B3 tradition, these being in charge of organised long-distance prestige-goods trade. It is thus characteristic that all the Hallstatt residences are located with reference to easy access to and control over major communication and trade routes. Together they occupied the crucial corner of southwest Europe where the Rhine, the Rhône and the Danube meet. Brun (1988b, Carte 4–5) has further demonstrated that the Hallstatt D residences encompassed an earlier Late Urnfield cultural province. We have already introduced the major

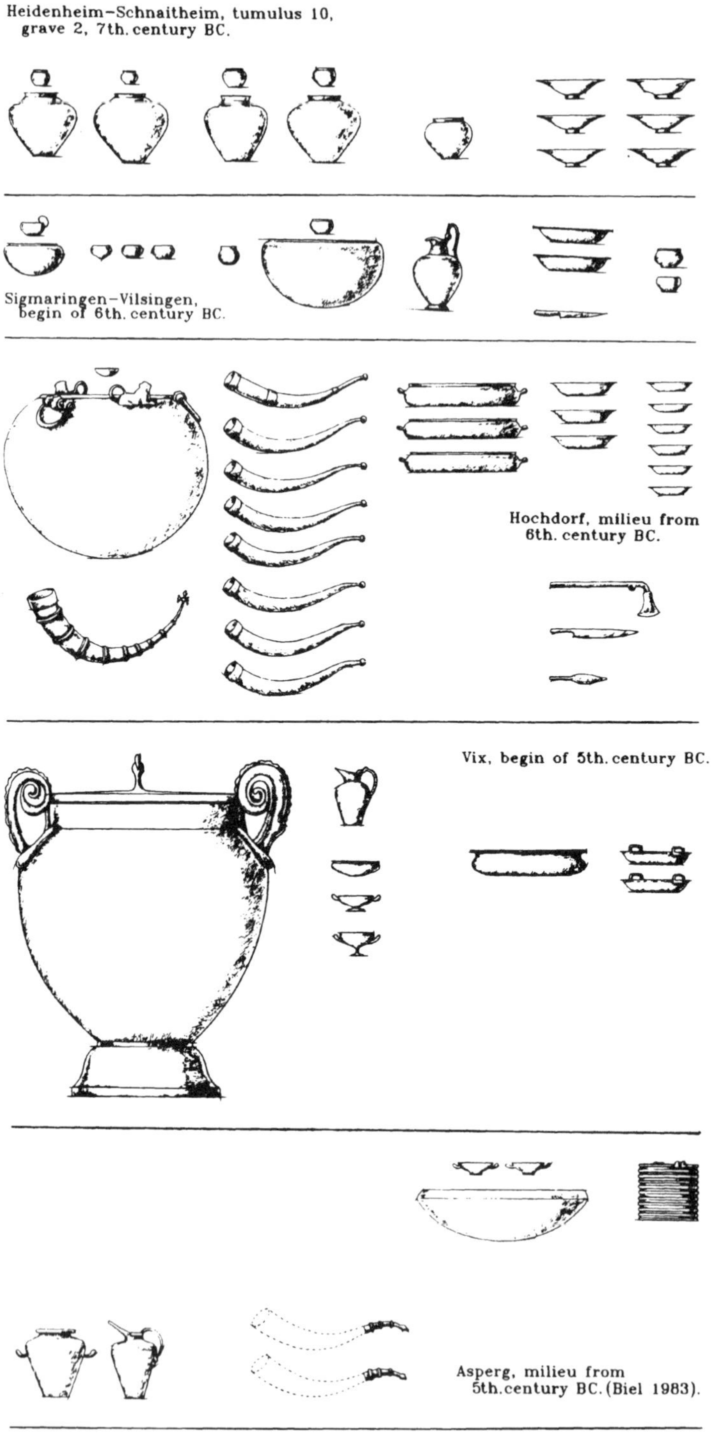

Heidenheim–Schnaitheim, tumulus 10, grave 2, 7th. century BC.

Sigmaringen–Vilsingen, begin of 6th. century BC.

Hochdorf, milieu from 6th. century BC.

Vix, begin of 5th. century BC.

Asperg, milieu from 5th. century BC. (Biel 1983).

Fig. 130 Grave inventories from a selection of princely burials of the Late Hallstatt period.

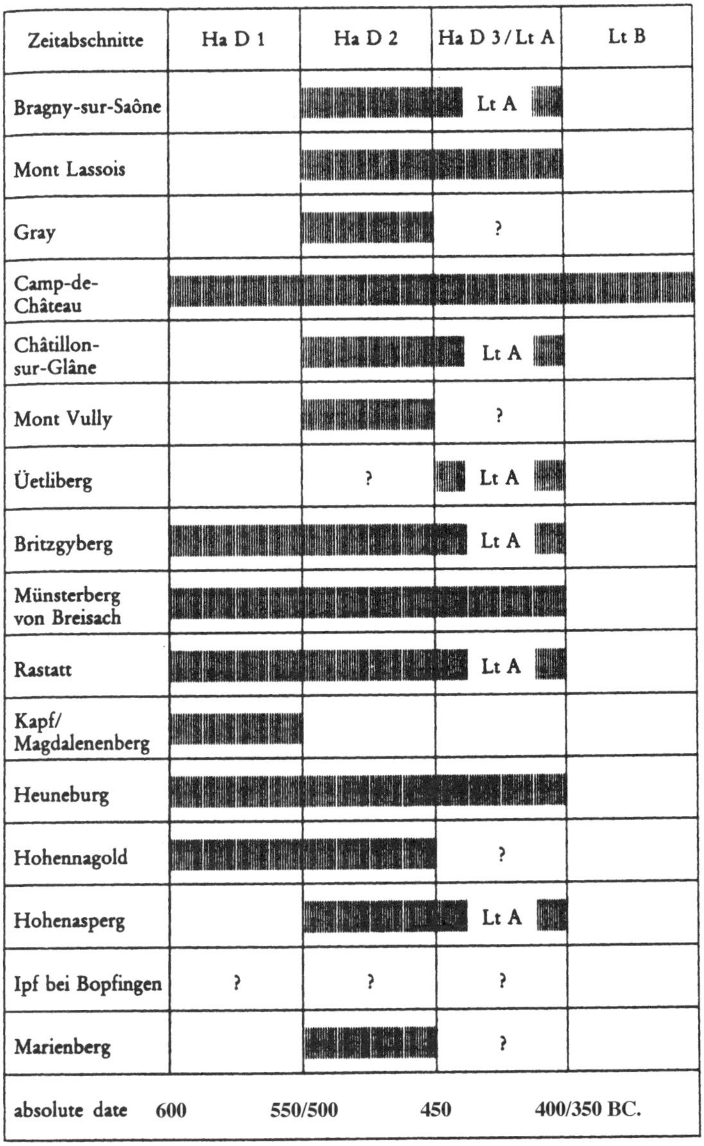

Zeitabschnitte	Ha D 1	Ha D 2	Ha D 3 / Lt A	Lt B
Bragny-sur-Saône		▓▓▓▓▓	Lt A ▓	
Mont Lassois		▓▓▓▓▓▓▓		
Gray		▓▓▓	?	
Camp-de-Château	▓▓▓▓▓▓▓▓▓▓▓▓▓▓▓▓▓▓▓▓▓▓			
Châtillon-sur-Glâne		▓▓▓▓	Lt A ▓	
Mont Vully		▓▓▓	?	
Üetliberg		?	▓ Lt A ▓	
Britzgyberg	▓▓▓▓▓▓▓▓▓▓▓		Lt A ▓	
Münsterberg von Breisach	▓▓▓▓▓▓▓▓▓▓▓▓			
Rastatt	▓▓▓▓▓▓▓▓▓▓		Lt A ▓	
Kapf/ Magdalenenberg	▓▓▓			
Heuneburg	▓▓▓▓▓▓▓▓▓▓▓▓			
Hohennagold	▓▓▓▓▓▓▓		?	
Hohenasperg		▓▓▓▓▓	Lt A ▓	
Ipf bei Bopfingen	?	?	?	
Marienberg		▓▓▓	?	
absolute date	600	550/500	450	400/350 BC.

Fig. 131 Chronological table of the Hallstatt royal residences and burials. The proposed continuity into Lt A is debated.

questions to be considered in the following section: the nature and impact of foreign trade, the internal structure of the Hallstatt residences and their larger economic and political background.[7]

There is a certain chronological and geographical development in the internal rise and fall of the Hallstatt residences (Spindler 1983, 83) and the rich burials, which corresponds to local shifts in political dominance (Figure 131). The Heuneburg on the Danube and a group of chiefly burials around it, such as those at Magdalenen-

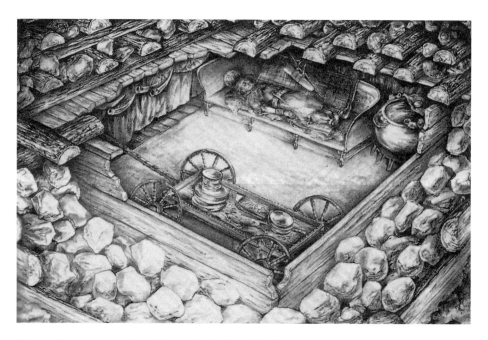

Fig. 132 Reconstructed view of the burial chamber of the Hochdorf prince.

berg and Hohmichele, belong to Ha D1 (Riek and Hundt 1962; Spindler 1971–80). The Heuneburg became the first major political centre of the eastern group of chiefly residences. It was burned down three times after being attacked, but was rebuilt after the first two destructions. The first destruction, in the mid 6th century BC, seems to have been disastrous – after that its political influence crumbled and it dwindled to being a local chiefly residence. A new group of chiefly burials emerged around Hohenasperg, further to the north on the Neckar, which persisted from Ha D2 (550 BC) well into the middle of the 5th century. To this belonged the most famous burial of them all (because it was not looted), Hochdorf (Ha D1/2) (Biel 1985) (Figure 132), along with Grafenbügel and Bad Cannstatt, of Ha D3, and Klein Aspergle of La Tène A (Kimmig 1988b).

Further southwest, on the upper Rhône and Rhine, we encounter another group of residences, one or two beginning in Ha D1, but all settled from Ha D2 (Pare 1989a), Mont Lassois with the princely burial at Vix from Ha D2/3 being the most famous, again because it was not looted in antiquity (Joffroy 1954, 1957; 1960). Its Rhodian krater, 2 m high, weighed 208.6 kg and holds 1,100 ls. After 450 BC new groups of warrior burials with wagons and Etruscan imports, especially *Schnabelkannen*, emerged on the Rhine–Moselle north of the Hallstatt residences, which now de-clined. Another group appeared in northeast France on the Marne, northwest of the Vix group, and a final group in Czechoslovakia (Endert 1984; Haffner and Joachim 1984; Soudská 1984). Traditionally they define the beginning of La Tène, but their development cannot be separated from that of the Ha D residences and the princely burials, although they are not comparable in richness to the latter. Let us first consider a royal residence and its burials.

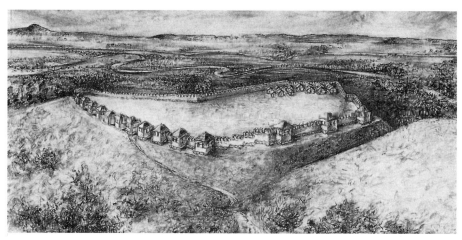

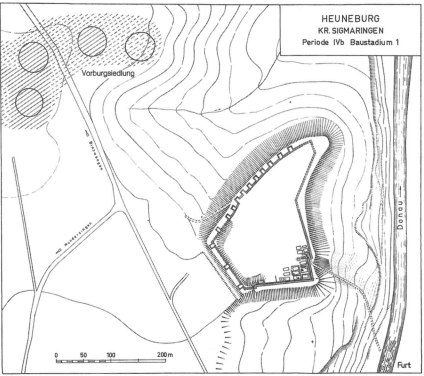

Fig. 133 Ground plan and aerial view of The Heuneburg in its classical 'Greek' phase.

The princely or royal Hallstatt residences can only be fully illustrated at The Heuneburg (Gersbach 1981; Kimmig 1983), due to the extensive excavations (Figure 133), but we must assume that it was typical of other residences as well, at some of which excavations have also taken place, especially at Mont Lassois (Joffroy 1960). Most of them, however, are covered by present-day occupation. Their primary functions seem to have been political-economic. A centralised production of various

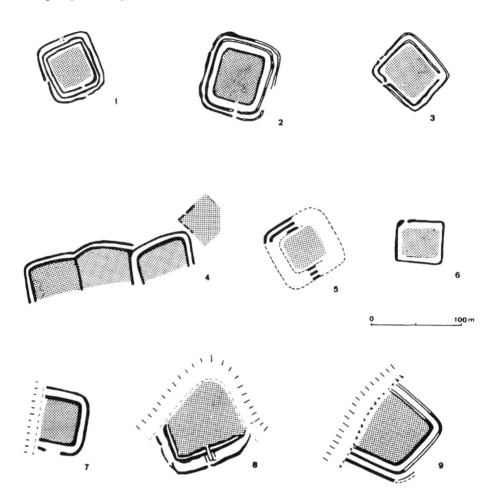

Fig. 134 Hallstatt period (chiefly) farmsteads in the Landshut region, Bavaria.

prestige goods for local needs, from metalwork to high-quality pottery, was carried out, just as commodities and tribute from the dependent vassals were collected here, some of it being traded southwards. The population was thus linked to performing the economic and military functions of the royal families and their vassals. It seems probable that the elite themselves had their living quarters or estates outside the walls. A few large enclosed farmsteads are known from Bavaria (Figure 134), and from an elaborate house preserved under a barrow at The Heuneburg-Talbau, with the unusual feature, for Europe North of the Alps at this date, of being divided into several rooms.

At The Heuneburg we can trace the settlement's history in greater detail (Kimmig 1983). The fortifications enclosed 3.2 ha, and with regular rebuildings as a result of three catastrophic destructions by fire its history is well illustrated. It had previously been settled during the Middle Bronze Age, but was abandoned in the Urnfield period. During the first period of reoccupation (termed phase IVc) at the beginning

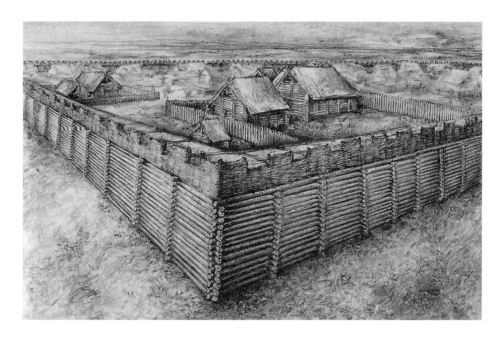

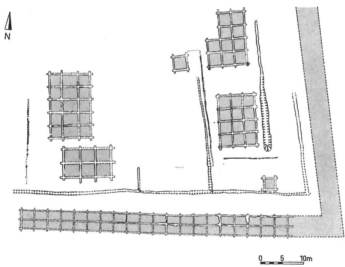

Fig. 135 Ground plan and reconstructed view of the early Heuneburg (period IVc) fortification with palisaded 'farmsteads'.

of Ha DI around 600 BC (or the late 7th century) (Parzinger 1982), the houses were still in the tradition of open-land farms, although laid out according to a plan (Figure 135). The defensive walls were also in traditional timber/earth construction. But soon after (phase IVa–IVb), at the beginning of the 6th century, a Greek defence system with rectangular bastions was employed, unique in Central Europe, just as was the use of sun-dried bricks for its construction (Figure 136). This was the climax of The

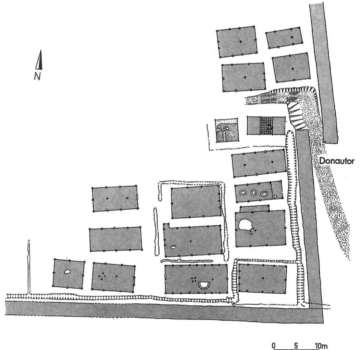

Fig. 136 Ground plan and reconstructed view of the southeastern corner of The Heuneburg in its classical, 'semi-urbanised' phase with the mudbrick fortification.

Heuneburg, when a large settlement even existed outside the walls. The interior settlement consisted of small, identical, houses for craft production, while larger (chiefly and perhaps trading) building complexes appeared outside the fortifications. The new defence system must have demanded a Greek or Italian architect. Also, the layout of houses inside the fortifications was clearly planned. Regular rebuilding of the settlement took place every ten to fifteen years, so five times during this prosperous phase. It ended dramatically, when the fort was attacked and burned down.

This destruction probably coincided with the plundering of the Hohmichele, which took place fifty years after its construction (in the beginning of Ha DI), according to dendrochronology. However, the dendrochronological dating of its construction has been adjusted three times, from 577 BC down to 551 and now recently back to 622 BC (Biel 1988a, note 25), from which we may then subtract fifty years, which does not correspond too well to the first burning catastrophe, normally placed around 550 BC, which should then fall around 570 BC. Historically, a correspondence seems more plausible, as the plundering could hardly have taken place secretly during the reign of the Heuneburg elite. Much of the exterior settlement was given up. When the fort was rebuilt, it was in the old style with traditional timber and earth walls, just as the houses returned to the traditional larger farmhouse type. No central planner was available any more. Once again, around 500 BC (or perhaps correspondingly earlier, around 530?), at the end of phase IIIa, The Heuneburg was sacked and burned down. Several cemeteries ceased to be used, but a rebuilding took place, the last occupation continuing until this was also sacked and burned in 450 BC (end of phase Ib) and The Heuneburg was abandoned – the population perhaps migrating southwards to northern Italy.

At The Heuneburg streets and houses were laid out systematically, to judge by the small group of houses that has been excavated. I hesitate to employ the term urban. To use this term demands a clear division of function in planning and the performance of administrative and political services. As The Heuneburg and similar centres were linked to a court located outside the settlement and were largely concerned with their economic activities, we should probably compare the Hallstatt residences with African royal courts or with later Viking trading/production settlements such as Hedeby. It is probably not until the oppida that we can speak of urbanisation, with a multifunctional population centre serving a larger region, although this is much debated (Audouze and Büchsenschütz 1989, 233ff).

In the vicinity of The Heuneburg were two of the largest burial mounds in the Hallstatt area, Magdalenenberg (100 m wide and 16 m high) and Hohmichele (Riek and Hundt 1962; Spindler 1971–80), the latter possibly holding the founder of The Heuneburg, while Magdalenenenberg might represent the founder of another residence originally lying some 60–70 km from The Heuneburg. Unfortunately, their central chambers were plundered; at Magdalenenberg this occurred around 570 BC according to the latest dendrochronological adjustment. The Magdalenenberg exhibited the East Hallstatt tradition of burying clan members and the personal followers/retinue of the chief, as at Stična. Here we find typical warrior burials with lances, as well as female burials, one with an Iberian belt (Spindler 1983, Taf. 16). Burial VI at Hohmichele was of a man and woman, and contained a wagon and horse gear, a cauldron, a quiver, and rich textiles with gold and brocade, the latter the earliest case of silk in European prehistory. 'Totenfolge' – the placing of closely related persons (a wife or followers) in the burial or outside it – was a royal ritual practised by societies from the Scythians to the Hallstatt Culture, although it is rare there. The Heuneburg residence and surrounding barrows suggest a rich early centre, influenced, perhaps founded, by a royal prince and his followers from the East Hallstatt, migrating down the Danube. Such a source of inspiration is suggested by the Magdalenenberg clan mound, burials with quivers (an original Scythian or pre-Scythian influence?), as also in Hochdorf, as well as by some of the metalwork.

The Heuneburg is normally considered to be commercially linked to Massalia during its early phase and especially during the 'clay brick wall' period. However, with the possibility of a later dating (the dendrochronological adjustments must leave some scepticism about their reliability) its 'classic' phase might even overlap with the expansion of the Etruscans in the Po plain and the intensified commercial expansion of the Greeks in the Adriatic. The distribution of Hallstatt *fibulae* southwards into the Alps also suggests frequent interaction with Golasecca and northern Italy (Frey 1988). Attic pottery could just as well have come from here, and some of the most impressive imports, for example the Hochdorf bronze 'sofa' bear witness to links with Italy (Biel 1988b, Taf. A–B). According to this, Ha D2 could be linked to the commercial expansion of the Etruscans. It seems clear, however, that as soon as the first residence had been established, the process spread rapidly, through the building up of vassals and allies from The Heuneburg. A similar process apparently took place with the rise of the early residences on the Rhône and beyond. This leads on to the question of political structure.

The economic and political organisation of the Hallstatt residences cannot be separated, because their economic basis extended beyond the immediate boundaries of the central settlement. It demanded the operation of a political structure that was able to extract surplus and tribute from a larger area, extensive enough to sustain the chiefly residences and their operations, including military support, and big enough to provide products for the Greeks in quantities they considered worthwhile. What size the political structure was and how it worked are still a matter of debate. Two models are to hand, the first proposed by Frankenstein and Rowlands (1978). In a classic analysis of the structure of burial goods, they suggested it corresponded to a prestige goods organisation in which vassal chiefs were attached by prestige goods and bonds of loyalty to a paramount chief (see also Zürn 1970; for a summary see Spindler 1983, 358). The vassals would in turn pay tribute to the centre, in the form of commodities for trade – slaves, iron and gold (if it was panned for locally, still a matter of debate), while the centre produced the necessary prestige goods for local distribution. In this way the structure could expand to embrace a large area of vassals, sub chiefs etc., all served from one large royal residence – The Heuneburg, later Hohenasperg (Figures 137, 138). Such a structure would have made it possible for the Greeks and Etruscans to carry out administered trade from a few central residences. The model thus

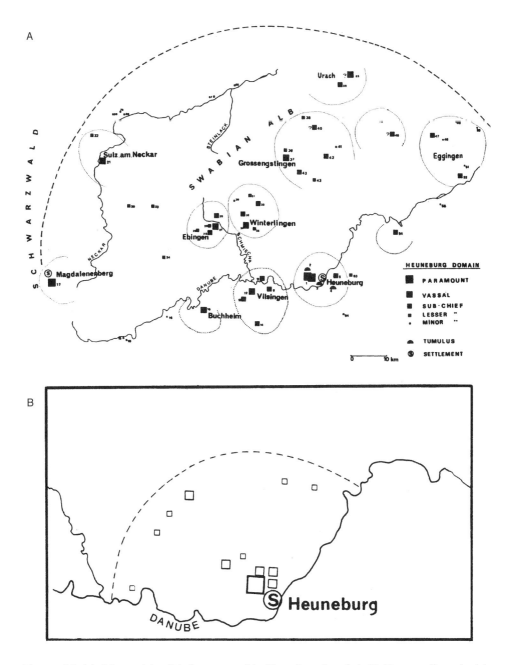

Fig. 137 Model of the spatial-political structure of the Heuneburg domain in Ha D1, according to burial wealth (A) and its crumbling in Ha D2–3 (B).

accounts both for the organisation of trade and for the internal organisation created to extract and provide the goods.

The other model, proposed by Heinrich Härke (1979), is based on the settlement evidence, and assumes each princely residence or royal court to represent an auton-

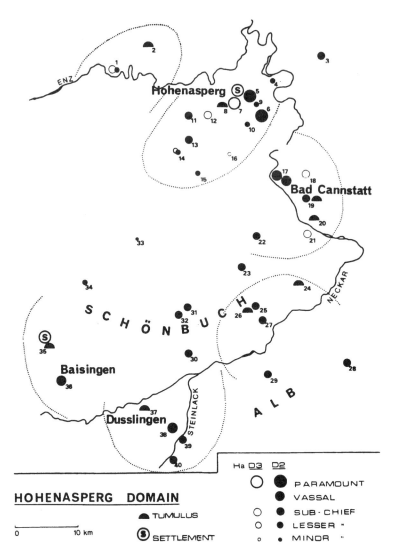

Fig. 138 Model of the spatial-political structure of the Hohenasperg domain in Ha D2–3, according to burial wealth.

omous political entity, surrounded by a smaller network of vassal chiefs. Seen from above, on a distribution map, there is quite a convincing pattern of residences being regularly spaced, each with a hinterland encircling 40–50 km (Figure 139). Examining a single centre (Figure 140), this still provides a convincingly regular local hierarchy. However, one model does not necessarily exclude the other: the Frankenstein–Rowlands model assumes a chiefly hierarchy, which could very well have the character of a confederation with a leading paramount chief or king. It did not mean that he was able to demand whatever he wished from his noble vassals; rather, it must be considered a relationship of mutual benefits based on the ideological and historical precedence of the Heuneburg royal family. Competition between the centres

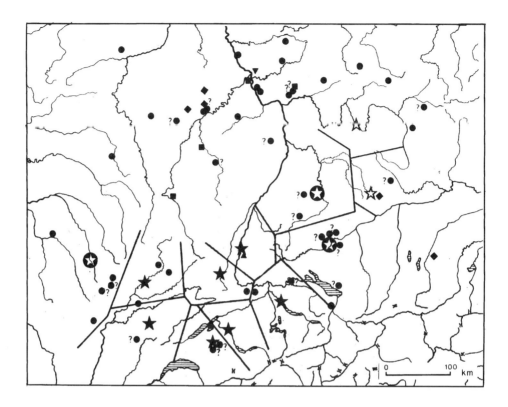

Fig. 139 Model of the political territories of the Ha D royal residences (*Herrensitze* or *Fürstensitze* shown by stars; other symbols represent various sizes of ordinary defended sites), based on weighted Thiessen polygons.

could easily end in hostilities, this being what happened around 550 and again around 500 BC when the residence was burned down, and some of the large royal burials were plundered by the conqueror. As secondary burials and some of the settlements stopped, although not at The Heuneburg itself, the hostilities must have had some impact. These events suggest that a well organised army, probably a new confederation of chiefs, stood behind the destruction. (Perhaps the first migrations into the Po Valley took place in conjunction with these events, to remove some of the competition.) This interpretation is supported by the fact that from now on the centre of wealth and trade definitely moved to Hohenasperg, where the Hochdorf prince was buried around the time of the second fall of The Heuneburg (the dating, however, is still debated, as the grave also contained older grave goods, produced a generation earlier). The Heuneburg shrank to a small centre surrounded by a group of vassals in its immediate vicinity (Figure 137b). The geographical scale of these changes suggests that the Frankenstein–Rowlands model is the most plausible for the political structure, while the settlement units taking part in it were based on local residences with a periphery of smaller chiefly settlements. Thus Härke's model represents the settlement structure, Frankenstein and Rowlands' the political configuration.

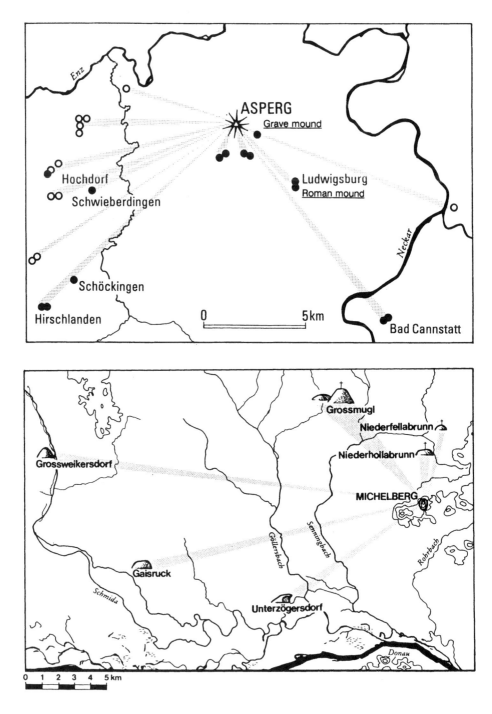

Fig. 140 The local structure of a royal residence and its princely burials and large tumuli at Asperg in Baden-Württemberg and at Michelberg in lower Austria.

   Trade and trade routes are inferred from the distribution of imports, in combination with historical knowledge of river transport and mountain passes. Ludwig Pauli (1974) has produced valuable analyses of the trade routes and suggested a development from a single monopolised route mainly carrying Greek products to a multiplicity of competing routes, as the Etruscans entered the scene (Pauli 1994) (Figure 141). The importance of Massalia from an early date has been demonstrated by Kimmig in several distribution maps of Rhodian vessels, wine amphorae etc., some of them reaching the Heuneburg area, although few in numbers (Kimmig 1982, Abb. 23, 27). However, actual penetration of the Rhône by the Greeks of Massalia was later in the 6th century, according to the pottery distribution (Kimmig 1982, Abb. 25–26). The organisation of trade must have demanded military support from Massalia/Etruscan towns and the princely residences along the route, combining river transport and overland transport using pack-donkeys. Since river transport was much cheaper than land transport (Spindler 1983, 320), the Rhône is assumed to have been of vital importance, also for products traded further along to the Danube/Neckar, even after the opening of the Alpine trade with the northern Etruscans. On the other hand, time and manpower were not scarce in the past, and security was probably the most important factor – river transport in small boats being less easy to defend than mobile land transport without severe limitations on the number of accompanying warriors to protect it.

   The commercial basis of the Hallstatt residences becomes abundantly clear when we consider the distribution of certain objects, especially iron bars and gold ornaments. Iron production was centred within the area of the Hallstatt residences, and the early La Tène chiefly burials (Figure 142). The distribution of gold ornaments in the same area gives a strong clue as to the importance of iron extraction and trade (but we should not exclude the possibility of local gold panning and production). To this we may add the products of the surrounding vassal territory. Härke has produced a highly interesting summary of the settlement evidence (Härke 1979, fig. 58). It suggests that the royal Hallstatt residences, mainly based on agrarian production together with some animal husbandry, were surrounded by settlements relying more heavily on animal husbandry. In the Hallstatt area samples of grain indicate the introduction of oats (for horses) and rye, which were more resistant than wheat to degraded soils. At the residences cattle dominated, while sheep were very scarce (Spindler 1983, ch. 7), whereas we can suppose them to be numerous at the smaller settlements in the mountainous areas, as in the Late Bronze Age, as is the case in one settlement (Spindler 1983, 310). The many smaller hillforts of the surrounding zone suggest a more warlike society. We know from Figure 129 that this was the former area of Ha C warriors, or at least part of it, and the later Early La Tène chiefly burials were also situated here. The group on the middle Rhine overlaps with the chiefly seats, and with another in northeast France. We are thus dealing with two social and economic systems, potentially in opposition, as well as potentially exploiting each other. They certainly could not have been unaware of each other. In an original contribution Daphne Nash (1985) has suggested that there existed a political-economic relationship between the two areas: the royal Hallstatt residences relied on

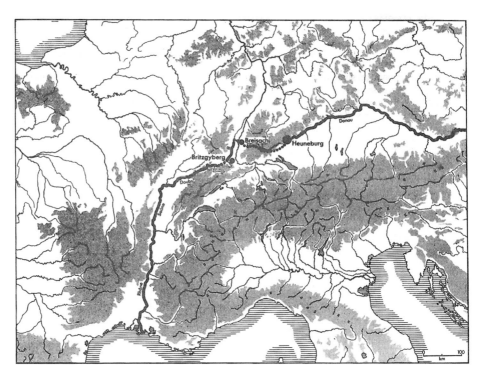

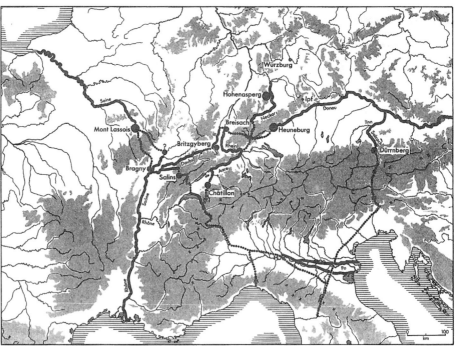

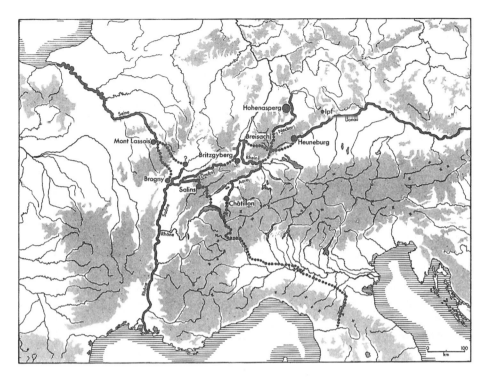

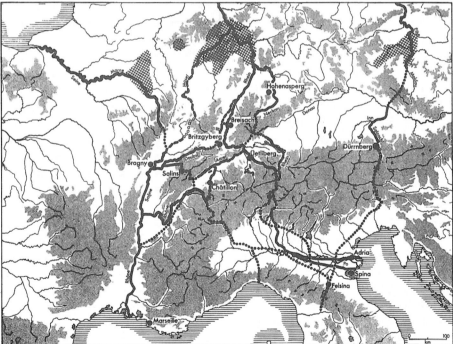

Fig. 141 The development of trade and communication networks in four stages from Early Hallstatt to Early La Tène in the Western Alps. The royal residences are named, while the Early La Tène wagon burials are hatched. River routes in solid line, land routes dotted.

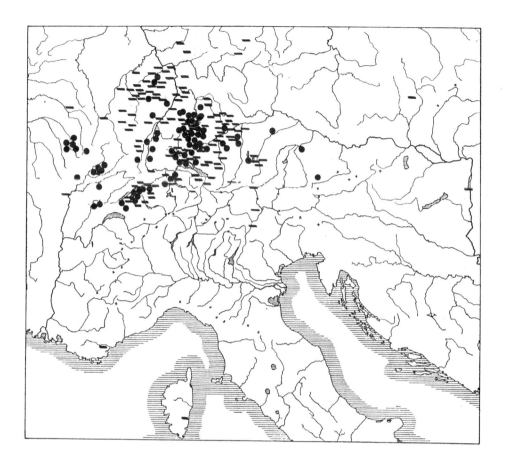

Fig. 142 Late Hallstatt gold finds (solid circle) and pyramid-formed iron bars of Late Hallstatt/Early La Tène.

the warring zone for slaves (through their raiding) and for mercenaries (spear burials). Härke has also suggested an economic relationship, with the warrior periphery providing animal products, hides and wool (1979, 240).

This evidence suggests that the polities of the prestige-goods model had the potential to develop a local relationship of centres and peripheries serving the centres at some distance. The contacts between the two zones were potentially dangerous, as the warrior periphery, or at least the mercenaries they provided, had to be kept satisfied, otherwise the Hallstatt residences themselves might be considered a tempting target. This delicate balance shifted at some time during the 5th century. But before turning to that we should briefly discuss another centre–periphery organisation.

What kind of relationship existed between the Greek/Etruscan traders and the Hallstatt chiefs? It conformed to the prestige goods model outlined above, which means that local chiefs adopted aspects of the 'civilised' elite lifestyle of the centre, symbolised by their luxury goods, ranging from wine to costly bronze vessels, pottery, cloth and furniture – just to mention the most common items in the princely burials and at The Heuneburg. This attraction was big enough to enable a trade based on prestige goods rather than money to develop, and one where out-of-date products were sometimes delivered, causing some chronological problems as well (meaning that some historical cross-datings may be a little too old). Although the real thing was preferred, there emerged skilled specialists able to imitate some of the imported prestige goods, as recently summarised by Kimmig (1982, 67 ff., Abb. 58–62). The high quality of these local copies suggests that Italian and Greek specialists were attached to the residences for short periods, and their context further indicates that the local imitations were luxury items controlled by the elite. In this way they still fulfilled the function of a prestige good; only in the final phase did experiments begin with an indigenous style, to be discussed in Chapter 7.

The Mediterranean lifestyle was closely linked to wining and dining (the banquet), but even the weapons demonstrate symbolic rather than actual leadership in war. We are far from the Ha C warrior chiefs, as hunts and the display of golden daggers now reflected the royal lifestyle of the Mediterranean and the Near East. Greek and Etruscan traders entered into a direct relationship with the Hallstatt centres, which borrowed craft specialists as one part of the trade. We should also envisage dynastic marriages being part of the maintenance of trade relations, as we know was the case on the Black Sea, where Scythian kings married both Greek and Thracian princesses. It is in this light that we should see the Vix burial, the anthropological type of which apparently diverges from the normal type known in the French Hallstatt area (Härke 1979, 184), as perhaps representing a Greek trader's or nobleman's daughter, married to the local king to strengthen their political alliance.[8] She brought with her the krater and other prestige goods as bridewealth (the krater presumably being an old family piece); they therefore belonged to her, and followed her into the grave. Likewise, the rarer Greek and Etruscan bronze vessels should be considered as diplomatic gifts (Fischer 1973), the visible aspects of the politics of trade, the bulk of which remains invisible.

The archaeological evidence of the West Hallstatt phenomenon is among the closest we can get to achieving a representative sample of a major social and economic transformation taking place within the framework of emerging centre–periphery relations. We only lack a thorough local settlement survey programme. It also has the advantage of being able to be related to some literary evidence, at least in the centres in Italy and the Mediterranean. Therefore it represents a laboratory – or a testing ground – for archaeological reconstruction and explanation: how far can we get, which hypotheses employ the data most convincingly, and what are the shortcomings where more research is needed?[9] The interpretations could also be used to generalise for areas with similar but more patchy evidence, such as the Balkans.

The eastern Hallstatt and the Balkans   During the 6th and early 5th centuries BC commercial relations with the Italic/Adriatic *koine* intensified and the princely, or royal, centres reached their zenith in the Central Balkans (Yugoslavia), reflected in elite burials with extraordinary wealth, mostly in the form of foreign imports, as at

Glasinac, Trebeniste, Atenica and Novi Pazar (Kromer 1986, Abb. 10–14; Palavestra in press). To the north there emerged a new pictorial tradition of metalwork – Situla art originating in Este and Bologna (Frey 1969), while to the south local traditions in metalwork continued alongside foreign imports (Figure 143). The Hellenisation or, more precisely, the acculturation to an Etruscan lifestyle must have been considerable in Slovenia, but it had of course already been underway since the 7th century. The exchange not only of goods but also of craft specialists, as well as dynastic marriages, was the basis of this development, turning Slovenia into a barbarian Etruscan province. Situla art illustrates the major social and ritual events associated with the royal life style: from war processions/games to hunts and banquets/feasts, which must have accompanied death rituals, dynastic marriages and other social events (Figure 143) (Kromer 1980). It also demonstrates symbolically, in scenes of women weaving, the high social standing of the female members of the elite (Eibner 1986). It was not only the elite that prospered. Another sign of general wealth and social integration is the spread of small luxury articles to many non-chiefly burials, suggesting that larger groups of craft specialists, merchants, warriors etc. were being drawn into the process of acculturation. It means that the circulation of goods and services was being extended to more of the population, an indication that a more stable and complex society was developing. It further suggests that the eastern Hallstatt had passed through the prestige goods phase, and was now entering a period of consolidation of the new social and economic order with less need for the elite to dispose of wealth in their graves.

   Another group of royal burials is found in the central Balkans, conforming more to the prestige-goods model of the West Hallstatt. It means that acculturation here was less developed – Greek and Italian prestige goods were lavishly employed in elite burials, such as the krater in the royal tomb of Trebeniste (Figure 144), probably coming from the same workshop as the Vix krater, and the remarkable gold mask, yet another indication of archaic Greek heroic ideology, if not actually looted from a Mycenaean grave. In an analysis of the central Balkan burials, Aleksandar Palavestra (1984) was able to define a group of princely burials sharing the same characteristics, including: (1) luxurious personal jewellery of amber, bronze, and gold; (2) some marks of rank, e.g. sceptres, armour etc.; (3) articles of amber; (4) imported dishes and bronze vessels for drinking and dining (banquets). A few burials also contained remnants of chariots and horse gear. The tomb constructions containing these burials were also uniform, including: (1) a tumulus over the burial, normally monumental; (2) interior stone chambers, either conical or square in shape; (3) secondary but rich burials in the mound. These findings indicate that the persons buried in them belonged to an elite, sharing an aristocratic ideology of burial ritual which distinguished them from other groups. The princely burials correspond closely to the West Hallstatt royal tombs in their adoption of the Greek and Italian life style, represented by imported prestige goods, as well as the employment of monumental barrows. As in the West Hallstatt they appear at some distance from the centres of civilisation in Italy and on the Adriatic coast, where Greek and Italian colonies were the ports of trade with which they had established political alliances. The Greek and

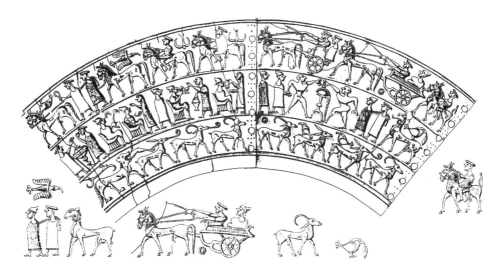

Fig. 143 Bronze bucket (*situla*) from Vace (Slovenia) of the 6th century BC, showing the most important scenes of the 'great festival', with processions of vehicles and horsemen, contests, and wining and dining accompanied by music. Similar scenes are depicted on wall paintings in Etruscan burial chambers.

Fig. 144 Large bronze krater from Trebeniste.

Italian imports were thus, as at Hallstatt, to be considered as diplomatic gifts (since they were exclusive), not only by the new Balkan elites stretching from Thrace via Macedonia into Yugoslavia (Frey 1991, Abb.1) (Figure 145), but also by the Greeks themselves. They were certainly not mass-produced products, and not until the late 6th and 5th centuries did the commercial relations become archaeologically more visible (Babic 1990; Winter and Bankoff 1989).

The economy of the central Balkan royal aristocracies was based on animal husbandry in the form of transhumance, and overland caravan trade. According to a recent analysis by Palavestra (in press) the royal tombs of the late Hallstatt period are

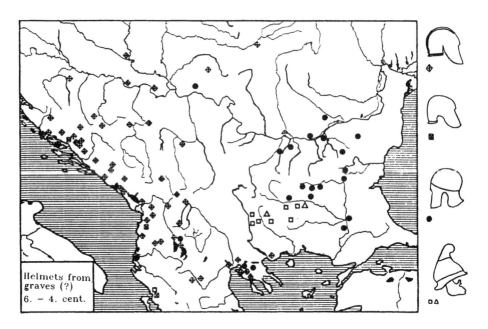

Fig. 145 Greek helmets in princely warrior graves from the 6th–4th century BC in the Balkans and eastern Europe/Thrace, often accompanied by other parts of Greek hoplite armour. The map indicates evolving centre–periphery relations between the Greek Mediterranean world and new warrior elites, employing Greek weapons as prestige goods.

located at old, historically attested, routes of transhumance and caravan trade, especially at crossroads, giving them a strategic advantage. As in the West Hallstatt they were in control of the main communication and trade routes, extracting taxes and tribute, as well as organising the more profitable trade ventures, or giving them military protection. This corresponds to a model of pastoral warrior aristocracy known from both Asia and North Africa, e.g. the Scythians and the historical Tuaregs: 'warrior aristocrats are entrepreneurs in the caravan trade and their clients are involved in wide-ranging pastoral transhumance' (Sáenz 1991, 100). The traded products were probably the 'classic' set, as known in medieval times: leather, wool, livestock, wax, honey, resin, timber, medicinal plants and slaves (the same categories can be documented for Scythian trade; see below).

The rise of the royal tombs has been connected by Yugoslavian archaeologists with the formation of historically attested tribes, as in the case of West Hallstatt.[10] It seems, however, that cultural traditions which had remained stable since the Cimmerian expansion were now changing. The period from the end of the 6th century BC to the middle of the 4th (when the Celtic intrusion and the rise of Macedonia as a great power occur) is, according to Palavestra (1984, 103):

> Characterised by the almost uniform rise of all ethnic cultural groups in the Balkan hinterland. The boundaries established between tribes in the 6th century BC with the aim of protecting their independence, customs and properties, were thrust wide open during the 5th century by the exchange of

raw materials and cultural goods . . . As a result the cultures of individual tribes became multifaceted – sumptuous and cosmopolitan in some places, poor and extremely archaic in others.

This description is a precise diagnosis of the social and economic consequences of the formation of new ruling elites and the subsequent breakdown of traditional norms of social organisation and interaction. Wealth was concentrated in fewer hands in strategic areas during the first phase, while later on some groups would prosper at the expense of others, creating local relations of centre and periphery, or even peripheries that had been cut off from contacts. We shall meet this picture again when returning to Central and northern Europe in the next chapter.

Royalty   In the preceding sections we have employed rather loosely a terminology of royal, princely and chiefly residences and burials. The analysis has given it some empirical flesh and blood, suggesting an archaic state structure of the prestige-goods type, by some called a complex chiefdom(see Chapter 3.2). Are there other criteria for describing these early centres as royal (princely) and their inhabitants as kings and princes? At least three factors justify the use of this terminology:

(1) The settlement evidence suggests that the central fortifications, (including the royal courts) formed a regular settlement hierarchy, from royal courts to chiefly centres and further down to open settlements in the lowlands, as well as highland settlements (sometimes in caves) for iron and salt extraction and herding. The fortified settlements were regularly spaced, suggesting the territorial control of rather large regions. The analysis of Frankenstein and Rowlands even suggests the formation of larger polities, linking chiefs to a centre up to 150 km away. If we accept the very large settlements such as The Heuneburg, Mont Lassois, Stična and Sopron as a royal level of sites, they must have controlled a large territory made up of units like those in Figures 114 and 139.

(2) The analyses of Frankenstein and Rowlands, and Palavestra, among others, have indicated that the group of rich burials share the same characteristics both in burial ritual and in grave goods, testifying to close dynastic alliances and contacts. In the Balkans the rulers were in control of overland caravan trade from the Adriatic coast, linking Italy and the central Balkans (Palavestra in press), as well as north–south trade between Pommerania and the eastern Hallstatt for amber (Palavestra 1987). To the west they controlled trade with the Greeks and the Etruscans.

(3) They share with royal burials from Gordion to Salamis all the basic traits of the burial ritual of kings, both in grave goods and in ritual. It means that they were familiar with the ideology and the political realities of kingship and wanted to signal that to their own followers and peers.

The nomadic connection: the Scythians
During the late 7th and 6th centuries Scythian warriors and mercenaries are ever present both in the textual and archaeological records from the Near East and in the archaeology of Central and northern Europe. Traces of the activities of the famous

Scythian archers, the characteristic arrowheads, are found embedded in defensive walls from Urartian/Assyrian towns such as Teishebaini in the east to anonymous Polish fortifications in the west. In the east, Scythian troops served as mercenaries and allies, after having been defeated, for the expanding Medes on their way towards Lydia, as they also later did for the Greeks, while in the west some of their tribes expanded into Central Europe in a series of conquest migrations. Soviet archaeologists have built up a detailed picture of the Scythians through a large number of excavations (e.g. Meliukova 1989).[11] What was the background to this remarkable expansion of new pastoral warring groups during the 7th–6th and 5th centuries?

On the Black Sea   The Scythians rose to power during the course of the decline of the Urartian/Assyrian Empires, at the same developing their cultural identity in the Scythian animal style, as described earlier. They were drawn into political conflicts as allies to the Assyrians, and an Assyrian princess was married to a Scythian king, demonstrating their importance. They gained control of some territories for brief periods during the vacuum left by the fall of Assyria in 614, and according to Herodotus (History 1.106) they controlled most of the Near East for twenty-eight years. With the political reorganisation of the Near East under the Medes they were expelled, retreating first to the Caucasus and later to the Black Sea area. Here they formed a strong kingdom, centred around the Dnieper, which controlled trade between the Greeks and the Scythian steppe tribes/chiefdoms. The newly founded Greek colonies, such as Olbia, and the rise of Scythian royal residences were clearly interlinked, and we are fortunate enough to have the rather detailed eye-witness reports of the Scythians given by Herodotus (Book IV),who visited Olbia in the 5th century BC (Berg 1979). His observations have been increasingly confirmed by Russian archaeological excavations during the past twenty-five years, as summarised by Renate Rolle in several works (1979; 1985; 1989).

Large royal tombs, some 100 m wide and 20 m high, surrounded by the smaller tombs of their followers and kin, demonstrate not only the wealth and power of the ruling elite, but also their ability to attract trade goods as well as craft specialists. The sheer volume of imported goods in some of these burials makes them resemble small warehouses, including wine cellars in special niches with amphorae once full of wine, some with residues still left in them. During the early phase, some of these imports could have been the spoils of war (booty), but later they were obviously the product of trade with the Greeks. The Scythian rulers had clearly adopted a Greek lifestyle, and intermarriage between Scythians and Greeks was not uncommon. This is in accordance with the archaeological discovery of defended royal urban settlements, as well as early Greek trade stations like Berezan, Nemirov and Olbia, holding estimated populations of 6,000–10,000 people, many of them non-Greeks, and including quarters for bronze- and ironworking. Their products were distributed by the Scythian kings in trade with the neighbouring tribes up to 500 km away. The evidence of animal bones as well as seeds demonstrates the importance of grain exports (various types of wheat, including bread wheat) from the 'agrarian Scythians', as Herodotus also mentions. In the early phase the settlements consisted mainly of small huts (6–14 m²), laid out on a simple street grid, only later to be replaced by stone-built houses (as at other Greek colonies, such as Massalia). Nemirov, a contemporary Scythian fortified residence, enclosed 110 ha, with an acropolis of 12.5 ha.

The early phase of commercial relations began during the late 7th century BC, when wine vessels dominated; trade intensified with the founding of Greek colonies from 600 BC onwards, continuing until the 3rd century. Imported goods consisted mainly of wine, Greek pottery, metal vessels, cosmetics, works of art, luxury clothing and finally weapons. All in all this displays the same variety as in the Late Hallstatt royal residences. According to literary evidence Scythian products provided in exchange included grain, fish (especially sturgeon), honey and wax, fur and leather, cattle, slaves and various medicinal/magical products. To this we should probably add iron and silver, as well as horses. The central organisation of trade is demonstrated by the clustering of Greek imports around the royal residences (Figure 146) (Rolle 1985, Abb. 3). It seems, however, that Greek imports were confined to the royal elite and their close vassals, while local products from Olbia and the royal Scythian workshops, which dominated production from the 5th century onwards, were extensively traded and exchanged with neighbouring tribes, a pattern reminiscent of the Hallstatt royal courts. Further parallels include royal defended urban-like residences, with quarters for artisans and craft specialists controlled and fed by the royal families.

Further north, in the forest steppe, Russian archaeologists have registered more than a hundred fortified settlements (*gorodisce*), with complex defensive walls (Skoryj 1989). A *gorodisce* at Bel'sk had a 33–km long wall enclosing a plateau with three individual fortifications controlling different river valleys, dating from the same period as the royal Scythian residences in the steppe zone on the Black Sea coast – the 7th to 3rd centuries BC. A similarly complex *gorodisce* is found at Kamenka in the Scythian steppe region on the River Dnieper, enclosing an area of 12 km². It held both an acropolis and large quarters for metalworking, extending over 900 ha. Iron production was especially prominent. Supplies of metalwork for most of the Scythian world in Europe could have originated here. Although there are urban-like settlements covering large areas, we must assume that the large enclosed areas also served to contain and protect the royal herds and horses, as well as serving as training grounds for the warriors. In Figure 147 the geographical location of royal Scythian burials and iron ores is shown, with the Kamenskoe *gorodisce* at the centre and Greek colonies on the coast. Kamenskoe was the royal residence during the 5th–4th centuries BC. It gives a good impression of the relations between royal Scythian settlements/burials and iron production, iron being easy to exploit as it lay close to the surface. Much was probably intended for export, but the need for iron among the Scythians themselves for weapons and body armour must have been quite enormous, considering their large armies.

The rise of the Scythian kingdoms during the 6th–5th centuries BC thus exhibits many parallels to the rise of the Hallstatt residences during the same period, including mining activities. It is perhaps surprising to learn that the Scythians, and pastoral

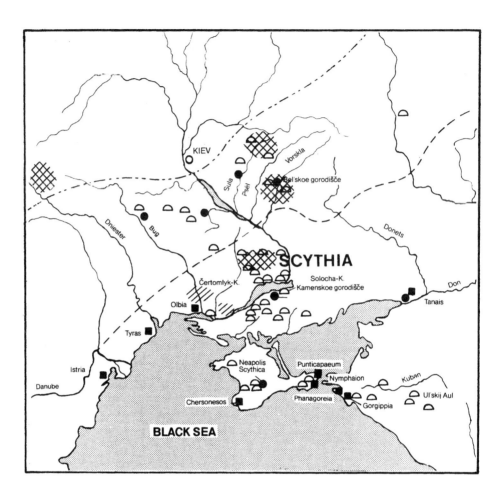

Fig. 146 Map of ancient Scythia: broken line with points = boundary between forest and steppe; broken line = boundary between forest steppe and grass steppe; square = main Greek urban settlements on the North coast of the Black Sea; solid circle = main fortified settlements dating from Scythian times; half circle = concentration of burial mounds; hatched = concentration of Greek imports.

chiefdoms, both before and after them, were basing much of their wealth on mineral exploitation, rich mines for copper and not least gold being located in the Caucasus and in the Altai/Kazakhstan, all three being areas with rich royal burials (Rolle 1979, ch. 3). Caravan routes connected the Central Asian mines with the Scythian kingdom on the Black Sea, which was said by Herodotus to have employed seven translators on the route, which may have led further on to China. The construction of large royal mounds, although an old steppe tradition, also conforms to the rise of new ruling elites, and may suggest that competition for rank and succession in the steppe region was always fierce. This is supported by the tradition of catacomb burials, that is burial chambers dug deeply into the black soil, making robbing laborious and dangerous. The many robbed graves, or attempts at robbing, suggest that new ruling dynasties were frequently seizing power, since such operations could hardly be carried out secretly, or in the dark by small groups, but had to be an official venture.

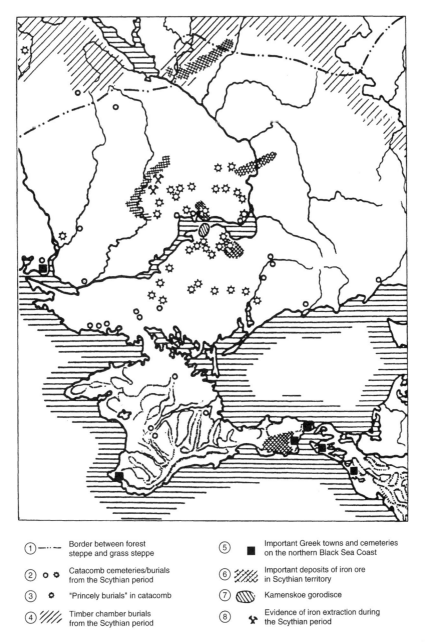

Fig. 147 Ancient Scythia in the 4th–3rd centuries BC, with sources of iron and iron production added.

The construction of the barrows and the catacombs demanded a large workforce, while timber and grass turfs were sometimes transported from far-away distances, whether for ritual reasons (an old homeland of the king?) or practical considerations (lack of local timber). According to both Indo-European legend and literary sources the dead king was transported around his territory for forty days in a wagon before his soul could be released. Large feasts accompanied the burial at Ordzonikidze (Figure 148); the animal bones from which fragments survived were calculated (using a conservative estimate) to have fed 1,300 people. Servants and horses were sometimes killed to follow their master. Large quantities of wine were also consumed, before the amphorae were smashed. Finally a stone stela was put on top of the barrow, this being an old custom in Eurasia.

The royal elite and the warrior class distinguished themselves not only in burial but also in lifestyle and living conditions. Being 10–15 cm taller than commoners, due to their healthy diet over several generations, they were 1.80 m or more in height, long skulled and of European type, very unlike the Mongols who began penetrating westward at this time and later came to dominate. The Scythian warriors spent most of their time on horseback, honing their professional warrior skills when not at war. Archaeological as well as textual evidence has taught us how well developed and organised Scythian warfare was. Warriors were equipped with weapons for attacking from all distances – from the bow and arrow to spears (carried in a combined quiver), the sword and finally axes and not least the whip. Their arrows, 'which promise a double death' according to Ovid, were poisoned (the double death) and widely feared. Twenty bow-shots a minute could be fired in the first phase of battle. Heavily armoured and mounted in organised phalanxes with their king taking part in the battle, and often buried after a heroic death in battle, they were the most efficient warriors of their time (Figure 149) responsible for sacking several Near Eastern towns. Scalps, or the heads of killed enemies, were their battle trophies, giving access to booty as a sign of bravery, and the skulls were worked into drinking cups. In all this they resembled the Celts, to whom we will come later. Their strength and renowned tactical skills were displayed when Darius of Persia led an enormous military campaign against the European Scythians during 513–12 BC to avenge the defeat and killing of Cyrus the Great in 529. By a series of tactical retreats Darius and his army were gradually lured into increasingly difficult terrain in which the Scythian troops were at home, finally forcing the Persian army to flee.[12]

Having outlined the historical and organisational background to the Scythian settlement on the Black Sea, which we must term an archaic state, it is easier to understand how and why they could penetrate deeply into Central Europe. The question is, how far?

East Central Europe   The regional displacements and westward migrations already described which took place during the early 6th century BC were reflected in Central Europe. Well-organised Scythian warrior groups expanded westward into Hungary during the 6th century, where their presence is mainly documented in new Scythian cemeteries from the so-called Szentes Verkerzug culture (Parducz 1952; 1954; 1955; 1965), displaying the characteristic Scythian complex – bow and arrow/quiver, horse harness, axe and dagger, and in female burials the characteristic mirror and earrings (Parducz 1974, maps therein). Scythian or pre-Scythian settlers had already appeared in the northern Carpathians (moving along the Dniester) and in Siebenbürgen, perhaps during the late 7th or early 6th century BC (Vasiliev 1976;

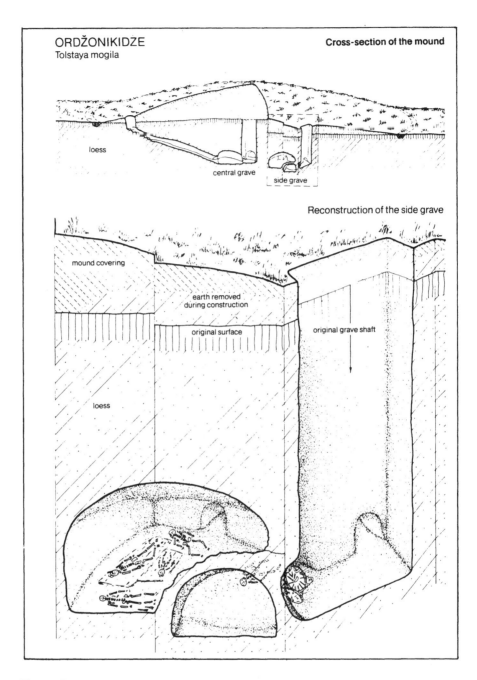

Fig. 148 Reconstructed view of Scythian royal burial at Ordzonikidze.

summarised in Chochorowski 1985; 1987), putting an end to the Hallstatt hillforts. From the middle to late 6th century large groups settled on the northern Hungarian plain, by some taken to represent the Sigynnians mentioned by Herodotus, although the horse trade is known to have started in the 7th century (Chochorowski 1987).

Fig. 149 High-ranking Scythians in full armour, based on archaeological finds. On the right is the prince from the Ordzonikidze kurgan (Figure 148).

This time not all of them stopped at the River Tisza, but continued westward and northward in a series of local conquests and migrations. A chronological sequence has been worked out (Chochorowski 1985, Tafel 4; 1987, fig. 7), suggesting that around 450 BC the expansion stopped and the groups consolidated within their territories and developed more peaceful relationships. From that time their former close relations with the mother-groups around the Black Sea seem to have ceased, and they continued a local development until the arrival of Celtic settlers in the 4th century BC.[13]

Kromer has recently presented a vivid picture of the opposition between the Late Hallstatt residences and the expanding Scythian war chiefs (Figure 150). By mapping the Hallstatt residences and the Scythian cemeteries it becomes apparent that they opposed each other, as during Ha B3/Ha C. Once again there appeared a buffer zone between the River Tisza and the Danube, although Scythian arrowheads suggest it was a battlefield, while the presence of some Scythian arrowheads in the defensive walls of Hungarian Hallstatt fortifications makes the warlike nature of their expansion clear. Being partly halted by the Hallstatt hillforts on the Danube they expanded north of the Danube through Moravia along the Oder into Silesia. A second expansion followed around 500 BC or shortly after, probably led by north Carpathian

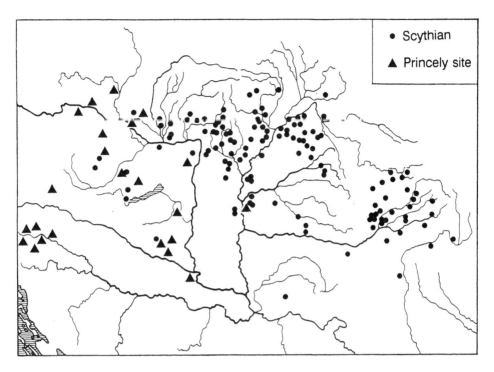

Fig. 150 Distribution of Scythian finds and princely sites of the Hallstatt culture in Central Europe.

groups, heading beyond the Vistula and roaming the area between the Oder and the Vistula (Figure 151).

The archaeological evidence for the presence of Scythians in the Lausitz territory has been analysed and discussed by Bukowski in some detail (1974; 1977a; 1977b; 1981; 1982), making the historical sequence rather clear, as outlined above. The contexts of finds fall into two main groups:

(1) In burials, testifying to a more regular presence of Scythians, at least enough of them to bury those warriors killed in battle (in cases where a single arrowhead was present the buried individual was presumably a local victim).

(2) Scythian arrowheads occur mainly in fortified settlements and around refuge caves. If we map both female and male equipment (for warfare), two distributions appear (Figure 152): a military frontier with only Scythian arrowheads and weapons, some in burials and others in conquered fortifications, and a zone a few hundred kilometres behind the frontier where we can add the presence of female burials, although a few occur in the frontier zone, suggesting that some family groups accompanied the warbands. A remarkable find of Scythian gold ornaments appeared in a bog in eastern Jutland several hundred kilometres away from the battlefields (Jensen 1969). What lay behind this deposition we shall never know, but a very direct link to the events in Poland must be assumed; it represents either the spoils of war brought back by auxiliary troops from Jutland, or, on the contrary, it was a marriage

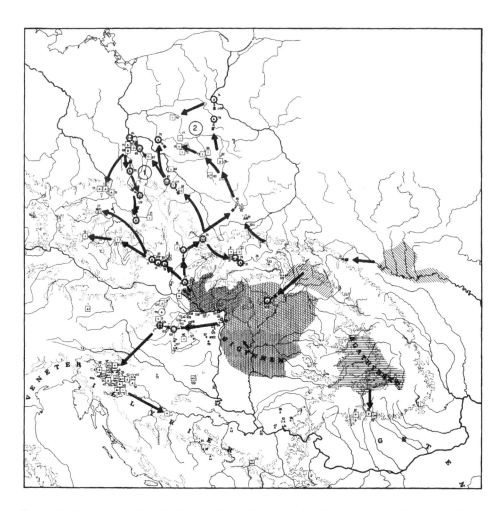

Fig. 151 Early expansion of the Scythians in Central Europe in the 6th century BC: hatched areas indicate local Scythian culture groups or tribes; squares = graves with Scythian finds, mainly arrowheads and axes; thick circles = fortified settlements with evidence of Scythian attack/presence, mainly arrowheads; triangles = caves and refuges with Scythian arrowheads. The solid arrows suggest the proposed route of expansion: 1 = early phase, 2 = later phase.

gift from the expanding Scythians to a Jutish king to secure the hinterland against support for the Lausitz hillforts.

There is thus no doubt about the presence of effective armies of mounted Scythian warriors destroying a chain of Lausitz fortifications along their route (Figure 151), even attacking refugees in their temporary cave shelters. It is characteristic that the military operations were aimed at some of the most important settlement groups in terms of trade and economic expansion – the first during the 6th century towards Silesia, which took part in the amber trade with the eastern Hallstatt, and the second against the Pommeranian area of amber production. We may assume that the Scythian presence added to the decline and disintegration of settlement and social

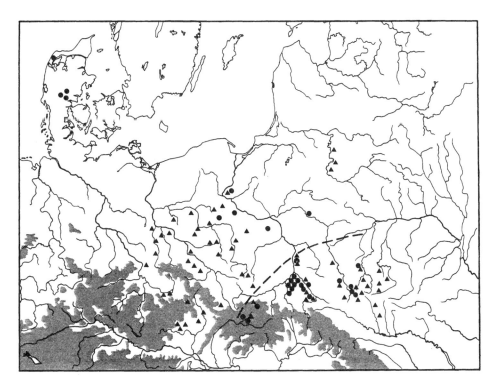

Fig. 152 Distribution of Scythian ornaments (circle) and weapons (triangle), with a suggested boundary (broken line) between permanent settlement areas and a northern frontier of military expeditions, mainly with male equipment.

organisation observable from Ha D2–3, just as the eastern amber trading network was disturbed, but only for a relatively short time. How do we interpret these events – as warriors groups on the lookout for booty due to pressure and crisis at home, roaming around for years, or as a much briefer, planned, military operation aimed at getting access not only to booty but also to trade? There are proponents of both interpretations. The lack of subsequent settlement expansion and migration perhaps favours the second hypothesis.

This leads us on to the East Hallstatt residences in Slovenia. Here we find another group of Scythian male burials, with horse gear and arrows, during the late 6th and early 5th centuries BC. They are found in quite high-ranking warrior burials, some with genuine Scythian equipment, others with local imitations. Rather than conquest, for which there is little settlement evidence, this pattern points to the employment of Scythian mercenaries in the service of the Hallstatt princes, e.g. at Magdalenska Gora, Stična and other residences, with the burials representing their chiefs or officers, while the local elite adopted some of the equipment as well. As there were regular contacts from an early time, this explanation seems likely.

The westward expansion of the Scythians was one element of the macrohistorical dynamics that linked events in the Near East with those in Central Europe. It demonstrates that the scale of historical processes – their causes and effects – goes beyond autonomous regional studies. What, then, were the consequences, and what structural regularities may we infer from tracing this chain of events? The answer to that cannot be given until we have discussed the fall of the royal Hallstatt centres and the changes taking place in western and northern Europe at the same time.

Conclusion 7

From the Black Sea through the Balkans to the northern Alps we encounter the same phenomenon: along the borders of the 'civilised' world there developed a new type of direct political and economic relations between centres and barbarian peripheries, based on an unequal exchange of prestige goods (and a new life style linked to them) for industrial products needed in the Mediterranean: iron, silver, amber and gold, plus horses, slaves and perhaps even mercenaries. These new possibilities were taken advantage of by entrepreneurial chiefs, using the new contacts and prestige goods not only to enrich themselves and their families but also to break down the old order and build up a new political structure that encouraged exploitation and demands for tribute to increase (Figure 153). These goals were achieved in the 'normal' ways: by demonstrating their new positions, contacts and life style in rich 'princely' burials, or *Prunkgräber* (Kossack 1974) , thereby distancing themselves from traditional values and probably also from traditional kin-based systems of rank. Their new social arrangements worked by attaching other chiefs to them as vassals, giving them access to the new wealth and life style, by employing warriors to secure their positions, and by redefining rituals to serve their needs. These rituals would later take on excessive forms, as contradictions and pressures rose.

Did it represent a 'hellenisation' of Europe? The answer is no. As pointed out by Büchsenschütz (1988b) for Central Europe, the differences between the two worlds were too great, which on the other hand was part of the attraction. This contradiction became fatal north of the Alps: the Mediterranean wine and olive economy, in combination with slave labour, allowed the formation of urban centres with an affluent middle and upper class of free, landowning citizens, craft specialists patronised by them, and also merchants. North of the Alps the traditional temperate farming economy was based on animal husbandry and grain growing, which in the long run could not sustain a growing elite, as neither could the ecology. The social and economic exploitation needed to acquire these foreign prestige goods, foods and habits had a price, not least if slave raiding was part of the system (Arnold 1988). Therefore Hallstatt society was unstable, as we shall see in the next section (in opposition to the preceding millennium, when Central Europe and the Mediterranean shared the same economy, with the exception of the Greek world). The situation was slightly different in the Balkans and on the Black Sea. The Balkan economy gradually adjusted to the Mediterranean, and here we find continuity right up to the 4th century, when Philip II of Macedon and the Celts put an end to royal elites in this part of the world as well. In the steppes the demographic and ecological balance (for both people and animals) was also delicate, but warfare and spatial mobility kept it stable in the long term, allowing the social structure to be reproduced endlessly.

The formation of centre–periphery relations along the border of the classical world

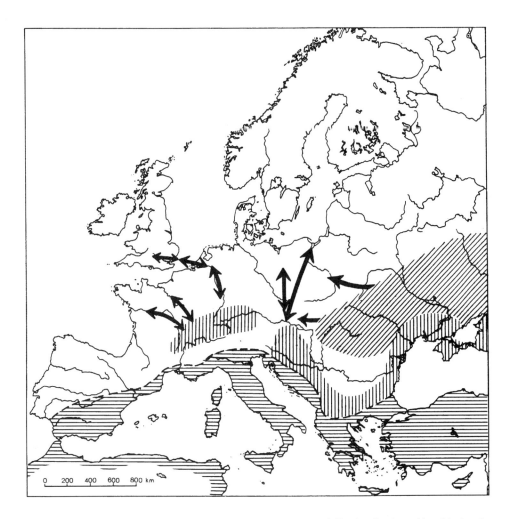

Fig. 153 Map of Europe showing the distribution of Mediterranean civilisation (horizontal hatching) and its primary periphery of royal barbarian burials and residences (vertical hatching). The Scythian area of influence is shown by oblique hatching. Solid arrows indicate major routes of trade and contact with the North European hinterlands.

(Figure 153) also had internal effects, as we have seen, leading to the formation of local relations of centre and periphery. It had at least two consequences: it introduced a higher level of political centralisation and exploitation, which meant that European societies entered a more dynamic stage in their development, characterised by frequent shifts of dominance, linked to local and regional competition and warfare. Also, revolts by exploited regions or population groups, the identity of these altering with migrations, were from now on familiar events. This new dynamic was illustrated by the two turbulent centuries of the Hallstatt phenomenon, from 600 to 400 BC, including its final decline and the takeover by the former periphery – a classic sequence, repeated many times throughout history. Another consequence of this development was the formation of larger zones of underdevelopment beyond the newly prosperous princely periphery (Figure 154). It meant that developments in the new 'tyrannies' of Central Europe stopped the flow of goods to northern and western Europe – sucked it up, so to speak – until these regions were able to establish new lines of exchange, or alternatively to break down the monopolies of the princely zone of 'tyrannies'. As we shall see in the next section this was actually what happened, once again demonstrating how fragile the new structures were, after all.

Thus the 6th to 5th centuries BC were a period of large-scale social transformations in Europe north of the Alps.

6.3 Transformation and decline

Shifts of dominance: the decline of the royal residences and the beginning of La Tène
The cultural and chronological transition between Late Hallstatt and Early La Tène also represents a geographical shift of centres of wealth in the West Hallstatt area. It thus offers an opportunity to illuminate the dynamics of centre and periphery relations within the Hallstatt Culture itself, as well as its relation to the centres in Italy and at Massalia during the period of change.

To begin with we have to confront a chronological problem: the nature of the transition between the Ha D3 and La Tène A periods has some bearing on the historical and social changes. According to one interpretation Ha D3, in the area of the royal residences, runs partly parallel with La Tène A, in the area of chiefly wagon graves on the Rhine and in France (Zürn 1974). The alternative view is that the shift between Ha D3 and La Tène A is synchronous in both regions (for a summary see Gersbach 1981, Abb. 10). In the recent publication of Klein Aspergle, a princely burial in the Hohenasperg domain of La Tène A, Kimmig (1988b, 276 ff.) concludes after a careful analysis that the transition to La Tène A takes place at the same time in both areas, around 450–440 BC, after a brief phase of experimentation (termed proto-La Tène), reflected, for example, in the last phase at The Heuneburg (which others like Pauli 1984a prefer to see as reflecting influences from the La Tène style on the now conservative Hallstatt area). Kimmig stresses the importance of the Late Ha D residences for the initial development of La Tène A, although there is also general agreement that the final development of the Early La Tène style took place outside the Hallstatt residences, in the areas of Early La Tène warrior and wagon burials – west of the Rhine in Rheinpfalz, Lothringen, Champagne and the Hunsrück Eifel (Figure 129). This is important for the interpretation of its social and ethnic signifi-cance, a question to which we shall return.

According to this latest chronology several of the Hallstatt residences were given up around 450 BC or shortly thereafter (e.g. Mont Lassois, Chatillon-sur-Glane and The Heuneburg), some, like The Heuneburg, after a violent destruction. Those that were not abandoned lost their importance (a summary is given in Spindler 1983, 83, where Ha D3 and La Tène A probably should be separated). Only at Hohenasperg and at Uetliberg near Zürich did princely burials appear in La Tène A, and Kimmig (1988b, 284) even points out the close connection between them in some of the burial goods. At the other residences the royal burials disappear, and so do the

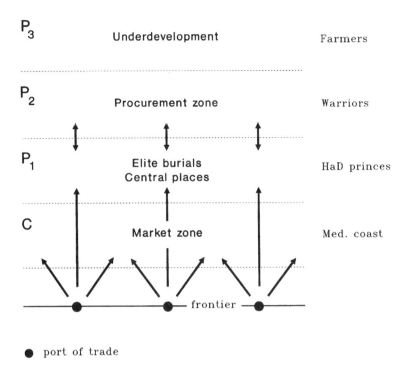

Fig. 154 Model of the structure of centre–periphery relations in Europe during the later Hallstatt period.

prestige goods from Italy and Greece. They are now found in less monumental, but still rich, warrior/wagon burials north of the Hallstatt residences (Lorenz 1985, fig. 6.2; Endert 1987). These burials represent the beginning of a new local style – La Tène – integrating the Mediterranean/Orientalising art styles into a new original design concept.

We can thus observe that after 450 BC the centres of rich burials with foreign imports moved geographically north of the Hallstatt residences, and at the same time a new cultural identity is beginning to form, to find its proper expression during the following period in the fully developed La Tène style. How are we to understand these changes?

First we should distinguish between the actual process of change and its causes. Ludwig Pauli (1980b; 1984a) and Bintliff (1984b) have most clearly put forward a scenario of internal revolts and opposition against the tyranny of the royal elites, whose exploitation had become too severe. Internal struggle mobilised the warrior retinues of the later La Tène A, which in the process destroyed the residences and took over the trade. Thus social and ecological overexploitation (internal causes) were the prime reasons for the loss of trade. Frankenstein and Rowlands (1978) instead stress a decline in the external trade relations, which undermined the ability of the Hallstatt kings to maintain political support among their vassals, again leading to internal competition and warfare (external causes).

A more complete understanding of the process of change from centre to periphery has been provided by Daphne Nash (1985). She takes as her point of departure the opposition between wealthy agrarian societies and more dynamic pastoral warrior societies, and describes their different organisation and social rationality as follows: 'The interdependence of the two principal forms of Celtic society was undoubtedly based upon their provision of complementary services for one another – the wealthier agrarian societies supplying wealth and opportunities for warfare, and the weaker warrior societies supplying military labour, slaves and raw materials' (1985, 50). She defines two centres of warrior expansion and their relation to Hallstatt residences: the Hunsrück–Eifel nobility (Haffner 1976; Haffner and Joachim 1984) linked to the Hohenasperg complex, and that of Champagne linked to the Mont Lassois complex (Endert 1984; 1987, Karte 5) (Figure 155). According to this model, the royal centres were able to expand their influence by creating a dynamic periphery of more distant warrior societies that raided their hinterlands to supply slaves to the centres for sale further on to Italy and Greece (Figure 156). They also served as mercenaries at the royal estates. In this way the royal centres were able to expand by exporting internal conflicts to the periphery, maintaining peaceful conditions at home. Instead they exploited their peasant populations, who were unarmed and therefore unable to revolt. It is clear that such a relationship was potentially dangerous if the goods fuelling it could no longer be supplied.

Nash argues that organised long-distance trade with Massalia declined at the end of Ha D as the interest of the Greeks in obtaining the products of Hallstatt chiefdoms dwindled in the face of changing economic and political conditions in the Mediterranean – among these were the consolidation of trade with Iberian towns and their own prosperous colonies in southern Italy, perhaps replacing some of the products delivered by the Hallstatt chiefs. The Celtic warriors may also have learned that they could sell their services as mercenaries more profitably to the Greeks and Etruscans themselves, and we know that they were already serving as mercenaries in the Hellenistic world by 390 BC. No matter what the underlying causes were the warrior Celts ran down the royal Hallstatt residences and now took over control of trade with the Etruscans (Figure 156B). The relationship was probably different from that of the Hallstatt chiefs, instead being based on personal contacts and service as mercenaries, bringing back home some of their spoils of war, at a time when the Etruscans were increasingly on the retreat. When there was finally no more to be gained from the relationship, they decided to take over and migrate, but this takes us too far forward in time.

Nash's model corresponds to our earlier finding that the settlements of the warrior periphery reflected another social and economic organisation (Figure 111), rooted in the former areas of Ha C warriors. It is therefore less important that there is perhaps no temporal overlap between Late Hallstatt D and Early La Tène, as one could have assumed five years ago, although Mont Lassois and Hohenasperg do continue into Early La Tène. Thus these relationships had old roots representing two basic organisational components in late-prehistoric Europe. For the first time it has been possible to elucidate their interaction over a time period in some detail, the implications of which we shall come back to. (According to our earlier model of the rise and

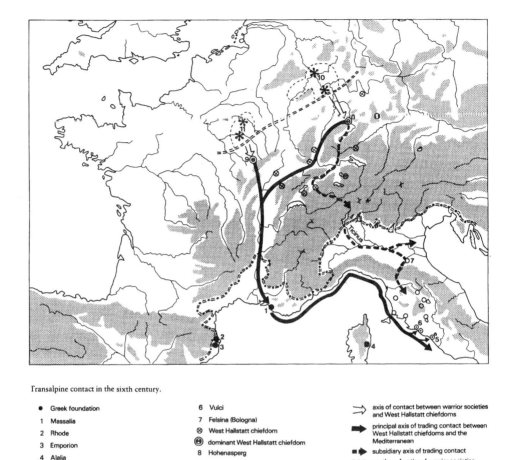

Transalpine contact in the sixth century.

●	Greek foundation	6	Vulci	→	axis of contact between warrior societies and West Hallstatt chiefdoms
1	Massalia	7	Felsina (Bologna)	➡	principal axis of trading contact between West Hallstatt chiefdoms and the Mediterranean
2	Rhode	⊗	West Hallstatt chiefdom		
3	Emporion	⊕	dominant West Hallstatt chiefdom	▪▶	subsidiary axis of trading contact
4	Alalia	8	Hohenasperg	= = =	southern frontier of warrior societies
○ ⊙	Etruscan city or outpost	9	Mont Lassois	=·=·=	frontier of generalised contact between Mediterranean cities and Celtic Europe
5	Caere	✳	centre of warrior expansion		
		10	Hunsrück-Eifel area		
		11	Champagne		

Fig. 155 Transalpine contacts in the 6th century BC between Mediterranean city states, Ha D residences and their warrior periphery.

consolidation of chiefly elites, it might have been expected that the Hallstatt residences consolidated their position during La Tène, with therefore less need to invest in rich burials, allowing the periphery to develop, this reflecting the expanding influence of the residences. As we have seen, however, this alternative is not supported by the archaeological evidence.)

How does this interpretation relate to Kimmig's conclusion that the very earliest La Tène style originated in the Late Hallstatt residences, or had its basis there, because only here existed the necessary number of skilled specialists and materials (gold, bronze, Italian imports)? Kimmig is absolutely correct. But it also follows that the only way the new centres of Early La Tène could have continued the development of the style was by taking over the specialists of the former residences. It links their decline and the rise of La Tène warrior peripheries intrinsically to each other.

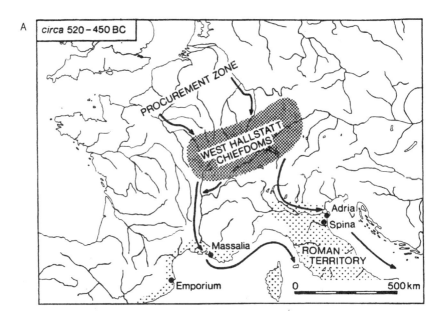

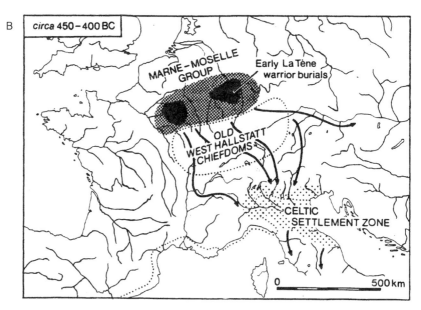

Fig. 156 Political-economic developments in Western Central Europe 550–400 BC. In (A) the arrows indicate movements of trade goods, reflecting a stable situation of centre–periphery relations; in (B) they represent migrations, indicating a situation of disruption and takeover by the former periphery.

The craft specialists of proto- or Early La Tène art were removed from the centres and spread out to work for the Celtic warrior chiefs (whether voluntarily or taken as 'booty'). It was only here that the development of a new, original, La Tène style – in opposition to the imitation of Hallstatt items, – developed. The warrior Celts allowed the artisans to experiment, in order to create a new cultural and artistic identity for themselves as a new dominant group. During the first phase this consisted of mixing Oriental/Scythian motifs (e.g. at Klein Aspergle, there is still a conflation of well-known motifs, with little sign of La Tène originality), but with a growing self-consciousness and opposition between the La Tène warrior societies and the Mediterranean world their style came to reflect this. La Tène art thus developed on the same basis as both Scythian and late Germanic art – as a self-conscious reflection of an independent identity in opposition to the former centres of domination. However, this discussion will be taken up again in the next chapter on the Celtic expansion. Before doing so we shall consider the effects of the development of the West Hallstatt culture on societies further north and west. Did they also experience decline and reorganisation and if so what was the cause?

The northeast: Biskupin and the decline of the Lausitz culture

The famous and extraordinarily well-preserved fortification of Biskupin from the 7th/6th century BC (Figure 157), with its systematic layout, was the result of a planned effort on the part of a large community of 1,000–1,200 people. It looks like a well-organised cooperative of equal farmers, yet I believe that it represented the final, critical, stage in the development of societies of the Lausitz culture, just before its disruption and fragmentation. Unfortunately a final publication for Biskupin itself has not yet appeared (preliminary reports are available, Kostrzewski 1950), but due to intensive and systematic excavations and research during the past twenty-five years on the Lausitz settlement system of Poland and the former DDR it is now possible to draw up a quite detailed picture of its development and final decline. It may further serve as a comparative case study for understanding the role of fortifications. In the following we shall concentrate on the final phase of the Lausitz culture based on case studies of the Billendorf Culture (Buch 1979; 1986b; 1989) and of the northern Lausitz culture in Poland (Ostorja-Zagorski 1974; 1980; 1982; 1983; 1986; 1989).

Through the duration of the Lausitz culture we can observe a development in the role and layout of fortified settlements, linked to increased settlement and population densities and changes in social organisation (Niesiolowska-Wedzka 1974). During the early phase (Ha B) the fortified settlements were large, and served as multifunctional centres for a larger group of open-land settlements. During Ha C there is a tendency towards smaller forts and a division of function – some hillforts served as central places, many being located on important communication lines, while others are situated at the periphery of settlement groups (defensively?). The fortifications seem to form clusters or groupings (confederations?). During the final phase of Ha D/Early La Tène the tendency towards smaller fortifications and smaller settlement units continues, but now they are in several areas in northeast Poland the only form of settlement, representing a remarkable concentration of population. It probably reflects the fragmentation or collapse of an earlier larger political structure of a more scattered and diverse settlement pattern, protected by a single centre. Now each community had to protect itself. The location of some hillforts in inaccessible places also suggests disruption. The Lausitz fortifications thus display a sequence of

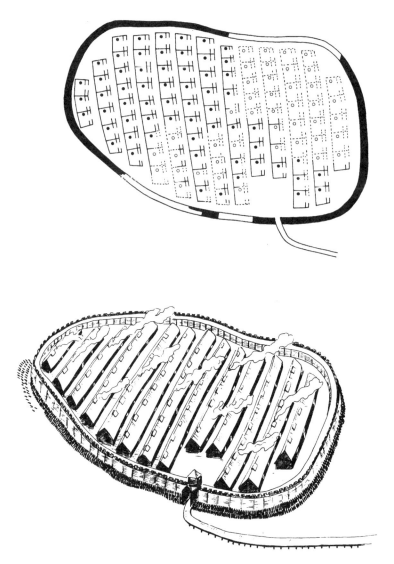

Fig. 157 Ground plan and reconstruction of the fortified village settlement at Biskupin in Poland from the late Hallstatt period.

changes in the functioning of forts – from central places of a large settlement area, towards groupings of fortifications in confederations (Gediga 1981) and the final fragmentation into many small tightly packed farming communities, such as Biskupin, apparently reflecting a period of social and economic crisis (Ostorja-Zagorski 1980). This general picture can be supplemented by detailed local studies of settlement organisation, economy and ecology in northern Poland and in the Billendorf culture.

The Billendorf culture was situated north of the eastern Hallstatt, and we have earlier described its role in the amber trade, leading to social and economic development, adopting many Hallstatt features during Ha C/early Ha D. Social hierarchy,

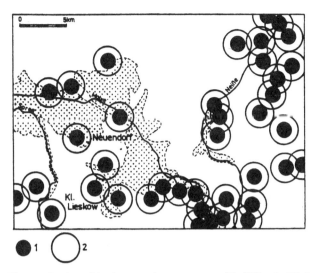

Fig. 158 Section of the dense settlement system of the Billendorf Culture, with proposed subsistence areas for farming (black inner circle) and forestry (outer circle).

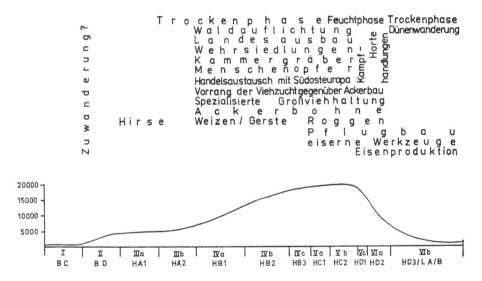

Fig. 159 Summary diagram showing changes in social-economic and ecological conditions during the rise and decline of the late Lausitz culture in the Billendorf group.

economic specialisation, e.g. cattle farming, and the introduction of iron testify to a development of social and economic complexity, which, however, in the end could not be sustained by the economy. In its latest phase the Billendorf culture displays a remarkable decline, which has been traced in detail by Buch (Figures 158, 159). It was due to a complex combination of factors, but among the most important were over-exploitation of soils, leading to degradation, loss of productivity and the spread of sand dunes during the decline of the 5th century. Soils in the open land of the

Lausitz culture are in many areas quite light, and therefore not resistant to intensive use. As demographic growth had been rapid (a tripling in 400 years) the settlement system exploited all suitable land, though avoiding areas with few natural water resources or deep-lying groundwater (Buch 1979, Abb. 2). The smaller community fortifications were apparently employed during the latest settlement expansion, taking in the last suitable tracts of land under increasing social and economic pressure. By the middle to late 6th century Scythian raids had destroyed some of the eastern fortifications, and cut off the amber trade, but since the western settlements that were not affected by the Scythian raids still declined later, we must give internal causes the priority. After 550/500 BC (Ha D2/Early La Tène) the crisis accelerated, leading to warfare, disruption of fortifications and depopulation. The fortified settlements were no longer properly maintained, and by La Tène times the population had settled in small hamlets, and some may eventually have migrated. The economy was now based on agriculture rather than cattle husbandry. In the process of change the Billendorf culture disappeared by adopting the new cultural identity of the Jasdorf culture, which was linked to this kind of social organisation, prevailing in the north European lowlands during La Tène.

A similar process has been documented in northern Poland by Ostorja-Zagorski, employing palaeo-economic data. Here also the Hallstatt period corresponded to an era of rapid social and economic development and prosperity, followed by decline, fragmentation and reorganisation after 500 BC. It can be demonstrated that the economy of the fortified settlements was based on specialised intensive farming, a kind of garden cultivation, in order to extract the necessary produce for the densely populated settlements (Figure 160). Legumes were widely cultivated, the most common being the pea. Beans and lentils were also grown. Climatic changes and the decline of productivity reduced the productive potential, and thereby undermined the economic organisation of the closely packed fortified farming communities, as their catchment areas could no longer sustain them. At Biskupin the changes in climate after 700 BC, when the fortification was settled (from 650 to 500 BC according to dendrochronology, Miklaszewska-Balcer 1991) led to a rise in the groundwater level of 2 m, which was disastrous for both the settlement and its subsistence basis. With the decentralisation of settlement after the fortified settlement communities gave up, the population adopted the Pommeranian culture (see Chapter 6.1), as it was already linked to such a social and economic organisation.

In the Lausitz area east of the Oder cultural developments were linked to those of the eastern Hallstatt. Here long-distance exchange (the amber route) and increasing populations were able to expand their productivity and maintain a centralised social organisation, though under increasing economic and social pressure from Ha D2/3. After adopting still smaller and more densely packed fortified settlements, which developed a highly refined farming technique, widespread collapse and fragmentation occurred after 500/450 BC. A more extensive land-use pattern based on family farms, as in the northwest European lowlands, came to dominate from La Tène onwards, leading to a concomitant change in material and spiritual culture. One may raise the question of whether some of the rather drastic population falls observed

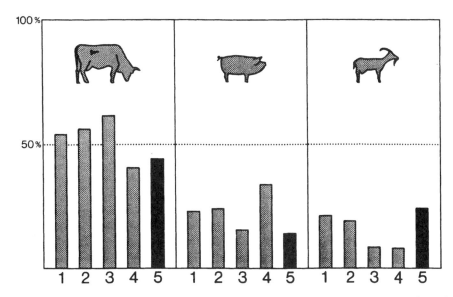

Fig. 160 Animal bones at Lausitz settlements of Biskupin type showing the relative proportions of cattle, pig and sheep/goat.

after 500 BC could have been directed towards the Hallstatt residences. Some of the changes were facilitated, however, by taking over the social and cultural identity of the Jasdorf culture, to be described in the next section.

The west: Danebury and the development of English hillforts
In the Atlantic and Nordic zones of Ha C, with the exception of the Thames valley, swords and new traditions in metalwork ran parallel to the continuation of traditional metalwork of BF III and Montelius V, whose late phase of Nordic ornaments in the grand style continued into the early phase of Ha C (Höchmann 1987), while in France the Hallstatt sword appears in a few of the latest hoards of the Carps Tongue tradition of BF III (Pautreau 1989, 242). Ha C culture was adopted by the local elites, as it expanded from the West Hallstatt core areas (Roymans 1991, 36), reflected in imitations of the Hallstatt sword in England (Burgess 1979), rather than these being a prototype, as suggested by Schauer (1971). Only from the mature Ha C (around 700 BC) do the shifts in ritual traditions and in metalwork manifest themselves.

In the Atlantic zone, from Ireland to France, the large composite hoards disappear and are replaced by many fewer and smaller hoards of regular sets of weapons/axes, in Britain termed the Llyn Fawr phase (Burgess 1979; Thomas 1989). In France the large Armorican axe hoards are another feature of this period; most of the axes in hoards are unused, in this respect resembling some of the English axes. The distribution of metalwork in southern England displays an interesting regional displacement: the Bronze Age tradition of deposition moved to Wessex, in southern England, while foreign Hallstatt and related metalwork concentrated in the Thames area, the traditional centre. It seems that bronze was distributed to the periphery, or simply taken over, while iron production dominated the Thames area. Wessex developed contacts with France, e.g. Armorican axes, both being areas of retarded Bronze Age tradition. Axes seem to take on a new function as primitive currency, becoming ritualised. Hillforts, such as Danebury, Maiden Castle, etc.,were founded, and the whole of southern England seems to experience a development of social and economic organisation (Cunliffe 1982a), which was to continue until the 1st century BC, as well as trade with northwestern France (Cunliffe 1982b). A new distinctive pottery style also developed to identify the new network. While the Thames area had formerly held a monopoly of trade, two parallel networks now developed: a Hallstatt C network between the Thames and Belgium and an archaic Bronze Final network between Wessex and northwestern France, based on hillforts and pastoral production. Recent evidence from the Thames area confirms this picture: the complex Late Bronze Age settlement system, integrating lowland and highland production, collapsed by Ha C. It was replaced by a more localised settlement system with lowland grazing in the central settlement area and fields around that, integrating the former regional division of production within the local settlement structure (Miles personal communication). From Middle La Tène onwards centralisation takes over, as a few hillforts grow at the expense of several smaller ones that are abandoned. These developed hillforts, surrounded by an organised landscape of individual farms and field systems, are exemplified by Danebury, a nearly completely excavated hillfort – the Heuneburg of England (Cunliffe 1983).

In several influential works during the late 1970s and early 1980s Barry Cunliffe has promoted a new understanding of the development of hillforts in southern England and the adjacent French coastal regions (1976; 1982b; 1983). This is based on the systematic inventory of hillforts in Britain carried out during the past twenty-five years, as well as excavations in and around Danebury, which represent a complete sequence of a hillfort and its environment (Cunliffe 1983). This led to, and was itself part of, an upsurge of theoretical and methodological discussions about the interpretation of hillforts and their role during the same period (Cunliffe and Rowley (eds.) 1976; Green, Hazelgrove and Spriggs (eds.) 1978; Burnham and Kingsbury (eds.) 1979; Grant 1986). The hillforts of southern England developed between 700 and 100 BC, beginning in Wessex and expanding northwards and westwards after 400 BC (Cunliffe 1982b, fig. 3). During the period 600–400 BC densely packed hillforts emerged in Wessex, in the Danebury area with distances of only 10 km between each (Figure 161). At Danebury all its later characteristics are present from the beginning – granaries, round houses along the sides and a central rectangular cult house, a significant difference from the normal round houses for living. Cult and square settings belonged together, as later seen in the *viereckschanzen*. By 400 BC a major reorganisation and geographical expansion of hillforts had taken place: in the settled areas, such as Danebury, their numbers dwindled, with the remaining sites having their fortifications strengthened, as well as their distribution becoming even more dense (Figure 162). Thus the first phase of local competition between smaller entities concluded with a strengthening of political centralisation and leadership. This is the period of complex hillforts, which continued down to 100 BC, after which time many

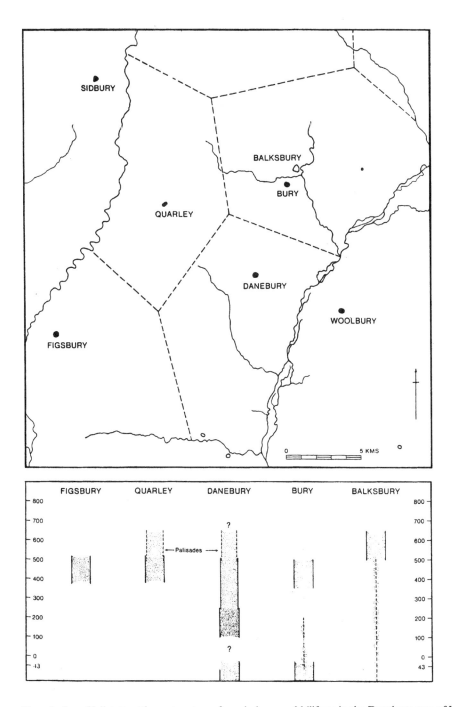

Fig. 161 Late Hallstatt settlement system of regularly spaced hillforts in the Danebury area of Wessex. Below, chronological chart showing the major phases during which the fortifications were maintained.

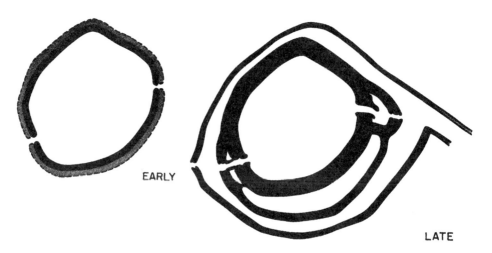

EARLY

LATE

Fig. 162 The development of Danebury from a simple to a complex hillfort.

were given up, as trade moved to the Thames The commercial and political centres were reduced to a few large forts, such as Maiden Castle, taking on the functions of oppida (Cunliffe 1988, 98 ff. and 147 ff.). Whether one should see it as a decline or a final centralisation is probably open to debate.

The excavations at Danebury have made its functions reasonably clear: according to Cunliffe it represented a centre for the collection of tribute, in the form of grain storage, production and trade, both local and cross-Channel. Granaries that had gone out of use were employed for occasional burials. Air photos and smaller excavations have established that the surrounding farm landscape was one of field systems and regularly spaced farm buildings (Figure 163). All in all this was a densely packed and intensively exploited landscape, with an emphasis on grain growing. There is no sign of elite residences within the fortifications, instead the elite lived on large farms outside the walls (Audouze and Büchsenschütz 1992). Other forts, especially the earlier ones before 600 BC, which were often larger, suggest a heavier emphasis on animal husbandry. Thus agriculture came to play an increasingly important role over time, as a basis for maintaining the forts and their activities, among them a retinue of warriors to defend the stronghold, and labour crews to maintain the fort. Enslaved clients probably made up the labour force, if they were not sold as slaves during the late phase, when trade with the Romans became more prominent. This might be one of the reasons for the geographical spread of hillforts after 400 BC, as groups tried to protect themselves against slave raiding, and instead enter into a social and economic relationship with the leading coastal forts.

The territorial organisation of the hillforts within a political territory is displayed in the emergence of local pottery groups, linking the formation of ethnicity, political centralisation and cultural identity closely to one another (Figure 164). It further confirms the competitive situation, clearly defining 'us' against 'them'. In his interpretation of the social and political structure Cunliffe applied written sources, both Caesar and late medieval Irish texts, to construct a model of a hierarchical social

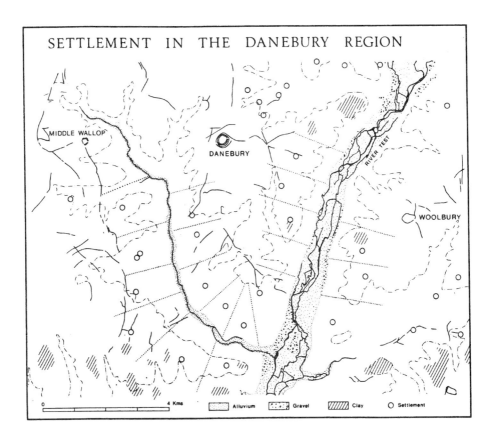

Fig. 163 The local context of a hillfort: Danebury and its surrounding landscape of regularly spaced settlements; the dotted lines represent theoretical boundaries between different farms.

order conforming to the pattern on the ground in the overall layout of the evidence, where hillforts provided a legal and religious focus for the community as well as an economic centre (Figure 165). According to Cunliffe (1983, 154):

> If this is really what was happening at Danebury, it would explain the enhanced storage capacity, the temples, the metal-working activity, the emphasis on weaving, the iron ingots and salt containers, and the weight standards. Individually these classes of evidence could be explained away and it could be argued that much of the activity is also found on contemporary farmsteads. This is so, but all the evidence taken together and the sheer intensity of activity at Danebury in the late period compared to what was going on in the countryside around, provides very strong circumstantial evidence to suggest that developed hillforts like Danebury performed an important redistributive function in articulating the exchange systems in society.

This interpretation has come under critical examination in recent years, as it should (Hazelgrove 1986; Grant 1986; Collis 1986; Hill 1993 and 1996): the value of the

A

B

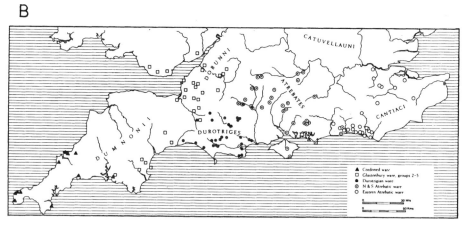

Fig. 164 Pottery styles in southern Britain, suggesting a development from smaller (A) to larger (B) cultural and political entities. A = 5th–3rd centuries BC, B = 1st century BC–1st century AD.

literary evidence has been doubted on source critical grounds, although as a hypothesis it may be just as good, or better, than any more freely constructed hypothesis. After all the past twenty years have given archaeological confirmation to an astonishing number of early writers from Herodotus to Caesar, to a degree that no traditional historians raised in the source critical tradition would have dared to expect. The

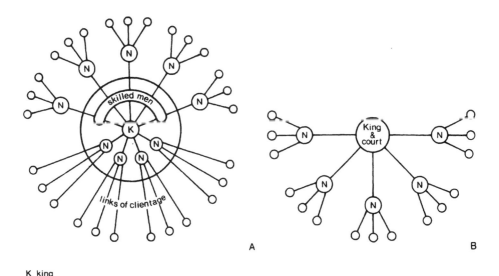

K king
N noble
○ freemen farmers

Fig. 165 Alternative models of the social structure at Danebury: (A) assumes the king, his followers, and some nobles reside in the fort; (B) assumes that only the king and his followers are resident.

central-place interpretation and its hierarchical implications for leadership are now also questioned. However, given the knowledge we have about the complexity of social organisation around the time of the birth of Christ, it demands a historical background of some length – and that is exactly what the hillfort sequence offers. When we add to this the comparative sequences from Lausitz and the West Hallstatt, I find Cunliffe's interpretation convincing.

The north: Grøntoft and the development of family farms and villages

Let us now turn again to northern Europe, which displays a diverging pattern of development. In the Nordic area paired sets of twisted neck-rings became the standard deposition during Ha C, now solely on moors, pointing to its ritual character. The old Nordic style gradually died out and was replaced by cruder ornaments in the form of large hollow rings (Schacht 1982), twisted neck-rings, and some simple iron neck-rings, more like bars than rings (Baudou 1960, Karte 36–37). In burials the Hallstatt toilet equipment was introduced, as well as new pin types (Baudou 1960, Karte 24, 42–43). During Ha C there are still some depositions of horse gear (*phalera*) and axes, but there is much to suggest that the specialist workshops disappeared during Ha D. It has further been proposed that most of the large lurs, the most complicated and costly bronze instruments, in both terms of casting and use (for ritual processions), were deposited during this late period (Ha C–D), reflecting disruption and unrest in connection with the decline of ritual authority. From Ha D there are virtually no signs of southern imports, in opposition to the lands east of the Oder, and depositions are rare, except for a group of solid twisted neck-rings. The late neck-rings are all extremely worn, confirming that lack of bronze was the real problem behind the decline of specialist production, not elite consolidation and a changed pattern of deposition. It is strongly reminiscent of a 'Dark Age', where burial traditions, ritual and metalwork changed, as well as settlement and the social organisation of production.

A new dominant ideology emerged from these changes: with the decline of chiefly prestige-goods production and long-distance exchange the whole rationality of society had to alter. The large and complex rituals associated with Bronze Age social organisation were linked to the integration of ritual and rank, which made it difficult for ambitous chiefs to manipulate them – the rituals set limits, and the whole community participated in them. It gave them a double function: they maintained the eternal status of a ranked society as well as constraining its further development. With the standardisation of ritual depositions, and finally their decline, we must envisage that this represented a similar change in the ritual role and authority of the chiefs. The chief and his followers, living in large longhouses and with freely grazing herds, now disappeared. Instead the farmer and the wider community become ritually visible: urnfields appear over a large area of northwestern Germany and Jutland, termed the Jasdorf culture (Lorenzen and Steffgen 1990 with summary of literature), indirectly inspired by Hallstatt D material culture in pins and small ornaments; later it took on La Tène influences. This culture became the new identity for the lowland societies of northwestern Europe from 600/550 BC onwards down to the Roman period. In opposition to the area east of the Oder, it reflected the formation of a new regional identity involving little contact with the Hallstatt culture, which had already ceased by late Ha C. Now the transformations following from this break of cultural interaction were being completed. However, the changes that took place during these centuries, especially after 600 BC, were also rooted in new conditions of production (for summaries see Kristiansen 1980; Hedeager and Kristiansen 1988; Hedeager 1992; Jensen in press).

During the Late Bronze Age the ecological balance had changed towards less productive open pastures, characterised by soil degradation (Figure 166). Settlement clustered, and the houses became smaller, adapted to individual families. By 500/450 this change in social organisation, settlement and production had taken place, reflected in the appearance of Celtic fields all over northwestern Europe (Müller-Wille 1965). At the same time small villages with family farms keeping stalled cattle appeared (Figures 167 and 168), allowing the collection of dung for fertilising the fields. It was a means of restoring productivity after 2,000 years of unregulated crop rotation and overgrazing by large free-roaming herds, which had degraded the soils. Now rotation and grazing were controlled, and land ownership, or rights of disposition, was the basis of wealth and power. In burial ritual communal urnfields with little or no indications of status difference reflect the new social organisation, in which chiefs were invisible (Figure 167). A few votive depositions of large neck-rings suggest that chiefs might still have existed. The ideology is one of equality, which may of course not have been real, but none the less was close to the truth, as the settlement evidence shows. It shared many basic traits with Urnfield society. With this new social organisation as a basis, settlement expansion began onto the heavier

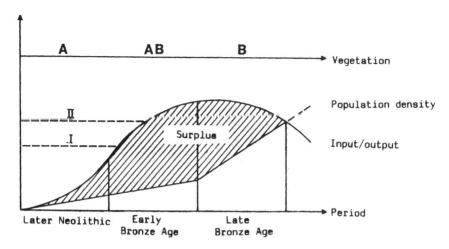

Fig. 166 Model of the relationship between population density/settlement density, ecological change and surplus production from the Late Neolithic to the transition to the Iron Age in southern Scandinavia: A = open secondary forest with grassland; B = open grassland with scattered secondary forest.

soils, and it did not stop until the time of the birth of Christ, when the landscape was completely filled out, and a new chiefly elite once again emerged.

During these centuries of the Pre-Roman Iron Age many local traditions developed, several of them later recognised by classical writers. This new territoriality was probably due to several factors: a decline in the intensity of long-distance exchange (a few Etruscan vessels from the 5th century were kept in circulation through the gap and placed in burials when trade was resumed during the late 2nd century BC), a social organisation linked to land rather than to movable wealth, and perhaps also a mobilisation of political and ethnic identity at the level of farming communities, the new building block of society. Some political and religious leadership must have been linked to these new territories, but it is not visible in the archaeological record until the last two centuries BC, although the remarkable deposition of a long boat and its warriors' weaponry in 350 BC at Hjortspring in south Jutland (Kaul 1988) confirms that organised armies/retinues, although small, were operating at this time. Sixty-nine lances (two to each man), just over fifty wooden shields, eleven swords and several sets of chain-mail give an idea of the organisation. There appears to have been a small group of officers and their retinues – each warrior bringing his personal equipment, as the weapons are not standardised. Local chiefs and their retinues joining together to form a larger warband was the usual model of mobilisation.

Conclusion 8

Settlement variation
We have now traced three regional sequences of hillfort development, and one of farmsteads and villages. This presents an opportunity for comparison and discussion of apparent regularities and their causes.

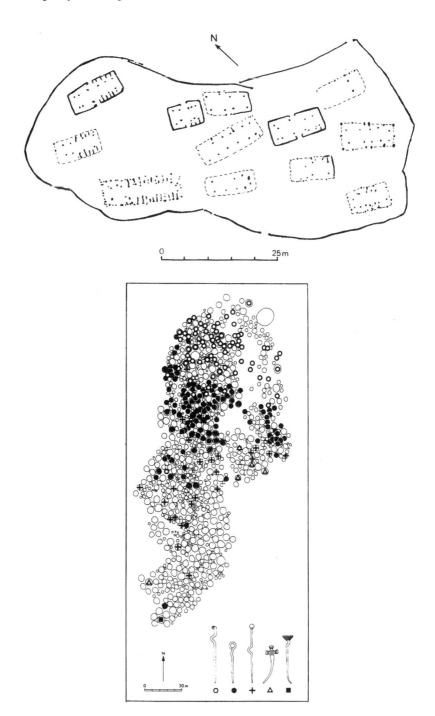

Fig. 167 Ground plan of Pre-Roman village at Grøntoft, western Jutland, and urnfield cemetery with simple grave goods.

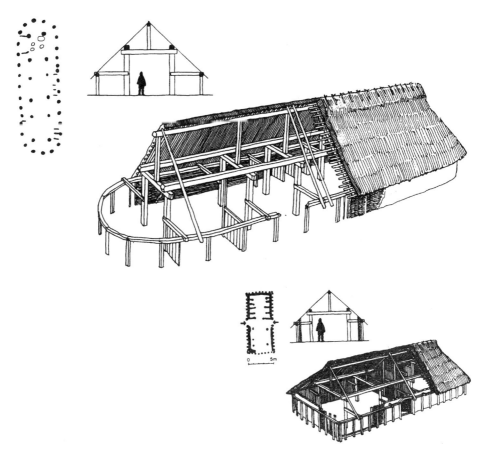

Fig. 168 Ground plan and reconstruction of Bronze Age clan house, (300 m²) and Early Iron Age family farm (100 m²), reflecting the fundamental social and economic changes taking place in the North European lowlands and Southern Scandinavia between the Bronze and Iron Ages.

The Heuneburg and similar Late Hallstatt residences represent a brief episode. They were based on a direct centre–periphery relationship of trade, and exploited their own hinterlands for these purposes. Both factors led to its destruction. The economy and the political organisation were not yet geared to establishing such a clear division of labour and social classes, supported by warriors and peasants. In reality there were two choices: to become Hellenised – by adopting the Mediterranean economy and social organisation – or to retain social and economic independence, like the early La Tène warrior chiefs who took over the area. The Hallstatt residences did neither, for only by Late La Tène was the economy geared to sustain larger 'urban' populations, having adopted some Mediterranean technologies and techniques, although part of that was transmitted by the Hallstatt residences. This was their historical mission.

Biskupin and the Lausitz forts illustrate a long-term historical process of hillfort development; in the initial phase under conditions of settlement expansion and demographic growth, in the later phase characterised by blocked expansion, continued demographic growth and ecological degradation. These contradictory trends resulted in the collapse of central authority under increasing economic and political stress, in some areas leading to a packing of the whole population into small, fortified, settlements. Such a development, from redistribution to simple reproduction, is known from other times and places in history, from the Far East (Friedman 1975) to Peru (Earle *et al.* 1987), where it is linked to devolutionary processes of blocked expansion in areas with too little productive capacity for state formation – the main alternative in such circumstances (Carneiro 1970). The Lausitz peasant forts were probably not totally autonomous, although nearly self-sufficient, but we have yet to see central chiefly residences. In the end fragmentation was completed by migration and the settlement expansion of family groups that were able to sustain themselves under the altered ecological conditions. The Lausitz forts took part in long-distance trade between Pommerania and the eastern Hallstatt and the Etruscans, but in opposition to the Hallstatt residences this was an indirect relationship, and central settlements did not depend on it for their survival.

Danebury and the southern English hillforts represent another long-term sequence, but this time apparently without a final decline; instead they give way to a few central oppida in the end. The sequence here is therefore reversed – from many smaller hillforts towards more complex and larger hillforts, in the end taken over by just one or two. It represents an evolution of central authority and 'protection', making the many early hillforts obsolete, as they arose in a situation of local competition and warfare. 'Industrialisation'/cross–Channel trade and a development from a pastoral towards an agrarian economy was probably the background to this successful development, which only slowed shortly before the Roman occupation.

Finally, the northwest European sequence exemplified the transformation of a Bronze Age chiefly, tribal settlement into individual family farms and villages with a regulated land-use. It was a response to two millennia of ecological transformation and the degradation of land by free-grazing herds of cattle/sheep and crop rotation. The new organisation of production provided more labour to feed the stalled animals and to fertilise the fields, as well as the development of new agrarian technologies, including the formation of hay meadows to replace forest products. This new organisation represented the beginning of a long-term sequence of settlement expansion, intensification and a gradual development of political centralisation from the 1st century BC. The northwest European sequence further shows how a decentralised settlement system without fortifications may support the development of a centralised political organisation, which culminated only in the 1st millennium AD, and which came to characterise much of Europe north of the Rhine/Danube.

The three sequences (Figure 169) illustrate several of the theoretical developments of hillforts proposed by John Collis (1982). They probably exemplify historical regularities to be found elsewhere in the world, and in both later and earlier periods of European history. Only in one case, that of the Hallstatt residences, were trade and craft production seen as causally linked to the formation of the fortified settlements. In the other situations internal forces of social, demographic and ecological developments were responsible for both the rise and decline of central settlements, as

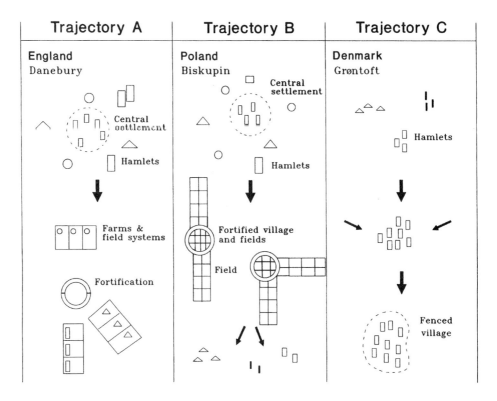

Fig. 169 Three settlement trajectories from Late Bronze Age to Early Iron Age in northern Europe.

vigorously argued by Bintliff (1986). It demonstrates the special nature of prestige goods trade as part of direct centre–periphery relations. But – and there is a but – without the need for a centralised organisation of industrial production, long-distance trade and local redistribution, there would be no need for central settlements. Wealth and specialist production are always linked to them except in their decline (the Biskupin phase).

I suggest there are two variants: one where control is physically linked to the central settlement, all industrial production taking place within its boundaries; and one where control is more developed, allowing some industrial production outside the fortified settlement, lower down the ranks, as in the Heuneburg and Danebury sequences. In the first variant the elite lived within the fortification, on an acropolis. In the second they settled on large estates outside the walls. With reference to the Grøntoft sequence, I also suggest that if control can be maintained by other means, e.g. strong retinues of mobile warriors, there is less need for fortified settlements, as in lowland northern Europe and in Central Europe during Hallstatt C and Early La Tène. In such a social environment only small chiefly residences can be fortified. It probably reflected an ability to mobilise warriors in critical situations, along chiefly lines of kinship and clientship. Celtic migrations were never directed towards northern Europe, perhaps for the very same reasons, although others were equally strong, as we shall see in the next chapter. This brings us to the impact of pastoral warriors.

Although the Scythian expansion had some effect on developments in the eastern Hallstatt and Lausitz, we can hardly attribute all changes to them, as has often been argued. They influenced warfare, both as mercenaries and by military organisation. They may have helped to set in motion internal contradictions already under way, and their presence could well have been used by the Early La Tène warrior elites in internal struggles. This would account for the indisputable Scythian component in Early La Tène art (Fischer 1988; Kruta 1988; Buchholz 1980), although political alliances could produce the same effects. However, the few Scythian arrowheads in the western Hallstatt (Sulimirski 1961, Abb. 1) can be taken to support a military presence (despite some claims of local origins, such arrowheads are too specifically linked to Scythian warfare and military practice to have been produced locally or traded). In Asia Minor they are the only trace of their large military campaigns, and the historically well attested raids west of the Danube by the Huns in the 5th century AD (Werner 1956), and by the Hungarians in the 9th and 10th centuries (Schulze 1985, Abb. 4–9), did not produce enough evidence to allow such conclusions on purely archaeological grounds. Only by comparison with these historically documented sequences can a similar relationship to the Scythians be suggested during the 5th century BC. It leads on to a consideration of the relationship between warrior societies and agrarian societies.

Agrarian and warrior societies
We can now begin to see the outlines of another regularity during the 1st millennium BC – that between stable agrarian societies, often with a hierarchical settlement structure, including hillforts, and more mobile warrior societies, with less need for fortified settlements. On a larger regional and macro-historical level it is represented by the contradictory relationship between pastoral warriors of the steppe and Central and western European agrarian societies – the border zone of both battles and mutual relationships always being in Hungary, at the River Tisza. It represents a macro-historical regularity, from the Late Neolithic Kurgan culture through the Cimmerians, Scythians, Sarmatians, Huns and Hungarians, to the Mongols and Turks, all of whom strongly influenced developments in Europe beyond the Danube, by periodic conquest migrations, or by the diffusion and takeover of new weapons and military strategies – thereby stimulating internal dynamics, as happened during Ha B3, with consequences in Ha C and perhaps also in La Tène A. At the local level this opposition between warrior societies and stable agrarian societies was played out in the relationship between the Late Hallstatt residences and the Early La Tène warrior chiefs, exemplifying the actual process of change. During the later 1st millennium such shifts took place several times, as outlined by Härke (1982). I shall attempt to demonstrate later that these shifts were part of a long-term regularity in prehistoric Europe, which explains some of its resistance to becoming 'civilised'.

Thus, prior to the Celtic migrations, large-scale changes in settlement organisation, economy and social organisation had taken place throughout northern Europe, as a response to a demographic and ecological crisis, which in combination with the decline of long-distance prestige-goods exchange and a worsening of the climate led to the collapse of Bronze Age society and its ritualised chiefly organisation in the lowland zone of northern Europe. It represented the culmination of processes that had been under way for several generations, and which had now reached the land's social and ecological carrying capacity. During the 5th century BC northern Europe saw a new social and economic organisation based on land ownership and mobile armies. It meant there was less need for fortified central places, just as tribute was paid to local chiefs rather than to a centre. As there was little industrial production and trade beyond local and regional needs, none of the conditions for fortified settlements was present.

Cause and effect

When discussing which factors were responsible for the social transformations taking place in lowland northern Europe, it is difficult to establish the priority of external against internal causes, in part because the chronological synchronisation between the Hallstatt culture and northern Europe is still not quite secure. It seems, however, that the social and economic transformations towards a more decentralised economy based on family farms and land divisions were completed in the north by the beginning of La Tène. Everything from farmhouses to rituals signals equality and communality – the domestic unit of production, the family farm, had become the basic component of social organisation, and was therefore now ritually and socially visible. The same development came to characterise the Celtic migrations from 400 BC, which raises the question of whether these democratic movements were some-how interlinked by more than social and economic long-term forces of change.

The Age of Tyranny was the Greek's way of describing the two hundred years of royal rule, before the establishment of democracy in Athens around 500 BC. It is indeed remarkable how democratic ideologies swept over the ancient world from Athens to Italy (Rome later sent a delegation to Athens to learn about their constitution), northern Europe and finally the Hallstatt residences. Was this accidental; or did the events in Central and Northern Europe reach Greece as a whisper – or was it the other way round? We have seen earlier how the ideology of royal elites was able to spread from the Mediterranean to Central Europe. The period from 700 to 450 BC can be seen as the era of royal and despotic rule in Central Europe, the Mediterranean and the Near East, because conditions for its development were available at that time. It seems that in the same way it created the conditions for its own decline, by carrying exploitation too far in an environment that could not yet sustain an emerging state structure. But the Hallstatt residences also indirectly influenced northern and western Europe, by cutting off exchange with the northern periphery. From now on the evolutionary trajectories of Europe north and south of the Alps were separated. This division came to influence the course of later history profoundly from the Roman Empire onwards.

Transformation and expansion: the Celtic movement, 450–150 BC

7.1 The archaeological context of population movements

Migration in retrospect

With the Celtic migrations we approach a period of documented population movements. As such phenomena have been widely criticised in archaeology during the past twenty-five years, it is necessary to contextualise the concept historically and theoretically, in order to legitimise its reintroduction and integration into modern archaeology.

Diffusion and migrations are phenomena on a continuous scale of cultural and social interaction and change. Throughout the 1960s and 1970s such studies concentrated on developing our knowledge of the basic forms of such interaction – from reciprocal exchange through elite exchange/prestige-goods exchange to trade (Earle and Ericsson 1977; Renfrew 1975). It has, however, become increasingly clear that a prerequisite for such studies is a better understanding of the social formation and constitution of culture as a spatial phenomenon. From acknowledging the complexity of the problem (Hodder 1978), during the 1980s we have seen an increasing number of studies trying to delineate some of the mechanisms by which material culture is constituted and maintained as part of social and political strategies (e.g. Hodder 1982a; 1982b).

Since diffusion and migrations were among the most criticised explanatory concepts of so-called traditional archaeology; modern archaeology has not yet come to terms with them, either in archaeological or in theoretical terms. This section is a preliminary attempt to incorporate the geographical movement of social groups into the conceptual and explanatory framework of archaeology.[1] How do we delineate various types of migrations against such phenomena as elite exchange, trade and marriage alliances? Also, how do we account for such phenomena in structural and evolutionary terms? Before answering these questions it will be useful to discuss the background to the present situation in more detail.

Throughout the 1960s and 1970s a number of studies demonstrated the archaeological inconsistencies and inadequate theoretical status of prehistoric migrations and diffusion (Adams 1968; Binford 1968; Clark 1966; Malmer 1962; Myhre and Myhre 1972; Renfrew 1973; Vajda 1973–74). Although a number of studies that combined historical and archaeological sources could demonstrate convincing regularities between ethnic groups and material culture (Hachmann, Kossack and Kuhn 1962), this proved impossible in other cases (Clarke 1968, ch. 9; Hachmann 1970), just as the ethnographic record showed no clear pattern (Hodder 1978b). It seemed increasingly difficult to establish reliable criteria that could be used more generally (e.g. Thompson 1958; Crossland and Birchall 1974; Rouse 1986). On the other hand it could be shown that an internal framework of social and economic change often accounted more convincingly for the evidence as part of an autonomous development (summarised in Renfrew 1973). Functional adjustments to various forms of social and ecological stress, in combination with international information exchange adapted to local needs, were seen as regulating factors (e.g. Renfrew and Shennan 1982; Bintliff 1985). This soon relegated the concepts of migration and diffusion from the realm of serious archaeological discussion within the new archaeology of the 1960s and 1970s. Today it is implicitly accepted that migrations played no significant role in the course of European prehistory (e.g. Champion *et al.* 1984), also demonstrated in a recent work of Colin Renfrew (1987). Some points of critique should be raised against this approach:

(1) Modern archaeology has convincingly demonstrated that material culture is complex and rarely reducible to an overlapping pattern of cultural traits (Clarke 1968, fig. 58), which was a basic notion that lay behind the traditional concept of culture, language and ethnicity. However, it is still implicitly believed that a migration presupposes an unchanged geographical movement of recurrent cultural traits, otherwise it is refuted (Shennan 1978). Thus the new archaeology has, paradoxically, maintained the traditional notion of culture as a one-dimensional phenomenon in its critique of migrations. One reason for this is, of course, the refusal to take population movements seriously, since they were not considered relevant to explaining social change. Therefore the concept was not dealt with in a systematic way. But I believe there is more to it.

(2) Just as the old parallelism between cultural change and migrations was rooted in a modern notion of national and political history, with cultures and migrations replacing nations and battles, so it can be argued that the prevailing parallelism between social change and peaceful internal development is rooted in post-World War II decolonisation and the development of modern middle-class welfare society, with international information exchange and internal social change substituting for international cooperation (United Nations, EU etc.) and social reforms. Culture, ethnicity and migrations were thus seen as linked to the political ideology that led to the disasters of two 'world wars' (Klejn 1974; Jensen 1988). A new theoretical framework was therefore needed which was in accordance with the political ideology dominant after World War II. It became one of evolution, progress and peaceful internal development. I propose that these changes in the modern ideological climate explain some of the reluctance of modern archaeology to deal with the traditional concepts of culture, ethnicity and migrations. This, however, has had some serious consequences.

(3) A theoretical and methodological framework without devices for identifying and interpreting the movement of social and/or ethnic groups, normally subsumed under the general term migration, is unlikely to make convincing progress in other fields of

social and cultural interaction. To exclude one phenomenon of social and cultural change in favour of others distorts our general ability to identify and explain such change. A framework of social change should thus include both conflict and harmony, migrations and information exchange. Migrations may both be a result of, and may result in, social and economic disruption, including geographical displacement and warfare. The incorporation of the study of migrations into modern archaeology, however, makes it necessary to make certain theoretical claims. First, it should be made clear that any such study should be contextualised, culturally and structurally. There exist no universal categories that allow the identification and explanation of such phenomena. Second, any such study must be evaluated against the historical background preceding it. Only in this way can changes be identified and explained. Third, a migration, of whatever kind, is always a symptom, not a primary cause, and so it has to be explained within a broader framework of social organisation, contradiction and change.

To proceed from here it is therefore necessary to work out some comparative guidelines for identifying and explaining population movements (see Kristiansen 1989; Anthony 1989). As a first approximation I shall classify some types of migration, in order to give an idea of the scale and variation. Later I shall narrow the focus towards the nature and structure of Celtic migrations.

Contexts and types of population movements
We have until now employed the traditional concept 'migration'. As it brings so many simplistic and value-loaded associations with it, one might prefer to use the more neutral expression 'population movements' to stress the diversity of such movements – from individuals through select groups of traders and warriors to whole populations. In the following we are mainly concerned with movements of larger groups of people. Although 'large' remains a relative word, it serves to differentiate between individual movements of marriage partners, mercenaries, traders or settlers and the coordinated movement of a group of people, whether voluntarily or forced, to occupy a new area. It marks a not easily definable difference between 'interaction' and 'takeover' (or at least an attempt to take over) by moving in larger groups of people, whether farmers, traders, warriors or all three at the same time. There are obviously intermediate stages of various types of domination.

   Identification   The first problem confronting any study of such phenomena is that of identification. This includes three elements:

1 Intrusion of an alien group (resettling);
2 A migratory route (connection);
3 A mother culture (origin).

Historically the process operates in the opposite order to this, but identification in the archaeological sense is mostly reversed, beginning where the process stops; and for very good reasons, since the replacement of one culture by another is often the most conclusive evidence an archaeologist can come up with (e.g. the Single Grave culture). As previously indicated, it may take many forms, from virgin settlement to various types of cultural mixing, the processes involved in which are still badly known.

Migratory routes are the most difficult to trace, due to the selective mechanisms at work (Schlette 1977). In several well documented cases both the mother culture and the final region of settlement can be traced, whereas the route is represented only by scattered finds (e.g. the Bastarnae: Babes 1988; the Cimbric/Teutonic migrations: Seyer 1976, Abb. 51; several Germanic migrations: Krüger 1977; the Langobards: Werner 1962). Thus it is clear that without literary sources a number of well-known migrations could not have been identified archaeologically, at least not in our present stage of knowledge (e.g. the Cimbric/Teutonic, and several North American and African historical migrations). This, however, also depends on the scale and nature of migrations, to which we shall now turn.

Types of population movements In the following we shall distinguish between full-scale and select movements. Other criteria may be employed, such as speed and directionality, but they belong with a later archaeological discussion about the nature of migrations, e.g. differences between settlement expansion and population movements, and the possibility of distinguishing between them (Neustupny 1981).

(1) The full-scale movement of social groups may be differentiated into three types:

A Forced displacement by states/empires;
B Social conflict/tribal competition (political dominance/conquest);
C Ecological/economic pressure and crisis.

The full-scale movement of tribal groups, including children, livestock etc., is not very well documented in prehistory, except for Caesar's description of the Helvetii and some Viking migrations. It should be pointed out that even such large migrations did not normally deprive a region of its population, but rather represented the combined effect of several groups or settlement units joining together, as was the case in the Viking period. We should not therefore expect, *a priori*, major displacements or a decline of settlement in those regions providing the people, although it may sometimes occur. The Viking period did not see any reduction of settlement, whereas the Migration period in Scandinavia saw in some regions a decline in the order of 10 per cent (Carlsson 1977; 1984).

Causes include the political displacement of opposition ethnic groups, a policy followed by all empires throughout history (the Jews in Babylonia, Celtic and Germanic tribes by the Romans, etc.), internal social conflict/exclusion (e.g. Erik the Red and his group leaving for Greenland, and part of the Polynesian expansion), political subordination or the threat of it by intruding dynasties (several Iron Age migrations), social and ecological constraints (the Corded Ware/Single Grave culture in Jutland, the Cimbric/Teutonic migration from Jutland), and planned migrations to take up new land (the Helvetii, as described by Caesar; several of the Pueblo cultures in the American Southwest).

(2) Select movements of social groups may be divided into at least four variants:

A Conquest;
B Mercenaries;
C Trading stations/colonies;
D Labour/stigmatised groups.

Migrations of select social groups were probably as widespread in prehistory as in history. They include the intrusion of foreign chieftains/kings and their retinue, who took over control – so-called conquest migrations (Renfrew 1987, 131ff.). Examples include the recurrent influx of nomadic groups into Europe, from the Scythians through the Huns to Ghengis Khan, part of the Tumulus expansion of the Middle Bronze Age, part of the Celtic and Viking expansion and the widespread feature of intruding dynasties in the myths of origin of African kingdoms. This may result in either a fast acculturation or an influx of larger groups from the home base of the new leaders, which could explain part of the Nordic Bronze Age expansion. In this way successful conquest migrations may lead to a migration of larger population groups, as described above. Mercenaries probably also belong here, since on return they often bring with them strong influences, such as the Germanic mercenaries employed in the Roman army.

From historical sources we have ample evidence of such military/political movements and takeovers (for a comparative discussion see Webb 1975), which have often left only slight traces in the archaeological record (e.g. the Huns as documented by Werner 1956; or the Vikings). This is not at all surprising, given the nature of such migrations. What may often betray their impact, however, are place names, since they symbolise the political/administrative takeover of a region. Thus place names are probably a good indicator of successful conquest migrations.

Another type is represented by trading stations/colonies, which are often characterised by the same lack of clear archaeological identification, or by a mixed cultural assemblage, such as the Vikings in Russia. Only when the colonising group represents a higher civilisation than the local society are differences easy to recognise, e.g. Mycenaeans/Greeks and Phoenicians in the Mediterranean (Kimmig 1982; Niemeyer 1984).

Finally there are the eternal migrations of stigmatised ethnic groups taking up specific tasks, such as blacksmiths/potters, trade and barter (Jews/Gypsies), labour (slaves), which should be seen as a more permanent structural outcome of large-scale processes of ethnic displacement and exploitation in empires throughout history.

From the above observations a certain processual development in the type of migration may be suggested, with the tribal migrations of the Neolithic mainly caused by ecological/demographic problems, to trade and conquest migrations/ further migrations of conquered peoples from the Bronze Age onwards. This also implies a differential impact upon material culture. Such a scheme was recently proposed by Renfrew (1987, 131), although he preferred to fix the evolutionary fault line for elite domination at the beginning of the Iron Age. We should, however, be cautious not to apply excessively simplistic models. Tribal chiefdoms may very well have migrated from an early stage according to a model of elite domination, just as migrations without any rational demographic or ecological background may be found, e.g. to seek mythical origins or just to explore new lands. In most cases that we know of, there was already a degree of familiarity with the new lands through exchange, trade, alliances or explorations (Helms 1988b).

The process of population movements Having given a broad, rather descriptive, outline of migrations, I shall now focus on possible structural and causal regularities, relying mainly on a recent comparative study by Anthony (1990): 'From a processual perspective, examining constraints and regularities in longer-term patterns of behaviour, migration can be viewed as a process that tends to develop in a broadly predictable manner once it begins.' According to this, most migrations are 'performed by specific subgroups (often kin recruited) with specific goals, targeted on known destinations and likely to use familiar routes'. If this is so, it should be possible to explain the Celtic movements in terms of their social and historical background. Before attempting this, I shall give an outline of some recurrent features of migrations.

A migration begins with a decision to migrate. It includes a plan for where to go, who is going to leave, and by which route. Thus migrations were always directed towards a known destination, at least in their first phase. Scouts were often sent out to gather information about the route and its possibilities. This whole process is most clearly described by Caesar for the migration of the Helvetii (*Gallic Wars* II.3–6). The structure of a migration depended on the level at which the decisions were taken. At a family or local level migrations tended to be short distance, following kinship lines, and therefore representing a kind of settlement expansion. Long-distance migrations were always promoted by chiefs or other leading groups, and involved careful planning. The motives varied from demographic and economic pressure to planned conquest. Ideological/mythical reasons were often put forward, hiding the social reality of pressure and competition. To give an example: a warrior ideology demanded warfare, a highly efficient outlet for social and demographic tensions, which might even bring with it opportunities to send out larger groups of people to settle.

Migrations are almost always a movement in two directions: the initial migration, which is followed by a counterstream moving back to the place of origin, bringing with it new ideas, prestige and booty. The returnees come to represent an important home base for maintaining and developing exchange relations with the migrated groups. They, on their side, often maintained strong ideological bonds with their lands of origin (there are several examples from the Migration period, such as the Herules or the Goths). It means that between migrating groups there would often develop various lines of communication, and the exchange of people and goods. Thus, a migration from one culture/ethnic group to another would often lead to an introduction of the foreign culture into the territory of the migrating culture – in opposition to what one perhaps would expect. One famous example is the Gundestrup silver cauldron. According to one hypothesis it was produced in Thrace and deposited as a gift to the gods in Himmerland (the land of the Cimbri) in northern Jutland, at the time of their migrations (Kaul *et al.* 1991; alternatively Hachmann 1990). At the same time a large number of Celtic prestige goods were introduced into Denmark, leading to a period of intensified exchange. In situations of centre–periphery relations, e.g. migrating groups of mercenaries, the returning groups would use their new wealth and knowledge to achieve status positions at home. Using a parallel with modern migration studies, typical return migrants do not invest in modernisation at home, but rather use their wealth in a traditional manner to acquire land and prestige goods.

Finally, migrations tend to accelerate. Modern studies show that migrants are often people who have migrated before, and who spread the knowledge. It means that migration is a process, not an event. A new spirit of being on the move, of prospects of a better future or of gaining wealth and honour, may develop during a certain time period, leading people to migrate. This attitude is known from all documented periods of large-scale migrations – from the 19th century AD migration to America back to the Viking period. Further, the migrating groups tend to be young, and more willing to take risks, and so offer a perfect outlet for a warrior society.

7.2 The social and historical context of Celtic population movements

Warrior ideology, ethnicity and migrations
With this background we can begin to adjust the two variables to each other: Celtic society at the time of the migrations; the structure and conditions of migration. The Celtic warrior societies, as they can be approached by us, mainly through their burials during La Tène A with two-wheeled war chariots, weapons and prestige goods, originated in a historical tradition going back to Hallstatt C and to the Cimmerian/Scythian traditions of warfare. It can therefore come as no surprise that many features were shared between them. Also, later European warrior groups took up traits and strategies from steppe pastoral warriors, e.g. the Huns and the Hungarians. Warrior societies of this type also share certain basic social and ideological features that represent an important background for understanding both the Celtic and later Germanic migrations (Hedeager 1992). The ideology of a warrior aristocracy is expansionist. Their war leaders were chosen (from among the elite) for their prowess in actual warfare (in opposition to the Hallstatt chiefs, one might suspect). They represented a landowning elite, but one which had enough wealth and time to learn and perform the professional skills of warfare as a full-time, noble and honoured task. However, the surplus needed in order to keep such a system going was not obtained solely through agriculture. War, plundering and conquests were necessary means to feed and reproduce the system, which became expansive in order to survive. Through the spoils of war the war lord attached able warriors to himself – wealth not only had to keep coming in, it also had to keep circulating, until deposited

in burials. So war is a necessary attribute of warrior societies, because a warrior not only lived for it and from it, it was also the only honourable way to die. If we hypothesise that only those who died in battle were buried with their weapons, much variation in the frequency and distribution of warrior burials would be explained. Perhaps the chiefs were an exception, for their need to boast their new positions acquired through conquest and warfare were just as decisive. In this way the frontier of new elites and their retinues can be traced in the distribution of their burials. We shall test this hypothesis in the next section.

Thus tribal rule had been superseded, perhaps rather supplemented, by one based on war leaders and their retinues, cross-cutting traditional bonds of kinship loyalty.[2] Young sons of farmers had another possible way of earning wealth and later land, by serving a chief or a war king, who might reward them with land or gold. And since the system had to be highly expansionist to survive, it tended to lead to conquest migrations, which, if successful, could easily accelerate. This is the so-called Military Democracy of Engels, or the 'decentralised archaic state'.

To this we may add another important dynamic, that between the Mediterranean city states and the Celtic warrior elites (after the fall of the Hallstatt residences, which had earlier taken care of that). The Mediterranean city states had fuelled some of the prestige goods needed for developing the Early La Tène warrior chiefdoms, probably as much through personal contacts as through trade, although slaves were a well-known trade commodity, as also for the Scythians. Slave trading would also tend to create centres of strong war leaders or kings sending out raiding warrior groups to capture slaves. If this traffic between the Mediterranean and the early Celtic warrior elites stopped, as it apparently did after 400 BC, the warrior societies were forced to seek other solutions for their survival, conquest migrations being an obvious choice.

Migrations, as we have seen, put certain demands on their participants in terms of organisation, but also in ideological terms, which have been somewhat neglected. Hedeager has recently described this for the Germanic migrations (Hedeager 1992): 'The migrations created a new form of political community which was founded upon neither ethnic nor genetic connections. The early medieval nation was composed of groups that were brought together for political reasons and which thereby conclusively ruptured the old Germanic tribal groupings.' It meant that the new Germanic confederations or kingdoms, created by conquest migrations, were polyethnic in structure. This is true of both the Ostrogoth kingdom ruled by King Ermanaric in the 4th century AD and that under King Theoderic in Italy in the 6th century. Marching along as Ostrogoths were also Finns, Slavs, Heruli, Alans, Huns and Sarmatians. What bound these groups together was the shared ideological identification of a tribe and a people. Ethnicity was traded and taken on, as in the melting pot which came to symbolise the USA. They all belonged to a recognised family, and the myth and charisma of their war leaders were shared by the group. During these turbulent centuries kingdoms were not primarily territorial, but were defined by the people belonging to them, with shared faith and oaths to their kings and warleaders. Kingdoms and peoples originated together.

To symbolise this new identity the Germanic style was developed; it became a symbol of the new communities of political confederations or 'nations'. I would argue that we can replace Germanic with Celtic in all of the above; as we shall see they correspond to each other in nearly all respects, with the Celtic migrations and art style developing under conditions very similar to those prevailing more than half a millennium later.

Having described both the general structure of migrations and the dynamics of Celtic warrior elites, it comes as no surprise that their early, well-attested migrations conform well to all the prescriptions we have outlined: they followed a well-known route, towards a rewarding destination in northern Italy, the reasons were internal competition and population pressure, and they led a return movement of people and goods and cultural influences, assimilated by Celtic artists who increasingly freed themselves from direct imitation, creating a new cultural identity, which served to unify the diverse groups following in the wake of the migrations under an ethnic banner. They combined conquest migrations with the permanent settling of larger population groups.

The background to the first Celtic migrations

In the following I shall not describe La Tène culture and society in detail – there are many books which do that (e.g. Pauli 1980a; Bittel, Kimmig and Schiek 1981; Lorenz 1986; Ross 1986; Moscati 1991; Megaw and Megaw 1989, 259–75 for a good thematic bibliography). My aim is to use the Celtic movements as a case study in migrations: their causes, their identification, their social organisation and ethnicity. This will help us to understand not only the Celtic movement, but also similar or related processes of social change, such as the Urnfield culture of the late 2nd millennium BC, to which we shall return in the concluding chapter. According to the above definition of ethnicity, I use Celts and Celtic synonymously with La Tène culture, as an ethnic and cultural identification.[3]

From Czechoslovakia to northeastern France Celtic warrior chiefs were buried with two-wheeled war chariots during the late 5th century BC, concentrated in three regional or local groups (Gustin and Pauli 1984; Duval 1988, fig. 2) (Figure 170). The grave goods show that trade with Italy was still maintained, two-handled *stamnoi* and beaked flagons (*Schnabelkannen*) being the most popular (Figure 170). The pattern points to the movement of more ordinary trade goods, rather than exclusive diplomatic gifts, perhaps suggesting a changed organisation of trade and exchange. This zone of strong warrior aristocracies, without large fortified residences, continued traditions developed in Ha C. In opposition to the Hallstatt elite, their burials appeared in cemeteries together with their kinsmen and followers, as in Ha C. Local warrior elites, perhaps in some sort of confederation with the centres of chariot burials, had replaced the centralised archaic states of Hallstatt D. A clear sign of the new warring style was the appearance of the two-wheeled war chariot, replacing the four-wheeled status wagons of Ha D and Ha C (Figure 171).

Caesar was so impressed when he was attacked by chariots, still in existence during his campaigns in England, that he gave a vivid description of their use (*Gallic Wars*, 4. 33):

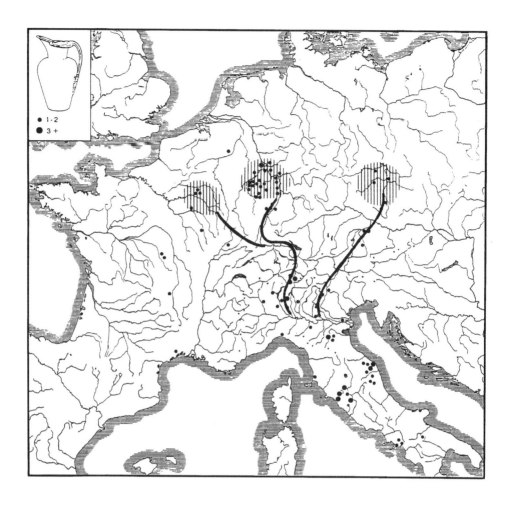

Fig. 170 The distribution of Etruscan beaked bronze flagons (*Schnabelkannen*) in Western Europe, showing a concentration in the three main areas of Early La Tène chiefly wagon burials (hatched); solid lines indicate migrating and trading routes from Northern Italy.

In chariot fighting the Britons begin by driving all over the field hurling javelins, and generally the terror inspired by the horses and the noise of the wheels are sufficient to throw their opponents' ranks into disorder. Then, after making their way between the squadrons of their own cavalry, they jump down from the chariots and engage the enemy on foot. In the meantime their charioteers retire a short distance from the battle and place the chariots in such a position that their masters, if hard pressed by numbers, have an easy means of retreat to their own lines. Thus they combine the mobility of cavalry with the staying power of infantry; and by daily training and practice they attain such proficiency that even on a steep incline they are able to control the horses at full gallop, and to check and turn them in a moment. They can run along the chariot pole, stand on the yoke, and get back into the chariot as quick as lightning.

Fig. 171 Reconstruction of a Celtic war chariot drawn by a pair of horses.

This description really incorporates all the ingredients of aristocratic warrior life and its social and economic demands of daily practice, well-bred, trained horses, chariot builders and aristocratic charioteers – that is, the whole chiefly following needed to reproduce a class of chiefly warriors.

How are we to understand the concentrations of wagon and weapon burials during Early la Tène in the three areas? They represented chiefly centres surrounded by less stratified warrior peripheries of more ordinary spear burials. This seems a reasonable possibility, but does not tell us much about the social dynamics behind the formation of such relationships. Two factors were important: like the Scythian royal elites, the Celtic elites are found in areas of rich iron ores (Driehaus 1965, Abb. 3, 5; Pauli 1974, Abb. 2), which could be used internally (the Etruscans probably had the iron they needed locally) to link vassals and allied warrior chiefs to them by giving access to iron and smiths. The warrior ideology, on the other hand, demanded constant feuds and raids, which were organised at increasingly greater distances from the chiefly centres, e.g. for capturing slaves both for internal use and eventually also for reselling to Italy with the growing demand in the Po valley. Slaves were at any rate already a substantial part of society by this time, captives being a necessary outcome of raids, and could be employed as labour to expand the activities of the successful centres. Intensification in the centre and outward aggressive expansion to increase its power base could not continue endlessly – at some point expansion was blocked and more stable relationships had to be built up. Internal competition would increase, as well as hierarchy, until an outlet had to be found (another alternative was to urbanise, but this was not chosen). Migration in this situation was simply a geographical extension of a well-known strategy of short-distance expansion. Population increase within the chiefly centres is shown by new cemeteries, just as settlement studies in micro-regions on the Rhine show clustering of settlement during La Tène (Simons 1989, Abb. 68–69).

Thus the rich chariot burials formed the visible top of densely settled warrior societies clustered around the princely barrows and along the major trade routes and alliances (Figure 155). The rise of Bohemia can be linked to the reopening of contact through the Dürrnberg at Hallein, a salt-mining community with a specialist production, which had competed successfully with Hallstatt (Pauli 1980c; 1984b). Once again we see the ability of Celtic warrior chiefs to exploit industrial resources, as in the case of the Scythians, as well as profiting from the trade. All the evidence, including literary sources, points to the exchange of raw materials, such as iron, gold, amber, salt and slaves for prestige goods (Timpe 1985; Frey 1985). Hallstatt and Bohemia represented the eastern limit of Early La Tène culture proper, corresponding to the old border between the eastern and western Hallstatt, although exchanges took place with more distant regions (Lorenz 1978; 1985).

Among the three centres of chiefly chariot burials, that on the Rhine was the richest. The Rhine elite patronised those craft specialists that were creating Early La Tène art, according to Megaw and Megaw (1989, 56), based upon plant motifs and early triscles, as well as incorporating Scythian elements, some of which also came from Italy (Frey 1980). Italian flagons were carved in the new style when they arrived at the Rhine, and some were reassembled and recreated in La Tène style. Foreign was good, but not without a Celtic mark on it, transforming it into a Celtic chiefly identity. An independent identity was taking form. Megaw has suggested that products from here were exchanged as gifts in alliance formations with centres in Bohemia and Champagne, leading to the formation of regional variations of Early La Tène art there (Megaw 1973; 1979; 1985) (Figure 172). Others have proposed that each centre maintained its own craftsmen, responsible for creating local variation. Craft specialists were exchanged rather than their products (Schwappach 1976), as regional preferences in style motifs in the east and west also demonstrate some overlap between the two areas (Schwappach 1976, figs. 4, 5). The existence of travelling artisans has also been proposed (S. Champion 1985), reflected in the production of nearly identical fibulae in widely separated areas (Figure 173).

Other similarities, from burial rituals to grave goods, produce the same picture: some individual preferences by craftsmen in each of the three centres, as well as a major overlap, testifying to close interchiefly contacts between them. The ability of

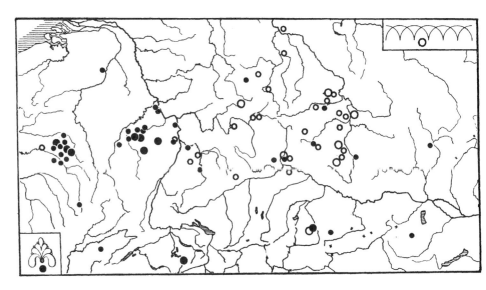

Fig. 172 Two characteristic motifs of Early La Tène A art ('Premier style') – palmettes and arcs, with a western and eastern distribution in the chiefly centres of Early La Tène warrior burials.

Fig. 173 Early La Tène fibulae of Münzingen-Andelfingen type, inlaid with coral, in Central Europe, indicating intensive interaction.

the chiefly centres to maintain lines of exchange both with north Italy and between each other, their ability to patronise groups of crafts specialists who were able to transform Oriental (Greek-Italian) and Scythian stylistic influences into a new original, artistic language, reflecting the self-consciousness of their masters – all this indicates to me that these early centres were well organised warrior kingdoms, based on chiefly landed (fortified) estates, surrounded by farms and small villages (Haffner 1976, 148 ff.), industrial production and trade, and tribute from their clients, combined with raiding and conquest. This adds up to a decentralised archaic state, much like the Germanic or Scythian kingdoms. The studies of Lorenz (1978 and1985) and Haffner (1976, 148 ff.) make it possible to hint at the internal structure of the royal and chiefly elite in burials, especially those of the Marne and Rhine/Moselle groups. At the top we find the princely chariot burials, while weapon graves with spears concentrate around and among them, to represent their retinues and local chiefs. Sword graves are rare, belonging with the upper group of chariot burials. Less richly furnished warrior graves dominate the area between the Rhine and the Danube. The warrior burials are on the whole a minority in the cemeteries, making up a chiefly elite and their retinues. Among them we may distinguish royal burials with golden rings (although not always of gold), armrings or torcs, the classic royal symbols, as known from the Scythians to the Germanic kings. They occur in only 10 per cent of sword graves, indicating their exclusive status. They may also, as in later Germanic times, be found in burials without weapons, suggesting that royal status was not solely linked to the function of active warrior.

It was from these early La Tène kingdoms that the first migrations towards Italy set out. The intensity of connections between northern Italy and the Hunsrück-Eifel at the Rhine suggests that we should expect the first migrations to originate here, as the centre of external contacts and the area with the most competition. However, we must also ask if conditions in the Mediterranean had changed in such a way as to invite migrations.

Developments in the Mediterranean were, as always, playing a crucial role. Collis (1984a) described the period 500–250 BC as 'The Tide Ebbs', signalling that the intensity of economic expansion and trade with Central Europe declined during this period, when Rome started its march towards empire, and Philip II and Alexander the Great established a shortlived Macedonian eastern empire, which fragmented after Alexander's death in 323 BC. Traditional city-state economies, and trade partnerships between them, were giving way to militarism and the formation of larger political and economic entities, employing coins and markets, a shift which was felt in Central Europe after 400 BC. At that time the Rhône route had declined, while local competition and warfare had taken over, reflected in a series of small, heavily fortified, settlements, some with Greek-inspired constructions and houses with stone foundations, into which the whole population seems to have concentrated (for summaries see Kimmig 1983, 25 ff.; Collis 1984b, 112 f.; Cunliffe 1988, ch. 3; Py 1989). Each settlement had a ritual shrine devoted to the skull cult, the most famous being that at Entremont. Their meaning is unknown, probably relating to ancestor worship, reflecting the changes in burial ritual and communal ritual that took place during middle and late La Tène (Bruneaux 1988). To this we may add that the Celts were known for taking the skulls or scalps of enemies as trophies, like the Scythians, and the skull cult might also reflect a ritualisation of the impact of endemic warfare – a ritual of tension, as we shall discuss later (see also note 7). Although French researchers consider these proto-urban settlements, or proto-oppida, to reflect a process of hellenisation, the lack of imports north of Vienna on the Rhône, and the process of nucleation and fortification, more closely resemble the 'Biskupin phase' (see Chapter 6.3), characterised by political fragmentation and warfare, only changing during the 3rd and 2nd centuries with the reopening of trade. Alternatively it could be argued that these 'oppida' were under the political control of Massalia and other Greek ports of trade in the Gulf of Lions (Kimmig 1983, Abb. 19), paying tribute in the form of meat and staples. This is supported by Figure 174, which shows that an influx of wine/amphorae during the late 6th and 5th centuries BC corresponds to a steep decline in meat consumption, reflecting the extracting of tribute (grain and meat) from Massalia in exchange of wine and amphorae, among other things, to replace the dwindling revenues of trade. After the 4th century BC pottery production for containing liquids and staples declines and remains at a low level during the following two centuries, indicating a prolonged period of economic decline and/or political subordination to Massalia. Economic revival does not begin until 100 BC.

The Po valley had thus become the meeting-place between La Tène mercenaries, traders and middlemen, and the Etruscans, as reflected in the distribution of Late Hallstatt and Early La Tène *fibulae*, some burials and inscriptions in North Italy and the distribution of a selection of favoured Etruscan products and their local imitations north of the Alps, in the three centres of Early La Tène chiefly warriors (Figure 170). The Celts apparently organised much of the trade themselves, as well as travelling into the Po valley on a regular basis. The first preconditions for a migration were thus fulfilled – a known destination and a familiar route.

Let us now lend an ear to how classical writers refer to the first Celtic migrations (Figure 175) (cited after Pauli 1985a). Pliny the Elder gives a brief account (Naturalis Historia):

> It is stated that the Gauls, imprisoned as they were by the Alps as by a then insuperable bulwark, first found a motive for overflowing into Italy from the circumstance that a Gallic citizen from Switzerland named Helico, who had sojourned at Rome on account of his skill as an artificer, had brought with him when he came back some dried figs and grapes and some samples of oil and wine; and consequently we may pardon them for having sought to obtain these things even by means of war (XXII 2.5).

Pompeius Trogus came from Gallia Narbonensis, and his work is cited in small parts in later sources, the Celtic migrations being mentioned twice (Historiae Philippicae):

> For these Gauls, however, the reason for their coming to Italy and seeking new lands was internal discord and bitter dissension at home; when, wearying of this, they had come into Italy, they expelled the Etruscans from their lands and founded Milan, Como, Brescia, Verona, Bergamo, Trento and Vicenza (XX 5.7–8).

> For their native lands could no longer contain the Gauls with their swelling numbers, they sent 300,000 men to seek new territories, like an offering of the first fruits of spring. Some of these settled in Italy, where they captured and

Kg of meat per 100 vases

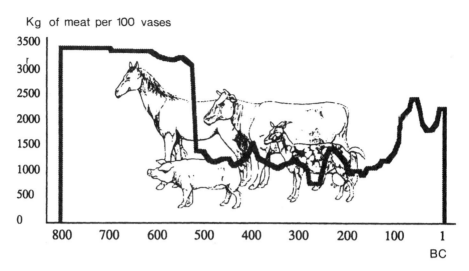

Fig. 174(A) The consumption of meat at oppida in the Nîmes region of Languedoc, during the period 800 BC to 1 BC, calibrated against the quantity of household pottery.

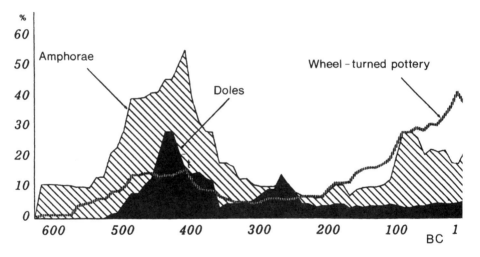

Fig. 174(B) The changing frequency of amphorae for wine, doles (grain containers) and wheel-turned pottery from 600–1 BC at oppida in the Nîmes region of Languedoc.

burned even the city of Rome; some, led by the birds (for the Gauls are experienced above others in the study of augury), spread through the head of the Adriatic and settled in Pannonia (xx 4.1–3).

Finally, Livy (born in Padua) is rather more detailed in his historical account. First he offers an explanation from a southern viewpoint (Livy: *Histories*, v. 33.2–6):

The story runs that this race, allured by the delicious fruits and especially the wine – then a novel luxury – had crossed the Alps and possessed themselves of

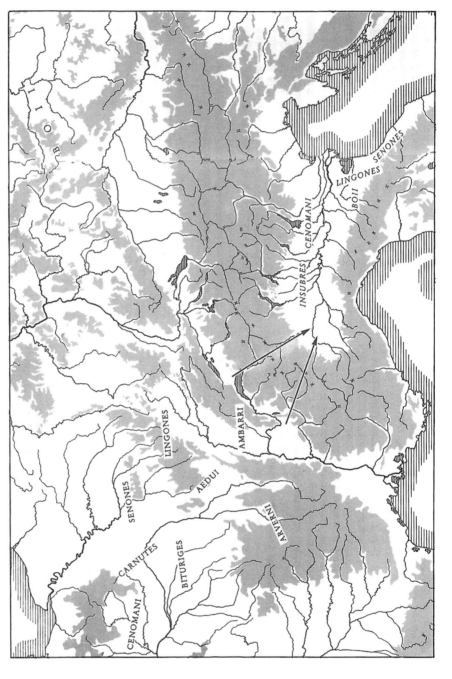

Fig. 175 The Celtic tribes which invaded Italy, mentioned by Livy and Polybius (italic script), and by Julius Caesar (Roman script).

lands that had before been tilled by the Etruscans; and that wine had been imported into Gaul expressly to entice them, by Arruns of Clusium, in his anger at the seduction of his wife by Lucumo. This youth, whose guardian he had been, was so powerful that he could not have chastised him without calling in a foreign force. He it was who is said to have guided the Gauls across the Alps, and to have suggested the attack on Clusium. Now I would not deny that Arruns or some other citizen brought the Gauls to Clusium, but that those who besieged Clusium were not the first to have passed the Alps is generally agreed. Indeed it was two hundred years before the attack on Clusium, and the capture of Rome, that the Gauls first crossed over into Italy; neither were the Clusini the first of the Etruscans with whom they fought; but long before that the Gallic armies had often given battle to those who dwelt between the Apennines and the Alps (v. 33.2–6).

After this description, which points to the employment of Celtic mercenaries, as well as frequent hostilities before the final migrations, a Celtic source is cited:

Concerning the migration of the Gauls into Italy we are told as follows: while Tarquinius Priscus reigned at Rome, the Celts, who make up one of the three divisions of Gaul, were under the domination of the Bituriges, and this tribe supplied the Celtic nation with a king. Ambigatus was then the man, and his talents, together with his own and the general good fortune, had brought him great distinction; for the Gauls under his sway grew so rich in corn and so populous, that it seemed hardly possible to govern so great a multitude. The king, who was now an old man and wished to relieve his kingdom of a burdensome throng, announced that he meant to send Bellovesus and Segovesus, his sister's sons, two enterprising young men, to find such homes as the gods might assign to them by augury; and promised them that they should head as large a number of immigrants as they themselves desired, so that no tribe might be able to prevent their settlement. Whereupon to Segovesus were by lot assigned the Hercynian highlands; but to Bellovesus the gods proposed a far pleasanter road, into Italy (v. 34.1–4).

The descriptions of Livy fill out the rather general and simplistic explanations offered by Pliny and Pompeius Trogus, and we have no reason to doubt their accuracy, except for the mistake about the time period, which he places two centuries too early. The causes cited appear again and again in historical descriptions of migrations from less complex to more complex societies: internal competition/population pressure, young aristocrats being send out to find new land (conquest migration) and a taste for Etruscan wealth (rather than life style). We further hear that Celtic artisans might travel to Italy, as shown by the *fibulae*, although several occur in female burials, perhaps representing cross-Alpine marriages – or possibly the slave trade (Frey 1988). Also the reappearance of some hoards of goldwork on the trade routes and near the chiefly centres suggests frequent communications, sometimes disrupted by attacks (Figure 176). But by the early 4th century young Celtic princes and their

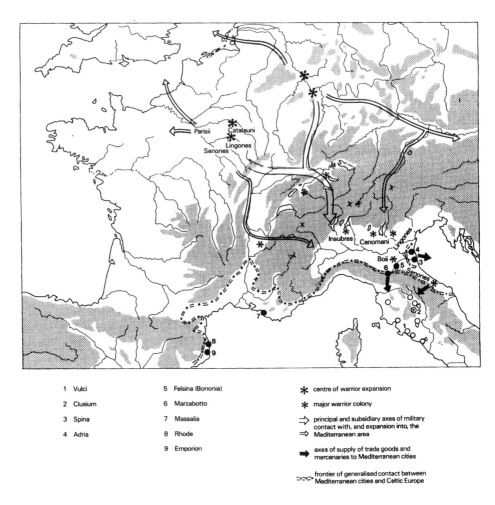

1	Vulci	5	Felsina (Bononia)	✳	centre of warrior expansion
2	Clusium	6	Marzabotto	✳	major warrior colony
3	Spina	7	Massalia	⇒	principal and subsidiary axes of military contact with, and expansion into, the Mediterranean area
4	Adria	8	Rhode		
		9	Emporion	➡	axes of supply of trade goods and mercenaries to Mediterranean cities
				⌐⌐⌐	frontier of generalised contact between Mediterranean cities and Celtic Europe

Fig. 176 Celtic territorial expansion in the 5th century BC.

followers headed for Italy along routes well known to them and by 387 the Celts had sacked Rome, settling in the Po valley until they were defeated by the Romans after 200 BC (the Boii were defeated 191 BC).

We should take a more detailed look at the organisation of these early migrations: the king's sister's sons are close relatives in traditional kinship systems, which are often patrilineal and based on cross-cousin marriage. The young princes were thus possible competitors for the throne, along with the king's own sons. In warrior societies it is normal practice to send out young sons to establish new settlements, in this way transforming internal competition into external expansion. The only differences here are the scale and distance of the operation. We are also informed that the Celts formed one division of Gaul, and they were ruled by a king, supplied by the Bituriges, who later lived south of the eastern Loire (Nash 1976, fig. 6). This might with some pushing correspond to an identification with the Marne group of chiefly burials, forming a kingdom, although somewhat more northerly. But other Gaulish tribes were also identified by classical writers, among them the Senones and the Boii, coming from the neighbouring region to the Bituriges (Figure 175). It seems that the Italian migrations drew upon several tribes of a large region, from the Marne in the north to the Auvergne in the south (Kruta 1986, figs. 3–5). But what is the archaeological evidence for the Celtic migration?

By Late La Tène A the wagon burials come to a (partial) halt in all the La Tène A centres – in the Marne group, in the Moselle/Rhine group, although a change in burial custom may in part be responsible here (Haffner and Joachim 1984, 76), and in Bohemia (Soudská 1984). Although chariot burials continued in the Moselle/Rhine group, the riches had disappeared, the last princely burial being Waldalgesheim, which gives its name to the migration style of the Middle La Tène, which I define as La Tène B and early C, lasting until the time of the oppida (Waldhauser 1987, Tabelle 1). As the north Italian Celts came from Gaul, the other chiefly centres must have provided most of the Celtic migrations towards east Central Europe, to which we turn in the next section, as the new style of expansion apparently developed in the centres just before and after the migrations.

The archaeology of northern Italy does not show massive evidence of a migration, probably because the Celts quickly adopted Etruscan culture. Classical writers have pointed out which areas were settled and controlled by the different tribes (Figure 175); these seem to be reflected in some differences in material culture and burial ritual. They also stress, as usual, their primitive habits and greed for gold and prestige goods. Polybius wrote just after the Celts' arrival in the 4th century BC (Nash 1978, 457):

> They lived in unwalled villages, and without knowledge of any of the other arts of civilisation. As they made their beds of straw and leaves, and fed on meat, and followed no pursuits but those of war and agriculture, they led simple lives . . . Each man's property consisted of cattle and gold, as these were the only things that could be easily carried with them when they moved from place to place whatever their circumstance, and changed their dwellings to suit their choice.

The description resembles the comments of Tacitus four hundred years later about the Germans. Cemeteries in which local La Tène and Italian objects are mixed are common (Lollini 1979), and Megaw has pointed out (Megaw and Megaw 1989, chap. 2) the rapid mixture of La Tène and Etruscan art, demonstrating both the Celts' creativity and their ability to adopt. However, the tribal territories are still recognisable in material culture in the 3rd century (Kruta 1986, fig. 8). A series of similar objects, grouped in the Po valley, in Switzerland and in the chiefly centres on the Moselle and the Marne and in Czechoslovakia, indicate a rapid spread of workshop products between these geographically widely separated centres, suggesting that contacts were intense (return migrants, artisans, mercenaries and traders), supplying Celtic artisans with new inspiration for their next great achievement – the development of the vegetational, or Waldalgesheim, style (Kruta 1979; 1982, fig. 1; Peyre 1982).

In other areas of expansion north of the Alps, however, Celtic culture dominated, making it possible to identify the areas of expansion in opposition to indigenous culture. Among these early areas of Late La Tène A expansion we can identify one in Yorkshire in northeastern England. Endert (1986) has by a careful comparative analysis demonstrated that it originated in a small group of chariot burials in the Ardennes in Belgium, which came to a complete stop at the same time. This suggestion is supported by additional ritual evidence (Wilhelmi 1987–88, Abb. 3). In Yorkshire the chariot burial tradition continued throughout La Tène, and it later transmitted Celtic influences to northern Ireland, which we shall discuss later.

The number of tribes taking part in the migration towards Italy, their battles and political domination, in combination with the observed contacts between northern Italy and the three centres of Early La Tène, give the impression of an organised action, or series of actions, directed from centres that were more than an agglomeration of individual warrior chiefs – they would be more accurately classed as kingdoms or confederations. One might suggest that the conquest of Italy could be seen as a well-organised attempt at political expansion on a grand scale, with the dual aim of gaining more secure access to its riches and solving problems at home, as was also the case with the later Viking raids and migrations. However, the new dynamic created by this soon meant that control of the conquest migrations slipped out of the hands of the early centres. As in the Viking period the kings lost some of their authority to upwardly mobile and ambitious chiefs, who attract large groups of followers and retinues as the reward of conquest and settling in new lands.

The expansion of Celtic ethnicity and populations during the 4th and 3rd centuries BC
The first successful migrations started a wave of new migrations, beginning a chain reaction that continued during the following two centuries. The reasons for this were not only a new entrepreneurial spirit of seeking new lands, although that was real enough, but also the further development of a heroic warrior ideology, as larger groups were now mobilised in the chiefly retinues, including both cavalry (the aristocracy) and infantry (Ross 1986, ch. 3, especially 48f.; Karl Peschel 1985). They often comprised warriors from different tribes, as in the battle of Telamon in 225 BC, which included Insubres, Boii and Gaesatae. A change to a form of social organisation adapted to distant settlement expansion and conquests took place, giving room for greater social mobility. This allowed large groups of young warriors, the sons of farmers, the chance of a warrior career, thereby becoming part of the chiefly group. Here we find the other rationale of migration – a certain democratisation allowing for social mobility. Finally, the migrations always resulted in a permanent settlement of a farming population, leading to an intensification of agrarian techniques and craft production. In reality we have to do with an expansion of farming into more fertile lowland river valleys. It allowed new opportunities for former peasants and younger sons of farmers with no possibility of inheriting land at home. The combined effect of these prospects represented a strong social and ideological mix, once set on the move.

A dynamic force had been set free, with chiefly groups of Celtic warriors leading large groups of armed farming populations and craft specialists, whose sons were trained as warriors, so beginning a series of conquest migrations into east Central Europe. The new settlements and cemeteries exemplify the social changes taking place under the selective pressure of migration, as well as the expansion of a successful social and cultural identity or ethnicity. As we shall see, Celtic culture spread far beyond the limits of the actual migrations, and even within the central areas of migration many local tribes and groups gave in and joined the Celtic nation. Its successful ideology of expansion, fuelled by a cult of the heroic warrior, is well described by classical authors. From a safe distance they followed and recorded the conquests of the Celts with a mixture of horror (the head-taking and human sacrifices) and admiration (their bravery and military efficiency, their strong-willed women), reaching a climax in Caesar's campaigns against Gaul (Rankin 1987). Let us consider two aspects of the migrations: their social organisation from initial settlement to oppida formation, and their material culture (compared to the written evidence). First I must present a brief historical summary, as recorded by the classical sources (Rankin 1987; Szabo 1986).

During the 4th century BC Celtic expansion was directed towards neighbouring regions from Bohemia and eastwards into the Carpathians, where they pushed the pastoral frontier eastwards beyond the Carpathians (Szabo 1986; 1988; Wozniak 1976). In the early 3rd century the Balkans were colonised (the area of Yugoslavia, (Gustin 1985)), probably from the Carpathians and the rivers Danube and Sava which had been settled already in the late 4th century BC (Jovanovic 1979). Celtic migrants and mercenaries were engaged by the Hellenistic states, e.g. the Athenians and Spartans in 367 BC. They were in the Balkans in 358 BC, according to Pompeius Trogus, battling the Illyrians, and in 335 Alexander received a Celtic delegation after their penetration of the lower Danube. 'With the end of the 4th century BC, the Celts had moved from the background of Herodotean rumour and material for analogical anecdote into the midstage of Greek history, in which they proved to be more terrible than earlier primitivising romantic imagination had ever imagined' (Rankin 1987, 48). By 298 BC they had established the kingdom of Tylis in Bulgaria, and by 279 they had overrun the kingdom of Macedonia, invaded Greece, and sacked the temple at Delphi. Some of the tribes are said to have taken booty back to their homelands near Toulouse in France, as returning migrants, thereby explaining much of the incredible identity in material culture over vast areas. These 3rd-century migrations, or, more accurately, mobile Celtic armies, included warrior groups even from distant Celtic tribes in Gaul, and some of the returning migrants and their followers can be identified archaeologically in Gaul, more specifically in the Marne region (Kruta 1986, figs. 6, 7). The late 3rd and early 2nd centuries brought Celtic expansion to a halt, and they were now defeated in several battles, from Asia Minor (defeat of the Galatae 240–30) to Italy, the crucial battle being at Telamon in 225, followed by the successive defeats of the Insubres in 222 BC, and the Boii in 191 BC, causing the Boii to migrate to the Danube.

During the same period Celtic mercenaries fought in Hellenistic armies in Sicily, Greece, Egypt and Asia Minor, their presence marked archaeologically only by occasional stray finds, but recorded in classical sources. Some of their more wide-ranging campaigns in Greece and later in Asia Minor were obviously short-lived conquest migrations. Sometimes the Celts were called in in support of local kings, as happened in 278 BC, when King Nikomedes of Bithynia invited the Galatians, as they were later named, to Asia Minor, where they stayed for nearly 100 years (Rankin 1987, ch. 9). Several of these tribes originally came from southern France. More permanent Celtic traces in the form of cemeteries were left in areas of more permanent settlement, extending along the Danube, but only sporadically represented in Greece (Maier 1973, Abb. 1). Here the effect of a rapid acculturation by a superior culture makes an archaeological evaluation of their impact in the Mediterranean difficult. It is during these two centuries that most of the descriptions were produced by classical writers and artists, including sculptures, such as the famous Dying Gaul – a naked warrior wearing a torc. The latter item became widely adopted among chiefly warriors and retinues, another example of the democratisation of status symbols and the possibility of individuals achieving a higher status.

From La Tène B onwards there are small inhumation cemeteries over large areas of Central Europe. They were generally smaller than the La Tène A cemeteries, containing 30–40 burials representing a group of farmsteads. They demonstrate a new ritual identification of warriors and farmers, furnished with the products of classical La Tène style, but with no, or very few, imports and without chariots. Warrior burials are prominent, with swords, lances and shields, and sometimes also spurs, these indicating mounted warriors (Figure 177). They are easily recognisable as an intruding element in areas of expansion, because of their maintenance of a distinctive Celtic material culture. The same changes also occur within the major La Tène centres, where they represent internal expansion. This demonstrates that the change in burial ritual and probably also social organisation had also penetrated the old centres. Well-published and well-analysed cemeteries from Czechoslovakia (Waldhauser 1987), Switzerland (Sankot 1980), the Carpathians (Bunja 1982) and Yugoslavia (Gustin 1985) will be employed here to exemplify the social organisation of the pioneer phase of expansion and the changes following on from consolidation.

In Czechoslovakia a number of grave-goods combinations can be defined, with weapons, ankle rings and bracelets/arm rings pointing to high status. These results have been linked to anthropological analyses of age and sex, allowing a comparison of burial equipment combinations with the age structure of the deceased (Figure 178). It displays some interesting variations: weapons may accompany even old men in the grave, suggesting a warrior oligarchy, or alternatively that even these older men were under arms during the pioneer phase. At the other end of the scale males without grave goods died between thirty and forty years of age, suggesting a lower status and a less healthy life style. Males with *fibulae* but no weapons are generally older, perhaps former warriors or farm owners. With respect to females, a succession in age from a pair of arm rings (dying young) through ankle rings (thirty to forty years at death) to a single arm ring (several between fifty and sixty years old) suggests that age groups were also identified by ornaments, although status may be a factor as well, with good health, longer life expectancy and high status going together. In the later period

Fig. 177(A) Late La Tène Celtic warrior reconstructed on the basis of grave 1178 at Wederath and classical accounts.

Fig. 177(B) Reconstruction of Middle La Tène female dress with fibulae and bronze belt.

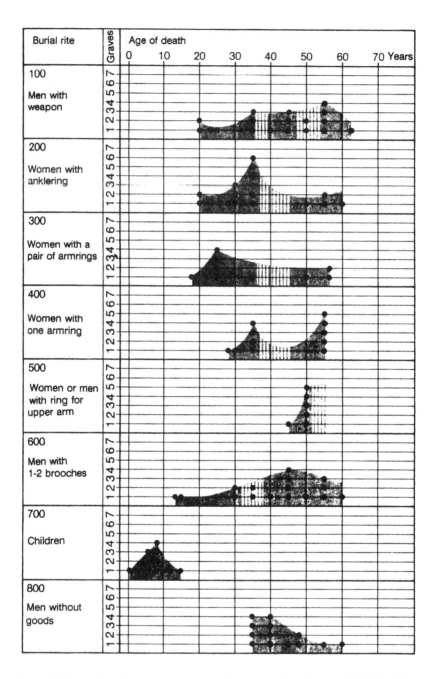

Fig. 178 The relationship between age at death, grave goods and sex at Middle La Tène cemeteries in Bohemia.

warrior burials with swords became rarer, suggesting either a centralisation of status, or less warfare.

Settlement groups have been totally excavated in micro-regions due to brown coal production, yielding an unusual glimpse of a complete settlement system

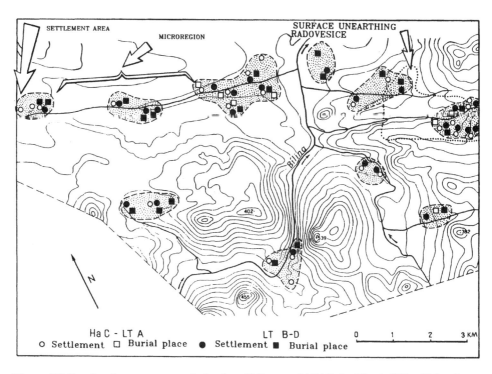

Fig. 179(A) Local settlement structure during Late Hallstatt and Middle La Tène in Bilina, Bohemia.

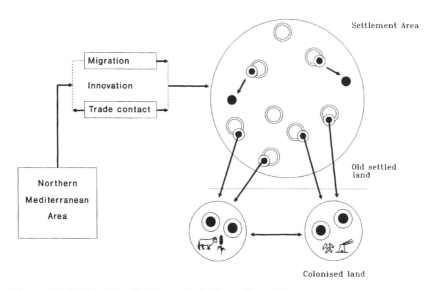

Fig. 179(B) Model of later La Tène colonisation in Central Europe.

(Waldhauser 1984b). The overall settlement structure consists of densely settled areas with empty buffer zones between them (Figure 179) Within a settlement group, clusters of smaller farms, shifting location every twenty years within a small area, demonstrate a stable micro-settlement pattern throughout La Tène. A cemetery belonged to each cluster (Figure 178). Discontinuity was most pronounced from La Tène A to La Tène B, suggesting some intrusion and also social changes. There existed a division between single farms and small villages. Stable settlements (villages) normally performed specialist functions – metalworking and other industrial production (also in Gaul, see Büchsenschütz 1988a). An increase in industrial production, and a development in agrarian techniques and crafts, took place during the 3rd and 2nd centuries BC. The local production and distribution system has been reconstructed by Waldhauser (in press), demonstrating the rise of central settlements and an intensification of craft production for agriculture during Middle La Tène, leading up to a major reorganisation in Late La Tène with the formation of oppida. A similar settlement pattern and development can be demonstrated on the Rhine (Simons 1989, ch. 6 Abb. 66–69) (Figure 180).

In the Carpathians a similar analysis of the flat grave inhumation cemeteries of Middle La Tène has been carried out (Bujna 1982). We find the same basic structure – warriors with weapons, sword, shields and spears being a dominant group of 18 per cent, half of them with swords, and many with metal belts. They are matched by a group of rich female burials (12 per cent) with metal belts, *fibulae* and rings (Husty 1989). In a second class amounting to 28 per cent we find warriors with just a spear and no belt, and women without metal belts but with many beads. Several burials with specialist tools belong to artisans. A third group had only dress accessories for both men and women (23 per cent), and a final group had only pottery (19 per cent). So even within these small community cemeteries there were significant differences in burial equipment, entailing clear elements of social differentiation. Once again we see a leading group of warrior chiefs and their retinue of ordinary warrior burials, plus specialists and commoners. There are, however, some interesting changes over time (Bujna figs. 36–41). Warrior burials are frequent in the early phase, then fall in number (maybe reflecting peaceful consolidation) and rise again towards the end of the cemeteries' period of use (possibly showing a new wave of unrest), perhaps reflecting the reorganisation leading up to oppida formation and new emigrants from northern Italy. Rich female burials gradually decline in number except in two regions. During the same period the frequency of poor graves of the third category increases. Bujna (1982) interprets the sequence as one of slightly increasing social differentiation, although it was still a more homogenous population than during La Tène A.

The Yugoslavian cemeteries of Middle La Tène display the same forms and combinations as in the Carpathians and Central Europe, and they cluster around the lowland river valleys – the Drava, Sava and Danube (Gustin 1985, Abb. 27–28). Their settlement and material culture can be clearly defined geographically against the remaining indigenous population outside their territory – the Illyrian settlements, which imported Celtic swords and adopted some Celtic cultural features (Gustin 1985, Abb. 29–30). The raids into Greece and Macedonia were organised from the Celtic settlement in Yugoslavia, although both Boii and Belgae are said to have participated (Jovanovic 1979). Finally, there are well-analysed cemeteries from Switzerland, which once again demonstrate the same divisions in burial goods and rituals,

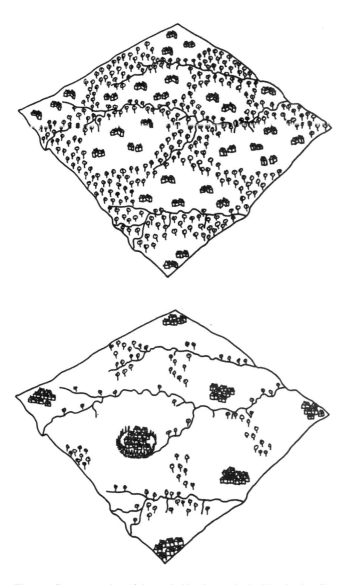

Fig. 180 Reconstruction of the settled landscape in the Merzbach valley area c. 700 BC and 100 BC.

suggesting that some general rules were followed throughout the Celtic area of Europe (Sankot 1980), due to frequent movement of goods and especially of people during the expansion period (migrants and return migrants).

From La Tène B onwards Celtic art reached a climax, displaying a homogeneity over large areas that is astonishing. The same is true of individual objects, such as *fibulae* and swords. We also observe an expansion of decoration: sword scabbards and lances are decorated in La Tène style, as well as helmets. The warrior and his weapons were important symbols of Celtic identity and military success, and were therefore decorated. Intense communication between the different migrating groups, returning migrants and travelling mercenaries, is the only possible explanation for the remarkable similarities that characterise this period. And to this we may add one necessary precondition: the conscious and proud production of, and identification with, a pan-European Celtic identity, a Celtic Nation of different tribes. The artistic creativity reflected the challenge of social change and freedom, as well as the need to create and maintain a Celtic identity as a symbol of a shared destiny. Thus, the historical and archaeological sources are in full accord in Central Europe: the migrations of new settlers under the banner of Celtic culture defined themselves clearly against local culture through material culture in burials. In Greece and the Mediterranean the archaeological identification is not so clear-cut, suggesting that migrations into more developed cultures lead to fast acculturation, just as mobile armies leave only scanty traces. The combination of warrior groups and farmers is a diagnostic feature of migrants expanding for land, founding new settlements and cemeteries. This is the only type of migration certain to leave identifiable traces.

A wider distribution of grave goods characterises the expansion phase, and although it may look less hierarchical, this is not necessarily the case: a distribution of goods may also reflect a wealthier and more integrated society, allowing new social classes, farmers and young warriors, a more central place in production and in burial ritual. Or, alternatively, by virtue of their importance in the phase of expansion and pioneer settlement, they managed to gain a more independent position, controlling more of their own production and its distribution, which the chiefly elite simply had to accept. Cause and effect are not easy to determine in circumstances of rapid change. The warrior elite probably made up a warrior oligarchy, as encountered later in the oppida phase (see also note 2). The age structure at some well analysed cemeteries may give some hints (Figure 177): warriors are still distinguished in burials at an old age, in opposition to periods of more stable princely rule. It may suggest a leading group of older warriors, an oligarchy, at least at the local settlement level. We cannot exclude the existence of kings simply because of the lack of royal graves. There are two reasonable alternatives: they might be consolidated, not being ritually visible, or they had stayed at home, in the old Early La Tène kingdoms.

To the west, in the Atlantic zone, the nature of Celtic expansion is difficult to evaluate, as literary sources are fewer and the archaeology is less clear-cut. Place names and archaeology often go hand in hand, as well as other philological evidence, but they should be separated, as the origin of La Tène culture and the Celtic language are two different phenomena. There is no way to account for the strong presence of Celtic languages in western Europe by reference to La Tène culture. As pointed out by linguistics (Tovar 1986), the Celtic language had older roots in Iberia (see also Almagro-Gorbea and Lorrio 1987, Almagro-Gorbea 1991, 13), in England and in Ireland (Mallory 1991a; Koch 1991). It has been convincingly demonstrated in several recent studies that proto- or common Celtic entails the basic terminology of the social and economic organisation of later Bronze Age society (Mallory 1991, Koch 1991). Thus the geographical distribution of both linguistic and archaeological evidence points towards the Atlantic Bronze Age as the formative zone of Celtic language (Ruiz-Galvez 1991; Cooney and Grogan 1991; Waddell 1991). It expanded during Hallstatt C, defined by the western Hallstatt, which formed the social and ideological background of La Tène Culture.

In general the massive expansion of La Tène culture, beyond the borders of Celtic ethnicity, was late in northern and western Europe, confined to the 2nd and 1st centuries BC, but with a few 3rd-century finds as well. It seems to have been related to the expansion of trade and the formation of oppida, in combination with local intensification of farming and development of social hierarchy (see May 1976 and Champion in press for eastern England; Klindt-Jensen 1953, Frey 1986 and Pearson 1989 for northern Europe). Some late cross-Channel migrations are well documented in both written sources and archaeologically (Rodwell 1976; Hazelgrove 1987; Cunliffe 1988), being part of intensive trade and population movements north of the expanding Roman frontier. The flourishing of later La Tène culture in eastern England and Ireland, however, was probably due to trade (e.g. the rich hoards and workshops at Snettisham, reported in Clarke 1954; Stead 1991) and perhaps some small-scale migrations of artisans and traders, supported by earlier migrations to Yorkshire. La Tène culture was adapted to local and regional traditions, as demonstrated by the useful classification and mapping of La Tène material by Raftery (1984, maps 13, 16–17; 1989). We might perhaps rather think in terms of some Irish and English migrants/mercenaries going to the Continent, resulting in Celticised returning migrants bringing back La Tène culture and workmanship, as was the case with the Cimbric and Teutonic tribes of northern Europe (discussion Warner 1991; Raftery 1991).[4] In fact the expansion of La Tène culture to the west corresponds largely with the termination of Celtic expansion in east Central Europe and the Balkans, and their defeats from Asia Minor to northern Italy. In Iberia the expansion of Celtic culture and its local adaption into Celtiberian followed a similar path, its distribution being mainly the former Atlantic core areas of northern and western Iberia (articles in *Revista de arqueologia* 1991: Los Celtas en la Peninsula Iberica).

Also in northern and northwestern Europe we find a series of La Tène swords and La Tène influences on local cultures and *fibula* production (Hachmann 1960; Wilhelmi 1981; Frey 1986), demonstrating an increasing acculturation from late La Tène onwards (Pre-Roman III). It culminated in the production of fine La Tène wagons, probably by visiting or migrating Celtic artisans, which were employed by the elite in burials or as votive offerings (Harch 1988). Locally it reflected the formation of a new warrior elite buried with La Tène swords and living in chiefly farms (Hedeager 1992, 193ff.), which had taken over not only certain elite aspects of La Tène culture, but also its social and ideological content, including the formation of retinues. In the east Germanic area, between the Oder and the Vistula, a new cultural formation, the Przeworsk culture, emerged on the basis of strong La Tène influences from LT C (Dabrowska 1989). Despite these cultural and political interrelations, there remained a sharp cultural borderline between the two Celtic and Germanic cultures, with evidence for this in material culture distributions from pottery to oppida (Hachmann, Kossack and Kuhn 1962) (Figure 181). The division was linked to their different levels of social organisation, the gap accelerating from

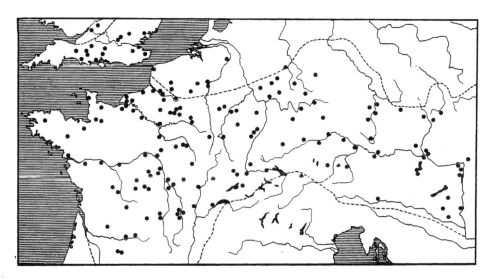

Fig. 181 Celtic oppida (black circle) and the distribution of wheel-turned pottery (broken line).

the 2nd century BC, placing the Germanic peoples in the role of a periphery to the urbanised Celtic societies.[5] The consequences of this evolutionary divergence, which was rooted in the changes that took place during the 6th and 5th centuries BC, were played out in full during the Roman expansion. This stopped at the border between the two cultures and societies, and even left a small Celtic buffer zone up against the Germanic people (Hedeager 1978b, fig. 18).

Urbanisation and the rituals of tension

Rituals are a sensitive barometer of the social conditions of existence, and therefore the correlation between certain categories of rituals, and particular processes of social change deserves fuller study. I have earlier suggested that there were regularities in the rise and consolidation of elites and the way in which wealth and monuments are employed in the process (Figure 32). It is important to stress again here that rituals and the deposition of various objects should be studied as a historical process of change. During the five centuries of Late Hallstatt/La Tène major social changes and displacements took place. Pauli has devoted a whole book to a study of the use of amulets in burials and their significance (1975). He observes that during the period of major social changes from Hallstatt to La Tène amulets were numerous in burials. They reflect the expansion of new magic-religious beliefs, taken up in the first place by individuals, as a means of protection against the risks and uncertainties of everyday life. This might later take on a more formalised structure of a (new?) religion. Parallels can be drawn with other times and places: during the expansion of the Urnfield culture various types of amulets became widespread (Kossack 1954b). The expansion of the Thraco-Cimmerian culture was also accompanied by a whole repertoire of amulets, employed in both sanctuaries (in Greece) and burials (in

Macedonia). Similar phenomena can be observed during periods of war and unrest in medieval and late historical times (e.g. the social and political changes during the Reformation period in 16th-century Europe).

Two conclusions can be drawn from these sequences: the spread of new social and economic strategies, eventually in combination with migrations, is often accompanied by new popular religious movements that expressed the ideology of the strategy and helped to mobilise larger groups of people. Deposition in burials or sanctuaries may suggest a more personal occupation with ritual (amulets); individuals have to protect themselves and their families in periods of migration and settlement expansion. Local and household rituals are more important in these circumstances than large communal rituals. Such a shift can be observed over most of the north European lowland area at the beginning of the Pre-Roman Iron Age after 500 BC, as household food sacrifices in pots became widespread at the expense of former communal rituals of hoard deposition (Becker 1971). In periods of centralisation, on the other hand, communal rituals develop to sustain the new higher order of organisation. There may eventually be attempts to replace local and family rites by these communal rituals. Increasing social stress will normally result in more excessive rituals, including human sacrifices. In African kingdoms in Kongo during the slave-raid period, large numbers of people were said to have been sacrificed and eaten by the king in the final phase of increasing stress and decline of royal authority. During this period (from the late 17th through the 18th and 19th centuries) local slave raiding warrior chiefs ruled the countryside, taking the scalps of their enemies and displaying them. Kingship becomes highly ritualised and without real power. From the late 19th century there then follows the forced colonisation and urbanisation (Ekholm 1985). Some of this historical sequence would seem to echo the La Tène period in its relation to the Mediterranean world, as described above. We are, however, mainly concerned with its final phase in this section.

Around 150 BC urbanisation spread across the Celtic world north of the Alps, starting in Central Europe in La Tène C2 (Bren 1976; Collis 1984b, 6–9) and spreading westwards within fifty years (Nash 1976; 1978; Collis 1982, 6–10). An early phase is also found in southern France around the Rhône valley (Cunliffe 1988, ch. 3), as well as in Manching. It had been preceded by an intensification of agriculture and industrial production, and a demographic increase, these being necessary but not sufficient preconditions for centralisation. It also happens so rapidly, with a few exceptions such as Manching, that other explanations have been sought. All cemeteries went out of use, with the exception of those in the central Rhineland, northeast France and southeastern England, including the old La Tène A centres (Collis 1975; Haffner 1989b, 44 ff.). Many farms were given up, when people moved into, or were moved to, the oppida. Was it a peaceful or a violent process? The rituals may give some indication.

But let us first briefly recapitulate the proposed causes (Nash 1976; 1978; Waldhauser 1984a; Collis 1984b; Frey 1984). Major changes affecting Celtic society took place during the 2nd century BC:

(1) Opportunities for mercenary service gradually came to an end with the expansion of the Roman Empire, and groups of mercenaries returned home, leading to social tensions, as well as bringing new experiences with them.

(2) As warring activities and migrations had come to an end, the conflicts could no longer be exported. This led to competition and internal warfare. People in need of protection became clients of nobles, building up large retinues and groups of followers/slaves. The Helvetian chief Orgetorix had a following of 10,000 slaves or freedmen and a multitude of clients. The early use of simple, high-value coins during the 3rd and 2nd centuries BC was linked to this development.

(3) Wealth therefore had to be gained through the intensification of production and trade with the Romans. In Gaul this took the form of exchanging slaves for wine, which also spurred slave raids and local warfare. Iron, gold and amber were other important products (Timpe 1985). The massive influx of Roman imports into Gaul and southern England from the mid-2nd century BC corresponds to this new development (Cunliffe 1988; Hazelgrove 1987).

(4) Finally, Rome was expanding, and had already expelled the Celts from northern Italy, which became Gallia Cisalpina. This development held promise of trade and diplomatic relations on the one hand (Fitzpatrick 1989), but also fear of its continuation. Measures for active resistance had to be taken, which might also at the same time facilitate trade with the Romans.

This combination of factors worked together to enforce quite rapidly, at least from an archaeological perspective, the agglomeration of large groups of the population in oppida, most importantly artisans and craft specialists, in the late phase under the leadership of groups of oligarchical nobles. It created a period of internal conflict and social stress. Although the change appears rapid, it may well have been facilitated by a gradual development of social hierarchy during late Middle La Tène (the creation of larger retinues and groups of clients), which was concealed by the 'democratic' burial ideology. As pointed out in Chapter 2.1, by the point at which a change can be observed archaeologically, it has already happened, and the processes leading up to it should be traced in the preceding period. In some areas opposition was strong enough to prevent the new system emerging, or at least to soften it, e.g. in Belgium/Holland on the Rhine and in southeastern England, where burial traditions also continued. In an illuminating study of northeastern France and the Netherlands Roymans (1987; 1990) has demonstrated how these divergent developments of opposition created a borderline on the Lower Rhine between traditional warrior societies opposing the new developments, and an area of oppida formation in France/Hunsrück Eifel (Roymans 1987, fig. 10.3). Even in the Middle Rhine/Moselle (Hunsrück-Eifel) group where oppida were adopted, although only in small numbers, the old royal warrior aristocracies remained in power, as reflected by a new series of rich Late La Tène chariot burials with Roman imports (Roymans 1987, figs. 7.2, 7.6; Hazelgrove 1987, fig. 10.6). During the process of oppida formation, craftsmanship and La Tène art of course declined, while at the same time an enormous increase in the volume of industrial production and trade can be observed,

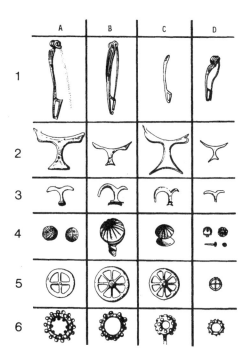

Fig. 182 Comparative chart of some Late La Tène items from oppida throughout Europe, demonstrating the intensity of contacts and the resulting similarity of production: A = Bibracte, France; B = Stradonitz, Czechoslovakia; C = Manching, southern Germany; D = Velem St Veit, Hungary.

e.g. reflected in the distribution of wheel-turned pottery, and the widespread similarities of objects (Figures 181, 182). In the oppida we normally find abundant evidence of trade with the Roman Empire, especially wine amphorae, as well as evidence of local craft production on a large scale. Low-value coins were now struck, facilitating the centralised distribution of basic commodities, as well as local trade between oppida and surrounding settlements (Nash 1978).

The oppida had three major functions: (1) defensive, to protect their central functions and the surrounding population (Figure 183); (2) administrative, to receive tribute, take care of local redistribution and long-distance trade; (3) industrial, to produce traditional commodities ranging from iron knives to fine pottery (Lorenz 1986) (Figure 184). These services were centred in different quarters of the oppida, corresponding to their definition as urban settlements. The use of coins points to a new level of economic transactions, at the same time restricting trade to the boundaries of the local mint (Allen 1980). So coins gave both control of trade and the possibility of more flexible exchange. The oppida further served to unify the different local economies, from downland to upland subsistence, within one political framework. As soon as the process of oppida formation started it spread in a chain reaction of competition and warfare. Nash (1978) has shown how archaic state formation (centralised as opposed to decentralised) was a function of the new social and economic order, enslaving probably hundreds of thousands of people during its one hundred-year existence, although these more horrible aspects of internal warfare and

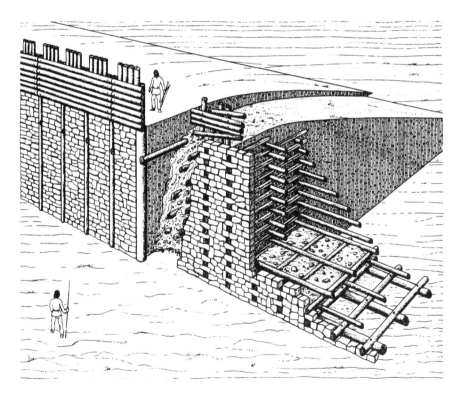

Fig. 183 Reconstruction of entrance and two period fortifications at Manching, Bavaria.

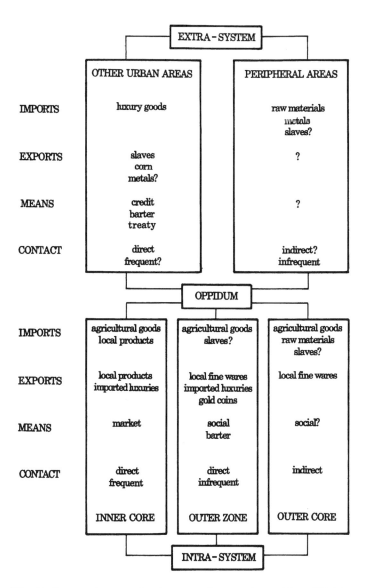

Fig. 184 Suggested nature of trade contacts between the oppidum of Colchester/Camulodunum and its hinterland and external areas.

slave raids are only documented in Gaul (Peschel 1990) (Figure 185). The rigid, class-divided, Celtic society of nobles, druids, commoners and slaves (Haselgrove 1987, fig. 10.3) was a result of the explosive development of the oppida, but it certainly built upon already existing components, whose potential for stratification was taken to their limit. But in the process the balance between them changed: the warrior leaders and their kings were replaced by groups of nobles, forming an oligarchy freed from warfare, in charge of trade and administration. Within the same group were the druids, whose rise to power must also have been a late phenomenon linked to oppida and state formation and the need for new types of communal ritual.

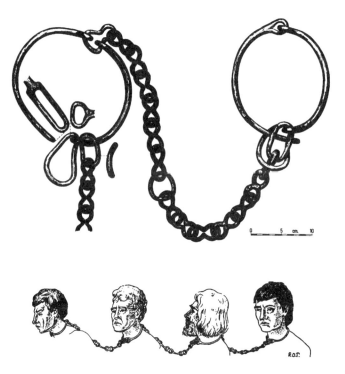

Fig. 185 Fragment of iron neck–chain and reconstruction of its use.

The conflicts referred to by Caesar between royal and oligarchical rule echoed the change in the social balance, reducing the traditional power of the warrior group, and leading to much internal warfare (Caesar BG 1.3–4, 1.31). Although Nash (1976; 1978) especially has underlined the gradual changes leading up to oppida formation: both archaeological and textual evidence point to the process itself being fast and violent. What light can the rituals throw on this question?

Significantly, it is at this time, when cemeteries come to a halt as well, that sanctuaries, and *Viereckschanzen*, appeared all over the Celtic world, but with a concentration in Central Europe and Gaul (Bittel, Schiek and Müller 1990; Büchsenschütz and Olivier 1989). Only in recent years has the nature and variation in late Celtic ritual come to our knowledge, due to modern excavation techniques (summarised in Bruneaux 1986 and 1988; Müller 1990). Although the formal components of sanctuaries and *Viereckschanzen* are rather similar, they should be differentiated on functional grounds (Büchsenschütz and Olivier 1989, Bruneaux 1988, ch. 2).

Viereckschanzen A small piece of land, 0.5–1 ha, was enclosed by a low wall and sometimes a trench for offerings; a wooden entrance and a simple house in a corner or in the middle (the temple) were normally the only constructional elements (Figure 186). Sometimes deep shafts were dug down 20–30 m, their function being unknown, although they are probably wells (furnished with planks at their sides), occasionally employed for ritual depositions. Most well known is the finding of a

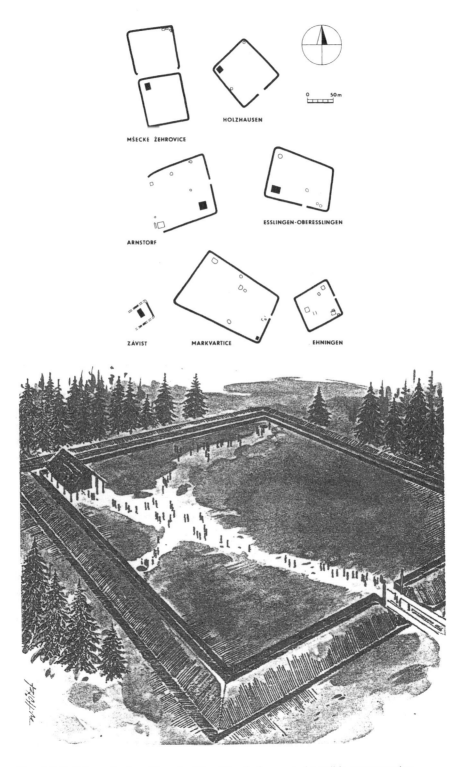

Fig. 186(A) Schematic plan of Late La Tène *Viereckschanzen* and possible reconstruction.

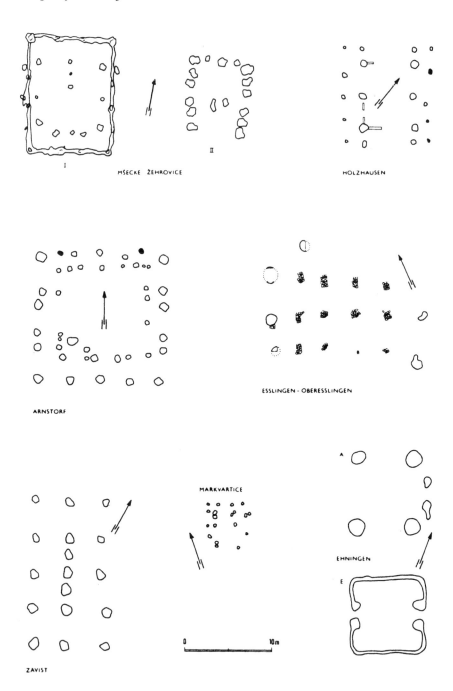

Fig. 186(B) Plans of the wooden structures inside the *Viereckschanzen*, considered as possible shrines.

group of wooden figures and animals in one at Felbach Schmiden, reflecting old Scythian traditions (Planck 1982). *Viereckschanzen* have mostly been regarded as sanctuaries or ritual shrines, due to the absence of settlement material in most of them. Sacrifices, however, are also absent, which has been ascribed to bone not

surviving due to poor conditions. In recent years these interpretations have come
under critical scrutiny, and other functions have been proposed, including communal meeting places and chiefly farms (Pauli 1991; Venclova 1993). Recent large-scale
excavations at Bopfingen in Germany of a larger surrounding area have revealed that
a *Viereckschanze* partly overlapped a chiefly settlement with the same layout, going
back to the earlier La Tène (Krause and Wielandt 1993). It suggests a linkage
between the chiefly farms, which are archaeologically badly known, and the construction of *Viereckschanzen* in late La Tène, in much the same way as the earliest
churches in the late Viking age were build by local Viking chiefs, sometimes inside
the chiefly farm itself (Jeppesen and Madsen 1988–89). It further stresses the central
function of *Viereckschanzen* at the local level in the social transformations taking
place during late La Tène.

Sanctuaries   in opposition to *Viereckschanzen*, sanctuaries are mostly linked to
an oppida, either inside as in Manching, or in the vicinity, as at Gournay (Rapin
1982) (Figure 187). They are mainly documented in the west (France, England),
often continuing into the Gallo-Roman period. Thus they rather represent a regional
ritual centre, corresponding to the political functions of the oppidum. Their basic
layout conforms rather closely to that of the *Viereckschanze*, an enclosure with a high
palisade and a ditch (Figure 187, upper part) and a quadrangular temple at the
centre. Deep pits for offerings were sometimes found within the sacred or enclosed
area, as in Gournay (Bruneaux 1988, 29). Ritual feasts and offerings took place at the
sanctuaries, including human sacrifices as well as weapons, as demonstrated at
Gournay (Figure 188), where the enclosure was located in the middle of an oppidum
(Rapin 1982; Bruneaux 1986, ch. 2). The role of druids and the function of the
sanctuaries were probably closely interlinked, representing a new ritual/legal medium for enforcing the new social and political conditions.[6] However, in some places,
like northern Gaul, sanctuaries preceded the formation of oppida, as they were
already functioning from the 3rd century BC.

Thus sanctuaries and *Viereckschanzen* were the focus of political and ritual activities at respectively local and regional levels, in a period that saw the creation of a new
social order and a new political and religious identity.[7] As stated by Bruneaux (1988,
142): 'The sanctuary is an indication of a people becoming aware of its unity and its
component parts. It reveals the emergence of the notion of citizenship.'

Other aspects of later Celtic rituals, such as skull cults and taking the heads of
enemies, were signs of a society under severe stress, taking to extreme ritual solutions
(many parallels can be cited from anthropology and history of similar reactions to
such stressful conditions, from Oceania (Kirch 1991), Burma (Friedman 1975),
Kongo (Ekholm 1985) to the Plains Indians of North America). The taking of enemy
heads as trophies was common during the migration period of middle La Tène,
whereas the skull cults belong rather with the later La Tène, where they are widespread, from both oppida (e.g. Manching: Lorenz 1986, 178ff. and Abb. 79) and
shrines/sanctuaries, where the heads were set up, sometimes in skull-niches in the
walls, as at the stone shrine at Roquepertuse.[8] The general occurrence of human

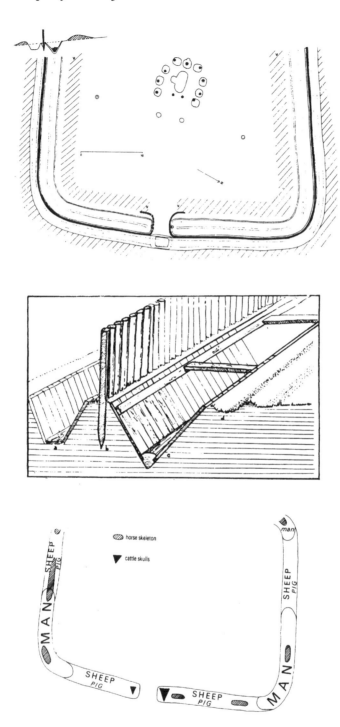

Fig. 187 Ground plan of the *Viereckschanze* at Gournay-sur-Aronde, France (above), reconstruction of palisade and ditch (middle), and the position of sacrificed bones placed in the ditches according to specific rules (below).

Fig. 188 Reconstruction of rituals in the early phase of Figure 187 at Gournay (above) and in the later phase (below).

bones in oppida, and systematic cutting marks bear witness to cannibalism, while other sites with systematic piling of human bones are taken to represent the new burial tradition, as in Ribemont-sur-Ancre (Bruneaux 1988, 21). It meant the dissolution of the individual, perhaps a significant indication of a new, class-divided social order.

The origins of *Viereckschanzen* and sanctuaries are unclear; proposals span from Mediterranean influences (Bruneaux 1988) towards indigenous traditions of rectangular burial structures and houses in the Hallstatt culture (Bruneaux 1988, 137 ff.; Lambot 1989; Pautreau 1990). What matters, however, is their renewed significance/ redefinition and use over most of the Celtic world from the beginnings of oppida formation. In the final phase of Celtic society a forced development of archaic state formation and urbanisation under increasing stress led to a cyclical process of political centralisation and fragmentation, internal warfare and stress. The traditional rule of warrior kings and their retinues was replaced by oligarchical rule under Roman inspiration (also drawn from the elite), in a process of internal conflict between 'traditionalists', maintaining old Celtic principles, and 'modernists' turning towards Roman and urban values, as happened many times during the following centuries along the expanding Roman frontier. The victory of the modernists, leading to oppida formation, made the later inclusion of Celtic culture within Roman rule much easier, whereas the Germanic people, who were now alone in maintaining the old warrior traditions, could not be incorporated. In the process farmers were especially liable to be enslaved or to lose their social and economic freedom, becoming clients of the nobles and kings. The emergence of communal rituals of animal and human sacrifices on a grand scale were part of this process of indirect social terror, making formerly more independent social groups, particularly farmers, ritually invisible (e.g. new invisible burial rituals), which corresponded to their new social standing.

Conclusion 9
The sequence from La Tène A (Early) through B/C1 (Middle) to C2/D (Late) represents a development from highland chiefly warrior societies, via migrations and the formation of downland farming communities (Figure 189), to centralisation in oppida which combined the two social and economic systems in an archaic state (Collis 1984b, figs. 10.1–2 and 10.8). The old La Tène A centres were mainly located on high ground, basing their economy on pastoral farming and control of iron sources and iron production, rooted in the warrior traditions of Hallstatt C times. By comparison, Middle La Tène migrations represented an expansion into more fertile lowlands suitable for intensive agrarian production, the old heartlands of the Urnfield culture. This produced an agrarian expansion and intensification. Both production and social organisation were decentralised. The migrations were led by large groups of warriors, and constituted a decentralised society adapted to migration and pioneer settlement. The new farming and warrior communities made themselves visible in burial ritual, suggesting their rise to the social status of a recognised group or class. The stimulus to migration was originally settlement expansion and conquest

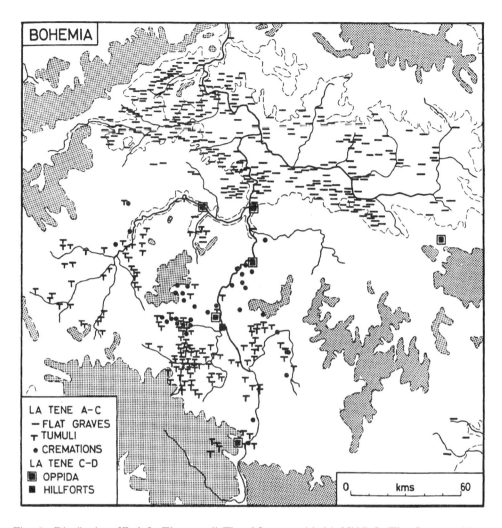

Fig. 189 Distribution of Early La Tène tumuli (T) and flat graves (circle), Middle La Tène flat graves (–), and Late La Tène oppida and hillforts in Bohemia (squares).

by young princes, in order to export internal conflicts out of the chiefly centres, and the first migrations may have been part of a coordinated effort to take over northern Italy. Soon they took on a dynamic of their own, out of the control of the former centres. New rewarding opportunities for large groups of young families, especially the sons of farmers and local warrior chiefs, became the backbone of expansion, leading to a period of social mobility. This was supported by the formation of a self-conscious Celtic national ethnicity, reflected in an easily identifiable material culture allowing the inclusion of new groups under a common cultural identity. In all these respects we may draw direct analogies to Germanic and later Viking migrations, which followed a similar pattern.

Processes of migration/settlement expansion and social and economic change were thus linked together, implying that we cannot interpret migrations as isolated events. The existence of written evidence, in combination with well-analysed and published archaeological finds, has allowed us to probe more deeply into the conditions and dynamics of migrations and their archaeological identification. The literary and archaeological evidence was seen to be in full agreement, and only briefer episodes of conquest migrations into the territory of more complex cultures proved difficult to identify archaeologically. We could also observe the effects of this sequence of changes in the relationship between La Tène culture and neighbouring groups in the north and west. During the migration period (Middle La Tène = La Tène B and early C), interregional exchange fell drastically and was reduced to random local exchange along the border zone, which meant, however, that La Tène cultural modes were to some extent followed. It appears that only with consolidation and the beginning of oppidum formation did interregional exchange with the north began to flourish, although it was facilitated by returning migrants from the Cimbri and Teutonic tribes (shown by the Gundestrup cauldron) and by a similar development of small-scale centralisation and warrior elites in the north. The distinction between a diffusion of La Tène culture through trade and exchange and its implanting due to migration is fairly easy to make. Local traditions in crafts and burial rituals continued in areas of exchange, while they were replaced in areas of migration.

With this case study as a platform, I shall make an attempt to reinterpret the expansion of the Urnfield culture in the concluding Chapter. But I suspect that major expansions in prehistory of new international cultures, such as the Battle Axe culture, when involving basic changes in burial ritual and settlements as well, were normally linked to some form of migration. The opposite explanation – that such major changes were due to peaceful exchange by sedentary societies – has yet to be supported by ethnographic and historical analogies. However, more selective social and ritual practices linked to the formation of new status positions, etc., may spread through elite exchange.

Some may find this view too historical and dramatic, with not enough emphasis on continuity. But we must remember that when 100 years are subsumed within a single archaeological period, it is no wonder that history appears to be dramatic, perhaps too dramatic, at the cost of continuity and everyday life. But drama and disruption were always essential ingredients in history, lifting it up into memory. Although history was shaped by the accumulating forces of everyday life, its traces and memories were often produced by the unusual and the dramatic. The archaeologist has to situate her- or himself between these two poles. During the past twenty-five years the weight has been on reconstructing the social and economic basis of historical change and action – this emphasis was much needed and with good reason. Now the time may be ripe to reintroduce history and the structural and evolutionary significance of major historical events, in so far as they can be reconstructed.

The emergence of the European world system in the Bronze Age and Early Iron Age: Europe in the 1st and 2nd millennia BC

8.1 The 2nd millennium: an interpretative and explanatory sketch

I have presented no final conclusion to the previous chapters, except for the partial conclusions numbered 1 to 9. A conclusion should be more than a summing up – it should provide new insights and hypotheses which can serve as a platform for future research. Throughout the chapters I have hinted at social and historical regularities in our data by comparison with other periods. I have further suggested that during the 1st millennium BC Europe entered into a kind of world system with the Mediterranean. In order to trace its origin we need to take a brief look at developments during the 2nd millennium. This may further provide the kind of comparative framework needed to generalise about the structures of interaction and processes of change described for the 1st millennium BC.

The role of the Mycenaeans

During the early 2nd millennium BC a network of long-distance trade in copper, silver, tin and textiles was in operation in the eastern Mediterranean and the Near East (Figure 190), as demonstrated by textual evidence (Larsen 1987a; Klengel 1978 and 1990, Abb. 3; Knapp 1991). It carried a large bulk of goods, especially silver, copper and textiles, with the quantities mentioned leaving no doubt as to the scale and organisation of trade. This can be compared to later historical city-state trade, such as Venetian or Dutch commerce (Larsen 1987a, 51 and note 7). Thus, before the rise of the Mycenaean culture the stimulus in trade and metalwork came from the Near East, based both on inland caravan routes, such as the well-known one connecting Assur and Kanesh in Asia Minor, and on sea trade, with Syria, Cyprus and Crete playing central roles (Crete: Klengel 1984; Cyprus especially from 1700 onwards: Knapp 1988). On Crete the palace system emerged around 1900 BC – at the same time as the development of a bronze metallurgy and the rise of metallurgical centres took place in Central and western Europe. These commercial trade networks spanning the Near East and the eastern Mediterranean serve as an illustrative background to the rise of the Mycenaeans and their role as middlemen between the western and eastern Mediterranean.[1] This is not to deny the role of internal development of settlement and economy (Bintliff 1977; 1982), but that does not explain the nature of Mycenaean culture and its role within this larger network; that is only poorly known, due to the sporadic archaeological evidence of metalwork in the Near East at this time (in general see Jahresschrift Frankfurt 1977; Hänsel 1982b). It also stresses that this early sea trade originated primarily in the Levant.

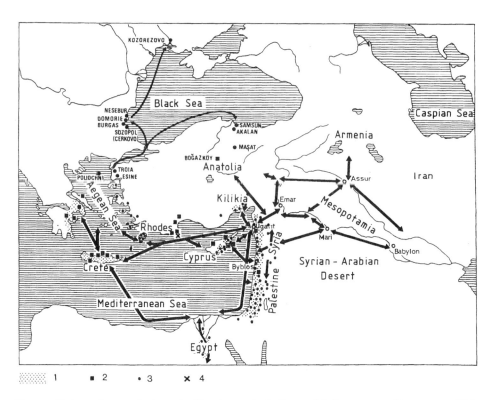

Fig. 190 Major trade routes in the 2nd millennium BC in the Eastern Mediterranean, with a suggested link to a Northwest Anatolian/Black Sea trade network: 1 = Finds of Mycenaean pottery; 2 = Finds of ox-hide ingots; 3 = Cypriotic potter; 4 = Cape Gelidonya shipwreck.

From the 17th century BC the Mycenaeans took over and developed the western fringe of the Near Eastern commercial networks, under strong influence from Minoan culture, as shown in imports (Cherry 1986, Fig. 2.1). Minoan culture both transmitted and integrated influences from the whole eastern Mediterranean, from Egypt to Asia Minor. That role was adopted by the Mycenaeans in relation to their trading partners and contacts in the western Mediterranean and Central Europe, although the situation was one of mutual inspiration, and mostly indirect in nature, as contact with European Bronze Age societies took place through middlemen. I shall thus consider the Mycenaeans in their role as transmitters and receivers of new influences between the east Mediterranean and Central Europe. I propose that they rose to power due to their ability to provide both parties with what they needed, creating a new competitive niche, which had only been sporadically exploited earlier by the kingdoms in Asia Minor and by the Minoans (Dickinson 1987). As argonauts in the western Mediterranean and traders along more well-known routes into the Black Sea (Buchholz 1983, Abb. 10) they established links with Early Bronze Age groups in both areas, the intensity of which increased over time, and changed in importance. The northern trade into the Black Sea was part of an old social and cultural network involving the coastal towns of Asia Minor; this was a potentially competitive relationship, as it later became in the Trojan war. It flourished during

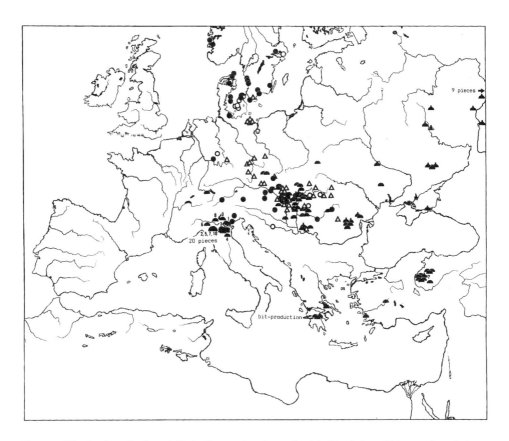

Fig. 191 Distribution of selected Early Bronze Age items (mainly Br. A2) testifying to the relations between Anatolia/the Aegean, East Central Europe and the Nordic area: black circle = variants of bronze axe with curved blade; triangle = shafthole axes of Krtenov type; open circle = Apa swords; half circle = tine cheek-pieces; halfcircle with extension = disc cheek-pieces. Depictions and finds of two-wheeled chariots show a similar distribution.

the Shaft Grave period between 1700 and 1450 BC and again from the late 13th century until the collapse of Mycenaean civilisation. From the mouth of the Danube lines of exchange were established with the rich bronze-producing cultures of the Carpathians (Figure 191), as shown by the distribution of a series of objects including double axes (Buchholz 1983), swords (Bouzek 1985, ch. 2) and carved bone objects, whose distribution along the coast of Asia Minor stresses the cultural *koine* of the Aegean/eastern Europe (Kull 1989), including horse gear and chariots (Hüttel 1977; 1982).[2] In the western Mediterranean trading posts or trading contacts were established in southern Italy, Sardinia and Corsica by the 17th century BC (Late Middle Helladic/early Late Helladic,), according to the most recent datings (Buchholz 1987, Abb. 69; Warren and Hankey 1989, Tabelle 3.1), by both Mycenaean and Cypriot traders (Figure 192) (Hase 1990, Abb. 22). At the same time fortified settlements appear (Peroni 1977, 192), later developing into trading sites or gateways (Smith 1987, 128ff.). The distribution of copper oxhide ingots (Figure 193) and Cypriot daggers in the same areas, and in France, is now taken by Harding

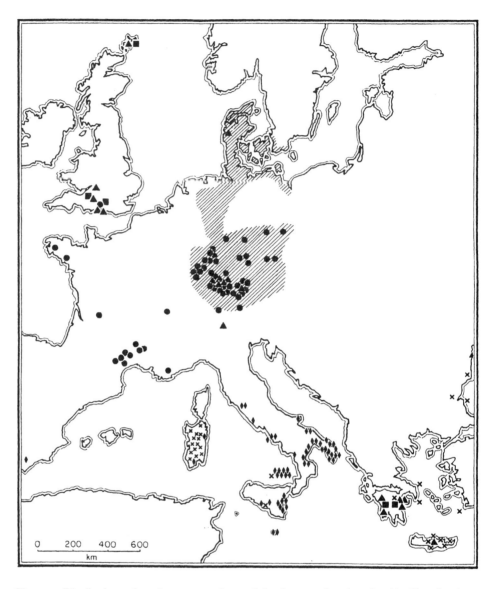

Fig. 192 Distribution of amber spacer-plates: (triangle = complex bored with V-perforations; square = end pieces with converging perforation; circle = all other types); ox-hide ingots (cross); Mycenaean pottery of LHI–LHIIIA date (rhombus); octagonally-hilted and early straight flange-hilted swords (hatched). The map suggests a West Mediterranean–Northwest European exchange system of regionally connected exchange circuits.

(1990) to indicate a circuit of trade stations in the western Mediterranean during this period. These connections were intensified from the 15th and 14th centuries BC onwards, when the Black Sea trade to Central Europe declined, and they culminated during the 13th century (Bietti Sestieri 1988; Vagnetti 1993). This developed into a more regular trading relationship with Italy, Sardinia (Vagnetti and Lo Schiavo 1989) and southern France around the Rhône, based on the exploitation of

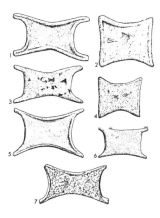

Fig. 193 Ox-hide ingots.

mineral resources, near to which the Greek settlements – or imports – concentrate (Hase 1990, Abb. 1–5).[3]

The development of Mycenaean culture, as reflected in burials and settlements, followed the 'normal' pattern – beginning with a series of richly furnished aristocratic burials of new royal elites (the Shaft Graves) between 1700 (1650 according to the standard dating) and 1500/1450 BC (Mylonas 1972; Kilian-Dirlmeier 1986), which was followed by an expansion and consolidation period, lasting until a major collapse around 1200 BC or shortly after (Dickinson 1987). The development of the palace system and the florescence of Mycenaean culture after 1500 was linked to their conquest of the Minoans, their former masters and source of inspiration. The palatial system and many rich burials in monumental chambers and barrows (the *tholoi*) scattered over the landscape indicate consolidation and the spread of wealth to new regional and local elites, the development of a more formal royal dynasty with vassals and local administrative centres (Figure 194) (Pelon 1976; Warren 1977; Kilian-Dirlmeier 1989).

We can thus distinguish three phases in the development of contacts between the eastern Mediterranean/Asia Minor and European Bronze Age societies: an early phase from 2000/1900 to 1700 BC, probably dominated by the Minoans and societies in Asia Minor; a second of closer contact corresponding to the Shaft Grave period and the rise of the Mycenaeans from 1700 to 1500; and a third of consolidation and more regular trade with Italian/west Mediterranean trade stations leading down to the fourth phase of collapse into a Dark Age after 1200 BC (also Sherratt and Sherratt 1991). During the early phase, contacts with Europe were apparently part of a traditional network of indirect contacts from the Balkans and the Black Sea area into Central Europe and the Aunjetitz culture of Br. A1 (Bouzek 1985, fig. 3). It was from the 17th century BC that trade developed and became more systematic, organised by the Shaft Grave kings. In a series of explorations, contacts were directed towards the Black Sea/east Central Europe and towards western Europe (Wessex/France). During the period of consolidation (1500–1200 BC) trade was mainly directed towards Italy and west Central Europe, and in the final phase once again towards east Central

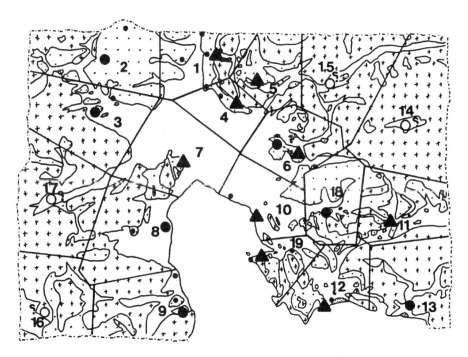

Fig. 194 Mycenaean sites in the Argive plain, Greece: major centres (triangles) form the centre of the Thiessen polygon cell network representing putative central-place territories; medium and minor sites are represented by large and small circles. Each cell holds an estimated population of 600–800.

Europe. At the same time Mycenaean activities also extended into the eastern Mediterranean (Harding 1984, fig. 53; Courtois 1987), although Syrian and Cypriot traders were also active in creating this pattern, as well as in the western Mediterranean (the Cypriot daggers and oxhide ingots, whose provenience has been determined by isotope analysis: Gale 1991b; Stos-Gale 1992, figs. 5–7). The historical sequence reflects a development from small-scale luxury trade in the early phase (tin, amber and gold) towards large-scale bulk trade in commodities – including copper – in the late period (Knapp 1990; Sherratt and Sherratt 1991).[4]

This brief outline just indicates the overall pattern of contacts. The literature is enormous, but I refer the reader to the two standard works, which summarise the evidence – Bouzek (1985), supporting wide-ranging contacts, and Harding (1984), who is more sceptical (also Krause 1988a, 145–180). My own position is more in line with Bouzek's, and recent discoveries (e.g. Gale 1991a) have tended to modify Harding's views (1990). As we shall see, the three phases outlined above also correspond to important changes in European Bronze Age societies. The real challenge is to evaluate the impact of these traces of contact and their effects on local cultures, and vice versa.

The rise of metallurgical centres
By 1900 BC alloys of copper and tin began to replace copper, and metallurgical techniques and the employment of bronze became more widespread. For the first

time large-scale copper mining and mining communities developed in Central Europe, a few centres of production supplying larger regions in Europe with standardised products, simple tools and ring ingots, as evidenced by trace analysis (Pittioni 1957). Fixed weights were employed for the products (Moosleitner 1988; Malmer 1992). The yearly output from some of these early mining areas has been estimated to be 10–20 tons.[5] We can identify two major areas of metalworking during the first half of the 2nd millennium BC, beginning in Br A1 and flourishing in A2, between 1700 and 1500 BC. To the west we find an Atlantic network in operation, and in Central and east Central Europe, along the Danube, and further north, was another network of bronze-producing societies, the Aunjetitz culture (Br A1) later to be followed by the Otomani culture, named after one of its sites. These cultures all had their roots in the widely distributed copper-using late Bell Beaker culture (Harrison and Gilman 1977; Kalicz and Kalicz Schreiber 1981; *Slovenskan Arch.* 1981; Shennan 1986a; 1986b). In the late Aunjetitz culture during Br A1 the first metallurgical centres developed in the Erzgebirge and the western Carpathians – their products, mostly simple axes and daggers, were widely spread. From Ireland, through Iberia, to Central Europe, early, rather small-scale, metallurgical centres of production developed, with chiefly burials appearing only in those few centres serving a wider area. An example is Leubingen, now dated to 1900 BC (Horst 1990), which was in charge of metal trade to the north, as reflected in numerous hoards of axes, ring ingots and daggers (Brunn 1959). It was not until 1700 BC (Br A2) that a real expansion in production began, resulting in a massive increase in the variety of products – now including all sorts of ornaments, swords and lances. From Bronze A2 to the beginning of B1 production flourished and long-distance networks developed. These Early Bronze Age societies had several things in common: they were based on intensive agriculture, this serving as an economic basis that allowed the development of mining, metal production and trade. They were favoured with a dry, warm climate, permitting the lowland cultivation of river valleys. These societies gradually developed a hierarchical and centralised settlement pattern of fortified, chiefly, residences surrounded by smaller open settlements. Thus the shift from A1 to A2 was marked by technological and social transformation, including the formation of a warrior elite and subsequent changes in warfare caused by the introduction of the long sword and the lance in Central Europe. It also represented an intensification of agriculture, reflected in new lake settlements, whereas valley slopes had been opened up during Br A1 (Brombacher and Dick 1987). Finally, larger regions to the north began an indigenous metal production, which created an increasing 'market' for the distribution of metal. The ideology of chiefly warrior elites had been adopted from the Mediterranean, and soon spread to larger areas, the consequences of this development being seen in the subsequent period.

For Iberia and the western Mediterranean the early Atlantic metalwork developed different regional traditions (Figure 195), with Brittany and Wessex as the centre of wealth display and of foreign contacts, recently summarised by Schauer (1984a, Abb. 1–7). Coastal contacts from Wessex/Brittany to Portugal and Spain were maintained, forming the background to many general similarities. As pointed out by Harding, a

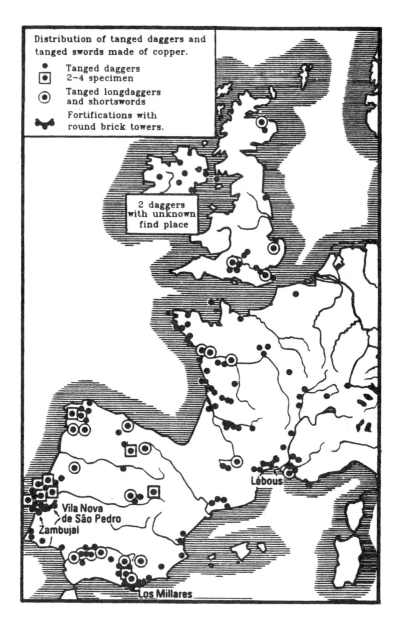

Fig. 195 The Atlantic Copper Age of the later 3rd millennium.

number of very specific Mycenaean status objects, such as the identical zig-zag mounts (belonging to sceptres) from Britain, France and Greece (Harding 1990, fig. 10), as well as the identical amber beads occurring in the same areas, must indicate the existence of a network of more regular contacts, which was able to carry not only valuables but also symbolic knowledge of elite status. A series of gold finds, and faience beads of Mediterranean origin or influence (Briard 1990), found in chiefly burials in the same area, point in the same direction (Figure 196). The point of entry

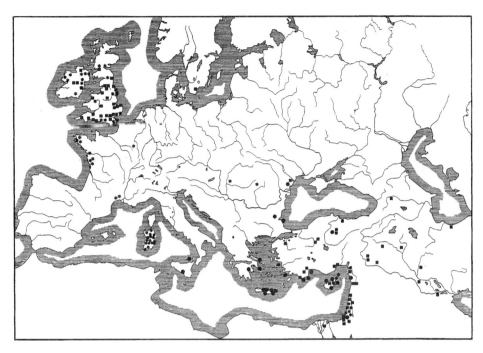

Fig. 196 Distribution of Early Bronze Age golden twisted earrings of East Mediterranean origin (star), ox-hide ingots (circle) and Arreton blades in Britain and related East Mediterranean pieces (square). The distributions slightly antedate and complement those in Figure 192.

was, apparently, southern France, with contacts from there reaching Brittany and southern England (Briard 1990, fig. 7). The emergence of chiefly tumulus barrows in Wessex and Armorica points to the rise of new chiefly elites, employing large-scale rituals at sites such as Stonehenge as a mobilising factor. The products of trade were gold and tin, so valuable that even small quantities could be profitably exchanged overland to the Mediterranean. Besides these exclusive products, metalwork developed according to local traditions, although some rather specific and short-lived technological improvements resulted from contacts with Cypriot or Mycenaean traders, such as the inlaid work on the dagger from Maris de Nantes (Schauer 1984a, Taf. I), sheet gold work and faience production (Taylor 1981). Mediterranean inspiration of a more general nature may also be seen in the metalwork, e.g. the Arreton daggers of southern England (Schauer 1984a, Abb. 35–37).

In Iberia stone towers surrounded by several circular masonry defence walls, spaced at regular intervals of 15 km, became the standard central settlement type in the lowlands (Chapman 1990, 237 ff.; Martín *et al.* 1993), while the uplands were dominated by large and complex stone-built settlements. This early Bronze Age settlement system was in operation during most of Br. A1–A2/B1, that is from 2200 to 1500 BC (Martín *et al.* 1993, 25ff.). The economy intensified, employing simple irrigation, and probably the vine–olive complex in the uplands (Gilman and Thornes 1985; Gilman 1991). Otherwise grain production and animal husbandry dominated in the open-land settlements, cattle/horse and sheep being exploited for their secondary products (Martín *et al.* 1993, 31f.). Both phenomena, interlinked as they were, point to developments in the local economy and hierarchy by El Argar and related cultures (Coles and Harding 1979, ch. 5; Gonzales, Lull and Risch 1992, ch. 4). The expansion of settlement into marginal areas also points in the same direction, e.g. La Mancha (Martín *et al.* 1993). Defensive considerations, in combination with the possibility of irrigation, determined the location of settlements – though settlements on high ground normally needed no defences. Thus power resided in the territorial control of production, apparently without any larger political centralisation (discussion in Gilman 1991; Martín *et al.* 1993, 41ff.; Harrison 1994; Nocete 1994 for an alternative view). Metallurgy and craft specialisation remained at a rather low level, exchange being local (Montero 1992). In all these respects, including the stone-built towers, they resemble settlement and society in the west Mediterranean islands, exemplified by the nuraghi on Sardinia (Webster 1991). Other products, such as ivory, were considered as prestige goods and exchanged widely. In Wessex, on the contrary, power resided in the chiefly operation of rituals and prestige goods trade of metalwork, creating for a brief period a chiefly hierarchy based on pastoral farming, organised around large-scale upland field systems and mineral exploitation (Fleming 1988; Earle 1991b). Thus Wessex and El Argar illustrate two alternative organisational strategies of the Early Bronze Age.

The flourishing of the Atlantic network was not due to any direct Mediterranean influences – it originated in the 3rd millennium (Harrison and Gilman 1977) and operated according to its own dynamics of coastal exchange, combining Atlantic and Mediterranean traditions (Figure 195). During the Early Bronze Age distinctive regional traditions in metalwork can also be identified below the general similarities. But from 1700 BC a more directional Mycenaean and Cypriot trade led to a growth in metalwork and the development of social hierarchy in Wessex/Brittany, whereas Iberia was apparently excluded from this.

In Central Europe there is a similar pattern of development: along the Danube and its tributaries, extending into Switzerland and eastern France, a series of rather small bronze-producing groups, with communal cemeteries, appeared during Br A1 (Hundt 1961; Ruckdeschel 1978; Krause 1988a; a summary is provided in Neugebauer and Neugebauer-Maresch 1990). They created small regional and local industries, which, however, shared a common repertoire of ornaments (pins) and weapons (axes and daggers). Their small village settlements or rather hamlets are exemplified by the Swiss lake dwellings, such as Mozartstrasse (Primas 1990) (Figure 197), as is their subsistence economy, based upon grain cultivation of mainly wheat, and cattle husbandry (Brombacher and Dick 1987).[6] Communal cemeteries, divided into clan segments, such as Gemeinlebarn, were common (Figure 198) (Neugebauer 1991, Abb. 35). A development from minimal ranking to more profound social and economic differentiation took place (Shennan 1975; 1986a), the more richly furnished chiefly males being taller than commoners with few grave goods (Teschler-Nicola 1987; Stadler 1988). With the decline of the Aunjetitz culture, the Carpathians became the centre of mining and bronze production, supplying large areas with their products.[7]

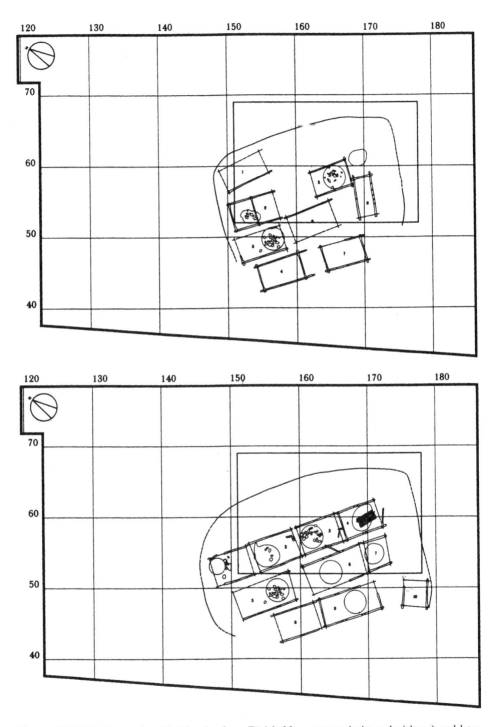

Fig. 197(A) Early Bronze Age (A2) hamlet from Zürich Mozartstrasse in its early (above) and later (below) phases.

Layer	10 20 30 40 50 60 70 80 90 %	10 20 30 40 50 60 %	10 20 30 40 50 60 70 80 %	
1u (Early B.A.)				648
1l (Early B.A.)				736
2 (Cord pottery)				789
3 (Horgen)				764
4u (Pfyn)				329
4m (Pfyn)				699
4l (Pfyn)				702
5 (Cortaillod)				1014
6 (Cortaillod)				1102

Layer	10 20 30 40 50 60 70 80 90 %	10 20 30 40 50 60 70 %	10 20 30 40 50 60 70 %	
1u (Early B.A.)				648
1l (Early B.A.)				736
2 (Cord pottery)				789
3 (Horgen)				764
4u (Pfyn)				329
4m (Pfyn)				669
4l (Pfyn)				702
5 (Cortaillod)				1014
6 (Cortaillod)				1102

Fig. 197(B) The relationship between wild animals and domesticated animals from the Neolithic to the Early Bronze Age at Zürich Mozartstrasse, based on the number of bones.

From Romania to Hungary and Moravia there emerged rich bronze-producing communities, centred on chiefly fortified settlements, and surrounded by open sites. I shall employ the term Otomani culture to cover them all, although different names have been assigned to the regional groups, including Veterov, Hatvan (an early phase), Vatina and Madarovce (Ordentlich 1969; Vladar 1973, 1977; 1982; Batora 1981; Bader 1982a; Kovacs 1982; Tocik 1982; Novotna 1988). They shared a common repertoire in metalwork, which was regularly deposited in hoards, and in burials within communal cemeteries, divided into clan and family groups. The central sites were regularly spaced, indicating political territories of some size. Both lowland and upland locations were common, overlooking central communication lines. Their size ranges from a few hectares to 10 or 15 ha, but they are generally smaller than Late Hallstatt fortifications (Figure 200). They were the centres in a hierarchical settlement system of both lowland and upland open sites, and in Romania supplemented by small circular fortifications on the plains, so-called atoll settlements or ring-forts, reminiscent of the Iberian type (Bader 1982b). In Slovakia several of the central settlements are well excavated. One of them, Spissky Sturtók, which was burned down and sealed, had an acropolis with a chiefly settlement that contained several hoards (Vladar 1977; Jockenhövel 1990). Buildings were laid out according to a 'town plan', with craft production being carried out in bronze, bone, amber, etc. (Figure 201). In Spišsky Sturtók there were more than twenty bronze hoards, in Barca three bronze hoards were found in one house, along with a gold

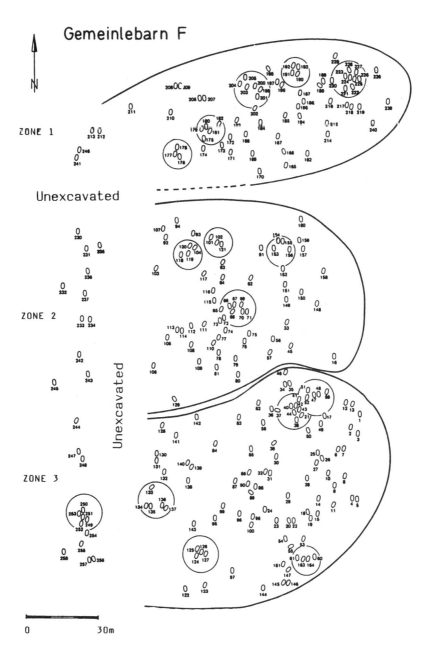

Fig. 198(A) The Early Bronze Age cemetery at Gemeinlebarn, divided into clan sections and family groups (circles).

hoard. Their primary functions as centres of production, redistribution and trade are evident. The recent excavations at the tell settlement of Feudvar at the river Tisza (Hänsel and Medovic 1991), dating to the first half of the second millennium BC (1800–1500 BC), has revealed interesting architectural features of wall decoration (Figure 202), as well as a system of small well-built houses forming house blocks,

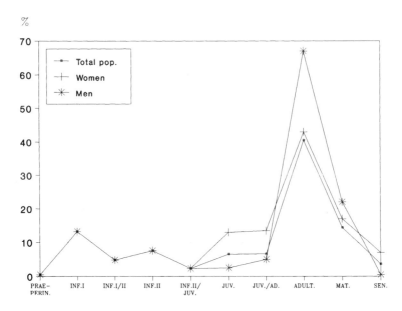

Fig. 198(B) Age structure of the buried population at Gemeinlebarn; note the rather low child mortality, compared to the Late Bronze Age.

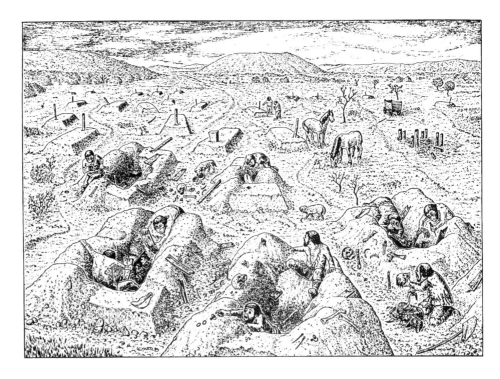

Fig. 199 Gemeinlebarn: reconstruction of Bronze Age grave robbing in the cemetery.

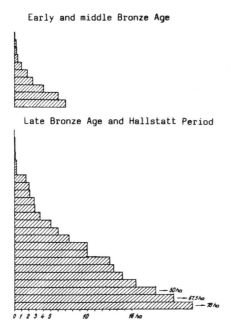

Fig. 200 The size of large fortified settlements in the Rumanian Carpathians during the Early and Middle Bronze Age and the Late Bronze Age and Hallstatt period.

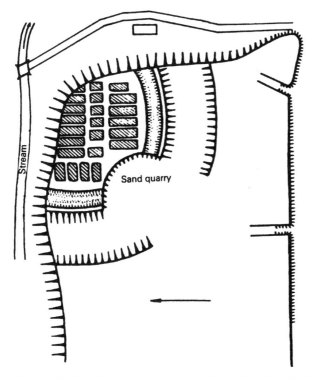

Fig. 201 The Early Bronze Age settlement at Barca, Slovakia. The fortified village consisted of three rows of two- and three-roomed houses.

separated by small streets 1–3 m wide (Figure 202) – all features of a developed social organisation.

A large number of features in the Otomani culture bear witness to Mycenaean/ Aegean influences, analysed in a series of works by Bouzek (1966), Vladar (1973), Vladar and Bartonek (1977) and Bader (1990). They vary from clear-cut imports or imitations of Mycenaean rapiers and swords (Hänsel 1973; Bader 1990, Abb. 24), through common traditions in bone carving, to the imitation of stone constructions in defensive walls and specific decorations on the hearths in the acropolis, and the employment of Mycenaean altars (Bouzek 1985, 71 ff; Bader 1990, Abb. 22, 23). All these 'civilising influences' are found in the central settlements, once again stressing their combined economic, political and ritual functions (Vulpe 1982). The fortified settlements were chiefly residences with attached specialists, rather than settlements for larger groups of people.

From the Otomani culture long-distance exchange relations were established with the Nordic region (Figure 191). Schauer has recently summarised the diverse evidence of these contacts (1985). It is characteristic that they change from one form to another. Only in east Central Europe can direct Mycenaean evidence be detected; from here impulses were transmitted in a variety of ways further northwards. To give one example: chariots are documented by cheek-pieces in the Otomani culture, and in a few simple drawings, e.g. on pots (Bader 1990, Abb. 25), by real chariots in burials north of the Black Sea (Figure 203), whereas in the Nordic region we find realistically drawn chariots, so precise in their constructional details that there must have been a real chariot or an absolutely accurate model to work from (Kristiansen 1987b, note 6) (Figure 203). We also find cast bronze wheels of a size and a detail demanding completely realistic prototypes, as the model wheels follow developments in wheel construction in Greece and Egypt, although knowledge of some of these complex characteristics may have been acquired later through the Tumulus culture (Kristiansen 1987b, note 6; Thrane 1990, figs. 2, 3).[8] We may assume, perhaps, that chariots in one form or another were rather common sights at the chiefly settlements of Central Europe, and were therefore not depicted, whereas their rarity in the north led to highly accurate imitations (Figure 204). Spiral ornamentation is another example, being employed in bone working or on pottery in the south and transmitted onto bronze in the north. This pattern of the transformation of Mycenaean influences reflects the difference between overland exchange via a series of networks in the north against more directional trade in the Mediterranean, where Mycenaean or Cypriot traders themselves reached Italy and the southern shores of France.

It should be made clear, however, that despite the adoption and transmission of Mycenaean symbols and ideology, the Otomani culture was not an imitation of Mycenaean civilisation, developing a metal industry with an originality of its own, and a hierarchical social organisation in accordance with this independent outlook. Thus, in both Atlantic Wessex and Central European Otomani indigenous bronze industries had developed *before* the time of Mediterranean/Mycenaean contacts.[9] The Mycenaeans were interested in gold and tin/copper (Davis 1985) as well as amber, accounting for the Nordic connection. Trade contacts were established on

Fig. 202 Reconstruction of houses and wall decorations at Feudvar, an Early Bronze Age tell settlement on the Danube.

the lower Danube at the Black Sea coast, indicated by a group of rich hoards with gold finds, including Borodino. As we have seen, there are some specific cultural traits which suggest that Mycenaean traders, or merchants from the coast of Asia Minor, visited some of their chiefly settlements.

The 200 years of contact between the Otomani culture and its western and northern peripheries had a profound effect on Nordic societies (Hachmann 1957),

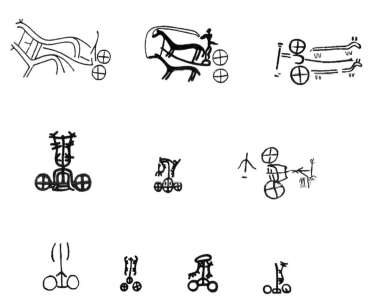

Fig. 203 Early Bronze Age engravings and depictions of two-wheeled chariots: with the exception of the two depictions on pots, above right from a burial at Velke Raskovce, Slovakia, and below that from a burial at Saratov, lower Volga, former USSR, the rest are from southern Scandinavia. Upper row: three-dimensional versions, middle row seen from above, and lower row more primitive imitations, most with solid wheels.

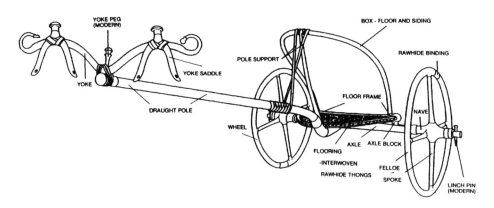

Fig. 204 Basic construction of light two-wheeled Egyptian war chariot; similar constructions were employed in the Otomani Culture and in Southern Scandinavia.

which around 1500 BC were ready to develop an original style of their own, and take a more active part in long-distance trade, not through the Otomani culture, but via the Tumulus culture, which now took over control of trade with the Mediterranean (Figure 192).

The expansion of warrior aristocracies

During the 16th century BC some major changes took place in the relationship between the old centres of metalwork and their peripheries. Within a brief period a new culture emerged in west Central Europe, which employed a new burial ritual: chiefly barrows for selected individuals and their families in highly visible locations on hills or at the heads of valleys. Grave goods were dominated by new weapon types (swords, lances, the bow and arrow) for the men, and rich ornaments and dress accessories for the women. From the Rhône valley to Denmark, and from the Rhine to the Tisza, the new social and ritual complex spread within a few generations and lasted until the 13th century DC (Holste 1953a; Ziegert 1963; Hänsel 1968; for recent literature see Furmanek and Horst 1990 and *Dynamique du Bronze Moyen en Europe Occidentale* 1989). Several factors were at work: a climatic change towards greater humidity and cooler weather triggering economic changes, a subsequent development of new social structures in western Europe, and finally a change in their relationship with the old centres of bronze production, facilitated by their increasing command of mining and metalwork as well as developments in social organisation. As a consequence a west European trade network gradually replaced the former Central or east Central European network. The nature of this shift in social and economic balance is still not fully understood, and several alternative interpretations have been presented.

Two main models have been discussed: one taking as its point of departure the decline of the Otomani fortified settlements and the concomitant appearance of a wave of hoards, the so-called Kosziderpadlas horizon. The Hungarian archaeologist Amalia Mozsolics has, in particular, proposed linking these phenomena together in a dramatic historical interpretation of Tumulus warriors penetrating eastwards, destroying the Otomani forts on their way. Her interpretation was supported by impressive publications of the Hungarian Bronze Age hoards (Mozsolics 1957; 1967; 1973). The other model instead stresses the transformation of local communities in combination with a spread of new social and ritual practices (Hänsel 1968; 1977; Vladar 1982). It is difficult to compare the different models, as they are not worked out systematically: the same archaeologists who promote gradual change in one case may elsewhere propose widespread migrations on rather shaky evidence. There is also a methodological opposition between the importance attached to small variations in metalwork and pottery when defining regional 'cultures', and the stressing of continuity, when similar or more drastic changes occur from one period to the next. The lack of theoretical and methodological consequences implies that it is necessary to develop a theoretical framework for understanding the change, based on the implications of the different social organisations before and after – a sedentary, hierarchical society against a mobile pastoral warrior society, to stress the oppositions strongly. With reference to our earlier characterisation and interpretation of warrior societies, we may assume that the Tumulus culture was expansive, due to its subsistence strategy demanding large pastures, and due to its warrior ideology, which promoted raiding and settlement expansion.

I propose the following scenario (Ozdani 1986; Kovacs 1981): during the 16th century BC (early Br B1) mutual relations between the Otomani and its neighbouring cultures intensified (Rittershofer 1983, 323 ff.), leading to both developments in bronzeworking (Primas 1977) and the adoption of an aristocratic warrior ideology.

This explains the similarities in material culture between the eastern and western Danube during Br B1 (Hänsel 1968, Beilage 1–5). It may be that some warrior groups were employed by the Otomani chiefs, but that was not a significant factor. The new ideology was adapted to a more decentralised social and economic environment of pastoral farming in the west, leading to dynamic social changes and the formation of a new warrior elite, which employed monumental burials and furnished them with weapons and symbols of wealth to stress their new positions. Several factors helped to promote this change: a climatic shift towards more humid conditions (see Chapter 2.2) caused many lowland settlements to be abandoned, e.g. lake dwellings, while it also affected Otomani lowland settlement. It favoured a change in subsistence towards animal husbandry and upland grazing, a suitable strategy for a mobile warrior society. It also meant that large heath and pasture lands in northwestern and northern Europe became economically profitable, leading to a rapid spread of warrior elites in the north, where palaeobotanical evidence documents the impact of animal husbandry and grazing (Hedeager and Kristiansen 1988; Andersen 1990). Finally, links were established to the south and to Greek and Cypriot traders, leading to the formation of long-distance trade networks between Jutland and the Rhône valley/northern Italy running through southern Germany and the Rhine, with amber and animal products moving southwards and Mycenaean prestige goods and ideology moving northwards. This interpretation makes the distribution of amber in tumulus burials and Mycenaean-Cypriot settlements in the western Mediterranean meet (Figure 192).

The decline of the Otomani culture was thus the result of a process of indirect centre–periphery dynamics, leading to the expansion of Tumulus Culture eastwards (and northwards), in a combined process of small-scale migrations/conquests and internal cultural change, as the economic underpinnings of the chiefly settlements were eroded and their northern exchange network was taken over by the new warrior elites. Many settlements seem to have been left peacefully, though others were burned down. At some, like Feudvar, the regular organisation of houses and streets was given up and replaced by a random distribution of houses (Hänsel and Medovic 1991, 77). Along the Danube metal depositions in bogs and burials retreat from the river valleys into the mountain valleys (compare Stein 1976, maps with Ruckdeschel 1978, maps). The Tumulus expansion stopped around the River Tisza, east and north of which local developments led to the formation of new regional groupings continuing to use communal cemeteries (Hänsel and Kalicz 1986; Benkovsky-Pivovarova and Enzersdorf 1989, Abb.1; Kemenczei 1989). At the cemetery of Mezocsat half the burials had been reopened and grave goods removed – is this a ritual tradition, or perhaps rather an expression of social change and a lack of bronze on the part of some groups, or even of systematic grave-robbing by intruders (Hänsel and Kalicz 1986, 50f.)?

The social organisation of the Tumulus culture is fairly well known, especially in the north, where differences in wealth have been analysed (Randsborg 1974), with various grave goods combinations (Larsson 1986; Ashing and Rasmussen 1989; Willroth 1989) and swords (Kristiansen 1984b) suggesting a distinction between ritual warrior chiefs, and young chiefly warriors employing more simple and effective swords as grave goods (Figure 205A, B). Schauer (1990) has pointed out the widespread similarities in weapon combinations, which reflect identical status distinctions over large regions. This all points to an aristocratic warrior elite without centralised political leadership, perhaps confederations of local chiefs. There are no large fortified settlements, and virtually no hoarding, in both respects a clear contrast to the Otomani culture. Chiefly settlements were densely occupied, consisting of large, well-built houses or halls, and in the north chiefly barrows or barrow groups are scattered over the landscape, forming larger groups or confederations of 30–40 km² in size (Rønne 1986, fig. 6–24). Similar groupings appear in southern Germany (see below). The widespread similarities in material culture and burial ritual indicate open networks of intense interaction from the Rhône to Jutland. Regional variations around common forms and traditions suggest that within such 'tribal' territories local traditions developed and their number increased over time, especially in female ornaments. Groups of similar swords in southern Germany and Denmark, however, suggest that warrior chiefs/bronzesmiths could travel over long distances, although of course a trade in weapons is a possibility. But the foreign swords are normally not buried with traditional Nordic status symbols, suggesting that they had a different status. It is also remarkable that this direct exchange between the two areas is paralleled in certain types of flange-hilted swords, and further represented by the later amber route, and by the historical cattle route between Jutland and southern Europe. Mary Helms' ethno-historical studies have demonstrated that long-distance travelling is an important part of 'chiefly culture', which maintains and recreates prestige by gaining access to distant knowledge and myth, as well as valuables (Helms 1986, 1988a, 1988b), Homer's epic of Ulysses' adventures being the archetypal tale of this chiefly ideology. We should therefore not exclude the possibility of chiefs travelling over these rather long distances with their warriors, amber and cattle. Southern Germany, the Hagenau and the Rhône valley are likewise characterised by close similarities in burials and metalwork (Koenig, Lambert, Piningre and Plouin 1989, fig. 2; Petrequin, Piningre and Dartevelle 1989; Kubach-Richter and Kubach 1989).

Studies of characteristic locally produced female ornaments indicate that marriage could take place between the Lüneburg area south of the Elbe and Zealand (Kristiansen 1987b). On the whole, female ornaments suggest more localised marriage patterns, but with some 'dynastic' marriages over longer distances. In southern Germany the well-published and analysed evidence allows the reconstruction of patterns of exchange and marriage alliances (Wels-Weyrauch 1989; Kubach-Richter 1990; Jockenhövel 1991): again we find local variations in burial and dress, forming local interaction groups (Figure 206), but also burials with 'foreign' equipment indicating marriages between groups over distances of up to 150 km (Figure 207). The stability of the size of local marriage groups suggests a social and political regularity, which we may compare with the analysis of Late Bronze Age networks already presented (Chapter 4). These are distances that were probably travelled more often by chiefs and their retinue, explaining the more widespread distribution of identical weapons,

Fig. 205(A) Nordic full-hilted chiefly sword, dagger and belt hook, plus wooden drinking cups from the 'Store Kongehøj' barrow with a preserved oak coffin and clothing; the decoration on the wooden drinking cup is lined with tin nails, a costly demonstration of status.

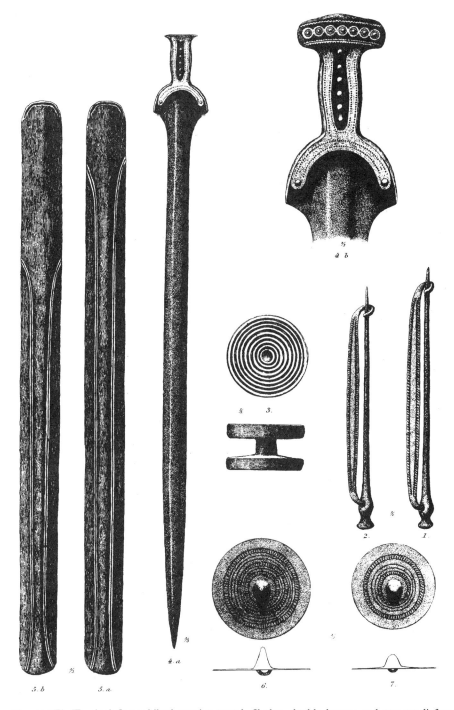

Fig. 205(B) 'Foreign' flange-hilted warrior sword, fibulae, double button and two tutuli from the 'Muldbjerg' barrow with a preserved oak coffin and clothing; the wooden hilt is engraved with small tin nails.

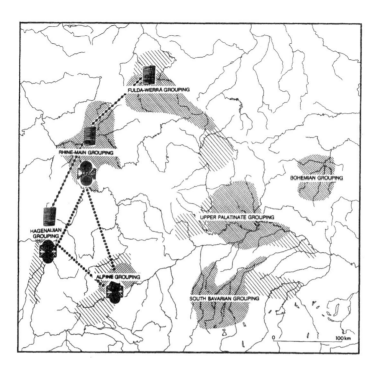

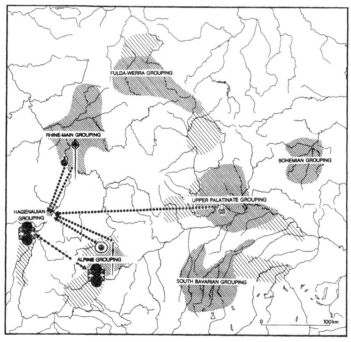

Fig. 206 Local settlement areas of the Tumulus Culture in Southern Germany: above: mapping of some common traits of the Hagenau female dress group originating in other South German groups; below: origin of 'foreign women' in burials of the Hagenau grouping (round dots) and influences from the Alpine grouping (rhombic dots).

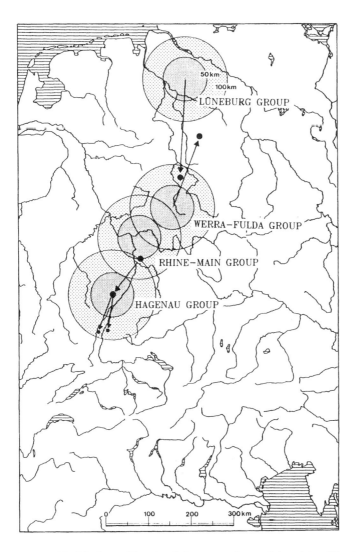

Fig. 207 Model of some Tumulus Culture groupings and the origin of 'foreign women' in burials.

as discussed above. It makes it easier to understand how new social and ideological ideas could spread rapidly over large distances – including the Mycenaean background to the warrior ideology of the Tumulus culture and its various manifestations in burial ritual, weapon types and status symbols. The full weapon combinations followed the Mycenaean, as can be seen by comparing Kilian-Dirlmeier's (1986) analysis of the Shaft Grave burial combinations with those of Schauer (1990) and myself (Kristiansen 1984b) of the Tumulus and Nordic weapon combinations.

The genuine Mycenaean imports, or direct imitations, of the 15th to 13th centuries, from flange-hilted swords to metal vessels and double-axe symbols, which are especially numerous in the north, represented the tip of an iceberg of heavy assimilation and transformation of an aristocratic warrior ideology (Kristiansen 1987b).

Some of the most direct influences were apparent in perishable materials, such as the wooden folding stools found quite widely in Denmark (Werner 1987), a royal symbol, or the Greek boar's-tusk helmet, which was commonly employed (Makkay 1982), wooden shields (Schauer 1990) and chariots. It is often forgotten that the ships on rock carvings are also clearly inspired by Mediterranean ship types in their lifted curved stems and general profile.

The development of new complex craft traditions in woodwork (folding stools, chariots and probably ship-building), weapon technology and burial rituals over large regions points to a much more massive interaction between Central European and Aegean/Mediterranean societies than normally thought, far beyond that of random trading contacts. Seen from Central Europe, Mycenaean culture could be considered to represent the ultimate development of the European Bronze Age chiefdoms. It is also essential to recognise that all these new accomplishments in weaponry and other status symbols were accompanied by information about their social and ritual significance, which helps to explain why Central European warriors could later take an active part in the large-scale historical changes that led to the collapse of the Mycenaean and Hittite Empires. Some of them were familiar with their culture, just as they were efficient warriors. But the difference in social organisation and economy was also clearly spelled out by the subsequent Dark Age. This leads us on to the next social and cultural watershed.

Reorganisation and intensification: the Urnfield expansion
The beginning of the Urnfield culture is no less debated than the beginning of the Tumulus culture, but the factors underlying it were perhaps even more complex. A series of external and internal changes took place during the late 13th/early 12th centuries BC (Br D), making it difficult to distinguish between cause and effect (in general see Müller-Karpe 1959; Bouzek 1985, ch. 3; for recent evidence see Brun and Mordant 1988; Plesl and Hrala 1987). Again we find an initial phase (Br D, comparable to Br B1), introducing changes that overlap with the old traditions, followed by the implementation of major social and economic changes, here from the late 12th/11th centuries (Ha A1) onwards. During the 13th century BC, Br D, contacts between Central Europe and Mycenaean culture were intensified both to the west and again in east Central Europe, leading to a development in metal craftsmanship in Central Europe and the formation of a new chiefly warrior elite. Soon after, there followed the collapse of the east Mediterranean palace system, and the influx of Central European and other warrior groups and tribes into Greece and Asia Minor. Internally urnfield cemeteries of local village farmers and their petty chiefs signalled both a religious and socio-economic shift towards intensive agriculture and the rise of farming communities. It correlated with a period of dry climate, favouring the cultivation of lowland river valleys, which now took place in most of Central Europe. In the following pages I shall describe the external and internal changes separately, before attempting a conclusion.

During the Early Urnfield period the rise of a new aristocratic warrior elite in Central Europe along the Danube to the Rhine can be seen. They employed monumental burials, exemplified by those at Caka (Tocik and Paulik 1960), Velatice (Paulik 1962), and Hart, this including a wagon (Müller-Karpe 1956), and they are distinguished not only by weapons, but also by Greek or Greek-inspired body armour (Paulik 1968; 1988), and beaten bronze vessels. Schauer (1984b) has demonstrated further similarities in grave goods between chiefly warrior burials during the Early Urnfield, suggesting wide-ranging and close contacts. The distribution of chiefly full-hilted sword types of the Riegsee type and related types of Br D and Ha AI supports the picture of close east–west contacts from the Carpathians along the Danube to the Rhine, originating in the east (Holste 1953b, Karte 5; Müller-Karpe 1961, Karte 1–2), where they are often found in hoards, while in the west they more often accompany burials (Torbrügge 1965, Abb. 6–7). The more plain and functional flange-hilted swords and spears of the chiefly retinue, or of local warrior chiefs, display a much broader geographical distribution. The rise of new groups of warrior chiefs along the Danube is also exemplified in the spread of common pottery types, and from Hallstatt AI common styles in personal adornments, such as pins and *fibulae*, as demonstrated earlier (Figure 31). From Ha AI onwards we can speak of similarities at all levels of material culture, as reflected in both urnfield cemeteries and settlements, although local variations can still be distinguished.

The rise of the new warrior elite, perhaps the culmination of the Tumulus culture, and the subsequent spread of a new common culture related to the formation of new farming settlements and their urnfields, has many similarities to the development from La Tène A to B. As during Early La Tène, a change took place in settlement location from upland to downland, and the formation of new pioneer village settlements (Krause 1990). In areas showing continuity from Tumulus to Urnfield culture it is seen as a narrowing and concentration of settlement along the river valleys (Hochstetter 1980). But we may also suggest more wide-ranging migrations. By comparison to the La Tène migrations those of the Urnfield Culture fulfilled the criteria for identifying migration in all respects: new cemeteries and settlements are founded with a new burial tradition (and a new religion e.g. Kossack 1954b; Matthäus 1981), and a new style in pottery is introduced. Metalwork is more widely distributed to local farming communities and although a centralised settlement hierarchy was in existence in the eastern Urnfield (Figure 208) the period of expansion is characterised by an apparently more egalitarian society, as during Middle La Tène. Settlement expansion continued during Ha AI–2 from the Rhine–Swiss group into France (Figure 41).

Although the overall tendency today is to stress continuity in settlement and culture between Tumulus and Urnfield culture (e.g. Sperber 1987) I find it difficult to maintain such a peaceful picture.[10] The parallels to La Tène suggest a similar development – the formation of new chiefly hierarchies, followed by a major reorganisation of settlement and economy, leading to the rise of strong, pioneer farming communities expanding into new habitats both locally and over longer distances, supported by warrior chiefs. The northern trade stopped for a longer period in the late 13th/12th centuries BC, reflected in a whole group of full-hilted swords being kept in circulation and being totally worn down. The earlier Urnfield sword types never

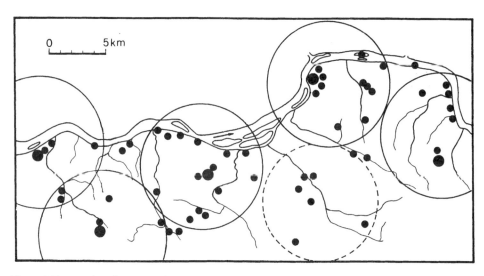

Fig. 208 Proposed settlement territories around fortified highland sites, surrounded by lowland, open, sites; a missing central site is suggested (dashed circle).

found their way north, for the same reason. Thus the settlement expansion was from the east towards the west, cutting off traditional lines of exchange with the north for a period. The densely settled Danubian/Pannonian region was probably hit by the dry climate, which left two possibilities: either to migrate along the Danube and its tributaries to settle in lowland areas with possibilities for intensive farming, or to migrate southwards towards the Balkans where transhumance could be practised. This latter possibility may account for the southward spread of a series of Central European Urnfield metal forms.

We shall consider two classes of objects, weapons and dress fasteners – representing warriors and women respectively – as a point of departure for understanding the relationship between Central Europe and Greece during the 13th and 12th centuries BC.

Dress fasteners, pins and *fibulae*, are among the most sensitive of objects chronologically and geographically, subject to rapid change and local trends in shape. Because they are personal, a part of the individual's clothing, they are not an object of trade, but linked to the person who wears them. Therefore they rarely move outside their local areas of production, except in cases of alliance formation with neighbouring cultures. When it happens that similar or closely related *fibulae* are found in areas far apart, we have good reason to assume a movement of people, if other changes point in the same direction. Comparative case studies of migrations from the Iron Age support this conclusion.

Weapons are easily spread and imitated if they represent new superior techniques and warrior ideologies, as was the case with the early full- and flange-hilted sword in northern Europe. None of these reasons, however, can explain why the later flange-hilted sword should be adopted in the Aegean, unless it was brought by people who produced and used them, since there were similar efficient weapons in the Aegean.

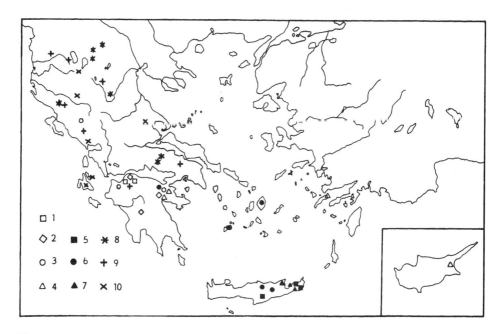

Fig. 209 Local schools of European-inspired weapons in Greece and Crete. 1–4 = Peloponnesian; 5–7 = Cretan; 8–10 = North Greek.

The flange-hilted Central European sword of Sprochoff's type II, which has been further classified by Schauer (1971) and summarised by Bouzek (1985), has a wide distribution, including the Aegean. A sequence of specific Central European and later types shows a gradually more southward distribution through the Balkans, Italy and into the Aegean (Bouzek 1985, figs. 59, 60, 62, 63), which is matched by spears of European inspiration (Bouzek 1985, figs. 66, 69). All in all they make up a quite massive distribution of European weapons in the Aegean (Figure 209) (Bouzek 1985, fig. 71). They followed two roads: one via Italy and another via the Balkans (Figure 210). The nature of these distributions is indicated by the *fibulae*, which follow the same pattern (Figure 211) (Bouzek 1985, 77–81). By comparison with the slighter evidence of Celtic mercenaries in the Mediterranean, not to speak of their raids into Greece, we must in this case of systematically patterned evidence, ranging from weapons to personal dress, assume a movement of people, probably warrior groups/mercenaries, during the 13th century (Br D), followed by more massive migrations from Ha AI onwards, as reflected by the later *fibula* types. This picture agrees well with other evidence of contacts during the 13th and 12th centuries.[11] It takes as its point of departure that a higher civilisation does not adopt the material culture of more primitive societies by its own will. For this to happen it presupposes a historical process by which the periphery is increasingly colonised and drawn into contact with the centre, *and* that the centre is weakened by internal conflict and partial collapse, thereby paving the way for the periphery to interfere. To elucidate these propositions I shall discuss in more detail the historical background to the dramatic changes during the 12th century BC in both the Mediterranean and Central Europe.

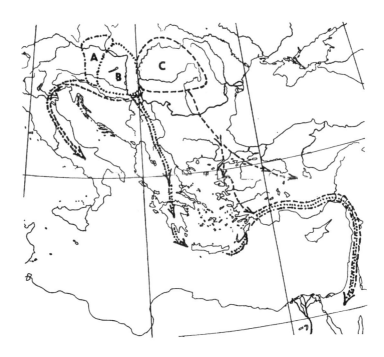

Fig. 210 Proposal for the earliest Urnfield migrations and their areas of origin: A = Velatice (old Italic) nation; B = Caka (old Dorian) nation; C = the Gava (proto-Thracian) nation.

During the 14th and 13th centuries BC Mycenaean culture strongly influenced social and economic developments in its near peripheries in northern Greece and Macedonia, illuminated by the well-excavated and published central site at Kastanas (Hänsel 1981 and 1982c; Hochstetter 1982). Here it led to major improvements in building techniques (the employment of clay bricks), and in the subsistence economy. In both pottery and material-culture similarities appeared in the area between the eastern Balkans, the Carpathians and the Black Sea (Gergova 1987), representing a secondary periphery of indirect cultural and political influence. At the same time trade and trading colonies in the western Mediterranean in Italy, including northern Italy (Figure 211), led to a spread of Mycenaean armour, which begins to appear in 13th-century princely burials in the secondary periphery in western and especially Central Europe on the middle Danube and in the Carpathians. Alternatively they could be interpreted as booty from return migrations into the Mediterranean and Greece; or, in a third view, as resulting from returning mercenaries. The parallel distribution of Peschiera daggers connecting the Carpathians, the Danube and the Po valley with the Aegean (Peroni 1956, Taf. 2–5) indicates that more regular contacts and movement of people (including metalworkers) and warriors took place, which is supported by a similar distribution of early violin-bow *fibulae*, as they presuppose a movement of people (Bouzek 1985, fig. 79) (Figure 211).

When the distributions of Central European and Mycenaean pottery and metalwork are combined there emerges a picture of a lively interchange of people and

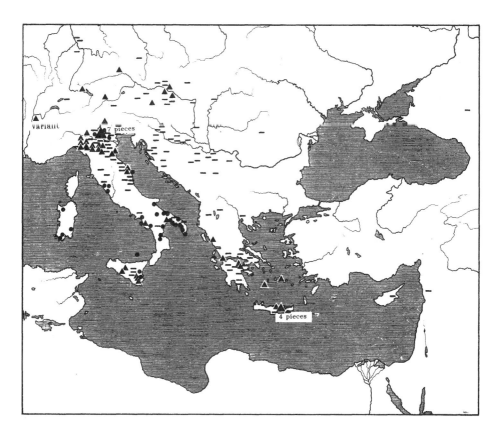

Fig. 211 The Greek/Balkan–Adriatic interaction zone, as defined by early Peschiera daggers (triangle), LHIIIC pottery and violin-bow fibulae.

technologies during the 13th century BC between the Carpathians/the Danube, northern Italy and Greece, and northern Greece/Macedonia and southern Greece, rather similar to the Late Hallstatt pattern. It signalled the emergence of a regional system of interaction (Harding 1984, 284ff.), in which process the closer periphery was integrated into the Mycenaean economy, reflected in the spread of Mycenaean pottery, which during LH IIIA and IIIB is very homogeneous from the west coast of Asia Minor to Italy (Podzuweit 1982, 71 f.). At Kastanas the introduction of Mycenaean pottery thus marked a complete change in material culture and economy (Hänsel 1981, 176 ff.). From the western colonies and the primary periphery in northeastern Greece goods and people began to move along traditional lines of political alliances, that were strengthened in the process, creating a secondary periphery, where Mycenaean body armour and skills in metal craftsmanship were adopted. Moving in the opposite direction we find that Central European warriors were increasingly employed as mercenaries in the Mediterranean during the late 13th century, and took part in the conquests around 1200 in Greece and later in the eastern Mediterranean (Bouzek 1985, fig. 102). The Italian–Adriatic sea route was probably paralleled by less strongly directional movements in the Balkans, which later led to the Dorian and other local migrations. At Kastanas there is rather solid evidence for the appearance of new groups of people with a new economy and material culture during the 12th century (Hänsel 1986). From the Balkans to Romania a series of hoard finds from the earlier Urnfield period, Ha A1, (Schauer 1974, Abb. 11) is thought by some authors to reflect migrations (Rusu 1982; Garasanin 1982; Vasic 1982).

Thus both in Asia Minor and in Greece a more primitive cultural complex with simple handmade pottery, open settlements and new burial rites replaced the former complex civilisations, indicating new dominant populations (for general surveys see Sandars 1978; Deger-Jalkotzy 1983). Both the written and the archaeological records are in full agreement that widespread destructions took place in the Aegean and Asia Minor after 1200 BC by people with a more primitive culture, mainly based on animal husbandry and transhumance (Bittel 1983; Schachermeyer 1983). Whereas the early phase of commercial contacts and movements during the 13th century derived from Central Europe and the northern Balkans, it seems fairly clear that the later Dorian migrations were much more local (Bartonin 1974), according to legend originating in Thessaly, just as the Phrygians of Asia Minor, according to literary tradition, should have come from Macedonia (Barnett 1967; Hammond 1976 and 1982).

We may conclude that by the 13th century BC Mycenaean civilisation had established close contacts with the Balkans and Italy in the western Mediterranean, whence the exchange of both goods and people took place with Central and north European Bronze Age societies. These had come to share military technology and combat techniques with the Mediterranean, their war chiefs employing full-hilted swords and protective armour, accompanied by retinues of spear-using warriors, also employing flange-hilted swords. Migrants, traders, mercenaries and goods moved regularly between the Danube, northern Italy/northern Balkans and the Aegean. A cessation of trade relations, or a crisis in the Mediterranean, would not go unnoticed in the warrior societies of Central Europe. They formed an indirect periphery to the Mediterranean cultures, and were employed as mercenaries, as later were the Celts, their social organisation and skills as warriors being of the same degree. This is in many ways a situation reminiscent of the development of Germanic societies prior to the migrations and the fall of the Western Roman Empire. I have only been able to hint at the historical and archaeological parallels that I take to support my interpretation; a more systematic comparative analysis of the Germanic, Celtic and Urnfield migrations is greatly needed for both historical and methodological reasons.

The Trojan War may be taken to symbolise the kind of competitive warfare over trade for which neighbouring Bronze Age tribes or kingdoms were mobilised that formed the background to the final collapse.[12] Thracians and other Balkan tribes are mentioned as taking part on the side of Troy, and the list of ships (*Iliad* Book II) records the mobilisation of the Greeks. It shows that war parties and troops from rather large regions were brought into the conflict, or hired as mercenaries, and it would obviously have had implications further inland. By drawing in neighbouring Bronze Age warriors in local feuds, Central European societies were being pulled into a more dynamic relationship with the Mediterranean, leading to the formation of large mobile warbands, who finally joined those still unknown states or groups who brought to an end the Mycenaean and Hittite civilisations, and whose subsequent settlements led to the Dark Age in the Aegean and Asia Minor. It resulted from a combined process of increasing interaction and acculturation between the Aegean and its neighbouring regions, including the European Bronze Age societies, which meant that when economic and demographic growth reached a critical limit in both areas, the balance tipped in favour of the periphery. This shift of balance may of course have been furthered by a period of climatic change, as suggested by Bouzek (1982), and perhaps reflected in the stratigraphical evidence at several sites, such as Tiryns, of disastrous floods around 1200 BC. Central Europe entered a prosperous phase of settlement expansion, new developments in metalwork and farming, which reached a climax around 1100 BC where we began our enquiry some chapters earlier. So the circle is closed, and we can begin to draw conclusions.

Conclusion 10

Having surveyed briefly the major sequences of change during the 2nd millennium BC we can detect a pattern reminiscent of the 1st millennium BC – a temporal and regional dynamic between expansive warrior societies and hierarchical sedentary societies, which could also be linked to changes in the relationship with the Mediterranean world. The Otomani culture had much in common with the consolidated Urnfield Culture, as well as sharing elements with the Hallstatt D royal residences, although on a smaller scale. The Tumulus culture likewise represented a west European shift towards a decentralised expansion of warrior elites with a dominant pastoral economy, comparable to the Hallstatt C warriors. Likewise, the early Urnfield chiefs can be compared to the early La Tène chariot burials, representing a phase of more centralised warrior regimes, preceding widespread settlement expansion and economic reorganisation based upon village communities. In both cases migrations and subsequent reorganisation of settlement took place in periods of political fragmentation in the Mediterranean, whereas centralised settlement systems and expansion of international trade took place in a period of Mediterranean expansion.

The social organisation of production, subsistence and settlement systems seems to correlate with these variations in social and political strategies, although the evidence is still scattered. In central-eastern Europe we encountered a densely settled landscape with packed settlements, and a high ratio of sheep/goat at Feudvar (Figure 212). In Italy, at Pitigliano in Etruria, and in Iberia a chronological sequence shows an increase of sheep/goat during the Early and Middle Bronze Age, in Italy with a steep decline of cattle, whereas the frequency of cattle remained low in Iberia (Figures 213, 214). These trends are reminiscent of central and northern Europe during the late Bronze Age, suggesting an earlier transformation of landscape and economy in southern Europe within a traditional farming regime. Also east-central Europe seems to have adapted to a heavily exploited landscape during the Early and Middle Bronze Age. In opposition to this we find in the Alpine region small-scale farming communities which only gradually developed a more intensive farming economy, as reflected in Mozartstrasse. Here hunting was still important until the

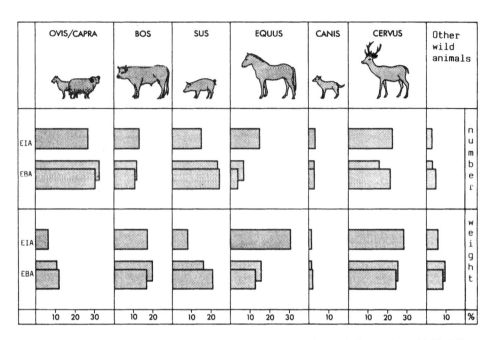

Fig. 212 Wild and domesticated animal bones at Feudvar, comparing Early Bronze Age with Early Iron Age.

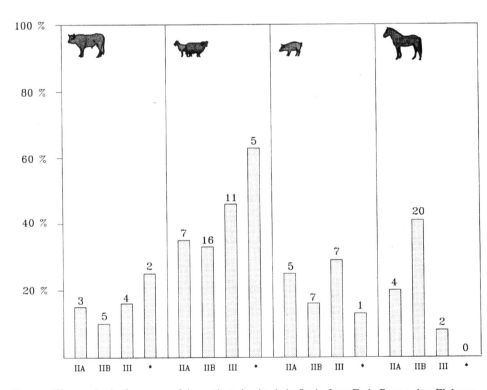

Fig. 213 Changes in the frequency of domesticated animals in Spain from Early Bronze Age El Argar (IIA), via a transition period (IIB), to Late Bronze Age (III) ; *, subsequent ages.

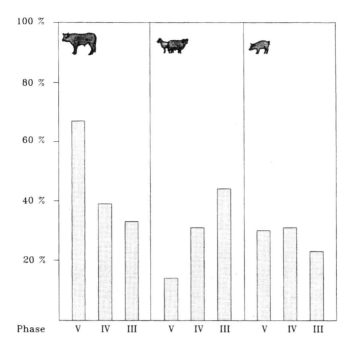

Minimum number of individuals
Italy

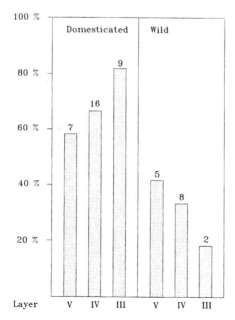

Fig. 214 Changes in the composition of domesticated animals at Pitigliano in Etruria, from Early Bronze Age (Br A2–3, Phase V) to Late Bronze Age (Br D, Phase III), showing the increasing dominance of sheep (above); during the same period the consumption of wild game declines (below).

3rd millennium (Figure 197B). Figure 215 further demonstrates the development in settlement size from Early/Middle to Late Bronze Age in the region, also seen in Padnal (Figure 216) . It is remarkable that wild game, especially deer, still played a role in the economy well into the Early and Middle Bronze Age in Etruria, and at Feudvar, here probably also to supply antler. The mortality curve at Gemeinlebarn (Figure 198B) differs from those of the Late Bronze Age, with a lower child mortality, suggesting more healthy living conditions. It is clear, however, that these scattered data should be supported by much more evidence before general statements can be made, but already now they indicate the potential of palaeodemography and zoology for reconstructing the Bronze Age economy. I have taken the evidence to indicate regional and chronological diversification that was linked to variations in social and political organisation.

In Section 8.4 I shall employ these historical sequences to construct a model of the European world system of the 2nd and 1st millennia BC that makes it possible to explain its 'behaviour' as a product of social and economic regularities. But first I shall discuss some social and cultural regularities to be extracted from the preceding chapters.

8.2 Some social and cultural regularities

Rules of marriage, inheritance and wealth deposition
Trends in the deposition of wealth in burials and hoards often follow a repetitive pattern, as demonstrated earlier (Figure 32A), linked to the rise and consolidation of elites. In the following pages I shall make an attempt to reconstruct in more detail some of the social and economic processes linked to these changes.

The rise of new elites often corresponds to an expansion phase of warrior chiefs, who demonstrated their new positions of power quite literally in burials. Therefore the early phases are dominated by male burials, and there is little stress on hoarding, as there had not yet developed ritual traditions linked to holy places (bogs and sanctuaries) which result from long-term settlement patterns and an agrarian economy. During the Tumulus culture, the Early Urnfield, Hallstatt C and the Early to Middle La Tène this was linked to a geographical expansion of the new social and economic strategies. Young sons of chiefs or kings were sent out to found new settlements, sometimes leading to migrations, as in the case of the Celts, sometimes to a series of small-scale conquest expansions of the new social and economic system, as in the case of the Tumulus culture. The subsistence strategy of the warrior societies was often, though not always, dependent on stock breeding, and therefore also more mobile than that of purely agrarian communities. It meant that wealth was mobile too, being linked primarily to cattle. Although some of the changes could spread along lines of alliance formation, in most cases the new strategy was so different from that of settled, hierarchical, agrarian societies that some degree of physical expansion was necessary to implement the changes. Conquest migrations were an integrated strategy of the social and economic landscape of Bronze Age Europe, as the necessary level of social and military organisation had already been achieved by the early 2nd millennium BC.

A

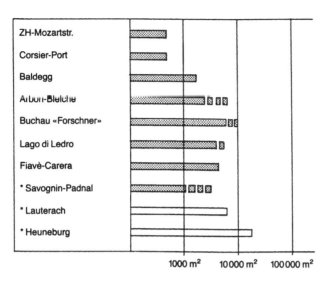

B

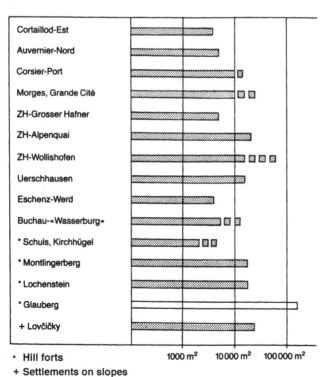

• Hill forts
+ Settlements on slopes

Fig. 215 The size of Bronze Age sites (A) in the Early and Middle Bronze Age, (B) Late Bronze Age.

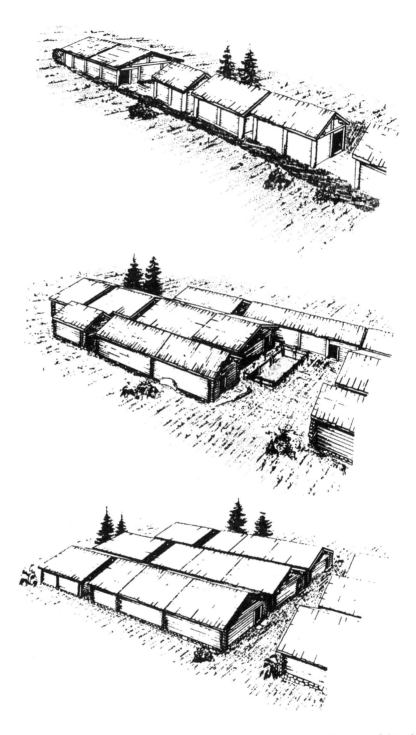

Fig. 216 Reconstruction of successive stages of the hamlet of Padnal, Savoigne, Grison from the end of the Early Bronze Age to the beginning of the Late Bronze Age.

Such expansion phases of new warrior elites, however, were normally rather brief, as barriers to expansion were reached after a few generations. They were followed by longer periods of consolidation, in the form of either a more massive reorganisation of the economy, sometimes including migrations, or the resettling of farming populations, as during the Urnfield and Middle La Tène. Rituals were directed more towards fertility (hoarding), the transmission of land and communication with the gods (community rituals at sanctuaries) to underpin in public the position of the elite.

It may therefore be suggested that changes of social and economic strategy were linked to changes in the use of wealth in burials and hoards in a predictable way. We may further assume that these strategies had to do with the way property and wealth were transmitted at marriage and death. Jack Goody has, in two important studies, spelled out the different strategies for transmitting property and wealth in Africa and Eurasia, based on a cross-historical analysis of ethnographic and historical records (Goody and Tambiah 1973; Goody 1976). In Eurasian societies of intensive farming and stratification, in-marriage is the rule to preserve property, linked to dowry at marriage. In more decentralised, expansionist, societies in Africa out-marriage is the rule, linked to the payment of bridewealth. The latter mostly consists of cattle and metal (moveable wealth), while dowry is linked to the inheritance of land (in this case a brideprice may often be paid from the groom to the bride, perhaps a relict of a former system). Other social features, such as monogamy/polygamy, can be linked to these strategies – polygamy being more common in societies with expanding networks, while monogamy and the use of adoption and concubines is the rule in stratified societies as a means of keeping property in the family. The consequences of the two strategies may also be seen culturally: in non-stratified societies preferring out-marriage 'groups tend to merge culturally even though they are politically distinct' (Goody 1976, 105). Before turning to the 2nd and 1st millennia let us briefly define bridewealth and dowry. According to Goody (1973, 17) there are basically two ways of exchanging women by marriage, that is bridewealth and dowry:

> *Bridewealth* passes from the kin of the groom to those of the bride; it forms a societal fund, a circulating pool of resources, the movement of which corresponds to the movement of rights over spouses, usually women. But *dowry* is part of a familial or conjugal fund, which passes down from holder to heir, and usually from the parents to the daughter. It is thus part and parcel of the transfer of familial property, but a process of transfer that includes women as well as men; that is, male property is transmitted to women as full heirs, semi heirs or residual heirs.

I believe it is possible to identify some of these patterns and strategies during the 2nd and 1st millennia BC (Figure 217).

During periods of expansion warrior elites dominated, reflected in burial ritual and wealth deposition, and in the appearance of international style zones, as during the Early Tumulus, Urnfield and Middle La Tène cultures. We can assume that kinship systems and marriage patterns were open (exogamous), favouring alliance formation

Social dynamics:

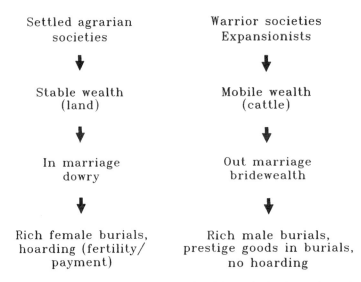

Settled agrarian societies	Warrior societies Expansionists
↓	↓
Stable wealth (land)	Mobile wealth (cattle)
↓	↓
In marriage dowry	Out marriage bridewealth
↓	↓
Rich female burials, hoarding (fertility/ payment)	Rich male burials, prestige goods in burials, no hoarding

Fig. 217 Models of marriage strategy and social organisation in agrarian and warrior societies.

between the expanding frontier and the chiefly centres, or simply as a means of establishing long-distance networks, as suggested by Mike Rowlands in his classic study of Late Bronze Age societies along the Atlantic façade (1980). Women were therefore exchanged out to maintain alliances, while moveable goods were exchanged in, which of course tended to level out over time, as both groups became receivers of marriage partners. The role of a woman became dependent on that of the man, being married into the man's family (patrilocal residence) to produce children = labour. Strong productive chiefdoms controlling the outward flow of women as well as the inward flow of bridewealth (tribute), labour and trade goods could in this way rise to power.

Thus in periods of expansion women are married out to establish alliances and to support expansion. They bring their personal wealth with them and can often be identified in burials through their different ornaments if they die young, as we saw in the case of the Tumulus culture (Figures 206 and 207), or during the expansion period of the Nordic Culture in the Late Bronze Age (Chapter 5.4). However, their position tends to be dependent on that of the man, and during the early phases of expansion they are often difficult to identify in burials for that reason. When expansion comes to a stop the inheritance of land becomes a major concern, as the most important way to build up and maintain wealth and economic power. This is done through marriage alliances, which will therefore tend to become much more localised (endogamous). Women increasingly come to inherit land, therefore property is granted personally to daughters by their parents as part of marriage. This is reflected in the appearance of rich female burials, as during the Hallstatt D period, the later part of the Tumulus culture, and in the later Urnfield culture. During the Nordic Bronze Age the deposition of female wealth in burials and hoards increased, to become dominant during the Late Bronze Age, which may well be taken to represent a long-term change in inheritance patterns. However, we cannot generalise over wide geographical regions, as local and regional sequences of expansion and consolidation may take place at different times. We find a similar sequence from the early Roman period of chiefly warrior burials to the late Roman period of rich female burials in northern Europe. It was these possibilities of keeping land inside the family by allowing women to inherit and marry within the family which the Christian church so successfully abolished, using it to gain that land for itself (Goody 1973 and 1983).

Thus I propose that the changing patterns of wealth deposition can be seen to reflect similar changes in social and economic organisation, periods of expansion and periods of consolidation being characterised by different rules of marriage, inheritance and economy, which can be seen in the balance between male/female and in the distances of marriage as a result of exogamous or endogamous strategies (Figure 218). I have presented a simplified picture of opposition between bridewealth and dowry; in actual historical sequences there will appear many overlapping or mixed situations. During the Bronze Age the tendency towards in-marriage and dowry was counterbalanced by the need to maintain alliances, which must have made a certain degree of out-marriage necessary, at least at the chiefly level. In such situations there might well develop mixed patterns of dowry and bridewealth, reflected in the use of brideprice between husband and wife. So when warrior and settlement expansion came to a stop, alliance politics took over, marrying women out. Behind these variations there is also a general long-term tendency to reduce wealth in burials during periods of consolidation, and expend some of it in ritual hoarding in sanctuaries, bogs or other holy places on behalf of the community.

Regional traditions, centre–periphery relations and the formation of cultural identity

Two types of interaction and change of cultural identity were at work during the 2nd and 1st millennia BC: indirect and direct centre–periphery relations. Indirect centre–periphery relations were based upon 'peer polity interaction' between regional traditions, leading to the assimilation of new social and ideological value systems, and some changes or imitations in material culture. But the overall tendency was towards integrating the new information into a well-known cultural idiom, or, on the basis of the new impulses, to create an independent version. This was seen in the Atlantic and the Tumulus/Nordic traditions, which reworked and so integrated the Mediterranean influences within their indigenous traditions. When the transmission of new information was part of a larger network of interacting regional systems from a higher culture, such as the Mycenaean or the Etruscan, we may talk about an indirect centre–periphery relation. Here the periphery maintained an independent social and economic system, and could even in certain respects be more developed than the centre – e.g. Central European mining and metalwork – but was dependent for the social reproduction of the elite on maintaining trade and prestige goods exchange, as was the case for the Nordic culture in relation to Central Europe. We may further assume that regional traditions were the result of continuous, overlapping circuits of exchange, based on open systems of marrying out (bridewealth) and long-distance

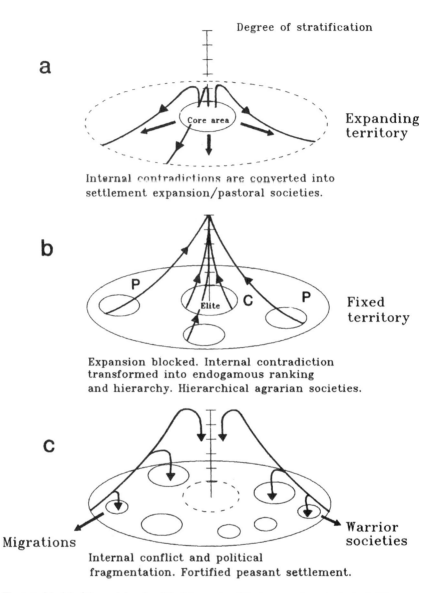

Fig. 218 Model of the social and political dynamics of the two marriage strategies in Figure 217.

chiefly trade and travels, as seen during both the 2nd and 1st millennia. Trade partnerships and personal relations and travels were probably the dominant mechanism of trade, the bulk of which involved no more than could be carried by a single person (several hoard containers suggest this), although some hoards indicate that a larger group of people (a protected caravan, or a sea journey) was employed on the expeditions. Voyages of several hundred kilometres could be undertaken, on land more typically 150 km, although longer expeditions by chiefly groups of warriors and specialists could be undertaken.

In opposition to direct centre–periphery relations only a few foreign objects are accepted. Although they may lead to the adoption of new social and ritual value systems, the foreign influences would normally be transformed into a regional cultural idiom, which explains why so few imports, whether Mycenaean or from neighbouring cultures, are found, although a massive impact may be attested indirectly, as in the case of Lausitz pottery influences on the Nordic Late Bronze Age. Imports are mostly found during the initial or final stage of a regional tradition. It suggests that major cultural changes are always linked to changes in social organisation, as evidenced during the rise and decline of the Nordic culture, the Tumulus and Urnfield cultures, the Hallstatt C warriors etc. Social strategies and their cultural/symbolic expressions were closely interlinked, maintaining a strong degree of autonomy once in operation. As they were linked to the maintenance of open systems of frequent interaction, we may also assume the regional traditions conformed to a kind of conscious national or tribal identity, and a common language group, to allow interaction. This was most clearly seen in border situations, where border maintenance was often strong, although 'middlemen' cultures might sometimes develop, as the Golasecca and Venetians in the Alps and the north German/Nordic local culture groups in the Late Bronze Age.

In contrast to this stand direct relations of centre–periphery, as in the case of the Phoenicians in Iberia, the Greeks/Etruscans and Late Hallstatt, and the Romans and Late La Tène. These are characterised by a direct commercial relationship, where industrial products and slaves are exchanged for prestige goods, ranging from metal vessels to wine, leading to a massive borrowing of new social and cultural values, sustained by foreign prestige goods. Often the periphery is dependent upon the centre for its political reproduction in such circumstances. Administered trade was probably the normal method of organisation for trade, including dynastic marriages between centre and periphery (the Vix princess, the Scythians), which ensured a heavy influx of new values. Such relationships came to characterise peripheral cultures from the Black Sea through the Balkans to Iberia during the Phoenician and Greek expansion between the 9th and 6th centuries, leading to a massive orientalisation of material culture.

We can observe three phases of orientalising influences in Europe:

> *The first* was linked to the Phoenician factories in Iberia, influencing both local cultures in a direct centre–periphery relationship and the regional cultures of the Atlantic tradition in a indirect centre–periphery relationship.
>
> *The second* major expansion came during the Greek colonisation of the Black Sea and the western Mediterranean during the late 8th/7th centuries, reflected in the orientalising phase in Italy and its impact especially on the eastern Hallstatt, as well as the development of Scythian art.
>
> *The third* orientalising phase was transmitted by the Etruscans and led to the formation of La Tène culture, although some indirect influence from Scythian art was also involved. During these historical sequences of Mediterranean expansion orientalising art and culture were transmitted to large areas and served as a platform for later Roman and Germanic artistic developments.

In cases of direct centre–periphery relations the periphery depended to a much larger degree for its social reproduction on the products from the centre, and might quickly collapse, as happened to the Late Hallstatt residences, if they were not able to transform their dependency into a new social and economic system based on the diffusion of technological and economic practices from the centre to wider regions, or to establish an oppositional culture based on indigenous values. The Hallstatt residences failed to do this, attempting to maintain a monopoly, whereas in Iberia and in the Late La Tène, the spread of new technologies and economic practices resulted in a major development in social organisation (the Tartessian/Iberian culture and the Oppida culture). Scythian and Early La Tène culture represent an example of the formation of a strong independent culture, taking certain foreign elements and developing them into a new cultural and ethnic identity of early state formation, in opposition to the centre. We may assume that during the formation of more territorial cultural identities in-marriage and dowry came to dominate property transfer and marriage alliances.

We may thus conclude that a more dynamic development and the formation of political ethnic identities resulted from the period of direct centre–periphery relations, the implication of which will be discussed in the following section.

Ethnicity, material culture and language

A renewed interest in the social mechanisms responsible for the maintenance of ethnic boundaries became predominant in archaeology during the late 1970s and the 1980s (Haaland 1977; Kleppe 1977; Hodder 1978b and 1982a), mainly influenced by the works of the Norwegian anthropologist Frederic Barth, who during the 1960s published a series of influential works (Barth 1967a) that led to a new approach towards ethnicity in social anthropology (e.g. Keyes 1981). However, these earlier ethno-archaeological studies have only to a limited degree been followed up by renewed studies on prehistoric material (some notable exceptions are Odner 1985; Olsen 1985), perhaps because of the methodological problems encountered (Chapter 2; Olsen in press), just as anthropological case studies can only give limited guidance to an understanding of long-term ethnic continuity and change. The ethnic trend was soon followed by a renewed interest in the relationship between language change and archaeology, triggered by Colin Renfrew's thought-provoking work from 1987. In this book the emphasis has been rightly shifted from the old question of equating culture, ethnicity and language to analysing the social processes of change, as they are believed to represent a more relevant point of departure (Renfrew 1987). Such an understanding, however, has two sides: we need to understand the relationship between ethnicity, material culture and language under stable conditions of continuity or gradual change in order to evaluate, by contrast, the more profound cultural changes and social transformations taking place in periods of rapid transformation. Finally, we would probably do well to separate the problems of identifying and understanding ethnicity and language, as they may fulfil different functions in society and therefore may not share the same conditions of survival. As a consequence of this approach I am not concerned with understanding either ethnic-

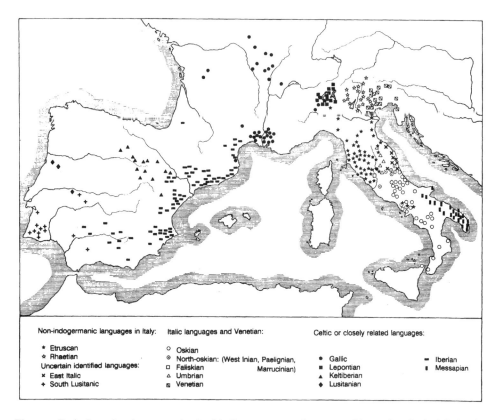

Non-indogermanic languages in Italy:

* Etruscan
☆ Rhaetian

Uncertain identified languages:

× East Italic
+ South Lusitanic

Italic languages and Venetian:

○ Oskian
⊕ North-oskian: (West Inian, Paelignian, Marrucinian)
□ Faliskian
△ Umbrian
▨ Venetian

Celtic or closely related languages:

● Gallic
■ Lepontian
▲ Keltiberian
◆ Lusitanian

— Iberian
▮ Messapian

Fig. 219 Early Iron Age languages in the Mediterranean, as documented by archaeological finds of writing.

ity or language, but with establishing a social and historical framework allowing for an assessment of their meaning (see discussion in Chapter 4.1). However, there are periods in which processes of social change and the formation of either an ethnic or a language identity seem to correlate in such a way that it is profitable to use them as a point of departure for discussion.

In Chapter 4.1 the question of the relationship between language and material culture was raised. It was proposed that some broad correlation existed, as shared cultural and social norms were supposed to have demanded a shared language. The question of ethnicity was considered more problematic, except in a general sense of a social and cultural identity and value system, defining 'us' against the 'other'. Its meaning had to be specified and historically contextualised, e.g. an elite culture versus that of commoners.

During the formation of city states in the Etruscan and Iberian cultures the use of writing occurs for the first time, allowing us to compare linguistic with archaeological evidence. Kimmig produced a map of early writing (Figure 219), delimiting the distribution of Iberian, Etruscan, Venetian, Celtic and other language groups, both Indo-European and non-Indo-European. The key observation is that there seems to be a nearly 100 per cent correlation with archaeologically defined culture groups, such as Golasecca, Este, Etruscan and Iberian. Even widely distributed types, such as axes (Stary 1982), exhibit local variations that conform to the language distributions in Italy, as do many other objects. We can observe a correlation between the production and distribution of culturally specific objects (Golasecca, Este, Etruscan and Iberian cultures) and a new use of language in material culture. It demarcated a territory within which a specific cultural code was used, which most probably reflected the formation of a political territory recognised by its inhabitants in this way. A politically defined ethnicity linked to state formation is probably what we see at work in these territorial distributions (Bentley 1981 and Nagata 1981 provide historical/ethnographic parallels). How far can we generalise from these specific historical observations (Figure 220)?

As we saw in the preceding chapter, the rise of royal residences represented a phase of rapid and fundamental social transformation, through the formation of centre–periphery relations, diplomatic gifts being gradually followed up by commercial transactions (Babic 1990). We observe in the Balkans that local territorial cultures formed around major chiefly residences or groups of chiefly residences. We may here assume a correlation between the definition of a political territory and the ethnic/cultural identity of its followers (Palavestra 1984; Vasic 1990), which, however, may have covered local resistance which is not easily recognisable. Whether or not such territories were also correlated with a certain language or dialect remains uncertain, as they were political formations, and it is only with some modifications that we can correlate these groups with the tribal names of the Illyrians, Macedonians etc., mentioned by Herodotus and other Greek authors, who were mainly referring to political and military elites rather than tribal or language groups (Fol 1991).[13] Thus, the first step in recognising ethnic or language groupings in material culture is to identify the social and political entities in the archaeological record – what segments of society are being represented.

These results provide some clues for discussing the formation of ethnicity during the Late Bronze Age, which I shall only hint at here. During the formation and expansion of the Urnfield culture in Central Europe and the Balkans between 1200 and 1000 BC Europe for the first time entered the historical scene, as these events were echoed in the collapse of the Mediterranean civilisations, leading to the Dark Ages in the Aegean and Asia Minor. Urnfield tribes, such as the Illyrians, Thracians, Daco-Mysians, Phrygians etc., are named by Homer in the *Iliad*, and when some of them later reappear in historical chronicles, e.g. Herodotus, we may assume that during the Late Bronze Age tribal groups or chiefs named themselves and thus had formed an ethnic identity that in some cases was carried forward (Garasanin 1982, 582 ff.; articles in Benac, Covic and Tasic 1991). The question we cannot answer yet is, by whom? Elites may take over or construct genealogies and 'ethnicities', as was the case with the Thracian kings (Fol 1991, 93). Thus it appears from the Etruscan and Iberian cases that the formation of an archaeologically identifiable ethnicity was the result of early state formation, which may have a different meaning to a tribal ethnicity, for example including larger groups beyond the actual centre of political power (Figure 221). So we should probably distinguish between political and tribal

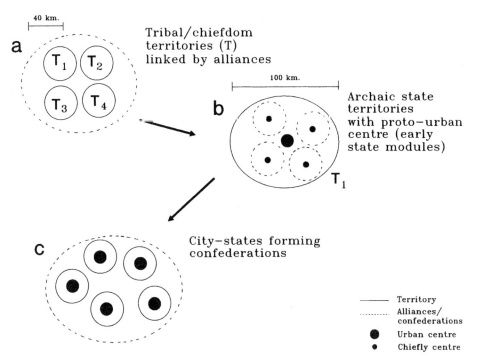

Fig. 220 Models of changing social and political organisation within a stable territory; case (b) tends to favour the development of a common language, whereas (a) and (c) are more open systems.

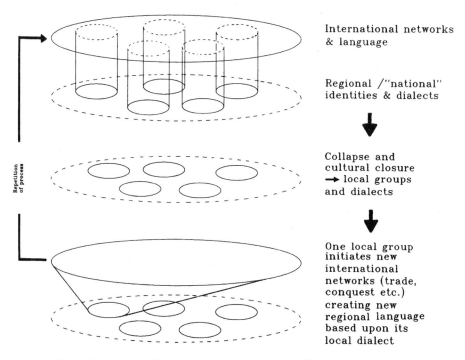

Fig. 221 Model of the process of language change through time within a tribal social organisation.

definitions of ethnicity, which need not always correlate with each other. On the other hand the political territories of the Early Iron Age were already visible in the Late Bronze Age (e.g. Villanova). We may therefore assume that the emergence of local and regional groups, ethnicity and some shared dialect or language are general phenomena linked to the formation of more hierarchical and bounded political structures, which emerged during the Urnfield period, but which may have existed as early as the Otomani culture.

This conclusion does not allow us to trace historically known ethnic groups back through time without severe reservations, due to the many social changes that took place throughout the Bronze Age, including some migrations. Few regions of Central Europe exhibit continuity throughout the Bronze Age; this is more frequent in marginal areas such as the Atlantic and Nordic regions. Only by linking language and ethnicity to social processes of change are we able to contextualise and explain the nature and role of such phenomena (Renfrew 1987). This does not exclude bilingual or multilingual situations, which must have been quite common in Bronze Age Europe in order to facilitate international exchange, especially in 'transit cultures' such as Este and Golasecca and similar groups in northern Germany and Poland during the 8th and 7th centuries. It also implies that we cannot assume any direct chronological connection between changes in material culture and language or ethnic change, except in very rare and well-documented cases. Culture is a code that may change or be applied for a variety of historical reasons – e.g. by an emerging elite (as in Ha D/La Tène A), without any language change, just as newcomers with a different ethnicity and language may adopt an existing material culture and its ethnicity. As cultural change is thus primarily a social and economic phenomenon we must first be able to explain archaeological changes within such a framework before any discussion of ethnicity and language can take place. If this simple rule had been followed in the past our knowledge of the late Bronze Age and Early Iron Age would have been a good deal better today.

In conclusion I propose some general criteria for assessing ethnic and language change (Figure 222):

(1) A homogenous material culture, whether belonging to an elite or to commoners, corresponds to a certain degree of ethnicity (group identification) and to at least one language or dialect (communication).

(2) Language and ethnicity are as general phenomena highly resistant to extinction. Their variation in this is considerable, however, and the rules of that variation are socially determined.

(3) Language is most resistant and culture most easily subject to change. Thus there is no direct relationship over time between changes in material culture and changes in language, or even ethnicity. Culture and social change occur regularly without major changes or the replacement of language, although ethnicity may take on new meanings.

(4) By contrast language change normally implies social and cultural change and often a change in ethnicity. A major language replacement demands either a new dominant population taking power through migration, settlement expansion or

Culture:	Ethnicity:	Language:
Adaptive & manipulating	Adaptive & manipulating	Stable & additative
Based on social strategies & traditions	Based on kinship & political relations	Based upon social reproduction

Fig. 222 Some principles of the learning and transmission of culture, ethnicity and language.

conquest by a strong state power (elite conquest is often not enough to initiate language replacement, but may often be reflected in place names, to signify a new administrative and political situation).

All of these principles can be seen at work during the four centuries of the Celtic and later Roman expansion in the western Mediterranean.[14]

8.3 Some evolutionary regularities

In this section I will suggest that the processes of cultural and social change during the second and first millennia BC were basically identical, due to similarities in organisational frameworks and in historical conditions of regional interaction, summarised in Figures 224 and 225. The internal properties or structural components of Bronze Age society generated a limited number of recurrent trajectories, which I shall first summarise.

Structural variants
We can distinguish between at least three different variants:

(*1*) *Sedentary centres of production and redistribution* developing in regions of high productivity, agriculturally and/or in terms of mineral resources/trade. Social hierarchies were based on accumulation and distribution of wealth to vassals/peripheries (Otomani and the Hallstatt princes). Settlement hierarchies developed around large fortified centres that served both as elite residences and as centres of production and tribute collection/redistribution from surrounding farming communities. These are normally well organised hamlets or villages each with their own village chief or local chief for a group of hamlets. In a more developed stage the chiefly or royal residences/ farms may be located outside the central settlement, reflecting a fuller political and military control (Ha D and La Tene C-D?). In such systems internal contradictions and competition are channelled into still more elaborate vertical lines of hierarchy and dependency, and into wealth consumption. If the hierarchies collapse, e.g. by losing their peripheries or by exhaustion of metal ores, the packed farming populations may migrate to take in new land, supported by warrior elites (e.g. the Urnfield culture and Middle La Tène), or develop into a type three trajectory.

(2) *Warrior societies* develop by transforming internal contradictions and competition into territorial expansion and competitive exchange and consumption
(Bonte 1979; Nash 1985). This creates a budding-off effect of continuous new
chiefdoms, linked by extensive prestige goods exchange (e.g. the Tumulus culture).
Although mixed farming is the economic basis, the subsistence strategy is extensive
and predominantly 'pastoral' (cattle/sheep husbandry), employed in exchange relations as moveable wealth (e.g. the Scythian 'Sigynnians' in Hungary, trading horses
to the Venetians in northern Italy, who sold them on to the Greeks). Settlements are
dispersed, centred around chiefly hamlets, period refuge fortifications and enclosures for cattle and sheep occur. Chiefly warriors may be employed as mercenaries by
the sedentary centres or by warring city states, as in the Celtic period, for payments in
prestige goods. In periods of crisis and decline they may either develop into bands of
raiders and mercenaries and/or they may take over control of peasant societies
(*militärische demokratie*), as happened in several regions during the Urnfield and La
Tène periods. In Late Urnfield times competitive warrior societies continued to
dominate the northern peripheries, while more stable hierarchies of warrior elites/
farming communities had developed in Central Europe. It might be suggested that
the Cimmerian influence during Late Urnfield, and the subsequent dominance in
Ha C of warrior elites, was due to a process much like the one described for Ha D to
La Tène A by Nash (1985).

(3) *Large peasant communities* living in highly organised, fortified settlements.
These develop in periods of blocked expansion, where competition and contradiction lead to warfare, contraction of settlement and political fragmentation. This
could be a result of demographic growth/overexploitation in regions of low productivity (the Lausitz culture) and/or a consequence of exclusion from larger networks of
centre–periphery exchange of goods necessary for social reproduction. The peasants
may disperse into smaller units to take in new land (migration). In regions of lower
demographic pressure settlements may be reorganised into small villages, which were
a suitable unit for settlement expansion and migration, characteristic of the Urnfield
and Middle La Tène periods.

Determinants and constraints
The development of these variants, which of course represent ideal types along a
continuum, was part of the reproduction of a single structure of cyclical transformations. The different strategies were both dependent on each other for their reproduction and potentially in opposition to each other, competing for dominance. Due
to the location of basic factors such as agricultural productivity, mineral resources
and the demands of more developed states in the Mediterranean, geographical
constraints and competitive advantages can be defined. But within that there was, as
we have seen, still room for both competition and some variation.
    It follows from this that no single factor may account for the observed structural
changes, although some elements, such as *climatic change*, may reveal striking parallels with shifts in settlement structure (Figure 223). This has been pointed out for

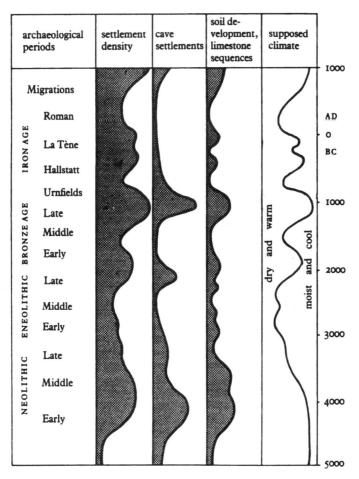

Fig. 223 Correlation of settlement density, number of cave settlements, soil development and supposed climatic changes in Central Europe; the figures are only approximate.

Central Europe by Bouzek (1982, fig. 4), while Burgess (1988) has recently presented an illuminating parallel between the second millennium BC settlement expansion and the final collapse of upland settlements in England and the sequence leading up to the medieval crisis and abandonment of settlement. Climate thus represents both the potential for, and constraints on, subsistence, but social and economic forces remain the prime movers when the environment is exploited not only close to, but often beyond, its carrying capacity, as defined by the cultural and economic rationality of prehistoric communities. In such situations a climatic fluctuation may trigger the collapse of an unstable economy. One of the lessons we may learn from the Bronze Age sequences is that demographic pressure and overexploitation of the environment were inherent features of prehistoric farming.

It should further be noted that a climatic change had different consequences depending on both environmental factors and subsistence strategies. A warm and dry climate, such as prevailed during the Early Bronze Age (Br A2/B1) and the Urnfield period in Central Europe, favoured intensive farming on lower fertile ground, while it might lead to drought and crisis in the steppe regions and in the Mediterranean, just as in some upland environments. This could lead in turn to local and regional displacements of settlement (e.g. farming communities leaving the Hungarian/Pannonian plains during the Urnfield drought). Alternatively, in periods of moist and cool climate there could be a change of subsistence strategy from downland to upland farming, as during the Tumulus or Hallstatt C periods). For these reasons it may often be difficult to distinguish between local changes in settlement (e.g. from upland to downland, or from one valley to another) and regional changes and migrations on a larger scale (see Furmanek 1985 for examples of local displacements). Thus pollen diagrams and settlement evidence testify to reductions in settlement and land-use in several areas of western Europe during Early Tumulus and Early La Tène, which quite evidently reflect the departure of some groups – but how far did they go? Only the combined textual and archaeological evidence of La Tène allows us to give an answer in that case; for earlier periods it can only be obtained through local and regional settlement projects in combination with pollen diagrams of land use and vegetation.

The location, exploitation and eventual exhaustion of *mineral resources* is another determining factor. Some of the shifting dominance of different areas producing bronze can thus be linked to the exploitation of new ores, e.g. those of the Alpine region during the Urnfield period. This could obviously lead to changes in commercial relations, although cause and effect are not always easy to determine. It follows from this that the systematic extraction and production of iron after 700 BC had significant social and economic consequences, and was consciously delayed in some regions, such as the Nordic, for the very same reasons. Since iron was widely available locally, in contrast to copper and tin, it democratised the production of subsistence tools and weapons, thereby shifting the focus of political power from the control of exchange to the control of land and its produce through tribute and taxation. In this way it undermined, in some areas, the traditional system of legitimation, based on exchange and ritualised rank, replacing it with one based on land and the direct control of production and producers, no longer defined as kin, but as farmers (denoting emerging social classes). This, however, was a gradual development, which had already started in the Early Bronze Age in east Central Europe, where bronze was available in large enough quantities to have the same effect locally, and it spread westwards during the Urnfield period. Although the spread of iron technology to many regions in Europe represented a threat to existing social formations, this was not the case in other areas, such as the Mediterranean. Here the production and exchange of prestige goods made of bronze did not cease abruptly after the introduction of iron. The full economic implications of iron were probably not realised in most of Europe until the subsequent millennium.

Finally, technical and organisational improvements in *production* and in *warfare* were decisive in defining a new framework for how many people could be sustained in an area (production), and how many people could be controlled/defended (military organisation). This again might extend the range of political control, leading to the formation of larger political units. I have mentioned above the implications of ironworking for opening up efficient farming tools to wider segments of society, e.g. the scythe and the creation of hay-meadows, although this was of course a gradual historical process. Technical improvements in farming could also raise the productive potential of a region, if coupled with efficient means of storage and distribution, as during the Urnfield and Middle La Tène periods. On the whole these were the two periods that saw the greatest improvements in farming techniques and practices (new crops, new tools etc.). None of these factors in themselves, however, created new conditions, unless they were coupled with corresponding social and economic developments. Most often their application arose out of social or economic needs rather than the other way round, as demonstrated in the case of the spread of iron working. Also, the introduction of new and more diverse crops, which characterised the Bronze Age, was often a response to new ecological and economic conditions created by intensive exploitation of the environment, e.g. the increased use of millet (Jäger and Lozek 1987).

However, most improvements in production during the Bronze Age and Early Iron Age were not revolutionary, but rather extended the range of available economic strategies and techniques, allowing for a more efficient adaptation to a wider range of environments, just as it provided a higher level of resistance to climatic and ecological changes.

With respect to military innovations and the organisation of warfare, the implications of metal weapons were more far ranging, as they created a new ideology of heroic war leaders, linked to the spread of the long sword and the lance in the earlier 2nd millennium BC. Thus from the Early Bronze Age onwards warfare changed direction and became both more efficient and also more ideological, as it was freed from traditional kinship hostilities. Instead it became organised around war leaders with a following of young warriors (these being early forms of retinue – see Kristiansen 1987a; Steuer 1982, ch. 7). War chariots and mounted warriors were most probably introduced during the Middle Bronze Age (Kristiansen 1987a, note 6), and at least from Urnfield times onwards the use of the thrusting sword testifies to mounted warriors, if not cavalry. The emergence of strongly fortified central settlements in the Early Bronze Age indicates that warfare had already taken on new dimensions, both in terms of internal political control and in the ability to defend and attack substantial fortifications, with the potential reward of gaining access to the revenues of tribute and trade from a larger area.

I therefore suggest that the nature of warfare, as it is known to us from the Early Iron Age, was already practised in its basic form by the beginning of the 2nd millennium BC. From this period onwards changes in weapon equipment and use occurred nearly simultaneously in the area from the Mediterranean to northern Europe, most probably also including some knowledge of military tactics and organisation.

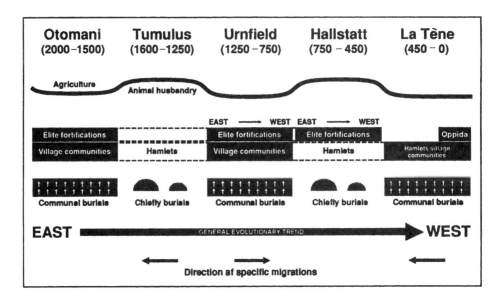

Fig. 224 Schematic outline of the dominant trends in settlement, subsistence and burial ritual from 2000–1 BC in Central Europe.

Evolutionary cycles and long-term regularities

In Figures 224 and 225, I have attempted to summarise the main regularities in the cyclical transformations of Bronze Age and Early Iron Age societies over some 2,000 years. The diagrams are descriptive, so I shall attempt to explain briefly some of the causal factors at work and their interplay.

In Figure 224 I suggest two types of regularities: one between a certain kind of social organisation and the structure of material culture (settlement and burial types), and one between a set of recurrent and interacting causal factors creating similar forms of social organisation. From a beginning in the early 2nd millennium BC I propose that European societies during the following two millennia oscillated between two dominant types of social organisation – one based on sedentary centres of metal production and distribution/redistribution controlled by an elite, another based on a more decentralised social and economic setting of warrior societies. While the first type had a basis of well-organised farming communities with a 'democratic' ideology reflected in communal burials with few social distinctions, the other type is characterised by a chiefly ideology of visible burials (often in mounds) and a more lavish display of wealth. The first type is essentially agrarian, and mainly linked to periods of warm, dry climate, whereas the second is primarily pastoral, based on animal husbandry, and corresponds to periods of cooler, more humid climate. These differences are reflected in the preference for site location. Downland settlements on the fertile soils alongside lakes and streams (e.g. pile dwellings) dominated during periods of sedentary agrarian settlements, while upland settlement locations were more common during periods of pastoral warrior societies. Some transhumance or exploitation of upland regions was an integrated part of the lowland agrarian settle-

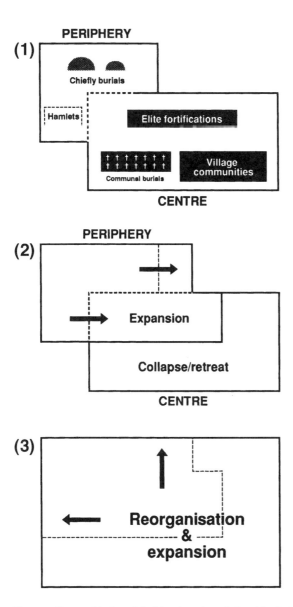

Fig. 225 Geographical model of the changing relationships between centres of metal production/agrarian production and warrior peripheries supplying special products and services.

ments, just as traditional farming was part of the economy of upland pastoral settlements. What we see reflected in the archaeological material is the dominant social and economic strategy, which according to palaeobotanical evidence also contains a good deal of prehistoric reality, but is not as clear cut as the archaeological record would imply.

Changes in the employment of wealth in ritual consumption which accompanied the cyclical transformations of the second and first millennia BC therefore offer important insights into the relationship between social strategies and their material correlates. The display of wealth in burials during the rise of new elites was in all cases followed by more 'egalitarian' traditions in burials. As could be demonstrated these changes represented shifts in the dominance of different social groups, and perhaps also different levels of social organisation, but not a real change from ranked to egalitarian societies. On the contrary they instead indicated the consolidation of elites, with less need to display their wealth and power, and the emergence of a peasantry socially and economically separated from the elite. It further meant that production and distribution of goods (e.g. ornaments and tools) was decentralised, or at least some of it, now taking place outside the centre in the villages. Rather than reflecting a more democratic and individualising society, this may signal that political control had taken on new and more efficient forms and therefore did not need to control production physically (e.g. Middle La Tène, and some regions during the Urnfield period). It corresponds to similar long-term trends observed in Denmark during the first millennia BC and AD (Kristiansen 1991). I therefore consider the discussion of whether the beginning of the Iron Age represented a significant change in economic and commercial possibilities for enterprising individuals to be some- what misleading, as it focusses too narrowly on a single period of change (Gosden 1985; Rowlands 1986; Wells 1989). Entrepreneurs always existed and operated according to prevailing social and economic conditions, becoming chiefs, military leaders, traders etc. From the Iron Age onwards social and economic conditions changed, defining a new context for enterprising individuals. To begin with it was not vastly different from similar changes taking place during the second millennium BC from the Otomani to Tumulus and Urnfield cultures. It was only in a long-term perspective that the potential of Iron Age social organisation for establishing more efficient systems of power and dependence unfolded, and even so it demanded the contribution of the Roman Empire.

Thus, the European societies of the 1st and 2nd millennia BC contained the building blocks of two social and economic strategies that were never totally separ- ated. In their basic or dominant forms they represented two different types of investment – in labour and land and in ritual – those aspects of material culture most visible to archaeologists. During periods of settlement expansion and agrarian inten- sification (Early Bronze Age, Urnfield period, middle La Tène) labour investments were directed towards land improvement, while ritual investments took the form of votive offerings and fertility cults. Whenever new warrior elites expanded and took over, investments were directed towards moveable wealth (animal husbandry and prestige goods) and ritual investments in burial monuments, and only rarely in votive depositions (hoards). As demonstrated in the previous chapter the two strategies were characterised by different rules of marriage and inheritance. The rise and expansion of farming communities were accompanied by new popular religions, as a mobilising force. So what we see during the Urnfield and La Tène expansions represents initial forms of world religions, being part of democratic movements in their expansionist phase. The cyclical change between warrior elites and farming regimes is in this perspective part of the tides and ebbs of tyranny and democracy in world history.[15]

Centre–periphery relations and world system regularities

The transformational succession between the two types of social organisation in Figure 224 depended on long-term regional changes on the one hand and interaction between regional systems or centres and peripheries on the other. Thus the sequence presented in Figure 224, which mainly relates to Middle/Central Europe, cannot be understood without reference to the larger geo-political context of which these societies were a part.

Figure 225 presents in schematic form the changing relationships between regional centres of metal/agricultural production and their peripheries, supplying special products (amber, lead, horses, slaves). This may in some periods develop into regional hierarchies.

1 May correspond to Br A2/B1 both in Central Europe and in the Mediterranean/Iberia.
2 May correspond both to the Tumulus culture and Late Hallstatt/Early La Tène in relation to the Mediterranean.
3 May correspond to the Urnfield and Middle La Tène periods.

If we try to extract some larger geo-political regularities from this scheme two types seem to emerge (Figure 226). Type One is characterised by the intensification of connections between the Near East/Mediterranean states, Central and northern Europe, forming a regional hierarchy of indirect centre–periphery relations. These are the periods in which new centres of production, distribution and trade between the Mediterranean and the rest of Europe appear (e.g. Otomani and Late Hallstatt), characterised by the demonstration of power and wealth in burials and hoards.

The second type follows on the collapse of centre–periphery relations, due to political fragmentation in the Mediterranean, or alternatively a reorientation of Mediterranean trade from south–north to east–west. These are periods of expanding farming communities in Central Europe (the Urnfield period/Mediterranean collapse and Middle La Tène/reorientation of trade), characterised by a more 'democratic' ideology, especially in burial ritual.

During the transition between these two geo-political systems, warrior societies appeared, either under influence from the eastern steppes or simply as an internal outcome of the changing balance between the centres and their peripheries, mainly due to declining supplies of exotic goods from the centres (the Tumulus culture, Hallstatt C and La Tène A). If we include the 1st millennium AD the same pattern can be observed. The Germanic expansion followed on the collapse of the Western Roman Empire, whereas the Viking expansion took place in a period of blocked north–south trade, due to the expansion of the Islamic/Arabian Empire in the Mediterranean. It can further be observed that during these periods of internal European expansion/colonisation, new indigenous art styles developed as a self-conscious response to the situation (Celtic, Germanic and Viking art), all based upon curvilinear motifs, including animal art.[16]

In such complex systems it is impossible to determine and define cause and effect as a one-way process. External and internal factors were interrelated, and in some

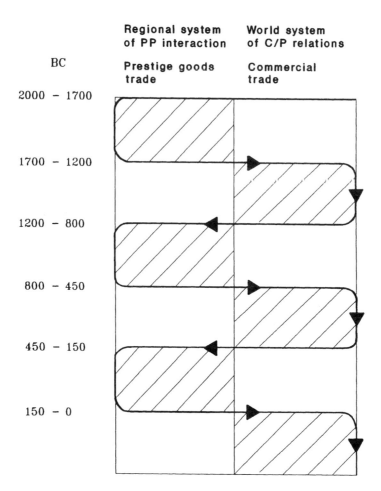

Fig. 226 Long-term cyclical shifts between European peer–polity interaction and world system centre–periphery relations between Europe, the Mediterranean and the Near East.

periods they clustered, leading to rapid changes and shifts in dominance. Some of these changes were evidently of world-historical scale, others operating within the regional boundaries of European Bronze Age societies (a scheme for world historical regularities is recently presented by Frank 1991, note 9). European Bronze Age societies of the 1st and 2nd millennia formed but one end of a supposed world system, in which dependency remained indirect, except in periods of recession and migrations. We should also be aware that local processes of evolution and devolution always occurred. Such local declines and rises were inherent features of the reproduction of larger regional systems. In the long run the balance between such multiple local processes determined the developmental potential of the regional system. Dominance, exploitation and the emergence of hierarchies, whether local or regional, were normally the result of multiple local processes of centre–periphery relations, which directed surplus towards dominant centres in a process of unequal exchange. But the mechanisms to extract surplus changed according to the nature of dominant social relations – whether they were warrior aristocracies (raiding, taking tribute and trading = wealth finance), sedentary agricultural communities (tribute = staple finance), or commercial centres of metal production and supply (trade = wealth finance). Ritual superiority also played a role in directing surplus to chiefly and ritual centres in many regions (Kristiansen 1987b). Thus it was the articulation of these strategies at local levels that determined the potential for regional dominance, e.g. in the form of regional confederations. Only in exceptional cases, such as the Late Hallstatt centres, would that give rise to larger polities and control from a single centre. On the other hand, it has to be admitted that such aspects of Bronze Age social organisation have been given little systematic attention. We may therefore be underrating their capacity to form larger polities.

The cyclical trends of evolution and devolution during the 2nd and 1st millennia BC suggest that developments in Bronze Age Europe were resistant to the formation of more rigid social differentiation and state formation. This was apparently due to inherent social and ecological constraints, in combination with the nature of interregional and international trade ties to the expanding centres of civilisation in the Mediterranean. Although much of Central Europe displayed the basic features of being in a transition to archaic state formation during the Bronze Age, regions of tribal warrior aristocracies, and areas of diminishing agricultural returns, tended to constrain developments towards state formation. But the balance between these developmental trends changed during the Bronze Age. This was reflected in a geographical shift of the cycle from the east (the Carpathian region), during the 2nd millennium, to the west (the Alpine region) during the 1st millennium. In this way, larger areas were encompassed by the processes of detribalisation. The basic layout of these centre–periphery relations is summarised in Figures 225 and 226. It meant that after 600 BC processes of archaic state formation could finally dominate and unfold, supported by the emerging city states and empires in the Mediterranean. The significant difference between the two cycles was that European Bronze Age societies were able to run along the civilisational frontier in the late 2nd millennium BC, while that was not the case nearly a thousand years later.

It follows from this that European social evolution did not progress in a unilinear fashion from simple to higher forms of social organisation, as has commonly been believed (Champion *et al.* 1984). The transition from Bronze to Iron Age has traditionally been considered a significant evolutionary leap. Colin Renfrew (1987) used this to justify his contention that migrations did not occur until the conquest migrations of the Iron Age, since they demanded a higher level of social organisation. However, with the exception of oppida and urbanisation in the 2nd and 1st centuries BC, developments during the first millennium were not significantly different from those of the second millennium. We have to project back the social complexity of the first millennium, and the notion of a European world system, another 1,000 years. And we also have to give up the modernist liberal myth that change and progress was always accomplished peacefully and freely, and that conflict, disruption and migrations did not occur in prehistory.

8.4 Concluding perspective – epilogue

We have come to the end of our inquiry and should therefore briefly address the questions raised in the introduction. Although answers have been given, we may here allow ourselves to reflect more generally upon the world historical implications of the conclusions reached. What makes the Bronze Age so special is linked to the nature of centre–periphery relations that characterised the 1st and 2nd millennia BC. By adopting the mastery of metallurgy, the rituals of status and the innovations of warfare from the east Mediterranean, but not the political and economic framework sustaining it, new social and economic dynamics were introduced to the societies of temperate Europe. These gradually transformed their social and ecological environment, yet without supplying the necessary economic innovations and technologies allowing a more centralised political system to emerge and to be maintained. New value systems were exported northward from first the Mycenaean and later the Greek/Etruscan world, in exchange for high value, small scale goods, such as tin, gold, amber from the most remote hinterland, and also horses and slaves from the closer periphery. The western Mediterranean in its turn represented the primary periphery to the commercial states in the Levant. Due to this structural balance Central and northern Europe were not urbanised and commodified until much later in history. As stated by Sherratt (1994):

> The contrast between the Bronze Age societies of Europe and the Near East, therefore, was a fundamental one: they were constructed on quite different principles. European societies were actively resisting commodification, not beginning a process of convergence. The economies of urban, state-organised societies had quite different properties from those of their predecessors and contemporaries with different forms of organisation . . . Europe lacked the concentrations of capital which would have allowed this structural differentiation; without external intervention, it was not even on the way to it . . . These factors explain why Bronze Age centralisation proceeded no further.

Thus wealth was invested in the traditional ways – it circulated for social and political ends, and was deposited for the same reasons in burials and hoards, no accumulation of capital took place – in opposition to the city states and empires of the east Mediterranean. They instead recirculated metal and invested in infrastructures such as roads, harbours, towns etc. This is a fundamental difference between pre-state and state societies.

Thus regional interaction between empires of productive irrigation agriculture in the Near East, commercial city states in the Mediterranean, nomads to the north, and ploughland agriculture and mineral exploitation in temperate Europe created a unique world system from approximately 2000 BC onwards. However, it distinguished itself from the modern world system by a number of basic features. Following Eden and Kohl (1993, 31) they are: 'the existence of multiple centres; logistical constraints impeding movements of materials, especially staples, along overland routes; the omnipresent military option to raid rather than trade; and technologies common to both peripheries and centres. These differences suggest that dependencies in the modern sense only rarely characterised centre–periphery relations in the ancient world.' The Bronze Age world system also contained a good deal of resistance to the expansion of traditional state and empire formation in temperate Europe and Asia, and it tended to check, or even halt, the civilisational process through counteraction on both the nomadic and agricultural peripheries (Mann 1986, ch. 2). During the first millennium BC the processes of state formation came, however, to dominate in most of Central Europe and the Mediterranean. This created an evolutionary division between northern and Central Europe, whose evolutionary trajectories became divided, although continuing to interact with each other. This dynamism between 'egalitarian' traditions in the north and more complex state formation in Central Europe was, during the first millennium BC, represented by Celts and Germans – whose ethnic identities, if they ever had a historical meaning outside the realm of classical writers, were the outcome of processes of centre–periphery relations and regional processes of social transformation. It is therefore meaningless, and historically unjustified, to use them more widely, and, even worse, to trace them up to our own time, as if the processes of history and changing social conditions did not matter.

On the other hand, there probably were basic structural constraints on long-term historical processes. It might be suggested that the structural divergencies created during the first millennium BC between northern Europe, Central Europe and the Mediterranean determined the later course of European history by establishing the structural foundations on which it came to rest, e.g. the limits of the Roman Empire in Europe. Later European history seems to have unfolded according to this structural framework, at least at the macro level. The question that remains to be answered is, what was the balance between world-historical processes of evolution and devolution against the forces of specific historical conditions? It can perhaps be argued that while most of the processes we have been discussing, from the formation of warrior elites to feudalisation, are general ones, it was their specific combination in a world system which generated the long-term trajectory that made possible the transformation of the European margin, and later periphery, into a centre. But I also believe that the specific regional conditions of Europe played a significant role. Its inability to cope with demographic growth, its agricultural constraints, its recurrent demographic and ecological crises, and its inherited pastoral warrior ideology of expansion, transforming internal competition and fragmentation into external expansion, preventing European empire formation, are conditions that can be traced back to the second and first millennia BC or even earlier.

Our inheritance from the Bronze Age is thus a structural one – during these two millennia a world-historical division was created between centralised Mediterranean states and decentralised north European societies, a division that still has a historical impact. But the Bronze Age may also teach us about our own foreignness – the peoples of the Bronze Age lived in a world that we will never fully understand, without understanding its otherness.

2 **Background to the archaeology**

1 Research environments: The 1st and 2nd millennia BC are normally divided into five periods in terms of academic specialisation: the Early Bronze Age (Br. A1–2/3), the Middle Bronze Age (Br. B–C), the Late Bronze Age (Ha A–B), the Early Iron Age (Ha C–D) and the later Iron Age (La Tène A–C). These divisions have generated a number of productive regional research groups that meet regularly, publish conference reports, etc., but which have rather little contact outside their research area. Such informal research groups exist for the Lausitz Culture (Bukowski 1988), the eastern and western Middle Bronze Age and Urnfield Cultures (east: Plesl and Hrala 1987; west: *Dynamique du bronze moyen en Europe occidentale* 1989; Brun and Mordant 1988), the Hallstatt Culture (east: Jerem 1986; west: Ulrix-Closset and Otte 1989; the Balkans: Benac *et al.* 1991), and the La Tène Culture (Duval and Kruta 1979; Pauli 1980a). Behind these culturally and chronologically defined research traditions we also see the effects of divisions determined by political conditions, language, and research traditions on a larger scale. To this we can add a Mediterranean research environment, with which I am less familiar, but which is also divided into different sectors, one major division being between classical studies, predominantly art orientated, and archaeological studies, with the emphasis on social and economic aspects (see Snodgrass 1987).

Most fundamental, however, has been the division of Europe into two political blocs, although contacts were maintained across the borders. There are also major language and research groupings centred around English (England, the Netherlands, and Scandinavia), German (Central Europe), and French, Spanish and Italian (the western Mediterranean), although French is also traditionally employed by many Central European scholars. There is much overlapping as well, and Scandinavia has changed from the German to the English tradition, although the change is not complete. The overall picture, however, is one of rather closed circles of research determined by a variety of both archaeological and political configurations, not to mention the overall dichotomy between 'traditional' and 'new' archaeology. Although there is at some levels interaction between the groups (e.g. UISSP committees and thematic conferences and books, and series such as *Prähistorische Bronzefunde*), and although there have been efforts recently to break through these arbitrary barriers to reach a more complete historical understanding of Bronze and Early Iron Age Europe (Wells 1984; Collis 1984a; Brun 1987; Cunliffe 1988), such attempts have been seriously hampered by the dominant research traditions. Therefore the historical significance of the Bronze Age has not yet been fully realised.

3 **Theoretical context**

1 I do not consider it productive to enter into the discussion between 'processualists' and 'post-processualists', as my position belongs in neither camp (for a discussion, see Kristiansen in press). The reader is referred to the initial debate between Hodder (1982b; 1986) and Binford (1986), which has been followed up by several debates after the publication of Shanks and Tilley's two books, 'the Black and the Red' (Shanks and Tilley 1987a and b),

especially in *Norwegian Archaeological Review* 22, No. 1, and *Scottish Archaeological Review*, Volume 7, 1990 and Volume 8, 1991.

2 French Structural Marxism represented one of the first serious critiques of traditional marxism characterised by evolutionary stage theory and by rather simplistic notions of economic determination (base–superstructure), at least in its general application in the communist world, and in evolutionary theory in North America, as represented by Leslie White, Elman Service and others. Maurice Godelier (1967) tried to develop a more dynamic and sophisticated marxist theory, in accordance with the theoretical structure of *The Capital*, rather than with the various theoretical formulations known as historical material-ism. It was further amplified by modern anthropological knowledge of pre-state societies, which added a 'substantivist' perspective (Sahlins 1974; Godelier 1977), just as it tried to incorporate some of the insights of Structuralism within a marxist framework, thereby making them operational. This led to a partial rejection of unilinear stage theory, for example by reviving the discussion of the Asiatic Mode of Production (see Chapter 3.2), and to a modification of the base–superstructure model. As stated by Godelier (1978, 763): 'To my mind, a society does not have a top and a bottom, or even levels. This is because the distinction between infrastructure and superstructure is not a distinction between institu-tions. Its principle, rather, is one of a distinction between functions.' The social relations of production could be dominated by and executed through kinship or any other institution. In this way dominant social relations may cross-cut traditional institutional boundaries or the subsystems of functional and ecosystem models. This echoes, quite naturally, one of Marx's formulations (1973, 107): 'In all forms of society there is one specific kind of production which predominates over the rest, whose relations thus assign rank and influence to the others.' According to Godelier (1978, 765) this opens up 'a vast new field of investigation, namely the search for the reasons and the conditions which, in history, have brought about shifts in the locus – and hence changes in the forms – of relations of production'.

These critiques were also applied to the American version of cultural evolution, rooted in ecological/adaptionist approaches, by Friedman (1974). However, Structural Marxism turned out to be constrained by its lack of historical perspective and by its perception of societies as closed or bounded entities, which to some extent was a function of its anthropol-ogical orientation. Ekholm (1980; 1981), and Friedman and Rowlands (1977), in a critique of this, have tried to develop a theoretical framework of social transformations as an articulation of both spatial and temporal processes of change, influenced by the world systems approaches of Braudel (1972) and Wallerstein (1974). It was situated within a redefined evolutionary framework seeing evolution and devolution as neither uni- nor multi-linear, but as a continuum in time and space, allowing for the interaction of multiple 'levels' of social organisation, whose developmental potential was determined by its place in the larger system. Thus according to Friedman and Rowlands (1977, 271): 'The structures of the larger systems are determined by the dominant relations of production that make them up, e.g. the internal potential demands of local systems and the spatial distribution of constraints that determine the relative potential for development of the individual units with respect to one another.' This approach allowed for a more open conception of society and evolution with a strong appeal to archaeology, (review Shennan 1987) and was soon applied in a number of works spanning from tribal systems (Kristiansen 1978; 1982) to archaic states (Gledhill and Larsen 1982), and the interaction between centres and peripheries in ancient world systems (Rowlands, Larsen and Kristiansen 1987).

3 Recent studies in later European prehistory have made important progress towards under-standing structural variability and evolutionary trajectories in pre-state, tribal societies (for a summary see Shennan 1987). This has been amplified by comparative studies and dis-cussions in North America (Hass 1980; Braun and Plog 1982; Saitta 1983; Bender 1985). It has been proposed that in Europe we are dealing with two variants of tribal structure, whose internal social and ideological properties were linked to differences in economy and ecology

(Renfrew 1974; Sherratt 1981; Shennan 1982; Kristiansen 1982; 1984a). They have also been described with reference to two significantly different kinship systems: one based on lineage society and one based on germanic community (Rowlands 1980; Thomas 1987). In a classic work Andrew Sherratt (1981) pointed to the combined effect of technological and economic changes for bringing about this transformation.

These variants of tribal structure which characterised temperate Eurasia during the fourth and third millennia have been labelled by Colin Renfrew (1974) as 'group-oriented' and 'individualising' chiefdoms. Others have stressed the relationship between ritual and social organisation – the Megalithic Culture being labelled a 'ritual authority structure' (Thorpe and Richards 1984), and the Corded Ware/Battle Axe cultures of the third millennium, to be followed by the Bronze Age cultures, a 'prestige goods economy' (Kristiansen 1982; see also Gilman 1981; Shennan 1986a; and Bradley 1984 for an illuminating regional study).

4 Regional systems: the social and cultural landscape in Europe in the Late Bronze Age 1100–750 BC

1 Some of these changes, like that of the Jutlandic Single Grave/Battle Axe culture in the Middle Neolithic, were due to migrations of new people, bringing with them new social and cultural norms (Kristiansen 1989); the radical new traditions are then visible behind the otherwise homogenous cultural distributions for nearly a millennium, until integrated into Bronze Age culture. So we may assume that ethnic identities can be very resistant, and will make themselves felt in cultural distributions, if they involve a whole population, rather than just conquerors, a question we will return to in Chapter 7.

2 The emergence of major regional traditions such as the Nordic, the Atlantic and the Urnfield –beyond reflecting the formation of new social and ideological value systems –must also have demanded a shared language in order to operate, or at least a shared language group within which communication could be maintained at certain standardised levels (e.g. pidgin language as defined by Sherratt and Sherratt 1988). By this I have not implied anything about the nature and causes of language change, only that at any given time within a specific cultural tradition there must have been some shared language relating to the meaning and operation of basic ritual and social institutions. We know that within the Nordic region regular chiefly relations could be operating between several regions –Jutland, southwest Norway, southern amd Middle Sweden –over long distances. Indeed, we should expect that the frequency of interaction in Bronze Age Europe, probably unparalleled in European prehistory and early history, would have levelled out language differences over large regions, whereas periods of contraction and closed circles of interaction would lead to the development of local language characteristics. These and related questions of language and ethnicity will be discussed in Chapter 8.

3 We are not considering the representativity of metalwork, as this has been extensively studied in Denmark (Kristiansen 1974a; 1985b; 1985c) and in some other European regions (e.g. Stein 1976, Abb. 13, 19–20). The main conclusion is that on a regional scale the distribution of metalwork can be considered as representative in terms of its history of recovery. Supplementary source critical studies have yet to be carried out to consider local variation.

4 Even early archaeologists, such as Worsaae, observed regularities in the combinations and find circumstances of Bronze Age hoards, suggesting regularity in the motives and causes of deposition as well. Worsaae (1866) interpreted most hoards as ritual, a view still favoured today by most researchers (for a recent exhaustive survey see Bradley 1990; and articles in *Arch. Korrespondenzblatt* 1985). Since the ritual hoarding of valuables is an unfamiliar category to modern perceptions, unlike burials, their interpretation has been difficult to come to terms with, although they represent an essential feature of European prehistoric societies, especially in the Bronze Age. Let us therefore consider some of the ways in which the analysis of hoards has been approached in recent years:

(a) Since Hundt (1955) convincingly proposed that during the Late Bronze Age hoarding represented an alternative way of depositing burial wealth after the introduction of urn burials (totenschätze), this interpretation has been widely accepted for personal hoards, as defined below.

(b) An important supplement to hoard interpretation was the analysis of recurrent sets of ornaments and weapons/tools, as carried out by von Brunn for northern Europe, defining regional groups corresponding to the groups defined by metal types (1968, Abb. 19–20; 1980). This approach has later been more widely applied (e.g. Kristiansen 1974b; Coombs 1975; 1989; Rowlands 1976; Stein 1976; Sasse 1977; Levy 1982).

(c) Analyses of the context of finds have often played a role in ascribing hoards to a single category: wet finds predominantly ritual, dry ones mainly secular. Whereas one may assume some connection between ritual depositions and depositions on moors and in lakes, since retrieval is not easy, the opposite is not the case. In an important study of the context of Danish Late Bronze Age hoards and single finds, Jørgen Jensen (1973) was able to demonstrate that most single finds were ritually deposited, which is today also believed to be true in other regions and has led to a more integrated study of metal deposition (e.g. Stein 1976; Willroth 1985; Larsson 1986). A special category of single finds is the river finds worked on by Törbrugge (1971; see also Wegner 1976; Kubach 1983; 1985), where a ritual motive is mostly favoured, although cargoes from river transport and warfare may sometimes occur (Muckelroy 1981). To this we may add another special category, that of caves (Schauer 1982b).

(d) In recent years the deposition or consumption of metalwork in hoards or graves has been studied quantitatively in relation to economic changes, regionally and temporally, in a number of studies (Randsborg 1974; Kristiansen 1978; 1984a). It can be shown that depositions are related to regional and temporal changes in economic conditions. It implies that all types of deposition should be studied, leading to a more integrated approach to Bronze Age metalwork (e.g. Barrett and Bradley 1980: Barrett and Needham 1988; Larsson 1988), linking deposition to social and economic organisation.

5 The above classifications are based on my records and partial analysis of north European hoards, and so are my statements about their cultural and chronological value. This is not the place to go into a more detailed documentation and analysis; hopefully there will come a time for that also.

6 The knowledge of settlement organisation is quite recent, compared to burials and hoards. It was not until after the turn of the present century that post-holes were recognised archaeologically at the Limes excavations (Eggers 1959, 220f.). The excitement it created is understandable: 'Im Halten sah auch ich im Sommer 1907 bei Dragendorff das erste Pfostenloch', wrote Kiekebusch, who excavated the first Urnfield village at Busch near Berlin at the beginning of the century (1911). Work followed on the well-preserved moor settlements, e.g. Buchau at Federseemoor, which came to typify a Late Bronze Age defended village (Reinerth 1936). The large Lausitz fortifications ('Heidenschanzen') also happened to become known through well-conducted excavations by Schuchardt among others at an early date (Eggers 1959, 223ff.), leading to a flourishing research tradition, so that Lausitz fortifications still remain the best known in Europe. Only in recent years have systematic excavations of fortified settlements revealed the widespread occurrence of defended central places during the Bronze Age in Central and western Europe (Chropovsky and Hermann 1982). Exceptionally, the Nordic/Baltic region did not employ fortified settlements.

In terms of house form there appear to be at least three regional traditions: a northwest European/Nordic one characterised by rather large three-aisled houses in small clusters of hamlets (Jensen 1987; Tesch 1993; Audouze and Büchsenschütz 1992, 132 ff.); a Central European one defined by two-aisled houses of *megaron* type/block-built houses (Rihovsky 1969; Brun 1981; Buch 1986b, Abb. 9; Torbrügge 1988, Tafel 3A, B) often in villages; and an English (Atlantic?) type of circular houses arranged in farmsteads or hamlets (Bradley 1978). Traditions of house building thus correspond to the larger regional cultural groupings discussed above (Audouze and Büchsenschütz 1989 (in French); 1992 (in English), give an excellent summary of house settlement types etc. for the whole Bronze and Early Iron Age).

7 At Cortaillod-Est, an Alpine Late Bronze Age settlement in Switzerland, sheep amount to 49.1 per cent, compared to cattle with 30 per cent (Chaix 1986). As the settlement was surrounded by large arable areas, we must imagine the systematic exploitation of upland grazing (Borello *et al.* 1986). An upland settlement at Vex-le-Chateaux, at 840 m altitude, had sheep dominating with 60–75 per cent, against cattle 18–30 per cent during Early, Middle and Late Bronze Age (Chaix 1990).

8 Early Urnfield 'pioneer' settlements seem to be small, consisting of a few farms (a hamlet) rather than organised villages (e.g. Krause 1990). It can often be difficult to establish how many of the houses in a settlement are contemporaneous. Here the 'Phahlbau' settlements offer unique opportunities of reconstructing sequences of houses. At Greifensee-Böschau a settlement of fifteen blockhouses was built in the year 1047/46 BC, and burned down immediately afterwards, representing one phase (Ebersweiler, Riethman and Ruoff 1987).

9 The recent find of a hoard of at least fourteen Herzsprung shields found in a bog in middle Sweden (Hagberg 1988), together with the find of nine bronze corselets from Marmesse in France (Mohen 1987), gives a rare glimpse of the organised distribution of valuable prestige goods. Their numbers must have been far greater than normally assumed – at least in the chiefly centres throughout Europe.

10 The dominant interpretation of human bones and skeletons at the large, fortified settlements as ritual (Salas 1990; Jelinek 1993) should be questioned, or at least modified. Considering the structure of Urnfield society, it is more likely that a combination of warfare (local conflicts), ritual sacrifice/cannibalism and the displacement of dead slaves would lead to the recurring features of unstructured human skeletons and dislocated human bones as evidenced at several settlements. When we do find clear evidence of unstructured displacement of human bones and skeletons, in contrast to the structured ritual of burials and votive offerings, we should be prepared to accept the evidence, rather than trying to force it into a pattern of ritual to which it does not conform.

5 Regional divergence: the Mediterranean and Europe in the 9th–8th centuries BC

1 Urartian bronzes have traditionally been thought to have been a major influence (Piotrovksy 1969) on the orientalising style. This, however, was mainly in terms of contacts northwards with the Caucasus. The orientalising style contained many nomadic or pastoral elements, due to the centre–periphery relations between Urartu-Assyria and the Cimmerians and Scythians (see Chapter 5). Recent research into the bronze industry of the Near East and Asia Minor has downplayed the role of Urartu (Seidl 1988) which should really be seen simply as characteristic of the royal prestige goods industries in the whole area, with the Phrygians as another good example (Muscarella 1988), leading to a remarkable similarity in the products found in royal contexts from Assyria to the eastern Mediterranean. However, due to different patterns of consumption in royal burials, and the general tendency of states to recycle rather than deposit metal, the survival of evidence is uneven (Winther 1988).

2 In his critique of the economic approach, Finley states (1973, 34), in his persuasive polemic style: 'To be meaningful, "world market", "a single economic unit" must embrace something considerably more than exchange of some goods over long distances . . . One must show the existence of interlocking behaviour and responses over wide areas . . . in the dominant sectors of the economy, in food and metal prices, for example and one cannot, or at least no one has.' Finley employs the traditional strategy of setting up an opposition which effectively blocks discussion of the intermediate stages between the two poles. As has been

shown in subsequent studies, several of Finley's premises were wrong (the nature of Near Eastern trade, e.g. Adams 1974; Larsen 1987b), just as the role of economic politics in the Archaic period has been stressed by Cartledge (1983), as well as trade in metals (Snodgrass 1983). It seem clear from the research of the past twenty years that Finley's model no longer gives an adequate representation of the Ancient economy.

3 Burgess (1991, 32ff.) has recently reevaluated the evidence for the Phoenician presence in Iberia during the Late Bronze Age. He reaches the same conclusion as Schauer (1983) that the Levant maintained contacts with Iberia even after the 12th-century collapse in the Mediterranean, originating from Tyre. At least from the early 10th century there is also supporting archaeological evidence (Almagro-Gorbea 1992). Most significant, perhaps, is the tholos Roca do Casal do Meiro, a burial chamber of East Mediterranean inspiration, with a so-called Cypriotic fibula and other grave goods, testifying to personal contacts between the eastern Mediterranean and the Atlantic coast at the beginning of the 10th century BC (Spindler and Veiga Ferreira 1973). The find further supports the proposal that fibulae of foreign inspiration or origin testify to personal relations.

4 It was Ernst Sprockhoff (1951) who first employed the name Phahlbau bronzes when defining their impact on the formation of Period V style in the north, and in tracing the rise of the North German/Baltic coastal area as a centre of metal production and consumption in this period. The stylistic impact had previously been discussed by Vogt (1942) and Hundt (1978), although a thorough analysis is still lacking. The Phahlbau style, also present on pottery, seems to represent an original reworking of stylistic trends from the Mediterranean, combining elements of Greek archaic (geometric) motifs with Urnfield motifs, in the north woven into the Nordic style. Geometric motifs were transmitted more widely in wood and bone-working, as seen in Denmark (Baudou 1960, Karte 51–52), whereas curvilinear motifs dominate on the bronzes.

5 This unique burial construction has parallels in the Cimmerian chiefly barrows of northern Caucasus (Machortych 1989), and the mat also in Hungary, where a grass mat was employed in a chamber in a large tumulus of Ha C (Vadasz 1983). Together with wagon/ horse gear, it stresses the impact of the Cimmerians, even in northern Europe.

6 By using the grave goods, or chiefly regalia, from the well-defined princely contexts at Seddin and Voldtofte we can by means of parallels identify other chiefly centres without monumental burials (Thrane 1983). On this basis we may conclude that distribution maps of phalerae and golden *eidrings* (Figure 97), lurs and costly ritual gear indicate a network of chiefly centres in southern Scandinavia and around the Baltic, some of which were served through the Seddin centre. Also belonging to the chiefly level, but probably a lower stratum, if not furnished with ornamentation or accompanied by gold rings, were razors and tweezers. The whole system was based on ritual and religious legitimation, as seen in the direct connection between the high chiefs and the performance of ritual, but a following of warriors must have been part of the operation of the system, perhaps demonstrated by the widespread distribution and deposition of spears, most effective in close combat (Schauer 1979), in bogs, sometimes a whole group together. The warriors of the chiefly following, however, are not visible in burials until the subsequent period.

7 The form of the three 'basins' in the unique tripartite vessel corresponds to the widespread use of similar symbols in silver vessels (*phialae*) from the Near East to the eastern Mediterranean (see Rogozen base motif no. 2, in Fol 1989, 140) and the form is repeated on the handles of Ha D *stamnois* (see Kleinaspergle in Kimmig 1988b, Taf. 14). Also the gold vessels correspond quite well to the general form language of the Early Iron Age, such as Stillfried-Hostomice and related forms (Mehrart 1952).

8 Thus there is continuity from Late Urnfield Ha B3 to Early Iron Age Ha C in this eastern region, both in fortifications and in pottery (Kromer 1986, Abb. 65–66), making it difficult to define a clear borderline between Ha B and C. Gabroviec (1966) therefore set the beginning of Ha C some fifty years later.

9 The Thraco-Cimmerian complex in Central Europe was recognised and described at an earlier stage than its Pontic/Central Asian counterpart, which explains some of the difficulties encountered in tracing its origins, a problem still felt (although Gallus and Horvath's original work (1939) still stands out as a readable classic). Another problem is that of language, most of the East European research being inaccessible to West European scholars, as it is only published in national languages, often without even summaries or figure captions in an international language. This, however, is unfortunately true of much European archaeology today, being a major obstacle to the development of a full understanding of a European prehistory in its wider cultural and geographical setting. The Cimmerian problem may teach us two lessons: first, it is a good example of the scientific rewards of systematic problem-orientated research over nearly two generations, in opposition to the mindless mapping of randomly selected types. The answers to the Cimmerian problem demand coordinated publication and classification over large geographical areas, and although no international research project has been formulated, the strength of the hypothesis has continued to initiate new and geographically expanding research, allowing us today to unfold the components of what we believe to be representative fragments of the whole cultural and social framework. Second, it demonstrates the potentials and problems of archaeological and historical sources. Without the latter we would not dare to propose anything concerning Cimmerian raids into Asia Minor (a few arrowheads are the sole archaeological testimony). This exemplifies the lack of archaeological evidence for warriors on the move. It also adds significance to the East European evidence.

6 The new economic axis: Central Europe and the Mediterranean 750–450 BC

1 Recent research has revealed that the Mälar region in central Sweden was an early centre of iron production (Hjärthner-Holdar 1993, fig. 7), linked to eastern contact in Russia/Ukraine, where the Mälar axes also originated (Hjärthner-Holdar 1993, figs. 2, 6).

2 Excavations, publications and research on the Hallstatt culture in Central Europe have in this generation produced remarkable results. They have been stimulated by regular symposia that have helped to coordinate research goals, as well as cooperation across national borders (e.g. Chropovsky 1974; Eibner and Eibner 1981; Jerem 1986; Ulrix-Closset and Otte 1989). Outside the central Alpine region, in western and southeastern Europe, research has only developed more recently. In the following I shall rely on the well-documented monographs, exhibition catalogues and conference reports, selecting certain themes for discussion and interpretation, rather than describing the whole culture. The division between eastern and western Hallstatt stems from their different geneses, the eastern group emerging already at the transition between the Late Bronze Age (Ha B2–3) and the Iron Age (Ha C), according to Central European tradition, while the western Hallstatt developed later and more abruptly from 750 BC (Ha C).

3 I shall stress one important observation not given enough attention by Jensen: high-value products, such as amber, are normally only consumed in the receiving areas, not in those delivering the product; here it was simply both too costly in exchange value foregone and too common. Amber thus disappears from local burials in Denmark when metal first makes its appearance, and only a few amber hoards datable to the Bronze Age testify to its systematic exploitation.

4 It has also been proposed that the Italian influences should reflect the presence of Etruscan traders, introducing the urban concept of Biskupin on their way. The arguments, based on archaeological and linguistic evidence have lately been summarised by Szafranski (1990). In the same seminar Bouloumie (1990), analysed the evidence from a southern perspective and finds no evidence of the presence of Etruscan traders. He rather sees the influences as a result of long-distance trade, resulting in frequent movements of people and goods over shorter distances, leading to the local adoption of new cultural and religious idioms.

5 Most recently a fortified 'Lausitz settlement' has been excavated in central Sweden, raising a

series of new questions about the nature of interaction between the two areas (Larsson 1993).

6 Later regional analyses have suggested that there was some geographical divergence between Ha B3 and Ha C, and continuity in burials between Ha B3 and Ha D (Hoppe 1986, Abb. 12, 87ff; Zürn 1987). In the more marginal areas of northwestern Europe, such as the lower Rhine and Thames, there is continuity of settlement areas (Roymans 1991, figs. 6, 13). In this region Ha B3/Ha C represents a demographic peak, where settlements expanded into lowland dune areas along the coast as well (Roymans 1991, fig. 24), suggesting an economy based largely on cattle husbandry and salt production. This may account for the central function of the Thames/Rhine line as the most important axis of exchange in northwestern Europe during Ha C (Roymans 1991, fig. 20).

7 In recent years a series of books have provided a good overview of the late west Hallstatt phenomenon: Härke 1979; Bittel, Kimmig and Schiek 1981; Fischer and Biel 1982; Kimmig 1982, 1983; 1988b; Spindler 1983; Biel 1985; *Les princes celtes* 1988.

8 The sex determination of the Vix burial has been contested, especially by Spindler (1983, 107), but has recently been firmly established as female (Langlois 1987), in relation to a reconstruction of the probable facial expression.

9 Recently Manfred Eggert (1988; 1991) has argued against the traditional German definitions and interpretations of the 'Fürstensitze' in the west Hallstatt, as representing an unreflected Eurocentric, historical model of the past. He points out that the foreign influences are relatively few and that indigenous developments are underestimated, due to the dominance of a similarly unreflected Mediterranean civilisational model. By using ethnographic models and by quantifying the labour investments in the building of the tumuli, an attempt is made to demystify the whole princely construction, although this perhaps may lead to an underestimation of the symbolic significance of power. In similar ways Michael Dietler (1989; 1990) has forwarded a new critical perspective on the relationship between the Mediterranean and Iron Age societies, to some extent based on ethnographic analogies, which assumes that imports were mainly employed in internal competition and politics, e.g. the use of imported wine for labour mobilisation. Thus they do not reflect the politics of Mediterranean states, but of the barbarian societies. Although such a perspective offers stimulating new ideas, and may indeed be much needed, Dietler underestimates the level of social and political organisation that characterised Bronze and Early Iron Age Europe in the 1st millennium BC. The social landscape of this period had nothing to do with tribal or Big-Man societies without coercive power, which means that some of the ethnographic parallels and the interpretative models following from them may appear somewhat misleading. However, I agree with the conclusion that 'it seems prudent for the moment to allow at least a little scepticism about the magnitude of Mediterranean influence in Hallstatt Europe' (Dietler 1989, 130). Pare (1991) also has stressed the importance of indigenous factors in the early phase of the West Hallstatt structure, pointing to a more dynamic perception of the changes from Ha D1 to Ha D3. This, however, is already taken into account in several of the previous models, especially by Frankenstein and Rowlands (1978). In conclusion, however, there is little doubt that these works signal a need for reconsidering internal conditions in future research (e.g. Woolf 1993).

10 A critical discussion of the problems of ethnicity, archaeology and their relation to each other was recently published (Benac, Covic and Tasic 1991). There is general agreement that the first millennium BC represents a crucial phase of social, cultural, and possibly also ethnic, transformation (Vasic 1991; Fol 1991; Velkov 1991), whereas links cannot be established in the Bronze Age, except in very broad, and therefore historically insignificant, terms (Covic 1991). These and related problems are taken up in Chapter 8.

11 Renate Rolle (1979; 1989) has in a series of works analysed and summarised the rich evidence; most recently, in 1991, a good overview has been given in articles from the

exhibition catalogue: *Gold der Steppe. Archäologie der Ukraine*, edited by Rolle, Müller-Wille and Schietzel in collaboration with Tolocko and Murzin.

12 This is most vividly described by Herodotus (IV. 126–127). In a classic exchange between Darius and the Scythian king, Idanthyrsus, the difference in political ideology is played out:

Darius sent a horseman to the Scythian king Idanthyrsus, and said: 'You are a strange fellow. Why do you keep flying from me when you might make a choice of courses? If you think yourself strong enough to oppose my power, stop wandering to and fro and stand and fight. If your mind tells you that you are the weaker, then, likewise, stop running away, give gifts –namely earth and water –to one who is your master, and come to words with me.'

To this the Scythian king, Idanthyrsus, answered: 'Persian, matters are thus with me. I have never fled from a man in fear in days past nor now. I am not fleeing from you. What I am doing now is no different from what I am wont to do in peacetime. I will also tell you why I do not instantly fight you. We have neither cities nor sown land among us for which we might fear –that they can be captured or destroyed –and so might be quicker to join in battle against you to save them. But if you must come to a fight with us quickly, there *are* our fathers' graves. Find them and try to ruin them, and you will discover whether we will fight or not –for the graves. Before that, we will not fight, unless some argument of our own takes possession of us. That is all I have to say to you about a fight. But for my *masters*, I count them to be Zeus, who is my ancestor, and Hestia, queen of the Scythians. These only. To you, instead of gifts of earth and water, I will send you such gifts as are fit to come your way. In answer to your claim to be my master, you will be sorry you said it.' That is the speech Darius got from the Scythians.

13 It should be mentioned that there is still some uncertainty about the chronology of pre-Scythian and Scythian settlement. Parzinger and Stegmann-Rajtar (1988) have recently proposed an early date for the first Scythian expeditions, in the earlier 6th century BC (Ha D). Their dating is based on a reanalysis of the finds from the hillfort of Smolenice-Malpir. Here the latest phase, including Scythian arrowheads, is no later than Ha D. Burials with Scythian material first appear at the same time.

Their interpretation of the Scythian finds from the hillfort, especially the many arrowheads at the fortification wall and in houses along the defences, is, however, not convincing. Everything points to a Scythian takeover of the fort in the early 6th century, after which it was abandoned. Even if the Scythian arrowheads in the houses were left by warriors inside the fort, it supports the suggestion of a period of Scythian control before leaving the fort. I am thus in full agreement with Bukowski (1977b, 254ff.) and others on the interpretation of a Scythian takeover and destruction. Acculturation, as proposed by Parzinger and Stegmann-Rajtar, has to be specified and explained, not simply used as a covering term.

7 Transformation and expansion: the Celtic movement 450–150 BC

1 A note of clarification: diffusion is a covering, descriptive, concept for the transmission and change of material culture that does not account for its underlying social mechanisms. Migration is likewise a covering concept for the movement of people, from whole populations to smaller groups. Here, too, the underlying social mechanisms are not accounted for.

2 The historical sources for the first migrating Celtic tribes that settled in northern Italy – Gallia Cisalpina – allow some insight into early Celtic social organisation, which has been excellently summarised by Christian Peyre (1979, ch. 3). An aristocracy with 'war kings' is attested, but nothing about the duration of these functions of war. Governing institutions included an aristocratic assembly and a public assembly (*publico concilio*) which among other things decided on declaring war. The population was organised in 'tribal territories' (*pagus, canton*), consisting of 112 groups (like the Suebi, which Caesar mentions consisted of 100). Each settlement unit (*vicus*) or village took part in major political decisions, where the

aristocratic assembly (*concilium*) represented a form of tribal confederation.

3 Celtic culture and language should be kept separate. Celtic culture, defined as La Tène culture, emerged in a specific area and time period as a response to specific historical circumstances, whereas the Celtic language both preceded and succeeded La Tène culture. There has been a tendency in recent years to derive uncritically Celtic culture and language from the Urnfield culture, inferring a Central European origin of Celtic and La Tène culture. This myth of origin has replaced an earlier hypothesis linking Celtic culture and language to the western Bell Beakers and the Atlantic Bronze Age tradition (for a good discussion of 'Celticity' see Renfrew 1987, ch. 9). I shall comment briefly on these two hypotheses:

The Central European Urnfield origin presupposes that Celtic language was brought to the west – England, Ireland and Iberia – through some form of migration.

The West European Atlantic origin presupposes that Celtic language was brought to Central Europe through some form of migration and later replaced by the Roman language.

With a few local exceptions there is as yet no evidence of massive Celtic migrations to England, Ireland and Iberia during La Tène, whereas the eastward migrations into Central Europe and even eastern Europe and the Balkans are archaeologically well documented, from cemeteries to settlements. On these grounds alone one must prefer a west European origin of Celtic, which, however, is discussed more fully in a subsequent section.

Ancient historians such as Herodotus (II, 33) refer to the Celts as living beyond the Pillars of Heracles at a time before the migrations. If accepted, this suggests southwestern Iberia as an original homeland of a Celtic-speaking people (evidence summarised and discussed in Garrito 1992).

4 The later survival of Celtic culture in Ireland once again demonstrates the role of the periphery as a refuge for social and cultural traditions being replaced by new dynasties or empires in the centre. It was strengthened by opposition to the Roman rule, adding a special significance to it as representing old traditions of independence. It also conformed well to the archaic traditions of pastoral farming and chiefly warrior societies going back to the Late Bronze Age, or even further. As the homeland of Celtic language was the Atlantic zone, both culture and language came to play a role of maintaining old traditions.

5 With the consolidation of Celtic social organisation in Central Europe, Germanic tribes sought a new outlet for expansion, leading to the formation of the Nordic–Pontic interaction zone, which was maintained for several centuries. Migrations and return migrations between southern Scandinavia/the Baltic and the Black Sea intensified, from the migration of the Bastardae 239–229 BC from Jutland/northwest Germany (Babes 1988) to the Goths from Sweden/Gotland (for a detailed account see Scukin 1989). It was only during the turbulent period of Roman intervention in Gaul that Germanic warbands and tribes interfered, leading to a series of battles and population movements (Wozniak 1979).

6 Caesar writes about the Druids: 'For they have the right to decide nearly all public and private disputes, and they also pass judgement and decide rewards and penalties in criminal and murder cases, and in disputes regarding legacies and boundaries . . . It is thought that this system of training was invented in Britain, and taken over from here to Gaul, and at the present time diligent students of the matter mostly travel there to study it' (taken from Ross 1986, 115).

7 Some classical sources (Poseidonius and Phylarchus of Naucratis) refer to chiefly public feasting taking place at specific fenced-in places and in halls: 'Louernius, the son of Bityes, a Galatian prince whom the Romans had conquered, wanted to bid for the leadership of his tribe. He used to drive over the plains in his chariot scattering gold and silver to the enormous crowd of people following. He fenced in a space twelve stadia square, set up wine presses in it and brought in vast quantities of food' (Rankin 1987, 65). Another account concerns Ariamnes of Galatia, referred to by Phylarchus (2nd century BC): 'Ariamnes announced that every year he would give a feast for all the Galatians. Throughout all Galatia

he divided out the countryside by measuring the roads, and built, at determined intervals, banqueting halls, each of which was capable of holding four hundred guests. Each had a large cauldron of stew which was kept boiling all the time' (Rankin 1987, 65). The physical remains of *Viereckschanzen* would seem to fit these descriptions quite nicely, as do their combined political-ritual functions.

8 Diodorus Siculus says of the practice of decapitating the enemy: 'They cut off the heads of enemies slain in battle and attach them to the necks of their horses. The blood-stained spoils they hand over to their attendants and carry off as booty, while striking up a paean and singing a song of victory; and they nail these first fruits upon their houses, just as do those who lay low wild animals in certain kinds of hunting. They embalm in cedar oil the heads of the most distinguished enemies, and preserve them carefully in a chest, and display them with pride to strangers, saying that for this head one of their ancestors, or his father, or the man himself, refused the offer of a large sum of money' (after Ross 1986, 51).

8 The emergence of the European world system in the Bronze Age and Early Iron Age: Europe in the 1st and 2nd millennia BC

1 During the past decade our conception of Bronze Age trade in the Mediterranean has changed, some would say drastically, from a traditional 'minimalist' position (Snodgrass 1991) to a recognition of the commercially well-organised nature of long-distance trade expeditions. This development has been based to a large extent on a programme of scientific analyses of the origins of metal, pottery, etc. (Gale 1991b; Jones and Vagnetti 1991; Stos-Gale and MacDonald 1991) in combination with sensational new finds, such as the large sunken cargo of Ulu Burun (Bass 1991). Much of this new evidence is presented in the proceedings of a recent conference on Bronze Age trade in the Mediterranean (Gale 1991a).

2 The interaction zone between the Aegean and the Black Sea area comprised the Pontic region, reflected in horse gear (Oancea 1976) and the appearance of the light two-wheeled chariot with spoked wheels (Piggott 1983, 91ff., fig. 47, better documented in recent Russian literature, Gening, Zdanovich and Gening 1992, figs. 106–108, with too crude a reconstruction) among the warrior elite (Kuznetsov 1992). Influences seem to have been reciprocal, as the metallurgical origin of the silver and gold vessels of the shaft graves was in the Troy area (Stos-Gale 1993), just as rapiers in the Trans-Caucasus area seem to be earlier than in the Aegean (Burger 1992).

3 Recent scientific analyses of pottery have demonstrated local production of Mycenaean pottery in Italy, as well as pottery from both Crete and Cyprus. Also local Italian ware has been found on Crete. As stated by Jones and Vagnetti (1991, 136): 'During the equivalent of LH IIIB and IIIC, analysis confirms a wide range of imported pottery from areas as diverse as West and Central Crete, mainland Greece, Rhodes and Cyprus. These imports are not restricted to fine wares, but also include large storage jars probably used as bulk transport containers . . . supporting the picture of extensive and regular trade linking the eastern and central Mediterranean.'

4 The Ulu Burun cargo of the 14th century BC had on board: 'six tons of copper, a substantial amount of tin, dozens of ingots of cobalt-blue glass, logs of Egyptian ebony, perhaps a ton of terebinth resin, more than half a dozen hippopotamus teeth, part of an elephant tusk, tortoise shells, a jar of orpiment (trisulphide of arsenic), ostrich eggshells, murex opercula, and spices and foodstuffs, including coriander, safflower, figs, grapes, sumac, almonds, a pithos of whole pomegranates, and amphoras of olives' (Bass 1991, 74).

5 Very few attempts have been made to reconstruct the actual organisation of mining and the scale of production since Pittioni's bold attempt for the Mitterberg area (1951; see Eibner 1982 for the technological processes). Pittioni suggested the development of specialised mining communities, working on a year-round basis, consisting of 180 people for one mining operation. Galleries would extend 100 m into the mountain. His figures for the organisation of deep mining probably mainly relate to the Urnfield period, although

production was already extensive from the Early Bronze Age (recent discussion by Shennan 1993). In opposition to the Carpathian/Alpine region, copper sources and production in the Atlantic region seem to have been on a much smaller scale (O'Brien 1990; Montero 1992). This picture has recently been revised for Wales (Dutton, Fasham and Jenkins 1994).

6 In many areas the Early Bronze Age represents the first stable agrarian economy and settlement, e.g. reflected in a continuous appearance of plantago and of cereals in pollen diagrams (Lise-Kleber 1990; Rosch 1990). In northern Europe the Early Bronze Age also represents an intensified and continuous exploitation of the landscape (Berglund 1991).

7 Systematic grave robbing characterises many of the Early Bronze Age cemeteries of central Europe (an exhaustive discussion is found in Neugebauer 1991, 123ff.; Batora 1991), just as many cemeteries came to a stop in west-central Europe before Early Bronze Age A2 (Krause 1988b). It must reflect a period of social change and unrest, which has been linked by some to the hoarding phase of the late Early Bronze Age (Br. A2). It could be linked either to the westward expansion of the Otomani culture during Br. A2 or to the later expansion of the Tumulus Culture during B1. However, it underlines the fact that social conflict and disruption on a larger regional scale were an inherent feature of Bronze Age society.

8 Given this background the suggestion of Ashbee (1989) that the Trundholm horse's head- and neck-decoration (trappings) represent a chamfrein become more probable, in spite of Littauer and Crouwel's critique (1991).

9 At the Singen cemetery in southwestern Germany, dated to Reinecke A1, four imported daggers of Armorico-British type had a high tin content of 5–9 per cent, in contrast to the local daggers. Later daggers show increasing use of tin. With a dating around 2000 BC it demonstrates that the use of tin alloying was directly related to influences from the Armorico-British region, and that this evolved around 2000 BC, before Mycenaean con- tacts, but only shortly before the expansion of the east Mediterranean trade. 'At present we can summarise that tin-metallurgy already existed in southern Germany during the phase Reinecke Early Bronze Age 1 in representative sites such as Singen under specific socio- logical and economic conditions and that the source at this time must have been in the Atlantic area' (Krause 1989, 29; see also Krause 1988a, 242f.).

10 At the hilltop settlement of Velim in Bohemia dating from the Late Tumulus/Early Urnfield period new, highly important information about social and ritual practices, including warfare, are being uncovered, e.g. due to excellent conditions of preservation for bone. In a recent presentation the findings of numerous disarticulated human bones in the filling of ditches, and numerous skeletons in pits, are interpreted as ritual (Hrala, Sedlacek and Vavra 1992, 300ff.). I find this interpretation untenable, reflecting an inherent dislike of the more brutal aspects of human existence, to be hidden under the term ritual. However, the excellent presentation of the excavation allows for an alternative interpreta- tion. The disarticulated bones in the fillings (features 1–5) could be a result of a rebuilding phase, in which former burials were levelled; alternatively they may reflect cannibalism. The latter interpretation is supported by a large ditch with numerous human bones (feature 30). However, the skeletons in pits (thirty-three individuals, male, female and children, have been uncovered in three pits up to now) are unquestionably victims of war. They were unstructured burials, the bodies having been thrown into the pits, one woman still holding her gold spirals in her hand (features 23, 27 and 30). Also a cluster of human skulls appeared in one of the pits. The pit was covered with traditional midden fill with human bones. These skeletons conform in every respect to criteria for war victims, including traces of head hunting, which along with cannibalism is linked to periods of endemic warfare and social stress in the ethnographic present. Traditional burials at the site mark the contrast even more clearly between the two phenomena, although the burials are without grave goods. Everything in the evidence points to a period of unexpected

disruption and warfare, also seen in the poorly constructed palisade, showing little familiarity with defensive constructions. Also here a ritual explanation has been proposed,
instead of a more natural or historical explanation. The extraordinary conditions of
preservation at Velim have revealed a rare glimpse of the social conditions of existence in
the final phase of the Tumulus culture, a disruptive period of social and ritual conflict (the
rise of the Urnfield tradition), where the traditional functions of the central settlement
(specialist production, tribute paying, rituals, etc.) gradually gave way to defensive considerations, until the final destruction and burning down of the settlement in the Early
Urnfield period.

11 As has been demonstrated in several studies, both swords and violin fibulae display local
variation (Kilian 1985; Harding 1992). The local production of violin fibulae, however, was
strongly influenced by contacts with neighbouring regions, e.g. reflected in import pieces.
Thus I am not proposing massive migrations, but a flow of people (warriors, traders and
their families), sometimes followed by smaller migrant groups. When this Aegean/Balkan/
Italian network collapsed some large-scale migrations undoubtedly accompanied it. An
example of this could be northern Italy and its relations with Hungary, which was part of
the regional network just described during Br. D (e.g. Peschiera daggers). According to
Peroni, Mycenaean influences were channelled via northern Italy to Hungary. However,
this is followed by a break in the middle of Ha1 in northern Italy: settlements are
abandoned (*terremare*), and a strong Hungarian influence follows in metalwork (Peroni
1989, 331ff., 544ff.). In fact the later revival of metalwork in Ha B2–3, which is often
referred to as the result of renewed Hungarian influence/migration, could represent a
continuation of this earlier integration (I am grateful to Professor Peroni for having detailed
these relations for me in personal communications).

12 The sequence of Mycenaean pottery at Troy suggests that the Trojan War took place
during LH IIIB2, the latter half of the 13th century. At this time there is a hiatus in the
sequence of imported Mycenaean pottery, LH IIIB2 pottery is absent, not only in Troy,
but at most sites on the west coast of Asia Minor. This can most probably be explained by a
termination of contact due to the hostilities. When Mycenaean pottery appears at Troy
again in LH IIIC, besides imported pottery, there is also local production of Mycenaean
pottery types (Podzuweit 1982, 82). I suggest this represents the Mycenaean takeover after
the defeat of Troy, which included migrants, artisans and traders.

13 In two recent works the Illyrian problem has been archaeologically and historically analysed and discussed (Parzinger 1991; Wilkes 1992). Although works of a high scholarly
standard, and with some critical consciousness, I have to declare my deep scepticism of
employing the term Illyrian outside its specific and rather narrow historical boundaries
(Parzinger 1991, 237ff. and Abb. 14) to cover the later prehistory of the wider Yugoslavian
region (Parzinger 1991, 206 & 237ff; Wilkes 1992, 38f). Parzinger (1991, Abb. 13) identifies
a number of local groups, defined by dress style in burials, dating between the 7th and 5th
centuries BC. They are thought to represent the formation of proto-Illyrian, but, more
importantly, they occur at the time of archaic state formation discussed above, and thus
correspond to the formation of a political territory.

14 Under certain conditions language and ethnicity can be seen to be rather closely linked
with material culture (here taking ethnicity in the general sense; in concrete cases it should
be socially contextualised). Such conditions can be demonstrated to prevail in cases of
settlement expansion and migrations, e.g. the Celtic, Roman, Slav and Viking expansions.
These examples demonstrate a number of recurrent features that may help us to clarify
further the relationship between ethnicity, language and material culture. They can be
summarised in the following preliminary observations, which may serve as propositions for
further research: (1) migrations and political expansion, such as in the case of the Romans
or the Turks, may rapidly establish a new dominant language over large regions, leading to
extinction or marginalisation of former languages (e.g. Celtic and Etruscan); (2) in the

initial or pioneer phase there is often a close correspondence between ethnicity and material culture due to the need to distinguish oneselves from resident populations (ethnic markers); (3) in the consolidation phase, if it occurs, such correspondences may quickly dissolve, being replaced by mutual acculturation. The most significant indication of political dominance of some length is therefore place names, as they demonstrate the ability to impose control and name-giving on a locality or region. If accepted these observations have a number of implications: (1) no a priori ethnic or linguistic continuity can be granted where major changes in material culture have taken place as a result of intruding state or empire formation; (2) consequently only a few regions in Europe may boast long-term ethnic and linguistic continuity. It makes the problem of tracing common proto- or archaic languages on archaeological grounds extremely complex, as recently illuminated by Sherratt and Sherratt (1988) and in an excellent overview of the Iberian evidence (Almagro-Gorbea and Ruiz Zapatero 1992).

15 There remained always throughout history a memory –sometimes preserved in myths, sometimes in philosophy –of democratic rights, enforcing a check upon tyranny and exploitation. State formation represents in that respect a crucial breaking-point by dividing populations into separate and 'natural' groups and classes. But even here the ethos of democracy survives and leads to recurring conflicts, such as those in both Greek and Roman history. One of the insights deriving from this study is the apparent world-historical pulse in the changes between elite culture and popular movements. Such a case is represented by the 5th century BC, characterised by the fall of 'tyranny' from Greece to Central and northern Europe. Was the call for democracy running as a silent whisper throughout Europe, preceding social and economic changes? Or were these events simply structurally linked, forming world-historical patterns of economic expansions and recessions? Both explanations are probably true.

16 During the past few years several archaeological works have appeared applying a world-system perspective, just as terms and concepts have been critically discussed (Patterson 1990 and in press; Peregrine 1992; Sherratt 1994; Eden and Kohl 1993). The originator of the 'dependency model' in Third-World studies, Gunder Frank, has in recent years turned his interests towards the reconstruction of the ancient world system originating in 3000 BC (Frank 1991 and 1993), as originally proposed by Ekholm and Friedman (1980; 1985). In several works he and his colleagues have attempted to delineate world-historical cycles of expansion and recession (Frank 1993; Frank and Gills 1993).

BIBLIOGRAPHY

Aaby, B. 1976 Cyclic climatic variations in climate over the past 5,500 years as reflected in raised bogs. *Nature* 263 (5575).

Adams, R. McC. 1974 Anthropological perspectives on ancient trade. *Current Anthropology.*

Adams, W. Y. 1968 Invasion, diffusion, evolution? *Antiquity*, 42.

Agostini, S., Coubray, S., De Grossi-Mazzorin, J. and D'Ercole, V. 1992. L'habitat et l'occupation du sol à l'Age du Bronze dans le Abruzzies: le cas du site de Celano. In C. Mordant and A. Richard (eds.).

Akurgal, E. 1968. *Urartäische und Altiranische Kunstzentren.* Türk Tarih Kurumu Yayinlarindan VI, Seri no. 9, Ankara.

Alexander, J. 1962 Greek, Italians and the earliest Balkan Iron Age. *Antiquity* 36.

Allen, D. F. 1980 *The Coins of the Ancient Celts.* Edited by Daphne Nash. Edinburgh University Press.

Almagro-Gorbea, M. 1986 Bronze Final y edad del hierro. In *Historia de Espana. Prehistoria.* Madrid.

Almagro-Gorbea, M. 1988a Representaciones de barcos en el arte rupestre de la peninsula Iberica. Aportacion a la navegacion precolonial desde el mediterraneo oriental. *Congreso internacional el estrecho de Gibraltar Ceuta.*

Almagro-Gorbea, M. 1988b Société et commerce méditerranéen dans la péninsule Iberique aux VII–Vᵉ siècles. In *Les Princes Celtes et la Méditerranée.*

Almagro-Gorbea, M. 1989 Arqueologia e historia antigua: el proceso protoorientalizante y el inicio de los contactos de Tartessos con el Levante mediterraneo. *Anejos de Gerion*, II. Edit. Universidad Complutense, Madrid.

Almagro-Gorbea, M. 1991 Los Celtas en la Peninsula Iberica. *Revista de arqueologia: Los Celtas en la Peninsula Iberica.*

Almagro-Gorbea, M. 1992 Los intercambios culturales entre Aragón y el litoral Mediterráneo durante el Bronce Final. *Aragon/Litoral Mediterráneo.* Intercambios culturales durante la Prehistoria. Diputación de Zaragoza.

Almagro-Gorbea, M. in press *Las estelas antropomorfas en la peninsula Ibérica. Tipologia, Dispersion, Cronoloigia y Significado.*

Almagro-Gorbea, M. and Dominingues de la Concha, A. 1988–89 El palacio de Cancho Roano y sus paralelos arquitectonicos y functionales. *Zephyrus* 41–42.

Almagro-Gorbea, M. and Lorrio, A. 1987 La expansion celtica en la peninsula Iberica: una aproximacion cartografica. In *Symposium los celtiberos.* Institucion Fernando el Catolico, Zaragoza.

Almagro-Gorbea, M. and Ruiz Zapatero, G. (eds.) 1992 *Paleoetnologia de la Peninsula Iberica.* Complutum, Numero 2–3, Madrid.

Ambros, C. 1986 Tierreste von der Heidenschanze in Dresden-Coschütz. In D.-W. Buch and B. Gramsch (eds.).

Ambrosiani, B. 1985 Das Mälargebiet und Balticum während der Spätbronzezeit und der älteren Eisenzeit. Acta Universitatis Stockholmiensis, Studia Baltica Stockholmiensis 1, 1985: *Die Verbindungen zwischen Skandinavien und Ostbalticum auf grund der archäologischen Quellenmaterialen.*

Ambrosiani, B. (ed.) 1986 *Die Bronzezeit im Ostseegebiet*. Rapport über das Julita-Symposium 1986. Kungl. Vitterhets Historie och Antikvitets Akademien, Konferenser 22, Stockholm.

Andersen, S. T. 1990 Pollen spectra from the Bronze Age barrow at Egshvile, THy, Denmark. *Journal of Danish Archaeology*, 9.

Andersen, S. T., Aaby, B. and Odgaard, B. V. 1984 Environment and man. Current studies in vegetational history at the geological survey of Denmark. *Journal of Danish Archaeology* 2.

Anderson, P. 1974 *Passages from Antiquity to Feudalism*. London: Humanities Press.

Anthony, D. 1990 Migration in archaeology: the baby and the bathwater. *American Anthropologist*, 92(4).

Anthony, D. and Brown, D. R. 1991 The origin of horseback riding. *Antiquity* 65.

Anthony, D. W. 1986 The 'Kurgan' culture, Indo-European origins and the domestication of the horse: a reconsideration. *Current Anthropology* 27(2).

Antiqua 15. 1986 *Chronologie*. Archäologische Daten der Schweiz. Veröff. der Schweiz. Ges. f. Ur- und Frügesch. Basel.

Archäologisches Korrespondenzblatt 11. 1981 *Bronzezeitlichen Feuchtbodensiedlungen im circumalpinen Raum*.

Arnold, B. 1988 Slavery in Late Prehistoric Europe: recovering the evidence for social structure in Iron Age society. In O. B. Gibson and M. N. Geselowitz (eds.), *Tribe and Polity in Late Prehistoric Europe. Demography, production, and exchange in the evolution of complex social systems*. Plenum Press.

Arnold, B. 1992 Villages du Bronze Final sur les rives du lac de Neuchâtel. In C. Mordant and A. Richard (eds.).

Arribas, A. 1964 *The Iberians*. London: Thames and Hudson.

Arteaga, O. 1987 Perspectivas espacio-temporales de la colonizacion fenicia occidental. Ensayo de approximacion. In A. Ruiz and M. Molinos (eds.), *Iberos*. Actas de las I Jornadas sobre el Mundo Iberic/Jaen, 1985. Ayuntamiento de Jaen/Junta de Andalucia.

Ashbee, P. 1989 The Trundholm horse's trappings: a chamfrein? *Antiquity* 63.

Ashing, P. and Rasmussen, M. 1989 Mange slags grænser. Et eksempel på regional variaton i sydvestdansk ældre bronzealder. In J. Poulsen (ed.) *Regionale forhold i Nordisk Bronzealder*. Århus.

Aubet Semmler, M. E. 1982 Zur Problematik des orientalisierenden Horizontes auf der Iberischen Halbinsel. In H. G. Hiemeyer (ed.)

Aubet, M. E. 1993 *The Phoenicians and the West. Politics, Colonies and Trade*. Cambridge University Press.

Audouze, F. and Büchsenschütz, O. 1989 *Villes, villages et campagne de l'Europe celtique*. Paris: Hachette.

Audouze, F. and Büchsenschütz, O. 1992 *Towns, Villages and Countryside of Celtic Europe*. Batsford.

Babes, B. 1988 Die Frühgermanen in östlichen Dakien in den letzten Jahrhunderten v.u.Z. Archäologischer und historische Belege. In F. Horst and F. Schlette (eds.) *Frühe Völker in Mitteleuropa*. Berlin: Akademie Verlag.

Babic, S. 1990 Graeco-barbarian contacts in the Early Iron Age in the Central Balkans. *Balcanica* 21. Belgrade.

Bader, T. 1978 *Epoca bronzului in nord-vestul Transilvaniei. Cultura pretracica si tracica. (Die Bronzezeit in Nordwestsiebenbügen)*. Bucuresti.

Bader, T. 1982a Die Entstehung der Bronzezeitlichen Kulturen in Nordwestrumänien. *Symposia Thracia*.

Bader, T. 1982b Die befestigten bronzezeitlichen Siedlungen in Nordwestrumänien. In V. Furmanek and F. Horst (eds.).

Bader, T. 1986 Neu Beiträge zu den mykenischen Schwertern vom Typ A aus Rumänien. *Zeitschrift für Archäologie* 20.

Bader, T. 1990 Bemerkungen über die ägäischen Einflüsse auf die alt- und mittelbronzezeitliche Entwicklung im Donau-Karpatenraum. In *Orientalische-ägäische Einflüsse*.

Bahn, B. W. 1990 Siedlungsgeographische Bemerkungen zur Bronzezeit im Mittelgebirgsbereich. In V. Furmanek and F. Horst (eds.).

Bailey, A. and Llobera, J. R. (eds.) 1981 *The Asiatic Mode of Production*. London: Routledge and Kegan.

Bandi, G. 1982 Spätbronzezeitliche befestigte Höhensiedlungen in Westungarn. In V. Furmanek and F. Horst (eds.).

Bandi, G. and Csermenyi, V. (eds.) 1983 *Nord-Süd-Beziehungen*. Historische und kulturelle Zusammenhänge und Handelsbezie-hungen die europäischen Bernsteinstrassen entlang vom I. Jahrtausend v.u.Z. bis zum Ende der römischen Kaiserzeit. Int. Koll. 1982 Bozsok-Szombathely. *Savaria* 16, Bull. der Museen des Komitats Vas.

Barker, G. 1988 Archaeology and the Etruscan countryside. *Antiquity* (237).

Barnett, R. D. 1967 Phrygia and the peoples of Anatolia in the Iron Age. *The Ancient Cambridge History*, Vol. II, Chapter xxx.

Barnett, R. D. 1982 Urartu. *The Ancient Cambridge History*, Vol. III, Part 1.

Barrett, J. and Bradley, R. (eds.) 1980 *The British Later Bronze Age*. BAR British Series 83 (ii). Oxford.

Barrett, J., Bradley, R. and Green, M. 1991 *Landscape, Monuments and Society. The Prehistory of Cranborne Chase*. Cambridge University Press.

Barrett, J. C., Fitzpatrick, A. P. and MacInnes, L. (eds.) 1989 *Barbarians and Romans in North-West Europe from the later Republic to late Antiquity*. BAR Int. Ser. 471, Oxford.

Barrett, J. and Needham, S. P. 1988 Production, circulation and exchange: problems in the interpretation of Bronze Age metalwork. In J. Barrett and I. A. Kinnes (eds.), *The Archaeology of Context in the Neolithic and Bronze Age: Recent Trends*. University of Sheffield.

Barth, F. 1956 Ecological relations of ethnic groups in Swat, North Pakistan. *American Anthropologist* 58.

Barth, F. (ed.) 1967a *Ethnic Groups and Boundaries. The Social Organisation of Culture Difference*. Oslo, Universitetsforlaget.

Barth, F. 1967b Introduction. In F. Barth (ed.).

Barth, F. 1967c Pathan identity and its maintenance. In F. Barth (ed.).

Bartoloni, G. 1989 *La Cultura Villanoviana. All'inizio della storia etrusca*. NIS: La Nuova Italia Scientifica, Roma.

Bartonin, A. 1974 The place of the Dorians in the late Helladic world. In R. A. Crossland and A. Birchall (eds.).

Bass, G. F. 1991 Evidence of trade from Bronze Age shipwrecks. In N. H. Gale (ed.).

Batora, J. 1981 Die Anfänge der Bronzezeit in der Ostslovakei. *Slovenska Archaeologia* 99(1).

Batora, J. 1991 The reflection of economy and social structure in the cemeteries of the Chlopice-Veselé and Nitra cultures. *Slovenska Archaeologia* 39, 1–2.

Baudou, E. 1960 *Die regionale und chronologische Einteilung der jüngeren Bronzezeit im Nordischen Kreis*. Acta Universitatis Stockholmiensis. Studies in North European Archaeology 1. Almquist & Wiksell, Stockholm.

Bech, C. W. 1983 Der Bernsteinhandel: Naturwissenschaftliche Gesichtspunkte. In G. Bandi and V. Csermenyi (eds.).

Bech, C. W. 1985 The role of the scientist: the amber trade, the chemical analysis of amber, and the determination of Baltic provenience. *Journal of Baltic Studies*, 16(3), special issue: Studies in Baltic Amber.

Becker, B. *et al.* 1985 *Dendrochronologie in der Ur- und Frühgeschichte*. Die absolute Datierung von Pfahlbausiedlungen nördlich der Alpen im Jahrringkalender Mitteleuropas. *Antiqua* 11. Veröff. der Schweiz. Ges. f. Ur- u- Frühgesch. Basel.

Becker, B., Jäger, K.-D., Kaufman, D. and Litt, T. 1989 Dendrochronologische Datierungen von Eichenhölzern aus den frühbronzezeitlichen Hügelgräbern bei Helmsdorf und Leubingen (Aunjetitzer Kultur) und an bronzezeitlichen Flusseichen bei Merseburg. *Jahresschrift mitteldeutsche Vorgesch.* 72.

Becker, B., Krause, R. and Kromer, B. 1989 Zur absoluten Chronologie der Frühen Bronzezeit. *Germania* 67.

Becker, C. J. 1971 Zur Frage der Eisenzeitlichen Moorgefässe in Dänemark. In H. Jahnkuhn (ed.) *Vorgeschichtliche Heiligtümer und Opferplätze in Mittel- und Nordeuropa.* Bericht über ein Symposium in Rheinhausen bei Göttingen vom 14. bis 16 Okt. 1968. Göttingen.

Becker, C. J. *et al.* 1989 Ein ungewöhnliches 'Depot' der jüngeren Bronzezeit von Spjald, Westjütland (with several contributions). *Acta Arch.* 60.

Beltz, R. and Wagner, E. 1899 *Vorgeschichte Mecklenburgs.* Berlin.

Benac, A. and Covic, B. 1957 *Glacinac II.* Katalog der Vorgeschichtlichen Sammlung des Landesmuseum in Sarajevo, Heft. 2.

Benac, A., Covic, B. and Tasic, N. (eds.) 1991 *Tribus paleobalkaniques entre la mer Adriatique et la mer noire de l'énéolothique jusqu'à l'époque Hellénistique.* I symposium Illyro-Thrace. Sarajevo-Beograd.

Bender, B. 1985 Prehistoric developments in the American midcontinent and in Brittany, northwest France. In T. D. Price and J. Brown (eds.) *Prehistoric Hunter-Gatherers.* New York: Academic Press.

Benes, J. 1987 Das Knovízer Gehöft in Liptice. In E. Plesl and J. Hrala (eds.).

Benkovsky-Pivovarova, Z. and Enzersdorf, M. 1989 Zu Entwicklungsprocessen der mittleren Bronzezeit in Nordostungarn und dem anliegenden Teil der Slowakei. *Archaeologia Austriaca* 73.

Bentley, G. Carter. 1981 Migration, ethnic identity, and state building in the Philippines. The Sulu case. In C. F. Keyes (ed.), *Ethnic Change.* University of Washington Press.

Benveniste, E. 1973 *Indo-European Language and Society.* London, Faber and Faber.

Berg, B. 1979 Dareios krig mot skyterna. Valda delar ur Herodots Historia Bok IV. In *Skyterna.* Statens Historiska Museum, Stockholm.

Berglund, B. 1969 Vegetation and human influence in south Scandinavia during prehistoric time. *Oikos* supplementum 12.

Berglund, B. (ed.) 1991 *The Cultural Landscape during 6000 Years in Southern Sweden.* Ecological Bulletins 41. Lund.

Berglund, J. 1982 Kirkebjerget – a Late Bronze Age settlement at Voldtofte, south-west Funen. *Journal of Danish Arch.* 1.

Bernabo-Brea, M. and Cremaschi, M. 1992 Les terramares dans la plaine du Pô. In C. Mordant and A. Richards (eds.).

Bernal, M. 1988 Black Athena denied: the tyranny of Germany over Greece and the rejection of the Afroasiatic roots of Europe 1780–1980. *Comparative Criticism* 8.

Bertilsson, U. 1987 *The Rock Carvings of Northern Bohuslän. Spatial Structures and Social Symbols.* Stockholm Studies in Archaeology.

Bertilsson, U. and Larsson, T. 1985 Economy and ideology in the Swedish Bronze Age. *Archaeological Review from Cambridge* 4(2).

Betzler, P. 1974 *Die Fibeln in Süddeutschland, Österreich under der Schweiz.* Prähistorische Bronzefunde 14(3).

Biel, J. 1985 *Der Keltenfürst von Hochdorf.* Stuttgart: Theiss Verlag.

Biel, J. 1987 Der Wagen aus dem Fürstengrabhügel von Hochdorf. In *Vierrädige Wagen der hallstattzeit. Untersuchungen zu Geschichte und Technik.* Römisch-Germanisches Zentralmuseum. Monographien Band 12. Mainz.

Biel, J. 1988a Die Hallstattkultur in Württemberg. *Archäologie in Württemberg.*

Biel, J. 1988b Influences méditerranéennes sur le site princier du Hohenasperg, près de Stuttgart. In *Les Princes Celtes el la Méditerranée.*

Bietti Sestieri, A. M. 1981 Economy and society in Italy between the Late Bronze Age and the

Early Iron Age. In G. Barker and R. Hodges (eds.), *Archaeology and Italian Society. Prehistoric, Roman and Medieval Studies*. Papers in Italian Archaeology II. BAR International Series 102. Oxford.

Bietti Sestieri, A. M. 1985 The Iron Age cemetery of Osteria Dell'Osa, Rome: evidence of social change in Lazio in the 8th century B. C. In C. Malone and S. Stoddart (eds.), *Papers in Italian Archaeology* IV. The Cambridge Conference. Part III: Patterns in Protohistory. BAR International Series 245.

Bietti Sestieri, A. M. 1988 The 'Mycenaean connection' and its impact on the central Mediterranean societies. *Dialoghi di Archeologia*, terza serie, anno 6, numero 1.

Bietti Sestieri, A. M. 1993 *The Iron Age Community of Osteria del' Osa. A study of socio-political development in central Tyrrhenian Italy*. Cambridge University Press.

Bietti Sestieri, A. M. and Santis, A. DE. 1985 Indicatori archeologici di cambiamento nella struttura delle comunita' laziali nell' VIII sec. a. C. *Dialoghi di Archeologia* 1.

Billamboz, A. 1997 Waldentwicklung unter Klima- und Menscheneinfluss in der Bronzezeit. In *Goldene Jahrhunderte. Die Bronzezeit in Südwestdeutschland*. Almanach 2, Landesmuseum Baden-Württemberg. Konrad Theiss, Stuttgart.

Billamboz, A., Keefer, E., Köninger, J. and Torke, W. 1989 La transition Bronze ancein-moyen dans le Sud-Ouest de l'Allemagne à l'exemple de deux stations de l'habitat palustre (Station Forschner, Federsee) et littoral (Bodman-Schachen I, Bodnsee). In *Dynamique du bronze moyen en Europe occidentale*.

Binford, L. 1968 Some comments on historical vs. processual archaeology. *Southwestern Journal of Anthr.* 24.

Binford, L. 1986 Data, relativism and archaeological science. *Man* (N.S.) 22.

Bintliff, J. 1977 The history of archaeo-geographic studies of prehistoric Greece, and recent fieldwork. In J. Bintliff (ed.), *Mycenaean Geography*. Proceedings of the Cambridge Coll., Sept. 1976. Cambridge.

Bintliff, J. 1982 Settlement patterns, land tenure and social structure: a diachronic model. In C. Renfrew and S. Shennan (eds.), *Ranking, Resource and Exchange. Aspects of the Archaeology of Early European Society*. Cambridge University Press.

Bintliff, J. 1984a The Neolithic in Europe and social evolution. In J. Bintliff (ed.), 1984c.

Bintliff, J. 1984b Iron Age Europe in the context of social evolution from the Bronze Age through to historic times. In J. Bintliff (ed.), 1984c.

Bintliff, J. (ed.) 1984c *European Social Evolution. Archaeological Perspectives*. University of Bradford.

Bintliff, J. 1989 Cemetery populations, carrying capacity and the individual in history. In C. Roberts, F. Lee and J. Bintliff (eds.), *Burial Archaeology, Current Research, Methods and Developments*. BAR British Series 211. Oxford.

Bittel, K. 1983 Die archäologische Situation in Kleinasien von 1200 v. Chr. und während der nachfolgender vier Jahrhunderte. In S. Deger-Jalkotzy (ed.).

Bittel, K., Kimmig, W. and Schiek, S. (eds.) 1981 *Die Kelten in Baden-Württemberg*. Stuttgart: Theiss.

Bittel, K., Schiek, S. and Müller, D. 1990 *Die keltischen Viereckschanzen*. Atlas Arch. Geländemäler in Baden-Württemberg, Band 1,1. Stuttgart: Konrad Theiss Verlag.

Bloch, M. 1977 The disconnection between power and rank as a process: an outline of the development of kingdoms in central Madagascar. In J. Friedman and M. Rowlands (eds.), *The Evolution of Social Systems*. Duckworth, London.

Boardman, J. (ed.) 1984a *The Cambridge Ancient History*. Plates to volume III, *The Middle East, the Greek World and the Balkans to the Sixth Century B.C.* New editions, Cambridge, New York, New Rochelle, Melbourne, Sydney: Cambridge University Press.

Boardman, J. 1984b The Greek World. In J. Boardman (ed.), *The Cambridge Ancient History*.

Bocquet, A., Marguet, A., Orcel, C. and Orcel, A. 1987 Datations absolues sur les stations littorales et l'âge du bronze final dans les Alpes du Nord. In P. Brun and C. Mordant (eds.): *Le groupe Rhin-Suisse-France orientale et la notion de civilisation des Champs d'Urnes*. Mémoires du Musée de Préhistoire d'Ile-de France no. 1, Nemours.

Bodilsen, I. 1987 Enkeltfund – votivfund i dansk bronzealder (summary: Single finds – votive finds in the Danish Bronze Age). *Kuml*.

Bökönyi, S. 1983 Trade of domestic animals between Pannonia and Italy. *Savaria* 16, Nord-Süd Beziehungen. Internationales Kolloquium 1982, Bozsok-Szombathely.

Bökönyi, S. 1986 Horses and sheep in east Europe in the Copper and Bronze Ages. In S. Skomal and E. Polome (eds.), *Proto-Indo-Europeans: The archaeology of a linguistic problem* (Studies in honour of Maria Gimbutas). Washington D.C.

Bonfante, L. (ed.) 1986 *Etruscan Life and Afterlife. A Handbook to Etruscan Studies*. Wayne State University Press. Detroit.

Bönisch, E. 1988 Hallstättische Bestattungssitten in der Lausitzer Kultur. In Z. Bukowski (ed.).

Bonte, Pierre. 1977 Non-stratified social formations among pastoral nomads. In J. Friedman and M. J. Rowlands (eds.), *The Evolution of Social Systems*. London: Duckworth.

Bonte, Pierre. 1979 Pastoral production, territorial organization and kinship in segmentary lineage societies. In P. C. Burnham and R. F. Ellen (eds.), *Social and Ecological Systems*. A.S.A. Monographs 18. New York: Academic Press.

Borello, M. A., Brachner, J. C., Chaix, L. and Hadorn, P. 1986 *Cortaillod-Est, un village du Bronze final 4*. Archéologie Neuchateloise 4, Saint-Blaise.

Bouloumie, B. 1988 Le symposion gréco-étrusque et l'aristocratie celtique. In *Les Princes Celtes et la Méditerranée*.

Bouloumie, B. 1990 Sur la question d'une éventuelle présence étrusque au bord de la Baltique. In T. Malinowski (ed.).

Bouzek, J. 1966 The Aegean and Central Europe: an introduction to the study of cultural interrelations, 1600–1300 B.C. *Pamatky Archeologickè*.

Bouzek, J. 1973 *Graeco-Macedonian Bronzes*. Prague, Charles University.

Bouzek, J. 1974 Macedonian bronzes. Their origins and relation to other cultural groups of the Early Iron Age. *Pamatky Archeologickè*.

Bouzek, J. 1978 Östlicher Mittelmeerraum und Mitteleuropa. Die bronzezeitlichen Beziehungen auf Grund der archäologischen Quellen. In W. Coblenz and F. Horst (eds.), 1978.

Bouzek, J. 1982 Climatic changes and central European prehistory. In A. Harding (ed.), *Climatic Change in Later Prehistory*. Edinburgh University Press.

Bouzek, J. 1983 Caucasus and Europe and the Cimmerian problem. *Sbornik Národniho Muzea v Praze*, Series A, 37(4).

Bouzek, J. 1985a *The Aegean, Anatolia and Europe: Cultural Interrelations in the Second Millennium B.C* Studies in Mediterranean Archaeology, vol. xxix, Göteborg: Paul Åströms Förlag and Prague: Academia, Publishing House of the Czechoslovak Academy of Sciences.

Bouzek, J. 1985b Relation between barbarian Europe and the Aegean civilizations. *Advances in World Archaeology*, Vol. iv. Academic Press.

Bouzek, J. 1988 Invasions and migrations in the Bronze Age Aegean: how to decipher the archaeological evidence. Paper presented at conference on *The Prehistory of the Aegean*, Athens, 1988.

Bouzek, J. 1989 The eastern Mediterranean and central Europe: the beginning of the Iron Age. In M. L. Sørensen and R. Thomas (eds.).

Bouzek, J. 1990 *Studies of Greek Pottery in the Black Sea Area*. Charles University, Prague.

Bouzek, J. 1993 Climatic changes: new archaeological evidence from the Bohemian Karst and other areas. *Antiquity* 67.

Bouzek, J., Koutecky, D. and Neustupny, E. 1966 *The Knoviz Settlement of North-West Bohemia*. Museum Nationale Pragae, Fontes Arcaeologici Pragenses, Volumen 10, Pragae.

Bowden, M. J. *et al.* 1981 The effect of climate fluctuations on human populations: two hypotheses. In T. M. L. Wigley *et al.* (eds.).

Bradley, R. 1978 *The Prehistoric Settlement of Britain*. London: Routledge and Kegan.

Bradley, R. 1984 *The Social Foundations of Prehistoric Britain. Themes and Variations in the Archaeology of Power*. London: Longman Archaeology Series, London–New York.

Bradley, R. 1988 Hoarding, recycling and the consumption of prehistoric metalwork: technological change in western Europe. *World Archaeology* 20(2).

Bradley, R. 1990 *The passage of arms. An archaeological analysis of prehistoric hoards and votive deposits*. Cambridge University Press.

Braudel, F. 1972 *The Mediterranean in the Age of Philip II*. London, Collins.

Braun, D. P. 1986 Midwestern Hopewellian exchange and supralocal interaction. In C. Renfrew and J. F. Cherry (eds.), *Peer Polity and Socio-political Change*. Cambridge University Press.

Braun, D. P. and Plog, S. 1982 Evolution of 'tribal' social networks: theory and prehistoric North American evidence. *American Antiquity* 47(3).

Breddin, R. 1986 Aussagen zur gesellschaftlichen Struktur anhand jungbronzezeitlicher Gräberfelduntersuchungen im Gebiet zwischen Elbe-Saale und Oder-Neiße. In *Veröffentlichungen des Museums für Ur- und Frühgeschichte Postdam* 20.

Bren, J. 1976 Earliest settlement with urban character in central Europe. In B. Cunliffe and T. Rowley (eds.), *Oppida in Barbarian Europe*. BAR Int. Ser. 2. Oxford.

Briard, J. 1965 *Les dépôts bretons et l'âge du Bronze Atlantique*. Rennes.

Briard, J. 1984 *Les tumulus d'armorique. L'age du bronze en France* 3. Paris: Picard.

Briard, J. 1988 La métallurgie du groupe Saint-Brieuc-des-Iffs. In P. Brun and C. Mordant (eds.), *Le groupe Rhin-Suisse-France orientale et la notion de civilisation des Champs d'Urnes*. Mémoires du Musée de Préhistoire d'Ile-de France no. 1 Nemours.

Briard, J. 1990 Les influences d'Egée et du Proche-Orient dans le Chalcolithique et l'Age du Bronze de la Bretagne. In *Orientalisch-ägäische Einflüsse*.

Broholm, H. C. 1946 *Danmarks Bronzealder*. Tredie Bind. Samlede Fund fra den yngre Bronzealder. Nyt Nordisk Forlag, København.

Brombacher, C. and Dick, M. (Jacocomet, S.) 1987 Die Untersuchung der botanischen Makroreste. In *Zürich 'Mozartstrasse'. Neolitische und bronzezeitliche Ufersiedlunge*. Band 1. Zürcher Denkmalpflege, Monographien 4.

Brown, N. 1988 A Late Bronze Age enclosure at Lofts Farm, Essex. *Proceedings of the Prehistoric Society* 54.

Brumfield, E. and Earle, T. (ed.) 1987 *Specialization, Exchange, and Complex Societies*. New Directions in Archaeology. Cambridge University Press.

Brun, P. 1981 L'habitat à l'Age du Bronze dans la moitié nord de la France. *Bulletin de la Société archéologique champenoise*.

Brun, P. 1984 Modèles diffusionnistes et systèmes chronologiques. In *Colloque transition Bronze final–Halstatt ancien*. 109 Congrès national des Sociétés savantes, Dijon, Archéologie t. II, Paris.

Brun, P. 1987 *Princes et princesses de la Celtique. Le premier Age du Fer (850–450 av J.-C.)*. Paris: Editions Errance.

Brun, P. 1988a L'entité 'Rhin-Suisse-France orientale': nature et evolution. In P. Brun and C. Mordant (eds.), *Le groupe Rhin-Suisse-France orientale et la notion de civilisation des Champs d'Urnes*. Mémoires du Musée de Préhistoire d'Ile-de France no. 1, Nemours.

Brun, P. 1988b Les 'Résidences princières' comme centres territoriaux: éléments de vérification. In *Les princes Celtes et la Méditerranée*.

Brun, P. 1991 Le Bronze Atlantique et ses subdivisions culturelles: essai de définition. In C. Chevilot and A. Coffyn (eds.).

Brun, P. 1993 East–West relations in the Paris Basin during the Late Bronze Age. In C. Scarre and F. Healy (eds.), *Trade and Exchange in Prehistoric Europe*. Oxbow Monographs 33, Oxford.

Brun, P. and Mordant, C. (eds.) 1988 *Le groupe Rhin-Suisse-France orientale et la notion de civilisation des Champs d'Urnes*. Mémoires du Musée de Préhistoire d'Ile-de-France No. 1, Nemours.

Bruneaux, J.-L. 1986 *Les Gaulois. Sanctuaires et rites*. Collection des hesperides. Editions Errance.

Bruneaux, J.-L. 1988 *The Celtic Gauls: Gods, Rites and Sanctuaries*. Seaby, London.

Bruneaux, J.-L. (ed.) 1991 *Les sanctuaires celtiques et le monde méditerranéen*. Actes du colloque de St.-Riquier (8 au 11 novembre 1990). Archéologie aujourd'hui. Dossiers de protohistoire No. 3. Editions Errance.

Brunn, W. A. von. 1958 Der Schatz vom Frankleben und die mitteldeutschen Sichelfunde. *Prähistorische Zeitschrift* 36.

Brunn, W. A. von. 1959 *Bronzezeitliche Hortfunde, Teil 1. Die Hortfunde der frühen Bronzezeit. Aus Sachsen-Anhalt, Sachsen und Thüringen*. Akademie Verlag, Berlin.

Brunn, W. A. von. 1960 Zur Nordwestgrenze der Lausitzerkultur. *Prähistorische Zeitschrift* 38.

Brunn, W. A. von. 1968 *Mitteldeutsche Hortfunde*. Römisch-Germanische Forschungen 29. Berlin: De Gruyter.

Brunn, W. A. von. 1980 Eine Deutung Spätbronzezeitlicher Hortfunde zwischen Elbe und Weichsel. *Bericht der Römisch-Germanischen Kommission*. 61.

Buch, D.-W. 1979 *Die Billendorfer Gruppe*. Veröff. des Museums für Ur- und Frühgeschichte Potsdam, Band 13. Berlin.

Buch, D.-W. 1982a Kulturelle Beziehungen der Billendorfer Gruppe zur Ostalpinen Hallstatt-Kultur und zum südöstlichen Raum. In M. Gedl (ed.) *Südzone der Lausitzer Kultur und die Verbindungen dieser Kultur mit dem Süden*. Krakow-Przemysl.

Buch, D.-W. 1982b Befestigte Siedlungen der Lausitzer Kultur im Norden der DDR. In V. Furmanek and F. Horst (eds.).

Buch, D.-W. 1986a Hallstattzeitliche Kammergräber der Lausitzer kultur und ihre sozialökonomische Hintergrund. In E. Jerem (ed.).

Buch, D.-W. 1986b Siedlungswesen und sozialökonomische Verhältniss bei den Stämmen der Lausitzer Gruppe. In D.-W. R. Buch and B. Gramsch (eds.).

Buch, D.-W. 1989 The transition from Bronze Age to Iron Age among the tribes of the western Lusatian culture. In M. L. S. Sørensen and R. Thomas (eds.).

Buch, D.-W. and Gramsch, B. (eds.) 1986 *Siedlung, Wirtschaft und Gesellschaft während der jüngeren Bronze- und Hallstattzeit in Mitteleuropa*. Internationales Symposium Potsdam 25 bis 29 April 1983 Bericht. Veröffl. des Museums für Ur- und Frühgeschichte Potsdam, Berlin.

Buchholz, H.-G. 1980 Kälbersymbolik. *Acta Praehistorica et Archaeologica* 11–12.

Buchholz, H.-G. 1983 Doppelaxte und die Frage der Balkanbezie-hungen des Ägäischen Kulturkreises. In A. Poulter (ed.), *Ancient Bulgaria*. Papers presented to the Int. Symposium on the Ancient History and Arch. of Bulgaria, Univ. of Nottingham, 1981.

Buchholz, H.-G. 1987 Spätbronzezeitliche Beziehungen der Ägäis zum Westen. In H. G. Buchholz (ed.), *Ägäische Bronzezeit*. Darmstadt: Wiss. Buchgesellschaft.

Buchner, G. 1979 Early orientalizing: aspects of the Euboean connection. In D. Ridgway and F. R. Ridgway (eds.), *Italy before the Romans*. Academic Press. New York, London.

Büchsenschütz, O. 1984 *Structures d'habitat et fortifications de l'âge du fer en France septentrionale*. Mémoires de la Société Préhistorique Française. Tome 18. Paris.

Büchsenschütz, O. 1988a Neu Forschungen zur Siedlungsarchäologie der Eisenzeit in Frankreich. *Zeitschrift für Archäologie* 23.

Büchsenschütz, O. 1988b Les habitats hallstattiens et la Méditerranéens. In *Les Princes Celtes et la Méditeranée*.

Büchsenschütz, O. 1991 Viereckschanzen et sanctuaires de l'Europe Celtique. In J.-L. Brunaux (ed.).

Büchsenschütz, O. and Olivier, L. (eds.) 1989 *Les Viereckschanzen et les enceintes quadrilatérales en Europe celtique*. Actes du 9ème colloque de l'A.F.E.A.F., Châteaudun 1985. Paris, Errance.

Buckley, V. (ed.) 1990 *Burnt Offerings. International Contributions to Burnt Mound Archaeology*. Wordwell Ltd, Academic Publications, Dublin.

Bukowski, Z. 1974 Characteristik der sogenannten skythischen Funde aus Polen. *Zeitschrift für Archaeologie* 8.

Bukowski, Z. 1977a Zum Charakter der sogenannten Vorskythischen Einflüsse im Gebiet der Lausitzer Kultur. In *Festschrift Marburg* 1977.

Bukowski, Z. 1977b *The Scythian Influence in the Area of Lusatian Culture*. Polish Academy of Sciences. Ossolineum.

Bukowski, Z. 1981 Die westliche Ausdehnung der sog. skythischen Einwirkungen in Mitteleuropa und ihr Charakter. In C. Eibner and A. Eibner (eds.).

Bukowski, Z. 1982 Der Charakter der sogenannten skythischen Einflusses in Südpolen. (Zusammenfassung). In M. Gedl (ed.), *Südzone der Lausitzer Kultur und die Verbindungen dieser Kultur mit dem Süden*. Krakow-Przemysl.

Bukowski, Z. 1983 Neue Ergebnisse zur Problematik der Ältersten Eisenbearbeitung und gewinnung im Bereich der Lausitzer Kultur. *Offa* 40.

Bukowski, Z. 1986a Der Beginn der Eisenverwendung bei den Stämmen der Lausitzer Kultur. In D.-W. Buch and B. Gramsch (eds.), *Siedlung, Wirtschaft und Gesellschaft während der jüngeren Bronze-und Hallstattzeit in Mitteleuropa*. v Internationales Symposium Potsdam 25 bis 29 April 1983 Bericht. Veröffl. des Museums für Ur- und Frühgeschichte Potsdam, Berlin.

Bukowski, Z. 1986b Bemerkungen zur Problematik des Frühen Eisens in Mittel- und Nordeuropa. Inga Serning in Memoriam. In B. Ambrosiani (ed.).

Bukowski, Z. (ed.) 1988 *Forschungen zur Problematik der Lausitzer Kultur*. Polska Akademia Nauk, Wroclaw, Warszawa, Krakow, Gdansk, Lodz.

Bukowski, Z. 1991 Zum Stand der demographischen und siedlungsgeschichtlichen Forschung zur Lausitzer Kultur im Stromgebiet von Oder und Weichsel. *Acta Praehistorica et Archaeologica* 22.

Bunja, J. 1982 Spiegelung der sozialstrucktur auf Latènezeitlichen Gräberfeldern im Karpartenbecken. *Pamatky Archeologické* 73.

Burger, G. 1992 Eine neue Beurteilung der Transkaukasischen (TK) Rapiere und ihre Rolle im Zirkumpontischen Gebiet. *Symposia Thracologica* 9. Bibliotheca Thracologica 11. Bucuresti.

Burgess, C. 1968 The later Bronze Age in the British Isles and north-western France. *The Archaeological Journal* 125.

Burgess, C. 1979 A find from Boyton, Suffolk, and the end of the Bronze Age in Britain and Ireland. In C. Burgess and D. Coombs (eds.), *Bronze Age Hoards. Some Finds Old and New*. BAR British Series 67. Oxford.

Burgess, C. 1988 Britain at the time of the Rhine-Swiss group. In P. Brun and C. Mordant (eds.), *Le groupe Rhin-Suisse-France orientale et la notion de civilisation des Champs d'Urnes*. Mémoires du Musée de Préhistoire d'Ile-de France No. 1. Nemours.

Burgess, C. 1991 The East and the West. Mediterranean Influence in the Atlantic World in the Later Bronze Age, c. 1500–700 BC. In C. Chevillot and A. Coffyn (eds.).

Burgess, C. and Coombs, D. (eds.) 1979 *Bronze Age Hoards. Some Finds Old and New*. BAR British Series 67. Oxford.

Burgess, C., Coombs, D. and Davies, D. G. 1972 The Broadward Complex and barbed spearheads. In C. Burgess and F. Lynch (eds.), *Prehistoric Man in Wales and the West – Essays in Honour of Lilly F. Chitty*. Adams and Dart, Bath.

Burnham, B. C. and Kingsbury, J. (eds.) 1979 *Space, Hierarchy and Society*. BAR Int. Ser. 59. Oxford.

Burnham, P. 1979 Spatial mobility and political centralization in pastoral societies. In *Pastoral production and society*.

Butler, J. J. 1986 Drouwen: end of a 'Nordic' rainbow? *Palaeohistoria* 28.

Calligas, P. G. 1988 Hero-cult in Early Iron Age Greece. In R. Hägg, N. Marnatos and G. C. Nordquist (eds.), *Early Greek Cult Practice*. Stockholm.

Canciani, F. 1970 *Bronze orientale e orientalizzantia Creta nell VIII e VII sec. A. C.* Rome.

Carlsson, D. 1977 Den folkvandringstida ödeläggelsen på Gotland. *Gotlandsk Arkiv*.

Carlsson, D. 1984 Change and continuity in the Iron Age settlement of Gotland. In K. Kristiansen (ed.), *Settlement and Economy in Later Scandinavian Prehistory*. BAR Int. Series 211, Oxford.

Carneiro, R. L. 1970 A theory of the origin of the state. *Science* 169.

Carpenter, T. H. 1991 *Art and Myth in Ancient Greece*. Thames and Hudson, London.

Cartledge, P. 1983 'Trade and politics' revisited: archaic Greece. In P. Garnsey, K. Hopkins and C. R. Whittaker (eds.).

Ceci, F. and Cifarelli, F. M. 1992 Aspects de l'occupation du sol dans le sud de l'Etrurie au IXe siècle avant Jésus-Christ. In C. Mordant and A. Richards (eds.).

Chaix, L. 1986 La Faune. In A. M. Borello *et al.*

Chaix, L. 1990 La Faune de Vex-le-Chateau, Valais Suisse, du Neol. Moyen au Bronze final. In M. David-El Biah.

Champion, S. 1985 Production and exchange in Early Iron Age central Europe. In T. Champion and J. V. S. Megaw (eds.).

Champion, T. 1982 Fortification, ranking and subsistence. In C. Renfrew and S. Shennan (eds.).

Champion, T. (ed.) 1989a *Centre and Periphery*. Comparative Studies in Archaeology. One World Archaeology 11. London: Unwin Hyman.

Champion, T. 1989b Introduction. In T. Champion (ed.).

Champion, T. 1994 Socio-economic development in eastern England in the first millennium BC. In K. Kristiansen and J. Jensen (eds.).

Champion, T., Gamble, C., Shennan, S. and Whittle, A. 1984 *Prehistoric Europe* Academic Press.

Champion, T. C. and Megaw, J. V. S. (eds.) 1985 *Settlement and Society. Aspects of West European Prehistory in the First Millennium B.C.* Leicester University Press.

Chapa Brunet, T. 1986 Escultura Iberica: una revision de sus interpretaciones. *Trabajos de prehistoria*, 43.

Chapman, R. 1990 *Emerging Complexity. The Later Prehistory of South-east Spain, Iberia and the West Mediterranean*. Cambridge University Press.

Chernykh E. N. 1976 Metallurgische Bereiche der jüngeren und späten Bronzezeit in der UdSSR. *Jahresber. des Inst. für Vorgesch. der Univ. Frankfurt a. M.*

Chernykh, E. N. 1978 *Gornoe delo i metallugiiya v drevney shey Balgaru* (Mining and metallurgy in ancient Bulgaria), Sofia.

Cherry, J. F. 1986 Polities and palaces: some problems in Minoan state formation. In C. Renfrew and J. F. Cherry (eds.).

Cherry, J. F. 1988 Pastoralism and the role of animals in the pre- and protohistoric economies of the Aegean. In C. R. Whittaker (ed.).

Chevillot, C. and Coffyn, A. (eds.) 1991 *L'Age du Bronze Atlantique. Ses facies, de l'écosse a l'Andalousie et leurs relations avec le Bronze Continental et la Méditerranée*. Actes du 1er Colloque du Parc Archéologique de Beynac. Publications de l'association des musées du Sarladais. Beynac.

Chevillot, C. and Gomez, J. 1979 Roues de char et statuettes en terre cuite de Chalucet (Saint-Jean-Ligoure, Haute-Vienne). Leur signification culturelle. *Bull. de la Société Préhistorique Française* 76.

Childe, V. G. 1930 *The Bronze Age*. Cambridge University Press.

Childe, V. G. 1942/1985 *What Happened in History*. Penguin Books.

Childe, V. G. 1957 *The Dawn of European Civilization*. 6th edition, revised. Paul Kegan, London.

Childe, V. G. 1958 Retrospect. *Antiquity* 32.

Chochorowski, I. 1985 Die Rolle der Vekerzug-Kultur (VK) im Rahmen der skythischen Einflüsse in Mitteleuropa. *Praehistorische Zeitschrift* 60.

Chochorowski, I. 1987 Herodots Sigynnen im kulturellen Milieu der frühen Eisenzeit auf der ungarischen Tiefebene (Zusammenfassung). *Przeglad Archeologiczny* 34.

Chropovsky, B. (ed.) 1974 *Symposium zu Problemen der jüngeren Hallstattzeit in Mitteleuropa*. Verlag der slowakischen Akademie der Wissenschaften, Bratislava.

Chropovsky, B. and Herrmann, J. (eds.). 1982 *Beiträge zum bronzezeitlichen Burgenbau in Mitteleuropa*. Berlin, Nitra.

Claessen, H. J. M. 1978 The early state: a structural approach. In H. J. M. Claessen and P. Skalnik (eds.), *The Early State*. The Hague, Paris, New York: Mouton Publishers.

Claessen, H. J. M. and Skalnik, P. 1978 The early state: models and reality. In H. J. M. Claessen and P. Skalnik (eds.), *The Early State*. The Hague, Paris, New York: Mouton Publishers.

Clark, G. 1966 The invasion hypothesis in British archaeology. *Antiquity* 40.

Clarke, D. 1968 *Analytical Archaeology*. London, Methuen.

Clarke, R. R. 1954 The early Iron Age treasure from Snettisham, Norfolk. *Proc. Prehistoric Society*, 20.

Clastres, P. 1977 *Society Against the State*. Oxford: Basil Blackwell.

Cleere, H. 1989 *Archaeological Heritage Management in the Modern World*. One World Archaeology 9. Unwin Hyman. London.

Coblenz, W. 1967 Zu den bronzezeitlichen Metalfunden von der Heidenschanze in Dresden-Coschutz und ihrer Rolle bei den zeitlichen und funktionellen Deutung der Burgen der Lausitzer Kultur. *Arbeits und Forschungsber. zur Sächsischen Bodendenkmalpflege* 16/17.

Coblenz, W. 1978 Zu den befestigten Siedlungen der Lausitzer Kultur in der DDR. In W. Coblenz and F. Horst (eds.).

Coblenz, W. 1981 Bemerkungen zur Hallstatt- und zur westlichen Lausitzer Kultur. In C. Eibner and A. EIbner (eds.).

Coblenz, W. and Horst, F. (eds.) 1978 *Mitteleuropäische Bronzezeit*. Beiträge zur Archäologie und Geschichte. Akademie-Verlag Berlin.

Coffyn, A. 1985 *Le Bronze Final Atlantique dans la Peninsula Iberique*. Publication du Centre Pierre Paris 11. Paris.

Coffyn, A., Gomez, J. and Mohen, J.-P. 1981 *L'apogée du bronze atlantique*. L'âge du bronze en France 1. Paris: Picard.

Cohen, R. 1978 State origins: a reappraisal. In H. J. M. Claessen and P. Skalnik (eds.), *The Early State*. The Hague, Paris, New York: Mouton Publishers.

Coldstream, J. N. 1982 Greeks and Phoenicians in the Aegean. In H. G. Niemeyer (ed.).

Coldstream, J. N. 1983 The meaning of the regional styles in the eighth century B.C. In R. Hägg (ed.), *The Greek Renaissance of the Eighth Century B.C.*: Tradition and Innovation. Acta Univ. Atheniensis Regni Sueciae Series in 4, xxx, Stockholm.

Coles, J. M. 1962 European Bronze Age shields. *Proc. Prehist. Society*.

Coles, J. 1982 Metallurgy and Bronze Age Society. In *Studien zur Bronzezeit*. Festschrift für Wilhelm Albert v. Brunn. Mainz/Rhein: Verlag Phillip von Zabern.

Coles, J. and Harding, A. 1979 *The Bronze Age in Europe*. London: Methuen.

Collis, J. 1975 *Defended Sites of the Late La Tène*. BAR Suppl. Series 2, Oxford.

Collis, J. 1982 Gradual growth and sudden change – urbanisation in temperate Europe. In C. Renfrew and S. Shennan (eds.).

Collis, J. 1984a *The European Iron Age*. London: Batsford.

Collis, J. 1984b *Oppida: Earliest Towns North of the Alps*. Department of Prehistory and Archaeology, University of Sheffield.

Collis, J. 1986 Central place theory is dead: long live the central place. In E. Grant (ed.).

Comsa, E. 1988 Die Viehzücht im Bronzezeitalter auf rumänischem Gebiet. *Slovenska Archaeologica* 36(1), Bratislava.

Coombs, D. 1975 Bronze Age weapon hoards in Britain. *Archaeologia Atlantica*.

Coombs, D. 1979 A Late Bronze Age hoard from Cassionbridge Farm, Watford, Hertfordshire. In C. Burgess and D. Coombs (eds.).

Coombs, D. 1988 The Wilburton complex and B.F. II in Atlantic Europe. In P. Brun and C. Mordant (eds.).

Coombs, D. and Bradshaw, J. 1979 A carp's tongue hoard from Stourmouth, Kent. In C. Burgess and D. Coombs (eds.).

Cooney, G. and Grogan, E. 1991 An archaeological solution to the 'Irish' problem? *Emania* 9. Bull. of the Navan Research Group. Belfast.

Courtois, J.-C. 1987 Enkomi und Ras Shamra, zwei Aussenposten der mykenischen Kultur. In H.-G. Buchholz (ed.), *Ägäische Bronzezeit*. Darmstadt.

Covic, B. 1991 Die Bronzezeit im 'illyrischen' Raum und das Problem der ethnischen Zuschreibung archäologischer Funde. In A. Benac, B. Covic and N. Tasic (eds.).

Cowen, J. C. 1955 Eine Einführung in die Geschichte der bronzenen Griffzungenschwerter in Süddeutschland und angrensenden Gebieten. *Bericht der Römisch Germanischen Kommission* 36.

Crossland, R. A. and Birchall, A. (eds.) 1974 *Bronze Age Migrations in the Aegean. Archaeological and Linguistic Problems in Greek Prehistory*. Noyes Press.

Crouwel, J.H. and Morel, J. 1981 *Chariots and Other Means of Land Transport in Bronze Age Greece*. Allard Pierso Series, Amsterdam.

Crumley. C. L. 1974 *Celtic Social Structures*. University of Michigan, Ann Arbor.

Cunliffe, B. 1976 The origins of urbanization in Britain. In B. Cunliffe and T. Rowley (eds.).

Cunliffe, B. 1978 *Iron Age Communities in Britain. An Account of England, Scotland and Wales from the Seventh Century BC until the Roman conquest*. (2nd edition). Routledge and Kegan Paul, London.

Cunliffe, B. 1982a Britain, the Veneti and beyond. *Oxford Journal of Archaeology* 1(1).

Cunliffe, B. 1982b Settlement hierarchy and social change in southern Britain in the Iron Age. *Analecta Praehistorica Leidensia* 15.

Cunliffe, B. 1983 *Danebury. Anatomy of an Iron Age Hillfort*. London: Batsford.

Cunliffe, B. 1988 *Greeks, Romans and Barbarians. Spheres of Interaction*. London: Batsford.

Cunliffe, B. and Rowley, T. (eds.) 1976 *Oppida in Barbarian Europe*. BAR Suppl. Series 11, Oxford.

Curtis, J. (ed.) 1988 *Bronze-working Centres of Western Asia c 1000–539 B.C*. London, Kegan Paul.

D'Altroy, T. N. and Earle, T. K. 1985 Staple finance, wealth finance and storage in the Inka political economy. *Current Anthropology* 26(2).

Dabrowska, T. 1989 Bemerkungen zur Entstehung der Przeworsk-Kultur. *Praehistorische Zeitschrift* 63. Band, Heft. 1. Berlin and New York.

Dabrowski, I. 1968 *Zabytki metalowe epoki brazu. Miedzy dolna Wisla a Niemnem*. (Metal artefacts from the Bronze Age found between the lower Vistula and the Niemen). Wroclaw-Warszawa-Krakow.

Dabrowski, J. 1989 The social structures of the Lusatian culture at the transition from Bronze to Iron Age. In M. L. S. Sørensen and R. Thomas (eds.).

Daniel, G. 1975 *150 Years of Archaeology*. Duckworth. London.

David-el Biali, M. 1990 L'âge du Bronze en Valais et dans le Chablais vaudois. *Jahrbuch d. Schweizerischen Gesellschaft f. Ur- und Frühgeschichte* 73.

Davis, E. 1985 The gold of the shaft graves: the Transsylvanian connection. *The Temple University, Aegean Symposium*.

De Grossi Mazzorin, J. 1985 I resti faunistici dell'insediamento protostorico di Pitigliano-Mulino Rossi (G.R.). In E. Pellegrino *L'insediamento protostorico di Pitigliano. Campagne di scavo 1982–83.* Pitigliano.

De Grossi Mazzorin, J. and Di Gennaro, F. 1992 L'habitat et l'occupation du sol à l'Age du Bronze en Etrurie Meridionale. In C. Mordant and A. Richards (eds.).

Deger-Jalkotzy, S. (ed.) 1983 *Griechenland, die Ägäis und der Levante während der 'Dark Ages' vom 12. bis zum 9. Jh. v. Chr.* Österreichische Ak. der Wissensch, Wien.

Dehn, W. 1980 Einige Bemerkungen zu hallstattzeitlichen Trensen Sloweniens. *Situla* 20/21, Ljubjana. (Festschrift Staneta Gabrovca).

Demoule, J.-P. 1989 D'un âge à l'autre: temps, style et société dans la transition Hallstatt/La Tène. In M. Ulrix-Closset and M. Otte (eds.).

Demoule, J.-P. and Ilett, M. 1985 First-millennium settlement and society in northern France: a case study from the Aisne Valley. In T. Champion and J. V. S. Megaw (eds.).

Dergachev, V. 1989 Neolithic and Bronze Age cultural communities of the steppe zone of the USSR. *Antiquity* 63(241).

Dickinson, S. 1987 *The Origins of Mycenean Civilization.* (SIMA 49). Göteborg.

Dietler, M. 1989 Greeks, Etruscans, and thirsty barbarians: Early Iron Age interaction in the Rhone Basin of France. In T. Champion (ed.).

Dietler, M. 1990 Driven by drink: the role of drinking in the political economy and the case of Early Iron Age France. *Journal of Anthropological Archaeology* 9.

Dietz, S. 1982 Naturen og mennesket og Etruriens forhistorie. In *Etruskernes verden.* Exhibition catalogue, the National Museum, Copenhagen.

Dietz, S. 1992 *The Argolid at the Transition to the Mycenaean Age. Studies in the Chronology and Cultural Development in the Shaft Grave Period.* The National Museum of Denmark. Copenhagen.

Dincauze, D. F. and Hasenstab, R. J. 1989 Explaining the Iroquois: tribalization on the prehistoric periphery. In T. Champion (ed.).

Dobiat, C. 1981 Die Hallstattnekropole bei Kleinklein im Sulmtal. In C. Eibner and A. Eibner (eds.).

Dobiat, C. (ed.) 1984 *Studien zu Siedlungsfragen der La Tènezeit.* Veröffentlichung des vorgeschichtlichen Seminars Marburg, Sonderband 3, Marburg.

Domingo, E. G. 1993 *Estelas, Paisaje y Territorio en el Bronce Final del Suroeste de la Peninsula Iberica.* Complutum 3, Madrid.

Drack, W. 1958–1964 *Ältere Eisenzeit der Schweiz.* Band 1–4. Materialhft. s. Ur- und Frühgesch. der Schweiz, Basel.

Drack, W. 1989 Die Schweiz zur Hallstattzeit. In M. Ulrix-Closset and M. Otte (eds.).

Driehaus, J. 1965 'Fürstengräber' und Eisenerze zwischen Mittelrhein, Mosel und Saar. *Germania* 43.

Dumezil, G. 1958: *L'idéologie tripartie des Indo-Européen.* Bruxelles, Berchem Latomus.

Dunning, C. 1992 Époque charnière dans un carrefour d'influences: le VIIIe siècle av. J.-C. a l' ouest du plateau Suisse. In C. Mordant and A. Richard (eds.).

Dusek, M. 1964 Waren Skythen in Mitteleuropa und in Deutschland? *Praehist. Zeitschrift* 42.

Dusek, S. 1973 K otazke vojenskej demokracie v pravekom vyvoji slovenska. (Zur Frage der militärischen Demokratie in der Urgeschichtlichen Entwicklung der Slowakei). *Slovenska Archeologia* 21(2).

Dutton, A., Fasham, P. and Jenkins. D. A. 1994 Prehistoric copper mining on the Great Orme, Llandudno, Gwynedd. *Proceedings of the Prehistoric Society* 60.

Duval, A. 1988 Des chars processionels aux chars de combat. In *Les princes Celtes et la Méditerranée.*

Duval, M.-F. and Hawkes, C. (eds.) 1976 *Celtic Art in Ancient Europe. Five Protohistoric Centuries.* London, New York, San Francisco: Seminar Press.

Duval, P.-M. and Kruta, V. (eds.) 1979 *Les mouvements celtiques du Ve au Ier siècle avant notre ère.* Paris: Edition du CNRS.

Duval, P.-M. and Kruta, V. (eds.) 1982 *L'art celtique de la période d' expansion IVᵉ et IIIᵉ siècles avant notre ère*. Centre de recherches d' historie et de philologie. Ecole pratique des hautes études IV section, Sciences hist. et phil. III hautes études du monde Greco-Romain 13, Geneve–Paris: Librairie Droz.

Düwel, K., Jankuhn, H., Siems, H. and Timpe, D. (eds.) 1985 *Untersuchungen zu Handel und Verkehr der vor und frühgeschichtlichen Zeit in Mittel- und Nordeuropa*. Teil I. Abh. der Akademie der Wiss. in Göttingen. Göttingen.

Dvorak, F. 1938 *Wagengraber der alteren Eisenzeit in Bohmen*. Praha.

Dynamique du Bronze moyen en Europe occidentale 1989 Actes du 113ᵉ congrès national des sociétés savantes, Strasbourg 1988, Commission de Pré- et Protohistorie. Paris: Editions du C. T. H. S. 1989.

Earle, T. 1978 *Economic and Social Organization of a Complex Chiefdom: the Halela District, Kaua'i, Hawaii*. Museum of Anthropology, University of Michigan, Ann Arbor, Anthropological Papers, Vol. 63. Ann Arbor, University of Michigan.

Earle, T. 1982 The ecology and politics of primitive valuables. In J. G. Kennedy and R. B. Edgerton (eds.), *Culture and Ecology. Eclectic Perspectives*. American Anthropological Association Special Publication 15. Washington DC.

Earle, T. 1987a Chiefdoms in archaeological and ethnohistorical perspective. *Annual Review of Anthropology* 16.

Earle, T. 1987b The economic bases of chiefdoms. Paper presented at the Center for Research in the Humanities, University of Copenhagen, spring 1987.

Earle, T. (ed.) 1991a *Chiefdoms: Power, Economy and Ideology*. School of American Research/ Cambridge University Press.

Earle, T. 1991b Property rights and the evolution of chiefdoms. In T. Earle (ed.).

Earle, T. *et al.* 1987 *Archaeological Field Research in the Upper Mantaro, Peru 1982–1983: Investigations of Inka Expansion and Exchange*. Monograph XXVIII, Inst. of Arch., Univ. of California, Los Angeles.

Earle, T. K. and Ericson, J.E. (eds.) 1977: *Exchange Systems in Prehistory*. New York and London, Academic Press

Ebersweiler, B., Riethmann, P. and Ruoff, L. 1987 Greifensee-Böcschau ZH: Ein spätbronzezeitliches Dorf. Ein Vorbericht. *Jahrbuch der Schweizerischen Gesellschaft für Ur- und Frühgeschichte 70*.

Ecsedy, I. 1979 *The People of the Pit-Grave Kurgans in Eastern Hungary*. Fontes Arch. Hungariae. Budapest.

Eden, C. M. and Kohl, P. 1993 Trade and World Systems in Early Bronze Age Western Asia. In C. Scarre and F. Healy (eds.), *Trade and Exchange in Prehistoric Europe*. Oxbow Monographs 33, Oxford.

Egg, M. 1980 Zum Helmfragment von Magdalenska gora. *Situla* 20/21. Zbornik posvecen stanetu Gabrovcu ob sestdesetletnici. Ljubbljana.

Egg, M. 1985 Die Hallstattzeitlichen Hügelgräber bei Helpfau-Uttendorf in Oberösterreich. *Jahrbuch Röm. Germ. Zentralmuseum Mainz*.

Eggers, H. J. 1959 Einführung in die Vorgeschichte. München: R. Piper and Co. Verlag.

Eggert, M. K. H. 1988 Riesentumuli und Sozialorganisation: vergleichende Betrachtungen zu den sogenannten 'Fürstenhügeln' der späten Hallstattzeit. *Archäologisches Korrespondenzblatt* 18, Heft 3.

Eggert, M. K. H. 1991 Die konstruierte Wirklichkeit: Bemerkungen zum Problem der archäologischen interpretation am Beispiel der späten Hallstattzeit. *Hephaistos*.

Eggert, M. K. H., Kurz, S. and Wotzka, H.-P. 1980 Historische Realität und archäologische Datierung: zur Aussagekraft der Kombinationsstatistik. *Praehistorische Zeitschrift* 55.

Eibner, C. 1974 Das Späturnenfelderzeitliche Gräberfeld von St. Andrä v.d. Hgt., p.B. Tulln, NÖ. *Aussagewert und Aussagegrenzen von Brandbestattungen für eine historische Interpretation. Archaeologia Austriaca Beiheft* 12.

Eibner, C. 1975 Die Erforschung der Urnenfelderzeit in den letzten fünfundzwanzig Jahren. *Mitteilungen der Österreichischen Arbeits-gemeinschaft für Ur- und Frühgeschichte* 25(2).

Eibner, C. 1982 Kupfererzbergbau in Österreichs Alpen. In B. Hänsel (ed.).

Eibner, C. 1983 Der Bereich der Mittleren Donau während der späten Bronze- und frühen Eisenzeit. In *Griechenland, die Ägäis und die Levante während der 'Dark Ages' vom 12. bis zum 9. Jh. v. Chr. Österreichische Akademie der Wissenschaften Sitzungsberichte* 418.

Eibner, C. 1986 Der Übergang von der Urnenfelderkultur zu Hallstattkultur in Ostösterreich. In E. Jerem (ed.).

Eibner, C. and Eibner, A. (eds.) 1981 *Die Hallstattkultur: Symposium in Steyr.* Land Oberöstereich, Linz.

Ekholm, Kajsa 1977 External exchange and the transformation of Central African social systems. In J. Friedman and M. J. Rowlands, The *Evolution of Social Systems*, London: Duckworth.

Ekholm, Kajsa 1980 On the limitations of civilization: the structure and dynamics of global systems. *Dialectical Anthropology*, vol. v.

Ekholm, Kajsa 1981 On the structure and dynamics of global systems. In J. S. Kahn and J. R. Llobera (eds.), *The Anthropology of Pre-capitalist Societies*, London: The Macmillan Press.

Ekholm, K. 1985 '. . . Sad stories of the death of kings': the involution of divine kingship. *Ethnos* 3–4 (History and Anthropology in Scandinavia).

Ekholm, K. and Friedman, J. 1979 'Capital', imperialism and exploitation in ancient world systems. In M. T. Larsen, *Power and Propaganda.* A Symposium on Ancient Empires, Copenhagen: Akademisk forlag, Mesopotamia 7.

Ekholm, K. and Friedman, J. 1980 Towards a global anthropology. In L. Blussé, H. L. Wesseling, and G. D. Winius (eds.), *History and Underdevelopment.* Essays on Underdevelopment and European Expansion in Asia and Africa, Leiden Centre for History of European Expansion and Edition de la Maison des Sciences de l'Homme, Paris.

Ekholm, K. and Friedman, J. 1985 Towards a global anthropology (enlarged version). *Critique of Anthropology* (5)1.

Ellison, A. 1981 Towards a socio-economic model for the Middle Bronze Age in southern England. In N. Hammond, G. Isaac and I. Hodder (eds.), *Patterns in Prehistory.* Cambridge.

Eluere, C. 1982 *Les ors préhistoriques.* L'âge du bronze en France 2. Paris: Picard.

Endert, D. van. 1984 Keltische Wagenbestattungen in Frankreich. In M. Gustin and L. Pauli (eds.).

Endert, D. van. 1986 Zur Stellung der Wagengräber der Arras-Kultur. *Bericht der Römisch Germanischen Kommission* 67.

Endert, D. van. 1987 *Die Wagenbestattungen der späten Hallstattzeit und der Latènezeit im Gebiet westlich des Rheins.* BAR Int. Series 355, Oxford.

Engels, Friedrich 1891 (1977) *Familiens, privatejendommens og statens oprindelse.* (Danish translation of 4th edition from 1891 of 'The origin of family, private property and the state' with a new large preface by Engels.) Copenhagen: Politisk revy.

Eogan, G. 1969 'Lock-rings' of the Late Bronze Age. *Proceedings of the Royal Irish Academy* 67, sect. C, No. 4.

Eogan, G. 1981 Gold discs of the Irish late Bronze Age. In D. O'Corrain (ed.), *Irish Antiquity.* Essays and Studies presented to Professor M.J. O'Kelly. Tower Books of Cork.

Eogan, G. 1990 Possible connections between Britain and Ireland and the east Mediterranean region during the Bronze Age. In *Orientalisch-ägäische Einflüsse in der europäischen Bronzezeit.* Römisch-Germanisches Zentralmuseum, Monographien Band 15.

Erbach-Schönberg, M.-C. 1985 Bemerkungen zu Urnenfeldezeitlichen Deponierungen in Oberösterreich. *Arch. Korrespondenzblatt* 15.

Facsar, G. and Jerem, E. 1985 Zum urgeschichtlichen Weinbau in Mitteleuropa. Rebkernfunde von Vitis vinifera L. aus der urnenfelder-, hallstatt- und latènezeitlichen Siedlung

Sopron-Krautacker. *Wissenschaftlichen Arbeiten aus dem Burgenland,* Bd. 71. Eisenstadt.

Feinman, G. and Neitzal, J. 1984 Too many types: an overview of sedentary prestate societies in the Americas. In M. Schiffer (ed.), *Advances in Archaeological Theory and Method,* Vol. VII. New York: Academic Press.

Fekete, M. 1983 Angaben zu Kontakten zwischen Italien und Transdanubien. *Savaria* 16. Nord-Süd Beziehungen. Internationales Kolloquium 1982, Bozsok-Szombathely.

Fekete, M. 1985 Rettungsgrabung früheisenzeitlicher Hügelgräber in Vaskeresztes (Vorbericht). *Acta Archaeologica Hungaricae* 37.

Ferguson, Y. 1991 Chiefdoms to city-states: the Greek experience. In T. Earle (ed.).

Finley, M.I. 1973 *The Ancient Economy.* London.

Fischer, F. 1973 Keimelia. Bemerkungen zur kulturgeschichtlichen Interpretation des sogenannten Südimportes in der späten Hallstatt-und frühe Latènekultur des westlichen Mitteleuropas. *Germania* 51.

Fischer, F. 1985 Der Handel der Mittel- und Spät-Latène-Zeit in Mitteleuropa aufgrund archäologischer Zeugnisse. In K. Düwel *et al.* (eds.).

Fischer, F. 1988 Celtes et Achéménides. In *Les Princes Celtes el la Méditerranée.*

Fischer, F. and Biel, J. 1982 Frühkeltische Fürstengräber in Mitteleuropa. *Antike Welt,* Sondernummer.

Fitzpatrick, A. P. 1989 The uses of Roman imperialism by the Celtic barbarians in the later Republic. In J. C. Barrett, A. P. Fitzpatrick and L. Macinnes (eds.).

Flannery, K. 1972 The cultural evolution of civilizations. *Annual Review of Ecology and Systematics* 3.

Fleming, A. 1972 The genesis of pastoralism in European prehistory. *World Arch.* 4.

Fleming, A. 1988 *The Dartmoor Reaves. Investigating Prehistoric Land Divisions.* Batsford, London.

Fogel, J. 1988 '*Import*' nordyjski na ziemiach polskich u schylku epoki brazu. (Nordischer 'Import' in die polnischen Länder in der Spätbronzezeit.) Univ. im. Adama Mickiewicza w Poznaniu, Seria arch. Nr. 30. Poznan.

Fol, A. 1988 Der geistige Umschwung in Hellas und Thrakien. In: *Der Thrakische Silverschatz aus Rogozen Bulgaren.* Ausstellungskatalog.

Fol, A. (ed.) 1989 *The Rogozen Treasure.* Sofia, Publishing House of the Bulgarian Academy of Sciences.

Fol, A. 1991 Der Stand der Forschungsarbeiten über die östliche Hälfte der Balkanhalbinsel bis zur Mitte des 1. Jahrtausend v. u. Z. In A. Benac, B. Covic and N. Tacic (eds.).

Fowler, D. D. 1987 The use of the past in the service of the state. *American Antiquity* 52 (2).

Frank, G. 1991 A plea for world system history. *Journal of World History* 2(1). University of Hawaii Press.

Frank, G. 1993 The Bronze Age world system and its cycles. *Current Anthropology,* 34(4).

Frank, G. and Gills, B. K. (eds.) 1993 *The World System. Five Hundred Years or Five Thousand?* Routledge, London and New York.

Franke, H. (ed.) 1987 *Skythika.* Vorträge zur Entstehung des skytho-iranischen Tierstils und zu Denkmälern des Bosporanischen Reichs anlässlich einer Ausstellung der Leningrader Ermitage in München 1984. Bayerische Akademie der Wissenschaften. Phil. - Hist. Klasse. Abh. Neue Folge, Heft 98. München.

Frankenstein, S. 1979 The Phoenicians in the Far West: A function of neo-Assyrian imperialism. In M. T. Larsen (ed.), *Power and Propaganda.* A Symposium on Ancient Empires. Mesopotamia 7. Copenhagen: Akademisk Forlag.

Frankenstein, S. 1994 Regional development in the First Millennium B. C. the Phoenicians in Iberia. In K. Kristiansen and J. Jensen (eds.).

Frankenstein, S. and Rowlands, M. 1978 The internal structure and regional context of Early Iron Age society in south-western Germany. *Bulletin of the Institute of Archaeology* 15, London.

Frederiksen, M. 1979 The Etruscans in Campani. In D. Ridgway and F. R. Ridgway (eds.), *Italy before the Romans*. Copenhagen: Academic Press.

Frey, H. 1966 Der Ostalpenraum und die Antike Welt in der frühen Eisenzeit. *Germania* 40.

Frey, O.-H. 1969 *Die Entstehung der Situlenkunst*. Studien zur figürlich verzierten Toreutik von Este. Römisch-Germanische Forschungen, Band 31, Berlin.

Frey, O.-H. 1976 Du Premier style au Style de Waldalgesheim. Remarques sur l' évolution de l' art celtique ancien. In P.-M. Duval and C. Hawkes (eds.).

Frey, O.-H. 1980 Die keltische Kunst. In L. Pauli (ed.).

Frey, O.-H. 1984 Die Bedeutung der Gallia Cisalpina für die Entstehung der Oppida-Kultur. In C. Dobiat (ed.), *Studien zu Siedlungsfragen der Latènezeit*. Veröff. des vorgeschichtl. Seminars Marburg. Sonderdruck 3.

Frey, O-H. 1985 Zum Handel und Verkehr während der Frühlatènezeit in Mitteleuropa. In K. Düwel *et al.* (eds.).

Frey, O.-H. 1986 Einige Überlegungen zu den Beziehungen zwischen Kelten und Germanen in der Spätlatènezeit. In Marburger Studien zur Vor-und Frühgeschichte, Bd. 7: *Gedenkenschrift für Gero von Mehrhart zum 100. Geburtstag*. Marburg.

Frey, O.-H. 1988 Les fibules Hallstattiennes de la fin du VIe siècle au Ve siècle en Italie du Nord. In *Les Princes Celtes et la Méditerranée*.

Frey, O.-H. 1989 Mediterranes Importgut im Südostalpengebiet. In M. Ulrix-Closset and M. Otte (eds.).

Frey, O.-H. 1991 Griechische Schutzwaffen und ihre Nachahmungen im illyrischen und thrakischen Gebiet. In A. Benac *et al.* (eds.).

Fried, M. 1960 On the evolution of social stratification and the state. In S. Diamond (ed.), *Culture in History*. New York: Columbia University Press.

Fried, M. 1967 *The Evolution of Political Society: an Essay in Political Economy*. New York: Random House.

Fried, M. 1978 The state, the chicken, and the egg, or what came first? In R. Cohen and E. R. Service (eds.), *Origins of the State: the Anthropology of Political Evolution*. Philadelphia: Institute for the Study of Human Issues.

Friedman, J. 1974 Marxism, structuralism and vulgar materialism. *Man* 9.

Friedman, J. 1975 Tribes, states and transformations. In M. Bloch (ed.), *Marxist Analyses and Social Anthropology*. London and New York: Malaby Press.

Friedman, J. 1976a Evolutionary Models in Anthropology. Unpublished Manuscript.

Friedman , J. 1976b Marxist Theory and Systems of Total Reproduction. Part 1: Negative. *Critique of Anthropology* 7.

Friedman, J. 1979 *System, Structure and Contradiction. The Evolution of 'Asiatic' Social Formations*. The National Museum of Copenhagen.

Friedman, J. 1982 Catastrophe and continuity in social evolution. In C. Renfrew, M. Rowlands and B. A. Segraves (eds.).

Friedman, J. 1985 The chicken in the egg and Captain Cook: an essay in transformational anthropology. In T. Vuyk (ed.) *Essays on Structural Change: the L. H. Morgan Society Symposium*, Leiden.

Friedman, J. 1989 Culture, identity and world process. In D. Miller, M. Rowlands and C. Tilley (eds.).

Friedman, J. and Rowlands, M. 1977 Notes towards an epigenetic model of the evolution of 'civilization'. In J. Friedman and M. Rowlands (eds.), *The Evolution of Social Systems*. London: Duckworth.

Furmanek, V. 1973 K nekterym spolecenskoekonomickym problemum doby bronzove (Zu einigen sozial-ökonomischen Problemen der Bronzezeit). *Slovenska Archeologia*. 21(2).

Furmanek, V. 1985 Zur ökonomischen Entwicklung bei den Stämmen der jüngeren Bronzezeit in der Slowakei. In F. Horst and B. Krüger (eds.), *Produktivkräfte und Produktionsverhältnisse in ur- und frühgeschichtlicher Zeit*. Historiker Gesellschaft der DDR, XI.

Tagung der Fachgruppe Ur- und Frühgeschichte vom 14. bis 16 Dezember in Berlin. Berlin: Akademie Verlag.

Furmanek, V. and Horst, F. (eds.) 1982a *Beiträge zum bronzezeitlichen Burgenbau in Mitteleuropa.* Berlin, Nitra 1982.

Furmanek, V. and Horst, F. 1982b Die sozialökonomischen Entwicklung der bronzezeitlichen Stämme in Mitteleuropa (eine übersicht). In V. Furmanek and F. Horst (eds.).

Furmanek, V. and Horst, F. (eds.) 1990 *Beiträge zur Geschichte und Kultur der Mitteleuropäischen Bronzezeit.* Berlin, Nitra.

Furmanek, V. and Ozdani, O. 1990 Kontakte der Hügelgräberkulturen und des Kulturkomplexes der südöstlichen Urnenfelder. In V. Furmanek and F. Horst (eds.).

Furmanek, V. and Stloukal, M. 1986 Einige Ergebnisse der archäologisch-anthropologischen Untersuchung des Gräberfeldes in Radzovce. In D.-W. Buck and B. Gramsch (eds.).

Furmanek, V. and Veliacik, L. 1987 Die Urnenfelderkulturen in der Slowakei. In E. Plesl and J. Hrala (eds.).

Furmanek, V., Veliacik, L. and Romsauer, P. 1982 Jungbronzezeitliche befestigte Siedlungen in der Slowakei. In V. Furmanek and F. Horst (eds.).

Gabrovec, S. 1966 Zur Hallstattzeit in Slowenien. *Germania* 44.

Gabrovec, S. 1974 Die Ausgrabungen in Sticna und ihre Bedeutung für die südostalpine Hallstattkultur. In B. Chropovsky (ed.).

Gailey, C. W. and Patterson, T. C. 1987 Power relations and state formation. In T. C. Patterson and C. W. Gailey (eds.), *Power Relations and State Formation.* Washington: American Anthropological Association.

Galanina, L. 1987 Die Kelermes-Kurgane als Quelle für die Erforschung der Kontakte Zwischen Skythen und der altorientalischen Kulturen. In H. Franke (ed.), *Skythika. Vorträge zur Entstehung des skytho-iranischen Tierstils und zu Denkmälern des Bosporanischen Reichs.* Bayerische Akademie der Wissenschaften. Phil.-Hist. Klasse Abh. Neue Folge, Heft 98. München.

Gale, N. H. (ed.) 1991a *Bronze Age Trade in the Mediterranean.* Papers presented at the Conference held at Rewley House, Oxford, in December 1989. Studies in Mediterranean Archaeology Vol. xc. Paul Åströms Förlag.

Gale, N. H. 1991b Copper oxhide ingots: their origin and their place in the Bronze Age metals trade in the Mediterranean. In N. H. Gale (ed.).

Gallay, A. 1981 The western Alps from 2500 to 1500 bc (3400 to 2500 BC), tradition and cultural changes. *Journal of Indo-European Studies* 9.

Gallay, A. 1986 Neolithicum und Frühbronzeit im Wallis: Anmerkungen und Tafeln. *Antiqua 15. Chronologie.*

Gallus, S. and Horvarth, T. 1939 *Un Peuple cavalier préscythique en Hongrie.* Budapest: Université Pierre Pázmány.

Gamito, T. J. 1988 *Social Complexity in Southwest Iberia 800–300 B.C. The Case of Tartessos.* BAR International Series 439. Oxford.

Gamito, T. J. 1992 The Celts in western Iberia. IX Congress international d'etudes celtiques. *Etudes celtiques,* CRNS, Paris.

Garasanin, M. 1982 The early Iron Age in the central Balkan area, c. 1000–750 B.C. *The Cambridge Ancient History* III, part 1. *The Prehistory of the Balkans, the Middle East and the Aegean World, tenth to eighth centuries B.C.* Cambridge University Press.

Garnsey, P., Hopkins, P. and Whittaker, C. R. (eds.) 1983 *Trade in the Ancient Economy.* Berkeley and Los Angeles: University of California Press.

Gathercole, P. and Lowenthal, D. (eds.) 1989 *The Politics of the Past.* One World Archaeology. London, Unwin Hyman.

Gebühr, M. 1987 Montelius und Kossinna im Himmel. *Archäologische Information* 10

Gediga, B. 1967 *Plemiona kultury luzyckiej w epoce bracu na Slasku snodkowyn.* (summary:

Tribes with Lusatian culture in Middle Silesia in the Bronze Age) Instytut historii kultury materialnej polskiej akademii nauk. Wroclaw-Warszawa-Krakow.

Gediga, B. 1979 Einige Kulturerscheinungen während der Lausitzer Kultur in Westpolen und ihre Verbindungen mit Westpannonien. *Mitt. der österreichischen Arbeitsgemeinschaft für Ur- und Frühgeschichte.* 29. Wien.

Gediga, B. 1981 Zur Entwicklung der hallstattzeitlichen Burgen der Lausitzer Kultur in Mittelschlesien. In *Die Hallstatkultur,* Symposium Steyr.

Gediga, B. 1982 Zur Frage der Besiedlungs- und Wirtschaftsveränderungen in der Bronze- und der Hallstattzeit. In J. Herrmann and I. Sellnow (eds.), *Produktivkräfte und Gesell-schaftsformationen in Vorkapitalistischer Zeit.* Berlin: Akademie-Verlag.

Gediga, B. 1988 Die Lausitzer Kultur – Definitionversuche. In Z. Bukowski (ed.), 1988.

Gedl, M. 1973 *Cmentarzysko halsztackie w kietrzu, pow. Glubczyce.* (Ein Gräberfeld aus der hallstattzeit in Kietrz, Kreis Glubczyce). Polska Akademia Nauk, Inst. Hist. Kultury Meterialnej, Ossolineum. Wroclaw, Warszawa, Krakow, Gdansk.

Gedl, M. (ed.) 1982 *Poludniowa strefa kultury Luzyckiej i powiazania tej kultury z poludniem* (Südzone der Lausitzer Kultur und die Verbindungen dieser Kultur mit dem Süden). Krakow-Przemysl.

Gedl, M. 1986 Späthallstattzeit in Schlesien. In E. Jerem (ed.).

Gedl, M. (ed.) 1991 *Die Anfänge der Urnenfelderkulturen in Europa.* Archaeologia Interreg-ionalis, Vol. XIII. Warsaw University and Jagellonion University Cracow.

Gedl, M. 1992 Besiedlungsdynamik in der spätbronzezeit an der Liswarta im westteil Klein-polens. *Archaeologisches Korrespondenzblatt* 22.

Gellner, E. 1988 *Plough, Sword and Book. The Structure of Human History.* Paladin. Grafton Books.

Gening, V. F., Zdanovich, G. B. and Gening, V. V. 1992 *Sintashta. Archaeological Sites of Aryan Tribes of the Ural-Kazakh Steppes.* Chelyabinsk.

Gerdsen, H. 1986 *Studien zu den Schwertgräbern der älteren Hallstattzeit.* Mainz/Rhein: Verlag Phillip von Zabern.

Gergova, D. 1982 Genesis and development of the metal ornaments in the Thracians' lands during the Early Iron Age 11th–6th century BC. *Studia Praehistorica* 3.

Gergova, D. 1987 The Thracien-Caucasian relations and the Thracian tribe Trerae. In E. Plesl and J. Hrala (eds.).

Gergova, D. 1988 Die Bedeutung der Schatzfunde in der Thrakischen Welt. In: *Der Thrakische Silberschatz aus Rogosen Bulgarien.* Ausstellungskatalog.

Gersbach, E. 1981 Neue Aspekte zur Geschichte des späthallstatt-frühlatenezeitlichen Für-stensitzes auf der Heuneburg. In A. Eibner and C. Eibner (eds.).

Geselowitz, M. 1988 Technology and social change: ironworking in the rise of social complex-ity in Iron Age Europe. In: B. Gibson and M. Geselowitz (eds.), *Tribe and Polity in Late Prehistoric Europe. Demography, Production, and Exchange in the Evolution of Complex Social Systems.* Plenum Press.

Gibson, B. 1988 Agro-pastoralism and regional social organization in early Ireland. In B. Gibson and M. Geselowitz (eds.), *Tribe and Polity in Late Prehistoric Europe. Demography, Production and Exchange in the Evolution of Complex Social Systems.* New York: Plenum Press.

Gibson, B. and Geselowitz, M. (eds.) 1988 *Tribe and Polity in Late Prehistoric Europe. Demogra-phy, Production and Exchange in the Evolution of Complex Social Systems.* New York: Plenum Press.

Gill, D. W. J. 1988 Expressions of wealth: Greek art and society. *Antiquity* 62(237).

Gilman, A. 1976 Bronze Age dynamics in southeast Spain. *Dialectical Anthropology* 1.

Gilman, A. 1981 The development of social stratification in Bronze Age Europe. *Current Anthropology* 22.

Gilman, A. 1987 Unequal development in Copper Age Iberia. In E. Brumfiel and T. Earle (eds).

Gilman, A. 1991 Trajectories towards social complexity in the later prehistory of the Mediterranean. In T. Earle (ed.).

Gilman, A. and Thornes, J. B. 1985 *Land-use and Prehistory in South-East Spain.* The London Research Seminar in Geography 8, Allen and Unwin.

Gilman, A. in press(a) Social evolution in southeast Spain.

Gilman, A. in press(b) The Iberian Peninsula: 6000 to 1500 B.C.

Gimbutas, M. 1965 *Bronze Age Cultures in Central and Eastern Europe.* The Hague: Mouton.

Gimbutas, M. 1979: The three waves of the Kurgan people into Old Europe, 4500–2500 B.C. *Archives suisses d'anthropologie générale, Geneve* 43(2).

Gimbutas, M. 1986 Remarks on the ethnogenesis of the Indo-Europeans in Europe. In Bernhard Kandler-Pálsson (ed.), *Ethnogenese europäischer Völker.* Stuttgart.

Girard, M. 1988 Analyse pollinique de la nécropole de Buno-Bonnevaux (Essonne). In P. Brun and C. Mordant (eds.), *Le groupe Rhin-Suisse-France orientale et la notion de civilisation des Champs d'Urnes.* Mémoires du Musée de Préhistoire d'Ile-de France no. 1, Nemours.

Gledhill, J. 1988 Introduction: the comparative analysis of social and political transitions. In J. Gledhill, B. Bender and M. T. Larsen (eds.).

Gledhill, J., Bender, B. and Larsen, M.T. (eds.) 1988 *State and Society.* The Emergence and Development of Social Hierarchy and Political Centralization. One World Archaeology 4. Unwin Hyman, London.

Gledhill, J. and Larsen, M. T. 1982 The Polanyi paradigm and a dynamic analysis of archaic states. In C. Renfrew, M. Rowlands and B. A. Segraves (eds.).

Gnoli, G. and Vernant, J.-P. (eds.) 1982 *La Mort, les morts dans les sociétés anciennes.* Cambridge.

Godelier, M. 1967 System, structure and contradiction in capital. *The Socialist Register,* ed. R. Milibrand and J. Saville. The Merlin Press. London.

Godelier, M. 1977 *Perspectives in Marxist Anthropology* (selection of articles). Cambridge Studies in Social Anthropology. Cambridge University Press.

Godelier, M. 1978 Infrastructures, societies and history. *Current Anthropology* 19(4).

Goetze, B.-R. 1984 Die frühesten europäischen Schutzwaffen. Anmerkungen zum Zusammenhang einer Fundgattung. *Bayerische Vorgeschichtsblätter* 49.

Goldmann, K. 1987 Überlegungen zur Demographie der Urnenfelderkulturen. In E. Plesl and J. Hrala (eds.).

Goldmann, K. 1990 Die mittlere Bronzezeit als Problem der Begriffs- und Zeitbestimmung. In V. Furmanek and F. Horst (eds.).

Goldschmidt, W. 1979 A general model for pastoral social systems. In *Pastoral production and society.* Cambridge University Press and Editions de la Maison des Sciences de l'Homme.

Gomez, J. 1983 Les traces de l'activité métallurgique à l'Age du Bronze et premier Age du Fer en centre-ouest, L'artisan dans la société. *Journées de Paléométallurgie.* Université de techn. de Compiegne, 22–23 fevr. 1983.

Gomez, J. 1984 Chars funéraires, chars rituels ou chars de combat? De la nature du pouvoir dans les sociétés du Bronze Final en France et dans l'aire de la culture des Champs d'Urnes d'Allemagne du sud et d'Europe centrale. In *Elements de pré- et protohistoire européenne.* Hommages à Jacques-Pierre Millotte. Annales Littéraires de l'Université de Besançon, Série Archéologie No. 32, Paris.

Gomez, J. de Soto 1991 Le fondeur, le trafiquant et les cuisiniers. La broche d'amathonte de Chypre et la chronologie du Bronze Final Atlantique. In *La Bronze Final Atlantique,* 1er coll. de Beynac.

Gonzalez Marcén, P., Lull, V. and Risch, R. 1992 *Arqueologia de Europa 2250–1200 A. C. Una introduccion a la 'Edad del Bronce'.* Historia Universal 6, Prehistoria. Editorial Sintesis.

Goody, J. 1973 Bridewealth and dowry in Africa and Eurasia. In J. Goody and S. J. Tambiah, *Bridewealth and Dowry,* Cambridge.

Goody, J. 1976 *Production and Reproduction. A Comparative Study of the Domestic Domain.* Cambridge Studies in Social Anthropology. Cambridge University Press.

Goody, J. 1983 *The Development of the Family and Marriage in Europe.* Cambridge University Press.

Gosden, C. 1985 Gifts and kin in Early Iron Age Europe. *MAN* 20.

Graham, A. J. 1982 The colonial expansion of Greece. In J. Boardman and N. G. L. Hammond (eds.), *The Cambridge Ancient History* III, Part 3: *The Expansion of the Greek World, eighth to sixth centuries B.C.*

Grant, E. (ed.) 1986a *Central Places, Archaeology and History.* University of Sheffield.

Grant, E. 1986b Hill-forts, central places and territories. In E. Grant (ed.).

Gräslund, B. 1965–66 Jungbronzezeitliche Fibeln-Schildsymbole? *Tor.*

Gräslund, B. 1967a The Hertzsprung shield type and its origin. *Acta Arch.*

Gräslund, B. 1967b Hethitische Schwerter mit Krummschneiden. *Opuscula Atheniensia* VII. Acta Inst. Atheniensis Regni Sueciae, Series in 4, XII, Lund.

Gräslund, B. 1985 Det enäggede svärdet och ridkonstens utvickling. *Tor* 20, Uppsala.

Gräslund, B. 1987 *The Birth of Prehistoric Chronology.* Dating Methods and Dating Systems in Nineteenth-century Scandinavian Archaeology. Cambridge University Press.

Green, D., Hazelgrove, C. and Spriggs, M. (eds.) 1978 *Social Organisation and Settlement.* BAR Int. Series 47. Oxford.

Greenfield, H. J. 1988 The origins of milk and wool production in the Old World: a zooarchaeological perspective from the Central Balkans. *Current Anthropology* 29(4).

Griesa, S. 1989 The 'Göritzer Gruppe'. Continuity from the late Bronze Age to the early Iron Age in GDR/Poland. In M. L. Sørensen and R. Thomas (eds.).

Gross, E. and Ruoff, U. 1990 Das Leben in neolitischen und bronzezeitlichen Dörfern am Zürich-und Greifensee. *Archäologie der Schweiz* 13.

Guidi, A. 1985 An application of the rank-size rule to protohistoric settlement in the middle Tyrrhenian area. In C. Malone and S. Stoddart (eds.), *Papers in Italian Archaeology IV.* The Cambridge Conference. Part III: *Patterns in Protohistory.* BAR Int. Ser. 245, Oxford.

Gustin, M. 1985 Die Kelten in Jugoslavien. Übersicht über das archäologische Fundgut. *Jahrbuch des Röm.-Germ. Zentralmuseums Mainz.*

Gustin, M. and Pauli, L. (eds.) 1984 *Keltski voz.* Posavski muzej Brezice, Knjiga 6.

Gustin, M. and Terzan, B. 1977 Beiträge zu den vorgeschichtlichen Beziehungen zwischen dem Südostalpengebiet, dem nordwestlichen Balkan und dem südlichen Pannonien im 5. Jahrhundert. In V. Markotic (ed.), *Ancient Europe and the Mediterranean.* Studies presented in honour of Hugh O. Hencken. Warminster.

Haaland, G. 1967 Economic determinants in ethnic processes. In F. Barth (ed.).

Haaland, R. 1977 Archaeological Classification and Ethnic Groups. *Norwegian Arch. Review* 10(1–2).

Haas, J. 1980 Troubles with tribes. An archaeological approach to an anthropological problem. Paper presented in the Symposium 'The Archaeology of Tribes' at the 79th Annual Meeting of the American Anthropological Association, December 4–7, 1980, Washington D.C.

Haas, J. 1982 *The Evolution of the Prehistoric State.* New York: Columbia University Press.

Habermas, J. 1968 (1973) *Erkenntnis und Interesse.* Mit einem neuen Nachwort. Suhrkamp Verlag Frankfurt am Main.

Hachmann, R. 1957 *Die frühe Bronzezeit im westlichen Ostseegebiet und ihre mittel- und südosteuropäischen Beziehungen.* Beiheft zur Atlas d. Urgesch., Hamburg.

Hachmann, R. 1960 Die Chronologie der jüngeren vorrömischen Eisenzeit. *Bericht der Römisch-Germanischen Kommission* 41.

Hachmann, R. 1970 *Die Goten und Skandinavien.* Berlin.

Hachmann, R. 1990 Gundestrup-studien. Untersuchungen zu den spätkeltischen Grundlagen der frühgermanischen Kunst. *Bericht der Römisch-Germanischen Kommission,* Band 71.

Hachmann, R., Kossack, G. and Kuhn, H. 1962 *Völker zwischen Germanen und Kelten.* Neumünster.

Haffner, A. 1976 *Die westliche Hunsrück-Eifel Kultur.* Röm. Germ. Forsch. 36.

Haffner, A. (ed.) 1989a *Gräber-Spiegel des Lebens.* Zum Totenbrauchtum der Kelten und Römer am Beispiel des Treverer-Gräberfeldes Wederath-Belginum. Mainz an Rhein: Phillip von Zabern.

Haffner, A. 1989b Das Gräberfeld von Wederath-Belginum vom 4. Jahrhundert vor bis nach 4. Jahrhundert nach Christi Geburt. In A. Hafner (ed.).

Haffner, A. 1989c Das spätlatenezeitliche Kriegergrab 1178 mit Feinwaage. In A. Haffner (ed.).

Haffner, A. and Joachim, J.-L. 1984 Die keltischen Wagengräber der Mittelrheingruppe. In M. Gustin and L. Pauli (eds.).

Hagberg, U. E. 1988 The bronze shields from Fröslunda near Lake Vänern, West Sweden. In B. Hårdh, *et al.* (eds.), *Trade and Exchange in Prehistory.* Studies in Honour of Bertha Stjernquist. Acta Arch. Lundensia. Series in 8, No. 16.

Hagberg, U.E. and Jacobzon, L. 1986 Bronssköldarna från Fröslunda- Ett europeisk praktfynd vid Vänern. *Västergötlands Fornminnesförenings Tidsskrift.*

Hägg, R. (ed.) 1983 *The Greek Renaissance of the Eighth Century B.C.: Tradition and Innovation.* Proceedings of the Second International Symposium at the Swedish Institute in Athens, 1–5 June, 1981. Acta Instituti Atheniensis Regni Suenciae, Series in 4, 30. Stockholm.

Hall, J. A. 1986 *Powers and Liberties. The Causes and Consequences of the Rise of the West.* Penguin Books Basil Blackwell.

Hall, J. A. 1989 Towards a theory of social evolution: on state systems and ideological shells. In D. Miller, M. Rowlands and C. Tilley (eds.).

Hammond, N. G. L. 1976 *Migrations and Invasions in Greece and Adjacent Areas.* New Jersey: Noyes Press.

Hammond, N. G. L. 1982 Illyrus, Epirus and Macedonia in the Early Iron Age. *The Cambridge Ancient History,* III, Part 1.

Hancar, F. 1966 Die bronzenen 'Pferdekopfszepter' aus der Hallstattzeit in archäologischer Ostperspective. *Arch. Austriaca* 40.

Hankey, V. 1987 The chronology of the Aegean Late Bronze Age. In P. Åström (ed.), *High, Middle or Low?* Acts of an International Colloquium on Absolute Chronology held at the University of Gothenburg 20th–22nd August 1987. Paul Åströms Förlag. Gothenburg.

Hänsel, B. 1968 *Beiträge zur Chronologie der mittleren Bronzezeit im Karpatenbecken.* Beitr. zur Ur- und Frühgesch. Arch. des Mittelmeer-Kulturraumes, Band 7–8, Bonn.

Hänsel, B. 1973 Eine Datierte Rapierklinge mykenischen Typs von der unteren Donau. *Prähist. Zeitschrift* 48.

Hänsel, B. 1976 *Beiträge zur regionalen und chronologischen Gliederung der älteren Hallstattzeit an der unteren Donau* I–II. Beiträge zur Ur- und Frühgesch. Arch. des Mittelmeer-Kulturraumes, Bd. 16–17. Bonn: Rudolf Hablet.

Hänsel, B. 1977 Zur historischen Bedeutung der Theisszone um das 16. Jahrhundert v. Chr. *Jahresber. des Inst. f. Vorgesch. der Universität Frankfurt a. M.*

Hänsel, B. 1981 Zum Spätbronzezeitlichen Geschehen im Raum nördlich der Ägäis. *Symposia Thracica A.* Int. Symp. über das Spätneol. und der Bronzezeit, Xanthi 4–10 Okt. 1981

Hänsel, B. 1982a (ed.) *Südosteuropa zwischen 1600 und 1000 v. Chr.* Prähistorische Arch. in Südosteuropa, Band 1, Berlin.

Hänsel, B. 1982b Südosteuropa zwischen 1600 und 1000 v. Chr. In B. Hänsel (ed.) *Südosteuropa zwischen 1600 und 1000 v. Chr.* Prähistorische Archäologie in Südosteuropa, Band 1, Berlin.

Hänsel, B. 1982c Burgenbau und Zentrumsbildung im spätbronzezeitlichen Südosteuropa nördlich der Ägäis. In V. Furmanek and F. Horst (eds.).

Hänsel, B. 1986 Interdisziplinäre Zusammenarbeit bei archäologischen Ausgrabungen am Beispiel einer Ausgrabung in Nordgriechenland (Kurzfassung).

Hänsel, B. and Kalicz, N. 1986 Das Bronzezeitliche Gräberfeld von Mezösát, Kom. Borsod, Nordostungam. *Bericht der Römisch-Germanischen Kommission*, 67.

Hänsel, B. and Medovic, P. 1991 Vorbericht über die jugoslawisch-deutschen Ausgrabungen in der Siedlung von Feudvar bei Mosorin (Gem. Titel, Vojvodina) von 1986–1990. *Bericht der Römisch-Germanischen Kommission*, Band 72.

Harbsmeier 1986 Danmark: nation, køn og kultur. *Stofskifte, tidsskrift for antropologi* 13. Tema: Denmark.

Harch, O. 1988 Zur Herkunft der nordischen Prachtwagen aus der jüngeren vorrömischen Eisenzeit. *Acta Arch.* 59.

Harding, A. (ed.) 1982 *Climatic Change in Later Prehistory*. Edinburgh University Press.

Harding, A. F. 1984 *The Myceneans and Europe*. London, New York: Academic Press.

Harding, A. 1987 Social and economic factors in the origin and development of the Urnfield cultures. In E. Plesl and J. Hrala (eds.), *Die Urnenfelderkulturen Mitteleuropas*. Symposium Liblice 21.–25.10. 1985. Praha.

Harding, A. F. 1989 Mycenaean relations with central and western Europe. In *Dynamique du bronze moyen en Europe occidentale*.

Harding, A. 1990 The Wessex connection: developments and perspectives. In: *Orientalische-ägäische Einflüsse*.

Harding, A. 1992 Late Bronze Age swords between Alps and Aegean. *Universitätsforschungen zur Prähistorischen Archäologie*. Band 8. Festschrift zum 50jähringen Bestehen des Institutes für Ur-und Frühgeschichte der Leopold-Franzens-universität Innsbruck. Rudolf Habelt, Bonn.

Harding, A. and Tait, W. J. 1989 'The beginning of the end': progress and prospects in Old World chronology. *Antiquity*, 63.

Härke, H. 1979 *Settlement Types and Settlement Patterns in the West Hallstatt Province*. B. A. R. International Series 57. Oxford.

Härke, H. 1982 Early Iron Age hill settlements in west central Europe. *Oxford Journal of Archaeology* 1.

Härke, H. 1989 Transformation or collapse? Bronze Age to Iron Age settlement in west central Europe. In M. L. Sørensen and R. Thomas (eds).

Harmatta, J. 1968 Früheisenzeitliche Beziehungen zwischen dem Karpatenbecken, Oberitalien und Griechenland. *Acta Arch. Hungarica* 20.

Harrison, R. J. 1988 *Spain at the Dawn of History. Iberians, Phoenicians and Greeks*. London: Thames and Hudson.

Harrison, R. J. 1994 The Bronze Age in northern and northeastern Spain 2000–800 BC. In C. Mathers and S. Stoddart (eds.), *Development and Decline in the Mediterranean Bronze Age*. Sheffield Arch. Monographs 8.

Harrison, R. J. and Craddock, P. T. 1983 A study of the Bronze Age metalwork from the Iberian Peninsula in the British Museum. *Ampurias* 43.

Harrison, R. J. and Gilman, A. 1977 Trade in the second and third millennium BC: between the Magrels and Iberia. In V. Markotic (ed.), *Ancient Europe and the Mediterranean: Studies in Honour of Hugh O. Hencken*. Warminster, Wilts., Aris and Phillips.

Hase, F.-W. von. 1969 *Die Trensen der Früheisenzeit in Italien*. Praehist. Bronzefunde XVI, 1. Bd.

Hase, F.-W. von. 1990 Ägäische Importe im Zentralen Mittelmeergebiet in späthelladischer Zeit (SH I-SH III C). In: *Orientalische-ägäische Einflüsse*.

Hatt, J.-J. 1988 Invasion ou acculturation? Conditions régionales de la diffusion de la culture des Champs d'Urnes en France. Maintien des traditions Champs d'Urnes et conséquences sur l'évolution de la religion. In P. Brun and C. Mordant (eds.), *Le groupe*

Rhin-Suisse-France orientale et la notion de civilisation des Champs d'Urnes. Mémoires du Musée de Préhistoire d'Ile-de France no. 1, Nemours.

Hawkes, C. 1976 Celts and cultures: wealth, power, art. In P.-M. Duval and C. Hawkes (eds.).

Hawkes, C. F. C. and Smith, M. A. 1957 On some buckets and cauldrons of the Bronze and early Iron Ages. *Antiquaries Journal* 37.

Hauser-Fischer, C. 1990 De Funde aus Spätbronze-Hallstatt und Latènezeit

Hayek, E. W. H. *et al.* 1989 Chemische Analyse von drei bronzezeitlichen Pechfunden. In: C. J. Becher *et al.*

Hazelgrove, C. 1986 Central places in British Iron Age studies: a review of some problems. In E. Grant (ed.), *Central Places, Archaeology and History.* Sheffield.

Hazelgrove, C. 1987 Culture process on the periphery: Belgic Gaul and Rome during the late Republic and early Empire. In M. Rowlands, M. T. Larsen, and K. Kristiansen (eds.).

Hedeager, L. 1978a Processes towards state formation in Early Iron Age Denmark. In K. Kristiansen and C. Paludan-Müller (eds.), *New Directions in Scandinavian Archaeology.* The National Museum, Copenhagen.

Hedeager, L. 1978b A quantitative analysis of Roman imports in Europe north of the Limes (0–400 A.D.), and the question of Roman-Germanic exchange. In K. Kristiansen and C. Paludan-Müller (eds.) *New Directions in Scandinavian Archaeology.* The National Museum, Copenhagen.

Hedeager, L. 1987 Empire, frontier and the barbarian hinterland: Rome and northern Europe from AD 1–400. In M. Rowlands, M. T. Larsen and K. Kristiansen (eds.), *Centre and Periphery in the Ancient World.* Cambridge University Press.

Hedeager, L. 1988 *Danernes land. Fra ca. år 200 f. Kr. – ca. 700 e. Kr.* København: Gyldendal og Politikens Danmarkshistorie, bind 2. Red. Olaf Olsen.

Hedeager, L. 1992 *Iron-Age Societies.* From Tribe to State in Northern Europe 500 BC to AD 700. Blackwell. Oxford.

Hedeager, L. and Kristiansen, K. 1988 Oldtid 4.000 f.Kr. – 1.000 e.Kr. In C. Bjørn (ed.) *Det danske landbrugs historie.* Odense: Landbohistorisk Selskab.

Hellström, P. 1980 Europas första smeder. In P. Hellström and A. Sandwall (eds.), *Trakerna.* Statens Historiska Museum, Stockholm

Helms, M. W. 1979 *Ancient Panama. Chiefs in Search of Power.* University of Texas Press, Austin and London.

Helms, M. W. 1986 Esoteric knowledge, geographical distance and the elaboration of leadership status: dynamics of resource control. Paper prepared for Conference on Ecology and Cultural Evolution in the Tropics, Ann Arbor, Michigan, 25–28 August 1986.

Helms, M. W. 1986 Thoughts on Public Symbols and Distant Domains Relevant to the Chiefdoms of Lower Central America. Paper to be published in volume on *Wealth and Hierarchy in Lower Central America*, Dumbarton Oaks, in press.

Helms, M. W. 1988 *Ulysses Sails. An Ethnographic Odyssey of Power, Knowledge, and Geographical Distance.* Princeton University Press.

Hencken, H. 1968 *Tarquinia, Villanovans and Early Etruscans.* American School of Prehistoric Research, Bulletin No. 23. Cambridge, Massachusetts.

Herity, M. and Eogan, G. 1976 *Ireland in Prehistory.* London: Routledge and Kegan.

Herodotus *The History.* Translated by David Green. University of Chicago Press 1987.

Herrman, F. R. 1966 *Die Funde der Urnenfelderkultur in Mittel- und Südhessen.* Römisch-Germanische Kommission Bd. 27. Berlin: De Gruyter.

Herrmann, J. 1982 Militärische Demokratie und die übergangsperiode zur Klassengesellschaft. *Etnographisch-Archäologische Zeitschrift,* 23.

Herrmann, J. 1988 Die Verterritorialisierung – ein methodisches und historisches Problem slawischer Wanderung, Landnahme und Ethnogenese. *Studia nad Etnogeneza Slowian* 1.

Hill, J. D. 1993 Can we recognise a different European past? A contrastive archaeology of later prehistoric settlements in southern England. *Journal of European Archaeology* 1(1).

Hill, J. D. 1996 Danebury and the hillforts of Iron Age Wessex: a return salvo. In T. Champion and J. Collis (eds.), *Recent Trends in Iron Age Archaeology*. Sheffield, J. R. Collis Publishers.

Hjärntner-Holdar, E. 1986 Early metallurgy in eastern Sweden. In B. Ambrosiani (ed.).

Hjärntner-Holdar, E. 1993 *Järnets och järnmetallurgiens introduktion i Sverige*. (The introduction of iron metallurgy to Sweden). Societas Archaeologica Upsaliensis. Uppsala.

Hobsbawm, E. and Ranger, T. (eds.) 1983 *The Invention of Tradition*. Cambridge University Press.

Hochstetter, A. 1980 *Die Hügelgräberbronzezeit in Niederbayern*. Bayerisches Landesamt für Denkmalpflege. Lassleben Kallmünz/Opf.

Hochstetter, A. 1982 Spätbronzezeitlichens und früheisenzeitliches Formengut in Makedonien und im Balkanraum. In B. Hänsel (ed.), *Südosteuropa zwioschen 1600 und 1000 v. Chr.* Prähistorische Arch. in Südosteuropa, Band 1. Berlin.

Hodder, I. (ed.) 1978a *The Spatial Organisation of Culture*. London: Duckworth.

Hodder, I. 1978b The spatial structure of material 'cultures': a review of some of the evidence. In I. Hodder (ed.).

Hodder, I. 1979 Social and economic stress and material culture patterning. *American Antiquity* 44.

Hodder, I. 1982a *Symbols in Action*. Cambridge University Press.

Hodder, I. (ed.) 1982b *Structural and Symbolic Archaeology*. New Directions in Archaeology. Cambridge University Press.

Hodder, I. 1986 *Reading the Past*. Current Approaches to Interpretation in Archaeology. Cambridge University Press.

Hoddinott, R. F. 1981 *The Thracians*. London.

Hodges, R. 1982 The evolution of gateway communities: their socio-economic implications. In C. Renfrew and S. Shennan (eds.).

Hodson, F. R. 1986 Methods for relating graves to social status: results from the Hallstatt cemetery. In E. Jerem (ed.).

Holste, F. 1953a *Die Bronzezeit in Süd- und Westdeutschland*. Handbuch der Urgeschichte Deutschlands 1, Berlin.

Holste, F. 1953b *Die bronzezeitlichen Vollgriffsschwerter Bayerns*. Münchener Beiträge zu Vor- und Fürhgeschichte, München.

Hoppe, M. 1986 *Die Grabfunde der Hallstattzeit in Mittelfranken*. Bayerisches Landesamt für Denkmalpflege, Band 55, Verlag M. Lassleben Kallmünz/Opf.

Horedt, K. 1974 Befestigte Siedlungen der spätbronze- und der Hallstattzeit im innerkarpatischen Rumänien. In B. Chropovsky (ed.), *Symposium zu Problemen der jüngeren Hallstattzeit in Mitteleuropa*. Verlag der Slowakischen Akademie der Wissenschaften, Bratislava.

Horne, D. 1984 *The Great Museum. The Re-Presentation of History*. Pluto Press. London and Sydney.

Horst, F. 1971 Hallstattimporte- und Einflüsse im Elb-Havel Gebiet. *Zeitschrift für Archäologie*. 5.

Horst, F. 1972 Jungbronzezeitliche Formenkreise im Mittelelb-Havel-Gebiet. *Jahresshcr. mitteldt. Vorgesch.* 56.

Horst, F. 1978 Die jüngbronzezeitlichen Stämme im nördlichen Teil der DDR. In W. Coblenz and F. Horst (eds.), *Mitteleuropäische Bronzezeit*. Beiträge zur Archäologie und Geschichte. Historiker-Gesellschaft der DDR, Berlin Akademie-Verlag.

Horst, F. 1982 Die jungbronzezeitlichen Burgen im nordwestlichen Teil der DDR. In V. Furmanek and F. Horst (eds.).

Horst, F. 1986a Ein jungbronzezeitliches Fernhandelszentrum im Gebiet von Brandenburg/Havel. In D. W. Buck and B. Gramsch (eds.).

Horst, F. 1986b Hallstattimporte und Einflüsse im Weser-Oder Raum. In E. Jerem (ed.).

Horst, F. 1989 Early Iron Age influences in the Weser-Oder area. In M. L. Sørensen and R. Thomas (eds.).

Horst, F. 1990 Bemerkungen zur chronologischen Einordnung der frühen und älteren Bronzezeit im mitteleuropäischen Raum. In V. Furmanek and F. Horst (eds.).

Horst, F. and Krüger, B. (eds.) 1986 *Produktivkräfte und Produktionsverhältnisse in ur- und frühgeschichtlicher Zeit.* Historiker-Gesellschaft der DDR, Berlin: Akademie-Verlag.

Horst, F. and Schlette, F. (eds.) 1988 *Frühe Völker in Mitteleuropa.* Berlin: Akademie Verlag.

Höchmann, O. 1987 Beiträge zur Datierung des Brandgrabes mit gegossenem Bronzebecken von Winzlar; Kr. Nienburg. *Jahrbuch des Römisch-Germanische Zentralmuseums Mainz* 34.

Hrala, J. 1990 Hügelgräberzeitliche Grundlagen für die Herausbildung der frühurnenfelderzeitlichen Kulturen in Böhmen. In V. Furmanek and F. Horst (eds.).

Hrala, J. 1992 Die Massenbestattung auf dem Brandgräberfeld der Lausitzer Kultur in Velk Osek. *Archeologické rozhledy* 44.

Hrala, J., Sedlacek, Z. and Vavra, M. 1992 Velim: a hilltop site of the Middle Bronze Age in Bohemia. Report on the excavation 1984–90. *Památky Archeologické* 83.

Hundt, H. J. 1955 Versuch zur Deutung der Depotfunde der nordischen jüngeren Bronzezeit. *Jahrbuch der Römisch-Germanischen Zentralmuseums Mainz* 2.

Hundt, H. J. 1956a Jungbronzezeitliches Skeletgrab von Steinheim, Kr. Offenbach. *Germania* 34.

Hundt, H. J. 1956b Spätbronzezeitliches Doppelgrab im Frankfurt-Berkersheim. *Germania* 36.

Hundt, H. J. 1961 Beziehungen der 'Straubinger' Kultur zu den Frühbronzezeitkulturen der östlich benachbarten Räume. *Kommission für das Äneolithicum und die ältere Bronzezeit. Nitra 1958.* Bratislava.

Hundt, H. J. 1978 Die Rohstoffquellen des europäischen Nordens und ihr Einfluss auf der Entwicklung des nordischen Stils. *Bonner Jahrbücher* 178.

Husty, L. 1989 Eine Mädchenbestattung mit mittellatenezeitliche Gürtelkette. In A. Haffner (ed.).

Hüttel, H.-G. 1977 Altbronzezeitliche Pferdetrensen. *Jahr. Ber. Des Inst. für Vorgeschichte der Univ. Frankfurt a. M.*

Hüttel, H.-G. 1982 Zur Abkunft des danubischen Pferd-Wagen-Komplexes der Altbronzezeit. In B. Hänsel (ed.).

Ijzereef, G. F. 1981 *Bronze Age Animal Bones from Bovenkarpsel. The excavations at Het Valkje.* ROB, Amersfoort.

Irons, W. 1979 Political stratification among pastoral nomads. In *Pastoral Production and Society.* Edition de la Maison des Sciences de l'Homme, Paris, and Cambridge University Press.

Jaanusson, H. 1981 *Hallunda. A Study of Pottery from a Late Bronze Age Settlement in Central Sweden.* The Museum of National Antiquities, Stockholm. Studies 1.

Jaanusson, H. 1988 Beziehungen zwischen den lausitzer und nordischen Kulturprovinzen während der jüngeren Bronzezeit. In Z. Bukowski (ed).

Jaanusson, H. and Jaanusson, V. 1988 Sea salt as a commodity of barter in Bronze Age trade of northern Europe. In B. Hårdh *et al.* (eds.), *Trade and Exchange in Prehistory.* Studies in Honour of Berta Stjernquist. Acta Arch. Lundensia. Ser. 8, No. 16.

Jacob-Friesen, G. 1968 Ein Depotfund des Formenkreises um die 'Karpfenzungenschwerter' aus der Normandie. *Germania* 46.

Jacob-Friesen, G. 1970 Skjerne und Egemose. Wagenteile südlicher Provenienz in skandinavischen Funden. *Acta Arch.* 40.

Jäger, K.-D. 1987 Zur Rolle der Ackerbohne *Vicia faba L.* in Landwirtschaft und Brauchtum der Urnenfelderbronzezeit in Mitteleuropa. In E. Plesl and J. Hrala (eds.).

Jäger, K.-D. and Lozek, V. 1982 Environmental conditions and land cultivation during the Urnfield Bronze Age in Central Europe. In A. Harding (ed.), *Climatic Change in Later Prehistory*. Edinburgh University Press.

Jäger, K.-D. and Lozek, V. 1987 Landesaufbau zur Urnenfelderbronzezeit und während des Mittelalters im östlichen Mitteleuropa. In E. Plesl and J. Hrala (eds.).

Jahresbericht des Instituts für Vorgeschichte der Universität Frankfurt a. M. 1975 Referate des Kolloquiums über die *Geschichte des 13. und 12. Jh. v. Chr.* am 3/4 Okt. 1975 im Frankfurter Inst. für Vorgeschichte.

Jahresbericht des Instituts für Vorgeschichte der Universität Frankfurt a. M. 1976 Referate des Fortsetzungskolloquiums über die *Geschichte des 13. und 12. Jahrhunderts v. Chr.* am 24. Februar 1976 im Frankfurter Inst. für Vorgeschichte.

Jahresbericht des Instituts für Vorgeschichte der Universitat Frankfurt u. M. 1977 Referate des Kolloquiums über die *Geschichte des 16. Jahrhunderts v. Chr.* am 1/2 Dezember 1977 im Frankfurter Institut für Vorgeschichte.

James, P. 1991 in collaboration with Thorpe, I. J., Kokkinos, N., Morkot, R. and Frankish, J. *Centuries of Darkness. A challenge to the conventional chronology of Old World Archaeology*. Jonathan Cape, London.

Jannsen, W. 1985 Hortfunde der jüngeren Bronzezeit aus Nordbayern. Einführung in die Problematik. *Arch. Korrespondenzblatt* 15.

Jazdzewski, K. 1984 *Urgeschichte Mitteleuropas*. Warszawa.

Jelinek, J. 1993 Dismembering, filleting and evisceration of human bodies in a Bronze Age site in Moravia, Czech Republic. *Anthropologie* 31(3).

Jensen, J. 1965a Ulbjerg-graven. Begyndelsen af den ældre jernalder i Jylland (The beginning of the Early Iron Age in Jutland). *Kuml*.

Jensen, J. 1965b Bernsteinfunde und Bernsteinhandel der jüngeren Bronzezeit Dänemarks. *Acta Archaeologica (Acta Arch.)* 36.

Jensen, J. 1966 Griffzungenschwerter der späten nordischen Bronzezeit. *Acta Arch.* 37.

Jensen, J. 1967a Et jysk ravfund. Ravhandelen i yngre bronzealder (Ein jütländischer Bernsteinfund). *Kuml*.

Jensen, J. 1967b Zwei Abfallgruben von Gevninge, Seeland, aus der jüngeren Bronzezeit (Periode IV). *Acta Arch.* 37.

Jensen, J. 1967c Voldtoftefundet. Bopladsproblemer i yngre bronzealder i Danmark. *Aarbøger for nordisk Oldkyndighed og Historie*.

Jensen, J. 1969 Ein thrako-kimmerischer Goldfund aus Dänemark. *Acta Arch.* 40.

Jensen, J. 1973 Ein neues Hallstattschwert aus Dänemark. Beitrag zur Problematik der jungbronzezeitlichen Votivfunde. *Acta Arch.* 42.

Jensen, J. 1981 Et rigdomscenter fra yngre bronzealder på Sjælland (A Late Bronze Age Centre of Wealth on Zealand). *Aarbøger for Nordisk Oldkyndighed og Historie*.

Jensen, J. 1982 *Nordens guld*. En bog om oldtidens rav, mennesker og myter. Gyldendal.

Jensen, R. 1986 The Bronze Age in eastern central Sweden – heaps of fire cracked stones and the settlement pattern. In B. Ambrosiani (ed.).

Jensen, J. 1987 Bronze Age Research in Denmark 1970–1985. *Journal of Danish Archaeology* 6.

Jensen, J. 1988 Ur-europæeren. In H. Boll-Johansen, and M. Harbsmeier (eds.), *Europas opdagelse*. Historien om en ide. Copenhagen.

Jensen, J. 1994 The turning point. In K. Kristiansen and J. Jensen (eds.), *Europe in the 1st Millennium BC*. Sheffield University.

Jeppesen, J. and Madsen, H. J. 1988–89 Stormandsgård og kirke i Lisbjerg (A nobleman's farm and church in Lisbjerg). *Kuml*.

Jerem, E. (ed.) 1986 *Hallstatt Kolloquium Veszprem 1984*. Budapest.

Jerem, E., Facsar, G., Kordos, L., Krolopp, E. and Vörös, I. 1985 A Sopron-Krautackeren feltart vaskori telep régészeti és környezetrekonstrukciós vizsgálata II (Summary: The archaeological and environmental investigation of the Iron Age settlement discovered at

Sopron-Krautackern II.) *Különlenyomat az archeologiai értesíto 112.* Évfolyam 1985. Évi I. Számából. Budapest.

Jockenhövel, A. 1971 *Die Rasiermesser in Mitteleuropa.* Prähistorische Bronzefunde VIII, I. Bd. München.

Jockenhövel, A. 1972 Westeuropäische Bronzen aus der späten Bronzezeit in Südwest-deutschland. *Arch. Korrespondenzblatt 2.*

Jockenhövel, A. 1974 Eine Bronzeamphore des 8. Jahrhunderts v. Chr. von Gellinghausen, Kr. Meschede (Sauerland), Mit Beitragen von Hans Beck, Hans Jürgen Hundt und Günter Lange. *Germania 52.* I. Halbband.

Jockenhövel, A. 1980 *Die Rasiermesser in Westeuropa.* Prähistorische Bronzefunde VIII, 3. Band. München.

Jockenhövel, A. 1981 Zu einigen Späturnenfelderzeitlichen Bronzen der Rhein-Main Gebietes. In *Studien zur Bronzezeit.* Festschrift für Wilhelm Albert v. Brunn. Mainz: Phillip von Zabert.

Jockenhövel, A. 1982 Jungbronzezeitlichen Burgenbau in Süddeutschland. In V. Furmanek and F. Horst (eds.).

Jockenhövel, A. 1986 Struktur und Organisation der Metallverarbeitung in urnenfelderzeit-lichen Siedlungen Süddeutschlands. In D.-W. Buch and B. Gramsch (eds.).

Jockenhövel, A. 1990 Bronzezeitliche Burgenbau in Mitteleuropa. Untersuchungen zur Struk-tur frühmetallzeitlicher Gesellschaften. In: *Orientalisch-ägäische Einflüsse.*

Jockenhövel, A. 1991 Räumliche Mobilität von Personen in der mittleren Bronzezeit des westlichen Mitteleuropa. *Germania 69.*

Jockenhövel, A. and Ostorja-Zagorski, J. 1987 Möglichkeiten einer Wirtschaftsarchäologis-chen Gliederung urnenfelderseitlichen Kulturgruppen Mitteleuropas? In E. Plesl and J. Hrala (eds.).

Joffroy, R. 1954 *La Tombe de Vix.* Fondation Eugène Piot. Monuments et Mémoires 48,1. Paris.

Joffroy, R. 1957 (1958) *Les sépultures a char du premier Age du Fer en France.* Revue Arché-ologique de l'Est et du Centre-Est 8.

Joffroy, R. 1960 *L'Oppidum de Vix et la civilization hallstattienne finale.* Publications de l'Université de Dijon 20. Paris.

Johnson, A. W. and Earle, T. 1987 *The Evolution of Human Societies. From Foraging Groups to Agrarian State.* Stanford University Press.

Jones, R. E. and Vagnetti, L. 1991 Traders and craftsmen in the central Mediterranean: archaeological evidence and archaeometric research. In N. H. Gale (ed.).

Jorge, S. O. 1988 Reflexoes sobre a Pre-Historia Recente do Norte de Portugal. *Actas do Colloquio de Arqueologia do Noroeste Peninsular,* vol. 1, SPAE, Porto.

Jorge, S. O. 1992 An approach to the social dynamics of northern Portugal's late prehistory. *Institute of Archaeology Bulletin, London,* No. 29.

Jovanovic, B. 1979 The formation of the Scordisci on the basis of archaeological and historical sources. In P.-M. Duval and V. Kruta (eds.).

Kahm-Brochnow, A.-R. 1988 *Die Bronzenadeln in Nordbayern. Die früh- und hügelbronzezeit-lichen Nadels mit Öse und Durchlochung.* Bad Dürrheim.

Kalicz, N. and Kalicz-Schreiber, R. (eds.), *Die Frühbronzezeit im Karpatenbecken und in den Nachbargebieten.* Internationales Symposium 1977 Budapest-Velem. Mitt. des Arch. Inst. der Ungarischen Akad. der Wiss. Beiheft 2, Budapest.

Karageorghis, V. 1984 Cyprus. In J. Boardman, (ed.), *The Cambridge Ancient History.*

Katicic, R. 1991 Die Quellenaussagen zur Paläoethnologie des zentralen Balkanraumes. In A. Benac *et al.* (eds.).

Kaul, F. 1988 *Da våbnene tav.* Copenhagen.

Kaul, F., Marazov, I., Best, J. and De Vries, N. 1991 *Thracian Tales on the Gundestrup Cauldron.* Najade Press, Amsterdam.

Kaus, K. 1981 Herrschaftsbereiche der Kalenderbergkultur. In C. Eibner and A. Eibner (eds.).

Kemenczei, T. 1982 Der spätbronzezeitliche Burgenbau in Nordungarn. In V. Furmanek and F. Horst (eds.).

Kemenczei, T. 1983) (Summary: Der früheisenzeitliche Hortfund von Prügny). *Communicationes Archeologicae Hungariae*.

Kemenczei, T. 1984 *Die Spätbronzezeit Nordostungarns*. Arch. Hungarica Series, Nova LI, Budapest.

Kemenczei, T. 1986 Zur Problematik der früheisenzeitlichen Geschichte Ostungarns. In D.-W. Buch and B. Gramsch (eds.).

Kemenczei, T. 1988a Der Pferdegeschirrfund von Fügöd. *Acta Archaeologica Hungaricae* 40.

Kemenczei, T. 1988b Zu den Beziehungen zwischen dem ungarischen Donau-Theissraum und dem NW-Balkan in der Früheisenz. *Folia Archaeologica* 39.

Kemenczei, T. 1989 Bemerkungen zur Chronologie der spätbronzezeitlichen Grabfunde im Fonau-Theiss Zwischenstromgebiet. *Communicationes Archaeologicae Hungariae*.

Kemenczei, T. 1990 Der ungarische Donauraum und seine Beziehungen am Ende der Hügelgräberbronzezeit. In V. Furmanek and F. Horst (eds.).

Kenk, R. 1986 *Grabfunde der Skythenzeit aus Tuva, Süd-Sibirien*. Materialien zur Allgemeinen und Vergleichenden Archäeologie, Band 24. München: Beck.

Keyes, C. (ed.) 1981 *Ethnic Change*. University of Washington Press.

Khazanov, A. M. 1978 The early state among the Scythians. In H. J. M. Claessen and P. Skalnik (eds.), *The Early State*. New Babylon, Studies in Social Sciences 32. The Hague, Paris, New York: Mouton Publishers.

Khazanov, A. M. 1984 *Nomads and the Outside World*. Cambridge University Press.

Kiekebusch, A. 1911 Die Ausgrabungen eines bronzezeitlichen Dorfes bei Busch in der nähe Berlin. *Praehist. Zeitschrift* 2.

Kilian, K. 1970 Zum Beginn der Hallstattzeit in Italien im Ostalpenraum. *Jahrb. Röm. Germ. Zentralmuseum Mainz* 17.

Kilian, K. 1985 Violinbogenfibeln und Blattbügelfibeln des griechischen Festlandes aus Mykenischer Zeit. *Prähistorische Zeitschrift*, 60 Band, Heft 2. Berlin and New York.

Kilian-Dirlmeier, I. 1985 Fremde Weihungen in Griechischen Heiligtümer von 8. bis zum beginn des 7. Jahrhunderts v. Chr. *Jahrbuch des Römisch-Germanischen Zentralmuseums Mainz* 32.

Kilian-Dirlmeier, I. 1986 Beobachtungen zu den Schachtgräbern von Mykenai und zu den Schmuckbeigaben mykenischer Männergräber. Untersuchungen zur Sozialstruktur in Späthelladischer Zeit. *Jahrbuch des Römisch-Germanischen Zentralmuseums Mainz* 33(1).

Kilian-Dirlmeier, I. 1989 Das Kuppelgrab von Vapheio: die Beigabenausstattung in der Steinkiste. Untersuchungen zur Sozialstruktur in späthellandischer Zeit. *Jahrb. Röm.-Germ. Zentralmuseums Mainz* 36.

Kimmig, W. 1949/50. Ein Grabfund der jüngeren Urnenfelderzeit von Singen am Hohentwiel. *Prähistorische Zeitschrift*, 34/35.

Kimmig, W. 1980 Zu einigen Späthallstattfibeln östlichen Zuschnitts von der Heuneburg. *Situla* 20/21, Ljubljana.

Kimmig, W. 1982 Die griechische Kolonisation im westlichen Mittelmeergebiet und ihre Wirkung auf die Landschaften des westlichen Mitteleuropa. *Jahrbuch des Römisch-Germanisches Zentralmuseums Mainz* 30.

Kimmig, W. 1983 *Die Heuneburg an der oberen Donau*. 2. völlig neubearbeitete Auflage. Führer zu archäologischen Denkmälern in Baden-Württemberg. Konrad Theiss Verlag.

Kimmig, W. 1988a La Heuneburg sur le Danube supérieur et ses relations avec les pays méditerranéens. In *Les Princes Celtes et la Méditerranée*.

Kimmig, W. 1988b *Das Kleinaspergle*. Studien zu einem Fürstengrabhügel der frühen

Latènezeit bei Stuttgart. Landesdenkmalamt Baden-Württemberg, Forsch. und Ber. zur Vor-und Frühgeschichte in Baden-Württemberg 30. Konrad Theiss, Stuttgart.

Kirch, P. 1987 Lapita and oceanic cultural origins: excavations in the Mussau Islands, Bismarck Archipelago, 1985. *Journal of Field Archaeology* 14.

Kirch, P. 1991 Chiefship and competitive involution: the Marquesas Islands of eastern Polynesia. In T. Earle (ed.).

Klejn, L. S. 1974 Kossinna a im Abstand von vierzig Jahren. *Jahresschrift für mitteldeutsche Vorgeschichte* 58.

Klejn, L. S. 1982 *Archaeological Typology*. BAR International Series 153. Oxford.

Klengel, H. 1978 Vorderasien und Ägäis. Ein Überblick über den bronzezeitlichen Handel. In W. Coblenz and F. Horst (eds.).

Klengel, H. 1984 Near Eastern trade and the emergence of interaction with Crete in the third millennium B.C. *Studi Micenei ed Egeo-Anatolici*. Fasc. XXIV. In memoria di Piero Meriggi. Roma.

Klengel, H. 1990 Bronzezeitlichen handel im vorderen Orient: Ebla und Ugarit. In *Orientalisch-ägäische Einflüsse in der europäischer Bronzezeit: Ergebrisse eines Colloquiums.* Römisch-Germanisches Zentralmuseum bd. 15. Bonn, Habell.

Kleppe, E. J. 1977 Archaeological material and ethnic identification. A study of Lappish material from Varanger. *Norwegian Arch. Review* 10(1–2).

Klindt-Jensen, O. 1953 *Bronzekedlen fra Brå* (The bronze cauldron from Brå). Jysk Arkæologisk Selskabs Skrifter, Bind III, Aarhus.

Kloss, K. 1986 Pollenanalytische Untersuchungen in einer Billendorfer Kulturschicht bei Lübben-Steinkirchen, Oberspreewald. In D. W. Buch and B. Gramsch (eds.).

Knapp, A. B. 1988 Copper production and eastern Mediterranean trade: the rise of complex society on Cyprus. In J. Gledhill, B. Bender and M. T. Larsen (eds.).

Knapp, A. B. 1990 Ethnicity, entrepreneurship, and exchange: Mediterranean inter-island relations in the Late Bronze Age. *The Annual of the British School at Athens,* No. 85.

Knapp, A. B. 1991 Spice, drugs, grain and grog: organic goods in Bronze Age East Mediterranean trade. In N. H. Gale (ed.).

Knez, T. 1974 Hallstattzeitliche Hügelgräber in Novo mesto. In B. Chropovsky (ed.).

Knez, T. 1981 Novo mesto in der Hallstattzeit. In C. Eibner and A. Eibner (eds.).

Koch, J. T. 1991 Eriu, Alba, and Letha: when was a language ancestral to Gaelic first spoken in Ireland? *Emania* 9. Bull. of the Navan Research Group, Belfast.

Koenig, M.-P., Lambert, G., Piningre, J.-F. and Plouin, S. 1989 La Civilisation des tumulus en Alsace et le groupe de Haguenau: aspects chronologiques et culturels. In *Dynamique du bronze moyen en Europe occidentale.*

Kohl, P. 1987 The ancient economy, transferable technologies and the Bronze Age world-system: a view from the northeastern frontier of the Ancient Near East. In M. Rowlands, M. T. Larsen and K. Kristiansen (eds): *Centre and Periphery in the Ancient World.* Cambridge University Press.

Kohl, P. 1988 Ethnic strife and the advent of iron. Paper delivered at the 'Völksbewegung und Klassenkämpfe – Triebkräfte früher Gesellschaftsentwicklung' Tagung Berlin, DDR, December 1988.

Kokabi, M. 1990 Ergebnisse der osteologischen Untersuchungen an den Knochenfunde von Hornstaad im Vergleich zu anderen Feuchtbodenfundkomplexen Südwestdeutschland. *Ber. der Römisch-Germanischen Komm.* 71(1).

Körber-Grohne, U. 1987 *Nutzplanzen in Deutschland*. Kulturgeschichte und Biologie. Theiss Verlag, Stuttgart.

Kossack, G. 1954a Pferdegeschirr aus Gräbern der älteren Hallstattzeit Bayerns. *Jahrbuch des Römisch-Germanischen Zentralmuseums Mainz* 1.

Kossack, G. 1954b *Studien zur Symbolgut der Urnenfelder- und Hallstattzeit Mitteleuropas.* Berlin.

Kossack, G. 1959 *Südbayern während der Hallstattzeit.* Römisch-Germanische Forschungen, Band 24. Berlin: Verlag Walter de Gruyter and Co.

Kossack, G. 1970 *Gräberfelder der Hallstattzeit an Main und fränkischer Saale.* Materialhefte zur Bayerischen Vorgeschichte, Heft 24. Verlag Mich. Lassleben Kallmünz.

Kossack, G. 1971 The construction of the felloe in the Iron Age spoked wheels. In J. Boardman and M. A. Brown (eds.), *The European Community in Later Prehistory.* Studies in honour of C. E. C. Hawkes.

Kossack, G. 1974 Prunkgräber. Studien zur vor- und frühgeschichtlichen Archäologie. In *Festschrift für Joachim Werner zum 65. Geburtstag.* Münchener Beitr. zur Vor- und Frühgeschichte.

Kossack, G. 1980 'Kimmerische' Bronzen. *Situla* 20–21, Zbornik posvecen Stanetu Gabrovcu ob sestdesetl etnici. Ljubljana.

Kossack, G. 1982 Früheisenzeitlicher Güteraustausch. *Savaria* 16, Bulletin der Museen Komitats Vas.

Kossack, G. 1983 Tli Grab 85. Bemerkungen zum Beginn des Skythenzeitlichern Formenkreises im Kaukasus. *Beiträge zur Allgemeinen und Vergleichenden Archäologie,* Band 5.

Kossack, G. 1986 Zaumzeug aus Kelermes. In *Hallstatt Kolloquium Veszprem 1984.* Mitt. Arch. Inst. Beiheft 3. Budapest.

Kossack, G. 1987 Von den Anfängen des skytho-iranischen Tierstils. In H. Franke (ed.), *Skythika.* Vorträge sur Entstehung des skytho-iranischen Tierstils und zu Denkmälern des Bosporanischen Reichs. Bayerische Akademie der Wissenschaften. Phil.-Hist-Klasse. Abh. Neue Folge, Heft 98. München.

Kossack, G. 1988 Pferd und Wagen in der frühen Eisenzeit Mitteleuropas-Technik, Überlieferungsart und ideeller Gehalt. *Münchener Beitrage zur Völkerkunde,* Band 1. Festschrift Laszlo Vajda. München: Hirmer Verlag.

Kossack, G., Behre, K.-E. and Schmid, P. (eds.) 1984 *Archäologische und naturwissenschaftliche Untersuchungen an ländlichen und frühstädtischen Siedlungen in deutschen Küstengebiet vom 5. Jahrhundert v. Chr. bis zum 11. Jahrhundert n. Chr.* Band 1, Ländliche Siedlungen. Acta Humaniora, DFG, Bonn.

Kostrzewski, J. (ed.) 1950a *Compte-rendu des fouilles de Biskupin en 1938–39 et 1946–48.* Poznan.

Kostrzewski, J. 1950b Les objects en bronze et en fer provenant de l'enciente fortifiée de la civilisation Lusacienne à Biskupin. In J. Kostrzewski (ed.).

Kostrzewski, J. 1958 Die nördliche Peripherie der Lausitzer Kultur. *Arch. Polona* 1.

Köszegi. F. 1983 World history and the Urnfield culture. *Savaria* 16. Nord–Süd Beziehungen. Int. Koll. 1982 Bozsok-Szombathely.

Koutecky, D. 1968 Zusammenfassung: Grossgräber, ihre Konstruktion, Grabritus und soziale Struktur der Bevölkerung der Bylaner Kultur. *Pamatky Arch.* 59.

Kovacs, T. 1981 Zur Problematik der Entstehung der Hügelgräber in Ungarn. *Slovenska Archeologia* 29(1).

Kovacs, T. 1982 Befestigungsanlagen um die Mitte des 2. Jahrtausends v.u.Z. in Mittelungarn. In V. Furmanek and F. Horst (eds.).

Krader, L. 1963 *Social Organisation of the Mongol-Turkish Pastoral Nomads.* The Hague, Mouton.

Krader, L. 1979 The origin of the state among the nomads of Asia. In *Pastoral Production and Society.* Edition de la Maison des Sciences de l'Homme, Paris, and Cambridge University Press.

Krause, E.-B. 1989 Zur Hallstattzeit an Mosel, Mittel- und Niederrhein Kulturelle Beziehungen zwischen der Laufelder Gruppe und dem Niederrhein während der frühen Eisenzeit. In M. Ulrix-Closset and M. Otte (eds.).

Krause, R. 1988a *Die endneolitischen und frühbronzezeitlichen Grabfunde auf der Nordstatterrasse von Singen am Hohenwiel.* Forschungen und Berichte zur Vor- und Frühgeschichte in Baden-Württemberg 32. Conrad Theiss, Stuttgart.

Krause, R. 1988b Ein alter Grabfund der jüngeren Frühbronzezeit von Reutlingen. Anmerkungen zur Frühbronzezeit Südwestdeutschlands. *Fundberichte aus Baden-Württemberg*, Bd. 13.

Krause, R. 1989 Early tin and copper metallurgy in south-western Germany at the beginning of the Early Bronze Age. In A. Hauptmann, E. Pernicka and G. Wagner (eds.), *Archäometallurgie der Alten Welt*. Beiträge zum Internationalen Symposium 'Old World Archaeometallurgy', Heidelberg 1987. Bochum.

Krause, R. 1990 Eine Siedlung der Urnenfelderzeit in Plaumloch, Gde Riesbürg, Ostalbkreis. *Fundber. Baden-Württemberg* 15.

Krause, R. and Wielandt, G. 1993 Eine keltische Viereckschanze bei Bopfingen am westrand des Rieses. Eine Vorbericht zu den Ausgrabungen und zur Interpretation der Anlage. *Germania.*

Kristensen, A. K. 1988 *Who were the Cimmerians, and where did they come from? Sargon II, the Cimmerians, and Rusa I.* The Royal Danish Academy of Sciences and Letters, Copenhagen.

Kristiansen, K. 1974a En kildekritisk analyse af depotfund fra Danmarks yngre Bronzealder (perode IV–V). Et bidrag til den arkæologiske kildekritik. (A source-critical analysis of hoards from the Late Danish Bronze Age (periods IV–V). A contribution to archaeological source criticism.) *Aarbøger for Nordisk Oldskyndighed og Historie.*

Kristiansen, K. 1974b Glerupfundet. Et depotfund med kvindesmykker fra bronzealderens femte periode. *Hikuin* 1. Århus.

Kristiansen, K. 1978 The consumption of wealth in Bronze Age Denmark. A study in the dynamics of economic processes in tribal societies. In K. Kristiansen and C. Paludan-Müller (eds.) *New Directions in Scandinavian Archaeology*, Studies in Scandinavian Prehistory and Early History 1. Copenhagen: National Museum Press.

Kristiansen, K. 1980 Besiedlung, Wirtschaftsstrategie und Bodennutzung in der Bronzezeit Dänemarks. *Prähistorische Zeitschrift* 55. Heft 1.

Kristiansen, K. 1981 A social history of Danish Archaeology (1805–1975). In Glyn Daniel (ed.), *Towards a History of Archaeology*. Thames and Hudson. London.

Kristiansen, K. 1982 The formation of tribal systems in later European prehistory: northern Europe, 4000–500 B.C.. In C. Renfrew, M. J. Rowlands and B. A. Segraves (eds.), *Theory and Explanation in Archaeology. The Southampton Conference.* New York: Academic Press.

Kristiansen, K. 1984a Ideology and material culture: an archaeological perspective. In M. Spriggs (ed.), *Marxist Perspectives in Archaeology.* Cambridge University Press.

Kristiansen, K. 1984b Krieger und Häuptlinge in der Bronzezeit Dänemarks. Ein Beitrag zur Geschichte des bronzezeitlichen Schwertes. *Jahrbuch des Römisch-Germanisches Zentralmuseums* 31.

Kristiansen, K. 1985a The place of chronological studies in archaeology. A view from the old world. *Oxford Journal of Archaeology* 4(3).

Kristiansen, K. (ed). 1985b *Archaeological Formation Processes. The Representativity of archaeological remains from Danish Prehistory.* The National Museum, Copenhagen.

Kristiansen, K. 1985c Bronze hoards from the Late Neolithic and Early Bronze Age; and Early Bronze Age burial finds. Both articles in K. Kristiansen (ed.).

Kristiansen, K. 1987a Center and periphery in Bronze Age Scandinavia. In M. Rowlands, M. T. Larsen and K. Kristiansen (eds.), *Centre and Periphery in Ancient World Systems.* Cambridge University Press.

Kristiansen, K. 1987b From stone to bronze: the evolution of social complexity in Northern Europe, 2300–1200 B.C. In M. Brumfield and T. K. Earle (eds.), *Specialization, Exchange and Complex Societies.* Cambridge University Press.

Kristiansen, K. 1989 Prehistoric migrations – the case of the Single Grave and Corded Ware cultures. *Journal of Danish Archaeology* 8.

Kristiansen, K. 1991 Chiefdoms, states and systems of social evolution. In T. Earle (ed.), *Chiefdoms – Economy, Power and Ideology.* Cambridge University Press.

Kristiansen, K. 1993 'The strength of the past and its great might', an essay on the use of the past. *Journal of European Archaeology* 1(1).

Kristiansen, K. 1994 The emergence of the European world system in the Bronze Age: divergence, convergence and social evolution during the first and second millennia BC in Europe. In K. Kristiansen and J. Jensen (eds.), *Europe in the First Millennium BC.* Sheffield.

Kristiansen, K. in press The theoretical cycle. A discussion of some universal oppositions in historical interpretation.

Kristiansen, K. and Jensen, J. (eds.) 1994 *Europe in the First millennium B.C.* Sheffield.

Kromer, K. 1958 Gedanken über den sozialen Aufbauder Bevölkerung auf dem Sulzberg bei Hallstatt, Oberösterreich. *Arch. Austriaca* 24.

Kromer, K. 1959 *Das Gräberfeld von Hallstatt.* Sansoni, Florence.

Kromer, K. 1980 Das Situlenfest. Versuch einer Interpretation der Dartellungen auf figural verzierten Situlen. *Situla* 20/21, Ljubljana.

Kromer, K. 1986 Das östliche Mitteleuropa in der frühen Eisenzeit (7.–5. Jh. v. Chr.). Seine Beziehungen zu Steppen Völkern und antikken Hochkulturen. *Jahrbuch des Römisch-Germanischen Zentralmuseums Mainz* 33.

Krüger, B. 1977: Zum Problem germanischer Wanderungen. In F. Horst (ed.), *Archäologie als Geschichtswissenschaft.* Studien und Untersuchungen. Schriften zur Ur-und Frühgeschichte 30. Akademie Verlag Berlin.

Kruta, V. 1979 Duchov-Münzingen: nature et diffusion d'une phase laténienne. In P.-M. Duval and V. Kruta (eds.).

Kruta, V. 1982 Aspects unitaires et facies dans l' art Celtique du IVᵉ siècle avant notre ère: l' hypothèse d' un foyer Celto-Italique. In P.-M. Duval and V. Kruta (eds.).

Kruta, V. 1986 Les Celtes des Gaules d'après l'archéologie. In K. H. Schmidt and R. Ködderitzsch (eds.).

Kruta, V. 1988 L'art celtique laténien du Vᵉ siècle avant J.-C.: le signe et l'image. In *Les Princes celtes et la Méditerranée.*

Kubach, W. 1978/88 Deponierungen und Mooren der südhessischen Oberrheinebene. *Jahresber. Inst. Vorgesch. d. Univ. Frankfurt a. M.*

Kubach, W. 1983 Bronzezeitliche Deponierungen im Nordhessischen sowie im Weser und Leinebergland. *Jahrbuch des Römisch-Germ. Zentralmuseums Mainz.*

Kubach, W. 1985 Einstück und Mehrstückdeponierungen und ihre Fundplätze. *Arch. Korrespondenzblatt* 15.

Kubach-Richter, I. 1990 Verbreitungsbilder bronzezeitlichen Arm- und Beinschmucks am Übergang von der Hügelgräber – zur Urnenfelderzeit – Beispiele für regional begrenztes Bronzehandwerk und weiträumige Kontakte. In V. Furmanek and F. Horst (eds.).

Kubach-Richter, I. and Kubach, W. 1989 Bronzezeitliche Hügelgräberkultur zwischen Rhein und Mosel. In *Dynamique du Bronze moyen en Europe Occidentale.*

Kull, B. 1989 Untersuchungen zur Mittelbronzezeit in der Türkei und ihrer Bedeutung für die absolute Datierung der europäischen Bronzezeit. *Praehistorische Zeitschrift* 64.

Küster, H. (ed.) 1988a *Der prähistorische Mensch und seine Umwelt.* Festschrift für Udelgard Körber Grohne zum 65. Geburtstag. Stuttgart: Theiss Verlag.

Küster, H. 1988b Urnenfelderzeitliche Planzenreste aus Burkheim, Gemeinde Vogtsburg, Kreis Breisgau-Hochschwarzwald (Baden-Württemberg). In H. Küster (ed.).

Kuznetsov, P. F. 1992 Disk cheek-pieces from the Late Bronze Age elite burials in the Volga region. *Symposia Thracologica* Nr. 9. Bibl. Thracologica Nr. 11. Bucuresti.

Kytlicova, O. 1967 Die Beziehungen der jung- und spätbronzezeitlichen Hortfunde südwärts und nordwärts des Erzgebirges. *Arb. u. Forsch. Ber. zu sächs. Bodendenkmalpfl.*, Bd. 16/17.

Kytlicova, O. 1975 Zur geschichtlichen Interpretation der böhmischen Bronzefunde von Beginn der Jungbronzezeit. *Jahresber. des Instituts für Vorgesch. der Universitäts Frankfurt a. M.*

Kytlicova, O. 1987 Ein Beitrag zur Gesellschaftlichen Gliederung und Eigenarten der böhmischen Urnenfeldergruppen. In E. Plesl and J. Hrala (eds.).

Kytlicova, O. 1988 K socialni strukture kultury popelni couych poli (zur sozialen Struktur der Urnenfelderzeit). *Pamatky Archeologicke* 79.

Lambert, G. and Millotte, J.-P. 1989 Sur les limites du groupe Hallstattien du Jura Franco-Suisse et de ses marges. In M. Ulrix-Closset and M. Otte (eds.).

Lambot, B. 1989 Les sanctuaires du bronze final et premier âge du fer en France septentrionale. In M. Ulrix-Closset and M. Otte (eds.).

Lamm, J. P. 1989 Hågafyndet tyvärr aktuelt igen. *Fornvännen* 84.

Lampe, W. 1982 *Ückeritz. Ein jungbronzezeitlicher Hortfund von der Insel Usedom.* Beiträge zur Ur- und Frühgeschichte der Bezirke Rostock, Schwerin und Neubrandenburg. Berlin.

Langlois, R. 1987 Le visage de la dame de Vix. In *Trésors des princes Celtes.* Paris.

Larsen, M. T. 1976 *The Old Assyrian City-State and its Colonies.* Mesopotamia 4. Copenhagen.

Larsen, M. T. 1987a Commercial networks in the Ancient Near East. In M. Rowlands, M. T. Larsen and K. Kristiansen (eds.).

Larsen, M. T. 1987b The Mesopotamian lukewarm mind. Reflections on science, divination and literacy. In F. Rochberg-Halton (ed.), *Language, Literature and History. Philological and Historical Studies Presented to Erica Reiner.* Chicago.

Larsen, M. T. 1988 Europas lys. In H. Boll-Johansen and M. Harbsmeier (eds.), *Europas opdagelse.* Historien om en ide. Copenhagen.

Larsen, M. T. 1989 Orientalism and Near Eastern archaeology. In D. Miller, M. Rowlands and C. Tilley (eds.).

Larsson, L. 1975 The Fogdarp find. A hoard from the late Bronze Age. *Medd. från Lunds Univ. Hist. Museum (MLUHM)* 1973–75.

Larsson, T. B. 1985 Multi-level exchange and cultural interaction in late Scandinavian Bronze Age. In K. Kristiansen (ed.), *Settlement and Economy in later Scandinavian Prehistory.* BAR Int. Ser. 211. Oxford.

Larsson, T. B. 1986 *The Bronze Age Metalwork in Southern Sweden. Aspects of Social and Spatial Organization 1800–500 B.C.* Archaeology and Environment 6. University of Umeå.

Larsson, T. B. 1988 A spatial approach to socioeconomic change in Scandinavia: Central Sweden in the first millennium B.C. In B. Gibson and M. Geselowitz (eds.).

Larsson, T. B. 1993 Vistad. Kring en befäst gård o Östergötland och östersjökontakter under yngre bronsålder. Studia Archaeologica Universitatis Umensis 4. University of Umeå.

Laszlo, A. 1977 Anfänge der Benutzung und der Bearbeitung des Eisens auf dem Gebiete Rumäniens. *Acta Arch. Hungaria* 29.

Laszlo, A. 1989 Les groupes régionaux anciens du Hallstatt à l'est des Carpates. La Moldavie aux XIIe–VIIe siècles av.n.è. In M. Ulrix-Closset and M. Otte (eds.).

Lattimore, O. 1979 Herdsmen, farmers, urban culture. In *Pastoral production and society.* Proceedings of the international meeting on nomadic pastoralism, Paris, 1–3 Dec. 1976. Cambridge University Press.

Layton, R. (ed.) 1988 *Who Needs the Past? Indigenous Values and Archaeology.* One World Archaeology 5. London, Unwin and Allen.

Lepage, L. 1988 Eléments R.S.F.O. dans la Haute Marne. In P. Brun and C. Mordant (eds.), *Le groupe Rhin-Suisse-France orientale et la notion de civilisation des Champs d'Urnes.* Mémoires du Musée de Préhistoire d'Ile-de France no. 1, Nemours.

Les Princes Celtes et la Méditerranée 1988 Rencontres de l'Ecole du Louvre. Paris: La Documentation Française.

Levinsen, K. 1989 The introduction of iron in Denmark. In M. L. S. Sørensen and R. Thomas (eds.).

Levy, Janet 1982 *Social and Religious Organisation in Bronze Age Denmark. An Analysis of Ritual Hoard Finds.* Oxford: BAR. International Series 124.

Lise-Kleber, H. 1990 Züge der Landschafts- und Vegetationsentwicklung in Pederseegebiet. Neolithicum und Bronzezeit. *Ber. Röm. Germ. Komm.* 71.

Littauer, M. A. and Crouwel, J. H. 1990 'The Trundholm horse's trappings: a chamfrein?' Reasons for doubting. *Antiquity* 65.

Litvinskii, B. A. 1989 The ecology of the ancient nomads of Soviet Central Asia and Kazakhstan. In G. Seaman (ed.), *Ecology and Empire. Nomads in the Cultural Evolution of the Old World.* University of Southern California, Los Angeles.

Liverani, M. 1987 The collapse of the Near Eastern regional system at the end of the Bronze Age: the case of Syria. In M. Rowlands, M. T. Larsen and K. Kristiansen (eds.), *Centre and Periphery in the Ancient World.* Cambridge University Press.

Lollini, D. G. 1979 I Senoni nell'Adriatico alla luce delle recenti Scoperte. In P.-M. Duval and V. Kruta (eds.).

Lopez, P. 1988 Estudio polinico de seis yacimientos del Surenste Espanol. *Trabajos de Prehistoria* 45.

Lorenz, H. 1978 *Totenbrauchtum und Tracht.* Untersuchungen zur regionalen Gliederung in der frühen Latènezeit. Bericht der Römisch-Germanischen Kommission 59.

Lorenz, H. 1985 Regional organisation in the western Early La Tène province: the Marne-Mosel and Rhine-Danube groups. In T. C. Champion and J. V. S. Megaw (eds.).

Lorenz, H. 1986 *Rundgang durch eine keltische 'Stadt'.* W. Ludwig Verlag.

Lorenzen, A. and Steffgen, U. 1990 Bemerkungen zur Leitformen der älteren vorrömischen Eisenzeit nördlich der Mittelgebirge. *Germania* 68.

Lorrio , A. J. 1991 Los Celtas en el Nordoeste. *Revista de arqueologia: Los Celtos en la Peninsula Iberica.*

Luka, L.J. 1966 *Kultura Wschodniopomorska na Pomorzu Gdanskim.* Biblioteka Archeologiczna, Tom 19. Wroclaw-Warszawa-Krakow.

Luka, L.J. 1969 Die Entstehung und Entwicklung der Ostpommerschen kultur der frühen Eisenzeit. *Ethn. Arch. Zeitschrift (EAZ)* 10.

Machortych, S. 1989 Kimmerier in Nordkaukasien. In R. Rolle *et al.* (eds.).

Maier, F. 1973 Keltische Altertümer in Griechenland. *Germania* 51.

Mair, L. 1977 *African Kingdoms.* Oxford: Clarendon Press.

Makkay, J. 1982 The earliest use of helmets in south east Europe. *Acta Arch. Hung.* 34.

Malinowski, T. 1983 L'ambre jaune baltique et le problème de son exportation pendant les premiers périodes de l'âge du fer. *Savaria* 16. Nord-Süd Beziehungen, Internationales Koll. 1982 Bozsok-Szombathely.

Malinowski, T. 1986 Über die Pommersche Kultur. *Zeitschrift für Archäologie* 20.

Malinowski, T. 1988a Les Caractères distinctifs de la civilisation Poméranienne. In Z. Bukowski (ed.).

Malinowski, T. 1988b Zur Geschichte der Stämme der Pommerschen Kultur. In F. Horst and F. Schlette (eds.), *Frühe Völker in Mitteleuropa.* Historiker Gesellschaft der DDR. Berlin: Akademie Verlag.

Malinowski, T. (ed.) 1990 *Problemy kultury Luzyckiej na Pomorzu.* Slupsk.

Mallory, J. P. 1989 *In Search of the Indo-Europeans. Language, Archaeology and Myth.* London: Thames and Hudson.

Mallory, J. P. 1991a Two perspectives on the problem of Irish origins. *Emania* 9. Bulletin of the Navan Research Group, Belfast.

Mallory, J. P. 1991b Migration and language change. Conference paper presented in Frederikstad, Norway, Dec. 1991.

Malmer, M. 1962 *Jungneolitische Studien. Acta Arch.* Lundensia Ser. 8(2), Lund.

Malmer, M. 1981 *A Chorological Study in North European Rock Art.* Antikvariska Serien 32, Stockholm.

Malmer, M. 1992 Weight systems in the Scandinavian Bronze Age. *Antiquity* 66.

Mandera, H.-E. 1972 Zur Deutung der späturnenfelderzeitlichen Hortfunde in Hessen. *Fundber. Hessen* 12.

Mandera, H.-E. 1985 Einige Bemerkungen zur Deutung Bronzezeitlicher Horte. *Arch. Korrespondenzblatt* 15.

Mann, M. 1986 *The Sources of Social Power*. Vol. 1. *A history of power from the beginning to A.D. 1960*. Cambridge Paperback Library.

Manning, S. 1988 The Bronze Age eruption of Thera: absolute dating, Aegean chronology and Mediterranean cultural interrelations. *Journal of Mediterranean Archaeology* 1(1).

Manning, S. W. and Weninger, B. 1992 A light in the dark: archaeological wiggle matching and the absolute chronology of the close of the Aegean Late Bronze Age. *Antiquity* 62(252).

Marazov, I. 1989 The gifts of the Odrysian kings. In A. Fol (ed.), *The Rogozen Treasure*. Sofia: Publishing House of the Bulgarian Academy of Sciences.

Marcenco, K. and Vinogradov, Y. 1989 The Scythian period in the northern Black Sea region (750–250 BC). *Antiquity* 63.

Marien, M. E. 1989 Aperçu de la periode hallstattienne en Belgique. In M. Otte and M. Ulrix-Closset (eds.).

Marinis, R. De 1988 Nouvelles données sur le commerce entre le monde méditerranéen et l'Italie septentrionale du VIIᵉ au Vᵉ siècle avant J.-C. In *Les Princes Celtes et la Méditerranée*.

Martín, C., Fernandez-Miranda, M., Fernandez-Posse M. D. and Gilman, A. 1993 The Bronze Age of La Mancha. *Antiquity* 67, No. 254.

Martins, M. 1988a *O povoado fortificado do Lago, Ainares*. Cadernos de Arqueologia Monograficas 1. Braga.

Martins, M. 1988b *A atânia de S Johao Vila Verde*. Cadernos Arq. Mon. 2. Braga.

Martins, M. 1989 *O Castro do Barbudo Vila Verdo*. Cadernos Arq. Mon. 3. Braga.

Martins, M. in press A Arqueologia dos castros no norte de Portugal: balanco e perspectivas de investigacao. *Trabathos de Antropologia e Etnologia*, Ponto.

Marx, K. 1973 *Grundrisse. Foundations of the Critique of Political Economy (Rough Draft)*. Penguin Books.

Matthäus, H. 1981 Spätmykenische und Urnenfelderzeitliche Vogelplastik. In *Studien zur Bronzezeit. Festschrift für Wilhelm Albert v. Brunn*. Verlag Phillip von Zabern. Mainz/ Rhein.

Matthäus, H. 1985 *Metallgefässe und Gefässuntersätze der Bronzezeit, der geometrischen und archaischen Periode auf Cypern*. Prähist. Bronzefunde II, 8.Bd.

May, J. 1976 The growth of settlement in the later Iron Age in Lincolnshire. In B. Cunliffe and T. Rowley (eds.).

Mazarakis, A. J. 1988 Early Greek temples – their origin and function. In R. Hägg, N. Marianatos and G. C. Nordquist (eds.), *Early Greek Cult Practice*. Stockholm.

McGuire, R. H. 1989 The greater Southwest as a periphery of Mesoamerica. In T. Champion (ed.).

Megaw, J.V. S. 1973 Style and style groupings in continental La Tène art. *World Archaeology* 3(2).

Megaw, J.V. S. 1979 Celtic art – products of travelling craftsmen or chieftainly vassals. In P.-M. Duval and V. Kruta (eds.).

Megaw, J. V. S. 1985 Meditations on a Celtic hobby-horse: notes towards a social archaeology of Iron Age art. In T. C. Champion and J. V. S. Megaw (eds.).

Megaw, R. and Megaw, V. 1989 *Celtic Art. From its Beginnings to the Book of Kells*. London: Thames and Hudson.

Mehrart, G. von 1952 Studien über einige Gattungen von Bronzegefässen. *Festschrift Röm. Germ. Zentralmuseum in Mainz* II. Mainz.

Meinander, C. F. 1985 Akozino, Achmylovo och mälaryxorna. *Finsk Museum.*

Meljukova, A. I. (ed.) 1989 *Stepii evropeiskai chasti CCCR f skifo-sarnatskoe vrenya.* Moscow

Mellink, M. J. 1964 (ed.) *Dark Ages and Nomads. Studies in Iranian and Anatolian Archaeology.* Istanbul, Nederlands Historisch-Archaeologisch Institut.

Mellink, M. and Masson, O. 1984 The native kingdoms of Anatolia. In J. Boardman (ed.), *The Cambridge Ancient History.*

Menke, A. 1972 *Die jüngere Bronzezeit in Holstein.* Topographisch-chronologische Studien. Karl Wachholtz Verlag, Neumünster.

Mihailov, G. 1984 The Thracians. In J. Boardman (ed.) *The Cambridge Ancient History.*

Miklaszewska-Balcer, R. 1991 Dating of the Lusatian culture fortified settlement at Biskupin (English summary). In J. Jaskanisa (ed.), *Prahistoryczny gród w Biskupinie.* Problematyka osiedli abronnych na poczatku epoki zelaza. Pánstwowe Muzeum Archeologiczne Biblioteka PMA. Warszawa.

Miller, D., Rowlands, M. and Tilley, C. (ed.). 1989 *Domination and Resistance.* One World Archaeology 3. London, Unwin Hyman.

Millotte, J.-P. 1988 La question des 'Champs d'Urnes' en France et sa place dans une perspective historique. In P. Brun and C. Mordant (eds.), *Le groupe Rhin-Suisse-France orientale et la notion de civilisation des Champs d'Urnes.* Mémoires du Musée de Préhistoire d'Ile-de France no. 1, Nemours.

Mogielnicka-Urban, M. 1986 Bemerkungen zur Verbreitung von Gefässen mit Merkmalen der Lausitzer Kultur im nordischen Kreis. In B. Ambrosiani (ed.).

Mohen, J.-P. 1979 La présence celtique de La Tène dans le sud-ouest de l'Europe: indices archéologiques. In P.-M. Duval and V. Kruta (eds.).

Mohen, J.-P. 1987 Marmesse. In: *Trésors des Princes Celtes.* Galeries nationale du Grand Palais 20 octobre 1987–15 février 1988. Edition de la Réunion des musées nationaux.

Mohen, J.-P., Duval, A. and Eluere, C. 1988 Les Grecs ont-ils tenté de coloniser les Celtes anciens? In *Les Princes Celtes el la Méditerranée.*

Montelius, O. 1885 Om tidsbestämning inom bronsålderen med särskilt hänsyn till Skandinavien. *Kongl. Vitterhets Historie och Antiquitets Akademiens Handlingar* 30. Stockholm.

Montelius, O. 1903 *Die ältere Kulturperioden im Orient und in Europa.* Part 1 separately published as: *Die Typologische Methode.* Stockholm.

Montelius, O. 1986 *Dating in the Bronze Age with Special Reference to Scandinavia.* Kungl. Vitterhets Historie och Antikvitets Akademien. Stockholm.

Montero, RUIZ I. 1992 Bronze Age metallurgy in southeast Spain. *Antiquity* 67(254).

Moory, P. R. S. 1984a Assyria. In J. Boardman (ed.), *The Cambridge Ancient History.*

Moory, P. R. S. 1984b Urartu. In J. Boardman (ed.), *The Cambridge Ancient History.*

Moosleitner, F. 1988 Vier Spangenbarrendepots aus Oberreching, Land Salzburg. *Germania* 66.

Mordant, C. 1989 Transgression culturelle et mouvements de population au XIVe–XIIIe siècles avant notre ère dans le Bassin parisien. Compétition culturelle et phénomène de lisière. In *Dynamique du bronze moyen en Europe occidentale.*

Mordant, C. and Gouge, P. 1992 L'occupation du sol au Bronze Final dans les valleés de l' Yonne et de la Haute-Seine. In C. Mordant and A. Richards (eds.).

Mordant, C. and Richards, A. (eds.) 1992 *L'habitat et l'occupation du sol à l'Age du Bronze en Europe.* Actes du colloque international de Lons-le-Saunier 16–19 mai 1990. Edition du Comté des Travaux Historiques. Paris.

Morris, I. 1987 *Burial and Ancient Society. The Rise of the Greek City-state.* Cambridge University Press.

Morris, I. 1989a Tomb cult and the 'Greek renaissance': the past in the present in 8th century BC. *Antiquity* 62(237).

Morris, I. 1989b Circulation, deposition and the formation of the Greek Iron Age. *MAN* 24(3).

Morris, M. 1988 Changing perceptions of the past: The Bronze Age – a case study. In J. Bintliff (ed.), *Extracting Meaning from the Past*. Oxford: Oxbow Books.

Moscalu, E. *et al.* 1989 Das Thrako-getische Fürstengrab von Peretu in Rumänien. *Ber. Römisch Germanische Kommission* 70.

Moscati, S. (ed.). 1991 *The Celts*. Bompiani, Milan.

Mozsolics, A. 1957 Archäologische Beiträge zur Geschichte der grossen Wanderung. *Acta Arch. Hung.* 8

Mozsolics, A. 1967 *Bronzefunde des Karpatenbeckens. Depotfundhorizonte von Hajdusamson und Kosziderpadlas*. Akademiai Kiado, Budapest.

Mozsolics, A. 1972 Beziehungen zwischen Italien und Ungarn während 'Bronzo recente' und 'Bronzo finale'. *Revista di scienze preihistoriche* 17(2) Firenze.

Mozsolics, A. 1973 *Bronze- und Goldfunde des Karpatenbeckens. Depotfundhorizonte von Forro und Opalyi*. Akademiai Kiado, Budapest.

Mozsolics, A. 1985 *Bronzefunde aus Ungarn, Depotfundhorizonte von Aranyos, Kurd und Gyermely*. Budapest.

Muckelroy, K. 1980 Two bronze age cargoes in British waters. *Antiquity* 54(211).

Muckelroy, 1981 Middle Bronze Age trade between Britain and Europe: a maritime perspective. *Proc. Prehist. Soc.* 47.

Muhly, J. D. 1991 The development of copper metallurgy in Late Bronze Age Cyprus. In N. H. Gale.

Müller, F. 1990 *Der Massenfund von der Tiefenau bei Bern*. Zur Deutung latènezeitlicher Sammelfunde mit Waffen. *Antiqua* 20, Basel.

Müller-Karpe, A. 1989 Ein keltischer Streitwagenkrieger des 3. Jahrhunderts v. Chr. In A. Haffner (ed.).

Müller-Karpe, H. 1955 Das Urnenfelderzeitlichen Wagengrab von Hart a. d. Alz, Oberbayern. *Bayerische Vorgeschichtsblätter* 21.

Müller-Karpe, H. 1959 *Beitrage zur Chronologie der Urnenfelderzeit nördlich und südlich der Alpen*. Römisch-Germanische Forschungen 22. Berlin: De Gruyter.

Müller-Karpe, H. 1961 *Die Vollgriffschwerter der Urnenfelderzeit aus Bayern*. Münchner Beiträge zur Vor- und Frühgeschichte 6. Munich: Beck'sche.

Müller-Karpe, H. 1962 Zur spätbronzezeitlichen Bewaffnung in Mitteleuropa und Griechenland. *Germania* 40.

Müller-Wille, M. 1965 *Eisenzeitliche Fluren in den Festländischen Nordseegebieten*. Siedlung und Landschaft in Westfalen 5. Münster.

Murphey, R. 1989 An ecological history of Central Asian Nomadism. In G. Seaman (ed.), *Ecology and Empire. Nomads in the Cultural Evolution of the Old World*, vol. 1. Proc. of the Soviet-American Academic Symposia in Conjunction with the Museum Exhibition 'Nomads: Masters of the Eurasian Steppe'. Los Angeles, Denver and Washington D. C.

Muscarella, C. W. 1988 The background to the Phrygian bronze industry. In J. Curtis (ed.).

Myhre, B. Magnus and Myhre, B. 1972 The concept 'immigrations' in archaeological contexts illustrated by example from West Norwegian Early Iron Age. *Norwegian Arch. Review* 5(1).

Mylonas, G. E. 1972 *Ho taplikos kyklos B ton Mykinon*. 2 vols. Athens: Archaeological Society.

Nagata, J. 1981 In defense of ethnic boundaries: the changing myths and charters of Malay identity. In C. F. Keyes (ed.), *Ethnic Change*. Washington University Press.

Nash, D. 1976 The growth of urban society in France. In B. Cunliffe and R. T. Rowley (eds.), *Oppida, the Beginnings of Urbanization in Barbarian Europe*. BAR, Int. Series 11, Oxford.

Nash, D. 1978 Territory and state formation in central Gaul. In D. R. Green, C. Hazelgrove and C. C. Spriggs (eds.), *Social Organization and Settlement*. BAR Int. Series 47

Nash, D. 1985 Celtic territorial expansion and the Mediterranean world. In T. C. Champion and J. V. S. Megaw (eds.), *Settlement and Society. Aspects of West European Prehistory in the First Millennium* B.C. Leicester University Press.

Navarette, M. I. Martinez and Garcia, J. M. Vicent 1983 La periodizacion: un analysis historico-critico. In *Homenaje al Prof. Martin Almagro Basch*. Madrid.

Needham, S.P. 1990 The structure of settlement and ritual in the Late Bronze Age of south-east Britain. Colloque international de Lons-le-Saunier, 16 19 mai 1990.

Needham, S. P. and Burgess, C. B. 1980 The Later Bronze Age in the Lower Thames Valley: the metalwork evidence. In J. Barrett and R. Bradley (eds.).

Neugebauer, J.-W. (ed.) 1988 *Die Bronzezeit im osten Österreichs*. Wien.

Neugebauer, J.-W. 1991 *Die Nekropole F von Gemeinlebarn, Niederösterreich*. Untersuchungen zu den Bestattungssitten und zum Grabraub in der ausgehenden Frühbronzezeit in Niederösterreich südlich der Donau zwischen Enns und Wienerwald. Verlag Phillipp von Zabern, Mainz am Rhein.

Neugebauer, J. W. and Neugebauer-Maresch, C. 1990 Überblick über die frühe und mittlere Bronzezeit in Ostösterreich. In V. Furmanek and F. Horst (eds.).

Neustupny, E. 1981 Mobilität der Äneolitischen Populatonen. *Slovenska Archeologia* 21.

Niemeyer, H. G. (ed.) 1982 *Phönizier im Westen*. Die Beiträge des Internationales Symposiums über 'Die phönizische Expansion im westlichen Mittelmeerraum' in Köln vom 24. bis 27 April 1979. Madriger Beiträge, Band 8. Mainz: Verlag Ph. von Zabern.

Niemeyer, N. G. 1984 Die Phönizier und die Mittelmeerwelt im Zeitalter Homers. *Jahrbuch des Römisch-Germanischen Zentralmuseums Mainz* 31.

Niesiolowska-Wedzka, A. 1974 *Poczatki i rozwoj grodow kultury Luzyckiej (Anfänge und Entwicklung der Burgen der Lausitzer Kultur)*. Polsak Akademia Nauk, Inst. Hist. kultury Mat. Wroclaq, Warszawa, Krakow, Gdansk.

Niesiolowska-Wedzka, A. 1987 Siedlungsformen 'städtischen Typs' der Bronze- und Früheisenz in Mitteleuropa/ Eine Übersicht. In E. Plesl and J. Hrala (eds.).

Nikolov, B. 1989 Historical and archaeological context. In A. Fol (ed.).

Nilsson, H. 1980 Antika författares berättelser om trakerna. In P. Hellström and A. Sandwall (eds.), *Trakerna*. Statens Historiska Museum, Stockholm.

Nocete, F. 1994 Space as coercion: the transition to the state in the social formation of La Campina, Upper Guadalquivir Valley, Spain, ca. 1900–1600 B.C. *Journal of Anthropological Archaeology* 13.

Nordbladh, J. 1980 *Glyfer och rum. Kring hällristningar i Kville* (English summary). University of Gothenburg.

Northover, J.-P. 1982 The exploration of long-distance movement of bronze in Bronze and Early Iron Age Europe. *Bull. Institute of Archaeology University of London* 19.

Novotna, M. 1987 Bemerkungen zur Deutung der Bronzehortfunde mit Bronzegefäßen aus der Slowakei. In E. Plesl and J. Hrala (eds.).

Novotna, M. 1988 Zu einigen terminologischen Fragen der Bronzezeit. *Universitas Comeniana, Zbornik Fil. Ped. Fak. Univ. Kom. Musaica*. Rocnik XXI

Nugent, S. 1982 'Civilization', 'society', and 'anomaly' in Amazonia. In C. Renfrew, M. J. Rowlands and B. A. Segraves (eds.).

Nyegård, G. 1983 *Dyreknogler fra yngre bronzealders bopladser i Sydskandinavien*. En studie over faunaøkonomi samt bearbejdede genstande af ben og tak. Upubliceret konferensspeciale. Københavns universitet.

O'Brien, W. F. 1990 Prehistoric copper mining in south-west Ireland. *Proceedings of the Prehistoric Society* 56.

O'Connor, B. 1980 *Cross-Channel relations in the later Bronze Age*. BAR, Int. Series 91, Oxford.

O'Connor, B. 1989 The Middle Bronze Age of southern England. In *Dynamique du bronze moyen en Europe occidentale*.

Oancea, A. 1976 Branches de mors au corps en forme de disque. *Thraco-Dacia. Recueil d'études a l'occasion du IIe Congrès international de Thracologie*. Bucharesti 1976.

Odner, K. 1985 Saamis (Lapps), Finns and Scandinavians in history and prehistory. Ethnic origins and ethnic processes in Fenno-Scandinavia. *Norwegian Arch. Review* 18(1–2).

Olausson, D. 1987 Piledal and Svarte. A comparison between two Late Bronze Age cemeteries in Scania. *Acta Arch.* 57.

Olivier, L. 1988 Le tumulus à tombe à char de Marainville-sur-Madon (Vosges). Premiers résultats. In *Les Princes Celtes et la Méditerranée.*

Olsen, B. 1985 Comments on Saamis, Finns and Scandinaviana in history and prehistory. *Norwegian Arch. Review* 18(1–2).

Olsen, B. and Robilinski, Z. 1991 Ethnicity in anthropological and archaeological research: a Norwegian-Polish perspective. *Archaeologica Polona.*

Ordentlich, J. 1969 Probleme der Befestigungsanlagen in der Siedlungen der Otomanikultur in deren rumänischen Verbreitungsgebiet. *Dacia* 13.

Ordentlich, J. 1970 Die chronologische Gliederung der Otomani-Kultur auf dem rumänischen Gebiet und ihre wichtigsten Merkmale. *Dacia* 14.

Orientalische-Ägäische Einflüsse 1990 *Orientalische Ägäische Einflüsse in der europäischen Bronzezeit:* Ergebnisse eines Kolloquiums. Römisch-Germanisches Zentralmuseum. Monographien, Band 15. Rudolf Habelt, Bonn.

Ostorja-Zagorski, J. 1974 From studies of the economic structure at the decline of the Bronze Age and the Hallstatt Period in the North and West Zone of the Odra and the Vistula Basins. *Przeglad Arch.* 22.

Ostorja-Zagorski, J. 1980 An attempt at reconstruction of economic transformations in the Hallstatt Period in the North and West Zone of the Oder and Vistula River Basins. In *Unconventional Archaeology,* Wroclaw.

Ostorja-Zagorski, J. 1982 *Przemiany osadnice demograficzne i gospodarcze w okresie halsztackim na pomorzu* (Settlement, demographic and economic changes in the Hallstatt period in Pomerania). Polska Akademia Nauk, Inst. Hist. Kultury Materialnej. Ossolineum, Wroclaw, Warszawa, Krakow, Gdansk, Lodz.

Ostorja-Zagorski, J. 1983 Aspekte der Siedlungskunde, Demographie und Wirtschaft hallstattzeitlicher Burgen von Biskupin-Typ. *Praehistorische Zeitschrift,* 58 Bd, Heft 2.

Ostorja-Zagorski, J. 1984 Biological-cultural changes in the Hallstatt Period in the microregion of Sobjejuchy near Znin, Bydgoszcz voivodship. *Archaeologia Polona,* 23.

Ostorja-Zagorski, J. 1986 Anthropogenic changes of the natural environment in the Late Bronze Age in the south-east Baltic Sea zone. In B. Ambrosiani (ed.).

Ostorja-Zagorski, J. 1989 Changes in the economic and social structures in northern Poland at the transition from the Bronze Age to the Iron Age. In M. L. S. Sørensen and Thomas, R. (eds.).

Otte, M. and Ulrix-Closset, M. (eds.) 1989 *La civilisation de Hallstatt.* Bilan d'une rencontre, Liège 1987. Etudes et Recherches Archéologiques de l'Université de Liège, No. 36, Liège.

Ozdani, O. 1986 Zur Problematik der Entwicklung der Hügelgräberkulturen in der Südwestslowakei. *Slovenska Archeologia* 34(1).

Palavestra, A. 1984 *Princely Tombs during the Early Iron Age in the Central Balkans.* Belgrade, Serbian Academy of Sciences and Arts, Institute for Balkan Studies.

Palavestra, A. 1987 Models of prehistoric amber trade in the central and western Balkans. *Balcanica* 18.

Palavestra, A. 1993 *Prehistoric Amber in Central and Western Balkans.* Serbian Academy of Sciences and Arts, Institute for Balkan Studies, Special Editions No. 52. Belgrade.

Palavestra, A. 1994 Prehistoric trade and the cultural model of princely tombs in the central Balkans. In: K. Kristiansen and J. Jensen (eds.).

Parducz, Z. 1952, 1954 and 1955 Le cimetière Hallstattien de Szentes-Vekerzug I–III *Acta Arch. Hungarica* 2–4.

Parducz, M. 1965 Graves from the Scythian age at Artand (county Hajdu-Bihar). *Acta Arch. Hung.* 17.

Parducz, M. 1974 Die charakteristischen skythischen Funde aus dem Karpartenbecken und die damit verbundenen ethnischen Fragen. In B. Chropovsky (ed.), *Symposium zu Problemen der jüngeren Hallstattzeit in Mitteleuropa*. Bratislava: Veda, Verlag der slowakischen Akademie der Wissenschaften.

Pare, C. F. E. 1987a Der Zeremonialwagen der Hallstattzeit – Untersuchungen zu Konstruktion, Typologie und Kulturbeziehungen. In *Vierrädige Wagen Der Hallstattzeit*. Monographien, Römisch-Germanisches Zentralmuseum, Mainz.

Pare, C. F. E. 1987b Der Zeremonialwagen der Urnenfelderzeit – seine Entstehung, Form und Verbreitung. In *Vierrädige Wagen der Hallstattzeit*. Monographien, Römisch-Germanisches Zentralmuseums, Mainz.

Pare, C. 1989a Ein zweites Fürstengrab von Apremont – 'La Motte aux Fées' (Arr. Vesoul, Dep. Haute-Saone). Untersuchungen zur Späthallstattkultur im ostfranzösischen Raum. *Jahr. Ber. Römisch-Germanisches Zentralmuseums Mainz* 36.

Pare, C. 1989b From Dupljaja to Delphi: the ceremonial use of wagons in later prehistory. *Antiquity* 63(238).

Pare, C. 1991 Fürstensitze, Celts and the Mediterranean world: developments in the West Hallstatt culture in the 6th and 5th centuries BC. *Proceedings of the Prehistoric Society* 57.

Parzinger, H. 1982 Zur Belegungsabfolge auf dem Magdalenenberg bei Villingen. *Germania* 64.

Parzinger, H. 1988 (1989) *Chronologie der Späthallstatt- und Frühlatène-Zeit*. Studien zu Fundgruppen zwischen Mosel und Save. VCH. Acta humaniora.

Parzinger, H. 1991 Archäologisches zur Frage der Illyrier. *Ber. der Römisch-Germanischen Kommission*, Band 72.

Parzinger, H. and Stegmann-Rajtar, S. 1988 Smolenice-Molpir und der Beginn skythischer Sachkultur in der Südwestslowakei. *Praehist. Zeitschr.* 63.

Pastoral Production and Society 1979 Proceedings of the international meeting on nomadic pastoralism Paris 1st–3rd Dec. 1976. Cambridge University Press/ Editions de la Maison des Sciences de l'Homme.

Patek, E. 1974 Präskytische Gräberfelder in Ostungarn. In B. Chropovsky (ed.), *Symposium zu Problemen der jüngeren Hallstattzeit in Mitteleuropa*. Bratislava: Veda, Verlag der slowakischen Akademie der Wissenschaften.

Patek, E. 1981 Die Anfänge der Siedlung und des Gräberfeldes von Sopron- Burgstall. In C. Eibner and A. Eibner (eds.).

Patek, E. 1982 Recent excavations at the Hallstatt and La Tène hillfort of Sopron-Varhely (Burgstall) and the predecessors of the Hallstatt Culture in Hungary. In D. Gabler, E. Patek and I. Vörös (eds.), *Studies in the Iron Age of Hungary*. BAR Int. Series 144, Oxford.

Patek, E. 1986 Zum Übergang von der Urnenfelderzeit zur Hallstattzeit in Transdanubien. Überblick über den heutigen Forschungsstand. In E. Jerem (ed.).

Patterson, T. 1987 Tribes, chiefdoms, and kingdoms in the Inca Empire. In T. Patterson and C. Gailey (eds.).

Patterson, T. 1990 Processes in the formation of ancient world systems. *Dialectical Anthropology*, 15.

Patterson, T. in press Archaeology, history, and the concept of totality.

Patterson, T. and Gailey, C. W. (eds.) 1987 *Power Relations and State Formation*. A Publication of the Archaeology Section/American Anthropological Association. Washington.

Pauli, L. 1971 *Studien zur Golasecca-Kultur*. Mitt. des deutsches arch. Inst. Romische Abt Bd. 19. Heidelberg: Kerle Verlag.

Pauli, L. 1974 'Der goldene Steig. Wirtschaftsgeographisch-archäologische Untersuchungen im östlichen Mitteleuropa. In G. Kossack and G. Ulbert (eds.), *Studien zur Vor- und frühgeschichtlichen Archäologie*. Festschrift für Joachim Werner zum 65. Geburtstag. München.

Pauli, L. 1975 *Keltischer Volksglaube. Amulette- und Sonderbestattungen am Dürrnberg bei Hallein und im eisenzeitlichen Mitteleuropa.* Münchener Bietrage zur Vor- und Frühgeschichte 28. Munich.

Pauli, L. (ed.) 1980a *Die Kelten in Mitteleuropa.* Kultur, Kunst, Wirtschaft. Salzburger Landesausstellung 1. Mai–30. Sept. 1980 in Keltenmuseum Hallein, Österreich. Salzburg.

Pauli, L. 1980b Die Herkunft der Kelten. Sinn und Unsinn einer alten Frage. In Pauli (ed.), *Die Kelten in Mitteleuropa.*

Pauli, L. 1980c Das keltische Mitteleuropa vom 6. bis 2. Jahrhundert v. Chr. In Pauli (ed.), *Die Kelten in Mitteleuropa.*

Pauli, L. 1984a Die westliche Späthallstattkultur. Aufstieg und Niedergang einer Randkultur der antiken Welt. In *Archäologie und Kulturgeschichte* 2, Symposium Saerbeck.

Pauli, L. 1984b Die Wagengräber auf dem Dürrnberg bei Hallein (Österreich). In M. Gustin and L. Pauli (eds.).

Pauli, L. 1984c *The Alps. Archaeology and Early History.* Thames and Hudson, London.

Pauli, L. 1985a Early Celtic society: two centuries of wealth and turmoil in Central Europe. In T. Champion and J. W. S. Megaw (eds.).

Pauli, L. 1985b Einige Anmerkungen zum Problem der Hortfunde. *Arch. Korrespondenzblatt* 15.

Pauli, L. 1986 La Società celtica transalpina nel V secolo a. C. In *Gli Etruschi a nord del Po. Ausstellungskatalog Mantova* 1986.

Pauli, L. 1991 Heilige Plätze und Opferbräuche bei den Helvetiern und ihre Nachbarn. *Archäologie der Schweiz* 14.

Pauli, L. 1994 Case studies in Celtic archaeology. In K. Kristiansen and J. Jensen (eds.).

Paulik, J. 1962 Das Velatice-Baierdorfer Hügelgrab in Ockov. *Slovenska Archaeologia* 10.

Paulik, J. 1988 K bojovnickemu vystroju v mladsej dobe bronzovej (zur Kriegerausrüstung in der jüngeren Bronzezeit). *Zbornik Slovenskeno Narodneho Muzea* 82, Historia 28, Bratislave.

Paulik, J. 1991 Karpaska kotlina na prahu historie. The Carpathian Basin on the history threshold. *Vlastivedny Casopis* 3, Rocnik xxxx.

Pautreau, J.-O. 1989 The transition from Bronze Age to Iron Age in France: economic, cultural and spiritual change (text in French), In M. L. Sørensen and R. Thomas (eds.).

Pautreau, J.-P. 1990 L'enclos protohistorique xxiii de la Croix Verte, Antran (Vienne). *Rev. archeol. Ouest, Supplément No. 2.*

Pearce, S. M. 1983 *The Bronze Age Metalwork of South Western Britain.* BAR British Series 120. Oxford.

Pearson, G. 1987 How to cope with calibration. *Antiquity* 61(231).

Pearson, P. M. 1989 Beyond the pale: barbarian social dynamics in western Europe. In J. Barrett, P. Fitzpatrick and L. Macinnes (eds.).

Peebles, C. S. and Kus, S. M. 1977 Some archaeological correlates of ranked societies. *American Antiquity* 42(3).

Pelon, O. 1976 *Tholoi, tumuli, et circles funéraires. Recherches sur les monuments funéraires de plan circulaire dans l'Égee de lAge du Bronze (III et II millénaires av. J-C).* Paris.

Perea, A. 1989 Cadiz: Orfebreria Fenicia. *Revista arqueologia, el Oro la Espana Preromana.*

Peregrine, P. N. 1992 *Missipian Evolution: A World-System Perspective.* Monographs in World Archaeology, No. 9. Prehistory Press. Madison.

Peroni, R. 1956 Zur Gruppierung mitteleuropäischer Griffzungedolche der späten Bronzezeit. *Badische Fundberichte* 20.

Peroni, R. 1977 Kulturverhältnisse auf der Apenninhalbinsel am Ende der Altbronzezeit. *Jahresbericht des Instituts für Vorgeschichte der Universität Frankfurt a. M.*

Peroni, R. 1979 From Bronze to Iron Age: economic, historical and social considerations. In D. Ridgway and F. R. Ridgway (eds.) *Italy before the Romans.* Academic Press.

Peroni, R. 1989 *Protostoria dell' Italia continentale. La penisola italiana nelle eta del bronzo e del ferro.* In *Popoli e civiltà dell' Italia antica* 9, Rome.

Peschel, Karin. 1985 Eisenfunde der Hallstattzeit im südlichen Mitteleuropa. In F. Horst and B. Krüger (eds.), *Produktivkräfte und Produktionsverhältnisse in ur- und frühgeschichtlicher Zeit.* Historiker Gesellschaft der DDR. Berlin: Akademie Verlag.

Peschel, Karl. 1985 Die Entwicklung der Produktivkräfte in der Hallstatt- und Latènezeit Mitteleuropas. In F. Horst and B. Krüger (eds.), *Produktivkräfte und Produktionsverhältnisse in ur- und frühgeschichtlicher Zeit.* Historiker Gesellschaft der DDR, Berlin: Akademie Verlag.

Peschel, Karl. 1990 Archäologisches zur Frage der Unfreiheit bei den Kelten während der vorrömischen Eisenzeit. *Ethnogr.-Archäol. Zeitschrift* 31.

Petrequin, P. 1988 Le groupe Rhin-Suisse-France orientale en France-Comté. Une Réévaluation des données sur l'âge du Bronze Final. In P. Brun and C. Mordant (eds.).

Petrequin, P., Piningre, J.-F. and Dartevelle, H. 1989 L'âge du Bronze moyen en Franche-Comté. In *Dynamique du bronze moyen en Europe occidentale.*

Petres, E. F. 1983 Neue Angaben über die Verbreitung der spätbronzezeitlichen Schutswaffen. *Savaria* 16. Bull. der Museen des Komitats Vas. Internationales Kolloquium 1982. Nord–Süd Beziehungen.

Petrescu-Dimbrovita, M. 1977 *Depozitele de brinzuri din România.* Bukarest.

Peyre, C. 1979 *La Cisalpine gauloise du IIIe au Ier siècle avant J.-C.* Etudes d'histoire et archéologie 1. Presses de l'Ecole Normale Supérieure, Paris.

Peyre, C. 1982 Y a-t-il un contexte Italique au style de Waldalgesheim? In P.-M. Duval and V. Kruta (eds.).

Piaskowski, J. 1986 Bemerkungen zu den Eisenverhüttungszentren auf polnischen Gebiet in ur- und frühgeschichtlicher Zeit. In F. Horst and B. Krüger (eds.).

Picard, C. 1982 Les navigations de Carthage vers l'Ouest. Carthage et le pays de Tarsis aux VIII–VI siècles. In H. G. Niemeyer (ed.).

Piggot, S. 1965 *Ancient Europe. From the beginnings of agriculture to classical antiquity.* Edinburgh University Press.

Piggot, S. 1983 *The Earliest Wheeled Transport. From the Atlantic to the Caspian Sea.* London: Thames and Hudson.

Pingel, V. 1980 'Balkanische' Bronzen der älteren Eisenzeit in Sizilien und Unteritalien. *Situla* 20/21. Zbornik posvecen stanetu Gabrovcu ob sestdesetletnici, Ljubljana.

Piotrovsky, B. 1969 *The Ancient Civilization of Urartu.* Translated from the Russian by James Hogarth. London: Barrie and Rockcliff.

Pittioni, R. 1951 Prehistoric copper-mining in Austria. Problems and facts. *Univ. of London Inst. of Arch. Ann. Report* VII.

Pittioni, R. 1957 Urgeschichtlicher Bergbau auf Kupfererz und Spurenanalyse. Beiträge zum Problem der Relation Lagerstätte-Fertigobjekt. *Arch. Austriaca Beiheft* 1.

Planck, D. 1982 Eine neuentdeckte keltische Viereckschanze in Felbach-Schmiden, Rems-Murr-Kreis. *Germania* 60.

Pleiner, R. 1980 Early Iron Age metallurgy in Europe. In T. A. Werttime and J. D. Muhly (eds.), *The Coming of the Iron Age.* New Haven, Conn., Yale University Press.

Pleinerova, I. and Hrala, J. 1988 Brezno. Osada lidu knovizske kultury v severozapadnich cechach. (Brezno. Die Siedlung des Volkes mit Knovizer Kultur in Nordwestböhmen). Okresni muzeum v Lounech Severoceske nakladatelstvi v Usti nad Labem.

Plesl, E. 1987 Die Urnenfelderkulturen Mitteleuropas. In E. Plesl and J. Hrala (eds.).

Plesl, E. 1990 Zur Frage der Herausbildung der Urnenfelderkulturen. In V. Furmanek and F. Horst (eds.).

Plesl, E. and Hrala, J. (eds.) 1987 *Die Urnenfelderkulturen Mitteleuropas.* Symposium Liblice 21.–25. 1985. Praha 1987.

Plesl, E. and Pleslova-Stikova, E. 1981 Die Beziehungen zwischen Karpatenbecken und Mitteleuropa in der urgeschichtlichen Entwicklung: der progressive Anteil ihrer Diskontinuität. *AFD Beiheft* 16, Beiträge zur Ur- und Frühgeschichte 1, Berlin.

Podborsky, V. 1970 *Mähren in der Spätbronzezeit und an der Schwelle der Eisenzeit*, Brno: University J. E. Purkyne.

Podborsky, V. 1974 Die Stellung der südmärischen Horákov-Kultur im Rahmen des danubischen Hallstatt. In B. Chropovsky (ed.).

Podzuweit, C. 1982 Die mykenische Welt und Troja. In B. Hänsel (ed.).

Primas, M. 1977 Zur Informationsausbreitung im südlichen Mitteleuropa. *Jahresber. Inst. Vorgesch. Frankfurt.*

Primas, M. 1989 Le Bronze moyen en Suisse. In *Dynamique du bronze moyen en Europe occidentale.*

Primas, M. 1990 Die Bronzezeit im Spiegel ihrer Siedlungen. In *Die ersten Bauern* 1. Phahlbaufunde Europas, Band 1 Schweiz. Sweizerisches Landesmuseum Zürich.

Primas, M. and Ruoff, U. 1981 Die Urnenfelderseitliche Inselsiedlung 'Grosser Hafner' im Zürichsee (Schweiz). Tauchausgrabung 1978–1979). *Germania* 59(1), 31–50.

Py, M. 1989 Economie des oppida d'après les documents de fouille. *Le Courrier du CNRS. Dossiers scientifiques.* No. 73. Archéologie en France Métropolitaine.

Raftery, B. 1984 *La Tène in Ireland. Problems of Origin and Chronology. Veröff. des Vorgesch. Seminars Marburg, Sonderband 2, Marburg.*

Raftery, B. 1989 Barbarians to the west. In J. C. Barrett, A. P. Fitzpatrick and L. Macinnes (eds.).

Raftery, B. 1991 The Celtic Iron Age in Ireland: problems of origin. *Emania* 9. Bull. of Navan Research Group, Belfast.

Rageth, J. 1986 Die Bronzezeit in Graubünden. *Antiqua* 15. *Chronologie.*

Randsborg, K. 1968 Von Periode II zu III. Chronologische Studien über die ältere Bronzezeit Südskandinaviens und Norddeutschlands. *Acta Archaeologica* 39. Copenhagen.

Randsborg, K. 1974 Social stratification in Early Bronze Age Denmark: a study in the regulation of cultural systems. *Prähistorische Zeitschrift* 49.

Randsborg, K. 1991(1992) Historical implications. Chronological studies in European archaeology c. 2000–500 B.C. *Acta Archaeologica* 62.

Randsborg, K. 1991 *The First Millennium A.D. in Europe and the Mediterranean.* Cambridge University Press.

Rankin, H. D. 1987 *Celts and the Classical World.* London: Croom Helm and Sydney: Areopagitica Press.

Rapin, A. 1982 Das keltische Heiligtum von Gournay-sur-Aronde. *Antike Welt.*

Rathje, A. 1979 Oriental imports in Etruria in the eighth and seventh centuries B. C.: their origin and implications. In D. Ridgway and F. R. Ridgway (eds.), *Italy before the Romans.* Academic Press.

Rausing, G. 1984 Bernstein und Weihrauch in der Bronzezeit. *75 Jahre Mannus und deutsche Vorgeschichte,* Bonn.

Reinecke, P. 1965 *Mainzer Aufsätze. Zur Chronologie der Bronze- und Eisenzeit.* (Reprint of series of classic articles between 1906 and 1909). Bonn: Habelt Verlag.

Reinerth, H. 1936 *Das Federseemoor als Siedlungsland des Vorzeitmennschen.* Leipzig.

Renfrew, C. 1972 *The Emergence of Civilisation, the Cyclades and the Aegean in the Third Millennium B.C.* Methuen.

Renfrew, C. 1973 *Before Civilization: The Radiocarbon Revolution and Prehistoric Europe.* London: Jonathan Cape.

Renfrew, C. 1974 Beyond a subsistence economy: the evolution of social organisation in prehistoric Europe. In C. Moore (ed.), *Reconstructing Complex Societies. An Archaeological Colloquium.* Supplement to the Bulletin of the American Schools of Oriental Research No. 20.

Renfrew, C. 1975 Trade as action at a distance: questions of integration and communication. In J. Sabloff and C. C. Lamberg-Karlovsky (eds.), *Ancient Civilization and Trade.* A School of American Research Book, University of New Mexico Press, Albuquerque.

Renfrew, C. 1987 *Archaeology and Language. The Puzzle of Indo-European Origins*. London: Jonathan Cape.

Renfrew, C. and Cherry, J. (eds.) 1986 *Peer Polity Interaction and Socio-political Change*. Cambridge University Press.

Renfrew, C. Rowlands, M. J. and Segraves, B. A. (eds.) 1982 *Theory and Explanation in Archaeology. The Southampton Conference*. New York, Academic Press.

Renfrew, C. and Shennan, S. (eds.) 1982 *Ranking, Resources and Exchange*. Aspects of the Archaeology of Early European Society. Cambridge University Press.

Revista de Arqueologia 1989 *El Oro en la Espana Preromana*.

Ridgway, D. 1980 *The Etruscans* University of Edinburgh, Dept. of Arch., Occasional papers, No. 6.

Ridgway, D. 1992 *The First Western Greeks*. Cambridge University Press

Ridgway, D. and Ridgway, F. R. (eds.) 1979 *Italy before the Romans. The Iron Age, Orientalizing and Etruscan periods*. London, New York: Academic Press.

Ridgway, F. R. 1979 The Este and Golasecca cultures: a chronological guide. In D. Ridgway and F. R. Ridgway (eds.), *Italy before the Romans*. Academic Press.

Riek, G. and Hundt, H. J. 1962 *Der Hohmichele*. Ein Fürstengrabhügel der späten Hallstattzeit bei der Heuneburg. Römisch-Germanische Forschungen, Bd. 25.

Rihovsky, J. 1965 *Das Urnengräberfeld von Kletnice*. Fontes Archaeologici Pragenses 8. Pragae.

Rihovsky, J. 1968 *Das Urnengräberfeld von Oblekovice*. Fontes Archaeologici Pragenses 12. Pragae.

Rihovski, J. 1969 Zur Kenntnis der Haustypen in der mitteldonauländischen Urnenfelderkultur. In: *Beiträge zu Lausitzer Kultur*. Berlin.

Rittershofer, K.-F. 1983 Das Hortfund von Bühl und seine Beziehungen. *Ber. der Römisch-Germanischen Komm.* 64.

Rivallain, J. n.d. *Contribution a l'étude du Bronze Final en Armorique*. Université de Haute Bretagne.

Rodwell, W. 1976 Coinage, oppida and the rise of Belgic power in south-eastern Britain. In B. Cunliffe and T. Rowley (eds.).

Rolle, R. 1977 Urartu und die Reiternomaden. *Saeculum*. Jahrbuch für Universalgeschichte, Band 28, Heft 1, München.

Rolle, R. 1979 *Totenkult der Skythen*. Teil 1: Das Steppengebiet. Vorgeschichtliche Forschungen Bd. 18 1,2. Berlin-New York.

Rolle, R. 1985 Der griechische Handel der Antike zu den osteuropäischen Reitenomaden aufgrund archäologischer Zeugnisse. In K. Düwel, H. Jankuhn, H. Siems and D. Timpe (eds.), *Untersuchungen zu Handel und Verkehr der vor- und frühgeschichtlichen Zeit in Mittel- und Nordeuropa*. Teil 1. Abh. d. Ak. d. Wiss. in Göttingen 143, Göttingen.

Rolle, R. 1989 *The World of the Scythians*. London: Batsford.

Rolle, R:; Müller-Wille, M. and Schietzel, K. (eds.) 1991 *Gold der Steppe. Archäologie der Ukraine*. Archäologisches Landesmuseum, Schleswig.

Romsauer, P. 1992 Interconnections between Europe and southeastern Europe in the 2nd–1st Millennium B.C. (Urnfield and Hallstatt periods). VI Symposium di Tracologia. *I Traci nel Mediterraneo*. Editrice Nagard. Roma.

Rønne, P. 1986 Stilvariationer i ældre bronzealder (Stilvariationen in der älteren Bronzezeit. Untersuchungen zu Lokalunderscheiden in der Verwendung von Ornamente und Funden der zweite Periode der älteren Bronze zeit). *Årbøger for Nordisk Oldkyndighed*.

Rösch, M. 1990 Veränderungen von Wirtschaft und Umwelt während Neolithicum und Bronzezeit am Bodensee. *Bericht der Römisch-Germanischen Kommission*, Band 71, 1.Teil.

Ross, A. 1986 *The Pagan Celts*. Batsford, London.

Roth, H. 1974 Ein Ledermesser der Atlantischen Bronzezeit aus Mittelfranken. *Arch. Korrespondenzblatt* 4.

Rötlisberger, F. 1986 *10000 Jahre Gletschergeschichte der Erde*. Aarau, Sauerländer.

Rouillard, P. 1991 *Les Grecs et la Pèninsule Ibérique du VIIIe au IVe siècle avant Jésus-Christ.* Publications du centre Pierre Paris (UA 991).

Rouse, I. 1986 *Migrations in Prehistory. Inferring Population Movement from Cultural Remains.* New Haven and London: Yale University Press.

Rowlands, M. 1976 *The Organization of Middle Bronze Age Metalworking.* BAR 31. Oxford.

Rowlands, M. 1980 Kinship, alliance and exchange in the European Bronze Age. In J. Barrett and R. Bradley (eds.), *Settlement and Society in the British Later Bronze Age.* BAR British Series 83. Oxford.

Rowlands, M. 1984a Conceptualizing the European Bronze and Early Iron Age. In J. Bintliff (ed.), *European Social Evolution – Archaeological Perspectives.* University of Bradford.

Rowlands, M. 1984b Objectivity and subjectivity in archaeology. In M. Spriggs (ed.), *Marxist Perspectives in Archaeology.* Cambridge University Press.

Rowlands, M. 1986 Modernist fantasies in prehistory? *MAN* 21 (followed by comments from Gosden and Bradley).

Rowlands, M. 1987a Centre and periphery: a review of a concept. In M. Rowlands, M. T. Larsen and K. Kristiansen (eds.), *Centre and Periphery in the Ancient World.* Cambridge University Press.

Rowlands, M. 1987b 'Europe in prehistory': a unique form of primitive capitalism? *Culture & History* 1. Copenhagen.

Rowlands, M. 1989 European barbarism and the search for authenticity. In Michael Harbsmeier and Mogens Larsen (eds.), *The Humanities between Art and Science. Intellectual Developments 1880–1914.* Akademisk Forlag, København.

Rowlands, M., Larsen, M. T. and Kristiansen, K. (eds.) 1987 *Centre and Periphery in the Ancient World.* Cambridge University Press.

Roymans, N. 1987 Tribale samenlevingen in Noord-Gallië. Doctoral dissertation. Amsterdam.

Roymans, N. 1990 *Tribal societies in Northern Gaul.* An Anthropological Perspective. Cingula 12, Amsterdam.

Roymans, N. 1991 Late Urnfield societies in the northwest European plains and the expanding networks of central European Hallstatt groups. In N. Roymans and F. Theuws (eds.), *Images of the Past. Studies in Ancient Societies in Northwestern Europe.* Amsterdam.

Ruckdeschel, W. 1978 *Die frühbronzezeitlichen Gräber Südbayerns. Ein Beitrag zur Kenntnis der Straubiner Kultur.* Antiquitas, Reihe 2, Band 11. Bonn: Rudolf Habelt.

Ruiz-Galvez, M. 1986 Navegacion y comercio entre el atlantico y el Mediterraneo a fines de edad del bronce. *Trabajos de Prehistoria* 43, 9–41.

Ruiz-Galvez, M. 1987 Bronce atlantico y 'cultura' del bronce atlantico en la peninsula Iberica. *Trabajos de Prehistoria* 44, 251–264. Madrid.

Ruiz-Galvez, M. 1989 La orfebreria del bronce final. El poder y su ostentacion. Revista arqueologia, *El oro en la Espana Preromana.*

Ruiz-Galvez, M. 1991 Songs of the Wayfaring Lad. Late Bronze Age Atlantic exchange and the building of the regional identity of the west Iberian Peninsula. *Oxford Journal of Archaeology* 10(3).

Ruiz-Galvez, M. 1994 The bartered bride. Goldwork, inheritance, and agriculture in the late prehistory of the Iberian peninsula. *Journal of European Archaeology* 2(1).

Ruiz-Galvez, M. (ed.) 1995 *Ritos de paso y puntos de paso. La Ria de Huelva en el mundo del Bronce Final Europeo.* Complutum-Extra 5. Universidad Complutense Madrid.

Ruiz-Galvez, M. and Galan Domingo, E. 1991 Las estelas del suroeste como hitos de vias ganaderas y rutas comerciales. *Trabajos de Prehistoria* 48.

Ruoff, U. and Rychner, V. 1986 Die Bronzezeit im schweizerischen Mittelland. *Antiqua* 15. *Chronologie.*

Rusu, M. 1963 Die Verbreitung der Bronzehorte in Transsilvanien vom Ende der Bronzezeit in die mittlere Hallstattzeit. *Dacia* N.S. 7.

Rusu, M. 1982 Bemerkungen zu den grossen Werkstätten und Giesserreifunden aus Sieben-burgen. In *Studien zur Bronzezeit*. Festschrift Wilhelm Albert v. Brunn. Mainz/Rhein.

Rychner, V. 1988 De l'Age du Bronze moyen au groupe Rhin-Suisse en Suisse occidentale: le phénomène métallurgique. In P. Brun and C. Mordant (eds.), *Le groupe Rhin-Suisse-France orientale et la notion de civilisation des Champs d'Urnes*. Mémoires du Musée de Préhistoire d'Ile-de France no. 1, Nemours.

Rychner, V., Egger, H., Gassmann, P. and Rychner, A. 1988 Dendrochronologie du groupe Rhin-Suisse dans la région neuchâteloise. In P. Brun and C. Mordant (eds.), *Le groupe Rhin-Suisse-France orientale et la notion de civilisation des Champs d'Urnes*. Mémoires du Musée de Préhistoire d'Ile-de France no. 1, Nemours.

Ryder, M. L. 1988 Danish Bronze Age wools. *Journal of Danish Archaeology* 7.

Rydzewski, J. 1980 Bevölkerungsstärke und Produktivitätsmöglichkeiten der Umwelt am Beispiel einer Siedlungskammer der Lausitzer Kultur in Wawrzenczyke bei Krakow. In F. Schlette (ed.), *Urgeschichtliche Besiedlung in ihrer Beziehung zur natürlichen Umwelt*. Halle.

Sáenz, C. 1991 Lords of the Waste: predation, pastoral production, and the process of stratification among the Eastern Twaregs. In T. Earle (ed.).

Sahlins, M. D. 1961 The segmentary lineage: an organisation of predatory expansion. *American Anthropologist* 63.

Sahlins, M. 1974 *Stone Age Economics*. Tavistock Publications, London.

Saitta, D. J. 1983 On the evolution of 'tribal social networks'. *American Antiquity* 48.

Salas, M. 1987 Zur Frage der jungbronzezeitlichen Höhensiedlungen in Südmähren. In E. Plesl and J. Hrala (eds.).

Salas, M. 1990 To the problem of human skeletal remains from the Late Bronze Age on Cézavy near Blucina. *Anthropologie* 28(2–3).

Saldova, V. 1974 Östliche Elemente in der westböhmischen Hallstattzeitlichen Hügelgräber-kultur. In B. Chropovsky (ed.).

Saldova, V. 1981 *Westböhmen in der späten Bronzezeit. Befestigte Höhensiedlungen*. Prag: Ok-rouhle Hradiste.

Sandars, N. 1976 Orient and orientalizing: recent thoughts reviewed. In P.-M. Duval and C. Hawkes (eds.).

Sandars, N. 1983 North and South at the end of the Mycenaean Age: aspects of an old problem. *Oxford Journal of Archaeology* 2.

Sandars, N. K. 1978 *The Sea Peoples. Warriors of the Ancient Mediterranean*. London: Thames and Hudson.

Sanders, W. T. and Webster, D. 1978 Unilinealism, multilinealism, and the evolution of complex societies. In C. L. Redman *et al.* (eds.), *Social Archaeology. Beyond Subsistence and Dating*. New York: Academic Press.

Sankot, P. 1980 Studien zur Sozialstruktur der nordalpinen Flachgräberfelder der La Tène-Zeit im Gebiet der Schweiz. *Zeitschrift Schweiz. Arch. und Kunstgeschichte* 37.

Sasse, B. 1977 Versuch einer statistischen Systematik der jungbronzezeitlichen Hortfunde im Mittelelbe-Saale-Gebiet. *Jahresschr. mitteldeutsche. Vorgesch.* 61.

Savory, H. N. 1949 The Atlantic Bronze Age in south-west Europe. *Proc. Prehist. Society* 15.

Schachermeyer, F. 1983 Die Zeit der Wanderungen im Spiegel ihrer Keramik. In S. Deger-Jalkotzy (ed.).

Schacht, S. 1982 *Die Nordischen Hohlwulste der frühen Eisenzeit*. Halle-Wittenberg.

Schauer, P. 1971 *Die Schwerter in Süddeutschland, Österreich und der Schweiz I* (Griffplatten, Grifffangel und Griffzungeschwerter). Prähistorische Bronzefunde, Abteilung IV, Band 2, München.

Schauer, P. 1974 Der urnenfelderzeitlichen Depotfund von Dolina, Gde. und Kr. Nova Gradiska, Kroatien. *Jahrbuch des Römisch-Germanischen Zentralmuseums Mainz*, 21.

Schauer, P. 1975 Die Bewaffnung der 'Adelskrieger' während der späten Bronze- und frühe

Eisenzeit. *Ausgrabungen in Deutschland 1950–1975.* Monographien des Römisch-Germanischen Zentralmuseums 1, Teil III.

Schauer, P. 1978 Die urnenfelderzeitlichen Bronzepanzer von Fillinges, Dep. Haute-Savoire, Frankreich. *Jahr. des Römisch-Germ. Zentralmuseums Mains* 25.

Schauer, P. 1979 Eine urnenfelderzeitliche Kampfweise. *Arch. Korrespondenzblatt* 9.

Schauer, P. 1979/80 Urnenfelderzeitliche Helmformen und ihre Vorbilder. *Fundber. aus Hessen* 19/20 – Festschr. U. Fischer.

Schauer, P. 1980 Der Rundschild der Bronze und frühen Eisenzeit. *Jahrbuch des Römisch-Germanischen Zentralmuseums Mainz* 27.

Schauer, P. 1981 Urnenfelderzeitliche Opferplätze in Höhlen und Felsspalten. In *Studien zur Bronzezeit.* Festschrift für Wilhelm Albert v. Brunn. Verlag Phillip Zabern, Mainz/Rhein.

Schauer, P. 1982 Die Beinscheinen der späten Bronze- und frühen Eisenzeit. *Jahrb. des Römisch-Germanischen Zentralmuseums Mainz* 29.

Schauer, P. 1983 Orient im spätbronze- und früheisenzeitlichen Occident. Kulturbeziehungen zwischen der Iberischen Halbinsel und dem Vorderen Orient während des späten 2. und des ersten Drittels des 1. Jahrtausends v. Chr. *Jahrb. des Römisch-Germanischen Zentralmusem Mainz* 30.

Schauer, P. 1984a Spuren minoisch-mykenischen und orientalischen Einflusses im atlantischen Westeuropa. *Jahrbuch des Römisch-Germanischen Zentralmuseums,* 31. Jahrgang.

Schauer, P. 1984b Überregionale Gemeinsamkeiten bei Waffengräbern der ausgehenden Bronzezeit und älteren Urnenfelderzeit des Voralpenraums. *Jahrbuch des Römisch-Germanischen Zentralmuseums* 31.

Schauer, P. 1985 Spuren orientalischen und ägäischen Einflusses im bronzezeitlichen Nordischen Kreis. *Jahrbuch des Römisch-Germanischen Zentralmuseums,* 32. Jahrgang.

Schauer, P. 1990 Schutz- und Angriffswaffen bronzezeitlicher Krieger im Spiegel ausgewählter Grabfunde Mitteleuropas. In V. Furmanek and F. Horst (eds.).

Schibler, J. 1987 Die Knockenartefakte. In: *Zürich 'Mozartstrasse'. Neolitische und bronzezeitliche Ufersiedlungen.* Berichte der Zürcher Denkmalpflege, Monographien 4. Kommissionsverlag: Orell Füssli Verlag Zürich.

Schlette, F. 1977: Zum Problem Ur- und frühgeschichtlicher Wanderungen und ihres archäologischen Nachweises. In F. Horst (ed.) *Archäologie als Geschichtswissenschaft.* Studien und Undersuchungen. Schriften zur Ur- und Frühgeschichte 30. Akademie Verlag Berlin.

Schmidt, K. H. and Ködderitzsch, R. (ed.) 1986 *Geschichte und Kultur der Kelten.* Heidelberg: Winter.

Schoknecht, T. 1990 Ein pollenanalytischer Beitrag zur Erforschung des bronzezeitlichen Siedlungs- und Wirtschaftsgeschehens in Mittelmecklenburg. In V. Furmanek and F. Horst (eds.).

Schortman, E. M. and Urban, P. 1992 Current trends in interaction research. In E. M. Schortman and P. Urban (eds.), *Resources, Power and Interregional Interaction.* Plenum Press. New York and London.

Schubart, H. 1982 Phönizische Niederlassungen an der Iberischen Südküste. In H. G. Niemeyer (ed.).

Schulze, M. 1984 Das Kriegergrab von Aspres-les corps. Untersuchungen zu den Ungarneinfällen nach Mittel-West- und Südeuropa (899–955 n. Chr.). *Jahrb. Römisch-Germanische Komm. Mainz,* 31.

Schumacher-Matthäus, G. 1985 *Studien zur Bronzezeitlichen Schmucktrachten in Karpatenraum.* Ein Beitrag zur Deutung der Hortfunde im Karpatenbecken. Marburger Studien zur Vor- und Frühgeschichte, Bd. 6.

Schwappach, F. 1976 L'art ornemental du 'Premier style' celtique. In P.-M. Duval and C. Hawkes (eds.).

Schwerin von Krosigh, H. G. 1989 Über die 'klassischen' Mälarbeile an Wolga und Oka in Mittelrussland. *Praehist. Zeitschr.* 64.

Scukin, M. 1989 *Rome and the Barbarians in Central and Eastern Europe. 1st Century B.C. – 1st Century A.D.* BAR International Series 542.

Scukin, M. and Eremenko, V. 1991 Zur Frage der Datierung keltischer Altertümer in Transkarpatengebiet der Ukraine und einige Probleme der Latène-Chronologie. *Acta Archaeologica Carpathica*, 30.

Seidl, U. 1988 Urartu as a bronzeworking centre. In J. Curtis (ed.).

Service, E. R. 1971 *Primitive Social Organization. An Evolutionary Perspective.* New York: Random House.

Service, E. R. 1975 *Origins of the State and Civilization. The Process of Cultural Evolution.* New York: Norton and Company.

Seyer, H. 1976: Die regionale Gliederung der Kulturen der vorrömischen Eisenzeit – Stammesgebiete -erste Wanderungen. In B. Krüger (ed.), *Die Germanen,* Band 1.

Shanks, M. and Tilley, C. 1987a *Reconstructing Archaeology: Theory and Practice.* Cambridge University Press.

Shanks, M. and Tilley, C. 1987b *Social Theory and Archaeology.* Cambridge: Polity Press.

Shefton, B. B. 1982 Greeks and Greek imports in the south of the Iberian Peninsula. The archaeological evidence. In H. J. Niemeyer (ed.).

Shennan, Stephen. 1978 Archaeological 'cultures': an empirical investigation. In I. Hodder (ed.), *The Spatial Organisation of Culture.* London: Duckworth.

Shennan, S. 1982 Ideology, change and the European Early Bronze Age. In I. Hodder (ed.) 1982b.

Shennan, Stephen. 1986a Central Europe in the third millennium BC: an evolutionary trajectory for the beginning of the European Bronze Age. *Journal of Anthropological Archaeology* 5.

Shennan, Stephen. 1986b Interaction and change in third millennium BC western and central Europe. In C. Renfrew and J. Cherry (eds.), *Peer Polity Interaction and Socio-political Change.* Cambridge University Press.

Shennan, Stephen 1987 Trends in the study of later European prehistory. *Annual Review of Anthropology* 16.

Shennan, Stephen 1989 Introduction: archaeological approaches to cultural identity. In S. Shennan (ed.), *Archaeological Approaches to Cultural Identity.* One World Archaeology 10. Unwin Hyman, London.

Shennan, Stephen 1993 Commodities, transactions and growth in the central European Early Bronze Age. *Journal of European Archaeology* 1(2).

Shennan, Susan. 1975 The social organization at Branc. *Antiquity* 49.

Sherratt, A. and Sherratt, S. 1988 The archaeology of Indo-European: an alternative view. *Antiquity* 62.

Sherratt, A. and Sherratt S. 1991 From luxuries to commodities: the nature of Mediterranean Bronze Age trading systems. In N. H. Gale (ed.), *Bronze Age Trade in the Mediterranean.* Studies in Mediterranean Archaeology, Vol. XC. Jonsered, Paul Åströms förlag.

Sherratt, A. 1981 Plough and pastoralism: aspects of the secondary products revolution. In I. Hodder, G. Isaac and N. Hammond (eds.), *Pattern of the Past. Studies in Honour of David Clarke.* Cambridge University Press.

Sherrat, A. 1984 Social evolution: Europe in the later Neolithic and Copper Ages. In J. Bintliff (ed.), *European Social Evolution.* Bradford: University Press.

Sherratt, A. 1987 Warriors and traders: Bronze Age chiefdoms in central Europa. In B. Cunliffe (ed.), *Origins.* BBC Publications.

Sherratt, A. 1994 Core, periphery and margin: perspectives on the Bronze Age. In C. Mathers and S. Stoddart (eds.), *Development and Decline in the Mediterranean Bronze Age.* Sheffield.

Sherratt, E. S. 1990 'Reading the texts': archaeology and the Homeric question. *Antiquity* 64, No. 245.

Shilov, V. P. 1989 The origins of migration and animal husbandry in the steppes of eastern Europe. In J. Clutton-Brock (ed.), *The Walking Larder. Patterns of Domestication, Pastoralism and Predation.* One World Arch. 2. London: Unwin Hyman.

Sievers, S. 1981 Die mitteleuropäische Hallstattdolche. In C. Eibner and A. Eibner (eds.).

Sievers, S. 1989 Die Waffen von Manching unter Berüchsichtigung des Übergangs von Lt C zu Lt D. Ein Zwischenbericht. *Germania* 67(1).

Sigfried-Weiss. A. 1979 *Der Ostalpenraum in der Hallstattzeit und seine Beziehungen zum Mittelmeergebiet.* Hamburger Beiträge zur Arch. 6. 1979.

Simon, K. 1985 Bronzemetallurgie der Hallstattzeit an Saale und mittlerer Elbe. In F. Horst and B. Krüger (eds.), *Produktivkräfte und Produktionsverhältnisse in ur- und frühgeschichtliche Zeit.* Berlin: Akademie-Verlag.

Simons, A. 1989 *Bronze- und eisenzeitliche Besiedlung in den Rheinischen Lössbörden.* Archäologische Siedlungsmuster im Braunkohlengebiet. BAR International Series 467. Oxford.

Skoryj, S. 1989 Die Skythen der Waldsteppenzone. In R. Rolle *et al.* (eds.).

Skydsgaard, J. E. 1988 Transhumance in Ancient Greece. In C. R. Whittaker (ed.).

Slovenskan Archeologia 29(1) 1981 *IX Internationales Symposium über das Äeneolithicum und die Bronzezeit im Donaugebiet.* Nitra-Nove Vazokany, 8.–12. OKt. 1979.

Smith, T. R. 1987 *Mycenaean Trade and Interaction in the West Central Mediterranean 1600–1000 BC.* BAR, int. Series 371. Oxford.

Snodgrass, A. 1971 *The Dark Age of Greece.* Edinburgh, University Press.

Snodgrass, A. 1980 *Archaic Greece. The Age of Experiment.* London: J. M. Dent and Sons Ltd.

Snodgrass, A. 1982 Les Origines du culte des héros dans la Grèce antique. In G. Gnoli and J.-P. Vernant (eds.).

Snodgrass, A. M. 1983 Heavy freight in Archaic Greece. In P. Garnsey, K. Hopkins and C. R. Whittaker (eds.).

Snodgrass, A. 1987 *An Archaeology of Greece. The Present State and Future Scope of a Discipline.* Sather Classical Lectures, Vol. 53 Berkeley, Los Angeles, London: University of California Press.

Snodgrass, A. 1989 The coming of the Iron Age in Greece: Europe's earliest Bronze/Iron transition. In M. L. S. Sørensen and R. Thomas (eds.).

Snodgrass, A. M. 1991 Bronze Age exchange: a minimalist Position. In N. H. Gale (ed.).

Sofri, G. 1975 *Det asiatiska produktionssättet. En marxistisk stridsfråga.* Stockholm: Bokförlaget Prisma. (Swedish translation from the Italian: Il modo di produzione asiatico, 1969).

Sørensen, M. L. 1987 Material order and cultural classification: the role of bronze objects in the transition from Bronze Age to Iron Age in Scandinavia. In I. Hodder (ed.), *The Archaeology of Contextual Meanings.* Cambridge University Press.

Sørensen, M. L. 1989 Period VI reconsidered: continuity and change at the transition from Bronze to Iron Age in Scandinavia. In M. L. Sørensen and R. Thomas (eds.).

Sørensen, M. L. and Thomas, R. (eds.) 1989 *The Bronze Age–Iron Age Transition in Europe. Aspects of Continuity and Change in European Societies c. 1200 to 500 B.C.* BAR International Series 483, Oxford.

Soroceanu, T. 1982 Hortfunde und befestigte Anlagen in Transsilvanien. In V. Furmanek and F. Horst (eds.).

Soudská, E. 1984 Gräber mit Wagen und Pferdegeschirr in Böhmen. In M. Gustin and L. Pauli (eds.).

Spencer, C. S. 1987 Rethinking the chiefdom. In R. D. Drennan and C. A. Uribe (eds.), *Chiefdoms in the Americas.* New York: University Press of America.

Sperber, L. 1987 *Untersuchungen zur Chronologie der Urnenfelderkultur im nördlichen Alpenvorland von der Schweiz bis Oberösterreich.* Antiquitas, Reihe 3, Band 29. Bonn: Rudolf Habelt.

Spindler, K. 1971, 1972, 1973, 1976, 1980 *Magdalenenberg – Der hallstattzeitliche Fürstengrab-hügel bei Villingen im Schwarzwald* 1–6. Villingen-Schwenningen.

Spindler, K. 1975 Grabfunde der Hallstattzeit vom Magdalenenberg bei Villingen im Schwarz-wald. *Ausgrabungen in Deutschland 1950–1975.* Monographien des Römisch-Germ. Zentralmuseums Mainz 1.

Spindler, K. 1983 *Die Frühen Kelten.* Stuttgart: Reclam.

Spindler, K. and Veiga Ferreira, O. 1973 Der spättbronzezeitliche Kuppelbau von der Roca de Casal do Meio in Portugal. *Madrider Mitteilungen,* 14.

Spriggs, M. 1988 The Hawaiian transformation of ancestral Polynesian society: conceptualiz-ing chiefly states. In J. Gledhill, B. Bender and M. T. Larsen (eds.), *State and Society. The Emergence and Development of Social Hierarchy and Political Centralization.* One World Archaeology 4. London: Unwin Hyman.

Sprockhoff, E. 1931 *Die Germanischen Griffzungenswerter.* Römisch-Germanische Forschun-gen 5. Berlin: De Gruyter.

Sprockhoff, E. 1937 *Jungbronzezeitliche Hortfunde Norddeutschlands* (Periode IV). Römisch-Germanischen Zentralmuseum zu Mainz, Katalog 12.

Sprockhoff, E. 1951 Pfahlbaubronzen in der Südzone des Nordischen Kreises während der jüngeren Bronzezeit. *Archaeologia Geographica ,* Beiträge zur vergleichenden geographi-sch-kartographischen Methode in der Urgeschichtsforschung. Jahrgang 2.

Sprockhoff, E. 1956 *Jungbronzezeitliche Hortfunde der Südzone des Nordischen Kreises* (Periode V). Römisch-Germanisches Zentralmuseum zu Mainz, Katalog 16.

Sprockhoff, E. 1957 Seddin – Sarajevo. *Vjesnik za arheologiju i historiju dalmatinsku* 56–59.

Sprockhoff, E. 1961 Zu den nordischen Bronzebecken der jüngeren Bronzezeit. *Ber. V. Kongress UISPP, Hamburg.*

Stadler, P. 1988 Möglichkeiten statistischer Untersuchungen im Vergleich Archäologie, An-thropologie und Zoologie. In J.-W. Neugebauer (ed.), *Die Bronzezeit im osten Österreichs.* Wien.

Stary, P. F. 1981 *Zur eisenzeitlichen Bewaffnung und Kampfesweise in Mittelitalien (ca. 9. bis 6. Jh. v. Chr.).* Marburger Studien zur Vor-und Frühgeschichte, Bd. 3.

Stary, P. F. 1982 *Zur hallstattzeitlichen Beilbewaffnung des circum-alpinen Raumes.* Ber. des Römisch.-Germ. Komm., Bd. 63.

Stead, I. M. 1991 The Snettisham treasure: excavations in 1990. *Antiquity* 65.

Stegman-Rajtar, S. 1986 Neuerkenntnisse zum Grab 169 vom Brno-Obrany (Mähren). In E. Jerem (ed.).

Stein, F. 1976 Bronzezeitliche Hortfunde in Süddeutschland. Beiträge zur Interpretation einer Quellengattung. *Saarbrücker Beiträge z. Altkde* 23.

Stepniak, T. P. 1986 *Quantitative Aspects of Bronze Age Metalwork in Western Poland. Long-distance Exchange and Social Organisation.* BAR International Series 317, Oxford.

Steponaitis, V. P. 1978 Location theory and complex chiefdoms: a Missippian example. In B. Smith (ed.), *Missippian Settlement Patterns.* New York: Academic Press.

Steuer, H. 1982 *Frühgeschichtliche Sozialstrukturen in Mitteleuropa.* Abh. der Akademie der Wissenschaften in Göttingen. Göttingen: Vandenhoeck and Ruprecht.

Stevenson, A. C. and Harrison, R. J. 1992 Ancient forests in Spain: a model for land-use and dry forests management in south-west Spain from 4000 BC to 1900 AD. *Proc. Prehist. Soc.* 58

Stjernquist, B. 1961 *Simris II. Bronze Age Problems in the Light of the Simris Excavations.* Acta Arch. Lundensia, Ser. in 4, Nor. 5. Lund.

Stjernquist, B. 1965–66 Models of commercial diffusion in prehistoric times. *Scripta Minora* 2.

Stjernquist, B. 1967 *Ciste a Cordoni.* Acta Arch. Lundensia, Ser. in 4, no. 6. Lund.

Stjernquist, B. 1988 Die Rippenciste. In W. Kimmig *Das Kleinaspergle.* Studien zu einem Fürstengrabhügel der frühen Latènezeit bei Stuttgart. Konrad Theiss Verlag, Stuttgart.

Stoddart, S. 1989 Divergent trajectories in central Italy 1200–500 B.C. In T. C. Champion (ed.), *Centre and Periphery. Comparative Studies in Archaeology*. One World Archaeology 11. London: Unwin Hyman.

Stos-Gale. Z. A. and Macdonald, C. F. 1991 Sources of metals and trade in the Bronze Age Aegean. In N. H. Gale.

Stos-Gale, Z. A: 1992 Isotope archaeology: reading the past in metals, minerals, and bone. *Endeavour* (N.S), 16(2).

Stos-Gale, Z. A. 1993 Lead isotope provenance studies – do they work? *Archaeologia Polona* 31.

Strøm, I. 1971 *Problems Concerning the Origin and Development of the Etruscan Orientalizing Style*. Odense University, Classical Studies, Vol. 2. Odense University Press.

Struwe, K. W. 1971 *Geschichte Schleswig-Holsteins. Die Bronzezeit Periode I–II*. Karl Wachholz Verlag Neumünster.

Struwe, K. W. 1979 *Geschichte Schleswig-Holsteins. Die jüngere Bronzezeit*. Karl Wachholz Verlag Neumünster.

Struwe, K. W. 1983 Zwei getriebene Bronzetassen der älteren Bronzezeit aus Schleswig-Holstein. *Offa-Zeitschrift* 40.

Stuchlik, S. 1990 Die Entstehung der Hügelgräberkultur zur Unstrutgruppe in Thüringen. In V. Furmanek and F. Horst (eds.).

Studenikova, E. and Paulik, J. 1983 *Osada z doby bronzovej v Pobedine* (Siedlung aus der Bronzezeit in Pobedun). Bratislava.

Sulimirski, T. 1961 Die Skythen in Mittel- und Westeuropa. *Bericht über den V. internationalen Kongress für Vor- und Frühgeschichte Hamburg 1958*. Berlin.

Sulimirski, T. 1970 *The Sarmatians. Ancient Peoples and Places*. London: Thames and Hudson.

Symposia Thracia 1982 *XI. Internationales Symposium über das Spätneolithicum und die Bronzezeit Xanthi 4–10 Oktober 1981*.

Szabo, M. 1988 La vaisselle métallique dans la cuvette des Karpates à l'époque des princes celtes. In *Les Princes Celtes et la Méditerranée*.

Szabo, M. 1986 Archéologie des Celtes continentaux: contribution a une division dans le temps et dans l'espace. In K. H. Schmidt and R. Ködderitzsch (eds.).

Szafranski, W. 1990 Kwestia pobytu Etruscow nad Baltykiem (La Question du séjour des Etruriens à la Côte de la mer Baltique). In T. Malinowski (ed.).

Tackenberg, K. 1971 *Die jüngere Bronzezeit in Nordwestdeutschland. Teil 1. Die Bronzen*. Veröff. der urgesch. Samml. des Landesmuseums zu Hannover. Hildesheim.

Tasic, N. 1971 The Bosut Group of the Basarabi Complex and the 'Thraco-Cimmerian' finds in Yugoslavian regions along the Danube and the Central Balkans. *Balcania* 2.

Taylor, J. 1981 Problems and parallels: an examination of wealthy graves in Early Bronze Age society in Wessex and Brittany. In *Enclos funéraires et structures d'habitat en Europe du nord-ouest*. Table ronde du CNRS, Rennes.

Taylor, R. 1982 Are hoards rubbish? Paper presented at the TAG conference, Durham.

Taylor, R. 1993 *Hoards of the Bronze Age of Southern Britain. Analysis and interpretation*. BAR British Series 228. Oxford.

Taylor, T. 1989 Iron and Iron Age in the Carpatho-Balkan region: aspects of social and technological change 1700–400 B. C. In M. L. Sørensen and R. Thomas (eds.).

Teichert, L. 1986 Tierknochenuntersuchungen der spätebronzezeitlichen Siedlung Zitz, Lkr.Brandenburg, in Vergleich zu Ergebnissen einiger zeitgleicher Fundorte. In D.-W. Buch and B. Gramsch (eds.).

Telegin, D. I. 1986 *Dereivka. A Settlement and Cemetery of Copper Age Horse-keepers on the Middle Dnieper*. BAR Int. Ser. Oxford.

Terzan, B. 1986 Zur Gesellschaftsstruktur während der älteren Hallstattzeit im Ostalpen-Westpannonischen Gebiet. In E. Jerem (ed.).

Tesch, S. 1993 *Houses, Farmsteads, and Long-term Change. A Regional Study of Prehistoric Settlements in the Köpinge Area, in Scania, Southern Sweden*. University of Uppsala, Dept. of Arch.

Teschler-Nicola, M. 1988 Bevölkerungsbiologische Aspekte der frühen und der mittleren Bronzezeit. In J.-W. Neugebauer (ed.).

Thevenot, J.-P. 1991 *L'Age du bronze en Bourgogne. Le dépôt de Blanot (Côte-d'or)*. Revue Archéologique de l'Est et du Centre-Est, Dijon.

Thomas, J. 1987 Relations of production and social change in the Neolithic of north-west Europe. *Man* 22.

Thomas, R. 1989 The bronze–iron transition in southern England. In M. L. Sørensen and R. Thomas (eds.).

Thompson, R. H. (ed.) 1958 *Migrations in New World Culture History*. University of Arizona, Social Science Bulletin No. 27.

Thorpe, I. J. and Richards, C. 1984 The decline of ritual authority and the introduction of beakers into Britain. In R. Bradley and J. Gardiner (eds.), *Neolithic Studies. A Review of Some Current Research*. Oxford: BAR British Series 133.

Thrane, H. 1958 Ein Depotfund der jüngeren Bronzezeit von Mandemark auf Møn. *Acta Arch.* 29.

Thrane, H. 1975 *Europøiske forbindelser. Bidrag til studiet af fremmede forbindelser i Danmarks yngre broncealder (periode IV–V)*. København: Nationalmuseet.

Thrane, H. 1977 Über die Verbindungen zwischen Odergebiet und Südskandinavien in der Bronzezeit, besonders Periode IV. In *Geneza kultury luzycjiej na terenie Nadodrza*. Wroclaw.

Thrane, H. 1980 Nogle tanker om yngre broncealders bebyggelse på Sydvestfyn. *Broncealder-bebyggelse i Norden*. Beretning fra det andet nordiske symposium for broncealderforskning, Odense 9–11 April 1980. Skrifter fra Odense Univ. nr. 28, Odense.

Thrane, H. 1981 Late Bronze Age graves in Denmark seen as expressions of social ranking – an initial report. In *Studien zur Bronzezeit*. Festschrift für Wilhelm Albert v. Brunn. Mainz/Rhein: Verlag Phillip von Zabern

Thrane, H. 1983 Indledende overvejelser af strukturudviklingen i Sydskandinavens broncealder. In B. Stjernquist (ed.), *Struktur och förändring i Bronsålderns samhälle*. Rapport från det tredje nordiska symposiet f r bronsåldersforskning i Lund 23–25 April 1982. University of Lund, Report Series No. 17.

Thrane, H. 1984 *Lusehøj ved Voldtofte – en sydvestfynsk storhøj fra yngre Broncealder*. Fynske Studier XIII. Odense.

Thrane, H. 1989 Pomeria and south Scandinavia during the Late Bronze Age, some provisional remarks. In *Problemy Kultury Luzyciej na Pomorzu*. Slupsk.

Thrane, H. 1990 Bronzezeitlicher Ackerbau – Beispiel Dänemark. In V. Furmanek and F. Horst (eds.).

Thrane, H. 1990b The Mycenaean fascination: a Northerner's view. In *Orientalisch-ägäische Einflüsse*.

Thrane, H. 1993 Lusehøj on Fyn. In S. Hvass and B. Storgård (eds.), *Digging into the Past. 25 years of Archaeology in Denmark*. Aarhus University Press.

Timpe, D. 1985 Der keltische Handel nach historischen Quellen. In K. Düwel, H. Jankuhn, H. Siems and D. Timpe (eds.).

Tinsley, H. M. and Grigson, C. 1981 The Bronze Age. In I. Simmons and M. Tooley (eds.), *The Environment in British Prehistory*. London: Duckworth.

Tocik, A. 1982 Beitrag zur Problematik befestigter Siedlungen in der Südwestslowakei während der älteren und zu Beginn der mittleren Bronzezeit. In V. Furmanek and F. Horst (eds.).

Tocik, A. and Paulik, J. 1960 Die Ausgrabung eines Grabhügel in Caka in den Jahren 1950–51. *Slovenska Arch.* 8(1).

Tonceva, G. 1980 Necropole tumulaire près du village Bellogradec du VIIe s. av. n.ère. *Thracia* 5.

Torbrügge, W. 1965 Volgriffschwerter der Urnenfelderzeit. Zur methodischen Darstellung einer Denkmälergruppe. *Bayerische Vorgeschichtsblätter*, Jahrg. 30, Heft 1/2.

Torbrügge, W. 1970/71 Vor-und Frühgeschichtliche Flussfunde. Zur Ordnung und Bestimmung einer Denkmälergruppe. *Ber. RGK* 51/52.

Torbrügge, W. 1979a *Die Hallstattzeit in der Oberpfalz I.* Auswerdung und Gesamtkatalog. Materialh. Bayer. Vorgesch. 39.

Torbrügge, W. 1979b Zum Übergang von der frühen zur mittleren Bronzezeit in Süddeutschland. *Arch. Korrespondenzblatt* 9, Heft 1.

Torbrügge, W. 1985 Über Horte und Hortdeutung. *Arch. Korrespondenzblatt* 15,

1orbrugge, W. 1988 Methodische Bemerkungen zur Urnenfelder- und Hallstattzeit in Thüringen und Nordbayern. In Z. Bukowski (ed.).

Torbrügge, W. 1990 Die mittlere Bronzezeit in Bayern. In V. Furmanek and F. Horst (eds.).

Tovar. A. 1986 The Celts in the Iberian Peninsula: archaeology, history, language. In K. H. Schmidt and R. Ködderitzsch, R. (eds.).

Trésors des Princes Celtes. Galeries nationale du Grand Palais 20 Octobre 1987–15 fèvrier 1988. Edition de la Réunion des musées nationaux.

Trigger, B. 1984 Alternative archaeologies: nationalist, colonialist, imperialist. *Man* (N.S.) 19.

Tsude, H. 1988 Land exploitation and the stratification of society: a case study in ancient Japan. *Studies in Japanese Language and Culture*. Joint Research Report No. 4. Faculty of Letters, Osaka University, Japan.

Turková, D. and Kuna, M. 1987 Zur Mikrostruktur der bronzezeitlichen Siedlungen. In E. Plesl and J. Hrala (eds.).

Turner, J. 1981 The Iron Age. In I. Simmons and M. Tooley (eds.), *The Environment in British Prehistory*. London: Duckworth.

Ulrix-Closset, M. and Otte, M. (eds.) 1989 *La civilisation de Hallstatt, bilan d'une rencontre*, Liège 1987. Etudes et Recherches Archéologiques de l' Université de Liège, no. 36, Liège. University of Arizona Social Bulletin No. 27.

Upham, S. 1987 A theoretical consideration of middle range societies. In R. D. Drennan and C. A. Uribe (eds.), *Chiefdoms in the Americas*. University Press of America.

Vadasz, E. V. 1983 Elözetes jelantes egy koranaskori halomsir feltarasaral Sütton (Vorbericht über die Erschliessung eines früheisenzeitlichen Hügels in Süttö). *Communicationes Archaeologicae Hungariae.*

Vagnetti, L. 1993 Mycenaean pottery in Italy: fifty years of study. In C. Zerner *et al.* (eds) 1993 *Proceedings of the International Conference Wace and Blegen. Pottery as Evidence for Trade in the Aegean Bronze Age 1939–1989*. Gieben, Amsterdam.

Vagnetti, L. and Lo Schiavo, F. 1989 Late Bronze Age long distance trade in the Mediterranean: the role of the Cypriots. In E. Peltenburg (ed.), *Early Society in Cyprus*. Edinburgh University Press in association with The National Museums of Scotland and The A.G. Leventis Foundation.

Vajda, L. 1973–74 Zur Frage der Völkerwanderungen. *Paideuma. Mitteilungen zum Kulturgeschichte*, Bd. 19–20.

Vandkilde, H. 1988 A Late Neolithic hoard with objects of bronze and gold from Skeldal, Central Jutland. *Journal of Danish Archaeology* 7.

Vandkilde, H. 1990 Metal analyses of the Skeldal Hoard and aspects of early Danish metal use. *Journal of Danish Archaeology* 9.

Vasic, R. 1982 Spätbronzezeitliche und älterhallstattzeitliche Hortfunde im östlichen Jugoslawien. In B. Hänsel (ed.).

Vasic, R. 1990 Graeco-Barbarian contacts in the early Iron Age central Balkans. *Balcanica* 21.

Vasic, R. 1991 Cultural groups of the early Iron Age in the west and central Balkans and the possibilities of their ethnical identification. In A. Benac *et al.* (eds.).

Vasiliev, V. 1976 Die Skythengruppe in Siebenbürgen. *Apulum* 14.

Veen, M. van der 1992 *Crop Husbandry Regimes. An Archaeobotanical Study of Farming in northern England 1000 BC–500 AD*. Sheffield Archaeological Monographs.

Veit, U. 1989 Ethnic concepts in German prehistory: a case study on the relationship between cultural identity and archaeological objectivity. In S. Shennan (ed.), *Archaeological Approaches to Cultural Identity.* One World Archaeology 10. Unwin Hyman, London.

Vekony, G. 1983 Veneter-Urnenfelderkultur-Bernsteinstrasse. In G. Bandi and V. Csermenyi (eds.).

Vekony, G. 1986 Zu einigen Fragen der Hallstattzeit der östlichen Transdanubiens. In E. Jerem (ed.).

Velkov, V. 1991 Ursprung und Entwicklung des Siedlungslebens im Altthrakien. In A. Benac *et al.* (eds.).

Venclova, N. 1993 Celtic shrines in central Europe: a sceptical approach. *Oxford Journal of Archaeology* 12(1).

Venedikov, I. 1980 Trakien. In P. Hellström and A. Sandwall (eds.), *Trakerna.* Statens Historiska Museum, Stockholm.

Venedikov, I. 1987 *The Vulchitrun Treasure.* Sofia.

Vierrädige Wagen der Hallstattzeit 1987 Monographien, Römisch-Germanisches Central-museum Mainz.

Vladar, J. 1973 Osteuropäische und mediterrane Einflüsse im Gebiet der Slowakei während der Bronzezeit. *Slovenska Archeologia* 21(2).

Vladar, J. 1977 Zur Problematik osteuropäischer und südostlicher Einflüsse in der Kulturent-wicklung der älteren Bronzezeit in Gebiet der Slowakei. *Slovenska Archeologia* 24(1).

Vladar, J. 1981 Zur Problematik der befestigten Siedlungen der ausgehenden älteren Bron-zezeit in der Slowakei. In C.-H. Frey and H. Roth (eds.), *Festschrift zum 50 jährigen Bestehen des Vorgeschichtlichen Seminars Marburg.* Marburger Studien zur Vor- und Frühgeschichte, Band 1.

Vladar, J. 1982 Die frühbronzezeitliche Entwicklung der Slowakei und das Aufkommen der befestigten Siedlungen. In V. Furmanek and F. Horst (eds.).

Vladar, J. and Batonek, A. 1977 Zu den Beziehungen zwischen des ägäischen, balkanischen und karpatischen Raumes in der mittleren Bronzezeit und die kulturelle Ausstrahlung der ägäischen Schriften in die Nachbarländer. *Slovenska Archeologia,* 25.

Vogt, E. 1942 Der Zierstil der späten Phahlbaubronzen. *Zeitschr. für Schweizerische Arch. und Kunstgesch.* Bd. 4.

Vulpe, A. 1965 Zur mittleren Hallstattzeit in Rumänien (Die Basrabi-Kultur). *Dacia* (N.S.), 9.

Vulpe, A. 1982 Beitrag zu den bronzezeitlichen kulturbeziehungen zwischen Rumänien und Griechenland. In B. Hänsel (ed.), *Südosteuropa zwischen 1600 und 1000 v. Chr.* Prähis-torische Arch. in Südosteuropa, Band 1. Berlin.

Waddell, J. 1991 The question of the celticization of Ireland. *Emania* 9. Bulletin of the Navan Research Group, Belfast.

Waldhauser, J. 1979 Beitrag zum Studium der keltischen Siedlungen, Oppida und Gräberfel-der in Böhmen. In P.-M. Duval and V. Kruta (eds.).

Waldhauser, J. 1984a Les fortifications celtiques de la période L.T. C D1 en Bohême. Oppida et castella. In A. Cahen-Delhaye *et al.* (eds.), *Les celtes en Belgique et dans le nord de la France. Les fortifications de l'âge du fer.* Revue du Nord, numéro spécial hors série.

Waldhauser, J. 1984b Mobilität und Stabilität der keltischen Besiedlung in Böhmen. In C. Dobiat (ed.).

Waldhauser, J. 1986a Kupfergewinnung und verhüttung in Böhmen und Mähren während der Späthallstatt- und Latènezeit (Forschungsstand). In D.-W. Buch and B. Gramsch (eds.).

Waldhauser, J. 1986b Struktur und Ökologie der keltischen Besiedlung während der Stufen HaD-LT D in Böhmen. In E. Jerem (ed.).

Waldhauser, J. 1986c Zur ökonomischen Entwicklung bei den keltischen Stämmen in Böh-men. In F. Horst and B. Krüger (eds.).

Waldhauser, J. 1987 Betrachtungen zu latènezeitlichen Gräberfelder in Böhmen. In *Keltische Gräberfelder in Böhmen.* Berich der Römisch-Germ. Komm. 68, Mainz.

Waldhauser, J. 1994 Ceramic variation, raw material supply and distribution areas during the last centuries B.C. /La Tène B2–D1) in Celtic Bohemia. In K. Kristiansen and J. Jensen (eds.).

Wallace, A. F. C. 1970: *The Death and Rebirth of the Seneca*. Alfred Knopf, New York.

Wallace-Hadrill, J. M. 1971 *Early Germanic Kinship in England and on the Continent*. Oxford at the Clarendon Press.

Wallerstein, I. 1974 *The Modern World System. Capitalist Agriculture and the Origins of the European World-Economy in the Sixteenth Century*. New York: Academic Press.

Wanzek, B. 1989 Bemerkungen zu den älterurnenfelderzeitlichen Hortfunde Ungarns. *Praehistorische Zeitschrift* 64.

Warmenbol, E. 1989 De l'âge du Bronze a l'âge du Fer en Belgique et dans le sud des Pays-Bas. In M. Otte and M. Ulrix-Closset (eds.).

Warner, R. B. 1991 Cultural intrusions in the Early Iron Age: some notes. *Emania* 9. Bull. of the Navan Research Group, Belfast.

Warren, P. 1977 The emergence of Mycenaean palace civilization. In J. Bintliff (ed.), *Mycenaean Geography*. Proceedings of the Cambridge Colloquium, Sept. 1976. Cambridge.

Warren, P. and Hankey, V. 1989 *Aegean Bronze Age Chronology*. Bristol.

Webb, M. C. 1975 The flag follows trade: an essay on the necessary interaction of military and commercial factors in state formation. In J. A. Sabloff and C. C. Lamberg-Karlovsky (eds.), *Ancient Civilization and Trade*. Albuquerque: University of New Mexico Press.

Webb, M. C. 1987 Broader perspectives on Andean state origins. In J. Haas, S. Pozorski and T. Pozorski (eds.), *The Origin and Development of the Andean State*. Cambridge University Press.

Webster, G. S. 1991 Monuments, mobilization and Nuragic organisation. *Antiquity* 65(249).

Wegner, G. 1976 *Die vorgeschichtlichen Flussfunde aus dem Main und aus dem Rhein bei Mainz*. Kallmunz: Michael Hassleben.

Welinder, S. 1974 *Kulturlandskabpet i Mälaromrâdet*. University of Lund, Dept. of Quaternary Geology. Report 5.

Welinder, S. 1976 *Ekonomiska Processer i Forhistorisk Expansion*. Lund: Acta Archaeologica Lundensia, Ser. in 8 Minore, No. 7.

Wells, P. 1980 *Culture Contact and Culture Change. Early Iron Age Central Europe and the Mediterranean World*. Cambridge University Press.

Wells, P. 1981 *The Emergence of an Iron Age Economy. The Mecklenburg Grave Groups from Hallstatt and Sticna*. Mecklenburg Collection, Part III. Cambridge, Massachusetts: Harvard University Press.

Wells, P. 1984 *Farms, Villages and Cities. Commerce and Urban Origins in Late Prehistoric Europe*. Ithaca and London: Cornell University Press.

Wells, P. S. 1989 Intensification, entrepreneurship, and cognitive change in the Bronze–Iron Age transition. In M. L. Sørensen and R. Thomas (eds.), *The Bronze Age–Iron Age Transition in Europe. Aspects of Continuity and Change in European Societies c. 1200 to 500 B.C.* BAR International Series 483. Oxford.

Wells, P. S. 1990 Iron Age temperate Europe: some current research issues. *Journal of World Prehistory* 4(4).

Wels-Weyrauch, U. 1989 Mittelbronzezeitliche Frauentrachten in Süddeutschland (Beziehungen zur Haguenauer Gruppierung). In *Dynamique du bronze moyen en Europe occidentale*.

Wels-Weyrauch, U. 1994 Im Grab erhalten, im Leben getragen Tracht und Schmuck der Frau. In A. Jockenhövel and W. Kubach (eds.), *Bronzezeit in Deutschland*. Archaeologie in Deutschland. Sonderhaft Theiss.

Werner, J. 1956 *Beitrage zur Archaeologie des Attilareiches*. München.

Werner, J. 1962 *Die Langobarden in Pannonien*. Bayerische Akademie der Wissenschaften.

Werner, W. M. 1985 Pferdetrensen aus Südosteuropa – eine Übersicht. *Archäologisches Korrespondenzblatt* 15.

Werner, W. M. 1987 Klappschemel der Bronzezeit. *Germania* 65(1).

Whitehouse, R. D. and Wilkins, J. B. 1989 Greeks and natives in south-east Italy: approaches to the archaeological evidence. In T. Champion (ed.), *Centre and Periphery. Comparative Studies in Archaeology*. One World Archaeology 11. London: Unwin Hyman.

Whittaker, C. R. (ed.) 1988 *Pastoral Economies in Classical Antiquity*. The Cambridge Philological Society.

Wickham, C. 1985 The uniqueness of the East. In T. J. Byres and H. Mukhia (eds.), *The Journal of Peasant Studies*. Special Issue on feudalism and non-European societies.

Wigley, T. M. L., Ingram, M. J. and Farmer, G. (eds.) 1981 *Climate and History. Studies in Past Climates and their Impact on Man*. Cambridge University Press.

Wigren, S. 1987 *Sörmländsk Bronsåldersbygd. En studia av tidiga centrumbildninar daterade med termoluminescens* (English summary). Theses and Papers in North European Archaeology 16.

Wilhelmi, K. 1981 *Die vorrömische Eisenzeit zwischen Sieg und Mittelweser*. Kleine Schriften aus dem vorgeschichtlichen Seminar Marburg, Hft. 8, Marburg.

Wilhelmi, K. 1987–88 Zur Besiedlungsgenese Englands und des nordwestlichen kontinents von 1500 vor bis Christi Geburt. *Acta Praehistorica et Archaeologica* 19–20.

Wilkes, J. 1992 *The Illyrians*. Blackwell.

Willerding, U. 1970 Vor- und frühgeschichtlichen Kulturpflanzenfunde in Mitteleuropa. *Neue Ausgrabungen und Forschungen in Niedersachsen* 5. Hildesheim.

Willerding, U. 1988 Zur Entwicklung von Ackerundkrautgesellschaften im Zeitraum vom Neolithicum bis in die Neuzeit. In H. Küster (ed.).

Willroth, K.-H. 1985 Aspekte älterbronzezeitlicher Deponierungen in südlichen Skandinavien. *Germania* 63(2).

Willroth, K.-H. 1989 Nogle betragtningerover de regionale forhold i Slesvig og Holsten i Bronzealderens perode II. In J. Poulsen (ed.), *Regionale forhold i Nordisk Bronzealder*. Århus.

Winter, F. and Bankoff, H. A. 1989 Diffusion and cultural evolution in Iron Age Serbia. In T. Champion (ed.).

Winther, I. 1988 North Syria as a bronzeworking centre in the early first millennium BC: luxury commodities at home and abroad. In J. Curtis (ed.).

Wolf, E. R. 1982 *Europe and the People without History*. Berkeley: University of California Press.

Woolf, G. 1993 The social significance of trade in Late Iron Age Europe. In C. Scarre and F. Healy (eds.), *Trade and Exchange in Prehistoric Europe*. Oxbow Monograph 33.

Worsaae, J. J. A. 1866 Om nogle Mosefund fra Broncealderen. *Aarbøger for Nordisk Oldkyndighed og Historie*.

Woytowitsch, E. 1978 *Die Wagen der Bronze- und frühen Eisenzeit in Italien*. Prähistorische Bronzefunde XVII, 1. Munich, C. H. Beck.

Wozniak, Z. 1976 Die östliche Randzone der Latènekultur. *Germania* 54.

Wozniak, Z. 1979 Der Besiedlungswandel in der germanischen Gebieten während der jüngeren Latènezeit und seine Bedeutung für die Geschichte der Kelten. In J.-M. Duval and V. Kruta (eds.).

Wüstemann, H. 1974 Zur Sozialstruktur im Seddiner Kulturgebiet. *Zeitschrift für Archäologie* 8.

Wüstemann, H. 1978 Zur Sozialentwicklung während der Bronzezeit im Norden der DDR. In W. Coblenz and F. Horst (eds.), *Mitteleuropäische Bronzezeit*. Beiträge zur Archäologie und Geschichte. Berlin: Akademie-Verlag.

Wylie, A. 1989 Matters of fact and matters of interest. In S. Shennan (ed.), *Archaeological Approaches to Cultural Identity*. One World Archaeology 10. Unwin Hyman, London.

Young, R. 1981 *Three Great Early Tumuli. The Gordion Excavations*. Final Reports Vol. 1. University of Pennsylvania. Univ. Museum Monographs 43.

Zaccagnini, C. 1977 Pferde und Streitwagen in Nuzi. *Jahresber. des instituts für Vorgeschichte der Universität Frankfurt A. M.*

Zaccagnini, C. 1987 Aspects of ceremonial exchange in the Near East during the late second millennium BC. In M. Rowlands, M. T. Larsen and K. Kristiansen (eds.).

Ziegert, H. 1963 *Der westlichen Hügelgräberkultur*. Berliner Beiträge zur Vor- und Frühgeschichte 7. Berlin.

Zürn, H. 1970 *Hallstattforschungen in Nordwürttemberg*. Veröff. des Stattl. Amtes f. Denkmalpflege Stuttgart, Reihe A, Hft. 16.

Zürn, H. 1974 Zur Chronologie der südwestdeutschen Späthallstattkultur und die Datierung der Fürstengräber. In B. Chropovsky (ed.).

Zürn, H. 1987 *Hallstattzeitliche Grabfunde in Württemberg und Hohenzollern*. Landesdenkmalamt Baden-Württemberg. Stuttgart: Konrad Theiss Verlag.

Zurowski, T. 1950 Les constructions de civilisation Lusacienne à Biskupin. Essai de reconstruction. In J. Kostrzewski (ed.).

INDEX

Page numbers in *italics* refer to illustrations.
Page numbers in **bold** indicate a main reference to the subject.

Recent Titles in the Series:

The Chaco Anasazi: sociopolitical evolution in the prehistoric southwest
LYNNE SEBASTIAN
ISBN 0 521 40367 7 hardback

Agriculture and the onset of political Inequality before the Inka
CHRISTINE A. HASTORF
ISBN 0 521 40272 7 hardback

Ancient Mesoamerica: a comparison of change in three regions: (*second edition*)
RICHARD E. BLANTON, STEPHEN A. KOWALEWSKI, GARY FEINMAN AND
LAURA FINSTEN
ISBN 0 521 44053 X hardback
ISBN 0 521 44506 6 paperback

Interpreting the axe trade: production and exchange in Neolithic Britain
RICHARD BRADLEY AND MARK EDMONDS
ISBN 0 521 43446 7 hardback

Ecology and ceramic production in an Andean community
DEAN E. ARNOLD
ISBN 0 521 43289 8 hardback

A Chesapeake family and their slaves: a study in historical archaeology
ANN E. YENTSCH
ISBN 0 521 43293 6 hardback
ISBN 0 521 46730 6 paperback

The archaeology of rank
PAUL K. WASON
ISBN 0 521 38072 3 hardback

The limits of settlement growth: a theoretical outline
ROLAND FLETCHER
ISBN 0 521 43085 2

An ethnography of the Neolithic: early prehistorical societies in southern Scandanavia
CHRISTOPHER TILLEY
ISBN 0 521 56096 9 hardback

Architecture and power in the ancient Andes: the archaeology of Public Buildings
JERRY MOORE
ISBN 0 521 55363 6